BEST PRACTICES

in School Psychology V

Alex Thomas  Jeff Grimes

NASP

VOLUME 5

BEST PRACTICES
in School Psychology V

Edited by

Alex Thomas
Port Clinton, Ohio

Jeff Grimes
Des Moines, Iowa

The National Association of School Psychologists
Bethesda, MD

Published by the National Association of School Psychologists

Copies may be ordered from:
NASP Publications
4340 East West Highway, Suite 402
Bethesda, MD 20814
(301) 657-0270
(301) 657-0275, fax
(866) 331-NASP, Toll Free
e-mail: *publications@naspweb.org*
www.nasponline.org

ISBN 978-0-932955-70-8

Volume 5

Printed in the United States of America

Third Printing, September 2010

10 9 8 7 6 5 4 3

Table of Contents

VOLUME 1

Section I. Professional Foundations

Appendices

VOLUME 2

Section II. Data-Based Decision Making and Accountability

VOLUME 3

Section III. Systems-Based Service Delivery

VOLUME 4

Section IV. Enhancing the Development of Cognitive and Academic Skills

Section V. Enhancing the Development of Wellness, Social Skills, and Life Competencies

VOLUME 5

Section VI. Interpersonal and Collaborative Skills

Section VII. Diversity Awareness and Sensitive Service Delivery

Section VIII. Technological Applications

VOLUME 6

Section IX. Professional, Legal, Ethical, and Social Responsibility

Section X. Scientific Method

Section VI
Interpersonal and Collaborative Skills

Volume 5 of *Best Practices in School Psychology V* supports an understanding of the competency *Blueprint III* emphasizing interpersonal and collaborative skills.

Description: School psychologists should demonstrate strong interpersonal skills, the ability to work effectively and collaboratively with people and agencies, and characteristics such as the ability to listen, adapt, tolerate ambiguity, and be patient in difficult situations.

101 Best Practices in Establishing Effective Helping Relationships

Julia E. McGivern
University of Wisconsin–Madison
Corey E. Ray-Subramanian
Northern Illinois University
Elana R. Auster
University of Wisconsin–Madison

OVERVIEW

Meeting the academic and social–emotional needs of today's students requires effective direct and indirect services at universal, targeted, and intensive tiers (e.g., see Tilly, chapter 2, vol. 1). At all tiers of services and in both direct and consultative roles, school psychologists work within the context of helping relationships with students, parents, and teachers. Recent attention in the field of psychology has been focused on the helping relationship as a critical ingredient of effective practice (e.g., Castonguay & Beutler, 2006; Creed & Kendall, 2005).

Working with students, parents, and teachers to facilitate positive outcomes in schools is an interpersonal process. *School Psychology: A Blueprint for Training and Practice III* (Ysseldyke et al., 2006) identified interpersonal and collaborative skills as foundational competencies that are "indispensable for school psychologists" (p. 15). The American Psychological Association (APA), in the report of the APA Presidential Task Force on Evidence-Based Practice (2006), noted that "Psychological practice is, at root, an interpersonal relationship between psychologist and patient" (p. 277). (In many psychological studies, research reports, and practice articles, the term *patient* is used to identify the recipient of services. However, unless quoting directly from another source, we will generally use the terms *client* or *consultee* when referring to the recipient of school-based services.) Erchul (2003) wrote about consultation, "Stripped to its essence, educational and psychological consultation consists of a problem-solving, interpersonal relationship that develops through periodic face-to-face contacts between consultant and consultee" (p.105).

Researchers investigating factors that influence treatment outcomes with youth and adults have found that both relationship variables and specific treatment techniques influence outcomes (Castonguay & Beutler, 2006; Norcross, 2002; Wampold, 2001). To maximize the effectiveness of psychological practice, school psychologists must capitalize on the power of both evidence-based interventions and factors known to improve the helping relationship. Recent research suggests that the treatment relationship may be particularly influential in work with youth because children and adolescents are often referred by adults for assessment and intervention and may be resistant to change (Shirk & Karver, 2003). Also, students referred for services in schools often have relationships with adults (especially teachers and parents) that are "impoverished and conflictual" (Pianta, 1999, p. 21), evidencing a need for supportive relationships with helpers.

Recognizing the impact of the helping relationship on treatment outcomes, Division 29 (Psychotherapy) of the APA formed a task force to identify variables within the helping relationship that contribute to client outcomes. In its work the task force identified variables found to be "demonstrably effective" (e.g., empathy) and "promising and probably effective" (e.g., positive regard) in facilitating positive client outcomes (Norcross, 2002). Recent studies have added to this body of work, providing a rich research base as a foundation for clinical practice. Several meta-analyses of relationship factors influencing the outcomes of youth treatment have been conducted (e.g., Karver, Handelsman, Fields, & Bickman, 2006), and additional task forces in psychology have worked to integrate the findings regarding evidence-based treatments and specific relationship factors (e.g., Castonguay & Beutler, 2006).

School psychologists practicing today can use evidence about helping relationships to improve outcomes for children and adolescents. Reliance on research findings is the foundation of science-based practice (see Tilly, chapter 2, vol. 1), and data-based decision making and accountability are functional competencies required by school psychologists (*Blueprint III*, Ysseldyke et al., 2006). Although the research base supporting effective relationship building is developing, it has limitations. Much of the direct service research to date has focused on adults; many studies are correlational, indicating a strong relationship but not necessarily causation among variables; many studies lack the statistical power necessary to detect small but meaningful effects; and most studies of relationship variables in direct services have been carried out in clinical settings rather than schools. In addition, relationship factors are complex and often confounded with other variables. Finally, Sheridan and Kratochwill (in press) note the paucity of research in the field of consultation regarding the effects of relationship variables on consultation outcomes. Yet there is much to be learned from examination of the findings of recent work regarding direct service and consultation.

Bridging the Research-to-Practice Gap

In its definition of evidence-based practice, APA stresses the need to rely on research along with clinical expertise. "Evidence-based practice in psychology (EBPP) is the integration of the best available research with clinical expertise in the context of patient characteristics, culture, and preferences" (APA Presidential Task Force on Evidence-Based Practice, 2006, p. 273). The purpose of this chapter is to help school psychologists bridge the research-to-practice gap (e.g., Riley-Tillman, Chafouleas, Eckert, & Kelleher, 2005). This bridge to evidence-based practice can be built through collaboration between the authors and readers of this chapter. In writing this chapter we have sought to identify evidence supporting specific relationship factors that improve student outcomes by summarizing the best available research regarding helping relationships and by

illustrating applications of research findings in practice through case examples.

The readers of this chapter can support the bridge by reflecting on the critical relationship factors discussed in the chapter; by examining the brief case examples and identifying additional factors that might be influential in each example; by analyzing the therapist factors they themselves bring to their work with clients, teachers, and parents; and by considering carefully the clients and consultees in their own practices.

At the end of each major section of the chapter we have identified questions for reflection to help extend the findings outlined in the chapter to the readers' practices.

BASIC CONSIDERATIONS

What Influences Outcomes

Why, as research clearly demonstrates, are some helpers more effective than others? Many factors have been found to influence the outcomes of direct and indirect services. Castonguay and Beutler (2006) classified these as technique factors, participant factors, and relationship (or interactive) factors. (Much of the research regarding treatment relationships has focused on direct service provision; however, many of the findings can be tentatively generalized to the practice of consultation. In general, when discussing direct service and consultation relationships, we will use the term *helping relationships*.)

- *Technique factors:* Those that derive from a practitioner's or consultant's model of practice (e.g., cognitive–behavioral theory, conjoint behavioral consultation). Although techniques are delivered within the context of a relationship, they are not considered a direct aspect of the relationship itself.
- *Participant factors:* Those that are unique to the client, consultee, or helper. These factors directly influence the relationship and consequently are of interest when examining helping relationships.
- *Relationship or interactive factors:* Those that operate at the intersection of client and therapist factors, such as race, gender, alliance, collaboration, and goal consensus. Some of these factors have been found to be critical to the helping relationship.

In addition, it is important to note that direct and indirect service outcomes are influenced by additional factors, such as barriers that prevent children, youth, families, and teachers from accessing school psychological services. When families cannot participate in consultation or intervention because of limited child care, transportation, or other barriers, student outcomes will suffer (e.g., McKay & Bannon, 2004; Sheridan & Kratochwill, in press).

Moderators and Mediators of Treatment Outcomes

Factors influencing the outcomes of interventions can be grouped in multiple ways. One perspective is to look at *moderators* and *mediators* of outcomes. Hinshaw (2002) described moderators of outcomes as variables that are measured prior to the treatment assignment (e.g., race or gender) that by definition are uncorrelated with treatment assignment. However, once treatment is completed, "moderator variables can identify subgroups of participants for whom treatment showed greater versus lesser effects" (Hinshaw, 2002, p. 2). Mediator variables, in contrast, occur after assignment to treatment (e.g., the helping relationship). Mediators are factors "through which treatment exerts its effects" (Hinshaw, 2002, p. 3). Some variables can function as either a moderator or mediator in different situations. For example, the alliance between the helper and the client/consultee is typically thought of as a mediator variable through which change occurs, but it could act as a moderator variable if a client and helper have already forged a positive therapeutic alliance that predisposes the client to perceive a new treatment positively. Identification of moderators and mediators of treatment can assist school psychologists in identifying characteristics of individuals (moderators) that render them more or less likely to benefit from specific interventions and variables (mediators) that influence the effectiveness of interventions. Table 1 identifies potential client, helper, and interactive factors that act as moderators and barriers to treatment that might influence treatment outcomes.

BEST PRACTICES

Below are examples of situations in which a school psychologist would likely work to develop a relationship with a student, parent, and teacher to facilitate positive student outcomes. These examples will be used throughout the chapter to illustrate application of research findings.

Anna (student): Anna is a ninth-grade student at Oakwood High School. Anna's mother is Caucasian and her father is Filipino. Anna has been a good student, but she has a history of stomachaches and nausea during the school year. Anna has missed 6 days of school in 3 weeks. Anna's mother called the school psychologist and

Table 1. Potential Factors Influencing Therapeutic Relationships and Outcomes

Moderating factors	Mediating factors	Barriers to intervention
Client factors • Age/developmental status • Functional impairment • Coping style • Expectations • Stage of change • Resistance	Client factors • Active participation in treatment • Homework completion • Self-efficacy • Goals	Client/consultee barriers • Student's and parents' schedules • Student/parent transportation • Parent child care • Teacher time
Helper attributes • Warmth • Genuineness or congruence • Trustworthiness	Helper strategies • Empathy • Positive regard • Communication strategies • Self-disclosure • Evidence-based strategies	Helper barriers • Knowledge and training • Resources • Time • System support
Interactive factors • Gender • Race/culture • Sexual orientation	Interactive factors • Therapeutic alliance • Goal consensus • Collaboration	Interactive barriers • Previous conflict • Competing goals

Note. Moderating factors: measured before treatment; factors that identify subgroups of participants most likely to benefit from treatment. Mediating factors: occur after assignment to treatment; factors through which treatment exerts its effects. Barriers to intervention: may arise before or during treatment; include client/consultee, helper, and system barriers. Source: Hinshaw (2002); McKay and Bannon (2004); Norcross (2002).

reported that Anna told her, "I'm worried about all the work I have to do in my classes. I'll never be able to keep up." Anna's mother also reported that Anna's friends aren't calling her anymore. The school psychologist saw Anna today, and when Anna entered the office Anna began to cry.

Mr. Singleton (parent): Sam Singleton, Mr. Singleton's son, is a kindergarten student at King Elementary School. He was evaluated a month ago by an Individualized Education Program team and was found to meet the criteria for autism. Sam's parents, both African Americans, are divorced. His mother agreed with the autism diagnosis, and his father, Mr. Singleton, did not. Mr. Singleton objected to the support of an educational assistant for Sam and said he did not want Sam to be singled out in school. Today Mr. Singleton met with the school psychologist to discuss Sam's progress. Mr. Singleton revealed his sadness and anxiety about Sam and asked to set up an appointment to talk about autism and what he can do to support Sam.

Ms. Walker (teacher): Ms. Walker is a Caucasian fifth-grade teacher at Centerville Middle School. She told the school psychologist that "Five or six students are disruptive during class. They constantly talk to each other and bother other students. We hardly get anything done." After observing in the classroom and collecting behavioral data, the school psychologist determined that the problem is more pervasive. Very few of the 26 students in her classroom comply with Ms. Walker's directives. Also, Ms. Walker is not using proactive classroom management strategies. The school psychologist has a meeting today with Ms. Walker.

Helper Factors That Facilitate Effective Relationships

Helper factors that influence relationships with students, parents, and teachers can be divided into two broad categories: personal attributes and broad trans-theoretical strategies that transcend the specific theoretical orientation of the helper.

Personal Attributes
Clients often attribute positive intervention outcomes to attributes of the therapist rather than to specific intervention techniques (Norcross & Lambert, 2006).

Personal attributes such as warmth, genuineness, and trustworthiness can help school psychologists develop effective relationships to promote positive student outcomes. Shirk and Karver (2006) noted that helper attributes such as warmth and genuineness may be crucial in facilitating clients' engagement in the intervention process. Many experts in this area of study argue that helper characteristics such as these are acknowledged by virtually all theoretical perspectives as necessary for client progress in treatment (e.g., Karver et al., 2006).

Warmth. Warmth is generally conveyed by helpers through nonverbal cues such as tone of voice, eye contact, facial expressions, gestures, and touch. Verbal responses that address a positive attribute about a client, or that involve immediacy (i.e., describing something as it occurs), can also convey warmth (Cormier & Nurius, 2003).

Genuineness (also sometimes referred to as congruence). Genuineness can be thought of as knowing oneself and communicating that self-awareness to the client. Genuineness has been found to be a critical element of the helping relationship (Castonguay & Beutler, 2006). It has been specifically identified as an essential component of effective relationship building with adolescents (Oetzel & Scherer, 2003). Adolescents relate best to helpers who are "real" and are candid with them and generally dislike helpers who adopt youthful mannerisms and act "cool" (Oetzel & Scherer, 2003). Genuineness is thought to contribute to effective helping relationships by facilitating closeness between the helper and the client. Nonverbal behaviors, spontaneity, and openness facilitate the communication of genuineness (Cormier & Nurius, 2003).

Trustworthiness. Trustworthiness has been described as a client's perceptions of the helper's interest, competence, and structuring of the work with the client (Cormier & Nurius, 2003). Trustworthiness relates to the client/consultee's confidence that the helper is indeed a person who can be counted on to operate in the client/consultee's best interests. Without trust, the helper is not likely to improve outcomes for clients/consultees. Trustworthy helpers increase the likelihood that clients will carry out intervention plans (Beutler, Moleiro, & Talebi, 2002). Sheridan and Kratochwill (in press), discussing trust in consultation relationships, noted "a positive atmosphere that promotes partnerships around learning is built on a foundation of trust."

Helper Strategies

In addition to drawing upon personal attributes to facilitate positive intervention outcomes for students, school psychologists can use specific strategies to build effective relationships in their direct work with students and in consultation with teachers and parents.

Empathy. Among the helper strategies that have been examined empirically, the use of empathy is the strategy found most consistently to positively influence the helping relationship and client outcomes. Empathy has been defined as the helper's ability to perceive "accurately the feelings and personal meanings that the client is experiencing and (communicate) this understanding to the client" (Rogers, 1980, p. 116). Thus, an empathic response reflects both the content and affective elements of the client's statements (Cormier & Nurius, 2003). An empathic response is illustrated below using the example of Anna.

> *Anna:* "Sometimes I just keep worrying about all the stuff I have to do. I feel like I can't breathe."
>
> *School psychologist:* "It sounds like you have a lot on your mind, Anna. It must be pretty scary when you feel like you can't catch your breath."

This response is considered empathic because the school psychologist acknowledged the content of Anna's statement (her numerous worries) and her feelings of fear or anxiety.

Helpers' use of empathy in professional helping relationships has been shown to have moderate effects on intervention outcomes for both adults (Bohart, Elliott, Greenberg, & Watson, 2002) and children (Karver et al., 2006). Examining direct interventions for social–emotional issues such as depression and anxiety, scholars have identified the use of empathy as a basic principle to promote positive change (Castonguay & Beutler, 2006). Failure to respond with empathy to depressed adolescents' expressions of emotion has been associated with poor bonds with helpers (Shirk, Karver, & Spirito, 2003).

The use of empathy is also a beneficial strategy for helpers who are serving as consultants. For example, it fits well within a model of consultee-centered consultation, which "emphasizes a nonhierarchical, nonprescriptive helping role relationship" (Lambert, 2004, p. 11). A key element of school-based consultee-centered consultation is the consultant's development of an understanding of the consultee's perspective of the client and the focal issue. This process requires reflective thinking on the part of the consultant and clarification from the consultee that may be achieved through the use of empathic statements. Below is an example of an empathic statement to a teacher.

> *Ms. Walker:* "These kids are really getting on my nerves with their disruptive behavior."
>
> *School psychologist:* "I can understand that you are frustrated with disruptions in the classroom while you are trying to teach."

Here, the school psychologist provided an appropriate empathic response that reflected both the content of Ms. Walker's statement (disruptions in her classroom) and her affect (frustration), without implying that the students' behavior is the underlying problem.

Empathy can also be used effectively with parents to indicate that the helper understands both the content and affect of a parent's communication.

> *Mr. Singleton:* "I don't want Sam to be different from the other kids. I know he is, but I feel so sad he can't just be a normal kindergartener."
>
> *School psychologist:* "Mr. Singleton, it is understandable you are sad that Sam needs special help. You just want him to be like other kids his age."

Positive regard. Positive regard, which is considered "a warm acceptance of each aspect of the client's experience as being part of that client" (Rogers, 1957, as cited in Farber & Lane, 2002, p. 176), is another strategy that helpers can use to build relationships and promote positive intervention outcomes. Cormier and Nurius (2003) identified five components of positive regard: (a) having a sense of commitment to the client, (b) making an effort to understand the client, (c) suspending critical judgment, (d) showing competence and care, and (e) expressing warmth to the client. Researchers have found that helpers' use of positive regard has a modest positive effect on intervention outcomes for adult clients (Farber & Lane, 2002). Despite the limited empirical research on the effects of using positive regard with children and adolescents to facilitate desirable intervention outcomes, many experts believe that, at the very least, conveying positive regard to students may help school psychologists develop effective helping relationships with them. While it may be relatively easy for school psychologists to convey a genuine sense of positive regard to most students, teachers, and parents, considering how to display positive regard in challenging situations or with resistant clients/consultees may be especially important to promote the development of effective helping relationships.

Related to positive regard is the concept of respect. Research indicates that displaying respect for clients and consultees is strongly related to retention in the helping relationship (e.g., Kerkorian, McKay, & Bannon, 2006).

Self-disclosure. In addition to empathy and positive regard, helpers' use of appropriate self-disclosure (i.e., statements that reveal something personal about oneself) has been found to be beneficial in facilitating positive helping relationships. Self-disclosure is considered most effective when it is used infrequently and for specific purposes related to developing the helping relationship or promoting positive intervention outcomes (Knox & Hill, 2003).

Knox and Hill (2003) identified seven types of helper self-disclosures: those based on (a) facts ("I have worked at this school for 8 years"), (b) feelings ("I also feel happy when I am with my family"), (c) insight ("I had a similar experience; I realized that I need to plan ahead more"), (d) strategy ("When I start to feel angry, I take deep breaths to stay calm"), (e) reassurance/support ("I think that would worry me, also"), (f) challenge ("I, too, am a single parent, so I understand the challenges involved"), and (g) immediacy ("As you were just talking, I realized that I feel uncomfortable when you raise your voice").

Although additional research is needed to better understand how helpers' use of self-disclosure influences their relationships with child/adolescent clients and parent/teacher consultees, there is ample research to suggest that careful attention to self-disclosures is warranted. Creed and Kendall (2005) found that a helper "emphasizing common ground" (p. 503) with children might damage the helping relationship. Creed and Kendall provide examples of self-disclosures that children might perceive to be disingenuous and that might lead children to find helpers insincere. For example: "You're the goalie for your hockey team? I played hockey for years!" (p. 504).

Below is an illustration of an appropriate and inappropriate self-disclosure with the example of Mr. Singleton. In the inappropriate self-disclosure, too much personal information is shared, risking a change in focus from the consultee's concerns to the helper's needs.

Mr. Singleton: "My ex-wife and I don't see eye-to-eye on what's best for Sam."

Inappropriate self-disclosure by school psychologist: "I understand how that feels. My husband and I argue all the time about how to raise our daughters. We've almost landed in divorce court over it!"

Appropriate self-disclosure by school psychologist: "I understand how that feels. My husband and I have sometimes had to work hard to understand each other's point of view about our daughters."

Feedback. Feedback has been demonstrated to be an influential helper strategy in both direct services and consultation. In the context of professional helping relationships, feedback is considered to be "information provided to a person from an external source about the person's behavior or its effects" (Claiborn, Goodyear, & Horner, 2002, p. 217). Researchers have identified four general types of feedback content: (a) observation or description of a client's behavior, (b) emotional reaction to a client's behavior, (c) inference about something not directly observable in a client, and (d) mirroring of client's behavior (Claiborn et al., 2002). Each of the four types of feedback content is illustrated below using the example of Anna.

Observation: The school psychologist says to Anna, "You were quiet in class today."

Emotional reaction: The school psychologist says to Anna, "I am happy that you came to see me today. I'm looking forward to getting to know you."

Inference: The school psychologist says to Anna, "During my observation of your class this morning, I sensed that you were unclear about the directions for the activity."

Mirroring: The school psychologist models for Anna the posture and affect that she exhibited during class today.

Research findings indicate that positive feedback is generally more acceptable to clients than negative feedback, and the acceptability of negative feedback to clients is enhanced when it is given in the context of a trusting relationship and preceded by positive feedback (Claiborn et al., 2002).

Within a consultation framework, providing frequent performance feedback to teachers has been shown to improve the integrity with which interventions are implemented and thus enhance student outcomes

(Noell et al., 2005). School psychologists can give teachers feedback that includes graphical representations of student outcome data and teacher intervention implementation data. Teacher feedback including intervention implementation data is particularly essential in maintaining intervention integrity (Noell et al., 2005).

Table 2 provides suggestions for using helper strategies with clients and consultees.

Reader Reflection

Consider the personal attributes (e.g., warmth, genuineness, trustworthiness) you bring to your contacts with clients and consultees:

- What are your interpersonal strengths?
- What attributes do you want to strengthen?

Consider the interpersonal strategies you use in your work with clients and consultees.

- Identify examples of your use of self-disclosure, empathy, and positive regard.
- Analyze the effectiveness of your use of these strategies with clients/consultees.

Client/Consultee Factors That Influence Helping Relationships

There are a number of client factors that exist prior to the establishment of a treatment relationship and which influence the development of the helping relationship. The unique characteristics that children and their families bring to treatment ultimately have an impact on the therapeutic relationship and consequently treatment outcomes (Karver et al., 2005). In fact, research has demonstrated that 30% of the variance in therapy outcomes can be accounted for by pretreatment characteristics (Norcross & Lambert, 2006).

Student Age/Developmental Status

Because school psychologists' primary clients are children and adolescents, it is particularly important to consider the role of a child's developmental status when forming relationships and planning interventions. When working with children directly and with parents and teachers in consultation regarding children, school psychologists must consider a child's developmental course. A child's development may deviate from typical

Table 2. Recommendations for Using Helper Strategies to Facilitate Effective Helping Relationships

Empathy: Involves responding to the content of the client's/consultee's statements and can improve intervention outcomes.
- Respond to both the content and affect of the client's/consultee's statements and presentation of affect
- Use empathy to respond to central messages of the client/consultee
- Be careful not to mind read or infer too much about how the client/consultee is feeling
- Avoid stating or implying that you know exactly how the client/consultee feels
- Seek clarification if you do not understand what the client is conveying
- Use nonverbal behavior to convey empathy (e.g., body position, facial expression, eye contact, head nodding)
- Provide empathy to all persons in conflict (students and teachers, parents and teachers, students and parents)

Positive regard: Includes demonstrating a sense of commitment to and acceptance of the client/consultee as an individual, which can facilitate development of helping relationships.
- Be on time for sessions and meetings
- Follow through with promises (e.g., identifying community resources, making follow-up phone calls)
- Express warmth through nonverbal and verbal cues
- Be clear about areas of professional competence and utilize appropriate resources, consultation, or training for areas outside of defined competence
- Refrain from passing critical judgment on the clients' decisions except when client safety is involved
- Make a concerted effort to understand the client/consultee and his or her perspective on the referral issue (e.g., culture, values and beliefs, personal experiences)

Self-disclosure: Can be used infrequently for specific purposes to promote positive short-term client outcomes.
- Use self-disclosure for specific purposes to facilitate the helping relationship or improve intervention outcomes
- Consider the content of self-disclosure carefully; self-disclosure becomes inappropriate when it is self-serving or includes information that is not acceptable for discussion in the context of a professional relationship
- Limit self-disclosure to infrequent use

Feedback: Can improve integrity of intervention implementation and help raise the client's awareness of factors influencing referral issues.
- Make negative feedback constructive so the client is given suggestions for how to change behavior
- Balance constructive feedback with positive feedback
- Give specific examples to illustrate important points
- Consider timing of feedback; be sensitive to times when the client/consultee may not accept feedback

development on numerous dimensions (e.g., biological, cognitive, emotional, and social) which may have an impact on functioning in domains such as emotional regulation, self-control, and behavioral autonomy (Holmbeck, Neff Greenley, & Franks, 2003). It is important to consider the impact of age and development on the ability of the child to develop a helping relationship and to participate in direct intervention. Often, interventions with young children are best implemented through consultation with parents and teachers. As Shirk and Karver (2006) pointed out, "It is unclear whether young children, in particular, understand the relationship between treatment goals, therapy activities, and the role of the therapist" (p. 480).

Table 3 provides recommendations for accounting for developmental status when building relationships with children and adolescents. Although the table describes suggestions across school levels, it is important

to recognize that development is a fluid process and that each student is unique. Additionally, it is important to note that children may regress to an earlier developmental stage in times of stress and conflict (Murphy & Christner, 2006).

Student Functional Impairment

Functional impairment refers to the severity of a problem as well as the areas of the student's life in which there is diminished functioning (e.g., classroom behavior, academic achievement; Beutler, Harwood, Alimohamed, & Malik, 2002). In developing a helping relationship with a student it is important to determine the student's level of functional impairment as research has shown that level of functional impairment relates to capacity to build helping relationships. Also, individuals with lower levels of impairment typically have more positive treatment outcomes (Norcross & Lambert, 2006).

Table 3. Strategies for Building Helping Relationships With Students

Age level	Recommendations for establishing a helping relationship
Preschool	• Involve parents in treatment; develop positive relationship with the parents • Demonstrate for the child that you have formed a working alliance with the parents to help the child see you as trustworthy • Provide a warm, friendly environment • Use strategies that are appealing to the client; consider incorporating games/toys into the intervention • Sit at the child's level during sessions • Tailor length of sessions to the child's ability to remain engaged • Recognize the child's language capacity; use concrete terms regarding assessment and intervention • Avoid strategies that require hypothetical thinking (e.g., role-playing) • Recognize that the child may have difficulty taking others' perspectives
Elementary/ middle school	• Provide a warm, friendly environment • Evaluate the importance of developing a therapeutic relationship with the child's parents to help the student perceive you as trustworthy • Provide empathy regarding the student's concerns • Involve the student in decision making (e.g., goal setting) • Recognize the increasing importance of the student's peer group and consider including peers in interventions • Consider using games with structured rules when getting to know students or teaching new skills (e.g., social skills) • Recognize the student's limited ability for abstract thinking; use examples when possible • Use strategies that emphasize identification of feelings
High school	• Respect the student's increasing need for autonomy and sense of identity • Provide empathy regarding the student's concerns • Avoid confrontation and passing judgment on the student's decisions (except when they impact student safety) • Recognize that peers are very important and consider incorporating the student's peers in treatment • Refrain from belittling the student's problem(s) and avoid providing false hope (e.g., "Every teenager goes through this. You will definitely get through it.") • Limit your use of self-disclosure to avoid appearing as if you are trying to impress the student • Demonstrate positive regard by establishing trust with the student; stress confidentiality in the treatment • Recognize that the student may be experiencing family conflicts and changing relationships with parents; determine the impact of involving parents in the treatment • Involve the student in treatment planning and decisions (e.g., goal setting and strategy selection) • Consider discussing the stage-of-change concept openly with the student; motivational interviewing strategies may be helpful with students of this age

Note. Source: Holmbeck et al. (2003); McConaughy (2005); Murphy and Christner (2006).

A student's level of functional impairment may be influenced by a number of factors, including (a) his or her level of social support, (b) problems with relationships at school and home, (c) comorbid conditions, (d) duration of the problem, (e) severity of the problem, and (f) cognitive impairment and difficulties with self-care (e.g., Beutler, Harwood, et al., 2002). Among these factors, research has demonstrated that social support is one of the most important correlates of functional impairment (Beutler, Harwood, et al., 2002; Demaray & Malecki, 2002). Higher levels of social support are typically associated with lower levels of functional impairment. Moreover, the student's self-reported level of distress and amount of perceived social support has been shown to have an impact on treatment outcomes (Beutler, Harwood, et al., 2002). Students with high levels of impairment may require a longer intervention or referral to community services. For students with low levels of social support, it may be helpful to consider implementing a group intervention that may assist in enhancing the student's social relationships (see Keenan & Tobin, chapter 94, vol. 4).

Example: Anna has missed a significant portion of the school year and is feeling overwhelmed. Although she appears to get along well with her parents, she does not have many peer social relationships. As part of Anna's intervention, it may be helpful to consider implementing a group intervention with other ninth-grade students with similar concerns about school to increase her social support.

Coping Style

Coping styles are defined as "habitual and enduring patterns of behavior that characterize the individual when confronting new or problematic situations" (Beutler et al., 2002, p. 147). Coping styles have been found to be heritable and relatively stable (e.g., Eysenck, 1967). Research with adult populations in treatment has demonstrated that a client's coping style moderates intervention outcomes (Beutler, Harwood, et al., 2002). Research with children (e.g., Shirk & Karver, 2003) suggests that coping style can influence a child's formation of treatment relationships and engagement in treatment.

Coping styles are often described as either internalizing or externalizing. These types are not dichotomous; rather, they exist on a continuum, and clients may display characteristics of both styles. An internalizing coping style is typically marked by withdrawal, introspection, and self-blame, whereas an externalizing

style is characterized by impulsivity, expressiveness, and a tendency to blame others (Eysenck, 1967; Shirk & Karver, 2003).

Studies with adult populations have shown that individuals with externalizing coping styles benefit from interventions that are focused on skill building and symptom change (Calvert, Beutler, & Crago, 1988). Individuals with internalizing coping styles often benefit from treatment that offers understanding, increases self-efficacy and perception of control over the situation, and is interpersonally oriented (Calvert et al., 1988; Castonguay & Beutler, 2006). Shirk and Karver (2003) found that children with externalizing disorders showed greater difficulty than children with internalizing disorders forming alliances and remaining in treatment. Shirk and Karver concluded that formation of treatment alliances with children with externalizing disorders may be both more difficult, due to hostility and interpersonal difficulties, and more critical.

Example: Anna displays an internalizing coping style. She may benefit from an intervention that focuses on understanding the conditions contributing to her difficulties and on the interpersonal issues that she is facing. Also, she may benefit from intervention that increases her self-efficacy in addressing these issues.

Understanding adult coping styles can also be beneficial for school psychologists. In a consultative relationship, it is important to recognize how a consultee (e.g., teacher, parent) approaches challenging situations. In particular, knowing the consultee's style of coping may assist the school psychologist in creating an acceptable treatment plan to benefit the target student. Finally, when children are faced with stress, they tend to observe the reactions of others to help them deal with the situation (Murphy & Christner, 2006). Therefore, knowledge of a family's coping style can help in understanding the child's own reaction to a given situation.

Stage of Change

An important client/consultee factor that influences helping relationships and outcomes is the attitude of the client/consultee toward change. Numerous theories of change have been developed that help explain the change process and factors that can influence a client's attitude toward change. One of most useful models is the trans-theoretical model (TTM) developed by Prochaska and colleagues (e.g., Prochaska,

DiClemente, & Norcross, 1992). A significant body of evidence with clients with addictive and heath-related behaviors suggests that clients move through the change process in stages through which they cycle in a spiral manner, and relapse and recycling through the stages is common. The TTM identifies six stages of change through which an individual may progress, from (a) precontemplation, in which a client has no intention to change, to (b) contemplation, in which a client is thinking of changing, to (c) preparation, in which a client is taking initial steps toward change, to (d) action, in which the client has made specific steps toward change, to (e) maintenance, in which a client attempts to safeguard changes already made, and, finally, to (f) termination, in which the client no longer requires treatment. Prochaska and Norcross (2002) warn against treating all clients as if they are in the action stage. Research regarding the TTM suggests that clients need different interventions at different stages of change.

Recent research regarding motivational interviewing (e.g., Miller & Rollnick, 2002) also suggests that clients in different stages of change require different interventions. Motivational interviewing theory asserts that clients move through phases in developing a commitment to change, from building motivation to change (phase one) to strengthening their commitment (phase two). The motivational interviewing literature indicates that when clients have not yet made a commitment to change, specific strategies to help them recognize the need for and benefits of change are required. Both the TTM and motivational interviewing rely on the construct of decisional balance to explain and facilitate change. Decisional balance theory suggests that people considering change weigh (consciously or unconsciously) the costs and benefits of change (Miller & Rollnick, 2002). Particularly when clients are in the contemplation stage of change, the goal of the helper is to assist the client in tipping the balance toward change. The TTM and motivational interviewing also both draw upon the concept of self-efficacy, the individual's assessment of his/her ability to perform a task (Bandura, 1997), in facilitating change. When clients are considering change, helping them believe they are capable of change can increase their commitment to change itself. The TTM model of change and motivational interviewing strategies are being increasingly applied to child/adolescent populations

Prochaska and Norcross (2002) and Miller and Rollnick (2002) suggested that not only do the specific strategies used by helpers across stages need to be

tailored to the individual client's stage of change, but the role of the helper requires adaptation as well. Table 4 describes the stages of change and helper roles and strategies that are appropriate for each stage.

Stages of change, as conceptualized in the TTM, have not been applied directly to consultation relationships, yet some models of consultation are stage based and clearly articulate the importance of the relationship-building phase in consultation. Some models of consultation, for example consultee-centered consultation (e.g., Lambert, 2004), place a high level of emphasis on the interpersonal nature of the consultation relationship and the importance of the relationship early in the consultation process.

Below are examples of application of stage-of-change principles in direct service and consultation:

> *Anna (student):* Anna may be in the preparation stage of change. She may have already attempted to reduce her anxiety unsuccessfully. She may need increased self-efficacy and assistance anticipating barriers.
>
> *Ms. Walker (teacher):* Ms. Walker may not yet be thinking of changing her own behavior. She is interested in changing the behavior of her students, but she may not be aware of the need to improve her classroom management. The school psychologist may want to provide empathy and help increase Ms. Walker's awareness of the scope of the problem.

Expectations and Preferences
Client/consultee expectations and preferences can influence the development of helping relationships and outcomes of interventions in both adolescents and adults (Dew & Bickman, 2005). Castonguay and Beutler (2006) noted that, particularly in clients with anxiety and substance abuse, clients with more positive expectations are likely to have more positive outcomes. Research has also indicated that parents with higher expectations for intervention outcomes perceive fewer barriers to treatment than parents with negative expectations (Kerkorian et al., 2006). These findings suggest that examining client/consultee expectations and addressing negative expectations may be influential for school psychologists in work with students, parents, and teachers. Conveying to clients/consultees that the helper has seen this problem before and that there are successful interventions available can increase the client's/consultee's hope and confidence that a solution is possible. Assessing client's/consultee's preferences for

Table 4. Client Stages of Change and Helper Roles and Strategies

Stage of change	Role of helper	Helper strategies
Precontemplation: The client has no intention to change behavior in the foreseeable future	*Helper acts as a nurturing facilitator:* • To understand why client is not considering change • To help motivate client to consider change	• Use empathy and reflective listening • Avoid arguments and advice • Identify pros and cons of the current situation • Provide a menu of options • Explore barriers • Instill hope; increase client self-efficacy
Contemplation: The client is aware a problem exists but is not yet committed to change	*Helper acts as a guide:* • To help the client understand problems • To help the client shift the decisional balance toward change • To help the client believe change is possible	• Ask questions to help the client clarify concerns • Assess how long the client has been contemplating change • Help the client identify risks and benefits of change • Provide accurate and relevant information and feedback • Affirm self-motivational statements • Help the client increase self-efficacy
Preparation: The client is intending to take action soon and has undertaken unsuccessful efforts in the past	*Helper acts as an experienced coach:* • To help the client anticipate or address barriers • To help the client believe change is possible	• Use careful listening and reflection • Help the client recognize ambivalence about change • Present a range of options to the client • Help the client evaluate options • Provide feedback on the client's choices • Instill hope and address self-efficacy
Action: The client has commitment to change and has taken overt behavioral action	*Helper acts as a consultant:* • To provide assistance as the client implements change plan • To help the client maintain commitment to change	• Help the client recognize conflicting feelings about change • Evaluate/revise the client's change plan • Provide affirmation about the client's accomplishments • Continue to instill hope and address self-efficacy
Maintenance: The client is working to maintain gains and/or prevent relapse	*Helper acts as consultant or coach:* • To help the client prevent relapse • To increase the client's recommitment to change in the face of relapse	• Help the client be aware of relapse potential • Encourage ongoing commitment to change • Increase self-efficacy if a relapse occurs • Help the client understand the change cycle

Note. Source: Prochaska and Norcross (2002); Miller and Rollnick (2002).

goals, outcomes, and service delivery types can assist the helper in providing services that are valuable to the client/consultee.

Table 5 summarizes client factors that influence the helping relationship.

Client/Consultee Factors That Interfere With Helping Relationships and Outcomes

Some clients and consultees do not appear motivated to address the concerns that brought them to treatment or consultation. Several factors can influence a client's/consultee's commitment to and participation in treatment and consultation.

Opposition or "resistance." Some clients and consultees, even those who have sought services, can appear hostile or withdrawn or may reject the helper's suggestions. They may do the opposite of what they are asked to do, withdraw from active participation in the helping process, or drop out entirely. There are multiple

perspectives on why clients or consultees might act this way. For example, social influence theory posits that clients may display "resistance" because they perceive the helper to be untrustworthy or not genuine. Reactance theory suggests clients may experience a threat to their freedom when interventions are suggested (e.g., Beutler, Moleiro, et al., 2002). Shirk and Karver (2003) found that adolescents resisted treatment when they perceived that their autonomy was threatened. These theories suggest that helpers must consider their own attributes and behaviors (e.g., genuineness, warmth, and trustworthiness) and examine client factors (e.g., level of functional impairment, type of coping style) that might influence the helping relationship and invoke client opposition.

Low motivation. Miller and Rollnick (2002) suggested that clients with little motivation to change (as is sometimes the case with students referred to school psychologists) are often in the precontemplation stage, and they may remain in this stage for different reasons.

Table 5. Client Factors That Influence Helping Relationships and Outcomes

Client factors	Assessment strategies	Intervention implications
Functional impairment (applies to clients) *Definition:* The severity of the client's problem(s) and the degree to which the client exhibits diminished functioning in daily life (Beutler, Harwood, et al., 2002)	• Complete record review • Conduct observation • Interview the student, parent, teacher • Use norm-referenced measures (e.g., cognitive/academic assessment; social–emotional scales)	• Provide longer treatment to students with higher levels of impairment • Provide group intervention to students with low levels of social support • Consider community referral for students with very high levels of impairment
Coping style (applies to clients and consultees) *Definition:* Habitual and enduring patterns of behavior that characterize the individual when confronting new or problematic situations; typically occur on a continuum of internalizing to externalizing (Beutler et al., 2002)	• Observe during work with the student • Interview the student, parent, teacher regarding past reactions to difficulties • Use norm-referenced measures (e.g., Locus of Control scale on BASC-2)	• Model appropriate coping • Match intervention to coping style • Focus intervention on interpersonal concerns of internalizing students • Use action-oriented interventions with externalizing students
Stage of change (applies to clients and consultees) *Definition:* The client's/consultee's intention to change; may range from lack of awareness of a problem and no intent to change to active efforts to change (Prochaska & Norcross, 2002)	• Ask the client/consultee about his or her commitment to change • Observe the client's/consultee's actions to identify discrepancies between verbalizations and actions	• Assess decisional balance; determine pros and cons of the current situation • Use motivational interviewing strategies • Increase the client's/consultee's self-efficacy beliefs • Affirm small successes
Expectations and preferences (applies to clients and consultees) *Definition:* The outcomes of services anticipated by the client/consultee and the desires of the client/consultee about the types of services (Castonguay & Beutler, 2006)	• Ask the client/consultee what he or she expects from the treatment or the consultation • Identify the client/consultee preferences for types of services • Consider the types and outcomes of previous services to evaluate possible expectations and preferences	• Facilitate positive expectations by addressing the client's/consultee's goals • Address the client/consultee preferences by providing the types of services desired • Reduce barriers to services

Table 6 presents four types of precontemplation and the helper strategies linked to each type.

Working with clients or consultees who are not interested in change may require careful examination of the reasons the client/consultee provides for avoiding change. In direct services the helper can assist the client in recognizing the benefits of change but must give the client the message that the client is in charge of the change process. In consultation relationships, the independence of the consultee must be acknowledged.

Table 6. Strategies for Use With Four Types of Precontemplation

Type of precontemplation	Definition and helper strategies
Reluctant precontemplation	Occurs when a client may not recognize a need for change and is comfortable with the current situation. The helper can provide listening, empathy, and feedback to help the client explore the possibility of change in a nonthreatening context.
Rebellious precontemplation	Signals that a client may have an interest in maintaining the status quo and does not like being told what to do. The helper can agree with the client that no one can make the client change. The helper can provide a menu of options for the client, including small incremental changes, and keep open the possibility of change.
Resigned precontemplation	Occurs when the client is overwhelmed by the problem and has given up on the possibility of change. The helper can explore barriers to change, gradually build confidence and self-efficacy, and affirm even small successes of the client.
Rationalizing precontemplation	Suggests the client can argue against reasons for change and appears to have all the answers. The helper can avoid letting the client talk about reasons for maintaining the status quo and can ask the client to articulate positives about the current situation. This sometimes leads clients to acknowledge negatives as well.

Note. Source: Miller and Rollnick (2002).

Reader Reflection

Consider your current clients and consultees:

- What attributes do they bring to their work with you that influence intervention outcomes?
- How do your clients'/consultees' stages of change influence your work together?
- How can you refine your practice to better incorporate client factors into treatment planning?

Interactive Factors That Influence the Helping Relationship

Interactive factors refer to qualities that influence the interaction between the client and the helper (Castonguay & Beutler, 2006). Particularly critical to client outcomes are the therapeutic alliance and factors of goal consensus and collaboration. Also of interest are personal factors, such as gender and race/ethnicity.

Alliance

The alliance between helper and client/consultee is a critical component of the helping relationship (e.g., Castonguay & Beutler, 2006). The term *therapeutic alliance* originated in the adult psychotherapy literature. However, the term *alliance* has been increasingly applied to relationships with child and adolescent clients and is applicable to the helping relationships school psychologists develop with parents and teachers in consultation. The therapeutic alliance is thought to reflect "the quality and nature of the interaction between the helper and client, the collaborative nature of that interaction on the tasks and goals of treatment, and personal bond or attachment that emerges in treatment" (Kasdin, Marciano, & Whitley, 2005, p. 726). This definition reflects the importance of the affective bonds between helper and client/consultee (e.g., mutual trust, liking, respect) and the cognitive aspects of treatment (goal consensus, commitment to treatment) that comprise helping relationships (Horvath & Bedi, 2002). Shirk and Karver (2006) proposed that the alliance refers to "the client's experience of the therapist as someone that can be counted on for help in overcoming problems or distress" (p. 480). When a strong alliance exists, the client sees the helper on his or her side, "allied against the problems that require treatment" (p. 480).

Most models of psychological treatment and consultation today recognize the importance of the alliance (e.g., Erchul, 2003; Norcross & Lambert, 2006). Nonbehavioral therapies see the alliance as a mechanism of change, a mediating factor through which client change occurs. Behavioral therapies may see the alliance as a moderator, an affective variable related to motivation in therapy (Shirk & Karver, 2003). Yet there is understanding across schools of direct intervention and consultation that a strong alliance between the helper and the client/consultee facilitates positive outcomes.

The alliance is related to engagement and participation in treatment tasks and retention in treatment. Research suggests that there is a need to form strong alliances with both parents and youth to influence youth treatment outcomes. Strong alliances with parents are related to retention in treatment, fewer cancellations and no-shows, and less premature termination. Strong alliances with youth have been shown to result in greater reduction in symptom severity due to greater motivation to work on problems, active participation in treatment and skill acquisition, and increased application of skills outside of treatment (Hawley & Weisz, 2005). When the helping relationship is positive, there is a greater chance that adolescents will remain in treatment and receive an appropriate amount of treatment. Helper characteristics, such as warmth and trustworthiness, facilitate development of the alliance with youth (Shirk & Karver, 2006).

Research has further demonstrated that youth stage of development may strongly influence the importance of the alliance. Because children and youth often do not self-refer for treatment and may not acknowledge the existence of problems, it may be critical for relationships with treatment providers to be positive. The alliance with adolescents is strongest when the helper respects adolescents' developmental need for increased autonomy (e.g., by emphasizing collaboration and confidentiality; Shirk & Karver, 2003). Negative therapist behaviors, such as a take-charge attitude early in treatment, can damage the therapeutic alliance with youth (Creed & Kendall, 2005).

Goal consensus and collaboration.

Collaborative involvement and goal consensus between the helper and the client/consultee significantly improve the therapeutic alliance (e.g., Creed & Kendall, 2005). Recent studies suggest that clients who perceive that treatment will be helpful, who believe their helpers' goals are consistent with their own, and who see the treatment process as collaborative will return for more treatment and will evidence more positive outcomes (e.g., Tryon & Winograd, 2002). Consultation research indicates that when consultees and consultants understand their roles, agree on goals, and work together as a team, outcomes are improved (Sheridan et al., 2004). As discussed by Schulte and Osborne (2003), collaboration has different meanings within different schools of consultation. There is consensus that collaboration between consultant and consultee is a positive aspect of the consultation relationship. However, how consultants and consultees conceptualize collaboration may differ. It is important for consultants to determine the preferences of families and teachers. For example, the degree to which families prefer collaboration over more directive services may vary. Table 7 identifies strategies for helpers to increase goal consensus and collaboration.

Gender, race/ethnicity, culture, and sexual orientation. As attributes of both clients and helpers, gender, race/ethnicity, culture, and sexual orientation are clearly variables that must be attended to in direct services and consultation. Race/ethnicity and culture may significantly influence a client's presentation of problem symptoms and the acceptability of certain interventions (e.g., APA, 2003). School psychologists in their roles as consultants must consider the beliefs, values, language, culture, and norms of the families with whom they work (e.g., Nastasi, 2005).

Direct intervention research has attempted to determine whether matching clients and helpers by gender and race/ethnicity leads to improved client outcomes. Research with adolescent substance abusers (e.g., Wintersteen, Mensinger, & Diamond, 2005) suggests that matching helpers and clients by gender may lead to greater retention in treatment. The authors hypothesized that in adolescence, when gender identification is at its peak, youth may seek affiliation with same-gender role models.

There is ample research demonstrating that minority adult clients prefer to see helpers of their own race/ethnicity, but studies of race/ethnicity matching have not found matching to lead to significantly improved outcomes (e.g., Sue & Lam, 2002). There is evidence, however, that racial matching in adults leads to greater service utilization and retention, which may indirectly influence treatment outcomes (Sue & Lam, 2002). In the Wintersteen et al. (2005) study of adolescents, racial mismatch did have a negative impact on the retention of clients in treatment, especially in dyads of Caucasian helpers and minority youth. Although practitioners in schools may have limited opportunity to match clients/consultees with same gender and race/ethnicity helpers, such matching, when possible, may facilitate retention in treatment. However, it will be important for helpers to consider individual client factors (e.g., client preferences, previous helping relationships, and cultural affiliation) that might increase the likelihood that race/ethnicity matching will influence outcomes.

Lott and Rogers (2005) cautioned that families who are "nonmainstream" may perceive significant barriers to working with school professionals. Some families may be disinclined to challenge professional judgments and may feel (sometimes correctly) that their knowledge is devalued and that they may face significant

Table 7. Strategies to Increase Goal Consensus and Collaboration

Goal consensus	Collaboration with clients	Collaboration with consultees
Working with students, parents, and teachers: • Identify client concerns • Ask questions to ensure accurate understanding of the client concerns • Attend to the client's/consultee's analysis of causes of concerns or problems • Address topics important to the client • Reach consensus on goals at the first interview if possible to facilitate the client/consultee's return • Include the student in teacher/parent interviews when appropriate	Working with student clients in direct services: • Establish a cooperative, friendly approach • Discuss goals frequently • Respect the student's values, beliefs, and preferences • Use shared decision making • Enlist active participation of the student • If using homework, focus homework on the client's concerns/problems • If using homework, review homework regularly	Working with parents and teachers in consultation: • Establish a cooperative, friendly approach • Clarify consultation roles • Discuss goals frequently • Use shared decision making • Respect the consultee's values, beliefs, and preferences • Respect the consultee's autonomy • Consider the consultee's preference for collaborative or directive approach • Avoid jargon • Establish the meetings at times and locations convenient for the consultee

Note. Source: Christenson and Sheridan (2001); Lott and Rogers (2005); Sheridan and Kratochwill (in press); Tyron and Winograd (2002).

racism and discrimination in the school system. As Lott and Rogers noted, "Consultants need to function as facilitators for parents who are not accustomed to advocating for the interests of their children, feel ill-prepared and frustrated in their attempts to do so, and who have often had negative educational experiences themselves" (p. 12). Overall, these findings suggest an ongoing need for multicultural training regarding specific preferences and needs of minority clients and specific competencies required of helpers (APA, 2003).

As Ortiz (2006) suggested, multicultural competence for school psychologists "lies not so much in understanding every unique or idiosyncratic characteristic of cultural groups but more in the ability to recognize when and where cultural issues might be operating in any aspect of practice" (p. 159). In a similar vein, Ingraham and Oka (2006) stressed the importance of avoiding reliance on client/consultee demographic variables, such as race and ethnicity, because these may "mask the variability in the underlying psychological and socioemotional influences on their approach, acceptability, adherence, and experiences with potential interventions" (p. 134). (For additional information on multicultural practice, see Jones, chapter 111, vol. 5.)

School psychologists today work with varied types of families, including families with parents and/or children who are gay, lesbian, bisexual, or transgender (GLBT). To establish effective relationships with GLBT parents and students, school psychologists must work at the system level to ensure that schools are inviting and safe places for all parents and children (Jeltova & Fish, 2005). In addition, they must examine their own individual practices to ensure the use of helper strategies, such as warmth, positive regard, appropriate language, and collaboration, to improve outcomes for children and adolescents.

Examples of strategies for building therapeutic alliances:

Anna: The school psychologist might (a) emphasize autonomy and confidentiality to meet Anna's developmental needs; (b) use warmth, empathy, and positive regard to communicate concern and respect for Anna; (c) address issues of importance to Anna; (d) identify intervention goals early in treatment; (e) use collaborative decision making to enlist Anna's active participation; and (f) consider whether gender or race/ethnicity matching will influence outcomes.

Mr. Singleton: The school psychologist might (a) explore whether racial/cultural issues are affecting the home–school partnership; (b) use warmth to help Mr. Singleton feel welcome at school; (c) provide empathy regarding Mr. Singleton's feelings about his son Sam's disability; (d) use positive regard to help Mr. Singleton understand that the school psychologist values Mr. Singleton's perspective; (e) clarify Mr. Singleton's concerns and goals; (f) stress the common goal of helping Sam; (g) address issues of importance to the family; and (h) use collaborative decision making when designing services.

Ms. Walker: The school psychologist might (a) use warmth to create a comfortable consultation environment; (b) use empathy to reflect understanding of Ms. Walker's frustration and the difficulties teachers face; (c) use positive regard to communicate respect of Ms. Walker as a teacher; (d) emphasize the common goals of helping students learn and helping Ms. Walker feel more efficacious; (e) respect Ms. Walker's analysis of the problem; and (f) use shared decision making to increase collaboration and to indicate respect for Ms. Walker's autonomy.

Repairing the Alliance
Even when helpers work to develop and maintain effective helping relationships, ruptures in the therapeutic and consultation alliance can occur. Ruptures can be defined as a tension or breakdown in the collaborative relationship (Safran, Muran, Samstag, & Stevens, 2002). Safran et al. conceptualize ruptures as consisting of disagreement about the tasks and goals and/or strains in the bond between members of the relationship. At these times helpers must examine the barriers to services, individual client factors, and helper behaviors to determine their impact on the relationship. Research suggests that direct discussion with adults about ruptures in the helping relationship may facilitate strengthening it; however, adolescents may perceive a direct approach as too confrontational and controlling (Creed & Kendall, 2005). Adolescents may benefit instead from recognition of their increasing autonomy and from an emphasis on collaboration (Oetzel & Scherer, 2003) and from helper empathy (Shirk & Karver, 2006). General strategies to use with adults include providing empathy and flexibility, reexamining the goals of consultation or intervention, and clarifying misunderstandings (Castonguay & Beutler, 2006; Safran et al., 2002). Table 8 identifies specific strategies to use with problems helpers frequently encounter in schools.

Table 8. Strategies for Strengthening Alliances With Clients and Consultees

Problem examples	Strategies
Client/consultee does not attend sessions	• Examine barriers to services • Examine expectations and preferences • Consider the referral issue: Is the appropriate issue identified? • Identify the client's/consultee's stage of change • Focus on collaboration
Client/consultee is passive, does not participate actively	• Match interventions to the stage of change • Use empathy to convey understanding • Identify the client/consultee's goals; increase the goal consensus • Examine the client's coping style • Use specific strategies to enlist commitment (e.g., motivational interviewing)
Client/consultee is angry or resentful of referral for services	• Use empathy to convey understanding • Express positive regard; avoid blaming and rejecting • Address the alliance directly (parents and teachers) • Do not address the alliance directly (adolescents) • Examine the client's coping style • Match interventions to the stage of change
Client/consultee does not follow through on homework or other goal-oriented actions	• Reexamine the goal consensus • Reexamine barriers • Clarify the referral issue • Identify the client's expectations and preferences • Review homework regularly

Note. Source: Beutler, Moleiro, et al. (2002); Shirk and Karver (2003); Karver et al., (2006).

Reader Reflection

• Identify one strong alliance you have developed with a client or consultee: What factors helped you develop this strong alliance?

• Identify one client or consultee with whom you have struggled to develop an alliance: What strategies might you use/have used to strengthen your alliance?

SUMMARY

The helping relationship provides a rich and crucial context within which school psychologists can influence student outcomes. Crafting strong, positive relationships with students, parents, and teachers will allow school psychologists to develop interventions that respect the individual characteristics, preferences, and needs of the client/consultee. In addition to considering individual client/consultee factors that influence the development of helping relationships, school psychologists can capitalize on their own attributes (such as warmth and genuineness) and strategies (such as empathy and positive regard) to create strong alliances with students, parents, and teachers. By developing caring treatment relationships while also selecting strategies with strong empirical support, the school psychologist will maximize the effectiveness of school-based practice.

REFERENCES

American Psychological Association, Presidential Task Force on Evidence-Based Practice. (2006). Evidence-based practice in psychology. *American Psychologist, 61*, 271–285.

American Psychological Association. (2003). Guidelines for multicultural education, training, research, practice, and organizational change for psychologists. *American Psychologist, 58*, 377–402.

Bandura, A. (1997). *Self-efficacy: The exercise of control.* New York: W.H. Freeman.

Beutler, L. E., Harwood, M. T., Alimohamed, S., & Malik, M. (2002). Functional impairment and coping style. In J. C. Norcross (Ed.), *Psychotherapy relationships that work: Therapist contributions and responsiveness to patients* (pp. 145–174). New York: Oxford University Press.

Beutler, L. E., Moleiro, C. M., & Talebi, H. (2002). Resistance. In J. C. Norcross (Ed.), *Psychotherapy relationships that work: Therapist contributions and responsiveness to patients* (pp. 129–143). New York: Oxford University Press.

Bohart, A. C., Elliott, R., Greenberg, L. S., & Watson, J. C. (2002). Empathy. In J. C. Norcross (Ed.), *Psychotherapy relationships that work: Therapist contributions and responsiveness to patients* (pp. 89–108). New York: Oxford University Press.

Calvert, S. J., Beutler, L. E., & Crago, M. (1988). Psychotherapy outcomes as a function of therapist-patient matching on selected variables. *Journal of Social and Clinical Psychology*, *6*, 104–117.

Castonguay, L. C., & Beutler, L. E. (Eds.). (2006). *Principles of therapeutic change that work*. New York: Oxford University Press.

Christenson, S. L., & Sheridan, S. M. (2001). *Schools and families: Creating essential connections for learning*. New York: Guilford Press.

Claiborn, C. D., Goodyear, R. K., & Horner, P. A. (2002). Feedback. In J. C. Norcross (Ed.), *Psychotherapy relationships that work: Therapist contributions and responsiveness to Patients* (pp. 217–233). New York: Oxford University Press.

Creed, T. A., & Kendall, P. C. (2005). Therapist alliance-building behavior within a cognitive–behavioral treatment for anxiety in youth. *Journal of Consulting and Clinical Psychology*, *73*, 498–505.

Cormier, S., & Nurius, P. S. (2003). *Interviewing and change strategies for helpers: Fundamental skills and cognitive-behavior interventions* (5th ed.). Pacific Grove, CA: Brooks/Cole.

Demaray, M. K., & Malecki, C. K. (2002). Critical levels of perceived social support associated with student adjustment. *School Psychology Quarterly*, *17*, 213–241.

Dew, S. E., & Bickman, L. (2005). Client expectancies about therapy. *Mental Health Services Research*, *7*, 21–33.

Erchul, W. P. (2003). Communication and interpersonal processes in consultation: Guest editor's comments. *Journal of Educational and Psychological Consultation*, *14*, 105–107.

Eysenck, H. J. (1967). *The biological basis of personality*. Springfield, IL: Thomas.

Farber, B. A., & Lane, J. S. (2002). Positive regard. In J. C. Norcross (Ed.), *Psychotherapy relationships that work: Therapist contributions and responsiveness to patients* (pp. 175–194). New York: Oxford University Press.

Hawley, K. M., & Weisz, J. R. (2005). Youth versus parent working alliance in usual clinical care: Distinctive associations with retention, satisfaction, and treatment outcome. *Journal of Clinical Child and Adolescent Psychology*, *34*, 117–128.

Hinshaw, S. P. (2002). President's message. Explanation in treatment research: Moderators and mediators. *Clinical Child and Adolescent Psychology Newsletter*, *17*(2), 1–3.

Holmbeck, G. N., Neff Greenley, R., & Franks, E. A. (2003). Developmental issues and considerations in research and practice. In A. E. Kazdin & J. R. Weisz (Eds.), *Evidence-based psychotherapies for children and adolescents* (pp. 21–41). New York: Guilford Press.

Horvath, A. O., & Bedi, R. P. (2002). The alliance. In J. C. Norcross (Ed.), *Psychotherapy relationships that work: Therapist contributions and responsiveness to patients* (pp. 37–69). New York: Oxford University Press.

Ingraham, C. L., & Oka, E. (2006). Multicultural issues in evidence-based interventions. *Journal of Applied School Psychology*, *22*, 127–149.

Jeltova, I., & Fish, M. C. (2005). Creating school environments responsive to gay, lesbian, bisexual, and transgender families: Traditional and systemic approaches for consultation. *Journal of Educational and Psychological Consultation*, *16*, 17–33.

Karver, M. S., Handelsman, J. B., Fields, S., & Bickman, L. (2005). A theoretical model of common process factors in youth and family therapy. *Mental Health Services Research*, *7*, 35–51.

Karver, M. S., Handelsman, J. B., Fields, S., & Bickman, L. (2006). Meta-analysis of therapeutic relationship variables in youth and family therapy: The evidence for different relationship variables in the child and adolescent treatment outcome literature. *Clinical Psychology Review*, *26*, 50–65.

Kasdin, A. E., Marciano, P. L., & Whitley, M. K. (2005). The therapeutic alliance in cognitive-behavioral treatment of children referred for oppositional, aggressive, and antisocial behavior. *Journal of Consulting and Clinical Psychology*, *73*, 726–730.

Kerkorian, D., McKay, M., & Bannon, W. M. (2006). Seeking help a second time: Parents'/caregivers' characterizations of previous experiences with mental health services for their children and perceptions of barriers to future use. *American Journal of Orthopsychiatry*, *76*, 161–166.

Knox, S., & Hill, C. E. (2003). Therapist self-disclosure: Research-based suggestions for practitioners. *Journal of Clinical Psychology*, *59*, 529–539.

Lambert, N. (2004). Consultee-centered consultation: An international perspective on goals, process, and theory. In N. Lambert, I. Hylander, & J. Sandoval (Eds.), *Consultee-centered consultation: Improving the quality of professional services in schools and community organizations* (pp. 3–19). Mahwah, NJ: Erlbaum.

Lott, B., & Rogers, M. R. (2005). School consultants working for equity with families, teachers, and administrators. *Journal of Educational and Psychological Consultation*, *16*, 1–16.

McConaughy, S. H. (2005). *Clinical interviews for children and adolescents: Assessment to intervention*. New York: Guilford Press.

McKay, M. M., & Bannon, W. M. (2004). Engaging families in child mental health services. *Child and Adolescent Psychiatric Clinics of North America*, *13*, 905–921.

Miller, W. R., & Rollnick, S. (2002). *Motivational interviewing: Preparing people for change* (2nd ed.). New York: Guilford Press.

Murphy, V. B., & Christner, R. W. (2006). A cognitive–behavioral case conceptualization approach for working with children and adolescents. In R. B. Menutti, A. Freeman, & R. W. Christner (Eds.), *Cognitive-behavioral interventions in educational settings: A handbook for practice* (pp. 37–62). New York: Routledge.

Nastasi, B. K. (2005). School consultants as change agents in achieving equity for families in public schools. *Journal of Educational and Psychological Consultation, 16,* 113–125.

Noell, G. H., Witt, J. C., Slider, N. J., Connell, J. E., Gatti, S. L., Williams, K. S., et al. (2005). Treatment implementation following behavioral consultation in schools: A comparison of three follow-up strategies. *School Psychology Review, 34,* 87–106.

Norcross, J. C. (Ed.). (2002). *Psychotherapy relationships that work: Therapist contributions and responsiveness to patients.* New York: Oxford University Press.

Norcross, J. C., & Lambert, M. J. (2006). The therapy relationship. In J. C. Norcross, L. E. Beutler, & R. F. Levant (Eds.), *Evidence-based practices in mental health: Debate and dialogue on the fundamental questions* (pp. 208–218). Washington, DC: American Psychological Association.

Oetzel, K. B., & Scherer, D. G. (2003). Therapeutic engagement with adolescents in psychotherapy. *Psychotherapy: Theory, Research, Practice, Training, 40,* 215–225.

Ortiz, S. O. (2006). Multicultural issues in school psychology practice: A critical analysis. *Journal of Applied School Psychology, 22,* 151–167.

Pianta, R. C. (1999). *Enhancing relationships between children and teachers.* Washington, DC: American Psychological Association.

Prochaska, J. O., DiClemente, C. C., & Norcross, J. C. (1992). In search of how people change: Applications to addictive behaviors. *American Psychologist, 47,* 1102–1114.

Prochaska, J. O., & Norcross, J. C. (2002). Stages of change. In J. C. Norcross (Ed.), *Psychotherapy relationships that work: Therapist contributions and responsiveness to patients* (pp. 303–313). New York: Oxford University Press.

Riley-Tillman, T. C., Chafouleas, S. M., Eckert, T. S., & Kelleher, C. (2005). Bridging the gap between research and practice: A framework for building research agendas in school psychology. *Psychology in the Schools, 42,* 459–473.

Rogers, C. (1980). *A way of being.* Boston: Houghton Mifflin.

Safran, J. D., Muran, J. C., Samstag, L. W., & Stevens, C. (2002). Repairing alliance ruptures. In J. C. Norcross (Ed.), *Psychotherapy relationships that work: Therapist contributions and responsiveness to patients* (pp. 235–254). New York: Oxford University Press.

Schulte, A. C., & Osborne, S. S. (2003). When assumptive worlds collide: A review of definitions of collaboration in consultation. *Journal of Educational and Psychological Consultation, 14,* 109–138.

Sheridan, S. M., Erchul, W. P., Brown, M. S., Dowd, S. E., Warnes, E. D., Marti, D. C., et al. (2004). Perceptions of helpfulness in conjoint behavioral consultation: Congruence and agreement between teachers and parents. *School Psychology Quarterly, 19,* 121–140.

Sheridan, S. M., & Kratochwill, T. R. (in press). *Conjoint behavioral consultation: Promoting family–school connections and interventions.* New York: Springer.

Shirk, S. R., & Karver, M. (2003). Prediction of treatment outcome from relationship variables in child and adolescent therapy: A meta-analytic review. *Journal of Consulting and Clinical Psychology, 71,* 452–464.

Shirk, S. R., & Karver, M. (2006). Process issues in cognitive-behavioral therapy for youth. In P. C. Kendall (Ed.), *Child and adolescent therapy: Cognitive-behavioral procedures* (3rd ed., pp. 465–491). New York: Guilford Press.

Shirk, S. R., Karver, M., & Spirito, A. (2003, November). *Relationship processes in youth CBT: Measuring alliance and collaboration.* Paper presented at the annual meeting of the Association for the Advancement of Behavior Therapy, Boston.

Sue, S., & Lam, A. G. (2002). Cultural and demographic diversity. In J. C. Norcross (Ed.), *Psychotherapy relationships that work: Therapist contributions and responsiveness to patients* (pp. 401–421). New York: Oxford University Press.

Tryon, G. T., & Winograd, G. (2002). Goal consensus and collaboration. In J. C. Norcross (Ed.), *Psychotherapy relationships that work: Therapist contributions and responsiveness to patients* (pp. 109–125). New York: Oxford University Press.

Wampold, B. E. (2001). *The great psychotherapy debate: Models, methods, and findings.* Mahwah, NJ: Erlbaum.

Wintersteen, M. B., Mensinger, J. L., & Diamond, G. S. (2005). Do gender and racial differences between patient and therapist affect therapeutic alliance and treatment retention in adolescents? *Professional Psychology: Research and Practice, 36,* 400–408.

Ysseldyke, J., Burns, M., Dawson, P., Kelley, B., Morrison, D., Ortiz, S., et al. (2006). *School psychology: A blueprint for training and practice III.* Bethesda, MD: National Association of School Psychologists.

ANNOTATED BIBLIOGRAPHY

Castonguay, L. C., & Beutler, L. E. (Eds.). (2006). *Principles of therapeutic change that work.* New York: Oxford University Press.

An excellent reference summarizing the principles of therapeutic change identified in psychological research. Participant and technique factors influencing outcomes with clients with a range of presenting problems are identified.

Karver, M. S., Handelsman, J. B., Fields, S., & Bickman, L. (2006). Meta-analysis of therapeutic relationship variables in youth and family therapy: The evidence for different relationship variables in the child and adolescent treatment outcome literature. *Clinical Psychology Review, 26,* 50–65.

Presents the findings of a meta-analysis of relationship factors influencing intervention outcomes with youth and families.

Norcross, J. C. (Ed.). (2002). *Psychotherapy relationships that work: Therapist contributions and responsiveness to patients*. New York: Oxford University Press.

Presents the work of the American Psychological Association Division 29's Task Force on Empirically Supported Relationships. It provides a comprehensive analysis of the effective and promising elements of the relationship between helper and client.

Sheridan, S. M., & Kratochwill, T. R. (in press). *Conjoint behavioral consultation: Promoting family-school connections and interventions*. New York: Springer.

Provides a description of the process of conjoint behavioral consultation, including a chapter on building the relationship between the consultant and the consultee.

102 Best Practices in Implementing Effective Problem-Solving Teams

Matthew K. Burns
Hilda Ives Wiley
Emily Viglietta
University of Minnesota

OVERVIEW

The role of a school psychologist has been debated for more than 50 years with entire books, journals, and conference proceedings dedicated to the topic. Practitioners report that opportunities to engage in activities beyond traditional special education eligibility assessments are highly related to increased job satisfaction, which suggests that consultation and provision of mental health services in the schools is the desired role of school psychologists (VanVoorhis & Levinson, 2006). The response-to-intervention (RTI) approach has been linked to enhanced outcomes for children (Burns, Appleton, & Stehouwer, 2005) and could be a venue for school psychologists to engage in more desirable professional activities (Canter, 2006). Participation in RTI procedures directly involves school psychologists in data-based decision making, consultation, and intervention implementation to such a level that the amount of time engaged in traditional special education evaluations decreases (Burns & Coolong-Chaffin, 2006).

Multidisciplinary problem-solving teams (PST) are a frequent component of RTI models that directly involve school psychologists (Burns & Ysseldyke, 2005), but the actual practices in which individual schools engage in the name of problem solving can vary significantly (Buck, Polloway, Smith-Thomas, & Cook, 2003). This inconsistency in implementation suggests a "significant flaw" in the PST model that could be a major obstacle in implementing RTI on a national level (Burns, Vanderwood, & Ruby, 2005, p. 101).

The origins of PSTs can be traced to the Prereferral Intervention Team (PIT) model presented by Graden and colleagues (Graden, Casey, & Bonstrom, 1985; Graden, Casey, & Christenson, 1985), later called Intervention Assistance Teams (Graden, 1989), which was defined as a collaborative problem-solving approach to increase teacher effectiveness and support students who were difficult to teach (Graden, Casey, & Christenson, 1985). Several names and different approaches to PIT have since evolved, with meaningful differences between them (Burns et al, 2005). Generally speaking, the different models of PIT followed these five basic steps: (a) request for consultation, (b) consultation, (c) observation, (d) conference, and, if needed, (e) formal referral for special education eligibility (Burns & Symington, 2002).

The essential differences between PITs and PSTs are that PSTs utilize a more systematic problem analysis approach and use data for different decisions than do PITs. Although PITs follow a consistent pattern of the aforementioned five steps, much variation within those steps can occur. However, PST members use procedures associated with behavioral consultation and tend to focus on behavioral analysis techniques (Bergan & Kratochwill, 1990). Data collected within the PST process are used to identify the interventions that lead to student success on an individual, class-wide, and/or school-wide basis, and can be used to determine if the intervention is successful or if special education services should be considered. Thus, PSTs are used to answer resource allocation questions, and PITs are used to screen children for special education eligibility. Although many schools may claim to operate a PST, they probably utilize a model that is more closely aligned with PIT.

PSTs do not rely on problem analysis alone in that they were developed from the concept of collaborative problem solving (Fuchs, Fuchs, & Bahr, 1990; Graden, 1989; Graden et al., 1985; Phillips & McCullough, 1990; Rosenfield & Gravois, 1996), which includes systematically conceptualizing a problem, analyzing factors that contribute to it, implementing interventions to address the problem, and evaluating the effectiveness of the interventions (Allen & Graden, 2002). These components represent a better framework for PSTs to successfully operate within RTI than the five steps of the PIT process because they can operate independent of timing and expected outcome (e.g., prereferral), could be easily applied to various school-based problems, and directly correspond with the RTI process that Tilly (see chapter 2, vol. 1) outlined as a science-based practice.

Although the PST model is intuitively appealing and conceptually sound (Burns et al., 2005), proposed educational practices also require data from applied experimental research to empirically demonstrate effectiveness (Ellis, 2001). A recent meta-analysis found strong mean effects for both system (e.g., reducing special education referrals, placements in special education, and student retentions) and student outcomes (e.g., student time on task, task completion, reading skills, and reduction in academic and behavioral difficulties; Burns & Symington, 2002). A collaborative team approach also reduced the disproportionate representation of minority students in special education (Gravois & Rosenfield, 2006). However, the meta-analytic procedures identified 72 relevant articles, but only 9 included data sufficient enough to warrant inclusion in the analyses (Burns & Symington, 2002) and few examined other relevant variables such as dropout rates, grade retention rates, and school climate.

Basic Considerations

Because PST implementation could be a significant obstacle to a national RTI implementation, we will next discuss the role that PSTs could serve within an RTI model and the potential barriers to PST implementation.

PST in RTI

Tilly (see chapter 2, vol. 1) has outlined three tiers of an RTI model that encompasses all students rather than just those with behavioral and/or academic difficulties. We believe that PSTs are a critical component of RTI

within and across all three tiers. Tier 1 involves quality core instruction and universal screening. A PST would assist in reviewing the screening data and identifying children in need of additional support, but could also serve in the decision-making for curriculum decisions and to closely match student needs and instruction and behavior policies and practices. Tier 2 involves supplemental instruction for the 10–15% of students who are not successful in the core curriculum. The PST could examine student data, decide the type of small group intervention needed and monitor progress of students receiving this intervention. The goal of this process is to identify interventions, not children. In other words, RTI seeks to find the instruction, intervention, and support needed for the child to be successful, not to identify children who require special education. The PST in all three tiers should focus on finding solutions and not identifying severe problems.

The PST could evaluate the severity of a child's needs and determine that support associated with Tier 2 is not sufficient and a more intensive intervention is needed. PSTs could also examine the progress of a child within a tier and determine that the child is making sufficient progress and could be better served in a lower tier (e.g., from Tier 3 to Tier 2). Chapter 15, by Powell-Smith and Ball (vol. 2) seems relevant, and readers are referred to that chapter for information on exiting students from a more intensive service. Finally, PST activities and decisions at Tier 3 involve identifying individual interventions for specific problems, which may require a level of support that can only be provided through special education. Thus, PSTs are a critical part of the special education eligibility process, and the interventions designed and implemented by the team are the key sources of data for eligibility determination (Tilly, 2002).

Potential Barriers

Although PSTs are being implemented with increasing frequency, several barriers to implementation often occur. As stated earlier, the implementation integrity of both the interventions used in the classroom and the PST process are critically important (Burns et al., 2005). Without proper training, teams tend to be inefficient and ineffective (Hayek, 1987). Problem solving does not always come naturally, and team members and educators can be taught to follow explicit steps. Though training may appear time consuming, the benefits of educating practitioners about problem solving and communication strategies eventually pay off. When the steps of problem solving are followed and success ensues, educators are more likely to believe in the process and share their approach with others (Bransford & Stein, 1984).

Although the literature regarding PSTs usually touts the use of a team, the actual format of the team is not widely agreed upon. Some argue against including special education personnel (Henry & Flynt, 1990; Pugach & Johnson, 1989), but teams that included school psychologists and/or special education teachers were found to be more effective than those that did not, perhaps because of specialized skills and training (Burns, 1999). The Pennsylvania Instructional Support Team model involves an instructional support teacher whose entire job is to oversee and facilitate the Instructional Support Team process (Kovaleski, Tucker, & Duffy, 1995). However, many districts may not have the resources to allocate to an entire position.

Within PSTs, the organization and assignment of member roles can also vary among models, with one of the largest differences being the choice of a broad participation model versus a case-manager model. Using the case-manager system, a specific facilitator for each student assumes leadership of the student's case, though the guidelines for choosing this facilitator can vary. Using the case-manager system as opposed to the broad participation model provides the team with a specific individual with whom to consult (Iverson, 2002). A survey that investigated PST leaderships across several states found that 59% of the respondents reported general education personnel were the mandated case manager, 45% reported elementary counselors, 47% reported special education teachers, and 31% reported school psychologists (Buck et al., 2003). However, respondents to this survey frequently reported more than one professional as team leaders. The most frequently endorsed choices for team leader/case manager presents problems because many general education teachers and elementary counselors are not adequately trained in relevant issues such as problem analysis and collaboration. Nonetheless, assigning management responsibilities to a person with a full-time appointment to that single school building is clearly advantageous.

Though problem solving has many team components, the majority of the work is conducted by the general education teacher. Thus, in order for the process to be effective, team members need to assure that the teacher has the necessary support and training to implement interventions and monitor intervention effectiveness. Teacher acceptance can be a slow process (Truscott,

Cosgrove, Meyers, & Eidle-Barkman, 2000) especially when addressing adaptations or classroom environmental changes (Schumm & Vaughn, 1991, 1992), but buy in is a critical component.

The implementation of interventions within PST requires time to see if those interventions are effective. While many team members view their goal as trying to intervene with student problems before considering special education, some teachers feel that teams try too hard to avoid special education (Meyers, Valentino, Meyers, Boretti, & Brent, 1996). Moreover, of the students placed in special education through a PST process, 22% were perceived to be "late" placements who did not qualify for special education services until 1 year after their problem was first brought to the team (Rock & Zigmond, 2001). Pennsylvania's Instructional Support Teams have a 50-school day time limit for instructional support, but most other RTI and PST models do not (Burns & Ysseldyke, 2005). These time-related concerns need to be addressed by researchers, policy makers, and educators as RTI and PST become more widespread.

Best Practices

There are many substantial barriers for schools to overcome if PSTs are to be an effective aspect of RTI. Fortunately, there are many well conceptualized and empirically supported components of the PST process including data-based decision making, collaboration, systemic interventions, problem analysis, parental involvement, and implementation integrity.

Data-Based Decision Making

Data are critical to instruction, intervention, and decision making, and data-based decision making is critical to school psychology (Ysseldyke et al., 2006), to RTI (Tilly, chapter 2, vol. 1), and to the PST process. However, because the PST can focus on student and systemic problems and solutions, individual student and system data are required.

Student Data
The instructional process involves decisions at several stages including planning instruction, managing instruction, delivering instruction, and evaluating instruction (Algozzine, Ysseldyke, & Elliot, 1997). Curriculum-based measurement (CBM; Deno, 1985) is ideally suited to measure the effectiveness of instruction and thus provides critical data to the PST process. The

effectiveness of, and implementation procedures for, CBM are well documented (see Fuchs & Fuchs, chapter 136, vol. 6; Hosp & MacConnell, chapter 22, vol. 2; Howell, chapter 20, vol. 2; Shinn, chapter 14, vol. 2). Thus, readers are referred to one of the many publications regarding this topic for further information.

Although CBM provides useful data, this tool alone will not provide sufficient information for the problem-solving process. Data are also needed to decide what, in addition to if, interventions are needed. Several studies suggest that issues such as matching instructional materials to student skills and needs are also important in developing interventions (Burns, in press; Daly, Martens, Kilmer, & Massie, 1996), and data are also needed to fully inform instruction. Gickling's model of curriculum-based assessment (CBA; Gickling & Havertape, 1981) seems ideally suited to address the instructional planning needs of the PST process (Burns, Dean, & Klar, 2004). Research has found that using CBA to match instructional material and student needs led to increased reading (Burns, 2002; Shapiro, 1992; Shapiro & Ager, 1992) and mathematics (Burns, 2002; Gickling, Shane, & Croskery, 1989) skills, and increased the learning rate of students identified as learning disabled to a point where they achieved a rate of growth that equaled expectations for children without disabilities (Burns, in press). Moreover, CBA data have been shown to have sufficiently reliability for instructional decision making (Burns, Tucker, Frame, Foley, & Hauser, 2000). Gravois and Gickling (chapter 30, vol. 2) address CBA, and readers are referred to it for further information about this assessment model. However, the assessment model used by PSTs should include both CBA to develop interventions and CBM to monitor the effectiveness of the interventions.

Systemic Data

Data regarding individual students are an obvious assessment focus within PST, but data that reflect a systemic perspective to education are also required. For example, PSTs may collect data regarding number of disciplinary infractions for all students during recess, total number of student absences within a particular grade, or the location of the school in which most reported incidence of student physical aggression occur. Moreover, the PST should focus on systemic data of the PST itself because many schools hastily implemented a PST or PIT approach in their interest to develop alternative services delivery programs and did not include an explicit evaluation component (Illback, Zins, Maher, & Greenberg, 1990). As described later,

correct implementation of the PST model is critical and should be assessed. Product assessments should also occur and could include variables such as the percentage of children in the school scoring at the proficient level on state accountability tests, number of students adequately responding to interventions, measures of teacher and parent satisfaction, and aggregated measures of individual student learning.

In addition to PST process and product data, PSTs should also collect and examine other systemic data such as the number of children retained in a grade each year, number of discipline referrals to the school office, number of student absences, frequency of severe behavioral incidents (e.g., student fights), and include measures of school climate such as the Comprehensive Assessment of School Environments (National Association of Secondary School Principals, 1987) or the Student Needs Survey (Burns, Vance, Szadokierski, & Stockwell, 2006). These data may be useful in informing decisions made by PSTs at Tiers 1 and 2 and should be part of the comprehensive assessment model.

Collaboration

Collaboration is a process by which two professionals engage in a nonhierarchical relationship to develop interventions (Rosenfield, 1987). Research on consultation has consistently supported a collaborative approach (Gersten, Morvant, & Brengelman, 1995; Houk & Lewandoski, 1996; Voltz, Elliott, & Harris, 1995; Wickstrom, Jones, LaFleur, & Witt, 1998). Although collaborative consultation is not without its critics (Erchul, 1999), it can lead to increased student learning and enhanced skills by those who engage in it, and it can directly affect systemic variables as well (Idol, Nevin, & Paolucci-Whitcomb, 2000). Thus, we endorse collaboration as a foundation for the PST process.

Collaboration in most PSTs is limited to conferences among a group of professionals, which is too limiting of a role. The standard procession of consultation within a traditional PIT or PST process involves a frustrated teacher seeking consultation from the PIT, which then suggests interventions for the already frustrated teacher to attempt, followed by a referral to the school psychologist to determine special education eligibility and needs. This process involves a shift in responsibility from the teacher to the team, back to the teacher, and then temporarily to the school psychologist. The results of the special education evaluation determines where the responsibility eventually ends in that if the child is determined to require special education services then the responsibility is shifted to the special education teacher, but a conclusion of ineligibility for special education results in a shift back to the referring and now hopelessly discouraged teacher.

Unlike the sequence described above, the PST process should involve a collaborative *sharing* of responsibility rather than a shift. This is best accomplished with immediate, supportive, effective, and lasting collaboration through the PST process shown in Table 1. It is important that the referring teacher feel sufficiently supported in the implementation process. Moreover, collaborative efforts before and after the conference reduce the length of time required at the meeting. The actual PST conference should require no more than 10–15 minutes for each child, as any additional time is usually spent "admiring" the problem rather than solving it (Allen & Graden, 2002, p. 568).

Although the number of professionals involved in a PST could vary among individual PST schools, key personnel to involve include the referring teacher, school psychologist, at least one other general education teacher, a special education teacher, and specialized personnel as needed (e.g., social worker, speech and language pathologist). While administrative support is an important variable for PSTs (Kruger, Struzziereo, Watts, & Vacca, 1989), it may not be necessary for the building principal to be a member of the team to obtain that support. However, it is highly preferable for the principal to be an active member of the PST. We also suggest that the school psychologist, a special education teacher, and one general education teacher be standing members of the PST, and that the building principal be an active supporter if not an actual member.

Perhaps more important than the professional positions of the PST member is the role of each in the PST process. We advocate for identifying a system facilitator who organizes meetings and monitors the steps of the process, a problem-solving facilitator who leads the brainstorming process within a PST conference, and a consultant who meets with the referring teacher before and after the conference. It is not necessary for the same person to always be the problem-solving facilitator or consultant, but one person should be designated as the system facilitator. Assignment of personnel to these roles should be dependent on skill rather than position, but school psychologists are ideally suited to serve as the consultant because of training in consultation, data collection, and behaviorally defining problems.

Problem Analysis

The first step in the problem-solving process is to adequately define the problem for which the student has been referred. The problem must be defined in a way that clearly directs the team to interventions. In a sense, the problem is often obvious to the team upon referral, but until the problem is operationally defined in meaningful and measurable terms, it is inappropriate and unwise to begin considering interventions.

According to Deno (2002), problem solving can be described as the attempt to eliminate the difference between "what is" and "what should be" (p. 38). Once identified, this difference represents the magnitude of the problem. In order to determine the "what is" aspect of the problem, it is important to obtain quantitative data regarding a student's performance. For example, instead of simply stating that a student is facing difficulty in reading and math, the general education teacher

Table 1. Problem-Solving Team Process

Event	Personnel	Activity	Timeline
1. Initial consultation	Referring teacher and consultant	• Behaviorally define problem • Collect baseline data • Brainstorm interventions	Within 2–5 days of initial request for assistance
2. Problem-solving team conference	Problem-solving team	• Conduct problem analysis • Brainstorm interventions • Assign implementation responsibilities to specific personnel	Within 2 weeks of the initial request for assistance
3. Follow-up consultation	Referring teacher and consultant	• Assess teacher's understanding of the intervention • Assess intervention integrity • Problem-solve unforeseen difficulties	Within 3–5 school days after the PST conference
4. Follow-up conference	Problem-solving team	• Examine intervention effectiveness data • Determine if student needs are being met • Identify different interventions as needed	Approximately 2 weeks after the follow-up consultation

could report the average number of words per minute that the student reads or the student's average scores on math homework, both of which could be compared to a standard derived from meaningful criteria or normative data.

Although the difference between "what is" and "what should be" defines the magnitude of the problem, it may not necessarily define the relative importance of the problem. It is crucial to remember that this difference has its roots in academic and social expectations (Deno, 2002). Depending on a variety of individual student characteristics, normative goals in some areas may not be realistic for some students, and may be less important than other goals. For example, a student referred for behavioral problems may have fewer positive peer relationships than what is considered normative. However, if the student's classroom behavior is extremely inappropriate, this behavior problem may bear more relative importance than does the student's number of friends. Once analyzed in relation to a student's individual characteristics and environmental surroundings, a problem may appear more or less relevant to the individual student's welfare.

Because a successful PST process should closely follow problem-analysis procedures, specific steps are necessary and should be documented. A consultant should meet with the referring teacher before and after the PST conference. In order to facilitate and document the process while enhancing communication through the problem-solving stages, we suggest using a form like the one presented in Figure 1. Although the proposed form is based on aspects of the forms used by the Minneapolis Public School Problem-Solving Team (Minneapolis Public Schools, 2002) and the Instructional Consultation Team (Rosenfield & Gravois, 1996), individual districts may need to make modifications based on their unique systems and needs.

Systematic Interventions

As stated above, PSTs were linked to improved systemic outcomes including reduced disproportional representation of minority children in special education (Gravois & Rosenfield, 2006). These findings are important to the practice of school psychology as the field continues to focus more on systemic issues in addition to interventions for individual children (Shapiro, 2000). PSTs are efficient and effective school psychological service delivery models, and systemic decisions are what separate PSTs from PITs. Thus, an effective PST needs to focus on systemic interventions in addition to

instructional and behavioral implications for individual children, and the evolution of school psychological practice would be enhanced by a systems focus for PSTs.

Perhaps successful outcomes associated with PSTs are the direct result of earlier intervention rather than traditional service delivery models. Thus, PSTs should discuss early intervention methods such as positive behavior support, Peer Assisted Learning Strategies (PALS; Fuchs, Fuchs, Mathes, & Simmons, 1997), and Success for All (Slavin & Madden, 2001) using problem-analysis sequence, which includes evaluating the effectiveness of the interventions. These, and other, class- or school-wide interventions would be matched to specific problems identified from data. For example, a class-wide mean mathematics fluency score that was below an instructional level criterion suggested a class-wide fluency problem that was successfully remediated with increased practice through peer tutoring (VanDerHeyden & Burns, 2005). Just as with the PST process for individual students, indicators of a successful intervention should be established a priori and baseline data collected.

A class-wide intervention that is linked to a specific problem could be considered a Tier 2 intervention within the RTI model discussed by Tilly (see chapter 2, vol. 1). However, PSTs should also consider Tier 1 issues as well. For example, the PST could select curricula, write school-wide behavior plans and procedures, evaluate and implement violence prevention programs, brainstorm methods to enhance parental engagement, and examine school climate. Although these decisions would not be interventions for specific problems, they should still be based on data. For example, in deciding what social skills curriculum to implement, the PST should examine research addressing the curricula being considered while examining the external validity of the data as compared to the student population, and evaluating the match between curriculum strengths and school needs.

Parental Involvement

Communication with parents throughout the entire problem-solving process is vital. When a child is first referred to the problem-solving team, his or her parents should be made aware that their child is experiencing difficulty at school if they have not already been contacted. The parents should be invited to participate in meetings, share strategies that they have seen work with their child, and have a say in the intervention that

Figure 1. Problem-Solving Team data collection form.

Student Name:	Grade:	Gender: Female Male
Parent(s):	Referring Teacher:	Date of Referral:

Teacher Concern:

Date of Initial Consultation:	Consultant:

Behaviorally Defined Problem:

Relevant Information From the Cumulative File:

Relevant Information Obtained From the Student:

Relevant Information Obtained From the Parent(s):

Baseline Data:

Interventions Attempted Before Problem-Solving Team Conference:

Date of Problem-Solving Team Conferences: First _____ Second _____ Third _____

Second Intervention:
Person Responsible and Timeline:
Date of First Follow Up:
Third Intervention:
Person Responsible and Timeline:
Date of Second Follow Up:
Data:

is selected for implementation. Though not all parents will choose to participate in team meetings, they should be welcomed, listened to, and considered equal partners if they do attend. If parents do not attend, either the teacher or related service provider should interview them before the conference, and follow up with a communication home to inform the parent of what was discussed and what intervention was selected. Parents should then be told how long the intervention will be conducted before the team will reconvene to evaluate the student's progress.

It is important that teams allow parents to exercise their due process rights and request a traditional evaluation if they feel that one is necessary and available data support the validity of such a request. Many parents are supportive of problem-solving strategies and prefer to first try and prevent their child's problems within the general education setting before considering special education services. Thus, as mentioned earlier in this chapter, it is helpful when a policy is in place that specifies the length of time for which an intervention can be implemented.

In addition to individual interventions and assessments, the parents should also be involved in systemic interventions developed through a PST process. Schools should be sure to invite a parent representative to the PST meeting in which systemic issues are discussed, should obtain data from parent perspectives when analyzing the problem and solution, and share the results of the intervention with all of the parents.

Implementation Integrity

Research has consistently demonstrated the importance of implementing interventions with integrity (Noell, Duhon, Gatti, & Connell, 2002; Noell, Gresham, & Gansle, 2002; Noell, Witt, Gilbertson, Ranier, & Freeland, 1997; Noell et al., 2005; Wickstrom et al., 1998). Implementation integrity provides the foundation for assessing student response within RTI (Noell & Gansle, 2006). In addition to implementing PST-developed interventions with integrity, PSTs should also examine the process with which interventions were developed by conducting a self-assessment of its process. In other words, it is important to adhere to both the intervention as designed and the problem-solving process as intended. Several best practices are listed above, but several more specific suggestions are available in the literature. We examined two sources (Kovaleski, 2002; Rosenfield & Gravois, 1996) and developed a 20-item self-evaluation. The items, listed in Figure 2, are endorsed as *yes* if the team consistently

Figure 2. Problem-Solving Team process fidelity checklist.

Item	Yes	No
1. Team meets on a consistent (e.g., weekly) basis.		
2. A request for assistance form is used to identify the problem and provide data before the meeting.		
3. The request for assistance form is brief, but provides adequate information about the problem.		
4. Documentation of consultant meeting with the teacher prior to problem-solving team meeting.		
5. Baseline data are collected and presented.		
6. Data are objective and empirical.		
7. Selected interventions are research based.		
8. Selected intervention is directly linked to assessment data.		
9. Start with interventions that have a high probability of success.		
10. Consulting personnel assist with implementation of intervention.		
11. Team develops specific implementation plan with the teacher.		
12. Parent information is discussed.		
13. Data collection plan is developed to monitor effectiveness and progress.		
14. Monitoring data are objective, empirical, and directly linked to the problem.		
15. A plan is developed to assess implementation integrity of the intervention.		
16. Follow-up consultation is scheduled between the teacher and one problem-solving team member.		
17. Follow-up meeting is scheduled.		
18. A case documentation form is used to track the team's activities.		
19. The building principal or administrative designee is present at the meeting.		
20. Problem-solving team members have designated roles (e.g., note taker, discussion facilitator).		

engages in this activity and *no* if not. Next, the team could examine the items listed as inconsistently implemented or absent and decide if and how they could address this recommendation. Adhering to the PST process with fidelity will likely enhance the outcomes associated with it.

Adherence to a practice requires that all involved understand it, which makes successful professional development a critical component of PSTs. Readers are referred to Stollar et al., chapter 53, vol. 3, regarding professional development, but we fully support the need for on-going inservice development and preservice instruction in school psychology training programs. Training should be directed toward collaboration techniques, problem analysis, establishing intervention goals, generating practical intervention plans that are directly linked to data, communicating effectively, and managing the process including team meetings.

SUMMARY

Problem solving and RTI are often used synonymously, which is an inaccurate application of the terms (Christ, Burns, & Ysseldyke, 2005). Conversely, some could implement a PST to develop interventions about individual students and assume that they have implemented RTI, but RTI is much more. In order to fully mesh the two complimentary concepts, PSTs and the resulting data should be used for many types of decisions including, but not limited to, special education eligibility. Combining both functions would likely assist in meeting the diverse needs of students while enhancing student learning, improving the resulting accountability data, directly linking research to practice in PK–12 schools, and providing school psychologists a venue to engage in desirable professional activities.

REFERENCES

Algozzine, B. S., Ysseldyke, J. E., & Elliott, J. (1997). *Strategies and tactics for effective instruction.* Longmont, CO: Sopris West.

Allen, S. J., & Graden, J. L. (2002). Best practices in collaborative problem solving for intervention design. In A. Thomas & J. Grimes (Eds.), *Best practices in school psychology IV* (pp. 565–582). Bethesda, MD: National Association of School Psychologists.

Bergan, J., & Kratochwill, T. R. (1990). *Behavioral consultation and therapy.* New York: Plenum Press.

Bransford, J. D., & Stein, B. S. (1984). *The IDEAL problem solver.* New York: W. H. Freeman.

Buck, G. H., Polloway, E. A., Smith-Thomas, A., & Cook, K. W. (2003). Prereferral intervention processes: A survey of state practices. *Exceptional Children, 69*(3), 349–360.

Burns, M. K. (1999). Effectiveness of special education personnel in the intervention assistance team model. The Journal of Educational Research, *92*, 354–356.

Burns, M. K. (2002). Utilizing a comprehensive system of assessment to intervention using curriculum-based assessments. *Intervention in School and Clinic, 38*, 8–13.

Burns, M. K. (in press). Creating an instructional level for reading by preteaching unknown words to children identified as learning disabled: Potential implications for response-to-intervention. *School Psychology Quarterly.*

Burns, M. K., Appleton, J., & Stehouwer, J. (2005). Meta-analytic review of responsiveness-to-intervention research: Examining field-based and research implemented models. *Journal of Psychoeducational Assessment, 23*, 381–394.

Burns, M. K., & Coolong-Chaffin, M. (2006). Response-to-intervention: The role of and effect on school psychology. *School Psychology Forum, 1*(1), 3–15.

Burns, M. K., Dean, V. J., & Klar, S. (2004). Using curriculum-based assessment in the responsiveness to intervention diagnostic model for learning disabilities. *Assessment for Effective Intervention, 29*(3), 47–56.

Burns, M. K., & Symington, T. (2002). A meta-analysis of prereferral intervention teams: Student and systemic outcomes. *Journal of School Psychology, 40*, 437–447.

Burns, M. K., Tucker, J. A., Frame, J., Foley, S., & Hauser, A. (2000). Interscorer, alternate-form, internal consistency, and test-retest reliability of Gickling's model of curriculum-based assessment for reading. *Journal of Psychoeducational Assessment, 18*, 353–360.

Burns, M. K., Vance, D., Szadokierski, I., & Stockwell, C. (2006). Student needs survey: A psychometrically sound measure of the five basic needs. *International Journal of Reality Therapy, 25*(2), 4–8.

Burns, M. K., Vanderwood, M., & Ruby, S. (2005). Evaluating the readiness of prereferral intervention teams for use in a problem-solving model: Review of three levels of research. *School Psychology Quarterly, 20*, 89–105.

Burns, M. K., & Ysseldyke, J. E. (2005). Questions about response-to-intervention implementation: Seeking answers from existing models. *The California School Psychologist, 10*, 9–20.

Canter, A. (2006). Problem solving and RTI: New roles for school psychologists. *Communiqué, 34*(5), insert.

Christ, T. J., Burns, M. K., & Ysseldyke, J. E. (2005). Conceptual confusion within response-to-intervention vernacular: Clarifying meaningful differences. *Communiqué, 34*(3), 1–2.

Daly, E. J., III, Martens, B. K., Kilmer, A., & Massie, D. (1996). The effects of instructional match and content overlap on generalized reading performance. *Journal of Applied Behavioral Analysis, 29*, 507–518.

Deno, S. L. (1985). Curriculum-based measurement: The emerging alternative. *Exceptional Children, 52,* 219–232.

Deno, S. L. (2002). Problem solving as "best practice." In A. Thomas & J. Grimes (Eds.), *Best practices in school psychology IV* (pp. 37–66). Bethesda, MD: National Association of School Psychologists.

Ellis, A. K. (2001). *Research on educational innovations* (3rd ed.). Larchmont, NY: Eye on Education.

Erchul, W. P. (1999). Two steps forward, one step back: Collaboration in school-based consultation. *Journal of School Psychology, 37,* 191–203.

Fuchs, D., Fuchs, L. S., & Bahr, M. W. (1990). Mainstream assistance teams: A scientific basis for the art of consultation. *Exceptional Children, 57,* 128–139.

Fuchs, D., Fuchs, L. S., Mathes, P. G., & Simmons, D. C. (1997). Peer-Assisted Learning Strategies: Making classrooms more responsive to diversity. *American Educational Research Journal, 34,* 174–206.

Gersten, R., Morvant, M., & Brengleman, S. (1995). Close to the bone: Coaching as a means to translate research into classroom practice. *Exceptional Children, 62,* 52–66.

Gickling, E. E., & Havertape, S. (1981). *Curriculum-based assessment (CBA).* Minneapolis, MN: School Psychology Inservice Training Network.

Gickling, E. E., Shane, R. L., & Croskery, K. M. (1989). Developing math skills in low-achieving high school students through curriculum-based assessment. *School Psychology Review, 18,* 344–356.

Graden, J. L. (1989). Reactions to school consultation: Some considerations from a problem-solving perspective. *Professional School Psychology, 4,* 29–35.

Graden, J. L., Casey, C., & Bonstrom, O. (1985). Implementing a prereferral intervention system: II, The data. *Exceptional Children, 51,* 487–496.

Graden, J. L., Casey, C., & Christenson, S. L. (1985). Implementing a prereferral intervention system: I, The model. *Exceptional Children, 51,* 377–384.

Gravois, T. A., & Rosenfield, S. A. (2006). Impact of instructional consultation teams on the disproportionate referral and placement of minority students in special education. *Remedial and Special Education, 27,* 42–52.

Hayek, R. A. (1987). The teacher assistance team: A prereferral support system. *Focus on Exceptional Children, 20,* 1–7.

Henry, N. A., & Flynt, S. E. (1990). Rethinking special education referral: A procedural manual. *Intervention in School and Clinic, 26,* 22–24.

Houk, J. L., & Lewandoski, L. J. (1996). Consultant verbal control and consultee perceptions. *Journal of Educational and Psychological Consultation, 7,* 107–118.

Idol, L., Nevin, A., & Paolucci-Whitcomb, P. (2000). *Collaborative consultation* (3rd ed.). Austin, TX: PRO-ED.

Ikeda, M. J., Tilly, W. D., III, Stumme, J., Volmer, L., & Allison, R. (1996). Agency-wide implementation of problem-solving consultation: Foundations, current implementation, and future directions. *School Psychology Quarterly, 11,* 228–243.

Illback, R. J., Zins, J. E., Maher, C. A., & Greenberg, R. (1990). An overview of principles and procedures of program planning and evaluation. In T. B. Gutkin & C. R. Reynolds (Eds.), *The handbook of school psychology* (2nd ed., pp. 799–820). New York: John Wiley.

Iverson, A. M. (2002). Best practices in problems-solving team structure and process. In A. Thomas & J. Grimes (Eds.), *Best Practices in School Psychology IV* (pp. 657–669). Bethesda, MD: National Association of School Psychologists.

Kovaleski, J. F. (2002). Best practices in operating prereferral intervention teams. In A. Thomas & J. Grimes (Eds.), *Best practices in school psychology IV* (pp. 645–655). Bethesda, MD: National Association of School Psychologists.

Kovaleski, J. F., Tucker, J. A., & Duffy, D. J. (1995). School reform through instructional support: The Pennsylvania Initiative, Part I. *Communiqué, 23*(8), insert.

Kruger, L. J., Struzziero, J., Watts, R., & Vacca, D. (1989). The relationship between organizational support and satisfaction with teacher assistance teams. *Remedial and Special Education, 16,* 203–211.

Meyers, B., Valentino, C. T., Meyers, J., Boretti, M., & Brent, D. (1996). Implementing prereferral intervention teams as an approach to school-based consultation in an urban school system. *Journal of Educational and Psychological Consultation, 7,* 119–149.

Minneapolis Public Schools. (2002). *Problem solving model.* Minneapolis, MN: Author. Retrieved August 31, 2006, from http://sped.mpls.k12.mn.us/sites/75af2ef0-c4b1-4638-be13-62253040cbcf/uploads/PSM_wksht_1_0700.pdf

National Association of Secondary School Principals. (1987). *Comprehensive assessment of school environments.* Reston, VA: Author.

Noell, G. H., Duhon, G. J., Gatti, S. L., & Connell, J. E. (2002). Consultation, follow up, and behavior management intervention implementation in general education. *School Psychology Review, 31,* 217–234.

Noell, G. H., & Gansle, K. A. (2006). Assuring the form has substance: Treatment plan implementation as the foundation of assessing response to intervention. *Assessment for Effective Intervention, 32*(1), 32–39.

Noell, G. H., Gresham, F. M., & Gansle, K. A. (2002). Does treatment integrity matter? A preliminary investigation of instructional implementation and mathematics performance. *Journal of Behavioral Education, 11,* 51–67.

Noell, G. H., Witt, J. C., Gilbertson, D. N., Ranier, D. D., & Freeland, J. T. (1997). Increasing teacher intervention implementation in general education settings through consultation and performance feedback. *School Psychology Quarterly, 12,* 77–88.

Noell, G. H., Witt, J. C., Slider, N. J., Connell, J. E., Gatti, S. L., Williams, K. L., et al. (2005). Treatment implementation following behavioral consultation in schools: A comparison of three follow-up strategies. *School Psychology Review, 34,* 87–106.

Phillips, B., & McCullough, L. (1990). Consultation-based programming: Instituting the collaborative ethic in schools. *Exceptional Children, 56,* 291–304.

Pugach, M. C., & Johnson, L. J. (1989). The challenge of implementing collaboration between general and special education. *Exceptional Children, 56,* 232–235.

Rock, M. L., & Zigmond, N. (2001). Intervention assistance: It is substance or symbolism? *Preventing School Failure, 45,* 153–161.

Rosenfield, S. A. (1987). *Instructional consultation.* Hillsdale, NJ: Erlbaum.

Rosenfield, S. A., & Gravois, T. A. (1996). *Instructional Consultation Teams: Collaborating for change.* New York: Guilford Press.

Shapiro, E. S. (1992). Use of Gickling's model of curriculum-based assessment to improve reading in elementary age students. *School Psychology Review, 21,* 168–176.

Shapiro, E. S. (2000). School psychology from an instructional perspective: Solving big, not little, problems. *School Psychology Review, 29,* 560–572.

Shapiro, E. S., & Ager, C. (1992). Assessment of special education students in regular education programs: Linking assessment to instruction. *Elementary School Journal, 92,* 283–296.

Schumm, J. S., & Vaughn, S. (1991). Making adaptations for mainstreamed students: Regular classroom teachers' perspectives. *Remedial and Special Education, 12,* 18–27.

Schumm, J. S., & Vaughn, S. (1992). Planning for mainstreamed special education students. *Exceptionality, 3,* 81–90.

Slavin, R. E., & Madden, N. A. (2001). *One million children: Success for all.* Newbury Park, CA: Corwin Press.

Tilly, W. D., III. (2002). Best practices in school psychology as a problem-solving enterprise. In A. Thomas & J. Grimes (Eds.), *Best practices in school psychology IV* (pp. 21–36). Bethesda, MD: National Association of School Psychologists.

Truscott, S. D., Cosgrove, G., Meyers, J., & Eidle-Barkman, K. A. (2000). The acceptability of organizational consultation with prereferral intervention teams. *School Psychology Quarterly, 15,* 172–206.

VanDerHeyden, A. M., & Burns, M. K. (2005). Using curriculum-based assessment and curriculum-based measurement to guide elementary mathematics instruction: Effect on individual and group accountability scores. *Assessment for Effective Intervention, 30*(3), 15–29.

VanVoorhis, R. W., & Levinson, E. M. (2006). Job satisfaction among school psychologists: A meta-analysis. *School Psychology Quarterly, 21,* 77–90.

Voltz, D. L., Elliott, R. N., & Harris, W. B. (1995). Promising practices in facilitating collaboration between resource room teachers and general education teachers. *Learning Disabilities Research & Practice, 10,* 129–136.

Wickstrom, K. F., Jones, K. M., LaFleur, L. H., & Witt, J. C. (1998). An analysis of treatment integrity in school-based behavioral consultation. *School Psychology Quarterly, 13,* 141–154.

Ysseldyke, J. E., Burns, M. K., Dawson, M., Kelly, B., Morrison, D., Ortiz, S., et al. (2006). *School psychology: A blueprint for the future of training and practice III.* Bethesda, MD: National Association of School Psychologists.

ANNOTATED BIBLIOGRAPHY

Ikeda, M. J., Tilly, W. D., III, Stumme, J., & Volmer, L. (1996). Agency-wide implementation of problem-solving consultation: Foundations, current implementation, and future directions. *School Psychology Quarterly, 11,* 228–243.

The PST model at the Heartland Area Education Agency 11 is one of the most widely known and referenced approaches to PST in the country, but few descriptions of the Heartland approach exist in the literature. This article describes specific steps within the PST model and provides case examples. More importantly, the authors contextualize the PST model within a large-scale implementation initiative. Therefore, this article is an important reference for anyone interested in implementing a PST approach at the district level.

Marston, D., Muyskens, P., Lau, M., & Canter, A. (2003). Problem-solving model for decision making with high-incidence disabilities: The Minneapolis experience. *Learning Disabilities Research & Practice, 18,* 187–200.

Describes the problem-solving model and how it was designed and also discusses the limitations of problem-solving research as well as barriers to the implementation of this model. The Minneapolis public schools use this model for intervention assistance, referral, evaluation, and eligibility decision making for students with academic difficulties. The implementation of the problem-solving model is driven by four themes: appropriateness of intelligence tests for eligibility determination, discriminatory procedures and outcome bias, allocation of school psychologist time, and linking assessment to instruction. Three steps are outlined to identify and support students with academic difficulties: classroom interventions, PST interventions, and special education referral and initiation of due process procedures. Learning disabilities prevalence data found that the percentage of the student population identified as learning disabled decreased from approximately 6% before the problem-solving model implementation to less than 3%. Moreover, student progress among children identified as learning disabled and those at risk who participated in RTI approximated the progress of children identified as on pace to pass the state accountability test.

Pawlowski, K. F. (2001). The instructional support team concept in action. In R. Sornson (Ed.), *Preventing early learning failure* (pp. 64–68). Alexandria, VA: Association for Supervision and Curriculum Development.

There are many descriptions of the Instructional Support Team process in the literature, but this chapter is the most comprehensive. The three basic steps of the Instructional Support Team are outlined as (a) an initial peer conference between the referring teacher and a consulting member of the Instructional Support Team, (b) the teacher concerns are behaviorally defined and addressed at a formal meeting of the Instructional Support Team, and (c) interventions are collaboratively designed and implemented by the classroom teacher and the instructional support teacher. The chapter, combined with others in the same book, provides a comprehensive depiction of the process and outcomes.

Rosenfield, S., & Gravois, T. (1996). *Instructional Consultation Teams: Collaborating for change.* New York: Guilford Press.

This is the most comprehensive discussion of the Instructional Consultation Team model including history, implementation, professional development, and institutionalization. Thus, this book is useful guide for anyone interested in the Instructional Consultation Team or using this approach as a basis for problem-solving teams. Instructional Consultation Teams are presented within a school-wide change process that includes planning and evaluating. Several sample forms and a simulation case are included.

103

Best Practice in Instructional Consultation and Instructional Consultation Teams

Sylvia Rosenfield
University of Maryland

OVERVIEW

Instructional consultation (IC) engages school psychologists in consultee-centered consultation with school staff on the most basic goal of schooling: enhancing the academic achievement of students. One of the major aspects of IC (Rosenfield, 1987), and its systemic delivery system, IC Teams (Rosenfield & Gravois, 1996; Rosenfield, Silva, & Gravois, 2008), is the ecologically driven focus on academic concerns, although other concerns are also addressed. In the context of the 2004 reauthorization of the Individuals with Disabilities Education Act (IDEA) and the No Child Left Behind Act, there is an increased emphasis on achieving academic outcomes for all students, including those who are often considered at risk for meeting standards. School psychologists' response to this context has been to evolve problem-solving models, such as described by Tilly (see chapter 2, vol. 1). IC Teams, as a consultee-centered approach to problem solving (Knotek, Kaniuka, & Ellingsen, 2008; Knotek, Rosenfield, Gravois, & Babinski, 2003), focuses on improving and enhancing staff competence as a route to both systems improvement and positive individual student outcomes.

In this chapter, the essential assumptions of IC and IC Teams, including how IC relates to *School Psychology: A Blueprint for Training and Practice III* (Ysseldyke et al., 2006; also see Ysseldyke et al., chapter 3, vol. 1), will be presented as basic considerations. A review of research supporting IC/IC Teams can be found in Rosenfield et al. (2008). The best practice section will describe the process for conducting

IC, focusing on the three central elements: (a) the problem-solving stages, (b) the communication and relationships skills, and (c) the use of evidence-based assessment and intervention strategies. Best practice in conducting IC Teams, which is the school-based delivery system for IC, follows, including the team structure, functions of the team, and the referral system. Because best practice also requires that any model of service delivery attends to issues of training and implementation, IC's approach to these components are included.

BASIC CONSIDERATIONS

Blueprint III delineates foundational and functional domains of practice that should be within the repertoire of school psychologists. IC is a problem-solving model that is directly related to the functional competence domain of "Enhancing the Development of Cognitive and Academic Skills ... [s]chool psychologists ... should know empirically supported components of effective instruction ... and they should ... work with others to improve instruction" (Ysseldyke et al., 2006, p. 19). In addition, the process of IC incorporates interpersonal and collaborative skills and data-based decision making, two additional functional competencies. Further, IC Teams, as a delivery system, is based on systems thinking. The *Blueprint III* model also addresses outcomes, and implementation of an IC Team in a school is designed to address both individual competence for all students and building competence of the system through both professional development of staff members and a systemic approach to school improvement.

Components

The original use of the term *instructional consultation* referred to consultation designed to "modify teacher behavior to enhance the learning of all students in a class" (Bergan & Schnaps, 1983, p. 105). The specific model of IC, developed by Rosenfield (1987), and its integration into a school-wide delivery system as IC Teams (Rosenfield & Gravois, 1996; Rosenfield et al., 2008), have extended this concept to a consultee-centered consultation framework that provides support to staff and students. IC Teams include the following components: (a) a stage-based process that embeds relationship and communication processes within the model; (b) an implementation design to support schools and school districts in facilitating change from initiation through to the institutionalization phase; (c) a formative and summative evaluation of the training, the implementation, and the outcomes as an ongoing commitment of the developers; and (d) a causal model incorporating past, current, and future research to guide research and development (see Gravois & Rosenfield, 2002; Rosenfield et al., 2008).

Importance of Underlying Assumptions

IC is, however, more than a set of procedures and activities. The assumptions underlying IC are ecological in nature and are central to integrity of the model's implementation. Failure to accept the assumptions leads to problems in the successful implementation of any service delivery or intervention model (Benn & Rosenfield, 2005), especially when the model challenges traditional beliefs. IC challenges the traditional deficit models that have been central to the training and practice of many school psychologists. Thus, a discussion of those assumptions becomes the starting point for the practice of IC.

IC begins with the assumption that the consultant and consultee actively construct and resolve the problem through their interaction: "The facts of a particular case are but a reflection of the values and prejudices of those persons describing that situation" (White, Summerlin, Loos, & Epstein, 1992, p. 350). Often, teachers, parents, and school psychologists assume that there is a problem to be diagnosed through the use of instruments, such as intelligence and processing tests, designed to examine and describe the student. They seek answers to questions about whether, for example, the child has an Attention Deficit Hyperactivity Disorder or is learning disabled, not recognizing that the very questions asked and

instruments used frame the type of problem that can be found. In IC, a different set of values and perspectives guide the process, based on an ecological view of problem construction. These assumptions guide the use of an ecological problem-solving process, addressing teacher concerns about students in their classrooms: (a) the school's mission is to support learning, not sort learners; (b) support should be provided at the classroom level; (c) the focus is on the instructional triangle, not just the student; and (d) embedded professional development is best practice.

School's Mission is to Support Learning

As schools increasingly move away from sorting and sifting students to accountability for academic outcomes, school psychologists have a valuable contribution to make at the classroom and system level rather than serving as the gatekeeper for special education. IC is not, in the usual sense, a prereferral model, since the primary goal of IC is to enhance learning rather than to focus on whether the student should be considered for or will require special education. When response to intervention is interpreted within the revision of IDEA as a problem-solving approach to finding the most effective way to enhance student learning within the classroom, IC can be considered a response-to-instruction approach.

Support at the Classroom Level

Given that the mission of IC/IC Teams is to support learning in the least-restrictive environment, it follows that support at the classroom level is a core value. Evidence confirms that early intervention and prevention for both academic and behavioral concerns are more effective and preferable to waiting until the problem requires intervention at more intensive levels. This is appropriate, moreover, "for children of any race or ethnic group, and children with or without an identifiable 'within-child' problem" (Donovan & Cross, 2002, p. ES-5), and this support should be provided within the setting in which the concerns first appear, beginning with the classroom. Thus, the teacher is a critical resource in enabling students to close gaps in achievement or behavior. As such, consultee-centered consultation that enhances teacher knowledge and skills is at the core of the IC model. It should also be noted, however, that IC is a problem-solving approach that has also been used by special education teachers and specialists for students who have been designated for services but about whom teachers still have concerns. For example, in one recent case, a teacher of a self-contained class for students with autism was able to work with an instructional consultant to resolve a concern. As in all cases, the focus of the service is to enable the staff to support the students more effectively.

Focus on the Instructional Triangle

When a student is experiencing academic problems, the focus is on the interactions between the student's entry-level skills, the instructional design or format, and the actual task with which the student is presented, rather than a search for an internal deficit within the student. The concept of the instructional triangle (see Figure 1) is in contrast with the traditional assessment paradigm that focuses predominantly on the student's characteristics. When assessment addresses student characteristics, the target is alterable learner variables (Bloom, 1976), such as the prior knowledge of the student, rather than IQ test scores. When the presenting concern of the teacher is behavior, the IC process includes an evaluation of whether students are able to engage successfully with classroom tasks and instructional methods, since behavior concerns are often the effect of student–task mismatch.

Teachers operationalize curriculum objectives into classroom materials and tasks, and their expectations for the students in their classroom are based on their evaluation of student work on these materials and tasks. Students who are unable to complete the work

successfully are considered to be at risk or in need of additional support. In IC, it is not just the performance on the task but the gap between the task and the learner's skills that is assessed, requiring an instructional assessment. (The term *instructional assessment* has now replaced the former label of *curriculum-based assessment*; see Gravois & Gickling, chapter 30, vol. 2). An instructional assessment enables the teacher to gain an understanding of what skills the student has and where the student can enter the curriculum at an instructional level. Improving the match between the learner skills and the task is the goal, so that the student can engage successfully with the material.

The instructional assessment method used by instructional consultants differs from curriculum-based measurement (CBM) in several ways. Screening and monitoring students using CBM does not target the specific learning needs of the students, so decisions based on a CBM can continue to reflect poor instructional matches unless additional assessments are done. For example, screening students for reading problems using fluency measures or instruments measuring level of skill is not sufficient to determine the specific academic needs of the student. Screening should be followed by an instructional assessment in the tasks that the student is expected to master in order to ensure an instructional match. Without the specificity of an instructional assessment on entry-level skills, implementing even an evidence-based program may not result in student progress if the level of the materials and instruction is not matched to the students' instructional levels.

The third point of the triangle is the instructional and management strategies that are implemented. Because IC is a consultee-centered consultation model that focuses on building teacher knowledge and skills, it provides an opportunity to introduce evidence-based interventions to the teacher through the collaborative process and to support teachers in their use. The instructional consultant combines knowledge of evidence-based interventions with the capacity to support teachers in their implementation. There is growing recognition of how difficult it is to move interventions from research to practice, and consultee-centered consultation is viewed as one way to address this concern (Rosenfield, 2000).

If classroom instruction is not affected by the consultation process, the student loses the benefit of productive engaged time in the classroom setting. Sending the student for interventions outside the classroom, without affecting and coordinating the instructional methods within the classroom, can result

Figure 1. The instructional triangle.

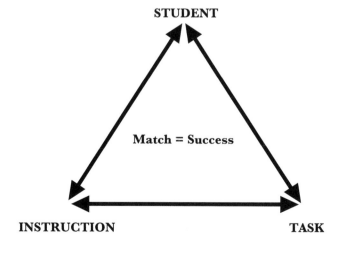

Note. Source: Gravois, Rosenfield, & Gickling, (2006).

in overloading the student with multiple tasks. What is equally problematic is that some portion of the tasks might not be at the instructional level. Further, valuable instructional time is lost as the student moves back and forth between instructional settings. Thus, IC emphasizes developing a good instructional match for the student in the classroom setting.

Embedded Professional Development

Building support at the classroom level also means that teacher professional development is a key aspect of the model. Current best practice in professional development values creating learning communities for teachers as a prerequisite for building learning communities for students. However, the learning community must also embed best practice (Benn & Rosenfield, 2005). Supporting teacher-reflective activities enables teacher skills to grow and improve student outcomes (Rosenfield et al., 2008). Referrals by teachers are viewed by instructional consultants as venues for teachers to consult and collaborate with colleagues about the problems of practice. As schools move away from sorting and sifting students to enhancing outcomes for all students, learning communities are increasingly viewed as important investments for school staff.

BEST PRACTICES

Conducting IC requires skill in the essential components of the process. The essential components include the capacity to build a collaborative working relationship, requiring effective use of communication skills, and to complete the steps of the problem-solving stages that comprise the process. Best practice of the IC Team requires attention to team maintenance and work functions. Finally, best practice requires that implementation be addressed, including training to facilitate integrity of implementation, and program evaluation to ensure that the model has both been implemented and has an evidence base. These aspects of IC/IC Teams are described in this section.

Core Components of Instructional Consultation as a Process

Three components are central to the IC process of the IC Teams model: (a) the relationship between the consultant and consultee, based in part on effective communication skills; (b) the stages of problem solving;

and (c) the assessment and intervention strategies to address learning and behavior problems.

Consultation Relationship

IC Teams, unlike most other team problem-solving models, is composed of both a case management and a team structure. Although IC Teams involves a multidisciplinary school team, the consultation process itself begins at the dyadic level between a teacher and a consultant, termed a case manager in IC Teams. At the center of the case management structure is a dyadic consultant–consultee relationship, essentially an "interchange between two or more professional colleagues, in a nonhierarchical relationship, working together to resolve a problem" (Rosenfield, 1987, p. 21).

Establishing a collaborative relationship between the case manager and teacher is core to the IC process. The relationship provides a space for teachers to reflect on their practice in a supportive environment and opens the possibility for them to examine the instructional environment for the student who has brought them to the table. For example, in a recent consultation case, a skilled and caring teacher was able to reflect with the consultant on her interactions with a child. She could comment at the conclusion of the process on the benefit of the interaction in reframing her understanding of the problem and her own part in both creating and resolving the concern that brought her to the problem-solving process. In front of a team there is often not the time to build this supportive environment for a teacher to be reflective, nor time to engage fully in all the steps of the problem-solving process. When case management is not available, there is often a press to develop interventions in the time allotted at a team meeting for any individual case. Teams may move too quickly to the intervention stage without adequate attention to definition and analysis of the problem.

Thus, building a working relationship is critical in IC because of the ecological focus and the focus on supporting the teacher. Teachers are informed from the beginning about the instructional triangle, making it clear that the process directly involves the nature of the teacher's work with the student. Without a working relationship in place, it would be difficult to examine and change the curricular, assessment, instructional, and management issues that will surface during the process.

The relationship in IC is collaborative, with the partners working shoulder to shoulder to resolve the concerns of the consultee rather than the consultant shouldering the problem. A working relationship is also one that allows the consultant and consultee to continue to work shoulder to shoulder in the face of potential differences that may arise in how the problem should be conceptualized and the intervention implemented. The consultant is, however, responsible for monitoring the quality of the relationship. Since the consultant is also responsible for ensuring that the stages of the problem-solving process are completed with integrity, a solid working relationship enables difficult situations to be negotiated. For example, consultation skill is required to work through the temptation to rush to intervention without a complete problem identification and analysis.

Communication Skills

The consultant's communication skills are essential to the quality of the relationship, as consultation is largely conducted through verbal exchanges (Rosenfield, 2004). It is through dialogue that the problem and solution are coconstructed. Skilled consultants are aware how much their language affects the relationship and problem solving, and develop skills in using language to facilitate the process. Instructional consultants-in-training are asked to tape their sessions with teachers. In listening to themselves on these tapes, many novice consultants recognize for the first time that the teacher's willingness to collaborate on problem solving is, in part, a function of the verbal interchanges during the sessions. Thus, attention needs to be paid to the quality of the consultant's communication and to examine the language used when problems arise in the problem-solving process.

Defining the problem in behavioral terms.
One of the key roles of the consultant is to support the teacher in constructing a problem definition that the teacher views as connected to the concern but that is also potentially resolvable within the classroom. If the teacher views the problem as an attention or memory deficit, the consultant helps the teacher to reframe the concern in terms of what the child is actually doing in the classroom to generate that perception. When a problem is defined in terms of learning and behavior rather than child deficit language, the teacher is more empowered to address the problem within the classroom (Rosenfield, 1987; Tombari & Bergan, 1978).

For example, a teacher brought a case to the consultant for problem solving because of concerns about a child's lack of work completion and poor handwriting. The teacher and parent had viewed the child as having poor motor skills. They were trying to find a computer for use in the classroom and were considering occupational therapy for the child. Using

communication skillfully, the consultant helped the teacher to develop a behavioral definition of the concern in terms of the student's handwriting skills. An instructional assessment of the child's handwriting revealed that he had difficulty forming his letters and was left-handed. He had never been taught to write as a left-handed person. The intervention included implementing an evidence-based program for handwriting and teaching him to write with strategies designed for left-handed students. The student's handwriting improved, and as he became more fluent, his work completion increased. As the child became more successful, the teacher's relationship with the child improved as well. Further, as a consultee-centered consultation process, the teacher now had a method for improving handwriting in the classroom and knew how to teach left-handed students to write. No out-of-classroom interventions were required. Through co-constructing a behavioral definition, the focus of the problem was changed.

Listening skills.
Communication strategies that are particularly useful in IC, and likely familiar to school psychologists from the helping skills literature, are listening skills such as clarifying, paraphrasing, and perception checking (Rosenfield, 1987, 2004). Without using such skills, consultants may develop and pursue hypotheses about problems based on their own interpretations rather than working collaboratively to understand the teacher's perception of the problem. In other words, consultants direct their questions to refining their own hypotheses rather than helping teachers to frame their concerns at the observable and measurable level. For example, if teachers say that they think the child has an attention deficit disorder because of the lack of work completion, school psychologists with a deficit model orientation will begin to frame questions to explore that possibility.

On the other hand, an instructional consultant is more likely to look for conditions under which work is completed or not, and whether the work is at the instructional level of the student. To explore the problem from the teacher's perspective, the instructional consultant would use listening skills, such as clarification, to specify the behavior that the teacher observes that leads to the inference that the student has an attention deficit disorder. The consultant would also check on the academic skills of the student with respect to the work in question, using clarifications and paraphrases to be sure that the consultant and consultee are congruent in their understanding of the behavior. Some preliminary research suggests that experienced instructional consultants use more clarification than novice ones (Benn & Rosenfield, in press).

Early in their training, novice instructional consultants often find the focus on using clarification and paraphrasing irritating, believing that it is time consuming and does not get them anywhere in diagnosing the "real" problem. With increasing practice, however, they come to recognize the value of communication skills and become more automatic in their use. Such skill development, however, does require specific attention to the language used in consultation, including taping sessions and feedback from supervisors or peers.

Problem-Solving Stages

The consultant and consultee collaborate to conduct a set of structured problem-solving stages. Each stage has specific tasks that need to be completed before moving on to the next stage. Without the scaffold of the stages and the work that each stage requires, many consultation interactions lack focus and accountability. Conversations with teachers in the hallway and in other informal settings are typical regularities for school psychologists, but such interactions are a limited vehicle for best practice in instructional consultation.

The stages of IC problem solving are (a) entry and contracting, (b) problem identification and analysis, (c) intervention design and planning, (d) intervention implementation and evaluation, and (e) closure. While the stages are linear, in that the business of each stage must be conducted before moving on to the next one, at any time it might be necessary to move back to an earlier stage. For example, a teacher may express concern about some aspect of the consultation process, and it might be necessary to re-contract, to determine if the teacher is clear about the process or committed to continuing, or if additional information in the intervention stage might require a new analysis of the problem (i.e., the problem identification stage may be need to be reinstituted). The stages are similar to those of behavioral consultation, but there are differences as well. Because these stages are so central to IC, a brief description of each stage follows.

Entry and contracting. Introduction of IC and IC Teams is done at two levels, to the school through entry and to individual teacher consultees through contracting. In entry, the school community is provided a basic awareness of IC/IC Teams as a component of the school psychologist's service delivery. Presentations

at staff meetings and written materials, including brochures and newsletters for teachers and parents, are common formats for this process. During this stage, information about referral procedures is disseminated so that staff can easily access consultation services; a simple one-page request for consultation with an indication of when the teacher is available to meet enables staff to access the process. When IC is introduced to a school district, systems-level entry is also advised (see Rosenfield & Gravois, 1996, for additional information).

However, no group presentation or written material about IC absolves the instructional consultant from the requirement of contracting with the individual consultee to obtain informed consent from the consultee to engage in the process. Contracting informs the consultee about the collaborative nature of the consultation relationship and the stages of the problem-solving process. The consultee can then make an explicit decision about whether or not to engage in the problem-solving process. This stage can be especially important for school psychologists, as the teacher may not really be clear about what is involved and may expect the school psychologist to test the student in the more traditional direct service paradigm.

The information that the consultant presents about IC during contracting includes the following:

- Informs the consultee about the stages of the problem-solving process
- Explains the instructional triangle (with its focus on alterable student variables, instructional methods, and tasks in the classroom)
- Clarifies the collaborative nature of the relationship
- Discusses time involvement
- Explains data collection that is typically involved
- Introduces the Student Documentation Form, the form that is used to guide and document the process (see Figures 2–4 in Appendix)
- Discusses the limits of confidentiality and the nonevaluative nature of the process (before engaging in consultation, it is critical for the consultant to clarify the school/school district policy on student and teacher confidentiality, so that the teacher can be accurately informed)
- If there is an IC Team in the school, discusses the function of the team in relation to the consulting process
- Concludes with a joint decision to move forward, including scheduling time and place, or concludes with a joint decision not to move forward but to leave the door open for a possible later collaboration

Problem identification and analysis. Once the consultant and consultee agree to move forward with problem solving, the problem identification and analysis stage begins. Although the consultee's initial description of the concern serves as a starting point, and is captured on front page of the Student Documentation Form, it is assumed that the participants will coconstruct the problem through their dialogue and data collection. A problem meaningful to the participants and respectful of their perspectives emerges from this stage. The problem will be framed in terms of the gap between current and desired performance and is defined in relation to the instructional triangle.

Communication skills play a major role in problem construction. The consultant avoids diagnostic and clinical jargon, focusing instead on the presence or absence of behaviors that led the teacher to decide that a referral was needed. Since speakers attune their concerns to their listeners (Rosenfield, 2004), teachers may focus when speaking to school psychologists on disorders such as attention deficit rather than academic concerns or specific classroom behaviors. Teacher concerns are reframed from initial, often high inference within-child concerns to specific behaviors within the ecology of the classroom that teachers feel more empowered to intervene.

The work of this stage is often completed over several sessions, depending upon the information that the consultee brings to the session and the complexity of the concerns. This work is done at the dyadic level rather than at the team level for several reasons. The quality of the assessment information obtained by teams is often fairly limited, a function of their time constraints, and not useful in providing data for setting specific goals or targeting interventions in relation to student instructional needs. Moreover, the dyadic consultation model allows teachers time to reflect on the problem within a collaborative relationship.

The following tasks are required to complete the stage: (a) specify the teacher's concerns in observable and measurable terms, defined as a *gap* between current and expected performance; (b) select a data collection method and establish a baseline with at least three data points; (c) identify the context of the problem within the instructional triangle; (d) decide if the gap is significant and requires intervention; and (e) establish short, intermediate, and long-term goals for the student.

Assessment strategies, usually instructional assessments and behavioral observation, are designed to supply information about the student's entry-level skills or behaviors, the task, and the instructional/ management strategies in use. An essential aspect of IC is the requirement that an instructional mismatch be ruled out even when the teacher's presenting concern is behavior. That principle is based on the assumption that students who are working at frustration level in the classroom instructional setting can be prone to behave inappropriately as well. For example, even if the teacher's initial concern is a student's lack of work completion or constant annoying of other students during reading lessons, the first hypothesis to be explored is the appropriateness of the reading tasks assigned in relation to the student's skills. Instructional assessment helps to identify whether a mismatch is present.

Instructional assessment is "a system for determining the instructional needs of a student based upon the student's ongoing performance within existing course content in order to deliver instruction as effectively and efficiently as possible" (Gickling, Shane, & Croskery, 1989, pp. 344–345). According to Stiggins and Conklin (1992), many "teachers either do not take the time or do not know how to make good use of assessment in presenting instruction, in evaluating it, and in making it more effective and meaningful" (p. 148). As a result, instructional assessment is a valuable tool in this stage. The five basic instructional assessment questions are:

- What does the student know?
- What can the student do?
- What does the student think?
- How does the student approach what he or she is unsure of?
- What can the teacher do next?

School psychologists are typically skilled in behavioral observation techniques, which are also tools for the instructional consultant. However, the IC process provides teachers working with instructional consultants opportunities for reflecting together on designing an observation in relation to the teacher's concern and jointly interpreting the data gleaned from the observation. Data gathered through the collaborative interactions between teachers and consultants during the problem identification, and later the intervention implementation stage, may help teachers gain a more objective perspective on the concern and better value the data gathered.

The Student Documentation Form (see Figures 2–4) serves several functions during the problem identification stage. The front cover of this four-page document provides a place for up to four initial statements of concern, a checkmark to ensure that instructional match has been evaluated, the behavior that will be addressed, and short/intermediate/long-terms goals, with a timeline for achieving the goals. Inside the form are two graphs on which baseline and later intervention data can be entered for two concerns (additional graphs can be added on separate sheets). Technical perfection in data collection may not be achieved, but over time teachers and consultants seem to develop a healthy respect for the process. They also recognize that the graphing of this case-specific data is valuable to their decision making.

Intervention planning. Jointly planning the intervention, based on the problem definition, is the next stage. The specificity of the IC problem definition process enables a targeted intervention. Sometimes this stage is easily completed. Teachers often can plan an intervention in their classroom once the initial problem that seemed unsolvable at the classroom level has been reframed through the problem identification and analysis stage. If the instructional assessment results document that work is not at instructional level for a student who was referred for being off task much of the time, then the intervention is targeted to developing tasks that better match the student's skills rather than focus on the behavior. Alternatively, collaborating with the teacher to clarify that a reading problem is a problem with comprehension skills might provide an opportunity for the teacher to learn new empirically supported strategies to teach comprehension to the target students and others in the classroom. Such strategies can then be tailored to fit that teacher's classroom context.

This stage is completed when the details of the intervention are described and the intervention is perceived as do-able by those responsible for implementation. The following questions must be answered:

- What is the description of the strategy?
- When and how often will it be implemented?
- Who will implement the intervention?
- What materials are required and are they currently available? (If not, how will they be obtained?)
- What data collection methods will be used to evaluate progress toward the student's goals?
- When will progress be monitored?

The Student Documentation Form provides a place for documenting the intervention design, including who will be responsible for the implementation.

Selecting a research-based intervention is the goal whenever possible. Research supports instructional strategies rather than interventions designed to fix processes that are deficient (e.g., Kavale & Forness, 1999). Thus, the interventions typically involve classroom personnel, including teachers, aides, and peers. Further, strategies need to be tailored to the demands of a particular classroom setting or student situation. Conditions that increase treatment integrity include ensuring that teachers have the necessary materials and that the persons designated to deliver the intervention are available.

Yet research-based interventions may still need to be modified in a particular case (Rosenfield, 2000). For example, behavioral contracting is a research-based intervention, but an effective contract may not be constructed on the first attempt. Building a student's sight word vocabulary may require modification of the number of new words introduced per lesson or the type of reinforcement used. Instructional consultants and consultees share the understanding that intervention plans may need to be modified based on data gathered to monitor progress toward goals.

Intervention implementation. It is during implementation that the feasibility and effectiveness of an intervention are determined. Classrooms are complex places. The collaborative working relationship allows the consultation dyad to problem solve during the uncertainty of the treatment implementation stage. This includes resolving the inevitable practical problems that arise during implementation, coping with treatment integrity issues, and supporting data collection on the effectiveness of the intervention. Consultants should be prepared for problems in these areas rather than view them as evidence of teacher resistance or failed problem solving. Consultation sessions are typically less frequent during this stage, but meetings to evaluate progress and treatment integrity should be scheduled at regular intervals.

During this stage, data continue to be collected, and evaluation of progress toward goal attainment is monitored. As short-term goals are attained within the designated time period, progress toward longer term goals can be addressed. If goals are not attained in a timely way, treatment integrity problems can be addressed, or the intervention can be changed or modified. Sometimes there is a need to return to the problem identification stage.

Resolution/termination. The last stage is formal closure of the problem-solving process and the working relationship with the teacher. Accountability requires a resolution/termination stage, culminating in a decision to continue or terminate working together. If the goals have been achieved and the problem is resolved to the partners' satisfaction, then the achievement can be celebrated. It should be clear to the consultee that the consultation process can be reengaged should new concerns emerge.

If progress toward goals is unsatisfactory, according to the data, it may be necessary to recycle back through the stages. For example, a more clearly defined behavior or additional data collection may be needed. Alternatively, the consultant–consultee dyad can ask for support from the building-level team or other resources, including other professionals (either internal to the school or in the community), or family members. In some cases, referral to special education becomes appropriate when the resources of general education and other remedial services do not meet the instructional or behavioral needs of the student. However, labeling students does not guarantee that appropriate services will follow, and much of the problem solving done during instructional consultation helps to focus the Individualized Educational Plan team on intervention planning. Even within special education, IC can play a role in supporting teachers and students.

If the teacher decides not to continue in the relationship, formal termination of the process should occur. One hazard of consultation is that the relationship may fade away through the press of time, personal concerns (such as an illness in the teacher's family or other major life event), unwillingness by one or both parties to confront relationship issues, or perceived or real lack of progress in resolving the referral concern(s). Explicitly addressing the reason for the teacher's withdrawal makes it possible to terminate the process while leaving the door open for future opportunities to consult on the current or other concerns.

Documentation

Documentation should be incorporated into any consultation service delivery system to demonstrate accountability. While this can be handled differently at the local level, documentation should provide a brief summary of the concern, relevant assessment data, a description of the interventions implemented, and the results. A summary form with instructional and management recommendations can be prepared for the student's next teacher. Maintaining records is important in the event of future concerns about a

particular student, and outdated records should be culled when appropriate. For individual accountability, consultants should examine how many consultee concerns are successfully addressed during the school year so that they can evaluate the effectiveness of their practice and target appropriate professional development.

A central document within the IC model is the Student Documentation Form, which has been discussed earlier in relation to the stages. Part of IC training involves use of the Student Documentation Form, which structures the process and provides a document for accountability. The format was designed in collaboration with school staff that had experience in implementing IC. This four-page folder is printed on card stock. As has been noted above, the cover page (Figure 2) includes space to write up to four initial concerns, to prioritize those initial concerns, to remind the dyad to evaluate the instructional match between the student's skills and the classroom task requirements, and to state short- and long-term goals. The inside of the form consists of two identical pages on which to provide an observable and measurable statement of the concern, to graph baseline and intervention data, and to describe the major components (who, what, when, materials needed) of the intervention design (Figure 3). The back cover of the form (Figure 4) provides space to summarize the consultation sessions and their outcomes.

The documentation process is multifaceted and comprehensive. However, fidelity in documentation is one measure of integrity in completing the steps of the IC problem-solving stages. In program evaluation of IC, the completed Student Documentation Forms enable schools to use goal attainment scaling, based on actual data on students' progress in relation to goals set, to evaluate the effectiveness of their work. However, use of the form requires training in the instructional consultation process, and by itself does not provide all the necessary skills to conduct IC.

IC Teams

It is possible to adopt IC as a delivery system as an individual practitioner. However, the IC process has also been embedded in a school-wide delivery system, IC Teams (Rosenfield & Gravois, 1996). The core component of IC Teams is a multidisciplinary team, each of whose members is trained in the IC process and is expected to serve as a consultant (called a case manager in the IC Team model) to classroom teachers. The team, led by a trained facilitator, represents major building stakeholders, including regular education teachers, administrators, special educators, and pupil services staff. The team meets weekly to assign new cases, monitors case progress, discusses cases that are not making progress, engages in embedded professional development, and attends to maintenance activities, including team evaluation. Team members do the majority of problem-solving work in dyadic consultation sessions with teachers separate from the team meetings. The rationale for using a case management system is that team meetings provide insufficient time for the work of the problem-solving stages; further, the large team meetings are not conducive to building high quality working relationships with teachers. However, the team can provide consultation to the teacher–consultant dyads when they need additional support or are not able to make progress at that level.

IC Teams have been implemented in multiple types of schools, geographically and demographically (urban, suburban, rural, and with different ethnicities; see Rosenfield et al., 2008, as well as www.icteams.umd.edu for updated information on school sites). Although IC Teams have been implemented in middle and high schools, elementary schools have been the site of most implementations. When implemented in secondary schools, case management with individual teachers appears to be more effective than grade-level meetings for similar reasons to their effectiveness in elementary schools. However, research on secondary school models and outcomes are in progress to examine how best to provide services at this level.

Training

Bringing an IC Team from initiation to implementation to sustainability within the school requires adherence to principles of school change; those principles are more fully described elsewhere (Rosenfield & Gravois, 1996). However, one critical component of effective implementation of IC Teams is comprehensive training (Gravois, Knotek, & Babinski, 2002; Rosenfield, 2002). An intensive training program has been designed to enable team members to grow from novice to competent consultants. Additional training is provided to team facilitators, who must acquire not only competence in the instructional consultation process but also skill in team facilitation (Rosenfield et al., 2008).

A team can be brought into operation when there is a skilled IC facilitator to lead it. One competence required for facilitators is skill in case management. Each aspiring team facilitator attends a 20- to 24-hour IC training institute and is then coached through a consultation case. Novice facilitators tape each consultation session of their first IC case in a school and then send the tapes to a coach. The coach responds by e-mail, using a structured coaching process. After developing basic IC skills, the facilitator-in-training received an additional 2-day institute in the skills of facilitation, including school change issues. Facilitators then attend a training institute with their teams. The facilitator guides team members through the problem-solving stages of IC with practice cases in their home school (see Rosenfield et al., 2008, for additional information about coaching and team training).

Program Evaluation

Program evaluation is integrated into every step of IC Team implementation. Training is evaluated for skill development of participants. Treatment fidelity of the IC process and team functioning is measured by the Level of Implementation Scale (Fudell, 1992), as revised by Rosenfield and Gravois (1996). Outcomes are also assessed for a variety of variables, including increases in professional collaboration, application of assessment and instructional practices, positive student behaviors, academic achievement, and decreases in inappropriate referrals for special education, especially for cultural and linguistic minority students. A review of the research and development of IC Teams is found in Rosenfield et al. (2008), and the impact on disproportional placement of minority students in special education is presented in Gravois and Rosenfield (2006).

Role of Parents in IC

A frequently asked question is the role of parents in the IC Team problem-solving process. An IC Team is based on consultee-centered consultation principles, and a major focus is on building the skills and knowledge of teacher consultees so that they can more fully support student growth. School staff are encouraged to view consultation as providing an opportunity for teachers to reflect on their practice and obtain support for improving aspects of the instructional triangle in their classroom, not just with the student whose concerns bring the teacher to the process, but with other students with whom the teacher works. Building a working relationship so that teachers feel comfortable in examining their practice is more difficult when parents, whose major concern is naturally their own child's progress, are present.

In most cases, communication with parents remains the function of the classroom teacher. As a result of engaging in the IC process, teacher–consultees can base their discussions with parents on specific academic and behavioral goals, have useful data to share, and may have introduced instructional modifications matched to the student's skill level. With these specifics in place, teachers report being able to provide recommendations to parents that are based on data. In some cases, for example, family members are able to provide additional structured practice activities that support the classroom interventions.

SUMMARY

IC is an early intervention, stage-based problem-solving process based on consultee-centered consultation principles. The purpose is to enhance teacher capacity to use data-based decision making and evidence-based interventions to address student academic and behavioral concerns in the classroom. Ecological assumptions are the foundation, leading the problem solving to focus on the instructional triangle of alterable student variables, instructional tasks, and instructional design. Variables taken from the instructional triangle are assessed to determine if there is an instructional match that facilitates student learning and if there is a gap between the student's current and expected performance that requires intervention. Evidence-based interventions are implemented if a gap exists. Data are used to evaluate progress and make decisions about additional resources needed, including those of special education in some cases.

In order to function as an instructional consultant, school psychologists must be comfortable with the ecological assumptions that sustain the model. They need skills in collaborative problem solving, including building a working relationship with the teacher and good communication strategies. The consultation process involves specific stages of problem solving, each with its own tasks. The stages include entry and contracting, problem identification, intervention planning, intervention implementation, and resolution/termination. When the concern has not been resolved, the stages can be recycled or additional resources accessed. Instructional consultants are competent in instructional and behavioral assessment and intervention, including the domains of instruction and classroom management.

Data-based decision making is a core component of instructional consultation, and documentation of the process is critical for accountability. The Student Documentation Form provides a format for this process, and also helps to structure the problem-solving stages. The form is integrated into program evaluation of the effectiveness of IC Teams (Gravois & Rosenfield, 2002).

The IC Team model was developed to provide a structured school-based service delivery system. Although case problem solving with teachers continues to be implemented at the dyadic level, the team serves other functions. The multidisciplinary team, led by a skilled facilitator, includes stakeholders that represent administration, regular and special education, pupil service staff, and others as determined by the school leadership. The team provides opportunities for embedded professional development of team members, for working on cases that have not made progress in the case-based consultation process, for examining school-wide problems that individual cases may highlight, and for evaluating the effectiveness of the implementation.

Research on the IC process and the IC Team has been largely based on program evaluation as the model has been developing since the 1980s (see Rosenfield et al., 2008, for the most updated review). Research and development of training, technical assistance, fidelity of implementation, and outcomes have led to current best practices on IC Teams. Outcome research has documented the effect of IC Teams on teacher satisfaction and professional development, student goal attainment, and special education referrals and placements, including the effect on disproportional placement of minority students in special education (Rosenfield et al., 2008). An experimental study, funded by the Institute for Education Sciences, is underway to evaluate experimentally the model of IC Teams.

IC Teams is congruent with *Blueprint III* domains, tiers, and outcomes. IC brings school psychologists into contact with teachers for the purpose of enhancing academic and behavioral outcomes for students within their classroom. There is an emerging evidence base, including demonstrating that IC Teams can be scaled up for use in schools in different geographic and demographic settings. Implementing IC Teams in schools has enabled many school psychologists to move from a narrow psychometric role connected to special education classification to a one that has an impact on the positive development of both teachers and students.

REFERENCES

Benn, A. E., & Rosenfield, S. (2005, August). *Analysis of problem-solving teams as communities of practice*. Poster presented at the annual meeting of the American Psychological Association, Washington, DC.

Benn, A. E., & Rosenfield, S. (in press). Analysis of instructional consultants' questions and alternatives to questions during the problem identification interview. *Journal of Educational and Psychological Consultation.*

Bergan, J. R., & Schnaps, A. (1983). A model for instructional consultation. In J. Alpert & J. Meyers (Eds.), *Training in consultation* (pp. 104–119). Springfield, IL: Thomas.

Bloom, B. S. (1976). *Human characteristics and school learning.* New York: McGraw-Hill.

Donovan, S., & Cross, C. (Eds.). (2002). Minority students in special and gifted education. Washington, DC: National Academies Press.

Fudell, R. (1992). Level of implementation of teacher support teams and teachers' attitudes toward special needs students. *Dissertation Abstracts International, 53,* 1399A.

Gickling, E. E., Shane, R. L., & Croskery, K. M. (1989). Developing math skills in low-achieving high school students through curriculum-based assessment. *School Psychology Review, 18,* 344–356.

Gravois, T. A., Knotek, S., & Babinski, L. (2002). Educating practitioners as instructional consultants: Development and implementation of the IC Team consortium. *Journal Educational and Psychological Consultation, 13,* 113–132.

Gravois, T. A., & Rosenfield, S. (2002). A multidimensional framework for the evaluation of instructional consultation teams. *Journal of Applied School Psychology, 19,* 5–29.

Gravois, T. A., & Rosenfield, S. (2006). Impact of instructional consultation teams on the disproportionate referral and placement of minority students in special education. *Remedial and Special Education, 27,* 42–52.

Gravois, T. A., Rosenfield, S., & Gicking, E. E. (2006). *IC Teams Manual.* Unpublished manuscript.

Kavale, K. A., & Forness, S. R. (1999). *Efficacy of special education and related services.* Washington, DC: American Association on Mental Retardation.

Knotek, S. E., Kaniuka, M., & Ellingsen, K. (2008). Mental health consultation and consultee-centered approaches. In W. Erchul & S. Sheridan (Eds.), *Handbook of research in school consultation: Empirical foundations for the field* (pp. 127–145). New York: Erlbaum.

Knotek, S. E., Rosenfield, S., Gravois, T. A., & Babinski, L. (2003). The process of orderly reflection and conceptual change during instructional consultation. *Journal of Educational and Psychological Consultation, 14,* 303–328.

Rosenfield, S. (1987). *Instructional consultation.* New York: Erlbaum.

Rosenfield, S. (2000). Crafting usable knowledge. *American Psychologist, 55,* 1347–1355.

Rosenfield, S. (2002). Developing instructional consultants: From novice to competent to expert. *Journal of Educational and Psychological Consultation, 13,* 97–111.

Rosenfield, S. (2004). Consultation as dialogue: The right words at the right time. In N. M. Lambert, I. Hylander, & J. H. Sandoval (Eds.), *Consultee-centered consultation: Improving the quality of professional services in schools and community organizations* (pp. 337–347). New York: Erlbaum.

Rosenfield, S., & Gravois, T. A. (1996). *Instructional consultation teams: Collaborating for change.* New York: Guilford Press.

Rosenfield, S., Silva, A., & Gravois, T. (2008). Bringing instructional consultation to scale: Research and development of IC and IC Teams. In W. Erchul & S. Sheridan (Eds.), *Handbook of research in school consultation: Empirical foundations for the field* (pp. 203–223). New York: Erlbaum.

Stiggins, R. J., & Conklin, N. F. (1992). *In teachers' hands: Investigating the practices of classroom assessment.* Albany, NY: State University of New York Press.

Tombari, M. L., & Bergan, J. R. (1978). Consultant cues and teacher verbalizations, judgments, and expectancies concerning children's adjustment problems. *Journal of School Psychology, 16,* 212–219.

White, L. J., Summerlin, M. L., Loos, V. E., & Epstein, E. S. (1992). School and family consultation: A language-systems approach. In M. Fine & C. Carlson (Eds.), *The handbook of family–school intervention: A systems perspective* (pp. 347–362). Boston: Allyn & Bacon.

Ysseldyke, J. E., Burns, M. K., Dawson, M., Kelly, B., Morrison, D., Ortiz, S., et al. (2006). *School psychology: A blueprint for training and practice III.* Bethesda, MD: National Association of School Psychologists.

ANNOTATED BIBLIOGRAPHY

Rosenfield, S. (1987). *Instructional consultation.* New York: Erlbaum.

Provides an extended description of the IC process, including the assumptions, the communication skills, and the stages, that are presented in this chapter.

Rosenfield, S., & Gravois, T. A. (1996). *Instructional consultation teams: Collaborating for change.* New York: Guilford Press.

The structure and implementation of IC Teams are presented. Includes forms useful for implementation of IC and IC Teams, as well as a copy of the Level of Implementation Scale–Revised.

Rosenfield, S., Silva, A., & Gravois, T. (2007). Bringing instructional consultation to scale: Research and development of IC and IC teams. In W. Erchul & S. Sheridan (Eds.), *Handbook of research in school consultation: Empirical foundations for the field* (pp. 203–223). New York: Erlbaum.

Provides a history of the development of the IC and IC Teams model, including the conceptual framework, the components of the model, and the research documenting the process and the outcomes.

APPENDIX

Figure 2. Student Documentation Form, cover page.

INSTRUCTIONAL CONSULTATION STUDENT DOCUMENTATION FORM

Student's Name _____ Grade _____ Date of Birth _____ Date Started _____

Teacher's Name_____ Case Manager _____ School _____

GOAL ATTAINMENT SCALE (GAS)

Step 1: Initial description of concern				
Step 2: Prioritize	**Importance 1 2 3 4** (student at instructional level? Y N)	**Importance 1 2 3 4** (student at instructional level? Y N)	**Importance 1 2 3 4** (student at instructional level? Y N)	**Importance 1 2 3 4** (student at instructional level? Y N)
Step 3: Observable/measurable statement of current perfor- mance (following baseline)	Date collected _____	Date collected _____	Date collected _____	Date collected _____
Step 4: Short-term goal: Expected performance in ___weeks (4–6 weeks)	Date consistently attained _____	Date consistently attained _____	Date consistently attained _____	Date consistently attained _____
Step 5: Interim goal: Expected behavior in ___weeks	Date consistently attained _____	Date consistently attained _____	Date consistently attained _____	Date consistently attained _____
Step 6: Long-term goal: Expected behavior in ___weeks	Date consistently attained _____	Date consistently attained _____	Date consistently attained _____	Date consistently attained _____

Figure 3. **Student Documentation Form, center page.**

OPERATIONAL DEFINITION OF ACADEMIC/BEHAVIORAL PERFORMANCE: Priority # _____
on GAS

What specific academic/behaviors will be recoreded?_____

_____

When will the behavior be recorded?_____

Where will the behavior be recorded?_____

KEY
☐ _____
☐ _____
☐ _____

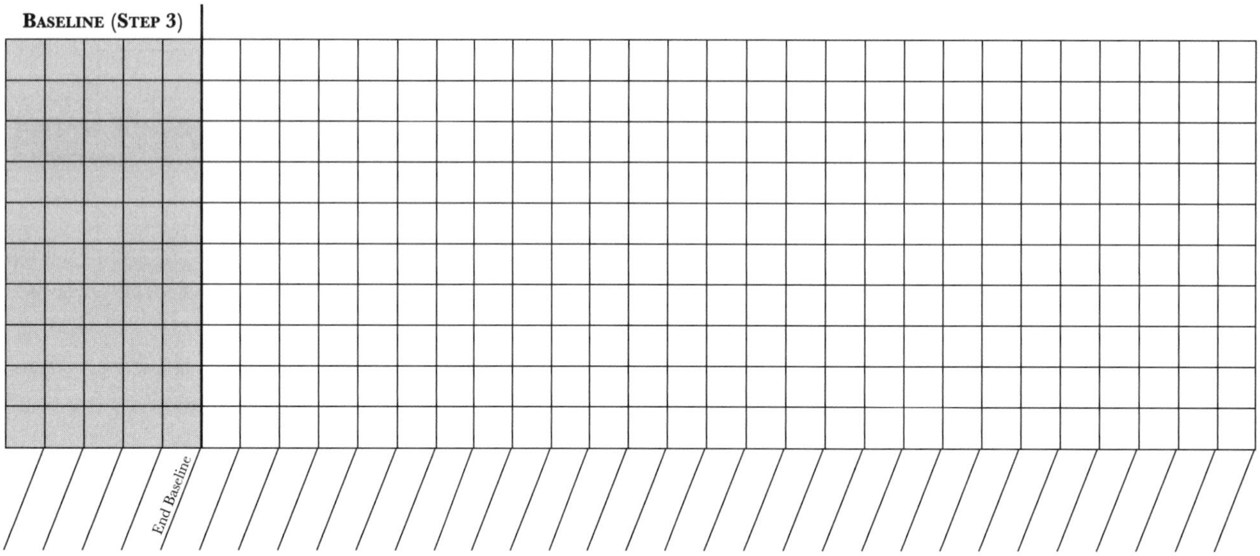

BASELINE (STEP 3)

End Baseline

Describe intervention design and materials	When and how often?	Persons responsible?	Motivational strategies?

Figure 4. **Student Documentation Form, back cover.**

Date	Summary of Meetings	Follow-Up Activities	Next Meeting Date and Time

104 Best Practices in Direct Behavioral Consultation

T. Steuart Watson
Miami University
Heather Sterling-Turner
The University of Southern Mississippi

OVERVIEW

Direct behavioral consultation is an extension of the behavioral consultation model first described by Bergan (1977) and subsequently elaborated on by Kratochwill and Bergan (1990). Briefly, behavioral consultation is a four-step problem-solving model where a consultant (i.e., school psychologist) helps a consultee (i.e., teacher) solve a client- (i.e., student) related problem. Behavioral consultation is conceptualized and practiced as an indirect service delivery model (for further discussion of the application of the four-step model in schools, see Kratochwill, chapter 105, vol. 5). There is a body of literature that shows behavioral consultation to be an at least moderately effective framework for delivering psychological services in the schools (Busse, Kratochwill, & Elliott, 1995) and as the preferred consultative model among school psychologists (Gutkin & Curtis, 1999). Because of the reported success of behavioral consultation, Sheridan and Kratochwill (1992) developed a consultation model called conjoint behavioral consultation in which a school psychologist works simultaneously with a parent and teacher (co-consultees) to solve a student-related problem. Like behavioral consultation, conjoint behavioral consultation has been reported to be a preferred model of service delivery by teachers (Freer & Watson, 1999).

Despite the reported success of behavioral consultation, legitimate criticisms have been raised regarding this model of service delivery. Noell and Witt (1996), for instance, listed five widely held assumptions about behavioral consultation that are not supported by empirical data: (a) psychological services delivered via a consultation model are more cost efficient than those delivered directly, (b) consultation conducted collaboratively is more effective than consultation whereby the school psychologist acts as an expert, (c) what is *said* during consultation is important for behavior change, (d) skills learned by the teacher during consultation will generalize to other situations and students, and (e) the school psychologist does not have to have direct contact with the student to effect behavior change in that student. Watson, Sterling, and McDade (1997) followed by adding four additional myths about behavioral consultation that, like the assumptions noted by Noell and Witt, are not supported by empirical evidence: (a) the *process* of behavioral consultation is based on a scientific analysis of behavior, (b) adherence to the process of behavioral consultation is important for treatment integrity and student outcome, (c) designing treatments that are acceptable to the teacher is important for enhancing treatment integrity, and (d) post-treatment acceptability is important.

In response to these assumptions and myths regarding the traditional process of behavioral consultation, Watson and Robinson (1996) described direct behavioral consultation, a variation of behavioral consultation. In direct behavioral consultation, the focus is on teaching *skills* to the teacher via direct interactions with the student throughout the consultation process. Admittedly, direct behavioral consultation is not an entirely new process as it is closely related to behavioral consultation and the methods and procedures for interacting with teachers and measuring behavior change are taken from the parent training, behavior analytic, and training applied psychology literature. It is distinguishable from other consultative models because of its focus on teacher skill acquisition through direct interactions with the student, measuring treatment integrity, measuring student outcome, and promoting generalization of teacher skills. For a graphic representation of the complete direct behavioral consultation model, see Figure 1.

Direct behavioral consultation fits within all tiers of a three-tier, school-based service delivery model. If the school psychologist is implementing a school-wide academic or social behavioral program (Tier 1), then some type of problem-solving process must be employed. For instance, if we are using a response-to-intervention (RTI) model, we must first determine what behavior we are going to measure, how it will be measured (e.g., curriculum-based measurement [CBM], Dynamic Indicators of Early Literacy Skills), and then staff must be trained to use the measurements correctly. Further, staff must be trained to analyze the results of the measurement and translate the analysis into educational programming.

All of these activities can be accomplished using the direct behavioral consultation model. Likewise, at Tier 2 (the targeted level), direct behavioral consultation can be used by school psychologists to assist personnel in making data-based decisions about student performance. Using the same RTI example, when the lowest performing 15% of students are identified, teachers must implement a more targeted intervention. Although teachers typically direct this process, school psychologists are often consulted to select and assist with implementation of the chosen intervention. For example, Peer Assisted Learning Strategies may be used for all children at this tier, which necessitates training in the procedure as well as in progress monitoring. Direct behavioral consultation is especially suited for this situation.

Finally, direct behavioral consultation is most often associated with application at Tier 3 (the intensive level), because most school-based consultation is focused on remediating deficits at the individual student level.

BASIC CONSIDERATIONS

Like behavioral consultation, direct behavioral consultation is a formal problem-solving process whereby a school psychologist seeks to assist a teacher with a student-related problem. The problem may be academic, social, or behavioral in nature. On the surface, the process of direct behavioral consultation does not differ substantially from behavioral consultation or its

Figure 1. A flow chart demonstrating the steps and major activities associated with the steps of direct behavioral consultation.

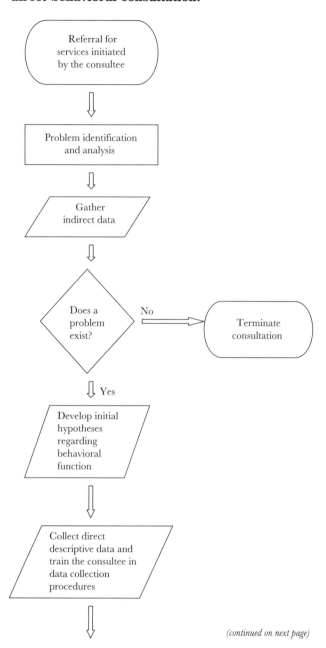

(continued on next page)

variants. Both models encourage (a) a structured problem-solving process to guide school psychologists and teachers; (b) operational definitions of target behaviors; (c) quantified intermediate and long-term goals; (d) and data collection pre-, during-, and post-intervention as an index of change by which to measure goal attainment. It should be made clear that behavioral consultation does not prohibit the activities that are hallmarks of direct behavioral consultation from occurring. However, these features of direct behavioral

Figure 1. (continued)

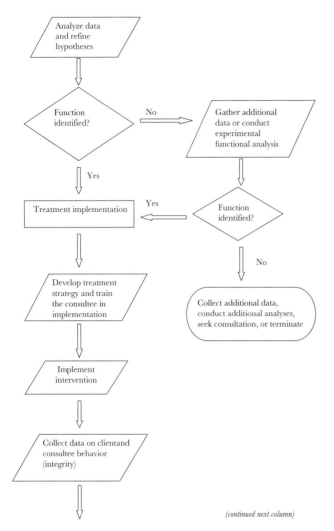

(continued next column)

Figure 1. (continued)

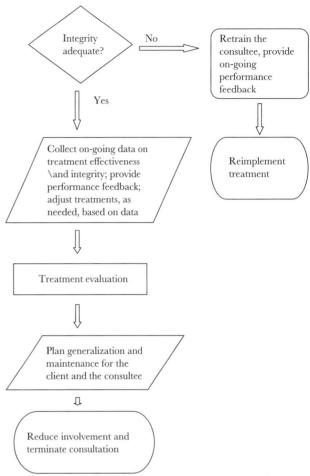

consultation are brought to the forefront of the model and are seen as crucial to each stage of the problem-solving process in all consultative relationships.

One difference between direct behavioral consultation and other models of consultation is that no division is made with regard to the focus of consultation. Other models of consultation have traditionally considered consultation occurring on a number of dimensions; most notably making distinctions between case-centered and teacher-centered (also referred to as technology training) modes of practice (for further discussion see Alpert,1995; Kratochwill & Pittman 2002; Caplan & Caplan, 1993). Case-centered consultation typically refers to a process in which a school psychologist helps bring about change in a client behavior through a mediator (teacher). This conceptualization is the more common view of a school psychologist–teacher consultative relationship. Technology training or teacher-centered consultation, on the

other hand, involves a consultative relationship in which the goal is to train or increase an existing skill in a teacher (Vernberg & Reppucci, 1986). In reality, school psychologists are often asking teachers to change their behaviors, sometimes substantially, to effect change in a client. Thus, direct behavioral consultation deems teacher training at all stages of the consultative process as an inherent part of case-centered consultation to ensure treatment integrity as well as to provide the teacher with a skill set he or she can employ in the future (generalization).

A second difference between direct behavioral consultation and other models of consultation is the *type* of data that drives the problem solving process. Direct behavioral consultation encourages the collection of direct measures of client behavior. Although school psychologists may employ teacher-collected measures as one source of data, these measures are corroborated with school psychologist–collected data. This is not to suggest that teachers are incapable of collecting data; however, there are two primary reasons to include school psychologist–collected data. First, given that very few teachers (and, presumably, even fewer parents) are trained in behavior analysis, teachers are unlikely to enter the consultative relationship with an adequate skill set to collect data in such a manner as to provide accurate information. This may be especially true with regard to behavioral function, a vital part of the problem identification and problem analysis stages of direct behavioral consultation. While one goal of direct behavioral consultation is to train teachers to view problems from a functional standpoint, direct observations of client behavior can avoid discrepancies that may result from differences in school psychologist and teacher understanding of behavior. For example, teachers may report that they ignore problem behavior in the classroom, but direct observations may reveal that teachers attend to the problem behavior in nonverbal ways (e.g., moving closer to the student) or actually providing attention (e.g., "You can keep doing that all you want. I'm just going to ignore you.").

A second important reason to collect direct observational data is to collect measures of treatment integrity; that is, the extent to which the independent variable (i.e., treatment) is implemented according to the prescribed procedures. There are two aspects of treatment integrity, which are important to interventions arising from consultation, accuracy, and consistency (Watson, 2004). Accuracy refers to implementing the intervention correctly. That is, were all the steps in the intervention protocol followed or what was the average percentage of steps implemented across a number of trials? Consistency refers to the percentage of time the intervention was implemented as a function of the number of opportunities available to implement the intervention. Both dimensions of treatment integrity are essential because a treatment could be implemented exactly as intended (100% accuracy), but if only done once every 10 times the opportunity arose (10% consistency), it would likely result in little to no behavior change. Conversely, an intervention could be

implemented with 100% consistency; yet each time was implemented with only 20% accuracy, which would also likely result in insufficient behavior change (see Table 1 for an illustration of the relationship between accuracy, consistency, and behavior change).

Although other models of consultation do not preclude the collection of measures of treatment integrity in this manner, direct observations are typically discussed as one option along with interviews and self-monitoring. The direct behavioral consultation model argues that direct observations of integrity, even through simple probe analyses, are crucial for ensuring the treatment plan is implemented as intended, as research has shown that teachers over report actual integrity (see, e.g., Robbins & Gutkin, 1994; Wickstrom, Jones, LaFluer, & Witt, 1998).

BEST PRACTICES

Problem Identification and Analysis

In most models of school-based problem-solving models, and certainly in behavioral consultation and its variants, the problem-solving process is broken down into four distinct stages: problem identification, problem analysis, plan (treatment) implementation, and problem (treatment) evaluation (Bergan & Kratochwill, 1990; Kratochwill & Bergan, 1990). These stages are usually associated with distinct interviews and specific objectives and tasks for each individual in the consultative relationship.

According to the behavioral consultation model (Bergan & Kratochwill, 1990; Kratochwill & Bergan, 1990), the goals of the problem identification stage of consultation are to define the problem behavior of interest, develop data collection measures, and establish discrepancies between the current problem behavior and a desired behavior (goal and objective setting). The primary method for accomplishing these goals is the school psychologist–teacher interview.

Table 1. A Diagram of the Predicted Relationship Between Levels of the Two Dimensions of Treatment Integrity (Accuracy and Consistency) and Behavior Change

		Accuracy		
		Low	Medium	High
		<40%	40–75%	>75%
Consistency	Low	Little to no behavior change	Little to no behavior change	Little to no behavior change
	Medium	Little to no behavior change	Moderate behavior change	Significant behavior change
	High	Little to no behavior change	Significant behavior change	Significant behavior change

The goals of the problem analysis stage of behavioral consultation include examining environmental and contextual variables related to the problem behavior and developing a plan by which to achieve the goals and objectives developed during the problem identification stage (for further discussion and description, see Bergan & Kratochwill, 1990, and Kratochwill & Bergan, 1990). As with problem identification, the problem analysis stage of consultation is typically conducted using interviews as a primary source of information. However, some school psychologists also use more objective measures, such as CBM and direct observation data to supplement their interview data.

In direct behavioral consultation, problem identification and analysis are not viewed as separate stages in the consultative process but are, instead, seen as inextricably intertwined, similar to the problem-solving process described by Edwards (1987). Although this distinction between direct behavioral consultation and behavioral consultation may be in effect splitting hairs, proponents of a direct behavioral consultation approach to consultation assert that without a proper analysis of data, including environmental factors, which contribute to the problem and which may assist in problem resolution, a school psychologist cannot be certain the problem has been correctly identified. A potential added advantage of viewing the process of consultation in this manner is that by developing hypotheses about behavioral function and refining hypotheses as data are continually collected the school psychologist and teacher may spend less time recycling through the consultative process.

Initial Problem Identification (Indirect Assessment)

The outset of the consultative relationship under direct behavioral consultation is akin to conducting a functional behavioral assessment (FBA) through indirect measures (for more detailed information on conducting functional behavior assessments see Steege & Watson, chapter 19, vol. 2). That is, the initial meeting between the school psychologist and teacher will likely take the form of an interview and involve the collection of other, supplementary data such as rating scales and records reviews. Data derived at this stage of consultation typically serve as a starting point from which the school psychologist can begin to develop hypotheses about the function of the client's problem behavior(s). In addition, interviews serve as a means by which to develop a working relationship with the teacher and lay out the framework for the process of consultation.

There is no one standard interview espoused for use in direct behavioral consultation. However, school psychologists are encouraged to use an interview that incorporates, at a minimum, the following information: (a) a precise, operational definition of the problem behavior including response dimensions such as frequency or rate; (b) times of the day and settings in which the problem behavior is most likely to occur; (c) other antecedents that may evoke the problem behavior; (d) consequences associated with the problem behavior; and (e) previously used strategies to address the problem behavior, whether successful or unsuccessful. In addition, school psychologists should be careful to collect information about antecedent and consequent condition that are *not* associated with problem behavior (i.e., making the problem behavior less likely to occur and/or producing desired behaviors), as this information is often useful in treatment development. The school psychologist may also want to include a client as a source of data, when appropriate, as he or she may provide insights as to what factors precipitate problem behavior as well as factors that may lead to desired behavior (e.g., an initial preference assessment).

Several published interview instruments that incorporate these essential elements of an FBA are available, including the Functional Assessment Interview (O'Neill, Horner, Albin, Storey, & Sprague, 1990), the Preliminary Functional Assessment Survey (Dunlap et al., 1993), and the Functional Assessment Interview Record (FAIR; Edwards, 2002). Although each of these instruments has research to support its use, one potential advantage of the FAIR is that it has separate forms for use with teachers (FAIR-T; Edwards, 2002) and parents (FAIR-P). The FAIR-T has also been modified to assess academic deficits only (FAIR-TA; Henry, 2000) and has a downward extension to assess environmental variables that may be unique to preschool settings (FAIR-Pre; Dufrene, 2005). Another potential advantage of the FAIR series is that they can be completed as a rating scale and followed up with an interview tailored to specific questions.

In addition to interview data, school psychologists may wish to employ rating scales as a source of data for examining potential factors impinging on the occurrence of problem behavior. Ideally, these scales should address behavioral function. As with interviews, there are many rating scales appropriate for use during problem identification and include several popular instruments such as the Motivation Assessment Scale (Durand & Crimmins, 1988), the Problem Behavior Questionnaire (Lewis, Scott, & Sugai, 1994), and the

Functional Analysis Screening Tool (Goh, Iwata, & DeLeon, 1996). School psychologists are cautioned, however, to never rely on rating scales as a primary or sole source of data. First, most rating scales, especially those specifically designed to assess behavioral function, cannot be administered repeatedly and, therefore, are poor indices of behavior change over time. Second, it is our experience that rating scale data often require follow-up interviewing and observation and clarification because of differences in most teacher's and school psychologist's conceptualization and understanding of behavior, particularly for those school psychologists who are trained in behavior analysis.

Direct Data Collection

Immediately following, or concurrent with, the collection of indirect sources of data, the school psychologist should begin to collect direct observational data of the student's behavior. Here again is a critical difference between direct behavioral consultation and behavioral consultation. Although behavioral consultation does not preclude a school psychologist from collecting data during problem identification, Bergan and Kratochwill (1990) wrote, "[i]t is generally not recommended that the school psychologist collect the data because it is not an efficient use of his or her time" (p. 61). Proponents of the direct behavioral consultation model would argue that the collection of data by the school psychologist actually may be a more efficient use of time in that relying solely on teacher report may not adequately capture the behavior of interest due to different understandings, conceptualizations, and interpretations of problem behavior (Sterling-Turner, Robinson, & Wilczynski, 2001; Sterling-Turner, Watson, & Moore, 2002; Watson & Robinson, 1996). In addition, the teacher may inadvertently and unknowingly be contributing to the maintenance of a problem behavior (Sterling-Turner, Robinson, & Wilczynski, 2001). By collecting observational data, the school psychologist may spend less time recycling through the consultation process because the probability of identifying the correct problem at the outset of consultation, identifying the most salient factors related to the problem during problem analysis (based on school psychologist–collected data and not the teacher report), and developing the most appropriate intervention based on these data is higher. That is, the school psychologist does not have to wait for treatment failure before collecting additional information to add to the understanding of the problem behavior.

As noted previously, just as school psychologists are not prohibited from collecting data under the traditional behavioral consultation model, the teacher is not disallowed from collecting observational data in the direct behavioral consultation model. Training the teacher in data collection methods is an essential component of direct behavioral consultation as originally conceptualized by Watson and Robinson (1996). It is unreasonable to assume that the school psychologist will be routinely available to collect data on a daily basis or for extended periods of time (i.e., multiple hours) on those days in which he or she is available to collect data. Further, in certain circumstances, teacher-collected data may be the only available source of information regarding the behavior(s) of interest (e.g., low frequency behavior; substantial reactivity to observers). Finally, because one of the goals of direct behavioral consultation is to provide the teacher with a skill set to use in the future, school psychologists must assist teachers in developing these skills. Given these factors, and because most teachers are not trained in data collection procedures, it's crucial to ensure that teachers are provided with a rationale for the importance of data gathering (e.g., not waiting until the day is over and providing estimates of what occurred, when it occurred, and why it occurred) and appropriate training in the systematic collection of data (Sterling-Turner, Robinson, & Wilczynski, 2001).

At times, based on direct observational data, the school psychologist will suggest that the teacher and school psychologist reconceptualize the definition of the problem behavior developed in the initial interview. For example, additional problem behavior may be discovered, which, if targeted, may effect change in the problem behavior that resulted in the teacher's seeking services. For instance, a third-grade student is referred because of repeated class disruptions. The teacher reports that the student is academically average and views the disruption as a behavioral compliance issue. The school psychologist observes the student and analyzes samples of academic work and discovers that problem behaviors occur most often during reading, particularly independent reading tasks. Coupled with a review of the school-wide academic screening data, the student falls on the borderline of a Tier 1/Tier 2 intervention. Based on this information, the school psychologist recommends to the teacher a more thorough investigation of reading skills as a means of reconceptualizing the nature of the disruption. That is, it appears less of a behavioral compliance issue and more of an academic skill deficit affecting behavior.

A thorough review of potential data collection methods are beyond the scope of this chapter but may include time-sampling procedures, narrative recording, or event recording. (See Hintze, Volpe, & Shapiro, chapter 18, vol. 2, on systematic direct observation of student behavior or Watson & Steege (2003) for further discussion on data collection methods and their relative strengths and weaknesses.) However, school psychologists are cautioned that the selection of the observation procedures should be done carefully in order to allow for the collection of relevant antecedent and consequent variables in addition to the targeted behavior(s). In addition, the data collection procedure should be chosen, most typically, with a particular data analysis procedure in mind. Finally, the data collected potentially can serve as baseline data.

Data Interpretation (Analysis)

Once some initial descriptive data are collected, the school psychologist can begin examining more fully the relationship between antecedents, behaviors, and consequences by examining patterns of behavior (i.e., the likelihood of environmental variables preceding or following targeted behaviors). There are several forms these analyses can take including simple narrative descriptions and conditional probability analyses (for additional discussion, see Sterling-Turner, Robinson, & Wilczynski, 2001; Watson & Steege, 2003). Although data collection methods will in part drive the selection of a data analysis procedure, the type of analysis (if done appropriately) does not matter as much as the end goal: to confirm or disconfirm initial hypotheses developed during the indirect and descriptive assessment phases.

At this point, there may be sufficient supportive data (i.e., convergent evidence) to suggest a behavioral function, at which point the school psychologist and teacher should move to the treatment development and implementation phase of direct behavioral consultation. Although descriptive data alone do not confirm a behavioral function (i.e., the data are only correlational) and some debate exists as to the correspondence between descriptive and experimental functional analyses, there are certainly research examples in which desired treatment outcomes were achieved when only descriptive data were included in the functional assessment (e.g., Clarke et al., 1995; Dunlap et al., 1993; Grandy & Peck, 1997; Kern, Childs, Dunlap, Clarke, & Falk, 1994; Mueller, Sterling-Turner, & Scattone, 2001; Repp & Karsh, 1994; Storey, Lawry, Ashworth, Danko, & Strain, 1994). Gathering direct descriptive data is part and parcel of the direct behavioral consultation process and likely contributes to its effectiveness as a service delivery model.

However, in those instances in which the results of a descriptive analysis are ambiguous or rival hypotheses exist regarding behavioral function, it is recommended that school psychologists use experimental analyses to verify hypotheses or examine temporally distant events (Ray & Watson, 2001). For example, a female kindergarten child is referred for excessive talking during center time. Observations indicated that when she is talking, she avoids her work and the teacher provides assistance on the task. In this case, it is unclear if the child is attempting to escape the task altogether, recruit teacher attention, or reduce task difficulty by receiving assistance from the teacher. By doing analyses in which each of these hypotheses is tested, a more clear relationship between antecedent variables (e.g., task difficulty), the child's behavior, and consequences (e.g., escape and attention) may be elucidated. A complete review of functional analysis methodologies is far too ambitious for this chapter but may include (a) a standard set of conditions such as those described by Iwata, Dorsey, Slifer, Bauman, and Richman (1982/1994), (b) hypothesis-driven procedures in which only those conditions hypothesized to contribute to the maintenance of problem behavior are assessed, (c) hierarchical methods (e.g., Cooper et al., 1992) in which variables hypothesized to be related to the occurrence of problem behavior are systematically assessed in order of easiest to most difficult to implement (and at times may be based on teacher preference), or (d) brief functional analysis (Derby et al., 1992; Northup et al., 1991).

Pragmatic concerns such as the availability of a space, availability of personnel, teacher cooperation, and time will undoubtedly have an impact on how a functional analysis is carried out. However, whenever possible, the school psychologist is encouraged to have the teacher implement the functional analysis conditions in order to create a set of conditions that most closely resemble the natural environment. Although some school psychologists may have concerns that a teacher will not be able to conduct these conditions, research has consistently shown that teachers in particular are amenable to training in functional analysis and implement conditions with high integrity following trainings (Broussard & Northup, 1995; Lalli, Browder, Mace, & Brown, 1993; Moore et al., 2002; Northup et al., 1991; Watson, Ray, Sterling-Turner, & Logan, 1999). Another advantage to having school psychologists implement functional analysis conditions is that it provides another opportunity for teachers to gain a greater understanding of environmental–behavioral relationships.

Treatment Implementation

Once all sources of data have been analyzed and the function of behavior identified, the school psychologist and teacher work together to develop an appropriate treatment that can be carried out in the classroom or other treatment setting(s). The school psychologist, because he or she has spent time analyzing factors related to the problem behavior and because of his or her training in applied behavior analysis techniques, will likely already have several recommendations to present to the teacher, if not a full treatment plan developed. As with planning any behavioral or academic intervention, the school psychologist should be careful to consider antecedent (e.g., response effort, establishing operations, and discriminative stimuli) and consequent variables that may have an impact on the teacher's performance. Input from the teacher should be sought regarding variables in the treatment setting that may facilitate goal attainment. The school psychologist should also assess the teacher's perceptions of variables that could impede goal attainment. As potential barriers are being discussed, the school psychologist can then work with the teacher to either modify the proposed treatment strategies or assist the teacher in finding ways to reduce the barriers.

One potential barrier to treatment success is a teacher's ability to implement the proposed intervention as intended. Before implementing the treatment, the school psychologist using direct behavioral consultation ensures that the person(s) responsible for implementing the treatment is well trained. Although other models of consultation do touch on the issue of teacher training, it is given less attention than other consultative process variables (e.g., assessing treatment acceptability, assessing power status among the parties).

Training issues in direct behavioral consultation are at the forefront of the model and are seen as crucial in the treatment implementation phase to ensure high implementation integrity. Numerous studies have shown that when behavior change agents (i.e., teachers) are taught via direct methods such as modeling and practice with feedback, their integrity is higher than when only given verbal instructions (Sterling-Turner & Watson, 2002; Sterling-Turner et al., 2002; Sterling-Turner, Watson, et al., 2001; Watson & Kramer, 1995). Sterling-Turner et al. (2002) demonstrated in a school-based

consultation study that using direct training as advocated by direct behavioral consultation resulted in higher levels of treatment integrity in four out of four teachers than when using verbal (didactic) instructions. Relatedly, higher levels of treatment integrity resulted in greater behavior change for three of the four students. It stands to reason that any procedure that increases the integrity of a well-designed and appropriate treatment will be more beneficial for the student than an otherwise appropriate treatment that is delivered with insufficient integrity. Without adequate integrity, no definitive decisions can be made about treatment effectiveness. Further, the school psychologist and teacher may spend less time recycling through the consultation process as high integrity will likely be associated with desired treatment outcomes (Noell et al., 2005; Sterling-Turner et al., 2002).

Once the teacher can implement the proposed intervention with sufficient integrity, the school psychologist and teacher should make plans for monitoring treatment effects. Ideally, the teacher will have been trained in a data collection system during the problem identification and analysis stage, and he or she will continue to collect these data as one measure of behavior change. The school psychologist will continue to collect direct observational data for the dual purpose of collecting data on client behavior change and, equally important, to assess the teacher's implementation integrity. The school psychologist should, based on the teacher's integrity, provide on-going performance-based feedback. Performance feedback has been shown to be a critical element in promoting on-going treatment integrity (Noell, Witt, Gilbertson, Ranier, & Freeland, 1997; Noell et al., 2000, 2005; Witt, Noell, LaFleur, & Mortenson, 1997).

In addition to assessing implementation integrity, an added advantage of school psychologist–collected data during treatment implementation is that it allows the school psychologist to identify other potential factors (e.g., lack of resources, instructional variables interfering with implementation needs) that may decrease the potential effectiveness of the intervention and make adjustments to the treatment plan accordingly. The school psychologist will likely be using some form of single-subject design to evaluate treatment effects. From a practice standpoint, single-subject designs, by their very nature, are amenable to changes in treatment procedures (e.g., adding a second treatment phase). Graphing data frequently will reveal the need to make treatment modifications (Barlow & Hersen, 1984; Edwards, 1987; Hayes, Barlow, & Nelson-Gray, 1999).

Perhaps notably absent from this and previous stages of the direct behavioral consultation model when compared to the behavioral consultation model is the assessment of pretreatment acceptability data. Direct behavioral consultation does not stipulate that acceptability data (i.e., teacher preference) cannot be included as a variable in making treatment selection decisions, such as in cases when two or more treatment options with equal probability of effecting the desired change in the client are available. Nor does the direct behavioral consultation model suggest that treatments should be created that are intentionally unacceptable to a teacher or without teacher input. However, there are insufficient empirical data to support the notion that treatment acceptability information leads to higher treatment integrity (as observed by direct measures of intervention agents' behavior) and/or relationship to direct measures of treatment outcomes (Noell et al., 2005; Sterling-Turner & Watson, 2002; Wickstrom et al., 1998). There are data, as noted previously, that training and performance feedback are crucial to promoting treatment, which, in turn, is associated with desired treatment outcomes. Therefore, we contend that school psychologists do not need to systematically assess teacher acceptability of treatment plans in all cases but, rather, spend their efforts engaging in practices that will result in a higher probability of goal attainment.

Treatment Evaluation

The school psychologist and teacher must agree at some point that it is time to reduce the school psychologist's involvement with a case. As with problem identification and analysis, in some respects there is no clear distinction between treatment implementation and treatment evaluation in the direct behavioral consultation model. Evaluation of progress is a dynamic process based on ongoing data-driven decision making, a hallmark feature of applied behavior analysis and single-subject designs. Thus, the school psychologist and teacher are constantly evaluating a client's progress toward a goal and making adjustments accordingly to increase the probability of goal attainment, whether these adjustments are made to the conceptualization of the problem, changing the goals of the consultation, increasing teacher skills in intervention implementation, or modifying the intervention plan.

When the school psychologist and teacher agree that the goal of consultation has been reached, as indicated by the data, consultation activities should be directed toward generalization and maintenance planning. As in behavioral consultation, the school psychologist and teacher have a number of options at this point including (a) leaving the intervention, as is, in place; (b) fading the intervention; or (c) discontinuing the intervention entirely. With regard to generalization planning, the school psychologist is encouraged to read both Stokes and Baer's (1977) and Stokes and Osnes' (1986) articles on generalization techniques. In addition to generalization and maintenance planning for client behaviors, the school psychologist should not terminate consultation before doing maintenance planning with the teacher as well. The school psychologist should ensure that the teacher has the requisite skills and resources to maintain the final plan before terminating the consultative relationship. In addition, the school psychologist should systematically plan, with the teacher, follow-up meetings in which data regarding continual client progress are presented and discussed.

Finally, before terminating consultation, the school psychologist should engage in some teacher skill-generalization activities as well. For example, the school psychologist could review the skills and techniques applied to the case and outline conditions and scenarios under which particular assessment and treatment components could be used again. In some instances, procedures developed for one student in a Tier 3 intervention are determined to be suitable for application at the class-wide level (Tier 2). A simple positive reinforcement program that was effectively used for one particularly problematic student is subsequently applied to every child in the class as a means of promoting positive social behavior. Ideally, the school psychologist will leave the consultative relationship with having provided the teacher with a skill set he or she can use in similar situations. Interestingly, two studies have shown that direct behavioral consultation results in greater generalization of skills than behavioral consultation (Freeland, 2003; Watkins-Emonet, 2001).

SUMMARY

Direct behavioral consultation is much like other consultative models in that it is a structured problem-solving process. However, it differs from other models of consultation in that it focuses on teaching skills to teachers via direct interactions with the student, that it actively promotes the development and measurement of treatment integrity, and that the ultimate indicator of success is student outcome and not adherence to the process or what is said *during* the consultative process. Previous research has shown direct behavioral consultation to be effective for accomplishing these goals and for promoting generalization of skills. What is unknown at this time, however, is the amount of effort required relative to other models of consultation. We can surmise that, initially, the direct behavioral consultation process may be a bit more time intensive because of the nature of the interaction between the school psychologist and teacher. Overall, we would expect less time required from the school psychologist because the direct behavioral consultation process focuses on teaching skills and promoting treatment integrity. These dual foci would likely result in less recycling through the consultation process due to lack of intervention effectiveness. That said, we believe there is a place for many of the different models of consultation referred to in this chapter and in this edition of *Best Practices*.

What is not known at this time is which consultation model works best, under what circumstances, with what type of teachers and presenting problems, and with consideration of teacher knowledge and skill. It is likely that these, and other variables, ultimately have an impact on the selection of consultation model in any given circumstance. We must also be careful to point out that we are not asserting that engaging in the direct behavioral consultation process will *always* produce the desired outcomes sought by the teacher. Sometimes, despite a school psychologist's, and teacher's, best efforts, the problem behavior targeted in consultation will not be resolved adequately and other avenues to reach a solution to a problem will have to be explored.

REFERENCES

Alpert, J. L. (1995). Some guidelines for school consultants. *Journal of Educational and Psychological Consultation, 6,* 31–46.

Barlow, D. H., & Hersen, M. (1984). *Single case experimental design: Strategies for studying behavior change* (2nd ed.). Boston: Allyn & Bacon.

Bergan, J. R. (1977). *Behavioral consultation.* Columbus, OH: Merrill.

Bergan, J. R., & Kratochwill, T. R. (1990). *Behavioral consultation in applied settings.* New York, NY: Plenum Press.

Broussard, C. D., & Northup, J. (1995). An approach to functional assessment and analysis of disruptive behavior in regular education classrooms. *School Psychology Quarterly, 10,* 154–164.

Busse, R. T., Kratochwill, T. R., & Elliott, S. N. (1995). Meta-analysis for single-case consultation outcomes: Applications to research and practice. *Journal of School Psychology, 33,* 269–285.

Caplan, G., & Caplan, R. B. (1993). *Mental health consultation and collaboration.* San Francisco: Jossey-Bass.

Clarke, S., Dunlap, G., Foster-Johnson, L., Childs, K. E., Wilson, D., White, R., et al. (1995). Improving the conduct of student with behavioral disorders by incorporating student interests into curricular activities. *Behavioral Disorders, 20,* 221–237.

Cooper, L. J., Wacker, D. P., Thursby, D., Plagmann, L. A., Harding, J., & Derby, K. M. (1992). Analysis of the role of task preference, task demands, and adult attention on child behavior in outpatient and classroom settings. *Journal of Applied Behavior Analysis, 25,* 823–840.

Derby, K. M., Wacker, D. P., Sasso, G., Steege, M., Northup, J., Cigrand, K., et al. (1992). Brief functional assessment techniques to evaluate aberrant behavior in an outpatient setting: A summary of 79 cases. *Journal of Applied Behavior Analysis, 25,* 713–721.

Dunlap, G., Kern, L., dePerczel, M., Clarke, S., Wilson, D., Childs, K., et al. (1993). Functional analysis of classroom variables for students with emotional and behavioral disorders. *Behavioral Disorders, 18,* 275–291.

Durand, V. M., & Crimmins, D. B. (1988). Identifying the variables maintaining self-injurious behavior. *Journal of Autism and Developmental Disorders, 18,* 99–117.

Dufrene, B. A. (2005). *Functional behavior assessment: A preliminary investigation of convergent, treatment, and social validity.* Unpublished doctoral dissertation, Mississippi State University, Starkville.

Edwards, R. P. (2002). A tutorial for using the Functional Assessment Informant Record for Teachers. *Proven Practice: Prevention and Remediation Solutions for Schools, 4,* 31–33.

Edwards, R. P. (1987). Implementing the scientist–practitioner model: The school psychologist as data-based problem solver. *Professional School Psychology, 2,* 155–161.

Freeland, J. T. (2003). Analyzing the effects of direct behavioral consultation on teachers: Generalization of skills across settings (Doctorial dissertation). *Dissertation Abstracts International, 63*(10-A), 3471.

Freer, P. J., & Watson, T. S. (1999). A comparison of parent and teacher acceptability ratings of behavioral and conjoint behavioral consultation. *School Psychology Review, 28,* 672–683.

Goh, H. L., Iwata, B. A., & DeLeon, I. G. (1996). *The functional analysis screening tool.* Poster session presented at the meeting of the Association of Behavior Analysts, San Diego, CA.

Grandy, S. E., & Peck, S. M. (1997). The use of functional assessment and self-management with a first grader. *Child and Family Behavior Therapy, 19,* 29–43.

Gutkin, T. B., & Curtis, M. J. (1999). School-based consultation theory and practice: The art and science of indirect service delivery. In C. R. Reynolds & T. B. Gutkin (Eds.), *The handbook of school psychology* (pp.598–637). New York: John Wiley.

Hayes, S. C., Barlow, D. H., & Nelson-Gray, R. O. (1999). *The scientist practitioner: Research and accountability in the age of managed care* (2nd ed.). Boston: Allyn & Bacon.

Henry, J. R. (2000). *Functional assessment: Determining maintaining variables of academic behavior*. Unpublished doctoral dissertation, The University of Southern Mississippi, Hattiesburg.

Iwata, B. A., Dorsey, M. F., Slifer, K. J., Bauman, K. E., & Richman, G. S. (1982/1994). Toward a functional analysis of self-injury. *Journal of Applied Behavior Analysis, 27*, 197–209, (Reprinted from *Analysis and Intervention in Developmental Disabilities*, 1982, *2*, 3–20.)

Kern, L., Childs, K. E., Dunlap, G., Clarke, S., & Falk, G. D. (1994). Using assessment-based curricular interventions to improve the classroom behavior of a student with emotional and behavioral challenges. *Journal of Applied Behavior Analysis, 27*, 7–19.

Kratochwill, T. R., & Bergan, J. R. (1990). *Behavioral consultation in applied settings*. New York: Plenum Press.

Kratochwill, T. R., & Pittman, P. H. (2002). Expanding problem-solving consultation training: Prospects and frameworks. *Journal of Educational and Psychological Consultation, 13*, 69–95.

Lalli, J. S., Browder, D. M., Mace, F. C., & Brown, D. K. (1993). Teacher use of descriptive analysis data to implement interventions to decrease student problem behaviors. *Journal of Applied Behavior Analysis, 26*, 227–238.

Lewis, T. J., Scott, T. M., & Sugai, G. (1994). The problem behavior questionnaire: A teacher-based instrument to develop functional hypotheses of problem behavior in general education classrooms. *Diagnostique, 19*, 103–115.

Lewis, T. J., & Sugai, G. (1996). Descriptive and experimental analysis of teacher and peer attention and the use of assessment-based intervention to improve pro-social behavior. *Journal of Behavioral Education, 6*, 7–24.

Moore, J. W., Edwards, R. P., Sterling-Turner, H. E., Riley, J., DuBard, M., & McGeorge, A. (2002). Teacher acquisition of functional analysis methodology: Didactic versus direct training. *Journal of Applied Behavior Analysis, 35*, 73–77.

Mueller, M. M., Sterling-Turner, H. E., & Scattone, D. (2001). Functional assessment of hand flapping in a general education classroom. *Journal of Applied Behavior Analysis, 34*, 233–236.

Noell, G. H., & Witt, J. C. (1996). A critical re-evaluation of five fundamental assumptions underlying behavioral consultation. *School Psychology Quarterly, 11*, 189–203.

Noell, G. H., Witt, J. C., Gilbertson, D. N., Ranier, D. D., & Freeland, J. T. (1997). Increasing teacher intervention implementation in general education settings through consultation and performance feedback. *School Psychology Quarterly, 12*, 77–88.

Noell, G. H., Witt, J. C., LaFleur, L. H., Mortenson, B. P., Ranier, D. D., & LeVelle, J. (2000). Increasing intervention implementation in general education following consultation: A comparison of two follow-up strategies. *Journal of Applied Behavior Analysis, 33*, 271–284.

Noell, G. H., Witt, J. C., Slider, N. J., Connell, J. E., Gatti, S. L., Williams, K. L., et al. (2005). Treatment implementation following behavioral consultation in schools: A comparison of three follow-up strategies. *School Psychology Review, 34*, 87–106.

Northup, J., Wacker, D. P., Sasso, G., Steege, M., Cigrand, K., Cook, J., et al. (1991). A brief functional analysis of aggressive and alternating behavior in an out-clinic setting. *Journal of Applied Behavior Analysis, 24*, 509–522.

O'Neill, R. E., Horner, R. H., Albin, R. W., Storey, K., & Sprague, J. R. (1990). *Functional analysis of problem behavior: A practical assessment guide*. Sycamore, IL: Sycamore Press.

Ray, K. P., & Watson, T. S. (2001). Analysis of the effects of temporally distant events on school behavior. *School Psychology Quarterly, 16*, 324–342.

Repp, A. C., & Karsh, K. G. (1994). Hypothesis-based interventions for tantrum behaviors of persons with developmental disabilities in school settings. *Journal of Applied Behavior Analysis, 27*, 21–31.

Robbins, J. R., & Gutkin, T. B. (1994). Consultee and client remedial and preventive outcomes following consultation: Some mixed empirical results and directions for future research. *Journal of Educational and Psychological Consultation, 5*, 149–167.

Sheridan, S. M., & Kratochwill, T. R. (1992). Behavioral parent/teacher consultation: Conceptual and research considerations. *Journal of School Psychology, 30*, 117–139.

Sterling-Turner, H. E., & Watson, T. S. (2002). An analog investigation of the relationship between treatment acceptability and treatment integrity. *Journal of Behavioral Education, 11*, 39–50.

Sterling-Turner, H. E., Robinson, S. L., & Wilczynski, S. M. (2001). Functional analysis of distracting and disruptive behaviors in the school setting. *School Psychology Review, 30*, 211–226.

Sterling-Turner, H. E., Watson, T. S., & Moore, J. W. (2002). Effects of training on treatment integrity and treatment outcomes in school-based consultation. *School Psychology Quarterly, 17*, 47–77.

Sterling-Turner, H. E., Watson, T. S., Wildmon, M., Watkins, C., & Little, E. (2001). Investigating the empirical relationship between training type and treatment integrity. *School Psychology Quarterly, 16*, 56–67.

Stokes, T. F., & Baer, D. M. (1977). An implicit technology of generalization. *Journal of Applied Behavior Analysis, 10*, 349–367.

Stokes, T. F., & Osnes, P. G. (1986). Programming the generalization of children's social behavior. In P. S. Strain, M. J. Guralnick, & H. Walker (Eds.), *Children's social behavior: Development, assessment, and modification* (pp. 407–443). Orlando, FL: Academic Press.

Storey, K., Lawry, J. R., Ashworth, R., Danko, C. D., & Strain, P. S. (1994). Functional analysis and intervention for disruptive behaviors of a kindergarten student. *Journal of Educational Research, 87*, 361–370.

Vernberg, E. M., & Reppucci, N. D. (1986). Behavioral consultation. In F. V. Mannino, E. J. Trickett, M. F. Shore, M. G. Kidder, & G. Levin (Eds.), *Handbook of mental health consultation* (pp. 49–80). Rockville, MD: National Institute of Mental Health.

Watkins-Emonet, C. E. (2001). Evaluating the teaching components of direct behavioral consultation on skill acquisition and generalization in Head Start classrooms (Doctoral dissertation). *Dissertation Abstracts International, 61*(10-B), 5547.

Watson, T. S. (2004). Treatment integrity. In T. S. Watson & C. H. Skinner (Eds.), *Encyclopedia of school psychology* (pp. 356–358). New York: Kluwer.

Watson, T. S., & Kramer, J. J. (1995). Teaching problem solving skills to teachers-in-training: An analogue experimental analysis of three methods. *Journal of Behavioral Education, 5*, 281–293.

Watson, T. S., Ray, K. P., Sterling-Turner, H. E., & Logan, P. (1999). Teacher-implemented functional analysis and treatment: A method for linking assessment to intervention. *School Psychology Review, 28*, 292–302.

Watson, T. S., & Robinson, S. L. (1996). Direct behavioral consultation: An alternative to traditional behavioral consultation. *School Psychology Quarterly, 11*, 267–278.

Watson, T. S., & Steege, M. W. (2003). *Conducting school-based functional behavioral assessments: A practitioner's guide.* New York: Guilford Press.

Watson, T. S., Sterling, H. E., & McDade, A. (1997). Demythifying behavioral consultation. *School Psychology Review, 26*, 467–474.

Wickstrom, K. F., Jones, K. M., LaFleur, L. H., & Witt, J. C. (1998). An analysis of treatment integrity in school-based behavior consultation. *School Psychology Quarterly, 13*, 141–154.

Witt, J. C., Noell, G. H., LaFleur, L. H., & Mortenson, B. P. (1997). Teacher use of interventions in general education settings: Measurement and analysis of the independent variable. *Journal of Applied Behavior Analysis, 30*, 693–696.

ANNOTATED BIBLIOGRAPHY

Freeland, J. T. (2003). Analyzing the effects of direct behavioral consultation on teachers: Generalization of skills across settings (Doctorial dissertation). *Dissertation Abstracts International, 63*(10-A), 3471.

Demonstrates that skill generalization across settings occurred as a result of using direct behavioral consultation as a method of service delivery. This was one of the first studies to explicitly examine the effects of a consultation model on generalization and supports not only the efficacy of the direct behavioral consultation model but also the general goals of school-based consultation.

Moore, J. W., Edwards, R. P., Sterling-Turner, H. E., Riley, J., DuBard, M., & McGeorge, A. (2002). Teacher acquisition of functional analysis methodology: Didactic versus direct training. *Journal of Applied Behavior Analysis, 35*, 73–77.

Compares indirect, didactic training to direct training with rehearsal and performance feedback for teachers' implementation of functional analysis in role-plays with a consultant as well as with referred children presenting with problem behaviors in the classroom setting. Results showed that direct training increased teachers' implementation integrity of functional analysis conditions.

Sterling-Turner, H. E., Watson, T. S., & Moore, J. W. (2002). Effects of training on treatment integrity and treatment outcomes in school-based consultation. *School Psychology Quarterly, 17*, 47–77.

Compares indirect, didactic training to direct training procedures for teachers' implementation integrity of interventions developed during consultation. Results showed that integrity was higher following direct training when compared to indirect training. Direct assessment of treatment outcomes (behavioral improvement) for referred children showed that greater improvements in child behavior were associated with higher treatment integrity.

Watkins-Emonet, C. E. (2001). Evaluating the teaching components of direct behavioral consultation on skill acquisition and generalization in Head Start classrooms (Doctoral dissertation). *Dissertation Abstracts International, 61*(10-B), 5547.

Shows that the direct behavioral consultation model was effective for skills training and subsequent skill generalization among preschool teachers. Unlike many other studies on consultation, this and related research has examined the efficacy of the direct behavioral consultation model for changing both consultee and client behavior.

105

Best Practices in School-Based Problem-Solving Consultation: Applications in Prevention and Intervention Systems

Thomas R. Kratochwill
University of Wisconsin–Madison

OVERVIEW

Consultation is a major approach for providing psychoeducational services to children and adolescents and has been identified as a practice guideline for problem solving and the delivery of evidence-based interventions (White & Kratochwill, 2005). Although past reviews of consultation suggest that it is becoming recognized as the most preferred and satisfying function of school psychologists (Gutkin & Curtis, 1999; Sheridan & Walker, 1999; Sheridan, Welch, & Orme, 1996), it will likely be a major part of response to intervention (RTI) through federal legislation that moves the practice of problem-solving consultation into widespread adoption in school psychology (Kratochwill, Clements, & Kalymon, 2007).

The purpose of this chapter is to review some of the fundamental features of problem-solving consultation in terms of the process of consultation and best practices in each phase of the consultation process. The relationship between problem-solving consultation and approaches to prevention and intervention is presented.

BASIC CONSIDERATIONS

Three major models of consultation that are used most frequently include mental health consultation, organizational development consultation, and behavioral consultation, but many more have been identified over the years (see Zins, Kratochwill, & Elliott, 1993). Although differences exist among these models, all emphasize problem-solving expertise of the consultant within a triadic relationship (consultant–consultee–child). The behavioral model of consultation emerged as an alternative to traditional service delivery approaches in applied settings (Reschly, 1988) and traditionally has strong ties to behavioral theory (e.g., Bergan & Kratochwill, 1990; Kratochwill & Bergan, 1990). Nevertheless, the model has expanded and new names have been invoked to describe the evolution in research and practice (see Gutkin & Curtis, 1999). The term *problem-solving consultation* is adapted here to replace the earlier term *behavioral* used in the previous version of this chapter (see Kratochwill, Elliott, & Stoiber, 2002), but other terms could be used as well (e.g., solution oriented, ecobehavioral). Many of the problem-solving models presented in this text can be traced to the problem-solving features of behavioral consultation (Bergan & Kratochwill, 1990).

Consultation is distinguished from the assessment and interventions that are used as part of the problem-solving process (White & Kratochwill, 2005). Although problem-solving consultation traditionally has been affiliated with behavior modification and intervention techniques from this theoretical school, a more current focus is to use a wide range of assessment and intervention technologies from diverse theoretical origins, especially if they are evidenced-based (see Gutkin & Curtis, 1999; Sheridan & Kratochwill, 2008). For example, school psychologists may apply more traditional behavioral principles and techniques in developing intervention programs and use behavioral methodologies to evaluate the effectiveness of these services. Likewise, school psychologists also may apply valid instructional principles such as pause time, pacing, teacher feedback, and/or homework instruction when developing an intervention plan to enhance the academic performance of underachieving students (Gettinger & Kohler, 2006). Whereas specific intervention strategies may vary across presenting problems, two identifiable features are most frequently associated with problem-solving consultation: (a) indirect service delivery and (b) a problem-solving approach. Each of these features extends into its use within prevention and intervention services.

The most widely recognized feature of consultation is its *indirect service* delivery approach (Bergan & Kratochwill, 1990; Sheridan & Kratochwill, 2008). Services can be delivered by a consultant (e.g., school psychologist) to a consultee (e.g., teacher and/or parent) who, in turn, provides services to a child in the school and/or community setting. Services can also be rendered to a group of teachers, administrators, or a problem-solving team. The indirect approach to service delivery generally is regarded as a distinct advantage of consultation, because it allows the psychologist to have an impact on many more mediators and especially children, than could be served by a direct service or treatment approach. In fact, the centrality of consultation in linking assessment and intervention practices is making consultative models increasingly prominent as a component of solution-focused service delivery systems such as RTI (see National Association of State Directors of Special Education [NASDSE], 2005).

Consultation involves a collaborative relationship in which the consultant is viewed as a facilitator. Emphasis is placed on the collaborative *problem-solving process*, which occurs during a series of interviews and related assessment and intervention activities. Throughout this process, the psychologist's role is to elicit a description of the problem, assist in analyzing the problem, coconstruct a plan for intervention, and establish a monitoring system once the program is implemented. The consultee's role is to clearly describe the problem, work with the consultant to implement the intervention program, observe progress, periodically evaluate the plan's effectiveness, and monitor the intervention. For the consultation process to be effective, both consultant and consultee should bring the following dispositions to the consultation process:

- A sense of preparedness and clear expectations
- A willingness to participate actively and openly in a collaborative work environment

- A capacity to assume a proactive role, especially with prevention programs and services

Goals of Consultation

Problem-solving consultation has two important goals: (a) to provide methods (prevention or intervention) for changing a system, classroom, or child's behavioral, academic, or social problem(s), and (b) to improve the system and/or consultee skills so the system or the consultee can prevent or respond effectively to future problems or similar problems in other children. Given these goals, consultation can be both a proactive and a reactive service. Although consultation-based interventions often have changed children's problem behaviors successfully (Sheridan et al., 1996; White & Kratochwill, 2005), the proactive goal of influencing a consultee's ability to handle future problems has not been observed consistently in research. The accomplishment of these goals requires consultees to participate in a general process for analyzing problems that results in an effective plan to resolve the problems. Successful consultants must demonstrate expertise in both coordinating and facilitating the problem-solving process and in implementing methods for monitoring whether the intervention is working.

Structure and Process of Consultation: Applications to the Individual, Group, and System

Consultation has been conceptualized as a series of stages that structure and focus the problem-solving interaction between consultant and consultees (Bergan & Kratochwill, 1990; Sheridan & Kratochwill, 2008). A heuristic five-stage framework for consultation can be applied to a system, group, or individual problem-solving process.

Traditionally, school psychologists have implemented consultation with classroom teachers in an effort to establish intervention programs in the regular classroom. This emphasis on interventions with teachers advanced the development of a knowledge base to prevent more serious behavioral problems in children and is one reason why the approach is recommended in RTI models (Gresham, 2006; NASDSE, 2005). School-based consultation services have expanded to include work with special education teachers, particularly teachers of emotionally impaired children (e.g., Gable et al., 1998; Kratochwill, Sheridan, Carrington Rotto, &

Salmon, 1991) and teachers from early intervention programs for preschool-age children (e.g., Barnett et al., 2006; Gettinger & Stoiber, 1999). In addition, consultation also has been used for many years to successfully remediate academic and socialization difficulties in school settings (Bergan & Kratochwill, 1990). Applications such as these have presented unique opportunities for school psychologists to increase contact with special education teachers while generally addressing more severe presenting problems in special needs children who often experience multiple difficulties. Hence, the role of consultant has become increasingly complex, with unique time demands and intervention needs that may vary according to the child's presenting problems and the teacher's level of expertise in areas such as behavior management and individualized instruction.

Although consultation with teachers to deal with problem reduction is an effective method of remediating school-based problems, this traditional focus fails to address the broader context and focus within which the child's problems may occur (Kratochwill & Pittman, 2002). For example, a withdrawn child who exhibits an absence of peer interactions at school likely will be unable to develop and maintain positive social relationships with neighborhood peers. Focusing exclusively on this child's social withdrawal in the school setting through teacher-only consultation restricts conceptualization, analysis, and intervention of the problem to a single target domain and setting. The broader behavioral interrelationships across environments should always be considered. First, consultation should focus on development of social competencies and not just the reduction of problematic behaviors. Second, problem-solving consultation should be extended to serve as a link among the significant settings in a child's life (primarily the home, school, and community environments; Sheridan & Kratochwill, 2008). This approach facilitates a comprehensive conceptualization of the problem while involving primary caretakers in the intervention process. In addition, although few investigators have assessed the generalization of intervention effects across settings, the potential benefits of broadening the focus of problem-solving consultation to encompass the interacting system in the child's life are apparent.

There are several methods that can be used to expand the scope of consultation. First, the focus of case problem solving needs to move beyond a target behavior focus where challenging behaviors are reduced to a focus that also includes building social competencies

(Stoiber & Kratochwill, 2000). For example, during the problem analysis phase the consultant can ask teachers and parents to complete measures on the academic functioning of students such as the Academic Competence Evaluation Scales (ACES; DiPerna & Elliott, 2000) to target academic enablers or skills for intervention. Figure 1 provides an illustration of the ACES subscales.

Another method of expanding consultation services entails involvement of parent–teacher pairs in problem solving. In conjoint consultation, parents and teachers together serve as consultees (Sheridan & Kratochwill, 1992; Sheridan & Kratochwill, 2008; Sheridan, Eagle, & Doll, 2006). The primary goals of this approach are to bridge the gap between home and school settings, maximize positive intervention effects within and across settings, and promote generalization of intervention effects over time. Continuous data collection and consistent programming across settings also are inherent with this approach. Conjoint consultation has been found to be an effective method of service delivery in

Figure 1. The clusters of skills, attitudes, and behaviors that contribute to academic competence.

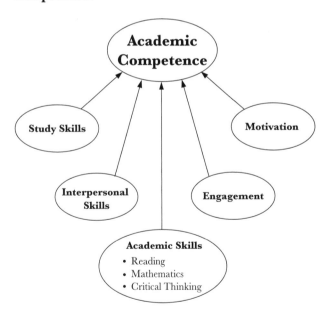

Note. From Kratochwill, T. R., Elliott, S. N., & Stoiber, K. C. (2002). Problem-solving consultation: In A. Thomas & J. Grimes (Eds.), *Best Practices in School Psychology IV* (pp. 583–608). Bethesda, MD: National Association of School Psychologists. Copyright 2002 by the National Association of School Psychologists, Bethesda, MD. Use of this material is by permission of the publisher.

enhancing social and academic competencies across home and school settings (see Sheridan & Kratochwill, 2008, for a comprehensive review).

Use of problem-solving consultation also has been extended beyond schools to address problems with individuals other than teachers, such as parents (Kratochwill & Pittman, 2002). Parent-only consultation may be applicable when a child's problematic behaviors are observed predominantly in the home and/or community settings but are not evident in the school environment. For example, parent consultation has been used to decrease the noncompliant behaviors of school-age children whose difficult behaviors were displayed at home and in public places but were not observed in the more structured classroom setting (e.g., Carrington Rotto & Kratochwill, 1994). In parent-only consultation, the traditional problem-solving consultation framework provides structure for involving parent(s) in the process of identifying and analyzing the problem as well as observing and evaluating intervention effects over time. Use of parent training provides structure for teaching parents specific skills, which enhance plan implementation. Necessary preparations for plan implementation include teaching parents specific behavior management skills and ensuring that the parents are adept at implementing these skills. Specific methods of promoting generalization of parent behaviors (i.e., skill implementation) across settings and situations to enhance specific child behaviors need to be implemented.

Another application of problem-solving consultation is at the system level and allows consultation services to occur to a wide variety of stakeholders who may be involved in implementation of a prevention system such as single and/or multitiered programs (see Kratochwill & Pittman, 2002). With implementation of a multitiered model where RTI has been integrated into the process, consultants must be knowledgeable about prevention science models as well as methods of progress monitoring (see Kratochwill et al., 2007; Kratochwill et al., in press). Most importantly, consultants should understand the limitations of a multitiered model as currently being advocated in much of the school psychology literature (e.g., the focus on a child deficit approach as opposed to a proactive social–emotional learning approach; see Kratochwill et al., 2007). In addition, the RTI approach, which was conceptualized as an intervention model to help address overrepresentation of minority students in special education (Heller, Holtzman, & Messick, 1982), may be limited unless other issues are addressed. To implement the RTI model to fully reduce

overrepresentation, a number of issues directly related to identifying racially diverse children with disabilities must be addressed (see Newell & Kratochwill, 2008). Specifically, Newell and Kratochwill advance the Critical Race Theory–Disabilities Studies framework as a potential theoretical approach to analyze social, economic, and ideological structures relevant to racially diverse groups (see Watts & Erevelles, 2004). When this framework is integrated with an RTI model there is greater potential to reduce racial discrimination and possibly reduce overrepresentation of minority students in special education through a consultative problem-solving approach.

BEST PRACTICES

Problem-solving consultation is a model for delivering assessment, prevention, and intervention services to children and schools via consultees through a series of structured meetings. A heuristic problem-solving framework provides structure for collecting information and affecting behavior change and can be applied to recent developments in the RTI movement (Gresham, 2006). Although the problem-solving structure is sequential and overt, it should not be interpreted as inflexible or irreversible. The activities of consultants and consultees are multifaceted, involving interviews, functional assessments, selection and implementation of evidence-based interventions, and evaluation of the interventions. Such activities generally require several interactions between the consultant and consultees, as well as ongoing consultee and client collaborative interactions.

Problem-solving consultation consists of a series of stages or phases that are used to implement the process of consultation, and each of these steps, with the exception of plan implementation, can involve a formal interview with specific objectives to accomplish. Best practices in problem-solving case consultation suggest that psychologists adhere to specific objectives and activities within each phase because each of these steps can be conceptualized as a practice guideline with evidence for its components (White & Kratochwill, 2005). The major components for each of these phases include establishing a consultant–consultee relationship, problem identification, problem analysis, plan implementation, and plan evaluation.

Stage 1: Establishing Relationships

The interpersonal relationship between a psychologist and consultees is assumed to play a major role in the use and effectiveness of consultation services. Thus, as with psychotherapy, issues of trust, genuineness, and openness have been deemed important qualities for both consultants and consultees (Sheridan & Kratochwill, 2008). Although competence in problem identification and plan implementation are necessary conditions of problem-solving consultation, they are not sufficient to facilitate effective consultative interactions. Integration of positive interpersonal skills and understanding with technical expertise are equally important to maximize consultant–consultee effectiveness. For example, characteristics such as acceptance through nonjudgmental statements, openness, nondefensiveness, and flexibility positively affect the interaction between consultant and consultees. These qualities are magnified in a consultative model of service delivery because of the predominance of an interview or verbal mode of information gathering and sharing. The dynamics of communication, both talking and listening, are the medium through which psychologists display their attitudes and beliefs about consultees. Personal characteristics, professional competencies, and modeling all are important elements in establishing and maintaining constructive and professional interactions in an individual and/or group relationship.

Consultation should begin with the *development of a relationship* between the consultant and the consultee(s). Collaborative consultants who develop positive working relationships with consultees may (a) experience less resistance to consultation process and intervention, (b) find their suggestions are readily accepted by consultees, (c) increase the probability that consultees will follow through on an intervention, and (d) increase the effectiveness of the consultation process for the consultee and clients. During this stage, it is critical that the consultant and consultee(s) have uncovered a shared need or goal to focus the consultation process and develop an intervention (e.g., setting up a multitiered service model). It is also during this stage that the consultant discusses with the consultee the stages of the consultation process, consultant and consultee roles, and shared responsibilities and ownership of the consultation outcomes, such as system change.

Sensitivity to issues of importance to consultees also contributes to the development of a positive consulting relationship. Variables commonly examined in intervention acceptability research (e.g., Elliott, 1988a; Witt & Elliott, 1985) and dimensions of helping emphasized by empowerment theorists (e.g., Dunst & Trivette, 1988; Witt & Martens, 1988) provide variables to consider consistent with consultation relevant to the enhancement of relationships with individuals or groups. For

example, acceptability researchers repeatedly have found that administration/management time and fairness of the intervention are important themes to virtually all teachers, and nonaversive approaches to intervention are valued highly by most teachers. Work by empowerment theorists applied to consultation suggests that (a) help is more likely to be perceived positively if it is offered proactively, (b) competence within teachers is best promoted by building upon their existing child management strengths rather than remediating deficits, and (c) use of existing resources in the school environment is preferred over the intervention or purchase of new resources (Witt & Martens, 1988). Thus, it is concluded that effective consultants overtly communicate awareness of these issues that are central to teachers' daily functioning and act cooperatively to design interventions. Such consultative actions may overcome many potential sources of resistance.

Resistance is a topic of considerable concern to practitioners and researchers alike and often has been conceptualized as something bad that resides within a person or institution. Yet, as observed by Wickstrom and Witt (1993), such a view of resistance may be overly simplistic and unnecessarily negative. Within the context of a consultant–consultee relationship, they define resistance as "including those system, consultee, consultant, family, and client factors which interfere with the achievement of goals established during consultative interactions making the construct very relevant to multilevels of prevention. Resistance, then, is *anything* that impedes problem solving or plan implementation and ultimately problem resolution" (p. 160). This definition stresses that resistance is part of a system context and is multidirectional; that is, it does not reside in only one part of the system.

Having reviewed the theoretical and empirical reports on resistance to intervention in both the psychotherapy and consultation literature, Wickstrom and Witt (1993) recommend two general tactics to respond to resistance. The first tactic they call "joining the consultee" and the second tactic they refer to as "emphasizing referent power." Joining the consultee involves understanding a consultee's attribution system for explaining a problem of concern and then using that attributional framework to build a link to an intervention. Emphasizing referent power involves a consultant working to become more similar to consultees. This tactic can be accomplished by using nonauthoritarian and noncoercive means of control, using cooperative modes of interaction, asking questions, and making suggestions for change in a tentative manner (Parsons & Meyers, 1984). Efforts to use the consultee's existing skills and preferences for interaction activities, thereby reducing the number of new aspects of an intervention, also is likely to make suggestions more acceptable, and thus less resisted.

Resistance at the system level requires that the consultant address a wide range of practical and logistical variables. For example, school psychologists must have the skills to consult and develop interventions, and this role requires training. Administrators must support the role of the consultant through public endorsement and resources. Alternate models of special education service delivery, such as RTI approaches (see NASDSE, 2005), may need to be embraced by the district and state. This process will require considerable effort on the part of the psychologist to change the student service system.

Implementation of consultation in a multitiered system raises special issues in terms of affecting the system as well as key stakeholders in the process. Fortunately, a growing body of literature has provided some guidance on increasing the probability that the multitiered system can be implemented through a consultation process. Specifically, in the prevention science literature, the Blueprints for Violence Prevention (hereinafter called Blueprints) was initiated with the goal to identify research-based violence prevention programs and to replicate these programs in a dissemination project (see Mihalic, Irwin, Fagan, Ballard, & Elliott, 2004). During the process of implementing these various programs, important issues came to the fore including conducting a site assessment, creating an effective organizational structure, having qualified staff including program champions in the effort, integrating the program into existing structures, ensuring implementation, fidelity, and providing training and technical assistance. Especially relevant in this process was the professional development effort (see Kratochwill, Volpiansky, Clements, & Ball, in press, for further information on professional development issues). Specifically, among the important issues learned from implementation of Blueprints, a number of important findings related to training teachers occurred (see Mihalic et al., 2004, pp. 7–8). Mihalic et al. found that trained teachers were more likely to implement and implement more of the prevention program than untrained teachers; fully trained teachers completed a greater percentage of programs with fidelity; trained teachers reported greater preparedness to teach the programs, teach them with greater fidelity, and achieve better student outcomes than untrained teachers; trained teachers were more effective and had more

favorable student outcomes than untrained teachers; and teachers without follow up and support over time failed to fully implement or continue to use the program. These findings have important implications for technology training consultation and specifically multitiered models. The lesson is that effective professional development must be part of a consultation process for implementation of single-focused and/or multitiered interventions (see Kratochwill et al., in press).

Stage 2: Problem Identification

Problem identification is the most critical stage of consultation because it results in the design and implementation of an effective plan. Traditionally, in case-centered behavioral consultation the focus was exclusively on identification of a target problem and elimination of that problem. More recently, an emphasis has been placed on teaching social and academic competencies in addition to dealing with a target problem (DiPerna & Elliott, 2000; Stoiber & Kratochwill, 2000). The interview represents a primary assessment technology for defining the problem and developing an understanding of the needs in social and academic competencies, although numerous other strategies may assist in defining the problem or issue (e.g., tests, rating scales and checklists, functional assessments, direct observations; Hurwitz, Rehberg, & Kratochwill, in press). During the problem identification interview, the consultant and consultee focus on describing and operationally defining concerns. In consultation a problem is a relative concept that becomes operationalized when consultees report a significant discrepancy between current and the desired levels of performance or circumstances. The determination of whether a significant discrepancy exists is not examined initially; however, once the current and desired levels of performance are defined objectively, this significant discrepancy becomes the focus. This approach to problem identification is based on the assumption that problems are the result of unsuccessful or discrepant interactions between and among persons or systems (e.g., child and teacher; child and parent; teacher, parent, and child; parent and school). Functional assessment strategies may be conducted to focus attention on the academic and social competencies that need to be taught and on the ecological context surrounding the concern, especially in the most intense level of services in a multitiered model (Stoiber & Kratochwill, 2001). Thus, the psychologist and consultees first analyze the issues within the ecological context. When baseline data support the existence of the specific problem, the psychologist and parent and/or teacher begin to jointly identify variables that might lead to problem resolution.

Consultation can involve a developmental or problem-centered focus. In developmental consultation the consultant establishes general, subordinate, and performance objectives. Usually these are obtained over a long period of time and in several series of interviews and are especially relevant to system change issues. In contrast, problem-centered consultation involves specification of problems that are specific and relate to one or a few primary concerns or goals. Relative to the developmental consultation process, problem-centered consultation is more time limited. Whether the nature of consultation is developmental or problem centered, the psychologist needs to achieve clear specification of problems, competencies, and goals. Typically, this process involves generating precise descriptions of the situation, carefully analyzing the conditions under which the problems occur, and establishing some indication of the level of persistence or strength of the problems.

During the problem identification phase, the goals of consultation should be established. One tool that can be helpful to establish goals and benchmarks is Outcomes: Planning, Monitoring, Evaluating (Outcomes: PME; Stoiber & Kratochwill, 2001). Outcomes: PME includes five steps (see Appendix C). The system embraces a focused goal setting and goal attainment scaling framework in which up to three goals and corresponding benchmarks are established. The system also includes a convergent evidence scaling format so that multiple outcome measures can be examined for correspondence on intervention effectiveness. Outcomes: PME is a useful tool for structuring and facilitating productive problem solving in consultation at both the case and system level.

The ACES (DiPerna & Elliott, 2000) and its corresponding intervention system, the Academic Intervention Monitoring System (AIMS; DiPerna, Elliott, & Shapiro, 2000), is another example of an approach to assessment and intervention that is consistent with a consultative problem-solving model. The ACES–AIMS approach utilizes teachers as the primary assessment and intervention agent for children experiencing difficulties with academic skills (reading, language arts, mathematics, and critical thinking) and academic enablers (interpersonal skills, engagement, motivation, and study skills). Both the ACES and

AIMS emphasize behavior rating and goal attainment scaling technology to identify and monitor behavior. Table 1 provides an overview of the use of both the ACES and the AIMS to facilitate enactment of a five-step problem-solving process. The ACES has been revised to include a Brief Academic Competence Evaluation Screening System (BACESS; see Elliott, Huai, & DiPerna, 2004). BACESS is especially useful in a multitiered system because it can be used to screen at the universal or primary level and identify students in need of early interventions for academic skill problems.

Another important objective of problem identification is establishing assessment techniques. Together, the consultees and psychologist agree on the type or kind of measures to be used, what will be recorded, and how this process will be implemented. There are a growing number of progress-monitoring tools that can be used to screen, assess baseline performance, and intervention outcomes (Albers, Glover, & Kratochwill, 2007a; Albers, Glover, & Kratochwill, 2007b; Kratochwill et al., in press).

Finally, certain procedural objectives must be met during the problem identification phase. One of the first objectives involves establishing times, dates, and formats for subsequent interviews and/or contacts with consultees to examine procedural aspects of the consultation process. For example, the psychologist may agree to contact the teacher and/or parent weekly or biweekly to determine whether data are being gathered properly or if any unique barriers have occurred.

Table 1. The Use of ACES, Goal Attainment Scaling, AIMS, and AIMS Forms Within a Five-Step Problem-Solving Process

Step 1. Identify academic concern(s)
- Student completes ACES

Step 2. Analyze academic concerns within the instructional environment
- Score ACES-college and analyze behaviors using ACES behavior classification framework
- Student intervention form

Step 3. Plan for intervention
- Determine desired behavior(s)
- Determine intervention goal
- Develop GAS to monitor intervention

Step 4. Implement intervention and monitor student progress
- Specify strategies to change target behavior
- Student completes GAS daily or weekly

Step 5. Evaluate intervention
- Student completes ACES a second time
- Review GAS and ACES data

Note. GAS = Goal Attainment Scaling. Source: DiPerna and Elliott (2000).

Stage 3: Problem Analysis

Problem analysis, the third major stage of consultation, focuses on the variables and conditions that are hypothesized to influence the system and/or the child's prosocial and challenging behaviors. Case-centered problem analysis is a natural extension of the problem identification stage, in that it essentially begins with the challenging behaviors and prosocial competencies of concern and focuses on establishing functional relationships between it and the antecedent or consequent events. Questions about who, what, where, when, and under what conditions or contingencies are all considered relevant and generally facilitate a better understanding of the problem behavior. In many cases, the problem analysis stage will require the psychologist to collect additional data about the child's challenging behaviors and social competencies. Thus, problem analysis may enhance refinement and consequently redefinition of the problem and the factor(s) that influence it.

After baseline data are collected on the areas of concern, the psychologist and consultees meet to decide jointly on factors that might lead to some resolution of the problem. In this regard, the consultation process will focus on variables that may be of relevance to case or system change. The problem analysis interview includes five major steps: choosing analysis procedures, determining the conditions and/or skills analysis, developing plan strategies, developing plan tactics, and establishing procedures to evaluate performance during implementation of any intervention program. Within the context of these phases, the psychologist might first analyze the factors that lead to potential solution of the problem and then develop a plan to solve the problem.

The psychologist focuses on conditions that facilitate attainment of the mutually agreed upon goals at the individual and/or system level. Generally, the following steps are necessary:

- Specifying whether the goal of intervention is to increase, decrease, or maintain conditions of the target issue and determining what conditions will be targeted
- Identifying setting events and antecedent/consequential conditions associated with conditions
- Determining what current conditions affect the goal by comparing the existing situation to related evidence-based prevention/intervention
- Identifying conditions not currently associated with the target issue but which nonetheless could influence solving the issue/problem

Through mutual problem-solving efforts, the psychologist and consultees must analyze the kinds of conditions necessary to achieve the goals of consultation during the problem analysis phase. In case-centered consultation, this process includes analyzing skills that the child does not possess and can include academic and/or social performance. In a multitiered system model, this process involves an analysis of system variables to put a prevention program in place (e.g., resources, staff time, professional development). Basically, the psychologist must work with the consultees to identify psychological and educational principles that relate to attaining the goals of consultation. It is beyond the scope of this chapter to outline these procedures in great detail. Rather, the reader is referred to a number of sources that can be useful to analyze overt behavioral and cognitive features that relate to system, instructional, and social functioning (e.g., Bergan & Kratochwill, 1990; DiPerna, Elliott, & Shapiro, 2000; Ysseldyke & Christenson, 2002).

The outcome of successful problem analysis is a plan to put into effect during the intervention implementation process. Development of this plan includes first specifying broad strategies that can be used to achieve the mutually agreed upon goals. The plan typically indicates *sources of action* to be implemented. Plan tactics are then used to guide implementation of the strategy and outline principles to be applied during the intervention. For example, if professional development is to be used, the person responsible for carrying out the plan and the conditions under which it will occur should be specified. During this phase, psychologists might also assess prevention/intervention acceptability before its implementation. A number of scales have been developed for assessment of pretreatment acceptability and readers are encouraged to consult this material (Elliott, 1988b; Witt & Elliott, 1985). Appendix A and Appendix B include two scales that can be used in the assessment of acceptability.

Finally, during problem analysis the psychologist and consultees must establish performance and assessment objectives that will be used during plan implementation. Typically, this procedure follows from a conditions analysis and involves specification of an assessment procedure previously used during baseline. For example, when plan implementation involves skill development, some agreed upon format for collection of data on performance related to the final objectives achieved is necessary.

Stage 4: Plan Implementation

Plan implementation follows the problem analysis stage and has dual objectives of selecting an appropriate prevention and/or intervention and implementing the program/procedures. Procedural details are essential at this stage, such as assigning individuals to various roles, gathering or preparing specific materials, or training individuals to implement the plan. The design and selection of appropriate interventions should be based on evidence-based interventions and require attention to issues of intervention acceptability, effectiveness, and consultee skills and resources (Kratochwill & Shernoff, 2004; Kratochwill & Stoiber, 2000a, 2000b). Many consumers and providers of psychological services are also demanding that interventions also be acceptable (i.e., time efficient, least restrictive, fair and/or low risk to the child; Elliott, 1988a, 1988b). Likewise, interest in interventions that are consistent with the teacher's/parent's child management philosophy and compatible with existing resources and skills of the individual delivering the intervention have also gained recent consumer interest and empirical support (Witt & Martens, 1988).

Plan implementation also involves discussing and actually carrying out the selected intervention. This substage may consume several weeks or months and is characterized by interactions between the consultant and consultees. These interactions may occur through brief contacts in which the psychologist monitors intervention integrity and side effects (Sanetti & Kratochwill, 2005), and possibly brainstorms with the consultee ways to revise the plan and its use. For case-centered consultation, DiPerna and Elliott (2000) developed a series of intervention record forms for teachers, parents, and students. These intervention records are based on the effective teaching literature and provide respondents opportunities to indicate "how helpful" and "how feasible" specific intervention tactics are likely to be with a given student. These intervention record forms are an example of trying to enhance the likelihood that the interventions selected are acceptable and will be able to be implemented by a consultee. The psychologist's role may also involve observations to monitor child and consultee behaviors or training sessions to enhance the skills of the individual who is executing the intervention plan.

During plan implementation the three major tasks that must be accomplished include skill development of consultees (if necessary), monitoring the implementation process, and plan revisions. Typically, the psychologist must determine whether the consultee has the skills to

carry out the plan. If skill development is required, the consultee must be offered some type of professional development or guidance (Kratochwill et al., in press). This training might be offered through direct instruction of the consultant, modeling the intervention by the consultant, videotape and self-instructional materials, or through formal training offered by others. Many evidence-based interventions are accompanied by a manual or protocol that can be used to train consultees or engage them in a self-instructional process of training.

A second task is to monitor data to determine if assessment is occurring as intended. Consultee records usually are examined to assess child outcome. This process usually will indicate to the psychologist when progress monitoring data are being gathered, how the performance of the child is being assessed, and what behaviors are being observed. It may also help the psychologist determine whether the plan is actually proceeding as designed. If little progress is observed, then it is advisable for the psychologist to meet with the consultees and revise the plan accordingly.

Monitoring plan implementation generally occurs in two ways. First, the prevention/intervention program is monitored on an ongoing basis. This progress monitoring is a continuation from the problem identification and problem analysis phases of consultation. A second type of monitoring activity involves an evaluation of the strategies that are associated with the plan implementation itself. It is essential for the psychologist and teacher/parent to ensure that the plan agreed upon is being carried out as designed. The psychologist may choose to monitor plan implementation and integrity by discussing the intervention plan with consultees. A second procedure that can be used to complement this strategy is to actually observe the plan in operation or to get the consultee to report integrity data periodically (Sanetti & Kratochwill, 2005). It is acknowledged that various individuals might serve in the role of intervention implementers. Nevertheless, it is very likely that the psychologist will use a variety of procedures to facilitate plan implementation that are compatible with resources and responsibilities in the school or setting.

Finally, changes should be made in the plan when necessary. If circumstances and/or the program are not changing in the desired direction, plan revision should occur. Generally, this outcome will require the psychologist and consultees to return to the problem-analysis phase to further analyze variables such as the setting, intrapersonal child characteristics, skill deficits or social competencies, and system barriers. Likewise, it may be necessary to return to the problem identification stage if it is determined that the nature of the problem has changed.

Stage 5: Plan Evaluation

Plan evaluation is the final stage of consultation with the objective of establishing a sound basis for interpreting outcomes of the intervention for the targeted issue or problem and providing a forum for evaluating plan effectiveness. The rigor of evaluation involved in research may not be used consistently in practice, but good evidence to verify outcomes should be routine in case-consultation efforts. Case study strategies provide one means for evaluating change in the child's progress (Kratochwill, 1985). The use of single-case research designs as recommended in some recent approaches to evaluation of RTI (e.g., Brown-Chidsey & Steege, 2006) are not likely to be used in practice (Kratochwill & Piersel, 1983). The procedures involving case study evaluation and discussed by Stoiber and Kratochwill (2001) are recommended. When the reported discrepancy between the child's behavior and desired level of functioning is reduced significantly or eliminated, academic and/or social competencies have been acquired, and the intervention is acceptable to both the teacher/parent and child, the consultant and consultees decide whether consultation should be terminated. Outcome criteria should include maintenance of the desired behavior over time and generalization across multiple settings and conditions. In theory, consultation is not concluded until the discrepancy between the existing and desired circumstances are addressed substantively and an acceptable maintenance plan is in place. Criteria such as overall improvement in the quality of life (social and academic) and system change can also be invoked but may require a developmental focus in case consultation. Therefore, it is often necessary to recycle through previous stages of consultation and reevaluate refined or newly implemented interventions.

Plan evaluation can be implemented through a formal plan evaluation interview and typically is undertaken to determine whether the goals of consultation have been obtained. The process of evaluation includes assessment of goal attainment, plan effectiveness, and implementation planning. The first major step in plan evaluation is to decide whether the actual goals previously agreed upon have been obtained. This decision is determined through discussion with the consultee and observation of the client's behavior. Again, the goal attainment framework of Outcomes: PME can be very useful to

make decisions about the goals of consultation and can be continued during this phase. The process of evaluating goal attainment first was initiated during problem identification where the objectives and procedures for measuring mastery were specified. When Outcomes: PME is used, specific benchmarks for each consultation goal are indicated. The data gathered since the problem identification phase should provide some evidence as to whether there is congruence between objectives and the problem solution. Basically, this step occurs on the basis of the data collected, but additional strategies might be invoked as well, such as social validation criteria specified in Outcomes: PME. That is, the psychologist will want to know, for example, whether the child reached some clinically established level of change and whether the intervention program brought the child's performance within a range of acceptable behavior as compared to normal or typical peers. Determination of the congruence between behavior and objectives generally leads the psychologist to conclude that no progress was obtained, some progress was made, or the actual goal was obtained.

Advances in the evaluation of intervention effects and consultation outcomes continue to appear in the research literature. Several of these advances have been used in the evaluation of community mental health services and supplement the case study and social validation strategies that have traditionally been used by consultants. Two of the most practical strategies are goal attainment scaling (see Stoiber & Kratochwill, 2001) and the Reliable Change index (RC; Jacobson, Follette, & Revenstorf, 1984). Both of these evaluation strategies are also used in the ACES–AIMS approach to academic interventions and can be generalized broadly.

Briefly, there are several different approaches to using a goal attainment framework. The basic tactic, however, is one where a consultee would be asked to describe five to seven levels of intervention outcome. The most unfavorable outcome described is given a -2 or -3 rating, a no change outcome is given a 0 rating, and the most favorable outcome is given a $+2$ or $+3$ rating. Ratings of -1 to -2 and $+1$ to $+2$ are ascribed to benchmark descriptions of outcomes that are situated between the most unfavorable and expected outcome and the most favorable and expected outcome, respectively. Outcomes: PME can be used to get daily or weekly measures on intervention progress, as well as final outcome perceptions from a consultee. Goal attainment scaling is a sensitive system because both over and under attainment of objectives can be rated. Outcomes: PME has specific application to prevention program application and can be very useful in RTI multitiered model implementation and evaluation.

The RC evaluation method was first proposed by Nunnally and Kotsche (1983) and is defined as the difference between post-test scores and pretest scores divided by the standard error of measurement. Typically an RC of +1.96 or greater is considered statistically significant, and more important, it is inferred that the intervention produced a reliable change in a person's behavior. The RC is designed to be used with data from rating scales or individualized tests where total pretest and post-test scores can be calculated. However, this metric for reporting intervention outcomes is affected by the reliability of the dependent measures. The dual criteria of social validation (social comparison and subjective evaluation) and RC can provide practitioners with a means for documenting educationally and statistically significant changes in behavior.

Once it has been determined that the problem has been solved, post implementation planning occurs to help ensure that the particular problem does not occur again. There are some alternatives available for the psychologist and teacher/parent in designing post implementation plans. One strategy is to leave the plan in effect. Typically, however, a plan that is put into effect will need to be modified (another alternative) to facilitate maintenance of program outcomes over time. There is considerable evidence in the intervention literature that specific tactics are needed to facilitate maintenance and generalization of intervention outcomes, and these tactics must be accomplished during this phase of consultation. Generalization may occur naturally, but more likely it will need to be programmed. Several factors have been identified that have a bearing on the generalization of skills (Haring, 1988; White et al., 1988). White et al. (1988) lists the strategies for facilitating generalization along with a definition and example. The summary is based on the seminal work of Stokes and Baer (1977) and can serve as a useful guideline for consultants.

Another major objective that should occur during the plan evaluation interview is discussion of post implementation recording. Generally, this procedure refers to the process of continuing record-keeping activities to determine whether the problem occurs in the future. Usually, the psychologist and consultees select periodic measures that are convenient to use and may maintain specific features of the original plan to facilitate this data collection process. The psychologist should consider conducting post-plan implementation acceptability assessment as well. These procedures can be implemented informally or more formally with acceptability instrumentation (Elliott, 1988b). Finally, the teacher/parent should notify the psychologist of any reoccurrence of the problem behaviors that might be indicated. These usually can be brought to the psychologist's attention and specific tactics set up to establish a system to analyze the problems.

SUMMARY

There has never been a time in our profession when consultation has been more relevant and appropriate for the provision of prevention and intervention services. Problem-solving consultation can be conceptualized as a five-stage approach that uses broad-based behavioral and collaborative methods as the basis for the consultation process. The major features of consultation include its indirect service delivery approach and problem-solving focus. Consultation has two principal goals. The first goal is to produce positive outcomes for a system, consultees, and clients indirectly through collaborative problem solving between a consultant (psychologist) and consultee(s) (e.g., teacher/parent, problem-solving team, administrators). A second yet equally important goal of consultation is to empower consultees with skills that will enable future independent problem solving at the system, classroom, and individual levels.

A growing body of research has accumulated on the positive outcomes of problem-solving consultation (Gutkin & Curtis, 1999; Sheridan & Kratochwill, 2008). Additionally, the practice of problem-solving consultation is expanding rapidly. In particular, there is a strong movement toward problem-solving consultation in school settings to the exclusion of traditional refer-test-place practices largely due to the RTI movement (Kratochwill et al., 2007). As psychologists have become interested in the integration of consultation with daily activities and child mental health in schools and homes, questions regarding the process and outcome of consultation have surfaced. Studies have examined the application of interventions in consultation to achieve changes in behavior and compared the effectiveness of consultation to other forms of service delivery.

Specifically, research documenting the effectiveness of consultation has been organized around four areas of investigation: (a) outcome research, (b) process research, (c) practitioner research, and (d) training research (White & Kratochwill, 2005). Research addressing outcomes of consultation document its effectiveness in remediating academic and behavior problems manifested by children in school settings (Bergan & Kratochwill, 1990; Sheridan & Kratochwill, 2008). Likewise, these same studies suggest that changes result in the teacher's and parent's behavior, knowledge, attitudes, and perceptions. Although consultation traditionally has been directed toward a single client (i.e., teacher), it can also be applied successfully with a number of mediators (e.g., peer consultation, conjoint consultation; see Kratochwill & Pittman, 2002). A collaborative problem-solving model whereby the consultant, teacher, and parents share information, value each other's input, and incorporate each other's perspectives in developing the intervention plan is considered to afford great benefits (Sheridan & Kratochwill, 1992). Little outcome research has been conducted on consultation problem-solving applications with groups and systems (Kratochwill & Pittman, 2002) and especially with multitiered models of prevention.

Typically, process research has focused on case-focused problem identification, since the consultant's ability to elicit a clear description of the problem has been identified as the best predictor of plan implementation and problem solution (e.g., Bergan & Tombari, 1975, 1976). Studies in this area also have focused on comparing consultation effectiveness with other forms of service delivery (Medway, 1979). It remains difficult to draw conclusions from the studies addressing variables associated with the process of consultation due to limitations in scope, theoretical base, and research methodology (Gresham & Kendell, 1987; White & Kratochwill, 2005).

Traditionally, studies on practitioner utilization have suggested that school-based case consultation is a preferred activity for school psychologists (e.g., Gutkin & Curtis, 1981; Meacham & Peckham, 1978). Most school psychologists do engage in consultation activities (Curtis, Walker, Hunley, & Baker, 1999), but many practitioners identify limitations to implementing consultation due to time constraints and lack of consultee commitment (Gresham & Kendell, 1987). Both individual consultant/consultee and system issues must be addressed to deal with those constraints.

Overall, problem-solving consultation is a rapidly growing area with increasing empirical support. Careful scrutiny of consultation will affect its future use as an alternative to traditional assessment and intervention practices in educational settings and may result in an emphasis on the development of increased formalized training in school psychology programs. In turn, these developments will contribute to the practice of school psychology and positively have an impact on the children, teachers, parents, and systems receiving psychological and educational services.

REFERENCES

Albers, C. A., Glover, T. A., & Kratochwill, T. R. (2007a). Introduction to the special issue: How can universal screening enhance educational and mental health outcomes? *Journal of School Psychology*, *45*, 113–116.

Albers, C. A., Glover, T. A., & Kratochwill, T. R. (2007b). Where are we, and where do we go now? Universal screening for enhanced educational and mental health outcomes. *Journal of School Psychology*, *45*, 257–263.

Barnett, D. W., Elliott, N., Wolsing, L., Bunger, C. E., Haski, H., McKissick, C., et al. (2006). Response to intervention for young children with extremely challenging behaviors: What it might look like. *School Psychology Review*, *35*, 568–682.

Bergan, J. R., & Kratochwill, T. R. (1990). *Behavioral consultation in applied settings*. New York: Plenum Press.

Bergan, J. R., & Tombari, M. L. (1975). The analysis of verbal interactions occurring during consultation. *Journal of School Psychology*, *14*, 3–14.

Bergan, J. R., & Tombari, M. L. (1976). Consultant skill and efficiency and the implementation and outcome of consultation. *Journal of School Psychology*, *14*, 3–14.

Brown-Chidsey, R., & Steege, M. W. (2006). *Response to intervention: Principles and strategies for effective instruction*. New York: Guilford Press.

Carrington Rotto, P., & Kratochwill, T. R. (1994). Behavioral consultation with parents: Using competency-based training to modify child noncompliance. *School Psychology Review*, *23*, 669–693.

Curtis, M. J., Walker, K. J., Hunley, S. A., & Baker, A. C. (1999). Demographic characteristics and professional practices in school psychology. *School Psychology Quarterly*, *28*, 104–116.

DiPerna, J. C., & Elliott, S. N. (2000). *The Academic Competence Evaluation Scales*. San Antonio, TX: The Psychological Corporation.

DiPerna, J. C., Elliott, S. N., & Shapiro, E. S. (2000). *The Academic Intervention Monitoring System*. San Antonio, TX: The Psychological Corporation.

Dunst, C. J., & Trivette, C. M. (1988). Helping, helplessness, and harm. In J. C. Witt, S. N. Elliott, & F. M. Gresham (Eds.), *The handbook of behavior therapy in education* (pp. 343–376). New York: Plenum Press.

Elliott, S. N. (1988a). Acceptability of behavioral treatments: A review of variables that influence treatment selection. *Professional Psychology: Research and Practice*, *19*, 68–80.

Elliott, S. N. (1988b). Acceptability of behavioral treatment in educational settings. In J. C. Witt, S. N. Elliott, & F. M. Gresham (Eds.), *The handbook of behavior therapy in education* (pp. 121–150). New York: Plenum Press.

Elliott, S. N., Huai, N., & DiPerna, J. C. (2004). *Brief Academic Competence Evaluation Screening System*. Unpublished manuscript.

Gable, R. A., Sugai, G., Lewis, T., Nelson, J. R., Cheney, D., Safran, S. P., et al. (1998). *Individual and systematic approaches to collaboration and consultation*. Reston, VA: The Council for Children With Behavioral Disorders.

Gettinger, M., & Kohler, K. M. (2006). Process-outcome approaches to classroom management and effective teaching. In C. M. Evertson & C. S. Weubsteub (Eds.), *Handbook of classroom management: Research, practice, and contemporary issues* (pp. 73–95). Mahwah, NJ: Erlbaum.

Gettinger, M., & Stoiber, K. C. (1999). Excellence in teaching: Review of instructional and environmental variables. In C. R. Reynolds & T. B. Gutkin (Eds.), *The handbook of school psychology* (3rd ed., pp. 933–958). New York: John Wiley.

Gresham, F. M. (2006). Response to intervention. In G. G. Bear & K. M. Minke (Eds.), *Children's needs III: Development, prevention, and intervention* (pp. 525–540). Bethesda, MD: National Association of School Psychologists.

Gresham, F. M., & Kendell, G. K. (1987). School consultation research: Methodological critique and future research directions. *School Psychology Review, 16*, 306–316.

Gutkin, T. B., & Curtis, M. J. (1981). School-based consultant: The indirect service delivery concept. In M. J. Grimes & J. E. Zins (Eds.), *The theory and practice of school consultation* (pp. 219–226). Springfield, IL: Thomas.

Gutkin, T. B., & Curtis, M. J. (1999). School-based consultation theory and practice: The art and science of indirect service delivery. In C. R. Reynolds & T. B. Gutkin (Eds.), *The handbook of school psychology* (3rd ed., pp. 598–637). New York: John Wiley.

Haring, N. G. (1988). A technology for generalization. In N. G. Haring (Ed.), *Generalization for students with severe handicaps: Strategies and solutions* (pp. 5–11). Seattle: University of Washington Press.

Heller, K. A., Holtzman, W. H., & Messick, S. (Eds.). (1982). *Placing children in special education: A strategy for equity*. Washington, DC: National Academies Press.

Hurwitz, J. T., Rehberg, E. A., & Kratochwill, T. R. (in press). Dealing with school systems and teachers. In M. Hersen & J. C. Thomas (Eds.), *Comprehensive handbook of interviewing: Vol. 2. Interviewing children, their parents, and teachers*. Thousand Oaks, CA: Sage.

Jacobson, N., Follette, W., & Revenstorf, D. (1984). Psychotherapy outcome research: Methods for reporting variability and evaluating clinical significance. *Behavior Therapy, 15*, 336–352.

Kratochwill, T. R. (1985). Case study research in school psychology. *School Psychology Review, 14*, 204–215.

Kratochwill, T. R., & Bergan, J. R. (1990). *Behavioral consultation in applied settings: An individual guide*. New York: Plenum Press.

Kratochwill, T. R., Clements, M. A., & Kalymon, K. M. (2007). Response to intervention: Conceptual and methodological issues in implementation. In S. R. Jimmerson, M. K. Burns, & A. M. VanDerHeyden (Eds.), *The handbook to response to intervention: The science and practice of assessment and intervention*. New York: Springer.

Kratochwill, T. R., Elliott, S. N., & Stoiber, K. C. (2002). Problem-solving consultation. In A. Thomas & J. Grimes (Eds.), *Best practices in school psychology IV* (pp. 583–608). Bethesda, MD: National Association of School Psychologists.

Kratochwill, T. R., Hoagwood, K. E., Frank, J., Levitt, J. M., Romanelli, L. H., & Saka, N. (in press). Evidence-based interventions and practices in school psychology: Challenges and opportunities for the profession. In T. Gutkin & C. Reynolds (Eds.), *The handbook of school psychology* (4th ed.). Hoboken, NJ: John Wiley.

Kratochwill, T. R., & Piersel, W. C. (1983). Time-series research: Contributions to empirical clinical practice. *Behavioral Assessment, 5*, 165–176.

Kratochwill, T. R., & Pittman, P. (2002). Defining constructs in consultation: An important training agenda. *Journal of Educational and Psychological Consultation, 12*, 65–91.

Kratochwill, T. R., Sheridan, S. M., Carrington Rotto, P., & Salmon, D. (1991). Preparation of school psychologists to serve as consultants for teachers of emotionally disturbed children. *School Psychology Review, 20*, 530–550.

Kratochwill, T. R., & Shernoff, E. (2004). Evidence-based practice: Promoting evidence-based interventions in school psychology. *School Psychology Quarterly, 18*, 389–408.

Kratochwill, T. R., & Stoiber, K. C. (2000a). Empirically supported interventions and school psychology: Conceptual and practice issues: Part II. *School Psychology Quarterly, 15*, 233–253.

Kratochwill, T. R., & Stoiber, K. C. (2000b). Uncovering critical research agendas for school psychology: Conceptual dimensions and future directions. *School Psychology Review, 29*, 591–603.

Kratochwill, T. R., Volpiansky, P., Clements, M., & Ball, C. (in press). Professional development in implementing and sustaining multitier prevention models: Implications for response to intervention. *School Psychology Review*.

Meacham, M. L., & Peckham, P. D. (1978). School psychologists at three-quarters century: Congruence between training, practice, preferred role, and competence. *Journal of School Psychology, 16*, 195–206.

Medway, F. J. (1979). How effective is school consultation? A review of recent research. *Journal of School Psychology, 17*, 275–282.

Mihalic, S., Irwin, K., Fagan, A., Ballard, D., & Elliott, D. (2004). *Successful program implementation: Lessons from blueprints* (NCJ 204273). Washington, DC: U.S. Department of Justice.

National Association of State Directors of Special Education. (2005). *Response to intervention: Policy considerations and implementation.* Alexandria, VA: Author.

Newell, M., & Kratochwill, T. R. (in press). The integration of response to intervention and critical race theory–disability studies: A robust approach to reducing racial discrimination. In S. R. Jimmerson, M. K. Burns, & A. M. VanDerHeyden (Eds.), *The handbook of response to intervention: The science and practice of assessment and intervention.* New York: Springer.

Nunnally, J., & Kotsche, W. (1983). Studies of individual subjects: Logic and methods of analysis. *The British Journal of Clinical Psychology, 22,* 83–93.

Parsons, R., & Meyers, J. (1984). *Developing consultation skills: A guide to training, development, and assessment for human services professionals.* San Francisco: Jossey-Bass.

Reschly, D. K. (1988). Special education reform: School psychology revolution. *School Psychology Review, 17,* 465–481.

Sanetti, L. H., & Kratochwill, T. R. (2005). Treatment integrity assessment within a problem-solving model. In R. Brown-Chidsey (Ed.), *Assessment for intervention: A problem-solving approach* (pp. 304–325). New York: Guilford Press.

Sheridan, S. M., Eagle, J. W., & Doll, B. (2006). An examination of the efficacy of conjoint behavioral consultation with diverse clients. *School Psychology Quarterly, 21,* 396–417.

Sheridan, S. M., & Kratochwill, T. R. (1992). Behavioral parent-teacher consultation: Conceptual and research considerations. *Journal of School Psychology, 30,* 117–139.

Sheridan, S. M., & Kratochwill, T. R. (2008). *Conjoint behavioral consultation: Promoting family–school connections and interventions.* New York: Springer.

Sheridan, S. M., & Walker, D. (1999). Social skills in context: Considerations for assessment, intervention, and generalization. In C. R. Reynolds & T. B. Gutkin (Eds.), *The handbook of school psychology* (3rd ed., pp. 686–708). New York: John Wiley.

Sheridan, S. M., Welch, M., & Orme, S. F. (1996). Is consultation effective: A review of outcome research. *Remedial and Special Education, 17,* 341–354.

Stoiber, K. C., & Kratochwill, T. R. (2000). Empirically supported interventions in schools: Rationale and methodological issues. *School Psychology Quarterly, 15,* 75–105.

Stoiber, K. C., & Kratochwill, T. R. (2001). *Outcomes: Planning, Monitoring, Evaluating.* San Antonio, TX: The Psychological Corporation.

Stokes, T. F., & Baer, D. B. (1977). An implicit technology of generalization. *Journal of Applied Behavior Analysis, 10,* 349–367.

Watts, I. E., & Erevelles, N. (2004). These deadly times: Reconceptualizing school violence by using critical race theory and disability studies. *American Educational Research Journal, 41,* 271–299.

White, J. L., & Kratochwill, T. R. (2005). Practice guidelines in school psychology: Issues and directions for evidence-based interventions in practice and training. *Journal of School Psychology, 43,* 99–115.

White, O. R., Liberty, K. A., Haring, N. G., Billingsley, F. F., Boer, M., Burrage, A., et al. (1988). Review and analysis of strategies for generalization. In N. G. Haring (Ed.), *Generalization for students with severe handicaps: Strategies and solutions* (pp. 15–51). Seattle: University of Washington Press.

Wickstrom, K. F., & Witt, J. C. (1993). Resistance within school-based consultation. In J. Zins, T. R. Kratochwill, & S. N. Elliott (Eds.), *Handbook of consultation services for children* (pp. 159–178). San Francisco: Jossey-Bass.

Witt, J. C., & Elliott, S. N. (1983). Assessment in behavioral consultation: The initial interview. *School Psychology Review, 12,* 42–49.

Witt, J. C., & Elliott, S. N. (1985). Acceptability of classroom intervention strategies. In T. R. Kratochwill (Ed.), *Advances in school psychology* (pp. 251–288). Hillsdale, NJ: Erlbaum.

Witt, J. C., & Martens, B. K. (1988). Problems with problem-solving consultation: A reanalysis of assumptions, methods, and goals. *School Psychology Review, 17,* 211–226.

Ysseldyke, J., & Christenson, S. (2002). *Functional assessment of academic behavior: Creating successful learning environments.* Longmont, CO: Sopris West.

Zins, J. E., Kratochwill, T. R., & Elliott, S. N. (Eds.). (1993). *Handbook of consultation services for children.* San Francisco: Jossey-Bass.

ANNOTATED BIBLIOGRAPHY

Bergan, J. R., & Kratochwill, T. R. (1990). *Behavioral consultation in applied settings.* New York: Plenum Press.

Provides an extensive overview of behavioral consultation research and practice. Provides detailed information for researchers and practitioners in the conduct of behavioral consultation. The text is accompanied by a companion self-instructional guide.

Sheridan, S. M., & Kratochwill, T. R. (2008). *Conjoint behavioral consultation: Promoting family–school connections and interventions.* New York: Springer.

Provides an overview of the process and procedures of conjoint behavioral consultation. Special emphasis is placed on consultant-family connections in problem solving.

APPENDIX A. BEHAVIOR INTERVENTION RATING SCALE

You have just read about a child with a classroom problem and a description of an intervention for improving the problem. Please evaluate the intervention by circling the number that best describes *your* agreement or disagreement with each statement. You *must* answer each question.

		Strongly disagree	Disagree	Slightly disagree	Agree	Strongly agree
1.	This would be an acceptable intervention for the child's problem behavior.	1	2	3	4	5
2.	Most teachers would find this intervention appropriate for behavior problems in addition to the one described.	1	2	3	4	5
3.	The intervention should prove effective in changing the child's problem behavior.	1	2	3	4	5
4.	I would suggest the use of this intervention to other teachers.	1	2	3	4	5
5.	The child's behavior problem is severe enough to warrant use of this intervention.	1	2	3	4	5
6.	Most teachers would find this intervention suitable for the behavior problem described.	1	2	3	4	5
7.	I would be willing to use this intervention in the classroom setting.	1	2	3	4	5
8.	The intervention would *not* result in negative side effects for the child.	1	2	3	4	5
9.	The intervention would be appropriate for a variety of children.	1	2	3	4	5
10.	The intervention is consistent with those I have used in classroom settings.	1	2	3	4	5
11.	The intervention was a fair way to handle the child's problem behavior.	1	2	3	4	5
12.	The intervention is reasonable for the behavior problem described.	1	2	3	4	5
13.	I liked the procedures used in the intervention.	1	2	3	4	5
14.	The intervention was a good way to handle this child's behavior problem.	1	2	3	4	5
15.	Overall, the intervention would be beneficial for the child.	1	2	3	4	5
16.	The intervention would quickly improve the child's behavior.	1	2	3	4	5
17.	The intervention would produce a lasting improvement in the child's behavior.	1	2	3	4	5
18.	The intervention would improve the child's behavior to the point that it would not noticeably deviate from other classmates' behavior.	1	2	3	4	5
19.	Soon after using the intervention, the teacher would notice a positive change in the problem behavior.	1	2	3	4	5
20.	The child's behavior will remain at an improved level even after the intervention is discontinued.	1	2	3	4	5
21.	Using the intervention should not only improve the child's behavior in the classroom but also in other settings (e.g., other classrooms, home)	1	2	3	4	5
22.	When comparing this child with a well-behaved peer before and after use of the intervention, the child's and the peer's behavior would be more alike after using the intervention.	1	2	3	4	5
23.	The intervention should produce enough improvement in the child's behavior so the behavior no longer is a problem in the classroom.	1	2	3	4	5
24.	Other behaviors related to the problem behavior also are likely to be improved by the intervention.	1	2	3	4	5

APPENDIX B. THE CHILDREN'S INTERVENTION RATING PROFILE

		I agree				I do not agree
1.	The method used to deal with the behavior problem was fair.	+	+	+	+	+
2.	This child's teacher was too harsh.	+	+	+	+	+
3.	The method used to deal with the behavior may cause problems with this child's friends.	+	+	+	+	+
4.	There are better ways to handle this child's problem than the one described here.	+	+	+	+	+
5.	The method used by this teacher would be a good one to use with other children.	+	+	+	+	+
6.	I like the method used for this child's behavior problem.	+	+	+	+	+
7.	I think that the method used for this problem would help this child do better in school.	+	+	+	+	+

Note. Developed by Witt and Elliott (1983).

APPENDIX C. OUTCOMES: PME PROCEDURAL CHECKLIST

Check all the steps completed

1. *Describe and establish the baseline of the behavioral or academic concern.*
   - ☐ 1. Behavioral or academic concern defined in observable, measurable terms.
   - ☐ 2. Baseline established on behavioral or academic concern.
   - ☐ 3. Situational analysis of concern conducted (e.g., routines, expectation, skill match, contingent relationships, adult/teacher support required).
   - ☐ 4. Student and situational assets to build on identified.
   - ☐ 5. Parental input about behavioral or academic concern obtained.

2. *Set meaningful goals and benchmarks.*
   - ☐ 6. Goal statement focusing on controllable, measurable behaviors written.
   - ☐ 7. Benchmarks specifying standard against which to compare and scaling format selected.
   - ☐ 8. Target date for goal attainment established.
   - ☐ 9. Standard or social-comparison criterion against which to measure progress selected.

3. *Plan the intervention and specify progress-monitoring procedures.*
   - ☐ 10. Intervention with empirical support or functional basis identified.
   - ☐ 11. Intervention strategies/steps developed and reviewed with the change agent(s) or interventionist(s), such as parent, teacher, language specialist, psychologist.
   - ☐ 12. Context, frequency, and resources needed to implement intervention determined.
   - ☐ 13. Progress-monitoring procedures specified, including individual responsible for implementing progress monitoring and individual responsible for collecting progress-monitoring data.

4. *Monitor progress and analyze data.*
   - ☐ 14. Goal scaled at beginning point, intervention with specified strategies implemented for specified time, goal scaled at ending point.
   - ☐ 15. Progress-monitoring data and goal-attainment data plotted.
   - ☐ 16. Evidence in support of child's progress documented.
   - ☐ 17. Reasons for positive and/or negative progress review.

5. *Evaluate intervention outcomes and plan the next steps.*
   - ☐ 18. Consensus on progress toward goal occurred based on convergent-evidence procedures.
   - ☐ 19. Intervention-quality and intervention-integrity data reviewed.
   - ☐ 20. Discrepancy between expected change and post intervention examined for significance.
   - ☐ 21. Sufficient monitoring data and convergent data established.
   - ☐ 22. Intervention goals and strategies revised, if indicated (e.g., due to poor progress).

106 Best Practices in the Use of Resource Teams to Enhance Learning Supports

Howard S. Adelman
Linda Taylor
University of California, Los Angeles

INTRODUCTION

Case-oriented work has long dominated school psychology. As a result, many school psychologists and their student support colleagues are not yet engaged in resource-oriented teams. In fact, some may say, "What's that got to do with my job?" Others may say, "What's that got to do with helping kids?"

Pursuit of best practices for carrying out resource-oriented functions is essential to end the marginalization that continues to seriously impede the contribution of student support staff and that leads to reductions in force. Teams focused on student support resources represent changes in school infrastructure that engage support staff in the type of analyses essential if school improvement planning and decision making are to create comprehensive systems of learning supports.

It is widely conceded that student supports tend to be fragmented and narrowly focused and reach only a small proportion of those in need. Moreover, sparse budgets lead school psychologists, counselors, social workers, nurses, and other support staff into counterproductive competition with each other and with community professionals working with schools. Clearly, changes are needed. Resource-oriented teams can play a major role in altering this unacceptable status quo.

As school psychologists know, what happens for students depend first and foremost on who makes decisions about resources and who plans the details for school improvements. As they also know, the reality is that prevailing infrastructure mechanisms marginalize the influence of those most directly concerned about addressing learning, behavior, and emotional problems. So, pursuit of best practices makes it essential to rethink school and district infrastructure to correct this deficiency. We have addressed this and related systemic change matters in detail elsewhere (Adelman & Taylor, 2006a; Center for Mental Health in Schools, 2005a, 2005b). The focus here is on resource-oriented mechanisms that are a permanent part of a school and district infrastructure. Such mechanisms are essential to school improvement, and they provide a vehicle for school psychologists and other student support staff to expand their focus to encompass the full continuum of interconnected systems of intervention. This is the key to moving from being seen as concerned only with providing services to a few of the many students who are not doing well to playing an essential role in ensuring all students have an equal opportunity to succeed at school.

Pioneering work across the country conceives resource-oriented mechanisms from the school outward (Center for Mental Health in Schools, 2004a, 2005c). That is, first the focus is on school-level resource-oriented mechanisms. Then, based on analyses of what is needed to facilitate and enhance school-level efforts, mechanisms are conceived that enable clusters or families of schools to work together. The objectives in doing so are to increase efficiency and effectiveness and achieve the financial benefits that can be garnered from combining resources in pursuit of shared and overlapping functions. From this perspective, system-wide mechanisms are (re)designed to support the work at each school and among clusters of schools (e.g., those in feeder patterns).

A resource-oriented mechanism at a school, for multiple school sites, and system-wide can provide oversight, leadership, resource development, and ongoing support for development of a comprehensive system of learning supports. Such mechanisms provide ways to (a) arrive at decisions about resource allocation; (b) maximize systematic and integrated planning, implementation, maintenance, and evaluation of student and learning supports; (c) outreach to create formal working relationships with community resources to bring some to a school and establish special linkages with others; and (d) upgrade and modernize the approach to providing student and learning supports in ways that reflect the best intervention thinking and use of technology. At each system level, these tasks require that staff adopt some new roles and functions and that parents, students, and other representatives from the community enhance their involvement. They also call for redeployment of existing resources as well as finding new ones.

OVERVIEW

All schools have some activity focused on specific concerns, such as learning problems, substance abuse, violence, teen pregnancy, school dropouts, and delinquency. Looked at as a whole, an extensive range of activity oriented to students' needs and problems are found in many school districts. Some programs are provided throughout a school district, and others are carried out at or are linked to targeted schools. The interventions may be designed to benefit all students in a school, those in specified grades, and/or those identified as having special needs. The activities may be implemented in regular or special education classrooms and may be geared to an entire class, groups, or individuals, or they may be designed as pull-out programs for designated students. They encompass efforts to improve classroom and school-wide climate and a range of curricular and clinically oriented activities.

While schools can use a wide range of persons to help students, most school-owned and school-operated services are offered as part of pupil personnel services. In large districts, school psychologists, counselors, social workers, and other specialists may be organized into separate units that straddle regular, special, and compensatory education that may result in programs and services that are planned, implemented, and evaluated in a fragmented and piecemeal manner.

Service staff at schools tend to function in relative isolation of each other and other stakeholders, with a great deal of the work oriented to discrete problems and with an over-reliance on specialized services for individuals and small groups. In some places, a student identified as at risk for grade retention, dropout, and substance abuse may be assigned to three counseling programs operating independently of each other.

Even in settings with relatively few services, such fragmentation not only is costly, it breeds counterproductive competition and works against developing cohesiveness and maximizing results. The problems inherent in all this have long been of concern to support staff and their professional organizations, as well as policy makers at state and federal levels (e.g., Fagan & Wise, 2000; Marx & Wooley, 1998).

Given the desire to deal with these matters, schools across the country that want to improve how they provide student support activity are pioneering the use of a mechanism that focuses specifically on how resources are used and enhanced (Center for Mental Health in Schools, 2004a). This mechanism differs in its functions from the case-oriented teams most schools have for reviewing individual student/family problems (e.g., a student support team, an Individualized Educational Plan team). The functions of such case-oriented teams include referral, triage, and care monitoring or management. In contrast, a student or learning supports resource-oriented team at a school takes responsibility for enhancing use of all available resources associated with addressing barriers to student learning and promoting healthy development.

Two metaphors help differentiate the two types of mechanisms and the importance of both. A *case-orientation* mechanism fits the starfish metaphor:

> The day after a great storm had washed up all sorts of sea life far up onto the beach, a boy sets out to throw back as many of the still living starfish as he could. After watching him toss one after the other into the ocean, an old man approached the boy and said, "It's no use your doing that, there are too many. You're not going to make any difference." The boy looked at him in surprise, then bent over, picked up another starfish, threw it in, and then replied, "It made a difference to that one!"

This metaphor, of course, reflects all the important efforts to assist specific students.

The *resource-oriented* focus is captured by a different metaphor:

> One weekend a group of school staff went fishing together down at the river. Not long after they got

there, a child came floating down the rapids calling for help. One of the group on the shore quickly dived in and pulled the child out. Minutes later another, and then another, and then many more children were coming down the river. Soon everyone was diving in and dragging children to the shore and then jumping back in to save as many as they could. In the midst of all this frenzy, one of the group was seen walking away. Her colleagues were irate. How could she leave when there were so many children to save? After long hours, to everyone's relief, the flow of children stopped, and the group could finally catch their breath. At that moment, their colleague came back. They turned on her and angrily shouted, "How could you walk off when we needed everyone here to save the children?" She replied, "It occurred to me that someone ought to go upstream and find out why so many kids were falling into the river. What I found is that the old bridge had several planks missing, and when children tried to jump over the gap, they couldn't make it and fell through into the river. So I got some folks to help fix the bridge."

Fixing and building better bridges is a good way to think about prevention, and it helps underscore the importance of taking time to improve and enhance resources, programs, and systems.

Clearly, as the emphasis on Tier 1, 2, and 3 service levels suggests, schools need to pursue case-oriented and resource-oriented functions. Since case-oriented teams are widely implemented, it seems essential to increase understanding of the importance of ensuring there also is the type of resource orientation that leads to an increased emphasis on prevention and responding as early after problem onset as feasible. Such an emphasis is critical in reducing the number of students who end up needing to be responded to as cases. It also can help school psychologists as they strive to play a greater role in school improvement planning and decision making.

Resource-oriented mechanisms have been designated by a variety of names including Resource Coordinating Team, Resource Management Team, and Learning Supports Resource Team. For purposes of this discussion, we will use Learning Supports Resource Team. We initially demonstrated the feasibility of such teams in the Los Angeles Unified School District (Lim & Adelman, 1997; Rosenblum, DiCecco, Taylor, & Adelman, 1995). Currently, the teams are being introduced in many schools across the country (Center for Mental Health in Schools, 2004a, 2005c).

Creation of resource-oriented mechanisms focused on learning supports at schools, for families of schools, and at the district level provides an often missing facet of the infrastructure (Center for Mental Health in Schools, 2005b). Where this facet is missing, certain functions may be given short shrift. Examples include analyses of how existing resources are deployed and clarification of how the various human and financial resources from public and private sectors can be woven together. When too little attention is paid to such functions, it hampers efforts to (a) weave together existing school and community resources; (b) enable programs and services to function in an increasingly cohesive and cost-efficient way; and (c) develop, implement, and evaluate over time a comprehensive system of learning supports.

Available evidence suggests that, by transforming current approaches for addressing barriers to student learning and promoting healthy development, resource-oriented mechanisms are vital in reducing marginalization and fragmentation of student and learner supports (Adelman, 1993; Adelman & Taylor, 1997a, 2006a; Gardner, 2005; Iowa Department of Education, 2004; Kretzmann, 1998; Kretzmann, McKnight, & Sheehan, 1997; Lim & Adelman, 1997; Rosenblum et al., 1995; U.S. Department of Education, 1996). Moreover, when such mechanisms are created in the form of teams, they also can be vehicles for building working relationships and can help solve turf and operational problems.

BASIC CONSIDERATIONS

Improving and enhancing resources, programs, and systems involve carrying out a variety of functions in a proactive way. These include providing leadership, capacity building, oversight for mapping and analyzing current resource use, establishing priorities for program development, making recommendations for resource (re)deployment and enhancement to improve programs and systems, and participating in decision making.

When resource-oriented mechanisms for learning supports are created, the intent is to maintain a focus on:

- *All students:* Using resources to address the diverse needs of the many as well as the few and doing so in ways that level the playing field and enable every student to have an equal opportunity to succeed at school

- *Building a school-site infrastructure:* Establishing and sustaining organizational and operational mechanisms that are linked into an effective and efficient infrastructure at the school site
- *Building infrastructure for a family of schools:* Connecting schools in a complex or feeder pattern to maximize use of available resources and achieve economies of scale
- *Connecting with the district central office infrastructure:* Ensuring that site-based and school cluster efforts are effectively linked to and nurtured by the central office
- *Connecting schools across districts:* Both appropriate and necessary, for example, in small rural school districts and where schools are organized into high school and elementary districts
- *Building school–community collaboratives:* Connecting school and community infrastructures and braiding school–community resources
- *Evolving a comprehensive, multifaceted, and cohesive system of learning supports:* Rethinking and deploying resource use in ways that evolve student support services into a comprehensive learning supports component that is treated as a primary and essential facet of school improvement

Team Composition

It is conceivable that one person could perform many of the basic resource-oriented functions. However, given the nature and scope of the work, it is preferable to have several stakeholders put their heads together and function as a formal Learning Supports Resource Team.

Some schools find the idea of establishing another team unappealing. In such cases, an existing team (e.g., student or teacher assistance teams, school crisis teams, healthy school teams, or school improvement teams) can perform resource-oriented functions. In adding the resource-oriented functions to another team's work, however, great care must be taken to structure the agenda so sufficient time is devoted to the additional tasks. For small schools, a large team often is not feasible, but a two-person team can still do much of the work. The point is to get started and build over time into the type of team that fits the setting. The key is not to lose sight of the functions the team needs to pursue and what needs to be accomplished.

The team meets as necessary. Frequency of meetings depends on how ambitious the group's agenda is and time availability. Initially, this may mean once a week. Later, when meetings are scheduled for every 2–3

weeks, continuity and momentum are maintained through interim tasks performed by individuals or workgroups. Because some participants may be at a school on a part-time basis, one of the problems that must be addressed is that of rescheduling personnel so that there is an overlapping time for meeting together. Of course, the reality is that not all team members will be able to attend every meeting, but a good approximation can be made at each meeting, with steps taken to keep others informed as to what was done. Well planned and trained teams can accomplish a great deal through informal communication and short meetings.

Where a new team is established, it might begin with only a few people. Then, as feasible, it can expand into an inclusive group of informed, able, and willing stakeholders. Although a resource-oriented team might be created solely around psychosocial programs, the intent is to focus on resources related to *all* major learning supports programs and services. Thus, the team tries to bring together representatives of all these programs and services. Because various teams at a school require the expertise of the same personnel, some people will necessarily be on more than one team. The following are the types of stakeholders who are candidates for such a team:

- Principal or assistant principal
- School psychologist
- Counselor
- School nurse
- School social worker
- Attendance and dropout counselors
- Safe and drug-free school staff
- Behavioral specialist
- Special education staff
- After school program staff
- Bilingual and Title I program coordinators
- Health educators
- Representatives of community agencies involved regularly with the school (e.g., community entities involved with physical and mental health, welfare and protective services, juvenile justice)
- Student and family representation (when appropriate and feasible)
- Others who have a particular interest and ability to help with the functions, including regular classroom teachers, noncertificated staff (e.g., front office, food service, custodian, bus driver, school resource officer).

For the team to function well, there must be a core of members who have or will acquire the ability to carry out identified functions and make the mechanism work (others are auxiliary members). They must be committed to the team's mission. Building team commitment and competence is an ongoing task. The team must have a dedicated leader/facilitator who is able to keep the group focused on the task and productive. It also needs someone who records decisions and plans and reminds members of planned activity and products. Whenever feasible, advanced technology (management systems, electronic bulletin boards and e-mail, clearinghouses) are used to facilitate communication, networking, program planning and implementation, linking activity, and a variety of budgeting, scheduling, and other management concerns.

A team forms small workgroups as needed to address specific concerns (e.g., mapping resources, planning for capacity building, addressing problems related to case-oriented systems), develop new programs (e.g., welcoming and social support strategies for newcomers to the school), implement special initiatives (e.g., positive behavior support), and so forth. Such groups usually are facilitated by a member of the resource team who recruits a small group of other stakeholders from the school and community who are willing and able to help. The group facilitator provides regular updates to the resource team on workgroup progress and brings back feedback from the team. Ad hoc workgroups take on tasks that can be done over a relatively short time period, and the group disbands once the work is accomplished. Standing workgroups focus on defined program areas and pursue current priorities for enhancing intervention in a given arena (e.g., helping to design cohesive approaches to provide supports for various student transitions, enhancing home and school connections).

Not an Isolated Mechanism, Part of an Integrated Infrastructure

Resource-oriented mechanisms at all levels cannot be isolated entities. The intent is for them to connect to each other and be part of an integrated infrastructure. We focus here on the school level. Extrapolations can be made from there.

A Learning Supports Resources Team must be a formal unit of a school's infrastructure. It must be fully connected with the other infrastructure mechanisms at the school (e.g., those associated with instruction and management/governance). Figure 1 illustrates relationships of such a team to other major infrastructure units.

Having at least one representative from the resource team on the school's governing and planning bodies (e.g., the principal's decision-making team, school improvement planning team) ensures the type of infrastructure connections that are essential if student and learning supports are to be maintained, improved, and increasingly integrated with classroom instruction. Of course, having an administrator on the team provides the necessary link with the school's administrative decision making related to allocation of budget, space, staff development time, and other resources. Moreover, as discussed below, where clusters or families of schools are working together, representatives from each of the schools meet together periodically (Adelman & Taylor, 2002; Taylor, Nelson, & Adelman, 1999).

A well-designed resource-oriented team complements the work of a site's governance body by focusing on providing on-site overview, leadership, and advocacy for all activity specifically used to address barriers to learning and teaching. However, for this to be the case, the team must be properly constituted, trained, and supported.

Establishing and building the capacity of resource-oriented mechanisms, of course, are not simple tasks. As a result, it is essential to think in terms of a phase-in process (Center for Mental Health in Schools, 2005a). Because establishing such a team involves significant organizational change, staff assigned to accomplish the tasks must have the skills of a systemic change agent. We designate this type of change agent as an *organization facilitator* (Adelman & Taylor, 2006a; Lim & Adelman, 1997; Rosenblum et al., 1995).

Anyone chosen to create organizational change must be assured the full administrative support and be specially trained as a change agent. The training must include developing expertise to help school sites, complexes, and districts implement and institutionalize substantively new approaches.

The work of an organization facilitator in establishing a Learning Supports Resource Team is highlighted in Appendix A. In brief, organization facilitators are catalysts and managers of change. As such, they strive to ensure that changes are true to the design for improvement and adapted to fit the local culture. Such a facilitator also must be an effective problem solver, responding quickly as problems arise and designing proactive strategies to counter anticipated barriers to change, such as negative reactions and dynamics, common factors interfering with working relationships, and system deficiencies. All this must be accomplished in ways that increase readiness and commitment to change while enhancing empowerment and a sense of community.

Figure 1. **Learning supports resource team as part of an integrated infrastructure at a school site.**

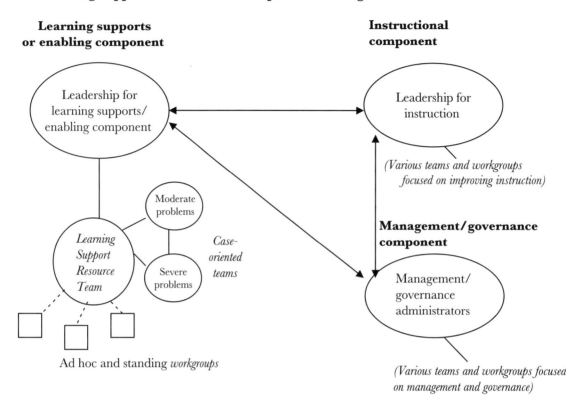

Note. Learning supports of enabling component leadership: Consists of an administrator and other advocates/champions with responsibility and accountability for ensuring the vision of the component is not lost. The administrator meets with and provides regular input to the Learning Supports Resource Team. *Learning Supports Resource Team:* Ensures component cohesion, integrated implementation, and ongoing development. It meets weekly to guide and monitor daily implementation and development of all programs, services, initiatives, and systems at a school that are concerned with providing learning supports and specialized assistance. *Ad hoc and standing workgroups:* Initially, these are the various teams that already exist related to various initiatives and programs (e.g., a crisis team) and for processing "cases" (e.g., a student assistance team, an Individualized Educational Plan team). Where redundancy exists, workgroups can be combined. Others are formed as needed by the Learning Supports Resource Team to address specific concerns. These groups are essential for accomplishing the many tasks associated with such a team's functions. For more on this, see http://smhp.psych.ucla.edu/pdfdocs/infrastructure/anotherinitiative-exec.pdf and http://smhp.psych.ucla.edu/pdfdocs/studentsupport/toolkit/aidk.pdf.

Organization facilitators also can help organize basic interdisciplinary and cross training to create the trust, knowledge, skills, and attitudes essential for the kind of working relationships required if the resource-oriented mechanism is to operate successfully. Because the work of resource-oriented teams involves promoting systemic changes at a school, an organization facilitator helps team members understand how to be effective agents of change as they work with a site's stakeholders to restructure programs and infrastructure mechanisms. This includes matters such as planning, implementing, and formatively evaluating stakeholder development (coaching, with an emphasis on creating readiness both in terms of motivation and skills; team building; providing technical assistance) and ongoing capacity building and support.

We have focused here on an organization facilitator as a change agent for one school. Such an individual, however, might rotate among a group of schools. In large school districts, a cadre of such professionals might be used to facilitate change across an entire district.

BEST PRACTICES

In keeping with the fundamental organizational principle emphasizing that structure (e.g., a resource-oriented mechanism) follows function, we discuss best practices for a Learning Supports Resource Team in terms of its major functions. After providing an overview, we explore in greater depth the core function of mapping and analyzing resources. Then, we highlight the role such a team can play in helping establish a comprehensive learning supports component. We conclude with a brief note about the type of data needed to guide and evaluate the work of a Learning Supports Resource Team.

Functions

When we describe a Learning Support Resource Team, some school staff quickly respond that they already have one. When we explore this with them, we usually find what they have is a *case-oriented team* (e.g., a student study team, student success team, student assistance team, teacher assistance team). To further clarify the difference between resource- and case-oriented teams, we will contrast the functions of each. In doing so, the intent is to highlight the differences in agenda, and the need for mechanisms to carry out both sets of functions listed in Table 1.

As noted already, the resource-oriented functions are pursued not just to enhance coordination but to make progress toward the overall aim of developing a comprehensive, multifaceted, and cohesive system of learning supports (i.e., a learning supports component). In pursuing its functions, the team provides what often is a missing link for managing and enhancing programs and systems in ways that integrate, strengthen, or stimulate new and improved interventions.

For example, such a mechanism can be used to (a) map and analyze activities and resources to improve their use in preventing and ameliorating problems; (b) build effective systems for referral, case management, and quality assurance; (c) enhance procedures for management of programs and information and for communication among school staff and with the home; and (d) explore ways to redeploy and enhance resources, such as clarifying which activities are nonproductive, suggesting better uses for resources, and establishing priorities for developing new interventions, as well as reaching out to connect with additional resources in the school district and community.

About Mapping and Analyzing Resources

Schools have a variety of programs and services to address barriers to learning and teaching, and these consume a significant amount of resources. The interventions range from Title I programs, through extra help for low-performing students, to accommodations for special education students. From what school administrators tell us, when the various sources of support are totaled at schools with substantial amounts of federal and special project funding, learning supports account for about 30% of the resources. However, because school leaders are mainly focused on enhancing instruction in direct ways, essential efforts to provide a well-designed learning supports system continue to be marginalized, and resources are deployed in a fragmented and often wasteful and ineffective manner. One result of marginalizing learning supports is that school improvement efforts continue to pay little attention to

Table 1. **Differences Between Case-Oriented Team Functions and Resource-Oriented Team Functions**

Case-Oriented Team Functions	Resource-Oriented Team Functions
• Triage • Referral • Case monitoring/management • Case progress review • Case reassessment	• Aggregating data across students and from teachers to analyze school needs • Mapping resources in school and community • Analyzing resources • Identifying the most pressing program development needs at the school • Coordinating and integrating school resources and connecting with community resources • Establishing priorities for strengthening programs and developing new ones • Planning and facilitating ways to strengthen and develop new programs and systems • Recommending how resources should be deployed and redeployed • Identifying where additional resources exist and developing strategies for accessing them • Social marketing

the need for and potential impact of rethinking how these resources can be used to enable student learning by doing more to address barriers (Adelman & Taylor, 2006b; Center for Mental Health in Schools, 2004b; McKnight, 1995; Taylor & Adelman, 2004).

Whatever the actual percentage of resources used for learning supports, the fact is that in too many locales these resources are expended in ad hoc, piecemeal ways (Marx & Wooley, 1998). A Learning Supports Resource Team can reverse this trend. The key to doing so involves mapping, analyzing, and managing resources with a clear emphasis on what needs to be done to help all students have an equitable opportunity to succeed at school (see Appendix B).

To determine high-frequency needs of a school, the team uses aggregated data about student learning and behavior. For example, a team at an elementary school may find that 30% of the third graders have problems reading or a high school team might find that 40% of the students are not graduating. Awareness of such needs raises the question of what resources already are being expended to address the problems (Academy for Educational Development, 2002; Bruner, Bell, Brindis, Chang, & Scarbrough, 1993; Dedrick, Mitchell, Miyagawa, & Roberts, 1997; Dewar, 1997; Kretzmann & McKnight, 1993).

Following initial mapping, the focus turns to analyzing how resources are currently used and considering how they might be redeployed to improve efforts to address barriers to learning and teaching. The goal is to develop specific recommendations for improving the work at each school through enhancing use of the school's resources and enhancing resources through collaboration among the family of schools and with neighborhood entities (McKnight & Kretzmann,1990). The tasks are to clarify what parts are in place, what is still missing, and how to braid and enhance resources to improve matters.

What Parts Are in Place

Discussion focuses on how effective and efficient current efforts are. Special attention is given to identifying redundant efforts, inefficient use of resources, and ineffective activities. With respect to what is seen as ineffective, analyses differentiate between activities that might be effective if they were better supported and more effectively implemented and those that are not worth continuing because they have not made a significant impact or because they are not well conceived. This facilitates generating recommendations

about what should be discontinued so that resources can be redeployed to enhance current efforts and fill gaps.

What Is Still Missing

Every school has a wish list of programs and services it needs. Analyses of mapping products provide an appreciation of major gaps and help put proposed programs, services, and initiatives into perspective of the vision for a comprehensive, multifaceted, and integrated approach to addressing barriers to learning and promoting healthy development. Thus, rather than making ad hoc choices from a long list of wishes, recommendations can be based on systematic analyses of what current efforts require enhancement and what gaps need to be filled.

How to Braid and Enhance Resources to Improve Matters

Analyses focus first on how resources are being used at a school. (Which are being used with the greatest impact and which are not? Is there redundancy? Ineffective activity? Programs where costs far outweigh benefits? Inefficiencies owing to lack of coordination? Are there promising programs that are under supported? Are there serious gaps in addressing high priority needs that have been identified by the school's governance body?) Based on the analyses, immediate priorities are set and recommendations are formulated with respect to how best to deploy and redeploy resources to have the greatest impact.

Essentially, the work involves conducting a gap analysis. That is, existing resources are laid out in the context of the adopted vision for a comprehensive, multifaceted, and integrated approach to addressing barriers to learning and promoting healthy development. This provides a basis for a discussion of matters such as: (a) what is working and whether certain activities should no longer be pursued (because they are not effective or not as high a priority as some others that are needed); (b) what are current priorities with respect to important areas of need and what resources might be redeployed and braided to meet the priorities, including enhancing existing promising practices and filling gaps; (c) what are strategies and time lines for improving the system of learning supports.

Having accomplished all this, the focus turns to how a family of schools (neighboring schools, especially those in a feeder pattern) might braid resources to address common concerns. At this juncture, the family of schools explores how community resources might be woven into the effort (Dedrick, Mitchell, & Roberts, 1994; Fisher & Kling, 1993; Kingsley, Coulton, Barndt, Sawicki, & Tatian, 1997). Schools in the same geographic (catchment) area have a number of shared concerns, and feeder schools often are interacting with students from the same family. Furthermore, some programs and personnel are (or can be) shared by several neighboring schools thus minimizing redundancy and reducing costs (see Appendix C).

Moving to the next level, recommendations are made for how to better use resources that the district and community agencies offer at central locations or to a few select schools. And, finally, the work turns to whatever extramural grants are available to schools, districts, and community entities to help turn the vision of a comprehensive, multifaceted, and cohesive system of learning supports into reality.

Tools to Aid in Mapping and Analyzing Resources

Mapping and analyzing resources is a major systemic intervention. There are many tools that can aid the process. Such tools are highlighted in the resource aids described at the end of this chapter.

One set of tools specifically designed to enhance school improvement planning for addressing barriers to learning and teaching are the self-study surveys developed by the Center for Mental Health in Schools at UCLA. These surveys focus on what currently is being done, whether it is being done well, and what else is desired. The set includes an overview Survey of System Status, which covers the leadership and coordination systems needed in developing an effective learning support component and surveys for each of the following six arenas for enhancing learning supports: (a) classroom-based efforts to enhance learning, engagement, and reengagement of those with mild-moderate learning, behavior, and emotional problems; (b) support for transitions; (c) prescribed student and family assistance; (d) crisis assistance and prevention; (e) home involvement in schooling; and (f) outreach to develop greater community involvement and support, including recruitment of volunteers. The set also includes a special survey focusing on school–community partnerships.

Self-study surveys can be used by any mechanism concerned with mapping and analyzing resources. For example, members of a Learning Supports Resource

Team initially might work separately in responding to survey items, but the major benefit comes from the shared understanding that arises during group discussions. The discussion and subsequent analyses also can provide a form of quality review.

As another tool in effectively mapping and analyzing resources and their deployment, it is helpful to have a broad framework of the scope and content of learning supports. An example of such a framework is illustrated in Figure 2. This matrix integrates a conceptualization of primary areas of focus for intervention and traditional levels (e.g., promotion and prevention, early intervention, and treatment; Tier 1, 2, and 3 service levels) but conceives of them as integrated systems of intervention.

Role of the Team in Helping to Establish a Comprehensive Learning Supports Component

Again, we stress that the ultimate aim of pursuing resource-oriented functions is not only to end the fragmentation of student and learning supports but also to end the marginalization of the whole enterprise (Adelman & Taylor, 1997a, 2006a). Toward these ends, Learning Supports Resource Teams can play a key role by rethinking and deploying resource use in ways that transform student support services into a comprehensive *enabling or learning supports component* that is treated as a primary and essential facet of school improvement (see Appendix D).

Major school improvement, of course, requires creating readiness, building consensus, and influencing action by key stakeholders for such a major systemic change (Adelman & Taylor, 1997b; Center for Mental Health in Schools, 2005a). The information arising from mapping and analyses of resources provides an important database that can be communicated to key stakeholders to help them understand the benefits of change (Kretzmann & McKnight, 1996; Mizrahi & Morrison, 1993). Also important to making effective change is the inclusion of the evidence base for moving in new directions (Center for Mental Health in Schools, 2004a, 2004b).

Data to Guide the Work and Evaluate Progress

All resource-oriented teams need data to enhance the quality of their efforts and to monitor their outcomes in

Figure 2. A unifying umbrella framework to guide rethinking of learning supports.

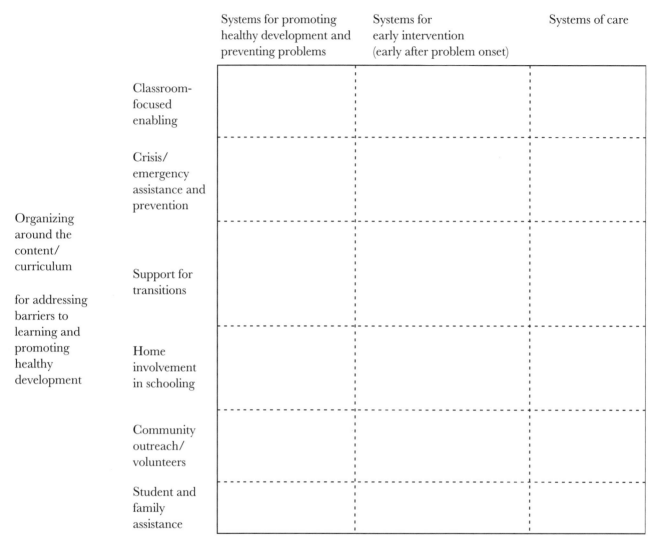

Note. Specific school-wide and classroom-based activities related to positive behavior support, prereferral interventions, and the eight components of the Center for Prevention and Disease Control's Coordinated School Health Program are embedded into the six content areas.

ways that promote appropriate accountability. While new teams often do not have the resources for extensive data gathering, sound planning and implementation require that formative evaluation data be amassed and analyzed. In the process, data can be collected that provide a base for a subsequent evaluation of impact. All

decisions about which data are needed should reflect clarity about how the data will be used.

The data for formative evaluation and team impact may already have been gathered from existing documents and records (e.g., base rate needs assessments, resource directories, budget information, census data, and reports from school, police, hospital, and other organizations). Where additional data are needed, they may be gathered using procedures such as checklists, surveys, semistructured interviews, focus group discussions, and observations. Of course, all data indicating that the team is having a positive impact should be widely shared as soon as it is available.

SUMMARY

Resource-oriented mechanisms are a key facet of school improvement efforts to transform and restructure daily operations for student and learning support. In some schools as much as 30% of the budget may be going to problem prevention and correction. Every school is expending resources to enable learning; few have a mechanism to ensure appropriate use of existing resources. Such a mechanism contributes to cost efficacy of learning supports activity by ensuring all such activity is planned, implemented, and evaluated in a coordinated and increasingly integrated manner. Creating resource-oriented mechanisms also is essential for braiding together school and community resources and encouraging intervention activity to function in an increasingly cohesive way. Furthermore, when such mechanisms are created in the form of a team, they also are a vehicle for building working relationships and can play a role in solving turf and operational problems.

One of the primary and essential tasks a learning supports resource-oriented mechanism undertakes is that of taking stock of school and community programs and services that are in place to support students, families, and staff. A comprehensive gap assessment is generated as resources are mapped and compared with data on the unmet needs of and desired outcomes for students, their families, and school staff. Analyses of what is available, effective, and needed provide a sound basis for formulating priorities and developing strategies to link with additional resources at other schools, district sites, and in the community and enhance resource use. Such analyses also can guide efforts to improve cost effectiveness.

In a similar fashion, a learning supports resource-oriented mechanism for a complex or family of schools (e.g., a high school and its feeder schools) and one at the district level provide mechanisms for analyses on a larger scale. This can lead to strategies for cross-school, community-wide, and district-wide cooperation and integration to enhance intervention effectiveness and garner economies of scale.

Minimally, a resource-oriented team can reduce fragmentation and enhance cost efficacy. On another level, this mechanism can provide leadership in guiding school stakeholders in evolving the school's vision, priorities, and practices for learning supports and working to enhance resources in an integrative way. That is, with appropriate leadership from student support staff, such a mechanism can play a key role in ending the marginalization of student and learning supports by transforming fragmented activity into a system of learning supports. In doing so, the focus needs to be on *all* school resources (including compensatory and special education, support services, adult education, recreation and enrichment programs, and facility use) and *all* community resources (including public and private agencies, families, businesses, services, programs, facilities, institutions of higher education, professionals in training, and volunteers including professional making pro-bono contributions).

The long-range aim is to weave all resources together into the fabric of every school and evolve a comprehensive component that effectively addresses barriers to development, learning, and teaching. As leaders and policy makers recognize the essential nature of such a component, it will be easier to braid resources to address barriers. In turn, this will enhance efforts to foster healthy development. When resources are combined properly, the end product can be cohesive and potent school–community partnerships. These partnerships are essential to fulfilling society's aims of closing the achievement gap and leaving fewer children behind.

REFERENCES

Academy for Educational Development. (2002). *Community youth mapping guide, toolkit, and informational video*. Washington, DC: Author.

Adelman, H. S. (1993). School-linked mental health interventions: Toward mechanisms for service coordination and integration. *Journal of Community Psychology, 21,* 309–319.

Adelman, H. S., & Taylor, L. (1997a). Addressing barriers to learning: Beyond school-linked services and full service schools. *American Journal of Orthopsychiatry, 67,* 408–421.

Adelman, H. S., & Taylor, L. (1997b). Toward a scale-up model for replicating new approaches to schooling. *Journal of Educational and Psychological Consultation, 8,* 197–230.

Adelman, H. S., & Taylor, L. (2002). So you want higher achievement scores? It's time to rethink learning supports. *The State Education Standard, 3,* 52–56.

Adelman, H. S., & Taylor, L. (2006a). *The school leader's guide to student learning supports: New directions for addressing barriers to learning.* Thousand Oaks, CA: Corwin Press.

Adelman, H. S., & Taylor, L. (2006b). *The implementation guide to student learning supports: New directions for addressing barriers to learning.* Thousand Oaks, CA: Corwin Press.

Bruner, C., Bell, K., Brindis, C., Chang, H., & Scarbrough, W. (1993). *Charting a course: Assessing a community's strengths and needs.* Des Moines, IA: National Center for Service Integration.

Center for Mental Health in Schools. (2004a). *Where's it happening?.* Los Angeles: Author. Retrieved August 11, 2006, from http://smhp.psych.ucla.edu/summit2002/wheresithappening.htm

Center for Mental Health in Schools. (2004b). *Addressing barriers to student learning and promoting healthy development: A usable research base.* Los Angeles: Author. Retrieved August 31, 2006, from http://smhp.psych.ucla.edu/pdfdocs/briefs/BarriersBrief.pdf

Center for Mental Health in Schools. (2005a). *Systemic change and school improvement: Designing, implementing, and sustaining prototypes and going to scale.* Los Angeles: Author. Retrieved August 31, 2006, from http://smhp.psych.ucla.edu/pdfdocs/systemic/systemicreport.pdf

Center for Mental Health in Schools. (2005b). *School improvement planning: What's missing?.* Los Angeles: Author. Retrieved August 19, 2006, from http://smhp.psych.ucla.edu/whatsmissing.htm

Center for Mental Health in Schools. (2005c). *Resource oriented teams: Key infrastructure mechanisms for enhancing education supports.* Los Angeles: Author. Retrieved August 31, 2006, from http://smhp.psych.ucla.edu/pdfdocs/Report/resource_oriented_teams.pdf

Dedrick, A., Mitchell, G., Miyagawa, M., & Roberts, S. (1997). *From model to reality: Community capacity building and asset mapping. Listen and learn . . . The answers are with communities.* Edmonton, Alberta: Author.

Dedrick, A., Mitchell, G., & Roberts, S. (1994). *Community capacity building and asset mapping: Model development.* Edmonton, Alberta: Community Development Caritas.

Dewar, T. (1997). *A guide to evaluating asset-based community development: Lessons, challenges and opportunities.* Skokie, IL: ACTA Publications.

Fagan, T. K., & Wise, P. S. (2000). *School psychology: Past, present, and future.* (2nd ed.). Bethesda, MD: National Association of School Psychologists.

Fisher, R., & Kling, J. (1993). *Mobilizing the community.* Newbury Park, CA: SAGE.

Gardner, S. (2005). *Cities, counties, kids, and families: The essential role of local government.* Lanham, MD: University Press of America.

Iowa Department of Education. (2004). *Developing our youth: Fulfilling a promise, investing in Iowa's future—Enhancing Iowa's systems of supports for learning and development..* Des Moines, IA: Author. Retrieved September 9, 2006, http://smhp.psych.ucla.edu/pdfdocs/iowa-systemofsupport.pdf

Kingsley, G., Coulton, C., Barndt, M., Sawicki, D., & Tatian, P. (1997). *Mapping your community: Using geographic information to strengthen community initiatives.* Washington, DC: U.S. Department of Housing and Urban Development.

Kretzmann, J. (1998). *Community-based development and local schools: A promising partnership.* Evanston, IL: Institute for Policy Research.

Kretzmann, J., & McKnight, J. (1993). *Building communities from the inside out: A path toward finding and mobilizing a community's assets.* Skokie, IL: ACTA Publications.

Kretzmann, J., & McKnight, J. (1996). *A guide to mapping and mobilizing the economic capacities of local residents.* Skokie, IL: ACTA Publications.

Kretzmann, J., McKnight, J., & Sheehan, G. (1997). *A guide to capacity inventories: Mobilizing the community skills of local residents.* Evanston, IL: Institute for Policy Research.

Lim, C., & Adelman, H. S. (1997). Establishing school-based collaborative teams to coordinate resources: A case study. *Social Work in Education, 19,* 266–277.

Marx, E., & Wooley, S. F. (Eds.). (1998). *Health is academic: A guide to coordinated school health programs.* New York: Teachers College Press.

McKnight, J. L. (1995). *The careless society–community and its counterfeits.* New York: HarperCollins.

McKnight, J., & Kretzmann, J. (1990). *Mapping community capacity.* Evanston, IL: Institute for Policy Research.

Mizrahi, T., & Morrison, J. D. (1993). *Community organization and social administration: Advances, trends and emerging principles.* Binghamton, NY: Haworth Press.

Rosenblum, L., DiCecco, M. B., Taylor, L., & Adelman, H. S. (1995). Upgrading school support programs through collaboration: Resource Coordinating Teams. *Social Work in Education, 17,* 117–124.

Taylor, L., & Adelman, H. S. (2004). Advancing mental health in schools: Guiding frameworks and strategic approaches. In K. Robinson (Ed.), *Advances in school-based mental health* (pp. 1–23). Kingston, NJ: Civic Research Institute.

Taylor, L., Nelson, P., & Adelman, H. S. (1999). Scaling-up reforms across a school district. *Reading and Writing Quarterly, 15,* 303–326.

U.S. Department of Education. (1996). *Putting the pieces together: Comprehensive school-linked strategies for children and families.* Washington, DC: Author.

ANNOTATED BIBLIOGRAPHY

Adelman, H. S., & Taylor, L. (2006). Mapping a school's resources to improve their use in preventing and ameliorating problems. In C. Franklin, M. Harris, & P. Allen-Meares (Eds.), *The school services sourcebook: A guide for social workers, counselors, and mental health professionals (pp. 977–990).* New York: Oxford University Press.

Emphasizes that to function well every system must fully understand and manage resources. Mapping is a first and essential step toward these ends and, done properly, it is a major intervention in efforts to enhance systemic effectiveness and change for addressing barriers to learning and teaching.

Center for Mental Health in Schools. (2005). *About infrastructure mechanisms for a comprehensive learning support component.* Los Angeles: Author. Retrieved August 26, 2006, from http://www.smhp.psych.ucla.edu/pdfdocs/infrastructure/infra_mechanisms.pdf

Explores one aspect of necessary infrastructure changes, namely, resource-oriented mechanisms that allow a learning support component to function and work effectively, efficiently, and with full integration with the other major components of school improvement.

Center for Mental Health in Schools. (2005). *Another initiative? Where does it fit? A unifying framework and an integrated infrastructure for schools to address barriers to learning and promote healthy development.* Los Angeles: Author. Retrieved September 11, 2006, from http://smhp.psych.ucla.edu/pdfdocs/infrastructure/anotherinitiative-exec.pdf

Highlights the fragmentation and illustrates the value of a unifying framework and integrated infrastructure for the many initiatives, projects, programs, and services schools pursue in addressing barriers to learning. Specifically highlighted are how initiatives can be embedded into a comprehensive framework and how existing infrastructure mechanisms can be integrated. Several tools are included.

Center for Mental Health in Schools. (2005). *Developing resource-oriented mechanisms to enhance learning supports: A continuing education packet.* Los Angeles: Author. Retrieved August 22, 2006, from http://smhp.psych.ucla.edu/pdfdocs/contedu/developing_resource_oriented-mechanisms.pdf

This set of training modules is designed as an aid for training leaders and staff about the importance of and how to establish effective resource-oriented mechanisms to advance development of a comprehensive, multifacted, and integrated learning supports (or enabling) component at every school.

Center for Mental Health in Schools. (2005). *Resource mapping and management to address barriers to learning: An intervention for systemic change.* Los Angeles: Author. Retrieved on August 29, 2006, http://smhp.psych.ucla.edu/pdfdocs/resourcemapping/resourcemappingandmanagement.pdf

Provides processes and tools for schools to use in taking stock of its resources related to addressing barriers to learning and rethinking how the resources can be used to greatest effect.

WEB RESOURCES

Resource-Oriented Mechanisms

Center for Mental Health in Schools at UCLA: http://smhp.psych.ucla.edu/

Has a great variety of relevant resources, including:

- *Resource oriented teams: Key infrastructure mechanisms for enhancing education supports.* http://smhp.psych.ucla.edu/pdfdocs/Report/resource_oriented_teams.pdf
- *Developing resource-oriented mechanisms to enhance learning supports.* http://smhp.psych.ucla.edu/pdfdocs/contedu/developing_resource_oriented-mechanisms.pdf
- *Creating the infrastructure for and enabling (learning support) component to address barriers to student learning.* http://smhp.psych.ucla.edu/qf/infrastructure_tt/infraindex.htm or http://smhp.psych.ucla.edu/qf/infrastructure_tt/infrastructurefull.pdf
- *Working collaboratively: From school-based teams to school–community–higher education connections.* http://smhp.psych.ucla.edu/pdfdocs/worktogether/worktogether.pdf
- *School–community partnerships: A guide.* http://smhp.psych.ucla.edu/pdfdocs/guides/schoolcomm.pdf
- *Addressing what's missing in school improvement planning: Expanding standards and accountability to encompass an enabling or learning supports component.* http://smhp.psych.ucla.edu/pdfdocs/enabling/standards.pdf

New Directions for Student Support and Systemic Change

- *New directions for student support: Some fundamentals*: Center for Mental Health in Schools. http://smhp.psych.ucla.edu/pdfdocs/newdirections/newdirections.pdf
- *Framing new directions for school counselors, psychologists,* and *social workers*: Center for Mental Health in Schools. http://smhp.psych.ucla.edu/pdfdocs/Report/framingnewdir.pdf
- *Organization facilitators: A change agent for systemic school and community changes*: Center for Mental Health in Schools. http://smhp.psych.ucla.edu/pdfdocs/Report/orgfacrep.pdf
- *Education systemic change tools*: National School Boards Association. http://www.nsba.org/sbot/toolkit/edsctls.html
- *Sustaining school and community efforts to enhance outcomes for children and youth: A guidebook and tool kit*: Center for Mental Health in Schools. http://smhp.psych.ucla.edu/pdfdocs/sustaining.pdf
- *Links to systemic perspectives*: The Network for Creative Change. http://www.chebucto.ns.ca/CommunitySupport/NCC/WWWPAGE.html

Mapping Resources

- *Addressing barriers to learning: A set of surveys to map what a school has and what it needs*: Center for Mental Health in Schools. http://smhp.psych.ucla.edu/pdfdocs/Surveys/Set1.pdf
- *Resource mapping and management to address barriers to learning: An intervention for systemic change*: Center for Mental Health in Schools. http://smhp.psych.ucla.edu/pdfdocs/resourcemapping/resourcemappingandmanagement.pdf
- *Mapping your school's resources*: Michigan Department of Education. http://www.michigan.gov/documents/4-5_107261_7.pdf

- *Community tool box:* University of Kansas Work Group on Health Promotion and Community Development, Lawrence, KS, and AHEC/Community Partners, Amherst, MA. http://ctb.ku.edu/
- *Building communities from the inside out:* Asset-Based Community Development Institute. http://www.northwestern.edu/ipr/publications/community/buildingblurb.html
- *Mapping community assets workbook:* Northwest Regional Education Laboratory. http://www.nwrel.org/ruraled/publications/com_mapping.pdf
- *Mapping community resources:* Community Technology Center's Network. http://www.ctcnet.org/index.htm
- *Resource mapping:* Learning Work Connection. http://www.ohiolearningwork.org/resourcemapping.asp

APPENDIX A. EXAMPLES OF ACTIVITY FOR AN ORGANIZATION FACILITATOR

Infrastructure Tasks

- Works with school governing bodies to further clarify and negotiate agreements about:

  - Policy changes
  - Participating personnel (including administrators authorized to take the lead for the systemic changes)
  - Time, space, and budget commitments

- Helps leaders identify and prepare members for a group to steer the process.
- Helps leaders identify members for the resource-oriented team.

Stakeholder Development

- Provides general orientations for governing and planning bodies.
- Provides basic capacity building for resource-oriented team.
- Ongoing coaching of team members (about purposes, processes).

  Example: At a team's first meeting, the organization facilitator offers to provide a brief orientation presentation (including handouts) and helps teams establish processes for daily interaction and periodic meetings. During the next few meetings, coaching might help with mapping and analyzing resources.

- Works with leaders to ensure presentations and written information about changes are provided to the entire staff and other stakeholders.

Communication (Visibility), Coordination, and Integration

- Determines if information on new directions (including leadership and team functions and membership) and about resources has been written and circulated; if not, the facilitator determines why and helps address systemic breakdowns; if necessary, effective processes are modeled.
- Determines if leaders and team members are effectively handling priority tasks; if not, the facilitator determines why and helps address systemic breakdowns; if necessary, effective processes are modeled.
- Determines if the following have been accomplished (and if not, takes appropriate steps):

  - Mapping of current activity and resources related to learning supports
  - Analyses of activity and resources to determine (a) how well they are meeting needs and how well coordinated/integrated they are (with special emphasis on maximizing cost effectiveness and minimizing redundancy); (b) what learning supports need to be improved (or eliminated); and (c) what is missing, its level of priority, and how and when to develop it
  - Information has been written and circulated about all resources and plans for change

- Determines the adequacy of efforts made to enhance communication to and among stakeholders and, if more is needed, facilitates improvements.
- Determines if systems are in place to identify problems related to functioning of the infrastructure and communication systems. If there are problems, determines why and helps address any systemic breakdowns.
- Checks on visibility of reforms and if the efforts are not visible, determines why and helps rectify.

Formative Evaluation and Rapid Problem Solving

- Works with leaders and team members to develop procedures for formative evaluation and processes that ensure rapid problem solving.
- Checks regularly to be certain that learning supports are enabling student learning and that there is rapid problem solving; if the data are not promising, helps school leaders to make appropriate modifications.

Ongoing Support

- Offers ongoing coaching on an on-call basis.

  Example: Informs team members about ideas developed by others or provides expertise related to a specific topic they plan to discuss.

- At appropriate points in time, asks for part of a meeting to see how things are going and (if necessary) to explore ways to improve the process.

- At appropriate times, asks whether participants have dealt with longer range planning, and if they have not, determines what help they need.

- Helps participants identify sources for continuing development/education.

APPENDIX B. ABOUT RESOURCE MAPPING AND MANAGEMENT

Why mapping resources is so important: To function well, every system has to fully understand and manage its resources. Mapping is a first step toward enhancing essential understanding and, done properly, is a major intervention in the process of moving forward with enhancing systemic effectiveness.

Why mapping both school and community resources is so important: Schools and communities share (a) goals and problems with respect to children, youth, and families; (b) the need to develop cost-effective systems, programs, and services to meet the goals and address the problems; (c) accountability pressures related to improving outcomes; and (d) the opportunity to improve effectiveness by coordinating and eventually integrating resources to develop a full continuum of systemic interventions.

What are resources: Programs, services, real estate, equipment, money, social capital, leadership, infrastructure mechanisms, and so on.

What do we mean by mapping and who does it: A representative group of informed stakeholder is asked to undertake the process of identifying what currently is available to achieve goals and address problems and what else is needed to achieve goals and address problems.

What does this process lead to: (a) Analyses to clarify gaps and recommend priorities for filling gaps related to programs and services and deploying, redeploying, and enhancing resources; (b) identifying needs for making infrastructure and systemic improvements and changes; (c) clarifying opportunities for achieving important

functions by forming and enhancing collaborative arrangements; and (d) social marketing.

How to do resource mapping: First, do it in stages (start simple and build over time). Clarify people/agencies who carry out relevant roles/functions. Next, clarify specific programs, activities, and services (including information on how many students/families can be accommodated). Then, identify the dollars and other related resources (e.g., facilities, equipment) that are being expended from various sources. Finally, collate the various policies that are relevant to the endeavor. At each stage establish a computer file and in the later stages create spreadsheet formats.

Use benchmarks to guide progress related to resource mapping.

APPENDIX C. DEVELOPING AND CONNECTING MECHANISMS AT SCHOOLS SITES, AMONG FAMILIES OF SCHOOLS, AND DISTRICT-WIDE AND COMMUNITY-WIDE

A multisite team can provide a mechanism to help ensure cohesive and equitable deployment of resources and also can enhance the pooling of resources to reduce costs. Such a mechanism can be particularly useful for integrating the efforts of high schools and their feeder middle and elementary schools. This clearly is important in addressing barriers with those families that have youngsters attending more than one level of schooling in the same cluster. It is neither cost effective nor good intervention for each school to contact a family separately in instances where several children from a family are in need of special attention. With respect to linking with community resources, multischool teams are especially attractive to community agencies that often do not have the time or personnel to make independent arrangements with every school.

In general, a group of schools can benefit from a multisite resource mechanism designed to provide leadership, facilitate communication and connection, and ensure quality improvement across sites. For example, a multisite body, or what we call a Learning Supports Resource Council, might consist of a high school and its feeder middle and elementary schools. It brings together one or two representatives from each school's resource team (see figure below).

The council meets about once a month to help (a) coordinate and integrate programs serving multiple schools, (b) identify and meet common needs with respect to guidelines and staff development, and (c) create linkages and collaborations among schools and with community agencies. In this last regard, it can play a special role in community outreach both to create formal working relationships and ensure that all participating schools have access to such resources.

More generally, the council provides a useful mechanism for leadership, communication, maintenance, quality improvement, and ongoing development of a comprehensive continuum of programs and services. Natural starting points for councils are the sharing of needs assessments, resource maps, analyses,

and recommendations for reform and restructuring. Specific areas of initial focus would be on local, high-priority concerns, such as addressing violence and developing prevention programs and safe school and neighborhood plans.

Representatives from Learning Supports Resource Councils would be invaluable members of planning groups (e.g., Service Planning Area Councils, Local Management Boards). They bring information about specific schools, clusters of schools, and local neighborhoods and do so in ways that reflect the importance of school–community partnerships.

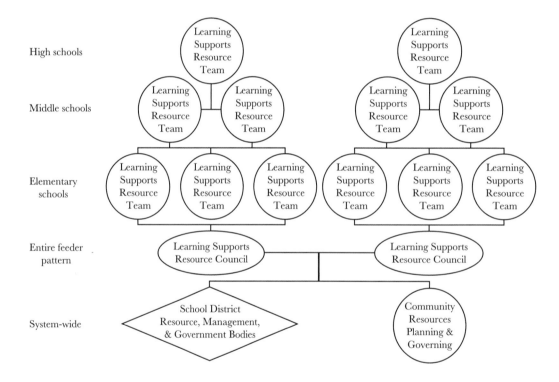

APPENDIX D. STEPS IN ESTABLISHING AN ENABLING OR LEARNING SUPPORT COMPONENT AT A SCHOOL

At any site, key stakeholders and their leadership must understand and commit to restructuring. Commitment must be reflected in policy statements and creation of an infrastructure that ensures the necessary leadership and resources.

Orientation and Creating Readiness

- Build interest and consensus for developing the enabling or learning support component.
- Introduce basic ideas to relevant groups of stakeholders.
- Establish a policy framework; that is, the leadership group at a school should make a policy commitment that adopts a comprehensive, multifaceted, and cohesive approach to enabling learning by addressing barriers to learning as a primary and essential component of school improvement.
- Identify a site leader (equivalent to the leader for the instructional component) to ensure policy commitments are carried out.

Start Up and Phase In: Building an Infrastructure and Putting It to Work

- Establish and provide leadership training for a steering group and other change agents to guide component development.

- Formulate specific start-up and phase-in plans.
- Build learning supports resource-oriented mechanisms into the infrastructure at all levels and train those who staff it.
- Organize learning support activity into a delineated set of intervention arenas and develop standing workgroups for each area to begin mapping and analyzing resources and formulating initial recommendations for enhancing intervention systems.
- Refine school infrastructure so that learning supports (enabling) component is fully integrated with the instructional and management components.
- Develop ad hoc workgroups to enhance component visibility, communication, sharing, and problem solving.
- Attempt to fill program/service gaps and pursue economies of scale through outreach designed to establish formal collaborative linkages with other schools in the feeder pattern and with district-wide and community resources.
- Establish a system for quality improvement and evaluation of impact.

Maintenance and Evolution: Toward Refinement, Increased Outcome Efficacy, and Creative Renewal

- Plan for maintenance.
- Develop strategies for maintaining momentum and progress.
- Generate creative renewal.

107 Best Practices in Collaborating With Medical Personnel

Steven R. Shaw
Amelia H. Woo
McGill University

OVERVIEW

Collaborating with medical professionals is fundamental to the practice of school psychology. Although vital to the profession, forging relationships between medical personnel and school psychologists presents both opportunities and challenges. These relationships better allow school psychologists to provide all three tiers of service delivery systems described in *School Psychology: A Blueprint for Training and Practice III* (Ysseldyke et al., 2006): targeted, intensive, and universal. Moreover, the foundational competencies described in this chapter are consistent with interpersonal and collaborative skills and professional, legal, ethical, and social responsibilities described in *Blueprint III*. School psychology is committed to providing increasingly comprehensive educational, psychological, and health services to all children (Nastasi, 2000; Talley & Short, 1995). Interdisciplinary collaboration is essential to achieving such comprehensive delivery of services.

Despite the potential to help improve student outcomes, collaboration between medical personnel and school psychologists does not take place as often as it could (Davis, Montford, & Read, 2005; Nastasi, 2004). To a large degree this is due to the systemic barriers and differences between the two professions (Shaw, Clayton, Dodd, & Rigby, 2004). Yet, these differences can and have been overcome in a variety of medical school programs that represent best practices in collaborating with medical personnel (Drotar, 1995).

Potential for Collaboration

Efforts focused on children are widely considered essential to achieving improved health for the general population (Drotar, Palmero, & Barry, 2004). Given the issues of uninsured and underinsured families in the United States and issues of access to healthcare in Canada, schools are important entry points for improving the current and future health of a society. Local schools are excellent settings from which to provide preventative healthcare to those who may experience poverty, homelessness, may have English as a second language, may be culturally or ethnically diverse, or otherwise may be difficult to access via traditional healthcare mechanisms. Moreover, schools have access to parents, have a variety of professionals on staff, and have expertise in instructional methods. Schools may also be the most cost-efficient location from which to provide preventative healthcare services (Power & Blom-Hoffman, 2004). This strong potential for effective provision of healthcare services has yet to be realized (Nastasi, 2004). The most common challenge is consistently effective collaboration between medical professionals in the community and schools. Transferring medical knowledge to the fertile ground of schools requires effective collaboration between medical and school professionals.

Although it is easy to think of the medical and education professions as two very different systems, there is much linking the two professions. Many times the boundaries between medical and educational service provision is not entirely clear. There are few medical issues that do not have some affect on the academic or social factors of schooling (American Academy of Pediatrics, Committee on Children With Disabilities, 2000). There are also many academic and social problems that have a medical basis (e.g., Attention Deficit Hyperactivity Disorder [ADHD]; Barkley, 1998;

Shevell, Majnemer, Rosenbaum, & Abrahamowicz, 2001). There is even more blurring of the boundaries between medical and educational professionals in the area of prevention and promotion programs, which tend to be educational in process but medical in content. Strong collaborative efforts between the educational and medical communities can result in improved community healthcare and improved educational outcomes.

Focus of Collaboration

There are two primary focuses of collaboration with medical personnel that require strong communication skills and knowledge of systemic issues. The first is a response to an individual child presenting with a medical issue. This is often a reactive approach to collaboration. Professionals come together on an ad hoc basis to assist one child with specific needs. The second is a coordinated effort to develop health prevention and promotion programs for the school population at large. This is a proactive approach requiring significant advanced planning and the establishment of collaborative relationships before such projects can begin.

Both situations require extensive communication, negotiation of role and function, and a spirit of collaboration to be successful. Most important, medical and school personnel need to acknowledge and address systemic barriers to effective collaboration.

Barriers to Collaboration

Most often barriers to collaboration are associated with impaired communication between the school and medical personnel (Drotar et al., 2004). When communication is impaired, children and their families are left to navigate the confusing and stressful process of aligning medical and school systems alone. Even less helpful, though, educators can find themselves in an adversarial relationship with medical personnel. For example, a physician might *demand* that the school provide special education or therapeutic services. In such a situation, educators may view the physician as arrogant, disrespectful of school policies, or ignorant of school law and regulation. Conversely, despite being prohibited by the 2004 reauthorization of the Individuals with Disabilities Education Act (IDEA) physicians might receive notes from teachers or principals *insisting* that they prescribe medication for a child because of behavior problems or receive a copy of

an Individualized Educational Plan (IEP), which is often filled with educational and legal jargon (Clay, Cortina, Harper, Cocco, & Drotar, 2004). Physicians might then view these educators as practicing medicine without a license, providing information irrelevant to children's medical issues, or misinforming parents (Drotar et al., 2004). These charges may contain a grain of truth. However, such perceptions interfere with the development of a potentially important relationship between educators and medical professionals (Shaw & Páez, 2002).

Although professional perceptions influence collaboration, there are also systemic barriers. The specific barriers to effective collaboration are the use of parallel diagnostic systems, differing decision-making processes, reimbursement, professional vocabulary, and differing conceptions of teamwork.

Parallel diagnostic systems. Physicians and educators use two different, but parallel, systems of diagnosis, service delivery, and treatment. Although there are many differences, there are just enough similarities between the two systems to create confusion for all professionals and parents. Physicians use the *International Classification of Diseases (ICD-10;* World Health Organization, 2005) and the *Diagnostic and Statistical Manual of Mental Disorders* (4th ed., text rev.) (*DSM-IV-TR*; American Psychiatric Association, 2000) criteria for making diagnoses. Educators use the guidelines set forth in IDEA, refined by regulation in each state, and implemented by each local educational agency. The confusion comes into play, for example, when a physician diagnoses a learning disability and educators find that the same child is not eligible for the learning disabilities classification within the special education system. In other words, students may be eligible for the diagnosis under the ICD-10 criteria but not eligible under the local regulations implementing IDEA. Or a physician may request educational assistance for a child with ADHD, yet educators do not believe special education services to be appropriate because there is limited evidence that the child's academic performance is impaired by ADHD (Foy & Earls, 2005). So who is right? Actually, both are. Physicians are making correct diagnoses *and treatment recommendations based on ICD-10* or *DSM-IV-TR* and recommending a medical model approach to treatment. Educators are correct in using state education department criteria for disability classification, local procedures to implement IDEA, following legally and educationally appropriate safeguards (especially regarding least restrictive environment), and developing an effective educational treatment plan.

Reimbursement. The adage that time is money is rarely truer than when working with medical professionals and school personnel. Physicians are under tremendous pressure to earn revenue to cover the massive overhead in any medical practice. As such, physicians are reinforced for spending as much of their time as possible engaged in activities that are likely to receive reimbursement from private insurance companies and/or the government. School visits, collaboration, prevention and promotion programs, and communication with school personnel are rarely reimbursed well, if at all. Some prevention and promotion programs have reduced the reimbursement issue by obtaining financial support from pharmaceutical companies or other sponsors to pay for materials and reimburse the time of medical professionals. Although this may help with the issues of reimbursement, other problems may arise, such as bringing the advertisement of products such as pharmaceuticals into the schools. Likewise, schools are under significant financial pressures in an era of shrinking budgets and growing school populations. Dedicating personnel to developing collaborative relationships with physicians can be quite difficult administratively. Both professions have financial considerations that can present major barriers to effective interdisciplinary collaboration.

Professional vocabulary. Educators and medical professionals are each armed with considerable professional vocabulary or jargon. This profession-specific vocabulary, although well known within each profession, can be a barrier to effective collaboration. When one professional cannot understand another, there is a tendency to dismiss the other professional as irrelevant (Foy & Earls, 2005; Shaw et al., 2004). Moreover, psychological and educational reports do not address the primary issues of medical professionals (i.e., disease states) and medical reports do not address the primary issues of educators (i.e., instruction). Yet, such reports can be complementary. Integration of medical and psychoeducational reports adds to a multifaceted assessment of the whole child. To be effective collaborators, profession-specific vocabulary needs to be minimized or explained. Removing profession-specific vocabulary is difficult but can be a major step to removing a barrier to effective collaboration.

Decision-making process. There are well-described differences between a medical model and an educational model of assessment and service delivery (Foy & Earls, 2005). The primary assumption of the medical model is that the problem is predominantly within the child (Shevell et al., 2001). The educational models tend to focus on the environment as the target for interventions (Lau et al., 2006). These differences may be in professional-specific vocabulary rather than true professional differences or barriers. For example, although physicians do not use the same vocabulary, they use a form of response-to-intervention model and least restrictive environment when a general practitioner uses a mild intervention to solve a problem and then assesses response before attempting a more invasive treatment. Physicians and educators are both turning to more evidence-based interventions. Physicians take family and medical histories and school psychologists frequently take medical histories. Both medical and educational fields have recognized the value of prevention and implement preventative programs. Although they seek the same goals, educational and medical models contain enough similarities and semantic differences to create confusion. However, the differences are likely exaggerated and represent similar decision-making processes yet with different professional vocabularies.

Teamwork. Teamwork involves negotiating and establishing the role and function of each member of the team. What are the expectations? What is the purpose of the team? Who will lead? What are the time demands? What will the end product be? These are not small issues given the differences in culture between medical and school professionals. Teams that have not invested time to negotiate these issues may find that teamwork is contentious, unsatisfying, and does not best serve children. First, both professions must understand that there are two equally legitimate and valid systems in place that can work together. Second, both professions need to appreciate that in many cases neither physicians nor educators can provide effective services to children alone. Teamwork is a requirement and not simply a refinement.

BASIC CONSIDERATIONS

There are two broad types of service provision requiring collaboration with medical professionals. The first type involves responding to individual children representing targeted or intensive interventions. The second type involves programmatic prevention and health promotion efforts representing universal interventions.

Both types of service delivery require specific collaborative skills when working with medical professionals.

Responding to Individual Children

The majority of school children experience few, if any, serious health or mental health concerns during their school careers. Yet, more than 10 million school children have some form of chronic health condition (American Academy of Pediatrics, Committee on Children With Disabilities, 2000). About 1 million school children have chronic health conditions that impair their daily functioning (Weinstein, 2006). When health and mental health concerns arise, however, management of children with health issues requires considerable staff time, home–school communication, and conferring with community health providers. These concerns may be as traumatic as addressing the needs of a child with a terminal illness (Bessell, 2001) or as transient as implementing homebound services while a child recovers from surgery or injuries (Maccionei & Ruben, 1989). Examples of this type of collaboration include monitoring medication management of children with ADHD (Barkley, 1998), educational planning for children recovering from head injury (Tyler & Mira, 1993), and transition to school for children experiencing prolonged hospitalization (Madan-Swain, Katz, & LaGory, 2004). In this type of collaboration, specific knowledge about the individual child, integrated with understanding of medical and educational systems, are required for a satisfactory outcome. Developing a collaborative relationship with medical personnel is critical in terms of supporting both the child's course of medical management and the child's learning and development.

Homebound instruction. Homebound instruction is an educational response to a temporary childhood health issue that is inconsistent with school attendance (Macciomei & Ruben, 1989). Homebound instruction varies widely by school districts. Most commonly homebound instruction involves having a certified teacher go to the child's home to provide in-home instruction from 1 to 10 hours per week. The purpose of homebound instruction is to assist children to keep pace with the academic progress of peers despite medical conditions that make school attendance impossible. Because children receiving homebound services have medical issues that disrupt their education and receive a fraction of educational contact hours of their school-base peers, there are pressures placed on the

parents to provide educational support. Homebound instruction is a triadic relationship between school, medical professional, and family. Teachers communicate lessons, assignments, and content to parents. Parents communicate their children's level of attention, energy, motivation, attitude, and other symptoms to teachers. Teacher and parent communication is strongly influenced by collaboration with medical personnel. Although the specific policies of homebound instruction vary across local educational agencies, nearly all involve consultation with physicians in order to determine eligibility. Medical information is required to estimate the duration of homebound instruction, accommodations that must be made during instructional activities, determination of when a return to school is appropriate, and potential threat to teachers and children due to contagion or violence. Communication among medical professionals, educators, and families is required to maximize the effects of homebound education and ease stress on parents.

Other Health Impaired. Other Health Impaired (OHI) is one of the designated special education categories under the 2004 reauthorization of IDEA. OHI is defined as a medical issue that has an adverse effect on school performance. Two important aspects of determining eligibility for OHI status are documentation of the existence of a medical problem and the probability that the medical problem has substantial impact on school performance. In addition, there must be evidence that the medical problem, or the school impact of the medical problem, is chronic. Recently, the OHI category has been used mostly for children diagnosed with ADHD (Foy & Earls, 2005). Given that ADHD requires both medical and behavioral monitoring in order to ensure effective treatment, collaboration between school psychologists and physicians is usually beneficial (Monastra, 2005).

Section 504 programming. Section 504 of the *Rehabilitation Act of 1973* is a civil rights law requiring that persons with a handicapping condition or suspected of having a handicapping condition have equal access to employment, education, and other aspects of community life. In schools, a Section 504 plan of accommodations is developed to ensure equal access to educational opportunities. In many cases, children served under Section 504 have medical issues. Collaboration with medical personnel is required to determine how a medical condition affects school performance and is essential in determining reasonable and appropriate accommodations (Madaus & Shaw, 2004). For example, developing an appropriate system of mobility for a child with quadriplegia or helping to improve the sound system for a child with a hearing aid are both dramatically improved when information from medical professionals is elicited and considered.

Monitoring medication effects. An increasing number of school children are prescribed psychotropic medications (Thomas, Conrad, Casler, & Goodman, 2006). An important part of the monitoring process of the effectiveness and unintended effects of medications is to monitor children's behaviors over the course of the day, both in school and at home. Although there are many techniques and methods for educators to monitor behaviors that take place in schools, all methods require coordination with medical personnel (see Carlson, chapter 86, vol. 4). School psychologists are well trained to conduct structured behavioral observations, interviews, and direct assessments. However, interpreting these data in light of dosage, unintended effects, family situation, and controlling for confounding environmental variables usually requires the combined efforts of a medical professional, school psychologist, and at least one family member.

Case management. The provision and monitoring of medical therapies for children require a delicate balance between the needs of medical personnel and educators. Many families who have children with severe or multiple disabilities participate in speech and language therapy, psychological counseling, occupational therapy, and/or physical therapy conducted both at school and privately or in a hospital setting (American Academy of Pediatrics, Committee on Children With Disabilities, 2000). Frequently, there are complaints that therapies conducted in one location may run contrary or interfere with therapies provided in another location (Thies, 1999). Given that there is rarely a formal case manager to coordinate services and to facilitate communication, parents often fill that role. Certainly, parents differ in their skills in facilitating coordination of services. Parents often do not tell school personnel that their child is receiving therapies through private or hospital-based sources because of a fear of being dropped by school-based services (Newacheck, Park, Brindis, Biehl, & Irwin, 2004). Although these parents appear to understand the administrative issues associated with the shortage of therapists available and subsequent rationing of therapy services, they are often unaware of the potential harm involved by intentionally disrupting communication

among therapists (Dunsmuir, Clifford, & Took, 2006). The importance of open communication (e.g., sharing progress notes, developing a shared set of goals and therapeutic techniques, and providing coordinated decision making) needs to be emphasized to parents. Such types of communication and collaboration have positive effects for children's outcomes or at least prevent negative outcomes caused by therapists working at cross purposes. Yet, in order to engage in this complex process, medical personnel and educators must overcome a significant number of systemic barriers.

School-based health clinics. School-based health clinics continue to be a small, but growing, venue for collaboration between medical personnel and school psychologists (Brown & Bolen, 2003). The scope of services offered in school-based health clinics varies widely. Some school-based health clinics are staffed with physicians, dentists, nurse practitioners, clinical psychologists, and social workers. This type of clinic is often referred to as a full-service school (Davis et al., 2005). Most school-based health clinics are staffed with nurse practitioners and a supervising physician, who is occasionally on site. Although school-based health clinics provide a valuable service in improving access to healthcare, perhaps the most valuable purpose is as an interdisciplinary platform from which to develop wide-reaching programs (Case & Matthews, 1983). For example, professionals from school-based health clinics collaborate with the mental health provider and school administrators to develop a program to address chronic pain among adolescents, with the ultimate goal of reducing absenteeism. Although controversial in many communities, a few school-based health clinics engage in sex education with the purpose of reducing sexually transmitted diseases (Case & Matthews, 1983; Weinstein, 2006). The variety of interdisciplinary programming possible through school-based health clinics is still being explored. However, all programming will require school collaboration with medical personnel.

Developing Prevention and Health Promotion Programs

The outcome of successful collaboration between educators and medical professionals is the development of detailed prevention and healthcare promotion programs being offered through schools (Nader, 1993; Power & Blom-Hoffman, 2004). In this type of collaboration, medical content knowledge is combined with a basic understanding of pedagogy. Promoting school health through education and prevention programs is a growing area of collaboration between school psychologists and physicians. For example, school programs have been designed and evaluated to improve nutrition and reduce childhood obesity (Blom-Hoffman & DuPaul, 2003), prevent accidents (Alexander & Roberts, 2002), increase seatbelt use (Alexander & Roberts, 2002), increase exercise and promote fitness (Simons-Morton, O'Hara, Simons-Morton, 1986), reduce violence and bullying (Whitted & Dupper, 2005), prevent sexually transmitted diseases and reduce pregnancy (Blake et al., 2005), and prevent alcohol and drug use (Sharma, 2006). Medical personnel including physicians, nurses, dietitians, physical therapists, and rehabilitation specialists have all made major contributions to the presentation content and methods of teaching such information to school children (Drotar et al., 2004). The complexity of developing and implementing a curriculum can be daunting. Certainly, an individual or even a small group of professionals can be overwhelmed by the details and scope of such projects. Often major prevention projects require coordination of parent groups, media outlets, law enforcement, charitable organizations, fire departments, and other government agencies. The most effective prevention programs have a strong community base and are interdisciplinary and multiagency in nature. Effective prevention programs result in fewer cases of obesity, less emergency room traffic due to accidents and overdoses, fewer cases of HIV, and less severe injuries due to seatbelt disuse. Educators will see fewer absences and spend fewer resources educating children with severe medical issues. Any health-related prevention program will likely be more effective with strong collaboration with medical personnel for knowledge and effective evaluation of outcomes.

BEST PRACTICES

This section includes two components: description of effective collaboration approaches and examples of programs requiring collaboration with medical professionals. The goal is to describe methods of overcoming barriers to effective collaboration and examples of how these skills have been applied.

Effective Collaboration

Respect professional boundaries. The first stage of collaboration is to respect the formal boundaries of the medical and educational practices as established by state certification, professional practice regulations, professional ethics, and licensure laws (Drotar, 1995). Physicians must refrain from demanding educational placement decisions or educational techniques. Schools must refrain from suggesting medication decisions or making medical diagnoses. However, information can easily be communicated across formal boundaries. For example, a teacher may state, "Since Jane started taking her medication, she has begun falling asleep in class." Or a physician may state, "Since Jane started in the gifted class, she has had severe abdominal pain with no known medical origin." Although information sharing (with parent permission) is important and needs to be encouraged, professional judgment and decision making about how to apply this information should be left solely in the hands of the appropriate professional.

Invite participation. Although respect for formal boundaries is important, there also must be an informal reaching across barriers. There are few activities that serve to develop interdisciplinary relationships as much as a physical presence (Talley & Short, 1995). When educators take time out of their busy schedules to attend a child's hospital discharge conference, they demonstrate a significant commitment to working as a collaborative team. When a physician takes time to attend a patient's IEP team meeting, the commitment to collaboration is equally clear. Realistically, though, tight schedules and pressures to earn clinical revenue make personal appearances difficult for many physicians. Thus, it is helpful to identify other means of participation. Inviting other professionals to review reports or provide written input regarding a child's progress is one of the best ways to reach across barriers without the time demands of a personal appearance (Drotar, 1995). Taking the initiative to invite the participation of others is critical to developing an interdisciplinary relationship.

Use liaisons. Because medical and educational systems have such different professional-specific vocabularies and reducing the use of such vocabulary is difficult, using a medical–education liaison as a translator of information is often helpful. The purpose of the liaison is to be able to translate jargon in order for the practitioners of the different professions to understand each other better. Usually the liaison is a person with training in both medical and educational environments (Shaw & Páez, 2002). Examples of professionals who are well prepared to act as liaisons are hospital-based teachers, school nurses, school social workers, and school psychologists. Translating jargon and understanding the specific individual and system needs of professionals in both medical and educational settings are valuable resources (Shaw & Páez, 2002).

Communicate effectively. The basics to effective communication are also important: Return phone calls in a timely manner. Educators must make themselves and their staff available by phone, fax, e-mail, or other methods. Remind teachers and other staff to communicate jargon-free and acronym-free. Having a brief fact sheet outlining the school's processes and procedures for collaborating with medical personnel and listing the names and contact information of appropriate staff is also helpful. This can easily be given to parents or sent directly to the medical professional's office.

Present the facts. There will also be times when educators will be expected to present their findings through either a telephone conversation or face-to-face contact. In these situations, it may be most helpful for school personnel to adopt a medical model of case presentation (Power, Shapiro, & DuPaul, 2003). This often serves to help organize large quantities of information into the pertinent positives and negatives. In other words, leave out all judgments and even extra information that is important but unessential to what needs to be addressed by the medical professional during their next encounter with the child (Shapiro & Manz, 2004). Following is a model for case presentations that may be helpful:

- The opening statement includes the patient's name, age, ethnic origin, native language, sex, and reason for referral.
- Address all *relevant* historical findings (i.e., history of brain injury, developmental delays, academic progress over time, social and behavioral history, or placement in a special education curriculum).
- List relative strengths and weaknesses of the target child as determined by assessment or direct observations compared to other children in the class.
- Describe the behavioral, cognitive, social, and academic requirements of the classroom.
- List the top three to four recommendations that comprise an immediate plan for how to help the child in light of the evaluation results. There will likely be more than three or four total recommendations in the report, but the main goal is to communicate interventions that need to be addressed by the physician. A quick statement summarizing the other

areas addressed in the recommendations might be helpful. (e.g., "Several suggestions were made regarding IEP goals that might help this child improve her handwriting.") This assures the physician that more environmental and systemic issues are receiving attention.

Engage parents and respect their boundaries. Ensure that parents have completed all appropriate release forms and understand the nature of the collaboration before it begins. Most parents believe that such an interdisciplinary relationship will help their child. However, some parents choose to keep medical and educational issues entirely separate. The parent's right to such a separation must be honored under the *1974 Family Education Rights Privacy Act* (20 U.S.C. § 1232g) and the *1996 Health Insurance Portability and Accountability Act* (Public Law No. 104-191). Yet, the school may request that parents provide any relevant information regarding treatment, medication, or symptoms to an appropriate staff member to support their child's academic needs. Sometimes, however, professionals need to understand that the answer may be, "No."

Engage the child and respect boundaries. The primary difference between elementary and secondary level children is the degree to which they can participate in the development of their own program. Often children are asked whether they approve of a plan after the team has developed the plan. A better method is to have the child be a central member of the team, developing programs from the start. For younger or lower functioning children, simply acquiring the experience in communicating preferences and gaining control can be productive for developing self-determination skills. In cases where the children are more mature and have higher skill levels, they can make significant contributions to their own transition and collaboration team. Such a simple investment of time with the child goes a long way toward ensuring the effectiveness of treatment plans. When children are enthusiastic participants in developing a treatment plan, the educators and medical professionals have a far easier task.

Examples of Programs Requiring Collaboration

Although there are many general practices that can help to facilitate collaboration between medical personnel and school psychologists, there are also specific opportunities for collaboration that nearly all schools can employ.

Establish a medical transition team. Responding to individual children with medical needs does not always have to be an ad hoc process. Collaborating with medical personnel to prepare and develop effective policies can prevent problems when the child with medical problems inevitably requires specialized services. Establishing a medical transition team can be extremely helpful. This interdisciplinary school–medical community team can assist in establishing homebound education procedures, hospital-to-school transition processes, processes for OHI and Section 504 eligibility determination and programming, and other medically related policies. The medical transition team can also be an advisory team to address specific concerns of children with medical issues. The medical transition team can include the medical liaison, a member of the school staff who is the point of contact with medical professionals. Most often, the medical liaison would be the school nurse. The configuration of the team might change slightly depending on the nature of the health problem. A core medical transition team composed of, for example, school nurse, administrator, school psychologist, and community medical professional could add members depending on the specific needs of the case. For instance, a special education teacher, physical therapist, and occupational therapist would necessarily be part of the team assisting a child recovering from traumatic brain injury. Advance planning and preparation development by a medical transition team can surmount systemic barriers presented when children with medical issues are present in a school setting.

Substance abuse prevention programs. The Safe and Drug-Free Schools office of the U.S. Department of Education has provided more than $8 billion to nearly every local educational agency in the United States to reduce the use of all tobacco and illicit drugs through education (U.S. Department of Education, 1998). Most medical professionals and other concerned parties consider tobacco, alcohol, and illicit drugs to be major health risk issues. A host of curricula have been developed and are implemented through the schools. Many of these programs have been developed by health professionals and health educators. Although 96% of local educational agencies report implementing at least some type of substance-use prevention program, only 10% have used curricula that are considered evidence based or have taken steps to evaluate the

effectiveness of the curricula (Weiss, Murphy-Graham & Birkeland, 2005). Most notable is the Drug Abuse Resistance Education (D.A.R.E.) curriculum (Weiss et al., 2005). Although D.A.R.E. is the most widely used program intended to prevent the use of illicit drugs, there is evidence that this program is ineffective in reducing the incidence or prevalence of drug use (Sharma, 2006).

Most commonly, prevention programs are packaged curricula administered by school personnel who have a minimum of training and minimal knowledge in the science of health risks posed by substance abuse. To a large degree high school children believe that educators are simply indoctrinating children through such programs rather than transmitting facts (Sharma, 2006).

Substance abuse and prevention programs can be effective, yet must be credible to children. Effective programs often have medical personnel, who are both knowledgeable of the healthcare ramifications of substance abuse and more credible to many children. Effective intervention programs appear to benefit from the inclusion of medical personnel such as school nurses, physicians, and rehabilitation professionals. Strong collaboration with medical personnel improves credibility in the eyes of many children and parents (Sharma, 2006).

Obesity prevention/intervention. Obesity prevention, diet, and fitness programs are growing in number in the public schools (Power & Blom-Hoffman, 2004). Unlike substance abuse prevention programs that frequently have political agendas influencing the program content and implementation (Lisnov, 1998), obesity prevention, diet, and fitness programs are usually developed locally.

Obesity prevention programs tend to be multidisciplinary in nature with strong interactive components. Programs have been developed by nutritionists, physicians, agricultural experts, dieticians, school psychologists, educators, and physical educators. Mentors, role models, natural helpers, family educators, school dieticians, and others provide strong support for behavioral change rather than simply providing information (Blom-Hoffman et al., 2004). In addition, some obesity prevention programs have targeted school lunches, school physical education programs, and other educational policies that can affect obesity.

Nearly all obesity prevention programs include medical specialists (e.g., physicians, nurses, dietitians), educators (e.g., classroom teachers, physical educators, school psychologists), and fitness professionals (e.g., community athletes, athletic trainers, and sports coaches).

Although some of the programs demonstrate effectiveness in reducing childhood obesity (Blom-Hoffman, Kelleher, & Power, 2004), many do not (Simons-Morton et al., 1986). The primary issue identified by multiple authors is that the programs were sound, but the implementation of the program lacked treatment integrity (e.g., Blom-Hoffman & DuPaul, 2003). There is potential for improved interdisciplinary collaboration with medical personnel in the community to increase treatment integrity.

SUMMARY

Despite differences in culture, vocabulary, training, and systemic pressures, medical personnel and educators have much in common. Interdisciplinary collaboration and open communication between medical personnel and educators are positive aspects of practice, which expands the scope of school psychology service delivery to include many of the most important issues facing school children.

Many school psychologists and many medical professionals value collaboration, and the benefits appear to be self-evident. However, despite the near universal support for collaboration efforts, the resultant teamwork sometimes falls short of the goals of improving student health and education outcomes.

Good intentions are not enough. Both medical and school professions need to understand the systemic barriers to collaboration and develop approaches to overcome them. The potential for an effective medical community and school relationship for individual children with medical needs and prevention and promotion programming for all children can be realized only when systemic barriers are surmounted.

REFERENCES

Alexander, K., & Roberts, M. C. (2002). Unintentional injuries in childhood and adolescence: Epidemiology, assessment and management. In L. L. Hayman, M. M. McMahon, & J. R. Turner (Eds.), *Health and behavior in childhood and adolescence: Cross-disciplinary perspectives* (pp. 145–177). New York: Springer.

American Academy of Pediatrics, Committee on Children With Disabilities. (2000). Provision of educationally related services for children and adolescents with chronic diseases and disabling conditions. *Pediatrics, 105,* 448–451.

American Psychiatric Association. (2000). *Diagnostic and statistical manual of mental disorders* (4th ed., text rev.). Washington, DC: Author.

Barkley, R. A. (1998). *Attention Deficit Hyperactivity Disorder: A handbook for diagnosis and treatment* (2nd ed.). New York: Guilford Press.

Bessell, A. G. (2001). Children surviving cancer: Psychosocial adjustment, quality of life, and school experiences. *Exceptional Children, 67,* 345–359.

Blake, S. M., Ledsky, R. A., Sawyer, R. J., Goodenow, C., Banspach, S., Lorhman, D. K., et al. (2005). Local school district adoption of state-recommended policies on HIV prevention education. *Preventative Medicine, 40,* 239–248.

Blom-Hoffman, J., Kelleher, C., & Power, T. J. (2004). Promoting healthy food consumption among young children: Evaluation of a multicomponent nutrition education program. *Journal of School Psychology, 42,* 45–60.

Blom-Hoffman, J., & DuPaul, G. J. (2003). School-based health promotion: The effects of a nutrition education program. *School Psychology Review, 32,* 263–271.

Brown, M. B., & Bolen, L. M. (2003). School-based health centers: Strategies for meeting the physical and medical needs of children and families. *Psychology in the Schools, 40,* 279–288.

Case, J., & Matthews, S. (1983). CHIP: The chronic health impaired program of the Baltimore city public school system. *Children's Health Care, 12,* 97–100.

Clay, D. L., Cortina, S., Harper, D. C., Cocco, K. M., & Drotar, D. (2004). Schoolteachers' experiences with childhood chronic illness. *Children's Health Care, 33,* 227–239.

Davis, T. K., Montford, C. R., & Read, C. (2005). Interdisciplinary teamwork in a school-based health center. *Nursing Clinics of North America, 40,* 699–709.

Drotar, D. (1995). *Consulting with physicians.* New York: Plenum Press.

Drotar, D., Palmero, T., & Barry, C. (2004). Collaboration with schools: Models and methods in pediatric psychology. In R. Brown (Ed.), *Handbook of pediatric psychology in school settings* (pp. 21–36). Mahwah, NJ: Erlbaum.

Dunsmuir, S., Clifford, V., & Took, S. (2006). Collaboration between educational psychologists and speech and language therapists: Barriers and opportunities. *Educational Psychology in Practice, 22,* 125–140.

Foy, J. M., & Earls, M. F. (2005). A process for developing community consensus regarding the diagnosis and management of Attention Deficit Hyperactivity Disorder. *Pediatrics, 115,* 97–114.

Lau, M. Y., Sieler, J. D., Muyskens, P., Canter, A., Vankeuren, B., & Maston, D. (2006). Perspectives on the use of the problem-solving model from the viewpoint of a school psychologist, administrator, and teacher from a large midwest urban school district. *Psychology in the Schools, 43,* 117–127.

Lisnov, L. (1998). Adolescents' perception of substance abuse prevention strategies. *Adolescence, 33,* 301–311.

Macciomei, N. R., & Ruben, D. H. (1989). *Homebound teaching: A handbook for educators*. Jefferson, NC: McFarland.

Madan-Swain, A., Katz, E. R., & LaGory, J. (2004). School and social reintegration after a serious illness or injury. In R. T. Brown (Ed.), *Handbook of pediatric psychology in school settings* (pp. 637–655). Mahwah, NJ: Erlbaum.

Madaus, J. W., & Shaw, S. F. (2004). Section 504: Differences in the regulations for secondary and post-secondary education. *Intervention in School and Clinic*, *40*, 81–87.

Monastra, V. J. (2005). *Parenting children with ADHD: 10 lessons that medicine cannot teach*. Washington, DC: American Psychological Association.

Nader, P. R. (1993). *School health: Policy and practice*. Elk Grove Village, IL: American Academy of Pediatrics.

Nastasi, B. K. (2000). School psychologists as healthcare providers in the 21st century: Conceptual framework, professional identity, and professional practice. *School Psychology Review*, *29*, 540–554.

Nastasi, B. K. (2004). Meeting the challenges of the future: Integrating public health and public education for mental health promotion. *Journal of Educational & Psychological Consultation*, *15*, 295–312.

Newacheck, P. W., Park, M. J., Brindis, C. D., Biehl, C. D., & Irwin, C. E. (2004). Trends in private and public health insurance for adolescents. *Journal of the American Medical Association*, *291*, 1231–1237.

Power, T. J., & Blom-Hoffman, J. (2004). The school as a venue for managing and preventing health problems: Opportunities and challenged. In R. Brown (Ed.), *Handbook of pediatric psychology in school settings* (pp. 37–48). Mahwah, NJ: Erlbaum.

Power, T. J., Shapiro, E. S., & DuPaul, G. J. (2003). Preparing leaders in child psychology for the 21st century: Linking systems of care to manage and prevent health problems. *Journal of Pediatric Psychology*, *28*, 147–155.

Shapiro, E. S., & Manz, P. H. (2004). Collaborating with schools in the provision of pediatric psychological services. In R. T. Brown (Ed.), *Handbook of pediatric psychology in school settings* (pp. 49–64). Mahwah, NJ: Erlbaum.

Sharma, M. (2006). Making effective alcohol education interventions for high schools. *Journal of Alcohol and Drug Education*, *50*, 1–4.

Shaw, S. R., Clayton, M. C., Dodd, J. L., & Rigby, B. T. (2004). Collaborating with physicians: A guide for school leaders. *Principal Leadership*, *5*, 11–13.

Shaw, S. R., & Páez, D. (2002). Best practices in interdisciplinary service delivery to children with chronic medical issues. In A. Thomas & J. Grimes (Eds.), *Best practices in school psychology IV* (pp. 1473–1484). Bethesda, MD: National Association of School Psychologists.

Shevell, M. I., Majnemer, A., Rosenbaum, P., & Abrahamowicz, M. (2001). Etiologic determination of childhood developmental delay. *Brain & Development*, *23*, 228–235.

Simons-Morton, B. G., O'Hara, N. M., & Simons-Morton, D. G. (1986). Promoting healthful diet and exercise behaviors in communities, schools, and families. *Family & Community Health*, *9*, 1–13.

Talley, R. C., & Short, R. J. (1995). *School health: Psychology's role: A report to the nation*. Washington, DC: American Psychological Association.

Thies, K. M. (1999). Identifying the educational implications of chronic illness in school children. *Journal of School Health*, *69*, 392–398.

Thomas, C. P., Conrad, P., Casler, R., & Goodman, E. (2006). Trends in the use of psychotropic medications among adolescents: 1994 to 2001. *Psychiatric Services*, *57*, 63–69.

Tyler, J. S., & Mira, M. P. (1993). Educational modifications for children with head injuries. *Teaching Exceptional Children*, *25*, 24–27.

U.S. Department of Education. (1998). Safe and drug-free schools program: Notice. *Federal Register*, *63*(104), 29901–29906.

Weinstein, J. (2006). School-based health centers and the primary care physician: An opportunity for collaborative care. *Primary Care: Clinics in Office Practice*, *33*, 305–315.

Weiss, C. H., Murphy-Graham, E., & Birkeland, S. (2005). An alternative route to policy influence: How evaluation affects D.A.R.E. *American Journal of Evaluation*, *26*, 12–30.

Whitted, K. S., & Dupper, D. R. (2005). Best practice for prevention or reducing bullying in the schools. *Children & Schools*, *27*, 167–175.

World Health Organization. (2005). *International statistical classification of diseases and related health problems* (10th rev., 2nd ed.). Geneva: Author.

Ysseldyke, J., Burns, M., Dawson, P., Kelley, B., Morrison, D., Ortiz, S., et al. (2006). *School psychology: A blueprint for training and practice III*. Bethesda, MD: National Association of School Psychologists.

ANNOTATED BIBLIOGRAPHY

Brown, R. T. (Ed.). (2004). *Handbook of pediatric psychology in school settings*. Mahwah, NJ: Erlbaum.

A comprehensive book concerning the provision of health care services to children and adolescents within a school setting. There are sections on prevention and health promotion, diseases encountered in school settings, developmental disorders and conditions, health issues related to development, and interventions within school settings.

Clay, D. L. (2004). *Helping schoolchildren with chronic health conditions*. New York: Guilford Press.

Contains brief descriptions of specific content areas. However, the most valuable aspect of this book is its many examples, worksheets, and handout templates.

Drotar, D. (1995). *Consulting with physicians*. New York: Plenum Press.

Effectively discusses the theories, reality, struggles, and practice of consulting with physicians. Although due for an update, this book remains the standard for understanding the major issues of collaborating with physicians.

Power, T. J., Shapiro, E. S., & DuPaul, G. J. (2003). Preparing leaders in child psychology for the 21st century: Linking systems of care to manage and prevent health problems. *Journal of Pediatric Psychology, 28*, 147–155.

A strong explanation of the need for interdisciplinary cooperation and professional collaboration in the provision of prevention and health promotion activities.

Section VII
Diversity Awareness and Sensitive Service Delivery

Volume 5 of *Best Practices in School Psychology V* supports an understanding of the *Blueprint III* competency emphasizing diversity awareness and sensitive service delivery.

Description: School psychologists must be able to recognize when issues of diversity affect the manner and nature of interactions with other people and organizations and must have the ability to modify or adapt their practices in to response those being served.

108 Best Practices in Working With Culturally Diverse Children and Families

Samuel O. Ortiz
Dawn P. Flanagan
Agnieszka M. Dynda
St. John's University

OVERVIEW

On the whole ... we are inadequately prepared to deal with cultural diversity.
—Honigmann (1963, p. 1)

Separating oneself from culturally based ethnocentric viewpoints inculcated from birth by way of natural social interaction is not easily accomplished. The very essence of what an individual believes, thinks, and does is a product of unique background and developmental experiences that are most often shaped and determined primarily by culture. Even simply understanding the manner in which all humans are profoundly defined by culture and how it has led directly to the acquisition of almost every precious truth and deeply held conviction requires considerable effort and insight. Matsumoto (1994) notes, "sometimes we cannot separate ourselves from our own cultural backgrounds and biases to understand the behavior of others" (p. 6). With continuing advances in technology (e.g., the Internet), there exist more opportunities to interact with individuals from other cultures. Although this increased exposure allows for learning and understanding about diversity, it also creates fertile ground for cultural misunderstandings.

Nevertheless, with respect to its impact on practice, school psychologists who work with students and families from diverse backgrounds must seek to understand the manner in which culture influences both their own view of others, and other's view of them.

Competence in being able to provide psychological services to children and families from diverse cultural and ethnic backgrounds is not merely a desirable skill but a necessity. Development of such skill is reinforced strongly by professional organizations including the National Association of School Psychologists (NASP) and the American Psychological Association (APA). In addition to providing a wide array of resources related to cultural competency on its website (http://www.nasponline.org/resources/culturalcompetence/), NASP promotes the importance of cultural competency in several ways. For example, *School Psychology: A Blueprint for Training and Practice III* (Ysseldyke et al., 2006) elevates skill in all aspects of cultural competency to one of the four foundational domains upon which the other domains of competency rest. This change reflects a recognition of the fact that cultural competence plays a part in all aspects of psychological service delivery. It is no longer viewed as an add-on to the psychologist's skill repertoire; rather, it is an essential tool that informs all professional activities and an area of skill that must be reinforced through professional preparation and training programs. The resources on the website, which even include a Self-Assessment Checklist for Personnel Providing Services and Supports to Children and Their Families, among other valuable materials, reflect NASP's commitment to culturally competent practice. In 2002, NASP formally stated in its strategic plan, as adopted by the delegate assembly, that "cultural

1721

competence is evident at the practice and association levels" and is one of the organization's major values. A similar commitment to cultural competency is held by APA. In 2002's *Guidelines on Multicultural Education, Training, Research, Practice, and Organizational Change for Psychologists*, APA reinforced its commitment to the training of psychologists in this light and the need for development of such skill by professionals. Clearly, the development of culturally competent psychological service delivery has become central to the mission of both NASP and APA and by default the responsibility of its constituency.

Cultural competence is neither a discrete skill nor a set of learned facts about a culture. Rather, cultural competence is reflected by the ability to recognize when and where cultural issues might be operating in the course of school psychology service delivery. That is, school psychology practice must be guided by activities that are effective for children and families who come from any cultural background and not be constrained for use with specific ones (Ortiz & Ochoa, 2005). Such a definition is aligned with the specification in *Blueprint III*, which identifies cultural competence as a foundational domain applicable to service delivery in a broad sense. It also maintains the focus on what a school psychologist does and not what he or she knows.

If a reasonable set of guidelines for engaging in best practices with culturally diverse children and families is to be suggested, then the first and foremost principle must be this one: that any individual's own culture greatly affects the way he or she views the world and others, including people from both within and outside the culture. In working with students, families, teachers, and administrators who come from cultural backgrounds and experiences quite different than those that typically comprise the U.S. majority, it is crucial to understand that these differences will affect the very things that school psychologists are often interested in; that is, learning, development, and behavior. It is equally important to recognize that there will be differences that are difficult to comprehend, appreciate, or accept and that such situations do not represent issues of right or wrong, good or bad, rational or irrational, but merely differences between people as a function of their unique cultural experience.

The task of delineating a framework for working with children and families from diverse cultural backgrounds hinges upon successful integration of a wide variety of practice-related topics. In order to work effectively with diversity in the schools, school psychologists need to develop full competence, rather than just sensitivity, in

the skills and knowledge bases related to these areas and be able to integrate them in a manner that guides cross-cultural interactions. Similar to the intentions and discussions presented in the previous version of this chapter in *Best Practices IV* (Ortiz & Flanagan, 2002) that were based largely on the preceding version (Flanagan & Halsell Miranda, 1995), this version also seeks to incorporate the increasing body of research in the area of diversity (Franklin, Harris, & Allen-Meares, 2006; Lynch & Hanson, 2004; Pedersen, 2004; Trimble, 2003). Much like other topics in school psychology that undergo change as a result of research (e.g., assessment), best practice in working with diverse children and families continues to evolve on the basis of a better understanding of cultural dynamics and understanding that emerges from such research. Indeed, what constitutes best practice in working with diverse children and families has undergone considerable change and remains a difficult skill to acquire and maintain. It is unfortunate, however, that school psychology training programs do not appear to provide sufficient direct supervision or instructional opportunities necessary to promote development of such competency (Geisinger & Carlson, 1998). The lack of culturally competent supervisors and trainers makes it difficult to incorporate such skills or knowledge into training regimens and school psychology curricula beyond the single course requirement needed to maintain accreditation. One training program that has demonstrated consistent success in this regard is San Diego State University, where cultural competency issues and training are infused throughout the curriculum and inform every area of education and practice, albeit such programs are rare. Consequently, the vast majority of school psychologists might be sent into the nation's increasingly diverse schools largely unprepared for interactions with diverse students, families, teachers, administrators, and fellow school psychologists. Responsibility for ensuring that they are indeed properly trained rests with both school psychology training programs where preservice experiences include the opportunity to interact with diverse children and families, as well as the school psychologist, who must find ways to continue developing competency.

This chapter is intended to address the latter need and provide school psychologists with some of the information they may need or seek as diversity is met in the schools. However, given the importance of cultural competence, and the potential difficulties in its development (e.g., resistance, ignorance of personal biases, cultural misunderstandings), it is recommended that school psychologists not rely solely on guidelines such as these for engaging in cultural learning. As with virtually all forms of psychological practice, direct mentoring and supervision are invaluable to the learning process.

BASIC CONSIDERATIONS

If the diversity of the U.S. population were constant and relatively unchanging, it is likely that competency in working with culturally diverse children and families would remain a distant priority and largely unnecessary for those rare cultural encounters. But this is not the case as the U.S. school-age population continues to change dramatically and is projected to continue this trend well over the next 4 decades (Kindler, 2002; U.S. Census Bureau, 2000).

Increasing Diversity

Figure 1 provides a summary of this shift in demographics and highlights the significant changes to follow, particularly for the Hispanic population, which is expected to reach 29.2% (almost double the current total of 16%) of the total school-age population by the year 2050. And although there is hardly a chapter on diversity issues that does not provide an abundance of demographic data to buttress the point, the statistics bear repeating here. By the year 2050, it is estimated that the U.S. population will increase approximately 50% compared to what it was in 2000 (U.S. Census Bureau, 2000). By itself, increased numbers of people are of little surprise. But the degree to which the increase is composed of diverse individuals is quite stunning.

Inspection of the data and the estimates upon which population projections are based indicate that the Asian and Pacific Islander population will increase by more than 267% from 1995 levels. The Hispanic population is projected to increase by 258%, African Americans by 83%, and Native Americans by 95%. By the year 2050, the Hispanic American population is projected to make up almost a quarter of the entire population (24%) and the African American population is projected to comprise about 14% of the entire population. Figure 2 summarizes the growth rates for the major ethnic groups in the United States.

Growth patterns are predicted to be variable, with the greatest increases expected in California, Texas, and Florida, as well as the southern and western portions of the United States (U.S. Census Bureau, 2000). Trends in the general population tend to reflect trends in the school population, and it is clear that school psychologists in every corner of the country will need to buttress their expertise in this area of practice. Figure 3 provides an illustration of the projected distribution of ethnic minority groups throughout the United States by 2050. Readers may wish to examine state-specific data concerning projected ethnic minority population growth for their school district.

The impact of increasing diversity is not limited to traditional definitions of the term that are based most commonly on "cultural" differences as reflected by the

Figure 1. Projected change in U.S. school-age population.

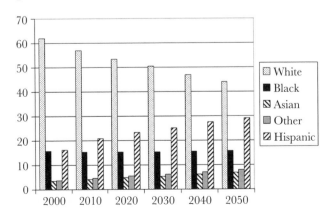

Note. Source: U.S. Census Bureau (2000).

Figure 2. Projected growth rates for major ethnic groups in the United States, 1995–2050.

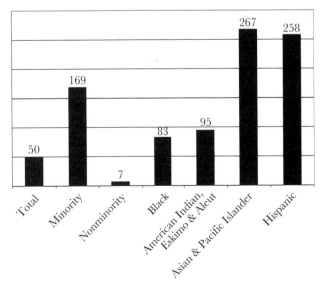

Note. Source: U.S. Census Bureau (2000).

Figure 3. Projected distribution of ethnic minorities in the United States by the year 2050.

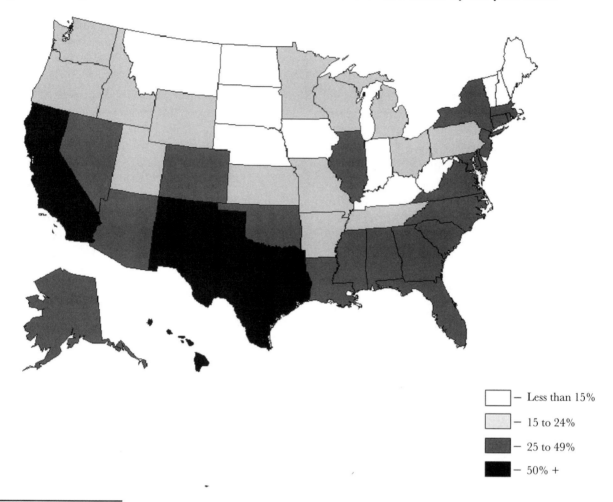

☐ — Less than 15%

▨ — 15 to 24%

▩ — 25 to 49%

■ — 50% +

Note. Source: U.S. Census Bureau (2000).

proxy variables of race or ethnicity (Rhodes, Ochoa, & Ortiz, 2005). For example, the very concept and composition of what constitutes a family are transforming, creating new cultural systems based on dynamics that have little to do with race or ethnicity. The percentage of traditional, nuclear families in the United States has been declining steadily while the percentage of single parent, stepparent, grandparent, adoptive, foster, and same-sex parent families has been increasing (Copeland & White, 1991; Franklin et al., 2006). Moreover, poverty has long been identified as a variable that meets most major definitions of culture and is an important influence in school performance (Hanson & Lynch, 1992). Similarly, people with disabilities represent a group whose experiences are becoming increasingly recognized as falling within the conceptual definitions of diversity and culture. Even diversity based on ethnic and racial

differences has undergone significant changes. As people from different cultures continue to intermarry, the relatively clear delineation of race or ethnicity and the concomitant cultural idiosyncrasies that often accompany them will begin to disappear as they are blended into the mainstream and are subsequently expressed in new and unique ways (Frisby, 1998; Sandoval, 1998a).

The need to be comfortable and competent in working with children and families that come from nontraditional, nonwhite backgrounds will increase in the future. This notion has been reinforced strongly in the vision for future school psychology practice in *Blueprint III* where cultural competence is now a foundational skill and no longer a supplemental skill. School psychologists will need to recognize when their own values and beliefs have an impact on their services to individuals whose backgrounds, experiences, and circumstances are distinctly different from their own. Failure to appreciate the manner in which one's own culture influences interactions with individuals from a different culture can often lead to conflict, miscommunication, and misunderstanding, having tremendous impact on the nature and effectiveness of service delivery (Ortiz, 2006).

Definitions

The phrase *culturally diverse* differs slightly from the phrase *culturally different*. Although there is much similarity between the two, the connotations of *diversity* are less severe than those of *different*. The term diversity almost begs an inclusive, pluralistic perspective whereas different seems to set the stage for exclusion. Thus, the phrase *culturally diverse* is preferable and will be used here. However, diversity does imply difference, and it is acknowledged that the basis for establishing diversity rests on the premise of some type of difference among individuals or groups. The key, then, is the nature of those differences. Cultural diversity does not represent differences solely or strictly on the basis of racial or ethnic heritage. Although these factors are often associated with cultural differences, they are not in fact the same, as will be discussed. In general, cultural diversity refers to the unique background and experiences that have influenced, to the greatest degree, an individual's development (e.g., physical, emotional, cognitive, social). It is the existence of particular environmental elements and their unique influence on an individual or a group that comprises the essence of culture. School psychology in the United States has traditionally been practiced within the context of U.S. mainstream culture. Therefore, cultural diversity refers to any individual or group whose backgrounds and experiences differ significantly from that reflected by the U.S. mainstream. This definition helps to avoid the error of treating culturally diverse children and families as coming from a unitary, monolithic heritage and keeps the focus squarely on the fact that any two people from any single culture are similar only in that their respective backgrounds differ from that of the mainstream and perhaps from the school psychologist. They may also differ significantly from each other. The following definitions are offered in an attempt to clarify the many dimensions along which cultural differences may exist. "Culture is the sum of all the forms of art, of love and of thought, which, in the course of centuries, have enabled man to be less enslaved" (Andre Malraux as quoted in Seldes, 1960).

Culture

It seems rather curious to have to point out that cultural diversity may exist as a function of cultural differences. What could be more obvious? Nevertheless, much confusion continues to surround the notion of culture probably because of its many connotations in the scientific literature and the popular vernacular. For example, culture may refer to the "characteristic patterns of living, customs, traditions, values, and attitudes that are associated with broad differences in intercontinental habitation or a society's level of technological sophistication" (Frisby, 1992, p. 533), as well as differences in language or religion. Those cultures that produce advances in technology and become industrialized are seen as "modern" whereas those that do not are seen as "primitive." Another definition of culture occurs when the term is included with a modifier that is intended to refer to a circumscribed group of individuals. The uses of phrases such as *deaf culture*, *culture of poverty*, *western culture*, and *culture of the school* are examples of culture defined in this manner (Frisby, 1998). Although the use of modifiers to specify particular groups of people may be valid in a general sense, it is important for school psychologists to understand that not every single individual from even the most circumscribed culture will display any or all of the features commonly associated with it. Individual differences do persist.

Perhaps the most common definition of culture revolves around the values, beliefs, and attitudes that are relatively unique to a given group of individuals and expressed in communal ways (Trimble, 2003). A good example of this definition was put forth by Matsumoto (1994), who described this elusive concept "as the set of attitudes, values, beliefs, and behaviors, shared by a group of people, communicated from one generation to the next via language or some other means of communication" (p. 4; see also Barnouw, 1985). Within the context of this definition, culture is seen as representing an element of consensus among a group of individuals regarding what is important and what will be maintained by the members and the children of the members of that group in particular. Examples of what may be important to merit transmission from generation to generation would include things such as language (including particular pronunciation patterns, regionalisms, or dialectical variations), religious practices, food preparation and cuisine, clothing and styles of dress, and values regarding interpersonal relationships. In this sense, culture is both a unique and shared experience that has idiosyncratic but predictable effects on virtually every aspect of development of its constituent members.

In sum, culture must not be viewed as "a rigidly prescribed set of behaviors or characteristics, but rather a framework through which actions are filtered or checked as individuals go about daily life" (Hanson, 1992, p. 3). Individuals of the same cultural background will definitely share certain tendencies, but they will not necessarily behave in exactly the same way. Other factors, including gender, age, socioeconomic status, area of residence, and level of education will also greatly affect behavior, beliefs, perceptions, attitudes, etc. (Hanson, 1992). Without question, the degree to which any individual follows the prescribed assemblage of cultural patterns under which they were raised varies considerably (Frisby, 1998; Hanson, 1992). When attempting to engage in best practices, school psychologists will need to remain aware of the subtleties inherent in any definition of culture. Lynch and Hanson (2004) provide several important summary statements that school psychologists need to keep in mind to avoid making generalizations that may be inappropriate or incorrect: (a) Culture is dynamic and ever changing; (b) culture, language, and ethnicity are not the only determinants of groups' shared beliefs, values, and behaviors; (c) differences within a culture are as great as differences between cultures, and are sometimes greater; (d) discussions about culture are *always* framed in terms of differences in relation to another group; and (e) everyone has a culture.

Race and Ethnicity

Although these terms are often used interchangeably, they are quite distinct and each carries its own separate meaning with respect to culture. Ethnicity is much narrower in scope than race and reflects "a micro-cultural group or collectivity that shares a common history and culture, common values, behaviors, and other characteristics that cause members of the group to have a shared identity" (Banks & Banks, 1993, p. 357; Trimble, 2003). The similarity between this definition of ethnicity and the previous definition of culture is noteworthy. On the whole, there is not much difference, but ethnicity tends to be even more confused with notions of race than culture. Race is simply a biological concept and refers to phenotypically distinct groups without reference to any other distinguishing qualities. For example, Hispanic, African American, and Native American constitute racial groups. But members of any given race may comprise a multitude of different ethnic and cultural groups. Likewise, members of a particular ethnic or cultural group may comprise a multitude of different races. Consider Puerto Ricans, for example, a well circumscribed ethnic group that is composed of a centuries long tri-racial heritage (native peoples, that is, the Taino and Western European Anglos; the Spanish/French/Portuguese explorers; and African, that is, people taken from their homeland for the purposes of slavery). Clearly, race and ethnicity are not the same thing. Race is much broader in scope than either culture or ethnicity and should not be equated with either. Rather, cultural traits represent the main attributes of an ethnic group whereas biological traits determine race (Banks & Banks, 1993). Racial categories such as Hispanic or Asian/Pacific Islander imply a uniformity of linguistic and cultural experiences that is not warranted. Mexicans and Cubans both speak Spanish, but not exactly in the same way. Japanese and Chinese are both Asian cultures but there are significant cultural differences and their languages are not mutually intelligible. Understanding that neither race nor ethnicity automatically implies that an individual has had a cultural experience that is similar, let alone identical to any other member of the same racial or ethnic group, prevents the school psychologist from making attributions or generalizations that are unfair and untrue (Constantine & Sue, 2006; Helms & Cook, 1999; Lynch & Hanson, 2004). This is particularly important in the assessment arena where interpretation is often based on notions of race or ethnicity without consideration of whether or not cultural experiences do in fact differ significantly from the mainstream (Ortiz & Dynda, 2005; Rhodes et al., 2005). Good decision making in working with culturally diverse children and families requires a solid grasp of the distinctive characteristics of race and ethnicity as limited markers of culture (Constantine & Sue, 2006).

Minority

The term *minority* has fallen out of favor as of late, perhaps in recognition of the fact that some previous minorities are now the majority. In California, for example, Hispanic children slightly outnumber Anglo children (California Department of Education, 1997). To call Hispanics a minority group is not only statistically inaccurate, it could be viewed as pejorative, a sort of semantic way of keeping diverse groups marginalized. As noted previously, the U.S. Census Bureau (2000) estimates that by the year 2050 the distribution of the population according to ethnic group in the United States may be such that no single group will represent a majority.

The term minority has historically carried implications regarding lack of privilege(s) or access to the mainstream, in particular the upper social strata. Members of minority groups have often been viewed as being disadvantaged (due to such factors as limited opportunity for educational or economic advancement) and treated unfavorably by the majority group (Helms & Cook, 1999). This notion continues to be reinforced by legislation. For example, the 2004 reauthorization of the Individuals with Disabilities Education Act again specifically excludes factors such as "environmental, cultural, or economic disadvantage" from being used as the basis for identifying a child with a specific learning disability (Section 602.30). The idea of economic disadvantage seems appropriate, but there is of course nothing inherently disadvantaged about being culturally diverse. In considering issues of culture, it is perhaps best to avoid most conceptions of it as related to minority group status, except in one way. When minority status has resulted in unfavorable treatment or systematic oppression of members by the majority in power, the effects of being rendered underprivileged in this way may adversely affect the psychological well-being of the group's family life (Tseng & Hsu, 1991) while simultaneously strengthening family or group bonds. But, again, it is the experience of the oppression that is responsible for the influence on development, and not the fact that an individual or family simply belongs to or identifies with any particular minority group.

Socioeconomic Status

The effects of socioeconomic status (SES) on the development of students and families, particularly within the school realm, have become so well known that it is not uncommon to refer to life under very low SES conditions as the *culture of poverty*. Several researchers have demonstrated that social class has a profound impact on essentially every variable that influences an individual's physical and psychological growth and development including educational attainment, occupational aspirations, lifestyle, selection of friends, activities, and social roles (Huang & Gibbs, 1992; MacMillian & Reschly, 1998; National Research Council, 2002; Oswald, Coutinho, & Best, 2002). Experience (i.e., being raised) in one socioeconomic stratum versus another tends to delineate the range of opportunities, the kind of choices, and the degree of challenges that are available to individuals and their families. It can even affect the quality of the schools, buildings, and teachers (MacMillian & Reschly, 1998; Oswald et al., 2002) to which the child is being exposed.

Race or ethnicity should no longer be equated directly with social class or culture. Although there might exist a correlation between race and SES, they are not linked by necessity or so easily circumscribed. Nevertheless, the U.S. mainstream continues to hold fast to notions that being White, heterosexual, nondisabled, and middle class reflects high status whereas being anything else reflects lower status (Helms & Cook, 1999). Consequently, impressionable children may learn to devalue themselves and their own culture as they attempt to assimilate into the mainstream, often in vain because of racially based differences in physical features that belie Anglo or Caucasian heritage (Ortiz, 1999, 2006). The desire to fit in is seen commonly in the schools where children often adopt anglicized nicknames and prefer to be called by those names as opposed to their given names (e.g., Johnny instead of Juan). Psychologists should therefore consider SES as an independent, albeit highly interrelated, cultural variable that influences development across a broad spectrum of individual functioning including, but not limited to, self-esteem, personal identity, acculturation, language preference, and academic achievement.

Acculturation

Much like the preceding discussion on culture, ethnicity, and SES, the manner in which acculturation influences all forms of behavior in children and families rests upon issues of differential experiences, not merely differences. According to Salvia and Ysseldyke (1991), "acculturation is a matter of experiential background rather than of gender, skin color, race, or ethnic background" (p. 18). The standard by which acculturation is measured depends greatly on context and purpose. In the United States, where evaluations of student performance or behavior are conducted in the schools, the de facto standard is represented naturally by comparisons with mainstream North American culture that implies English language proficiency and values reflecting predominantly Anglo or Western European views. Thus, whenever the experiences of an individual, family, or group differ markedly from those of individuals who comprise the U.S. mainstream, expectations regarding functioning, performance, or behavior must be examined within the context of level of acculturation (Ortiz & Dynda, 2005; Rhodes et al., 2005).

A number of authors have discussed ways of understanding acculturation in a variety of contexts. In his discussion of acculturation, Padilla (1980) describes a model that emphasizes cultural awareness, ethnic loyalty, and five dimensions of acculturative change (viz., language familiarity and usage, cultural heritage, ethnic pride and identity, interethnic interaction, and interethnic distance). Hoover and Collier (1985) described different sociocultural explanations for withdrawn, defensive, disorganized, and aggressive behaviors as exhibited by students that can be considered when referring culturally and linguistically different children for special education. Sattler (1998) described factors affecting acculturation (e.g., history of migration experience), ways in which people deal with acculturation (e.g., marginality, assimilation), and suggestions for questions that can be posed during diagnostic interviews to help assess for a client's level of acculturation (e.g., inquiring about the language the client uses to speak with various family members and friends).

Atkinson, Morten, and Sue (1989) outlined five levels of acculturation that describe the manner in which diverse individuals or groups react to the dominant culture. The first level, conformity, is characterized by behavior that devalues cultural differences while at the same time praising the dominant culture. Dissonance, the second level, is defined primarily as a time of intrapsychic conflict where personal views regarding cultural differences shift between degrees of acceptance and rejection. Resistance and immersion form the third level of acculturation and are evident in patterns of general behavior that begin to show appreciation for cultural differences coupled with a certain degree of disdain for the majority culture. Introspection is the fourth level and is best described as a process whereby individuals attempt to explore the basis of their attitudes, in particular those that represent a liking of themselves and their inherent cultural differences. And last, synergetic articulation and awareness comprise the fifth level of acculturation wherein individuals come to appreciate both the cultural differences that exist, as well as particular aspects of the majority culture. Patterns of acculturation tend to be related to familial generations. The level at which an individual may fall on the acculturation spectrum is related to such issues as whether they represent the first among their family to come to the United States (but were not born here), versus their children who were born and raised in the United States (who are often bicultural and bilingual), to their grandchildren who were born and raised comfortably in the U.S. mainstream (and often speak English only; Rhodes et al., 2005).

Acculturation is not, however, a natural or invariant process. Many individuals or groups may deliberately choose to cling tightly to precisely those things that provide them with a sense of identity, even if it retains a measure of cultural difference. For some, acculturation is viewed as the process of assimilation whereby the native values, beliefs, and customs are gradually lost and replaced by the values, beliefs, and customs of the dominant culture (Ortiz, 1999; Rhodes et al., 2005). Consequently, different members of the same family may be at different points in terms of their level of acculturation. For example, highly impressionable young children may feel no loss in assuming new and culturally different social roles than their middle-aged parents. This difference in acculturation may even create acculturative stress (i.e., tension and disharmony within the family) and disrupt the family hierarchy. It is not uncommon in first-generation families to see the role of parents and children reverse, particularly when the child has acquired better English language proficiency than the parent and begins to act as liaison between the family and mainstream society in certain social contexts (Huang & Gibbs, 1992; Ortiz, 1999, 2005; Tseng & Hsu, 1991).

Knowledge regarding the level of acculturation for a family and the individuals who comprise the family provides an important perspective from which the school psychologist can develop plans for service delivery. Given the varying degrees of acculturation that may be experienced by culturally diverse children, families, and educators and its attendant impact on the attitudes, values, and beliefs held by them, the importance of assessing and evaluating acculturation levels carefully prior to engaging in any service delivery activities should not be overlooked.

Stereotyping

Because there is a finite number of facts and information one can learn about a specific culture, generalizing is an important strategy that psychologists can use to help recognize unique characteristics of each culture. Although evaluating each family as its own entity is important, evaluating how they function within the context of their culture also provides a wealth of information about their functioning. Generalizations allow practitioners to develop a concept of cultural norms and some compass for what may or may not be clinically significant. Simply looking at each as unique may prevent us from acknowledging the influence of the cultural and group history. However, when these generalizations become a rigid set of rules that are applied to every individual from that specific culture, they can develop into prejudicial stereotypes. For example, notions that certain cultural groups are lazy, or do not value education, or do not care about time, are unfounded biases. These stereotypes seem to provide an exaggerated and inaccurate view of a specific individual and prevent practitioners from taking a closer look at the unique factors that may contribute significantly to the functioning of the individual as a whole. Determining whether one's decisions are being made on the basis of stereotypes is an important part of developing competence in working with diverse families (Ortiz, 2006; Pedersen, 2004).

Multicultural Training and Education

Despite the increasing diversity of the U.S. population, in particular within the schools, training and education toward cross-cultural competency development remains largely inadequate. With few exceptions, as noted previously, training programs that prepare individuals to work with diverse children and their families do not include large numbers of students from differing ethnic, cultural, and linguistic groups (Hanson, 1992; Lynch & Hanson, 2004). Multiculturalism, cross-cultural competency, and even bilingual assessment tend to enter the graduate school curriculum in the form of a single course, not always taught by individuals with significant professional training or education in these particular issues and not always including supervised experience with diverse children or families. In such cases, it will be the responsibility of school psychologists to engage actively in continuing education efforts even to the point of finding opportunities for mentorship or supervision.

Training and education directed toward development of competency in cultural skills and knowledge too often fall into a format perpetuated by books built upon the notion of "chapter cultures," that is, one chapter on African Americans, one chapter on Native Americans, one chapter on Hispanics, one chapter on Asian Americans, etc. Such instruction is destined for failure because true competency is unlikely to ever develop simply from reading a book (Frisby, 1998; Lynch & Hanson, 2004). In addition, the chapter cultures approach often inhibits a focus on cross-cultural similarities, which can be an important foundation for bridging differences and planning intervention. This is also one of the reasons why this chapter provides examples but does not discuss details regarding specific cultures. The intent is to keep the focus on the process of personal cultural learning that underlies competency in working with children and families from all cultural backgrounds. And, finally, such courses rarely emphasize the importance of understanding one's own culture

first before attempts are made to understand others (Lynch & Hanson, 2004). Consequently, as was discussed previously, failure to appreciate the manner in which one's own culture influences interactions with individuals from a different culture can often lead to difficulties in social interaction that negatively affect service delivery (McGoldrick, Giordano, & Garcia-Prieto, 2005).

The solution to the question of engendering true cultural competence is rather simple, but the implementation is admittedly difficult. Many training programs have already seen the value of recruiting students from diverse backgrounds in order to both provide the school system with a source for psychologists with the desperately needed cultural knowledge bases and the opportunity for students to gain experiences in cross-cultural transactions during their graduate training. Other programs have already worked on expanding university curricula to include an emphasis on multi-cultural education (Banks, 1993; Hanson, 1992), but the efforts must move beyond notions of single courses and seek earnestly to provide experiences commensurate with the needs and expectations found in the course of actual practice (Geisinger & Carlson, 1998). Graduate training programs also must make a commitment to hiring culturally diverse faculty members who have research and practical experience in working with culturally diverse populations. In the meantime, school psychologists and other service providers are expected to develop cultural competency largely on their own through continuing education efforts, a major reason supporting the need for a chapter such as this. Books, articles, workshops, and other continuing education opportunities on issues related to cultural competence will form the bulk of the education and training school psychologists will likely receive once they have graduated from their programs. But whatever methods are employed to gain the knowledge and skills necessary for effective service delivery, school psychologists must develop and maintain respect for the inherent difference and value of other cultures as well as the notion that differences do not always imply disorders (Hanson, 1992; Lynch & Hanson, 2004).

BEST PRACTICES

Cultural Competence: Knowledge

Cultural competence is based partly on skills and partly on knowledge bases. School culture represents primarily a knowledge base.

School Culture

To understand the school as a culture unto itself, one only needs to ask whether the abbreviations IEP, IDEA, LD, ED, MR, ESL have any meaning to the layperson not employed in schools. Worse yet, these abbreviations may have alternate meanings that could inhibit communication ever further. Schools have rules, expectations, and norms for all sorts of functioning including behavior, language, and attitudes. There is little, if anything, that occurs in the schools that does not reflect the U.S. mainstream culture in one way or another. Samuda, Kong, Cummins, Pascual-Leone, and Lewis (1991) recognized that:

> We took for granted, also, the cultural orientation of the WASP mainstream. The school was, in fact, a reflection of the middle-class societal norms and teachers were frequently the purveyors of information couched in terms of a collective mindset that almost totally disregarded any kind of minority sociocultural perspective. (p. vii)

The influence and the impact of the schools as a culture should not be minimized. Apart from the book learning that is taking place, much more is being learned in the school system. The very culture that gave rise to the public school system ensures that it teaches the values mirrored by society. Public school curricula are often based more on political and social agenda than on sound pedagogy. Examples of this include the passage of Proposition 227, known as the Unz Initiative, in California in 1998 (and later in Massachusetts and Arizona) that greatly limited the implementation of primary language programs, or the continued efforts in various states (e.g., Georgia) to introduce creationism as an alternative scientific explanation or direct replacement for evolution as the origin of life on earth.

But perhaps the best example of the politics of public school education can be seen in the impact, both positive and negative, that have surrounded passage of No Child Left Behind (NCLB). The desire to hold schools and districts accountable for the learning and progress of every student is a noble and worthy goal. But when high-stakes tests are used for this purpose, schools and classrooms tend to degenerate into test-preparation centers where critical thinking quickly becomes a lost art.

Such is the politics of public education. What is taught and tested in our schools is not there by mistake or chosen at random. It is chosen precisely and deliberately to espouse a particular point of view, a particular set of attitudes, beliefs, and ideology that mirrors the values held dearly by the mainstream culture (Spring, 2004).

The problem for the school psychologist is not that the dominant culture dictates the culture of the school. In fact, there have been significant advances in correcting some of the more egregious inequities perpetuated by culturally based ethnocentrism (e.g., the omission of historical and scientific contributions from non-White Americans, portrayals of Native Americans as uncivilized and obstacles to progress, views of slavery purely from political and economic viewpoints without regard to the toll on individual human beings and families). Rather, the problem for school psychologists lies in recognizing school as a culture and understanding the manner in which the system operates to inculcate a particular set of values in each and every student in attendance (Knauss, 2001; Lynch, 2004; Lynch & Hanson, 2004; Ortiz, 2006; Trimble, 2003). As diverse children are imbued with these values, the effects can be broad and far-reaching with potentially devastating consequences. Consider the following excerpt:

> Racism is often characterized, albeit facetiously, as an inherited disease—you get it from your parents. I guess I was lucky; I didn't get it from mine. Like so many other unsuspecting children, I went out and got it from a more authoritative source, school.... I was infected with a far more insidious strain that taught me to hate my *own* people because they were different than what society said they should be ... speaking Spanish simply wasn't allowed in school. Bilingual education was but a distant dream, and I was expected to learn English immediately upon entering kindergarten, never mind that my parents could barely speak it.... By second grade, my teacher placed me outside the classroom in a small group where I was teaching other Spanish-speaking children how to read in English. I distinctly remember feeling superior to these children aspiring to be as proficient as I was in English.... It wasn't that anyone ever said anything to me overtly, and it wasn't that my parents didn't value their own culture or language. There just always seemed to be a clear, unspoken norm that English was *better* than Spanish and that being White was *better* than being brown. It wasn't based simply on being different; it was a question of value. White culture was superior to all other cultures, including mine. (Ortiz, 1999, p.10, emphasis in original)

The possible effects of the culture of the school are indeed powerful ones. Best practices dictate that school psychologists fully understand the learning context that exists in each and every school and recognize that the context will differentially affect the learning and development of each and every student. Students whose backgrounds and cultural experiences are not consonant with the values taught in school may respond in ways that run counter to the typical educational expectations. Conversely, the very same children with diverse backgrounds and cultural experiences may respond in ways that are quite consistent with the public school system norms, as expressed in the quote above. In each case, the effects can be considerable (especially with respect to intrafamilial relations or school–family relations) and it will be incumbent upon the school psychologist to carefully assess the forces that have shaped the individual and have served as the underlying influences on their development, notably acculturative patterns, educational programming, and familial attitudes. When diverse children and their families are in need of educationally related services (e.g., counseling, assessment, consultation, behavior modification, instructional intervention), success will hinge in large part on the identification of the dynamics and similarities and differences in culture between the individual or family and the school.

Family Culture

There is probably no greater arena in which the influence of culture operates more directly than within the immediate family. It could even be said that each family represents a unique culture in and of itself (Frisby, 1998; Lynch & Hanson, 2004; McGoldrick et al., 2005). Development of a knowledge base that serves as the foundation for understanding the manner in which family systems work and how they represent cultural entities and transmit culture across generations is crucial to the proper selection and design of educational services by school psychologists (Helms & Cook, 1999; Leigh, 1998; Lynch, 2004; Ysseldyke et al., 2006). It is, however, well beyond the scope of this chapter to examine every aspect of families as cultural systems. Consequently, only a brief cross-cultural perspective of how family systems function will be presented, and the reader is referred to Tseng and Hsu (1991) for a more comprehensive discussion.

Family has been defined as "the basic sociocultural unit … the nest for the growth of an individual, the resource for social support, and the institution through which culture is transmitted" (Tseng & Hsu, 1991, p. 1).

Although it is not the only method by which culture is passed on to new generations, the family group nevertheless plays a significant role in cultivating the growth, development, and psychological well-being of its children (Lewis, Beavers, Gossett, & Phillips, 1976; Randall-David, 1989). Families, as groups, are likely to come into contact with school psychologists or other service providers when a school-age member of the family has or is suspected of having a disability. Contact may occur informally (e.g., telephone contact, home visit) or more formally through some type of prereferral process meeting or actual referral for special education evaluation. Depending on the background, experiences, and familiarity with the school system, engagements with the family may be welcomed or they may be seen as threatening (Hanson, 1992). For example, families from many Hispanic and Latino backgrounds typically view the school system as entirely capable of handling any and all situations with their children (Ortiz, 1999; Ruiz & Padilla, 1979). They generally seek not to interfere, and when called upon by the school or school staff, even for innocuous or positive reasons, Hispanic families, for example, may suspect that they are actually being summoned because of problems with their child (Ortiz, 1999). If so, they may feel a great deal of embarrassment because the behavior of one member of the family is seen as a reflection of the family as a whole and thus they often arrive at meetings with a strong sense of shame and obsequiousness at having to intrude upon the teacher's or psychologist's turf (Dana, 1993). Similarly, the respect for educators within Hispanic families is quite large, and they are unlikely to provide much discussion or feedback, let alone critique, of recommendations offered for intervention services (e.g., special education services). Hispanics tend to value the concept of *respeto*, where deference and status, as indications of respect, are accorded on the basis of such things as age, but also educational attainment (Lynch & Hanson, 2004). Thus, school psychologists should be careful not to mistake the strong sense of respect accorded to all educators as a sign of passivity or disinterest in their child's education. Rather, the respect is so strong that it precludes doing anything that even gives the slightest appearance of disrespect and it carries an almost ironclad sense of trust. The educator is viewed as the professional and to question his or her decisions would be unthinkable (Dana, 1993; Ortiz, 2006).

School psychologists may find themselves in a better position to provide culturally relevant services to families of different cultural backgrounds if they are able to understand the fundamental cultural aspects of family systems and function such as those just described. The particular aspects of family systems that may be most relevant to school psychologists would include variations related to marriage, residence, kinship, structure, power, and roles (Tseng & Hsu, 1991). McGoldrick et al. (2005) point out, for example, that with respect to family structure, African Americans will likely have at least some regular involvement with extended family members (see also Boyd-Franklin, 1989). For this reason, they emphasize the need for any service provider working with African Americans to take the time to learn about the relationships that children and immediate family members have with extended family members. In similar fashion, Falicov (2005) and Kusnir (2005) suggest that it is important to remember that in addition to nuclear family relationships and focus on interdependence, Latino family relationships generally include certain formalized kinship relations such as that of the *padrino* or godfather. This is important for school psychologists to know because a student's biological parents may not be the only ones who feel they have a stake in and the authority to make decisions about educational or school matters.

In summary, there are many different aspects of the family that need to be considered by the school psychologist from a cultural perspective. An understanding of the economic, political, ecological, social, and historical conditions that play a role in shaping a family's unique cultural patterns will aid in providing an individualized approach to service delivery, where intervention is tailored to the family's needs. Combined with knowledge regarding the school as a culture, a knowledge base regarding family as a culture will enable school psychologists to respond sensitively and effectively to families whose cultural practices differ from that of the mainstream or even their own.

Cultural Competence: Communication

In general, school psychologists who speak the same language(s) as the families they serve may have more effective interpersonal interactions than those who do not. The comfort level felt by parents or children who may not be fluent in English when given the opportunity to express themselves in their native language(s) is a substantial contributor to rapport (Helms & Cook, 1999; Lynch, 2004; Lynch & Hanson, 2004). Effective communication is not, however, based solely on verbal or signed interchanges, but very often on nonverbal or gestured expression as well. The need for competence in the former (verbal or signed communication) can often

be attained with the assistance of an interpreter/translator. Competence in the latter (nonverbal communication) will likely require application of a general knowledge base and perhaps even some cultural training from an individual familiar with the culture of the child and/or family to be served (Rhodes et al., 2005).

The amount of information that is communicated explicitly through verbal versus nonverbal means or contextual clues varies considerably from one culture to the next (Lynch & Hanson, 2004; McGoldrick et al., 2005). High-context cultures rely less on verbal communication, and meaning is derived typically through shared experience, history, and implicit messages. This tends to be the case with Asian, Native American, African American, and Latino cultures. For example, posture, eye gaze, and depth of bowing are all important nonverbal signals that have been refined through centuries by the Japanese and which convey meaning in powerful ways. In contrast, low-context cultures rely heavily on verbal communication, and meaning is derived primarily from direct, precise, and logical verbal interchanges. This tends to be used more in Anglo-European American, Swiss, German, and Scandinavian cultures (Lynch, 2004). The proliferation of political talk shows on both television and radio provide examples of the preference of low-context cultures for verbal communication.

Communication norms within the culture of the school appear to be reflective of the low-context modality. Not surprisingly, misunderstandings between school psychologists and families may arise when the normal level of context typically used by each to communicate on an everyday basis differs significantly. Individuals from high-context cultures, for example, Native Americans, may perceive specific verbal directions, detailed examples, and extensive elaboration as insensitive and mechanistic whereas individuals from low-context cultures (e.g., British) may become impatient if a speaker does not get to the point quickly and may not process gestures, environmental clues, or obscure phrases. School psychologists should attempt to observe family communication patterns, as appropriate, or consult with an individual who may be familiar with the culture of the family in order to determine what level of context the family uses to communicate. Ingraham (2000) discusses the use of a cultural broker who can be an intermediary between the school psychologist and family to bridge the cultural gap. This information will enable school psychologists to adjust their style of communication to match that of the families with whom they work, thereby increasing rapport and the likelihood of success with proposed interventions (Lynch & Hanson, 2004; Ortiz, 2006). See Lynch and Hanson (2004) for specific communication strategies the school psychologist can use to match the communication style of a family from a different communication style.

The use of an interpreter/translator can often assist considerably in managing communication between a school psychologist and a student or family. Interpreters/translators should be trained, however, specifically for the tasks they will be asked to perform (Rhodes et al., 2005). Finding an individual at the last minute and pulling him or her in to interpret at a meeting shows lack of planning and could easily be seen as disrespectful. In addition, the interpreter/translator should be knowledgeable of education-specific terminology and school law. Care should also be taken in matching the student's and the family's particular dialect. The expressions typically used by one cultural or ethnic group (e.g., Colombian) can differ markedly from the expressions used by another cultural or ethnic group (e.g., Nicaraguan) even though each ostensibly speaks the same language (Spanish). The dialectical and regional variations may well create a sense of discomfort, awkwardness, and even conflict because the common usage of certain words and expressions from one ethnic group may be quite offensive to members from different ethnic groups. For example, the concept of "now" is expressed by the word *ahorrita* in Mexico, but it means "later" in Puerto Rico. Conversely, the concept of "later" is expressed by the word *ahorra* in Mexico, but it means "now" in Puerto Rico.

Beyond these considerations, school psychologists must ensure that interpreters/translators are used properly. The interpreter/translator should be seated in a manner that facilitates communication between the school psychologist or other professional and the parent or child. The interpreter/translator should not be used as a representative for the school or as an advocate for the parent and should be trained only to interpret and not offer opinions (often a strong temptation because the parent tends to build rapport with the interpreter). When speaking, school psychologists should make it clear that they are speaking to the parent, not to the interpreter. Although it is awkward at first, the interpreter/translator should remain a background figure at all times, never the center of attention or the focus of the interaction. An interpreter/translator should also be licensed, follow the professional code of ethics, and be compensated appropriately.

As stated previously, verbal communication is not the only method of communication in which school psychologists should seek to develop skills. Nonverbal communication and miscommunication can have dramatic effects on the nature of the relationship between a school psychologist and members of a family. For example, prolonged eye contact between individuals from Hispanic cultures is considered disrespectful, and any eye contact between a child and an adult is equally disrespectful. Similarly, eye contact between two strangers in some Asian cultures is regarded as shameful (Lynch, 2004; Lynch & Hanson, 2004). Other nonverbal behaviors such as specific facial expressions, interpersonal distance (small for Hispanic and Asian cultures, larger for Anglo culture), type of physical contact permitted (e.g., a handshake, hug, slap on the back), and body language (e.g., standing with one's hands on one's hips is considered hostile in some Asian cultures) are influenced greatly by culture and differ as a function of age, gender, religion, and personal preference as well as professional status and economic background. In the absence of concerted effort and sustained study, the average school psychologist is unlikely to learn all the culturally appropriate ways of communicating and behaving. However, with assistance, consultation, and informed readings, it is very possible for school psychologists to acquire enough skill and knowledge related to the more salient patterns of nonverbal communication within a given culture. Particularly important are the behaviors and gestures that show respect (e.g., bowing in Asian cultures, using titles and calling others by surnames only; not using first names in Hispanic cultures; Lynch, 2004) and the often ritualized methods of greeting and dismissal. For example, in the United States, small talk often centers on the topic of weather, but in Puerto Rico it centers on general health concerns and aches and pains.

Mastery of even a few skills related to showing respect or saying hello or goodbye (e.g., bowing, shaking hands, waving) in an appropriate manner can pay large dividends in the success of school psychology service delivery. Behaviors such as these tend to put the family at ease. For example, Hispanics tend to begin any function with polite talk about issues not directly related to the purpose for the meeting. To get right down to business would cause some discomfort for Hispanics as the more common method of attending to matters of import is to first spend some time in small talk about other issues (e.g., the family, health, work), drink some coffee, and allow the conversation to turn naturally from personal things to the issue at hand. Japanese families may expect formal introductions with bowing in lieu of hand shaking, and tea. Engaging in such practices is not difficult, but may feel a little awkward to the school psychologist or other educator who feels time pressures bearing down on them. Engaging children and families successfully will require patience, effective listening skills, and a willingness to take the time necessary to establish mutual goals. Attempts to show deference, respect, and cordiality to diverse children and parents as well as diverse educators may not always be completely successful, but efforts and attempts to do so will likely be very much appreciated.

Despite the need to learn about some of the particulars of a culture and their manifestation in any given student or family, the most important component of effective communication is represented by the school psychologist's ability to view and appreciate the world from the family's perspective(s). Intervening effectively with students and families will come more from a genuine respect of their native values, beliefs, and attitudes than anything else that might be said or done, especially when their views run counter to beliefs that may be held so dearly. In such cases it must be remembered that school psychologists are not often in positions where they are designing interventions for themselves. Rather, the intervention is for others and they will only be successful in so far as they are culturally relevant to the children and families for whom they are intended.

Cultural Competence: Awareness

Cultural competence is not a discrete skill or set of facts. To view cultural competence in such a light would be a great disservice. As mentioned at the outset, cultural competence represents the integration of a wide variety of knowledge bases and specific competencies that encompass many aspects of work with diverse children and families. Cultural self-awareness represents the first step to developing skill and competency in cross-cultural service delivery (Helms & Cook, 1999; Leigh, 1998; Lynch, 2004; Ortiz, 2006; Pedersen, 2004). This was recognized at the beginning of this chapter where the ability to serve diverse children and families was stated to come from an appreciation of the impact of one's own culture(s) on perceptions of self and others from both within and outside the culture. School psychologists should strive to develop keen insight into how one's own values, beliefs, experiences, attitudes, languages, and customs have been molded by culture. Shweder (1986) put it succinctly: "[T]he best way to get inside yourself is to go outside yourself, and as any good ethnographic knows, if you cannot find yourself in the other, you are not going to find yourself at all" (p. 38).

Based on Guthrie's (1975) research, several important points emerged that described difficulties psychologists may experience when they try to understand a culture other than their own (Lynch & Hanson, 2004): (a) Cultural understanding in one's first culture is typically well established by the fifth year of life; (b) in general, children are able to learn new cultural patterns more easily than adults; (c) although values are determined by one's first culture, they may need to be revised to be effective in a second culture; and (d) not having a deep understanding of one's first culture often yields errors in interpreting the second culture.

The need to recognize school systems as cultural entities and the values that they infuse into the curriculum were discussed previously. The basis of the values being indoctrinated by society into children in the schools, and in children and families outside the school (e.g., through the media), comes from mainstream U.S. culture. Typical North American values are derived primarily from Western European influence and tend to emphasize individualism, independence, autonomy, interpersonal competition, mastery, equality, punctuality, materialism, progress, and a future orientation. Moreover, there are elements of our culture that value interactions that are more informal as opposed to formal, that display a high regard for individual achievement, and that foster pride in direct and assertive interactional communication styles (Helms & Cook, 1999; Leigh, 1998; Ortiz, 2006). School psychologists who understand the extent to which they identify with each of these values will be in a better position to determine how the values that they adhere to most strongly affect their practice (Leigh, 1998; Lynch, 2004). Moreover, they will be more likely to appreciate the influence that mainstream culture is having on the development and functioning of culturally diverse students, families, and colleagues.

Self-awareness involves recognition of differences in one's own world view from that of others and it serves as the first step toward developing competence in working with diverse families (Barrera, Corso, & Macpherson, 2003; Lynch, 2004). For example, school psychologists who tend to value independence and autonomy in young children or who believe in promoting the attainment of developmental milestones and correcting slight deviations from the norm may have considerable difficulty understanding why some Native American and Hispanic American parents seem to have a relaxed attitude toward their children's achievement of self-reliance (Joe & Malach, 2004; Zuniga, 2004). Similarly, school psychologists who tend to value individual achievement and interpersonal competition may find themselves at odds with families who come from a cultural background that values interpersonal affiliation, cooperation, and reciprocity (e.g., Hispanic American families). And finally, school psychologists who tend to believe that the source of a child's disability lies in physical phenomena rather than spiritual factors will need to work through the dissonance that may result from interactions with parents who are committed to spiritual rather than medical treatments (e.g., some Southeast Asian groups) or some fundamental forms of so-called mainstream religion (e.g., snake holding, immersion in water; Chan, 1986; Harry, 1992).

Clearly, the extent to which a school psychologist's own cultural values differ from those of other cultures as well as the extent to which adhering strictly to those values affects service delivery to diverse children and families is a necessary requirement for engaging in best practices. Honest and genuine cultural self-awareness and appraisal provides the foundation from which the cultural elements of others can be best understood and brought to bear on improving personal and working relationships with diverse students and families.

Data Gathering

School psychologists spend a significant amount of time in activities that are designed specifically to collect information that serves a variety of applied purposes including assessment, evaluation, consultation, and counseling. In all of these components of service delivery, specific information about cultural elements relevant to the purpose for collection helps significantly in being able to understand the values, beliefs, and behaviors operating to define functioning or behavior of any kind. Not only does such knowledge affect the manner in which any collected data might be interpreted, but it also influences the very nature of the data that are sought and collected in the first place and how these data are later defined and used (Hanson, Lynch, & Wayman, 1990). For example, when a school psychologist hypothesizes that poor academic work may be the result of a disability, all interview questions, all observations of behavior and performance, all meaning ascribed to information contained in school records, and all data from testing may be interpreted within the context of providing support, not refutation, of the presumption of dysfunction (Ortiz & Dynda, 2005). Cultural factors that may have significant relevance to and influence over the precise meaning of all of the data are dismissed, ignored, or left uncollected because the presumption steered data-gathering efforts in a particular manner that did not include or place much importance on such factors (Rhodes et al., 2005; Sandoval, 1998b). In order to avoid errors in practice of this nature, school psychologists should adhere to gathering culturally relevant information in line with the following principles:

- *Establish rapport and build trust:* School psychologists should use the increasing knowledge bases regarding displays of respect and appropriate greeting behavior and exiting behavior. Help the family to feel at ease and respected, and provide the opportunity for the family members to fully participate and contribute to the process of service delivery. Use interpreters/translators as necessary but ensure they are appropriately trained and consult with individuals who are familiar with the culture and languages relevant to the purposes of service delivery.

- *Identify the presenting problem:* School psychologists should listen carefully to the family's perception of any suspected problem and attempt to understand it from the family's perspective. The family may feel there is no problem at all. It is also necessary to determine the family's past efforts to resolve the problem and to elicit the family's present understanding of new intervention strategies and goals. Once these issues have been clarified, the school psychologist will be in a much better position to negotiate intervention strategies.

- *Learn the family system:* The structure of the family system must be assessed and determined to the maximum extent possible. Particularly important to evaluate are the areas related to family composition, family members' roles and responsibilities, family's interactional patterns, family's support system, family's childrearing practices, and the family's beliefs about the student's suspected handicapping condition and its source. Knowledge of the relevant aspects of the structure of the family system provides the basis for interventions that are appropriate and individually tailored to the particular needs and resources of the family.

- *Evaluate one's own cultural biases:* It is virtually impossible to form opinions and impressions that are free from the influence of one's own cultural influence. It will be important to school psychologists to examine how their own cultural experiences influence the conclusions drawn from the collected data. This task will become increasingly more important for those individuals whose culture differs significantly from that of the school psychologists.

- *Determine the influence of previous cultural information:* Appropriate generalizations about a culture can aid practitioners in determining whether an aspect described by the family is or is not a significant issue. However, taken too far, such stereotypes can inhibit school psychologists from looking at unique and idiosyncratic family and individual variables. Failure to distinguish general issues from specific differences will undermine efforts in delivering effective services and inhibit the development of necessary cultural competence.

SUMMARY

Until the affirmations provided by NASP's and APA's organizational commitments to cultural competence, little attention was given to developing cross-cultural competence and understanding the manner in which cultural differences affect school psychology service delivery. Achieving cultural competence is an intentional and challenging process that requires individuals to take risks, lower their defenses, and set aside their own beliefs in an attempt to appreciate another's point of view. It is expected and not uncommon for individuals who have just begun to foster development of cultural competence to have some encounters with diverse students or families that have proven to be uncomfortable or less than successful. The rapidly changing demographics of the U.S. population with respect to diversity leaves many school psychologists faced with the challenge of providing services to culturally diverse children and their families for which they may not be well prepared. The relative lack of substantial and systematic training, education, and supervision toward the development of cultural competence that exists in professional psychology creates a strong need for relevant information and useful strategies applicable to service delivery to diverse children and families.

The information and specific strategies offered here are meant to serve as a readily accessible compendium for school psychologists searching for assistance. Despite the existence of a chapter of this type, it must be recognized that acquiring cultural competency and skills is a lifelong process. Developing cultural competence does not happen overnight and one cannot expect to know everything there is to know about every culture.

However, through an open mind and a willingness to implement new ideas, acquisition of specific strategies that will enable school psychologists to work effectively and sensitively with culturally different families as well as enable families to feel comfortable about their interactions with service providers. Learning about another culture and developing the skills necessary to communicate effectively with its members is a process that begins with the very first family with whom school psychologists work and with deliberate effort improves steadily over time as cross-cultural interactions and experiences increase.

REFERENCES

Atkinson, D. R., Morten, G., & Sue, D. W. (Eds.). (1989). *Counseling American minorities.* Dubuque, IA: Brown.

Banks, J. A. (1993). The canon debate, knowledge construction, and multicultural education. *Educational Researcher, 22*(5), 4–14.

Banks, J. A., & Banks, C. A. (1993). *Multicultural education: Issues and perspectives* (2nd ed.). Boston: Allyn & Bacon.

Barnouw, V. (1985). *Culture and personality.* Chicago: Dorsey Press.

Barrera, I., Corso, R. M., & Macpherson, D. (2003). *Skilled dialogue: Strategies for responding to cultural diversity in early childhood.* Baltimore: Brookes.

Boyd-Franklin, N. (1989). *Black families in therapy: A multisystems approach.* New York: Guilford Press.

California Department of Education. (1997). *Guidelines for language, academic, and special education services required for limited-English proficient students in California public schools, K–12.* Sacramento, CA: Author.

Chan, S. Q. (1986). Parents of exceptional Asian children. In M. K. Kitano & P. C. Chinn (Eds.), *Exceptional Asian children and youth* (pp. 36–53). Reston, VA: Council for Exceptional Children.

Constantine, M. G., & Sue, D. W. (2006). *Addressing racism: Facilitating cultural competence in mental health and educational settings.* Hoboken, NJ: John Wiley.

Copeland, A. P., & White, K. M. (1991). *Studying families.* Newbury Park, CA: SAGE.

Dana, R. H. (1993). *Multicultural assessment perspectives for professional psychology.* Boston: Allyn & Bacon.

Falicov, C. J. (2005). Mexican families. In M. McGoldrick, J. Giordano, & N. Garcia-Prieto (Eds.), *Ethnicity and family therapy* (pp. 229–241). New York: Guilford Press.

Flanagan, D. P., & Halsell Miranda, A. (1995). Best practices in working with culturally different families. In A. Thomas & J. Grimes (Eds.), *Best practices in school psychology III* (pp. 1049–1060). Washington DC: National Association of School Psychologists.

Franklin, C., Harris, M. B., & Allen-Meares, P. (Eds.). (2006). *The school services sourcebook: A guide for school-based professionals.* New York: Oxford University Press.

Frisby, C. L. (1992). Issues and problems in the influence of culture on the psychoeducational needs of African American children. *School Psychology Review, 21*, 532–551.

Frisby, C. L. (1998). Culture and cultural differences. In J. Sandoval, C. L. Frisby, K. F. Geisinger, J. D. Scheuneman, & J. R. Grenier (Eds.), *Test interpretation and diversity: Achieving equity in assessment* (pp. 51–73). Washington, DC: American Psychological Association.

Geisinger, K. F., & Carlson, J. F. (1998). Training psychologists to assess members of a diverse society. In J. Sandoval, C. L. Frisby, K. F. Geisinger, J. D. Scheuneman, & J. R. Grenier (Eds.), *Test interpretation and diversity: Achieving equity in assessment* (pp. 375–386). Washington, DC: American Psychological Association.

Guthrie, G. M. (1975). A behavioral analysis of culture learning. In R. W. Brislin & W. J. Lonner (Eds.), *Cross-cultural perspectives on learning* (pp. 95–115). New York: John Wiley.

Hanson, M. J. (1992). Ethnic, cultural, and language diversity in intervention settings. In E. W. Lynch & M. J. Hanson (Eds.), *Developing cross-cultural competence: A guide for working with children and their families* (3rd ed., pp. 3–18). Baltimore: Brookes.

Hanson, M. J., & Lynch, E. W. (1992). Family diversity: Implications for policy and practice. *Topics in Early Childhood Special Education, 12*, 283–306.

Hanson, M. J., Lynch, E. W., & Wayman, K. I. (1990). Honoring the cultural diversity of families when gathering data. *Topics in Early Childhood Special Education, 10*, 112–131.

Harry, B. (1992). Developing cultural self-awareness: The first step in values clarification for early interventionists. *Topics in Early Childhood Special Education, 12*, 333–350.

Helms, J. E., & Cook, D. A. (1999). *Using race and culture in counseling and psychotherapy*. Boston: Allyn & Bacon.

Honigmann, J. J. (1963). *Understanding culture*. New York: Harper & Row.

Hoover, J. J., & Collier, C. (1985). Referring culturally different children: Sociocultural considerations. *Academic Therapy, 20*, 503–509.

Huang, L. N., & Gibbs, J. T. (1992). Partners or adversaries? Home–school collaboration across culture, race, and ethnicity. In S. L. Christenson & J. C. Conoley (Eds.), *Home–school collaboration* (pp. 81–109). Silver Spring: National Association of School Psychologists.

Ingraham, C. (2000). Consultation through a multicultural lens: Multicultural and cross-cultural consultation in schools. *School Psychology Review, 29*, 320–343.

Joe, J. R., & Malach, R. S. (2004). Families with American Indian roots. In E. W. Lynch & M. J. Hanson (Eds.), *Developing cross-cultural competence: A guide for working with children and their families* (3rd ed., pp. 109–140). Baltimore: Brookes.

Kindler, A. L. (2002). *Survey of the states' limited English proficient students and available educational programs and services 1999–2000 summary report*. Washington, DC: National Clearinghouse for English Acquisition and Language Instruction Educational Programs.

Knauss, L. K. (2001). Ethical issues in psychological assessment in school settings. *Journal of Personality Assessment, 77*, 231–241.

Kusnir, D. (2005). Salvadoran families. In M. McGoldrick, J. Giordano, & N. Garcia-Prieto (Eds.), *Ethnicity and family therapy* (pp. 256–268). New York: Guilford Press.

Leigh, J. W. (1998). *Communicating for cultural competence*. Boston: Allyn & Bacon.

Lewis, J. M., Beavers, W. R., Gossett, J. T., & Phillips, V. A. (1976). *No single thread: Psychological health in family systems*. New York: Brunner/Mazel.

Lynch, E. W. (2004). Developing cross-cultural competence. In E. W. Lynch & M. J. Hanson (Eds.), *Developing cross-cultural competence: A guide for working with children and their families* (3rd ed., pp. 19–40). Baltimore: Brookes.

Lynch, E. W., & Hanson, M. J. (Eds.). (2004). *Developing cross-cultural competence: A guide for working with children and their families* (3rd ed.). Baltimore: Brookes.

MacMillian, D. L., & Reschly, D. J. (1998). Overrepresentation of minority students: The case for greater specificity or reconsideration of variables examined. *Journal of Special Education, 32*(1), 15–24.

Matsumoto, D. (1994). *Cultural influences on research methods and statistics*. Pacific Grove, CA: Brooks/Cole.

McGoldrick, M., Giordano, J., & Garcia-Prieto, N. (2005). *Ethnicity and family therapy* (3rd ed.). New York: Guilford Press.

National Research Council. (2002). *Minority students in special and gifted education*. Washington, DC: National Academies Press.

Ortiz, S. O. (1999). You'd never know how racist I was, if you met me on the street. *Journal of Counseling and Development, 77*, 9–12.

Ortiz, S. O. (2006). Multicultural issues in working with children and families: *Responsive intervention in the educational setting*. In R. B. Mennuti, A. Freeman, & R. W. Christner (Eds.), *Cognitive behavioral interventions in educational settings: A handbook for practice* (pp. 21–36). New York: Routledge.

Ortiz, S. O., & Dynda, A. M. (2005). Use of intelligence tests with culturally and linguistically diverse populations. In D. P. Flanagan & P. L. Harrison (Eds.), *Contemporary intellectual assessment: Theories, tests, and issues* (2nd ed., pp. 545–556). New York: Guilford Press.

Ortiz, S. O., & Flanagan, D. P. (2002). Best practices in working with culturally diverse children and families. In A. Thomas & J. Grimes (Eds.), *Best practices in school psychology IV* (pp. 337–351). Bethesda, MD: National Association of School Psychologists.

Ortiz, S. O., & Ochoa, S. H. (2005). Intellectual assessment: A nondiscriminatory interpretive approach. In D. P. Flanagan & P. L. Harrison (Eds.), *Contemporary intellectual assessment* (2nd ed., pp. 234–250). New York: Guilford Press.

Oswald, D. P., Coutinho, M. J., & Best, A. M. (2002). Community and school predictors of overrepresentation of minority children in special education. In D. J. Losen & G. Orfiled (Eds.), *Racial inequity in special education* (pp. 1–14). Cambridge, MA: Harvard Education Press.

Padilla, A. M. (1980). The role of cultural awareness and ethnic loyalty in acculturation. In A. M. Padilla (Ed.), *Acculturation: Theory, models and some new findings*. Boulder, CO: Westview Press.

Pedersen, P. B. (2004). *110 experiences for multicultural learning*. Washington, DC: American Psychological Association.

Randall-David, E. (1989). *Strategies for working with culturally diverse communities and clients*. Washington, DC: Association for the Care of Children's Health.

Rhodes, R., Ochoa, S. H., & Ortiz, S. O. (2005). *Assessment of culturally and linguistically diverse students: A practical guide*. New York: Guilford Press.

Ruiz, R. A., & Padilla, A. M. (1979). Counseling Latinos. In D. R. Atkinson, G. Morten, & D. W. Sue (Eds.), *Counseling American minorities: A cross cultural perspective* (2nd ed., pp. 213–231). Dubuque, IA: Brown.

Salvia, J., & Ysseldyke, J. E. (1991). *Assessment* (5th ed.). New York: Houghton Mifflin.

Samuda, R. J., Kong, S. L., Cummins, J., Pascual-Leone, J., & Lewis, J. (1991). *Assessment and placement of minority students*. New York: C. J. Hogrefe/Intercultural Social Sciences.

Sandoval, J. (1998a). Test interpretation in a diverse future. In J. Sandoval, C. L. Frisby, K. F. Geisinger, J. D. Scheuneman, & J. R. Grenier (Eds.), *Test interpretation and diversity: Achieving equity in assessment* (pp. 387–401). Washington, DC: American Psychological Association.

Sandoval, J. (1998b). Critical thinking in test interpretation. In J. Sandoval, C. L. Frisby, K. F. Geisinger, J. D. Scheuneman, & J. R. Grenier (Eds.), *Test interpretation and diversity: Achieving equity in assessment* (pp. 31–50). Washington, DC: American Psychological Association.

Sattler, J. (1998). Clinical and forensic interviewing of children and families. In *Guidelines for the mental health, education, pediatric, and child maltreatment fields* (pp. 264–265). San Diego, CA: Author.

Seldes, G. (1960). *The great quotations*. New York: Lyle Stuart.

Shweder, R. A. (1986, September 21). Storytelling among the anthropologists. *New York Times Book Review, 7*(1), 38–39.

Spring, J. (2004). *The American school: 1642–2004*. New York: McGraw-Hill.

Trimble, J. E. (2003). Cultural sensitivity and cultural competence. In J. Prinstein & D. Patterson (Eds.), *The portable mentor: Expert guide to a successful career in psychology* (pp. 13–32). New York: Kluwer Academic/Plenum.

Tseng, W. S., & Hsu, J. (1991). *Culture and family: Problems and therapy*. Binghamton, NY: Haworth Press.

U.S. Census Bureau. (2000). *U.S. interim projections by age, sex, race, and Hispanic origin*. Washington, DC: Author.

Ysseldyke, J., Burns, M., Dawson, P., Kelley, B., Morrison, D., Ortiz, S., et al. (2006). *School psychology: Blueprint for training and practice III*. Bethesda, MD: National Association of School Psychologists.

Zuniga, M. E. (2004). Families with Latino roots. In E. W. Lynch & M. J. Hanson (Eds.), *Developing cross-cultural competence: A guide for working with children and their families* (3rd ed., pp. 179–218). Baltimore: Brookes.

ANNOTATED BIBLIOGRAPHY

Leigh, J. W. (1998). *Communicating for cultural competence*. Boston: Allyn & Bacon.

Predominantly geared toward social work practice. Nevertheless, both the information and the strategies offered for developing cultural competence are equally applicable to the school psychologist. There are excellent exercises and materials within that make it a very useful tool for advancing one's own competency.

Lynch, E. W., & Hanson, M. J. (Eds.). (2004). *Developing cross-cultural competence: A guide for working with children and their families* (3rd ed.). Baltimore: Brookes.

This updated version continues the same tradition of excellence in providing practitioners with information and guidance on providing culturally competent services to diverse children and families. It remains the number one resource for school psychologists on this topic. Part I introduces issues regarding provision of services to diverse families with a focus on developing intercultural effectiveness. Part II describes the history, values, and beliefs of the major cultural and ethnic groups in the United States. Part III offers suggestions and recommendations for working with diverse families.

McGoldrick, M., Giordano, J., & Garcia-Prieto, N. (2005). *Ethnicity and family therapy*. New York: Guilford Press.

Although geared primarily toward counseling and therapy services, this is a solid reference for culturally relevant information about practices with individuals from more than 40 different ethnic groups. In addition to discussing how various assumptions influence the relationship between the service provider and various ethnic groups, it also examines the patterns of parent–child and multigenerational relationships. Based on this information, a variety of culturally informed applications are recommended.

Pedersen, P. B. (2004). *110 experiences for multicultural learning*. Washington, DC: American Psychological Association.

The purpose of this publication is to demonstrate the relevance of cultural diversity in psychological topics. Provides instructors, students, and professionals with collections of simulations, exercises, and structured role-playing activities to improve cultural understanding, increase cultural sensitivity and awareness, and develop cultural competence. Overall, an excellent resource for engaging in activities to promote one's cultural competence and enhance service delivery.

109 Best Practices in Increasing Cross-Cultural Competence

Antoinette Halsell Miranda
The Ohio State University

OVERVIEW

"You must be the change you wish to see in the world."

—Mahatma Gandhi

Since the 1980s, fields of education and school psychology have actively attempted to address the rapidly changing demographics in the United States. According to the U.S. Census Bureau (2003), almost 32% of the U.S. population consists of people of color. School age demographics are even more dramatic. In 2004, 43% of public school students were considered to be part of a racial or ethnic minority group (National Center for Educational Statistics, 2006). This represents a 22% increase from 1972. Among students enrolled in elementary and high school, 57% were non-Hispanic White, 19% were Hispanic, 16% were non-Hispanic Black, and 4% were Asian and Pacific Islander. In 2002, Hispanic school enrollment surpassed African American student enrollment for the first time (National Center for Educational Statistics, 2006). Between 1979 and 2004, the number of school-age children who spoke a language other than English at home increased from 9 to 19%. Spanish is the most frequently spoken language outside of English in these students' homes. Students of color in the United States are also more likely to be poor and attend high poverty, segregated schools than their White peers. It is expected that these trends will continue.

Sue, Bingham, Porche-Burke, and Vasquez (1999) discuss the need for the profession of psychology to address issues of race, culture, and ethnicity. They advocate for a multicultural psychology in order to address the challenging issues of diversity. Multicultural psychology requires revolutionary change and can best occur through the implementation of cultural competence of all aspects of the profession (Sue et al., 1999). The field of school psychology has also recognized this need, and, as a result, numerous researchers have suggested that the discipline address this growing need to have culturally competent professionals (Gopaul-McNicol 1997; Ramirez, Lepage, Kratochwill, & Duffy, 1998; Rogers, Ponterotto, Conoley, & Wiese, 1992).

Unfortunately, while the U.S. school-age population is becoming increasingly diverse, the school psychology profession, for the most part, remains predominately Caucasian. The latest demographics of the profession continue to show that minority school psychologists are significantly underrepresented (Curtis, Chesno Grier, Walker Abshier, Sutton, & Hunley, 2002). It is expected that limited representation of underrepresented groups will continue to confront the field of school psychology. Because of this increasing disparity between students and practitioners, it is essential that training programs provide students in school psychology with the skills to respond effectively to diverse populations.

Since the 1980s, the two major organizations that represent school psychologists, the American Psychological Association (APA) and the National Association of School Psychologists (NASP), have attempted to address this issue in a variety of ways. Diversity issues are addressed in the standards of both professional organizations (APA, 1993; NASP, 2000), and they both have standing committees dedicated to addressing the issue. APA (2003) has also developed a detailed set of guidelines in their policy for multicultural teaching, research, and practice and has approved resolutions that address issues of diversity in graduate education in psychology (APA, 1987). NASP has a link on their website for culturally competent practice, which provides a mission statement espousing NASP's commitment to promoting inclusive educational environments. The "website was developed as a collection of resources to assist school psychologists, educators and parents in their efforts to enhance the mental health and educational competence of all children" (NASP, n.d.). In 1996, NASP established a minority scholarship fund that awards $5,000 scholarships. In 2006, NASP was able to award three of those scholarships to deserving students, and it has the goal of one day awarding five a year (D. Crocket, personal communication, March 28, 2006).

Historically, diversity has not been reflected in school psychology literature despite the growing recognition that school psychologists need to acquire the knowledge and skills to be able to work with culturally diverse populations. In an investigation of multicultural themes in school psychology literature over a decade and a half (1975–1990), Rogers Wiese (1992) found that only 9% of the total articles in the three major journals (*Psychology in the Schools*, *Journal of School Psychology*, and *School Psychology Review*) reflected multicultural content. With respect to the focus of the research, 77% of empirical research was on assessment issues and the school psychologist's role as psychoeducational evaluator. In contrast, only 3% of the articles dealt with the impact of issues of culture and ethnicity and the role of consultant and counselor, and no studies dealt with the impact on other roles such as supervisor and program coordinator. A recent study extending Rogers Wiese's work (1990/1999) found that the multicultural content of the four major school psychology journals has increased slightly from 9 to 10.8% (Miranda & Gutter, 2002). Six journal issues had diversity as a special topic, and these articles accounted for 25% of the total multicultural articles. Freeman (2006) looked at participant characteristics in articles that focused on evaluating intervention outcomes as published in four leading school psychology journals during 1990–2004. Their results demonstrated that samples used by researchers were diverse but not representative of the U.S. population.

Strides are being made in school psychology research, however, to develop the essential knowledge and skills to respond to the increasingly diverse population, it is imperative that the field of school psychology increases its literature base in the area of diversity, particularly as it relates to the potential influence of cultural factors within work settings. For example, as the field continues to move more toward intervention-based practice, it is important that more research on the effectiveness of interventions with diverse populations be conducted.

Several researchers have also expressed the need for more diversity training (Curtis, Hunley, Walker, & Baker, 1999; Loe & Miranda, 2005; Ramirez et al., 1998; Rogers et al., 1992). The challenge is how to train students to develop the skills they need to effectively work with diverse populations. How should school psychology students be trained in the area of diversity so that they become comfortable in discussing issues of diversity in their delivery of school psychology services, are able to understand differences across cultures as well as differences within cultures, are able to understand that there are more differences within groups than between groups, understand the difference between stereotypes and sociotypes, and understand how issues of diversity affect the practice of school psychology?

It is a challenge that trainers of school psychologists need to examine. So many programs do not, or only minimally, infuse the content into courses, and trainees often have limited access to minorities during their field experiences (Loe & Miranda, 2005; Rogers et al., 1992). Thus, many practicing school psychologists may not have been trained to work with children who are culturally different from themselves.

The purpose of this chapter is to provide a framework for school psychologists to recognize how culture can potentially influence the practice of school psychology and how to effectively work with children from a cultural perspective.

BASIC CONSIDERATIONS

In working with culturally diverse populations, it is important for practitioners to understand the complexity of the diverse student population and to view students from a multidimensional rather than a one-dimensional perspective. It is difficult to thoroughly explore the multifaceted dimensions of diversity in this chapter. Therefore, selected issues will be discussed.

Diversity is Complex

Early diversity training often focused on describing the cultures of ethnic minority groups. Unfortunately, presentations such as these did not allow for the wide variability that exists within cultures and did not take into consideration the complexity of cultures and the interplay of class and gender.

Since the 1980s, scholars of diversity "have created a rich body of knowledge extending across gender, social, and cultural lines, along with an unprecedented range of approaches for acquiring and interpreting information" (Quina & Bronstein, 2003, p. 3). We now live in a society where there are more opportunities than ever before to have contact with people who are culturally different from ourselves. Thus, instead of being an option, it is a necessity that practitioners develop a working knowledge of equity and diversity issues especially as they relate to education and psychology.

While *multicultural* was the term most frequently used in the 1980s and 1990s, there has been a movement toward using the terms *equity* and *diversity*. Regardless of the terms used, there is a recognition that all encompass more than just race and ethnicity, and includes sexual identity, socioeconomic level, disabilities, age, and religion.

For many years, gender, race, and ethnicity were viewed as biological characteristics. As such, early research that espoused racial differences, for example, viewed those racial differences as innate, stable, and unlikely to change. Thus, traits and characteristics were viewed as permanent, which often led to conclusions that problems resided within the individual person and absolved society from many of the "isms" (racism, sexism, classism).

More recently, research has provided evidence that a variety of behaviors as well as lifestyles can be found within each racial, ethnic, and gender group leading researchers to conclude that these behaviors are more social constructions (Gergen, 1985; Unger, 1995). This requires the researcher, practitioner, and graduate student to view culture in a more complex fashion, understanding that there is often the intersection of a variety of identities (Quina & Bronstein, 2003).

Early research in diversity often focused on group differences especially with respect to race. More recent research by multicultural scholars that includes both empirical as well as theoretical recognizes the inadequacy of relying on race as the explanation for differences between groups (Quina & Bronstein, 2003). There is an acknowledgement that a variety of factors such as ethnicity, social class, language fluency, education, and skin color interacts and at times supersedes race and gender as key variables that have an impact on behavior and academic attainment (Quina & Bronstein, 2003).

The Diversity Challenge Facing Schools

While we would like to hold on to the utopian view of education as the answer to social inequality, there is the harsh reality that schools, for a long time, have played a major role in sorting students of different backgrounds (Nieto, 2004). The sorting that most educators are familiar with is tracking. Research has shown that students from minority backgrounds are disproportionately tracked into remedial and lower level classes in high school and virtually absent in honors and advanced placement classes (Noguera, 2003). Researchers have come to understand that many variables contribute to the academic difficulties of minority children and that not all reside in the children and their families.

An area most often studied by researchers has been the lack of educational attainment by many groups. Often, simplistic explanations are forwarded such as, "Poverty causes academic failure," which is a classist view that is widely accepted (Nieto, 2004). While it is true that poverty can have a detrimental effect on student achievement, research has also provided evidence that poverty alone is not a sufficient explanation for the failure to learn (Taylor & Dorsey-Gaines, 1988). Research abounds that clearly demonstrate that schools can indeed help poor, minority children be academically successful (Carpenter, 2005; Matthews, 2005).

Over the years, many theories, such as the poverty theory, have been proposed to explain the lack of educational attainment of minority and poor students. However, no single theory adequately explains why some students succeed in schools and others fail. We have to resist the urge to latch on to simplistic theories and understand that school achievement or lack of it is a result of a number of intersecting variables. There also has to be an understanding of the sociopolitical context in which public education takes place that often affects minority and poor students more.

In an era of high-stakes testing and federal legislation (e.g., No Child Left Behind [NCLB]), educators have had to work harder to find ways to help all children succeed. The NCLB requirement that data be disaggregated to determine if certain groups are not succeeding has put front and center the lack of academic achievement of ethnic minorities, English language learners, economically disadvantaged, and students with disabilities. While this is not new knowledge to the education field, it is the first time that school districts have been held accountable for groups of students who in the past were left behind. "Due to the increasing amount of cultural and social diversity found in society and in our schools, educators must find the right balance which promotes a healthy school climate while also embracing some degree of cultural pluralism" (Beachum & McCray, 2004, p. 8). Many researchers believe and have demonstrated that understanding the cultural diversity of the students and developing culturally relevant practices will turn a student's cultural strengths into academic assets (Ladson-Billings, 2001). The task facing educators, which includes school psychologists, is finding successful ways to intervene with students who historically have underachieved in our public schools.

As school psychologists work toward becoming cross-culturally competent, it is important that they understand culture and its role in education. Culturally relevant school psychologists "understand that culture is a complex concept that affects every aspect of life [and they] are able to recognize their own cultural perspectives and biases" (Ladson-Billings, 2001, p. 98). Training programs that incorporate a strong diversity focus can provide practitioners with a diversity knowledge base that will assist them as they move toward providing culturally relevant practice to the students they serve.

Training Issues

Training in the area of cultural diversity is not simply learning about racial, cultural, and ethnic groups, as was the major focus of early cultural diversity courses. In fact, this type of training often teaches broad characteristics of groups viewed as absolute truth, which only serves to stereotype. Cultural diversity training should help students understand how issues of race, class, ethnicity, and sexual orientation are interrelated with politics, economics, and power.

Issues of diversity are complex issues and should not be relegated to one course. Understanding diversity issues from a historical, sociological, as well as psychological perspective is important. Trainers as well as practitioners must not be fearful to address and confront the most difficult and often taboo topics, such as race, oppression, and social justice.

Jacobs (1999) states that "race has become so toxic a topic in America that many of us are afraid to even touch it, at least in public, without some kind of industrial-strength protection" (p. 3). In order to make progress, we need to have open and honest discussions that will facilitate a better understanding about the issues and diminish our tendency to resort to understanding groups through stereotypes. A complete level of understanding takes time and commitment and a different worldview. "The ability to differentiate the general from the specific, the universal from the unique, is critical to effective work with children of all cultures and backgrounds (Gibbs & Huang, 1998, p. 362).

While a single course focused on diversity often provides an overview for students, it is equally important to infuse these issues throughout school psychology coursework. This can easily be done by using case studies that incorporate issues of diversity, choosing major textbooks and supplemental textbooks that are focused on diversity issues in education and psychology, as well as creating practicum experiences with diverse populations (if the training program is situated in an area that is diverse).

Presently, it is far more likely that school psychology practitioners have had some training in the area of diversity. Because diversity is such a complex and far reaching topic, continued professional development is one way for practitioners to continue to expand their knowledge base and develop effective practices that will benefit culturally diverse students.

BEST PRACTICES

Generally, practitioners who are not experts in issues of diversity may become overwhelmed with how to provide culturally relevant practice to such diverse populations. This section will highlight the process of cross-cultural competence as well as several methods that a practitioner can use as part of their culturally relevant practice. More important, these practices are not confined to specific diversity groups but are general and broad enough to be effective practice with all culturally diverse groups.

Cross-Cultural Competence

Many researchers in the field of cultural diversity talk about the development of cross-cultural competence (Baruth & Manning, 1999, Gopaul-McNicol, 1997; Pope-Davis & Dings, 1995), the development of skills that enable the professional to be "competent, sensitive, and knowledgeable of the critical factors related to issues of cultural diversity to best serve minority students" (Gopaul-McNicol, 1997, p.17). Lynch and Hanson (1998) describe cross-cultural competence as "the ability to think, feel, and act in ways that acknowledge, respect, and build upon ethnic, sociocultural, and linguistic diversity" (p. 50). The process of developing cross-cultural competence has been described by many, usually with some element of variation. However, all of them have in common three elements: personal awareness, knowledge of other cultures, and application of that knowledge.

Developing a Personal Awareness
A person must first understand his or her own cultural heritage to be able to work effectively with another

cultural group. Everyone has a culture. Members of the majority culture are often unaware of just how their culture has influenced their values, beliefs, and attitudes.

How we view the world is influenced by our experiences. Lynch and Hanson (1998) advocate searching our roots through an exploration of such things as our family's origin, time of immigration, reason for immigration, and family's settlement in the United States. Other potential influences are languages spoken, religion, politics, economics, and socioeconomic status. This goes beyond simply doing a genealogy. A significant aspect of this self-examination is an analysis of the socialization process during the developmental years. Exploring our own cultural heritage allows us to develop an understanding of how we have been socialized to view the world.

The socialization process is often influenced by family values, beliefs, behaviors, and customs that are associated with cultural norms. Part of that exploration also includes a critical look at how we were socialized to deal with people different from ourselves as well as our own experiences with race. For Caucasians, this process can be challenging because many have often not had to consciously think about what it means to be white in the United States. McIntosh (1988) terms this *White privilege*. She further states, "I think Whites are carefully taught not to recognize White privilege, as males are taught not to recognize male privilege…. I have come to see White privilege as an invisible package of unearned assets which I can count on cashing in each day, but about which was 'meant' to remain oblivious" (p. 2).

While the exploration process might be painful for some, it enables us to confront potential biases and prejudices that may have been a part of our socialization process. Knowing we have a bias allows us to consciously avoid acting upon those biases, particularly in our professional life. Having developed a self-awareness, practitioners now have a foundation for learning about other cultures.

Developing Knowledge of Other Cultures
There are a number of ways to develop a knowledge base about other cultures. Lynch and Hanson (1998) suggest that the four most effective ways are reading books, interacting with people from diverse cultures who can act as cultural mediators, participating in the daily life of another culture, and learning the language of the culture. Reading is probably the easiest and least threatening, though, and should not be the only means by which information is gathered. Literature can provide us with diverse views of culture. Biographies

and fiction provide more nuanced knowledge of cultures than history books. Reading and understanding the historical context of minority people can put many of the issues in perspective. Reading provides a broader perspective of cultures while helping the practitioner see the continuum of culture.

Interacting with people from diverse cultures who can act as cultural mediators is particularly helpful in learning more about beliefs, values, and practices. Cultural mediators help bring what we have read to life and provide opportunities to ask questions about what we have read and experienced. Nothing is more powerful than hearing the experiences from somebody who lives it. Nuances of culture and cultural practices can be learned through cultural mediators as well. Remember, however, that the cultural mediator is also sharing his or her culture through his or her own personal lens and may not be representative of others in their group.

Participating in the daily life of another culture or doing a cultural immersion experience is an excellent way to increase cross-cultural understanding. For many, it will be the first time they have experienced what it is like being a minority. Participation in the life of another culture allows us to increase our awareness and understanding of a group. For many, this activity will be a challenge, but part of developing cross-cultural competence is taking risks.

Learning the language of another culture takes one of the strongest commitments and probably is the most difficult to achieve particularly for adults. Language is considered important because so much of culture is reflected in language.

Applying the Knowledge
Considering culture in the practice of school psychology provides the practitioner with the opportunity to address issues of diversity in an effective and systematic manner with the goal of providing optimal services to a culturally diverse population. Having a personal awareness and a knowledge base of cultures are essential prerequisites to practicing school psychology cross culturally. Becoming cross-culturally competent requires emotional risks. It is not always easy when talking about these issues and confronting them. It is important to listen to people with very different ideas and experiences. This does not necessarily mean agreement needs to occur, but listening with an open mind allows the practitioner to include a different perspective. It may require us to relook, reconceptualize, reexamine, and rethink, and it is the beginning of practicing

school psychology in a cross-culturally competent manner.

In addition to building a knowledge base regarding cultures, it is equally important to build a knowledge base about equity and diversity issues that are applicable to many marginalized peoples. Two such concepts, identity development and dual socialization, may be helpful in our attempt to determine whether culture is a factor that is affecting the problem situation.

Identity development. Tatum (2003) believes that "identity development as integrating one's past, present, and future into a cohesive, unified sense of self is a complex task that begins in adolescence and continues for a lifetime" (p. 20). Culture shapes identity. "Identity is influenced by a culture's language, social structure, rituals, and taboos in terms of how one views situation and events, particularly outside of their culture" (Baruth and Manning, 1999, p. 30).

While identity development occurs throughout the life span, significant development occurs during adolescence. This search for personal identity during the adolescence years involves several dimensions, including religious beliefs, values and preferences, gender roles, career goals, and ethnic identities. "While all adolescents struggle with identity issues, not all adolescents think about themselves in racial terms" (Tatum, 2003, p. 53).

Research demonstrates that racial and ethnic identity is more important for ethnic minority individuals than for majority group individuals (Branch, 1999). School psychologists working in multicultural settings need to understand both culture and child/adolescent development. "Understanding one entity without understanding the other limits the [school psychologist's] ability to intervene, especially with [students] of differing cultural backgrounds" (Baruth & Manning, 1999, p. 31).

Research has documented the relevance of racial and ethnic identity theory (Cross, 1995; Helms, 1995; Branch, 1999). The identity models tend to be stage models, which have the "advantage of considering race-related adjustment as a dynamic process that can be modified" (Helms, 1995, p. 182). School psychologists working with middle and high school students may find identity development to be an important variable to consider.

Phinney and Tarver (1988) studied Black and White eighth graders from an integrated urban junior high school on the search for identity. They found that among the 48 participants, more than a third were considering the effects of ethnicity on their future. Not only were they considering it, but also discussing it with family and friends and learning more about their ethnic group. While both groups were beginning to think about ethnic identity, the results suggested that Blacks were more engaged in an active search. Tatum's (2003) research on Black youth in predominantly White communities yielded results consistent with Phinney and Tarver's (1988) findings. Tatum believes environmental cues that trigger an examination of racial identity become particularly evident in middle school.

While early research on racial and ethnic identity focused almost exclusively on Blacks and Whites, more recent research on identity development has expanded to include other diverse groups such as biracial; Asian; Latino; and gay, lesbian, bisexual, transgendered youth, adolescents, and adults. Interestingly, after 9/11, Arab Americans, many for the first time, began to think of themselves and their communities in terms of racial identity and are seeking out a place in the racial dialogue (Salih, 2006). This is due in large measure to the racial stereotypes that have emerged in America around people who look "Arab." Tatum (2003) reminds us that "our self-perceptions are shaped by the messages that we receive from those around us" (p. 54).

Identity development of minority adolescents, particularly African-Americans, is being more closely examined as it relates to academic achievement. NCLB legislation has forced educators to deal with the achievement gap that has existed for decades. A number of researchers are beginning to examine how racial identity development may affect academic achievement in middle and high school. This has become particularly important in research that is examining the achievement gap of African American students in predominately White schools where even middle class Blacks have an achievement gap (Ogbu, 2003). Research results are showing that the development of racial identity has an effect that is often complex and textured. Research also clearly demonstrates that educators are the least aware of this and rarely consider its impact on these students in these schools. Tatum (2001) states, " teachers and school administrators would do well to understand and acknowledge different stages of racial identity development, just as they are knowledgeable about adolescent sexuality and other aspects of adolescent development" (p. 133).

Dual socialization. As discussed before, culture occurs on a continuum and is influenced by the process of dual socialization. Dual socialization is "the process of bicultural socialization through which minority parents teach their children how to function in two distinct sociocultural environments" (DeAnda, 1984, cited in Gibbs and Huang, 1998, p. 12). This important concept helps explain some of the variability within cultural groups. DeAnda believes six factors influence the outcome of the process of dual socialization: "the degree of overlap or commonality between the two cultures with regard to norms, values, perceptions, and beliefs; the availability of cultural translators, mediators, and models; the amount and type of corrective feedback provided by each culture regarding a person's behaviors in the specific culture; the congruence of conceptual and problem-solving styles of the minority individual with those of the mainstream culture; the individual's degree of bilingualism; and the degree of similarity in physical appearance to the mainstream culture" (p. 12).

Individuals who are able to negotiate two cultures successfully are said to be bicultural. Sue and Sue (1977) identified three variables to assess minority students in determining the impact or influence of culture: culture bound, language bound, and class bound. These also influence the socialization process and can affect the continuum of biculturalism. Culture-bound variables include knowledge of the cultural background, attitudes, and norms. Language-bound variables are knowledge of the family's first language, immigration history, and acculturation level of the family. Class-bound variables include the family's socioeconomic status and its impact, community experiences, and the family's aspirations.

APA Multicultural Guidelines

To assist psychologists in becoming cross-culturally competent, the APA multicultural guidelines were developed after 40 years of attention to multicultural issues in a number of applied psychology subfields (Constantine & Sue, 2005). The development of the guidelines is a result of several iterations of the tripartite model of multicultural counseling competencies and the dedicated efforts of several leaders in the field of psychology who have been committed to recognizing and integrating issues of diversity within the psychology community.

These guidelines are grounded in six principles that "articulate respect and inclusiveness for the national heritage of all groups, recognition of cultural contexts as defining forces for individuals' and groups' lived experiences, and the role of external forces such as historical, economic, and sociopolitical events" (APA, 2003, p. 382). While most of the principles focus on the individual psychologist reflecting on his or her own

professional practice, two of the principles address organizational and social change that psychologists can engage in that will benefit clients, students, and society at large. The six principles (Constantine & Sue, 2005, p. 6–8) are as follows:

- Ethical conduct of psychologists is enhanced by knowledge of differences in beliefs and practices that emerge from socialization through racial and ethnic group affiliation and membership and how those beliefs and practices will necessarily affect the education, training, research, and practice of psychology.
- Understanding and recognizing the interface between individuals' socialization experiences based on ethnic and racial heritage can enhance the quality of education, training, practice, and research in the field of psychology.
- Recognition of the ways in which the intersection of racial and ethnic group membership with other dimensions of identity (e.g., gender, age, sexual orientation, disability, religion/spiritual orientation, educational attainment/experiences, and socioeconomic status) enhances the understanding and treatment of all people.
- Knowledge of historically derived approaches that have viewed cultural differences as deficits and have not valued certain social identities helps psychologists to understand the underrepresentation of ethnic minorities in the profession and affirms and values the role of ethnicity and race in developing personal identity.
- Psychologists are uniquely able to promote racial equity and social justice. This is aided by their awareness of their impact on others and the influence of their personal and professional roles in society.
- Psychologists' knowledge about the roles of organizations, including employers and professional psychological associations, are potential sources of behavioral practices that encourage discourse, education and training, institutional change, and research and policy development that reflect rather than neglect cultural differences. Psychologists recognize that organizations can be gatekeepers or agents of the status quo, rather than leaders in a changing society with respect to multiculturalism.

While these principles were designed to influence the planning and actualization of education, research, practice, and organizational change informed by diversity, the APA multicultural guidelines encourage psychologists to be leaders in social justice in their practice of psychology and active advocates of equity and diversity (Constantine & Sue, 2005).

There are six APA guidelines that are consistent with the three elements of developing awareness, knowledge, and skill in cross-cultural competence. For example, in APA Guideline 1, psychologists are encouraged to recognize that, as cultural beings, they may hold attitudes and beliefs that can detrimentally influence their perceptions of and interactions with individuals who are ethnically and racially different from themselves. The guidelines represent an acknowledgement that we live and work in a culturally diverse world and that our traditional models of training, research, and practice are no longer appropriate. These guidelines assist psychologists in developing and engaging in culturally relevant practice and can be considered a road map.

Ecological Perspective

The use of an ecological perspective as proposed by Bronfenbrenner (1979) fits nicely with the idea of viewing a child in a cultural context. An ecological perspective views the child as an active participant in a system that is connected at all levels. Deficits are not seen as existing within the child, which has been the traditional way of looking at children's problems, but instead aspects of the child's environment, ranging from the family and the school systems to the community andeven the larger society, are evaluated for their potential impact on the child. Many minority families, particularly those that live in poverty, experience a number of ecological stressors that have a negative impact on their children's lives. "The ecological perspective is especially relevant in analyzing the impacts of poverty, discrimination, immigration, and social isolation on the psychosocial development and adjustment of minority children and youth" (Gibbs & Huang, 1998, p. 6–7).

Ethnic Validity Model

While suggested guidelines are helpful for cross-cultural practice, methods for systematically considering ethnicity and culture with assessment and intervention are needed (Barnett et al., 1995). A model developed by Barnett et al. shows promise as a framework for assisting school psychologists in conducting culturally relevant practice. The ethnic validity model uses a problem-solving orientation that systematically considers cultural

differences. (This problem-solving model will not be detailed here; see Tilly, chapter 2, vol. 1).

There are three key elements to the ethnic validity model. The first key element is a problem-solving orientation that looks at problems in a holistic fashion. In addition, the foundation of the model includes establishing an advocacy role for the population being served and accepting, respecting, and understanding the cultural values, perspectives, and behaviors of the population being served (Barnett et al., 1995). Throughout the problem-solving model, professionals are always considering the cultural context as well as potential influences of culture on the problems situation.

The second key element is acceptability. This involves the participant's acceptability of the interventions that are being considered. There is a commitment to developing interventions that are compatible with the needs, values, and customs of the participant. Thus, a participant's culture could be considered a factor in determining intervention acceptability.

The third key element is teaming. As teams use the ethnic validity model, there are core features that support it: interaction and collaboration, ethnic group representation and participation, and distributed decision-making power. The ethnic group representation is seen as important in that it provides some measure of expertise with respect to culture. However, while this is an important feature, in reality it might be difficult to carry out. This will be particularly difficult in districts that are predominately White, where minority staff members are small in number. In addition, while there may be minority staff members, they may choose not to serve in the role of being an expert on their culture. Other alternatives may be the use of community people willing to be a part of the teaming process. However, logistically this may be difficult. Another solution would also be to have a consultant whose expertise is cultural diversity. While this person may not be present at the teaming process, he or she can act as a consultant in helping the team to evaluate their decisions within a cultural context.

Consideration of cultural variables should occur throughout all stages of the problem-solving model. Not considering cultural variables in the problem-identification stage could potentially result in the inaccurate identification of a problem, which could lead to an ineffective intervention. The consideration of culture is not new. The Individuals with Disabilities Education Act legislation requires teams to consider culture when working with children from diverse backgrounds. Because culture, race, and ethnicity are considered sensitive topics by many, practitioners are often afraid to bring these topics up for fear they themselves may be considered racist, because they feel uncomfortable discussing them, or they lack the knowledge base to address or explore the issues in any depth.

In addition, more research is needed on evidenced-based interventions with culturally different populations as most intervention studies are conducted with White, middle class, suburban populations (Freeman, 2006)

SUMMARY

As the population of the United States continues to be increasingly diverse, school psychology faces the challenge of preparing future school psychologists to practice in a culturally competent manner. This is particularly important given the fact that there have consistently been fewer than 10% of school psychologists in the field who are members of minority groups. It is essential that school psychologists learn to view each child in a cultural context with the goal of providing optimal services. In order to do this, school psychologists will need to become culturally competent. This involves developing a personal awareness, acquiring knowledge of other cultures, and applying the knowledge in skill-based practice. Being able to understand culture as a continuum as well as understanding cultural influences will, it is hoped, avoid stereotyping of groups.

Effective cross-cultural practice relies on the practitioner being able to both accept and respect human differences as well as the similarities. The problem-solving model, which is the basis of the ethnic validity model, shows great promise as a systematic process or model for considering ethnicity and culture in the culturally relevant practice of school psychology.

An ecological perspective is also beneficial because it encourages the practitioner to view the child as an active participant in a system that is connected at all levels.

Becoming culturally competent is a process that will present some challenges but many more rewards. It is essential, however, if our goal is to provide effective services to an increasingly diverse student population. Culturally competent practice is simply best practice.

REFERENCES

American Psychological Association. (1987). Resolutions approved by the national conference on graduate education in psychology. *American Psychologist, 42*(12), 1070–1084.

American Psychological Association. (1993). Guidelines for providers of psychological services to ethnic, linguistic, and culturally diverse populations. *American Psychologist, 48*, 45–48.

American Psychological Association. (2003). Guidelines on multi-cultural education, training, research, practice, and organizational change for psychologists. *American Psychologist, 58*, 377–402.

Barnett, D. W., Collins, R., Coulter, C., Curtis, M. J., Erhardt, K., Glaser, A., et al. (1995). Ethnic validity and school psychology: Concepts and practices associated with cross-cultural professional competence. *Journal of School Psychology, 33*, 219–234.

Baruth, L. G., & Manning, M. L. (1999). *Multicultural counseling and psychotherapy* (2nd ed.). Upper Saddle River, NJ: Prentice Hall.

Beachum, F. D., & McCray, C. R. (2004). Cultural collision in urban schools. *Current Issues in Education, 7*(5). Retrieved October 1, 2006, from http://cie.ed.asu.edu/volume7/number5/

Branch, C. W. (1999). Race and human development. In R. H. Sheets & E. R. Hollins (Eds.), *Racial and ethnic identity in school practices*. Mahwah, NJ: Erlbaum.

Bronfenbrenner, U. (1979). *The ecology of human development: Experiments by nature and design*. Cambridge, MA: Harvard University Press.

Carpenter, B. L. (2005). Urban Catholic schools excel academically, struggle financially. *School Reform News*. Retrieved October 1, 2006, from http://www.heartland.org/Article.cfm?artId=16672

Constantine, M. G., & Sue, D. W. (2005). The American Psychological Association's guidelines on multicultural education, training, research, practice, and organizational psychology: Initial development and summary. In M. G. Constantine & D. W. Sue (Eds.), *Strategies for building multicultural competence* (pp. 3–18). Hoboken, NJ: John Wiley.

Cross, W. E., Jr. (1995). The psychology of nigrescence: Revising the Cross model. In J. G. Ponterotto, J. M. Casas, L. A. Suzuki, & C. M. Alexander (Eds.), *Handbook of multicultural counseling* (pp. 93–122). Thousand Oaks, CA: Sage.

Curtis, M. J., Hunley, S. A., Walker, K. J., & Baker, A. C. (1999). Demographic characteristics and professional practices in school psychology. *School Psychology Review, 28*, 104–115.

Curtis, M. J., Chesno Grier, J. E., Walker Abshier, D. W., Sutton, N. T., & Hunley, S. (2002). School psychology: Turning the corner into the twenty-first century. *Communiqué, 30*(8). Retrieved June 29, 2006, from http://www.nasponline.org/publications/cq308demog.html

Freeman, E. (2006, March). *Sample diversity across intervention studies published in school psychology journals*. Poster session presented at the annual meeting of the National Association of School Psychologists, Anaheim, CA.

Gergen, K. (1985). The social constructionist movement in modern psychology. *American Psychologist, 40*, 266–275.

Gibbs, J. T., & Huang, L. H. (Eds.). (1998). *Children of color: Psychological interventions with culturally diverse youth*. San Francisco: Jossey-Bass.

Gopaul-McNicol, S. (1997). A theoretical framework for training monolingual school psychologists to work with multlingual/multicultural children: An exploration of the major competencies. *Psychology in the Schools, 34*, 17–29.

Gopaul-McNicol, S., & Thomas-Presswood, T. (1998). *Working with linguistically and culturally different children: Innovative clinical and educational approaches.* Boston: Allyn & Bacon.

Helms, J. E. (1995). An update of Helm's white and people of color racial identity models. In J. G. Ponterotto, J. M. Casas, L. A. Suzuki, & C. M. Alexander (Eds.), *Handbook of multicultural counseling* (pp. 181–198). Thousand Oaks, CA: SAGE.

Howard, G. R. (1999). *We can't teach what we don't know: White teachers, multiracial schools.* New York: Teachers College Press.

Jacobs, B. A. (1999). *Race manners.* New York: Arcade.

Ladson-Billings, G. (2001). *Crossing over to Canaan: The journey of new teachers in diverse classrooms.* San Francisco: Jossey-Bass.

Loe, S., & Miranda, A. H. (2005). The incidence of ethnic incongruence in school psychology services and practitioner's perspectives on cultural diversity training. *Psychology in the Schools, 42*, 419–432.

Lynch, E. W., & Hanson, M. J. (1998). *Developing cross-cultural competence* (2nd ed.). Baltimore: Brookes.

Mathews, J. (2005, August 11). Study finds big gains for KIPP; Charter schools exceed average. *The Washington Post.* Retrieved October 1, 2006, from http://www.kipp.org/presscenter.cfm?pageid=nav7

McIntosh, P. (1988). *White privilege and male privilege: A personal account of coming to see correspondences through work in women's studies* (Working Paper 189). Wellesley, MA: Center for Research on Women, Wellesley College.

Miranda, A. H., & Gutter, P. (2002). Diversity and equity research in school psychology: 1990–1999. *Psychology in the Schools, 39*, 597–604.

National Association of School Psychologists. (n.d.). *Culturally competent practice.* Retrieved June 26, 2006, from http://www.nasponline.org/culturalcompetence/index.html

National Association of School Psychologists. (2000). *Standards for the provision of school psychological services.* Washington, DC: Author.

National Center for Educational Statistics. (2006). *Participation in education: Elementary/secondary education.* Retrieved June 26, 2006, from http://nces.ed.gov/programs/coe/2006/section1/indicator05.asp

Nieto, S. (2004). *Affirming diversity: The sociopolitical context of multicultural education.* (3rd ed). Boston: Pearson Education.

Noguera, P. A. (2003). *City schools and the American dream: Reclaiming the promise of public education.* New York: Teachers College Press.

Ogbu, J. (2003). *Black American students in an affluent suburb: A study of academic disengagement.* Mahwah, NJ: Erlbaum.

Phinney, J. S., & Tarver, S. (1988). Ethnic identity search and commitment in black and white eighth graders. *Journal of Early Adolescence, 8*(3), 265–277.

Pope-Davis, D. B., & Dings, J. G. (1995). The assessment of multicultural counseling competencies. In J. G. Ponterotto, J. M. Casas, L. A. Suzuki, & C. M. Alexander (Eds.), *Handbook of multicultural counseling* (pp. 181–198). Thousand Oaks, CA: SAGE.

Quina, K., & Bronstein, P. (2003). Gender and multiculturalism in psychology: Transformations and new directions. In P. Bronstein & K. Quina (Eds.), *Teaching gender and multicultural awareness* (pp. 3–11). Washington, DC: American Psychological Association.

Ramirez, S. Z., Lepage, K. M., Kratochwill, T. R., & Duffy, J. L. (1998). Multicultural issues in school-based consultation: Conceptual and research considerations. *Journal of School Psychology, 36*, 479–509.

Rogers Wiese, M. R. (1992). Racial/ethnic minority research in school psychology. *Psychology in the Schools, 29*, 267–272.

Rogers, M. R., Ponterotto, J. G., Conoley, J. C., & Wiese, M. J. (1992). Multicultural training in school psychology: A national survey. *School Psychology Review, 21*, 603–616.

Salih, M. A. (July 29, 2006). Arab Americans: In search of identity. *Asharq Alawsat, Arab international daily* (English ed.). Retrieved October 26, 2006, from http://aawsat.com/englishs/news.asp?section=3&id=5800

Sue, D. W., & Sue, E. (1977). Barriers to effective cross-cultural counseling. *Journal of Counseling Psychology, 24*, 420–429.

Sue, D. W., Bingham, R. P., Porche-Burke, L., & Vasquez, M. (1999). The diversification of psychology: A multicultural revolution. *American Psychologist, 54*, 1061–1069.

Tatum, B. D. (2001). Family life and school experience: Factors in the racial identity development of black youth in white communities. *Journal of Social Issues, 60*, 117–135.

Tatum, B. D. (2003). *Why are all the black kids sitting together in the cafeteria?* New York: Basic Books.

Taylor, D., & Dorsey-Gaines, C. (1988). *Growing up literate: Learning from inner-city families.* Portsmouth, NH: Heinemann.

Unger, R. K. (1995). Conclusion: Cultural diversity and the future of feminist psychology. In H. Landrine (Ed.), *Bringing cultural diversity to feminist psychology* (pp. 413–431). Washington, DC: American Psychological Association.

U.S. Census Bureau. (2003). *State and county quick facts.* Retrieved June 26, 2006, from http://quickfacts.census.gov/qfd/index.html

ANNOTATED BIBLIOGRAPHY

Barnett, D. W., Collins, R., Coulter, C., Curtis, M. J., Erhardt, K., Glaser, A., et al. (1995). Ethnic validity and school psychology; Concepts and practices associated with cross-cultural professional competence. *Journal of School Psychology, 33*, 219–234.

Reviews models of ethnic validity and how the models can be used as a framework in the practice of school psychology. Also provides suggestions for incorporating ethnic validity in practice, training, and research.

Esquivel, G. B., Lopez, E. C., & Nahari, S. G. (2006). *Handbook of multicultural school psychology*. Mahwah, NJ: Erlbaum.

Provides a balanced view of the emerging field of multicultural school psychology. Theory, research, and practice are integrated throughout. Includes an interdisciplinary perspective and a focus on evidence-based interventions related to major competency areas.

Gibbs, J. T., & Huang, L. H. (Eds.). (1998). *Children of color: Psychological interventions with culturally diverse youth*. San Francisco: Jossey-Bass.

A must read for practitioners working with culturally diverse children. Provides an up-to-date analysis and guide to the unique problems and special needs of minority youth experiencing psychological and behavioral problems. An ecological perspective is the common thread through all the chapters and in the case studies.

McIntosh, P. (1988). *White privilege and male privilege: A personal account of coming to see correspondences through work in women's studies* (Working Paper 189). Wellesley, MA: Center for Research on Women, Wellesley College.

Looks at the privilege of "whiteness" and how it has advantaged a group of people and disadvantaged others. Presents a frank discussion of race and racism in American society and how we can attempt to even the playing field.

Tatum, B. D. (2003). *Why are all the black kids sitting together in the cafeteria?* New York: Basic Books.

A practical and enlightening book that answers some of the commonly asked questions about race and racism. It will help the reader move to a new understanding of what racism is, how it affects us, and provides suggestions for what can be done about it.

110 Best Practices in Working With School Interpreters

Queens College, City University of New York

OVERVIEW

There is a shortage of bilingual school psychologists. These shortages were recently discussed in the 2002 Futures Conference in School Psychology (Curtis, 2002) and in a special issue of *Psychology in the Schools* entitled "Addressing the Shortage of School Psychologists" (McIntosh, 2004). Accurate data are not available as to the number of bilingual school psychologists in the United States. However, recent surveys from the membership of the National Association of School Psychologists (NASP) reported that only 1 of 10 school psychologists fluently spoke a language other than English (Curtis, Hunley, Walker, & Baker, 1999) and only 8% of the members were of minority backgrounds (i.e., African American, Hispanic, Native American/ Alaskan Native, Asian/Pacific Islander or other; Curtis, Hunley, & Grier, 2004). Zhou et al. (2004) concluded that "school psychology remains an ethnically homogeneous profession that nonetheless provides services to a diverse population of students and families" (p. 443).

Our schools educate a significant number of students who are in the process of learning English as a second language and are from linguistically diverse backgrounds. According to Capps et al. (2005), 3.9 million linguistically diverse children were designated as English language learners (ELLs, or students who are learning English as a second language) in 2000. (The literature often uses the terms limited English proficient and English language learning students interchangeably. Both terms refer to students who are in the process of learning English as a second language. ELL is used throughout this chapter to refer to those students.) Data from the same year also showed that six out of seven children in grades 1–5 and two out of three students in

secondary schools lived in households in which all members over 14 years of age were ELLs (Capps et al., 2005). Kindler (2002) indicated that ELL students speak more than 460 different languages, with the majority speaking Spanish (79.2%), Vietnamese (2%), Hmong (1.6%), Cantonese (1%), and Korean (1%). Other languages spoken by significant numbers of ELL students (i.e., 10,000 or more) include Arabic, Armenian, Chinese, Chuukese, French, Haitian Creole, Hindi, Japanese, Khmer, Lao, Mandarin, Mashallese, Navajo, Polish, Portuguese, Punjabi, Russian, Serbo-Croatian, Tagalog, and Urdu (Kindler, 2002). In general, these data suggest that school personnel work with students and families who are unable to communicate effectively in English and are from very diverse language backgrounds.

Significant numbers of ELL students and families who speak many different languages concomitant with shortages of bilingual school personnel have led to the practice of using interpreters to bridge communication gaps. Finding ways to communicate with ELL students and their families is imperative as schools make efforts to provide a wide range of support services designed to meet these students' academic and mental health needs. The No Child Left Behind Act (NCLB) emphasizes the critical need to improve the academic performance of all students, including ELL students. Meeting the educational needs of these students requires using a variety of procedures (e.g., language samples, curriculum-based assessment, observations, interviews) to identify the ecological variables that have an impact on academic achievement and classroom functioning (e.g., instructional tasks designed to increase language proficiency, classroom management; Rhodes, Ochoa, & Ortiz, 2005). Intervention and prevention efforts in the form of instructional and behavioral consultation are particularly important for ELL students in order to address their learning needs (Esquivel, Lopez, & Nahari, 2007; Lopez, 2000, 2006). Prevention services such as consultation are helpful to teachers and other instructional staff to design effective instructional and behavioral interventions that are culturally responsive. The NCLB and the 2004 reauthorization of the Individuals with Disabilities Education Act also emphasize the importance of working collaboratively with parents to achieve positive academic outcomes. Communicating via interpreters is imperative in order for school psychologists and other school professionals to engage in meaningful dialogues with ELL students and their families about planning and implementing effective academic and mental health services.

The purposes of this chapter are to discuss the process of using interpreters and to provide practice guidelines for school psychologists working with interpreters. Recommended practices are provided for school psychologists working with interpreters within a wide range of professional roles (e.g., consultation, parent meetings to plan and implement interventions, assessment).

Defining Terms and Contexts

The term *interpreters* is routinely used for professionals who demonstrate expertise in translating the *spoken* language (Tribe & Raval, 2003). In contrast, translators engage in the process of translating the *written* language as when, for example, translating letters and legal documents. Although interpreters and translators are both used in school settings, the focus of this chapter is on interpreters. The term *translation* refers to the process of changing messages produced in one language to another language. The language from which one translates is referred to as the source language whereas the language into which the translation is made is the target language.

The contexts in which interpreters are used in schools vary. Results of surveys indicate that interpreters work with school psychologists during parent interviews, parent conferences, parent consultations, student interviews, and student assessments (Lopez, 1995; Lopez & Rooney, 1997; Lopez, Sawyer, Biedenkapp, Irigoyen, & Mitchelle, 2007; Ochoa, Gonzalez, Galarza, & Guillemard, 1996). In mental health settings, interpreters are used to translate during intake evaluations, interviews, and therapeutic sessions (Tribe & Raval, 2003).

Potentially, school psychologists can work with interpreters to deliver services at various levels of the three-tier model of school supports recommended in *School Psychology: A Blueprint for Training and Practice III* (Ysseldyke et al., 2006). The service delivery system in *Blueprint III* takes into consideration students' needs and recommends that we design interventions to match the severity of those needs. Providing systems (i.e., universal), targeted, and intensive interventions involve providing a wide range of services to ELL students that may include, for example, culturally responsive response-to-intervention supports (i.e., systems-level interventions for students in bilingual education programs to address curriculum and classroom management), consultation services focusing on specific English as a second language (ESL) strategies or adapting the classroom instruction for ELL students (i.e., targeted level), and newcomer support services (i.e., intensive interventions for recent immigrants struggling with issues of literacy and acculturation). Delivering services to ELL students at all three levels requires collecting culturally and linguistically appropriate assessment and problem-solving data for decision making, communicating with students about interventions, and establishing collaboration relationships with their parents to implement interventions and discuss treatment outcomes. These goals cannot be realized unless we are able to effectively communicate with ELL students and their families, a task that must be frequently achieved via school psychologists' work with school interpreters.

BASIC CONSIDERATIONS

Communicating via interpreters presents school psychologists with various opportunities and challenges. The discussion that follows addresses major issues related to working with interpreters. The last section of the chapter provides school psychologists with guidelines to address challenges and follow best practices.

Interpreters as Facilitators

Language interpreters facilitate communicative interactions between individuals who speak different languages, and this is without question the primary benefit of working with school interpreters. Working with interpreters is helpful when establishing trust and rapport with ELL students and their families. For example, in a qualitative investigation in which interpreters were used within the instructional consultation process, Lopez

(2000) found that the students and parents viewed the interpreters as facilitating their communication with the consultants and consultees. Several studies in the medical and mental health fields reported that clients expressed feeling better understood and helped by clinicians when communicating via interpreters (Morales, 2006; see Raval, 2003, for review). Interpreters who are viewed as resources within communities are instrumental in helping culturally different families to more readily accept assessment or intervention recommendations (Harvey, 1982; Raval & Smith, 2003).

Challenges of Working With Interpreters

Despite the potential benefits of improved communication and increased rapport, providing educational and psychological services via interpreters is a difficult task. The challenges faced when working via interpreters are related to several issues that include (a) characteristics intrinsic to the process of translation, (b) the complex nature of providing psychological services via an intermediary (i.e., the school interpreter), and (c) systemic barriers related to shortages of trained interpreters.

Characteristics Intrinsic to the Process of Translation

Translating is a complex task that requires high levels of proficiency in the source and target languages. For example, many words and concepts cannot be directly translated from one language to another (Langdon, 1994). Metaphors, puns, and jokes tend to lose their meaning when literally translated. The meanings of words and concepts sometimes change when translated because they may have more than one meaning in the target language. Variations in vocabulary due to regional differences render translations difficult because interpreters must have knowledge of the lexical variations used in specific regions or geographical areas (e.g., many Puerto Ricans call kites *cometas* whereas many Cubans call kites *papalotes*). The developmental levels of concepts change when translated from one language to another. Translation requires interpreters with excellent translation skills, including skills to communicate with students and families from various regional backgrounds (e.g., knowledge of lexical variations).

Some challenges are also intrinsic to the style of translation used by interpreters and the characteristics of the communicative interactions. In the author's experience, school psychologists typically ask interpreters to use a style of translation referred to as consecutive translation. In consecutive translation, speakers deliver

their messages in the source language and stop to allow interpreters to deliver the translations in the target language (Anderson, 1976). There are two forms of consecutive translation: continuous and discontinuous. In continuous translation, interpreters wait until the speakers have finished their entire message before delivering their translation. In discontinuous translation, interpreters deliver the translation at periodic breaks. According to Barik (1973), the number of translation errors made by interpreters increases as speakers increase their speech rates. The translation research also indicates that interpreters tend to omit more information if the message givers speak for a long period and do not allow interpreters to translate messages periodically (Barik, 1973). These data suggest that school psychologists should avoid speaking at a fast rate and should pause frequently to allow interpreters to translate messages when communicating via the consecutive translation style. In contrast to consecutive translation, simultaneous translation requires that interpreters translate *while* the speakers are delivering their messages. The process of simultaneous translation demands careful attention from interpreters and speakers because of the simultaneous nature of the translations, and it also calls for interpreters who are well trained in this method of translation.

In general, overcoming the challenges inherent to the translation process requires interpreters who have high levels of language proficiency and a wide range of knowledge and skills related to the process of translation. The implications for school psychologists are that they must also have an understanding of the translation process and specific skills to work with interpreters (e.g., meeting with interpreters prior to translation sessions to discuss terms that will be translated and translation style that will be used).

Complex Nature of Providing Psychological Services Via Interpreters

An even greater challenge for school psychologists is that of providing educational and psychological services through interpreters. As practitioners, school psychology training focuses on developing skills as clinicians, assessors, problem solvers, and interventionists. However, school psychologists are not just trained to use tools such as assessment instruments and specific interventions; in essence, they are trained to assess, intervene, and problem-solve via methods of observations and problem-solving skills. Language barriers are not barriers just to communication; language barriers also curtail school psychologists' ability to effectively establish trust and interact with clients because they are now dependent on language interpreters to transmit content (e.g., topic of discussion), intent (e.g., meaning behind message), and accuracy (i.e., clarity of message) in communicative interactions (Hale, 2002). Communication and language are central to the work of school psychologists and losing their ability to communicate directly with their clients often results in a sense of disconnectedness that is difficult to overcome.

Beyond the language barriers are also cultural barriers. Cultural differences in how school psychologists communicate and in their world views pose significant challenges in their work, even when they speak the same languages as their clients. Providing psychological services to culturally diverse children and families requires school psychologists to acknowledge cultural differences. However, knowledge and sensitivity are not sufficient as school psychologists must also demonstrate multicultural competencies and engage in culturally responsive practices (Lopez & Rogers, 2007). These caveats also apply to situations when they are working with interpreters.

Several investigations shed light into the barriers that clinicians encounter when providing educational and psychological services via interpreters. Raval and Smith (2003) interviewed mental health providers (e.g., clinical psychologists, social workers) and identified the following treatment barriers when working with interpreters: (a) losing important information in translations, (b) experiencing a slower and more labored pace in the therapeutic process, (c) feeling restricted about using a variety of questioning styles because of the technical aspects of translation (e.g., some questions and styles of questions were difficult to translate), (d) experiencing difficulties in establishing a "coworker alliance" with the interpreters because of power differentials (i.e., nature of unequal relationships between interpreters and clinicians) and issues of trust (e.g., clinicians' lack of trust in the interpreters' translations), and (e) feeling unsuccessful in establishing rapport with clients. The practitioners reported that the interpreters were sometimes uncomfortable with the topics discussed in the therapeutic sessions (e.g., male interpreters discussing specific issues with female clients, interpreters uncomfortable when discussing culturally specific taboo subjects), which made the process cumbersome. The clinicians felt that using interpreters had often resulted in using more simplified interventions and adopting more expert therapeutic roles (e.g., advice giving). Their perception was that the quality of the relationship that they established with the interpreters had a direct effect on the quality of the

services that the clients received (i.e., more positive relationships between clinicians and interpreters resulted in more positive outcomes and better therapeutic alliances with their clients).

Lopez (2000) also found that working with interpreters during consultation interactions with parents and students sometimes hindered the consultation process. A student from Ethiopia who spoke Amharic, for example, felt inhibited by having to communicate through an interpreter who was part of the student's community. The student felt uneasy in discussing many issues related to his family because he feared that the interpreter would violate confidentiality. Green et al. (2005) investigated the use of interpreters in healthcare facilities treating Chinese and Vietnamese patients and found that patients communicating via interpreters often had questions that they did not ask, especially about mental health issues. The researchers found that rapport between patients and clinicians was compromised when interpreters were used to deliver healthcare. Furthermore, they reported that the relationship between the patients' ratings of overall care was directly related to their ratings of the interpreters as patients who rated their interpreters "highly were more likely to rate the overall care provided highly …" (p. 1054). It is clear from the available research that the presence of interpreters has an impact on the relationships between clinicians and their clients, the clients' perceptions of the quality of care that they receive, and the clinicians' ability to provide quality care.

The barriers described by these researchers can be addressed by engaging in a variety of recommended practices. For example, time should be allotted for the interpreter and school psychologist, and the interpreter and student or family, to establish rapport (Lopez, 2000). Training interpreters and school psychologists together is helpful to address communication and rapport-building strategies that are relevant to the interpreter and the school psychologist (e.g., how to discuss topics that the interpreter may be uncomfortable with, how to build rapport with the student or family prior to starting a meeting; Hsieh, 2006).

Working via interpreters also has a direct influence on the dynamics of the interactions between clinicians, interpreters, and clients. According to Anderson (1976), because interpreters hold the key to the communication process in situations where individuals from different language backgrounds cannot communicate with each other, the interpreters' position is pivotal and has the advantage of power. Anderson adds that the interpreters' position of power "is inherent in all positions which control scarce resources" (p. 218). As such, interpreters may exert control by translating all that is said or part of what is said. Lopez (2000), for example, found that one of the interpreters working in the case study of a Polish student who was receiving instructional consultation services was unwilling to translate everything said in the interviews with the student and parents because the interpreter felt it was too time consuming.

The interpreters' feelings toward the clients and their reactions toward the issues being discussed may also interfere with their ability to deliver accurate translations. Nida (1964) acknowledges that interpreters may not be able to avoid a certain degree of personal involvement in their work and may attempt to change the content of the messages they translate to fit their own personal, political, social, or religious preferences. In general, all information obtained through interpreters must be carefully evaluated because of the mere fact that the information is filtered through the interpreters and the school psychologists are not able to judge the quality of the translation. Nida recommends providing school interpreters with opportunities to process their responses and reactions to the issues they face when translating. In school settings, that can entail providing training and supervision for interpreters. The debriefing sessions (i.e., meeting sessions between school psychologists and interpreters) discussed in the best practices section of this chapter can also be used to help interpreters to discuss their experiences and plan potential strategies.

Challenges of Using Interpreters in the Assessment Process

Perhaps one of the most challenging and controversial issues is the use of interpreters in the practice of translating tests. Test adaptation experts argue that test translations often result in significant changes in the underlying psychological constructs assessed by the translated version of the test (Bracken & Barona, 1991; Geisinger, 1994). Thus, test translations alter test validity for ELL subjects. According to Geisinger (1994), merely translating a test is not sufficient when "the new target population differs appreciably from the original population with which the assessment device is used in terms of culture or cultural background, country, and language" (p. 304). In such situations, the tests must be adapted through the following procedures: (a) translating the test questions, (b) reviewing the translated version through an editorial review committee, (c) adapting the draft instrument on the basis of the comments made by the editorial review committee, (d) pilot testing the instrument, (e) field testing the instrument, (f) standardizing the scores, (g) obtaining validation data, (h) developing a manual and documentation, (i) training users, and (j) collecting reactions from users (Geisinger, 1994). In regards to the establishment of validation data, Geisinger points out that the validity and reliability of the adapted measure must be established to "demonstrate that the instrument continues to assess the same qualities with the same degree of accuracy in the new population" (p. 308). That recommendation is supported by the Standards for Educational and Psychological Testing (American Educational Research Association, American Psychological Association, & National Council on Measurement in Education, 1999), which state that when a test is translated from one language or dialect to another, its reliability and validity should be established for the uses intended with the linguistic groups to be tested.

Bracken and Barona (1991) also argue that translating test items is problematic because test directions are frequently too "psychotechnical" or difficult to allow for easy translation and that versions of translated tests produced by practitioners and interpreters are rarely "sufficiently perfected" to provide equivalent meanings across languages. Although test translations are not recommended, several survey studies have found that school psychologists use interpreters to translate test questions either on the spot or before the testing session (Lopez, 1995; Lopez et al., 2007). On-the-spot translations involve the school psychologist reading testing questions to the interpreter and the interpreter translating them during the testing session for the student being assessed. The interpreter then translates the student's responses to the school psychologist.

Research in the medical and court translation literature is available showing that interpreters' errors can lead to serious consequences when decisions are made based on inaccurate translations (Berk-Seligson, 2002; Flores et al., 2003). Lopez (1994) argues that interpreters' translation errors can contribute to test validity issues by significantly changing the content of the test questions. In a study designed to examine interpreters' translation errors, interpreters with little or no previous experience and training in translation or in assessment issues were asked to translate questions from the Wechsler Intelligence Scale for Children–Revised (WISC-R) into Spanish. The WISC-R was chosen because it has an equivalent version that was translated and pilot tested in Spanish called the Escala de Inteligencia Wechsler Para Niños–Revisada (EIWN-R). The equivalent version in Spanish was used to examine the quality of the interpreters' translations and to code the types of translation errors that the interpreters made when translating the test questions. A translation error classification scheme developed by Barik (1971) was used to code the interpreters' errors. The results indicated that the interpreters sometimes omitted, added, and substituted words and phrases that significantly changed the content and the meaning of the test questions and directions. There were even situations in which the interpreters were unable to translate specific words because they did not have the appropriate vocabulary in Spanish.

Another practice used by school psychologists is to provide the interpreters with the testing manuals before translation sessions begin so that the interpreters translate the test questions prior to the assessment sessions (Lopez, 1995; Lopez et al., 2007). The assumption made is that if the translation is conducted prior to the assessment session, the quality of the translation will be better because the interpreters have more time to work on more accurate translations. However, the additional time factor will not necessarily result in better products because the practice of translating tests is problematic for several reasons. As previously discussed, equivalent words or concepts may not be found when translating from the source to the target language. Thus, the content of test items may change substantially. The developmental level of items or questions may also change when the items are translated into the target language (Langdon, 1994). Examples can be found in the translation of the WISC-R to the Spanish EIWN-R. When the questions in the Information subtest of the WISC-R were translated into Spanish and the translation was pilot tested, the test publishers found that the developmental levels of the questions changed based on the performance of the children who participated in the pilot testing. Neither the school psychologists nor the interpreters will be able to accurately judge the developmental level of the items simply based on their practical experiences (Bracken & Barona, 1991). The bottom line here is that school psychologists should primarily use tests with validated translations and/or nonverbal cognitive tools that do not need translation.

The challenges of using interpreters during assessment sessions are not limited to loss of validity in the process of translating questions for normed tests. The same barriers discussed above apply to situations in which school psychologists may work with interpreters to translate informal problem identification tools for consultation, such as instructions for structured language

samples and curriculum-based assessment tasks. The validity of those informal tools can also be significantly altered if errors are made when translating directions and if school psychologists assume that a task such as a reading inventory in English can be translated to identify reading strengths and deficits in a second language. When it comes to developing informal tools in a language other than English, school psychologists must work with skilled interpreters and bilingual education staff to clearly identify the purpose(s) of the informal tool, the skills that need to be assessed, the content of the informal task, and the criteria used to examine student functioning.

Once interpreters translate the questions in formal and informal assessment tools, they also translate the students' responses for the benefit of the school psychologists; thus, miscommunications can occur at that stage of the translation process. How is the school psychologist to know that the interpreter's translation is an accurate representation of the student's message in terms of content, grammatical organization, and emotional intent? Because of the nature of the translation process, interpreters must avoid delivering a literal translation and must filter the message so that the translation conveys the original intent of the senders. Since the school psychologist must solely rely on the interpreters' rendition of the students' message, interpreters must demonstrate highly proficient translation skills.

Thus far, the discussion has focused on challenges inherent to the translation process and to the nature of providing educational and psychological services to ELL students and their families. A prevalent theme throughout this chapter is the importance of locating and working with well-trained and competent interpreters. The next section of the chapter explores systemic barriers related to the current shortages of trained school interpreters.

Systemic Barriers Related to Shortages of Trained Interpreters

Given the complexity of the translation process and the nature of providing educational and psychological services to ELL students and their families, it seems imperative that school psychologists acknowledge the importance of working with trained interpreters. It is widely agreed within the field of interpreter training that interpreters must possess a number of important competencies (Tribe & Sanders, 2003). Table 1 provides an outline of the various competencies required by school interpreters and school psychologists (Lopez,

Table 1. Competencies for School Interpreters and School Psychologists

School interpreters
- High levels of proficiency in the source and target languages
- Knowledge about and skills in the process of translation
- An understanding of their roles as interpreters along with the abilities to remain objective and professional (e.g., confidentiality)
- Knowledge of educational contexts (e.g., education system, district policies, school policies, technical vocabulary such as diagnostic categories, instructional programs, psychological terms) and psychological issues relevant to providing translation services

School psychologists
- An understanding of the facilitators, barriers, and challenges of working with interpreters
- Skills in working with interpreters to establish rapport; conduct interviews, assessments, meetings, and consultation sessions via interpreters
- Skills in assessing and obtaining problem identification data via interpreters and in interpreting and reporting assessment data (formal and informal) collected via interpreters
- Skills in training interpreters to translate in educational and psychological contexts
- Skills in evaluating the validity of the information/data obtained via interpreters and the utility of the process

Shared competencies
- An understanding of the problems inherent in the translation process within educational and psychological contexts
- Knowledge of the cultural backgrounds of the students and families
- Knowledge of language development and second language acquisition
- Knowledge of cultural differences in regards to views of exceptionality, cross-cultural communication, child rearing, educational practices, and other issues relevant to working with ELL students and their families
- Knowledge of and skills in cross-cultural communication
- Knowledge and skills relevant to working together to provide educational and psychological services (e.g., briefing, debriefing) to students and families

1999). Since interpreters and school psychologists work together, Table 1 also reflects shared competencies.

In general, interpreters need to have (a) skills in language translation, (b) knowledge of the specific cultural backgrounds of the ELL students and families they work with, and (c) an understanding of the educational and psychological issues that school psychologists face in schools. Finding interpreters with all those skills is difficult and schools often end up with interpreters who fulfill only some of those competencies. Training is not readily available for school interpreters because training programs are typically geared for interpreters who work in business, medical, or court settings (Lopez & Rooney, 1997). There is also the challenge of locating trained interpreters who speak Twi, Urdu, or other languages that are not prevalent within specific communities. Sometimes, finding that one interpreter is like looking for a needle in a haystack.

Several school districts in the United States have developed training components for interpreters such as the Broward County, FL (Diane K. Wilen, personal communication, April 13, 2007) and the Salt Lake City, UT (Alicia Hoerner, personal communication April 13, 2007) school districts. In addition to providing training, these school districts have also developed procedures for identifying and working with interpreters who speak a variety of languages.

An important component in school settings, and especially in providing educational and psychological

services, is finding interpreters who have had training in following ethical guidelines. Rhodes et al. (2005) provide a helpful discussion of ethical guidelines for school interpreters that address issues of confidentiality, quality of the translation, neutral roles of interpreters, qualifications of interpreters, fees and payments for services, professional conduct, and continued education and training.

Yet, the greatest challenge may be that trained interpreters are not viewed nor recognized as valuable resources in schools. If trained interpreters are available, it is then often difficult to persuade school administrators to allocate funding to pay for them and time for school personnel to offer the interpreters training on issues relevant to translating in educational and clinical situations. Thus, school psychologists continue to rely on using mostly untrained interpreters or approach the process by simply placing the label of "interpreters" on bilingual colleagues (e.g., teachers, secretaries), students, students' family members, and individuals from the community who may feel reluctant about the interpreter role or may be simply unprepared to carry off the required tasks of that role (Lopez, 1995; Lopez et al., 2007; Ochoa et al., 1996).

School psychologists should advocate for ELL students and parents by working with administrators to make sure that funding is made available to locate trained interpreters. School psychologists can also organize and deliver training sessions so that interpreters gain knowledge and skills to provide translation services during educational and psychological services. Various experts recommend training the interpreters and school psychologists together to discuss issues related to roles and functions, and to explore strategies relevant to assessment, interviews, rapport building, and translation (Rhodes et al., 2005; Tribe & Sanders, 2003). Recent investigations focusing on examining cross-cultural competencies for school psychologists identified various specific competencies related to working with interpreters. The results of those studies reinforced the belief that knowledge and skills in this area are important to provide culturally responsive services to linguistically diverse students and their families (Lopez & Rogers, 2001; Rogers & Lopez, 2002).

Overcoming Challenges by Instituting Best Practices

The significant numbers of students who are unable to communicate effectively in English and the pronounced shortages of bilingual school psychologists mean that school interpreters have become important resources in efforts to provide educational and psychological supports to families from diverse language backgrounds. The process of providing services via interpreters is challenging to school psychologists because of the difficulties inherent within the translation process, the complex nature of providing educational and psychological services via interpreters, and systemic barriers relevant to locating trained interpreters in a variety of languages.

BEST PRACTICES

School psychologists work with interpreters during a variety of activities including interviews, conferences for intervention planning and implementation, parent consultations, and formal as well as informal assessment sessions (Lopez et al., 2007). A number of barriers were discussed that include challenges inherent to the process of translation and to providing educational and psychological services via interpreters. The next section of the chapter provides school psychologists with recommendations as to how to address these challenges in order to improve the quality of the services school psychologists provide to ELL students and their families.

Identifying the Needs of Students and Districts

The needs of the students, families, school psychologists and other school personnel can be identified in several ways. First, individual schools can identify the languages

other than English spoken by their ELL students and families. Data obtained by school districts (e.g., number of ELL students, languages used in the students' homes) may be helpful in this regard. School psychologists and other school personnel can conduct a needs assessment of their school buildings to identify the situations during which they need to use interpreters. Bilingual personnel can also conduct a needs assessment by surveying the ELL students and parents as to the types of situations during which they would like to have interpreters when communicating with school staff.

Defining Roles and Functions

Interpreters play important roles in school psychologists' efforts to deliver educational and psychological services to ELL students and their families. But, how should interpreters' roles be defined? This question concerns the complexity of the translation process and the nature of the services school psychologists provide to culturally and linguistically diverse clients (Berk-Seligson, 2002). On the one hand, some of the literature argues that interpreters should take narrow roles, that of language translators or linguistic conduits, by merely translating language (Avery, 2001). On the other hand, more current models of mental health translation propose that the conduit model is too simplistic because it does not recognize that interpreters are an integral part of working with clients and their presence adds a new dimension to the traditional clinician–client interaction. Raval (2003) argues that interpreters may also have valuable information to offer pertaining to cultural issues and differences. For example, interpreters who are knowledgeable about clients' cultural backgrounds and communication styles are helpful to school psychologists when exploring culturally relevant issues related to discipline, views of learning and mental health problems, attitudes about education and child rearing, and beliefs about psychological interventions.

The culturally interactive model proposes that interpreters can adopt more active roles as cultural brokers (i.e., by helping school personnel to bridge cultural differences with clients), cultural consultants (i.e., by helping school psychologists and other professionals to solve problems focused on cultural and linguistic differences), and even advocates (i.e., by advocating for the culturally and linguistically diverse clients that they work with as interpreters; Messent, 2003; Raval, 2003). There is no consensus at this time as to what should be the role of interpreters when working with school psychologists. However, given that the cultural interactive role model acknowledges the interactive role of interpreters and their potential pivotal role as cultural brokers, it is argued that defining the role of the interpreter solely as a language translator is not sufficient.

Avery (2001) argues that the roles of interpreters should be defined along a continuum that ranges from linguistic conversion to "actively assisting, when necessary, to overcome barriers to communication embedded in cultural, class, religious, and other social differences" (p. 7). Avery also clearly draws boundaries along this continuum of roles by arguing that "the interpreter is responsible for clear communication" and the clinician is responsible for the ultimate outcome (p. 10).

Adopting a more comprehensive definition of the roles of interpreters implies that school interpreters must receive training to prepare them to engage in a variety of roles. For example, interpreters in the roles of cultural brokers should have extensive knowledge about cultural differences, as cultural consultants they would need to demonstrate collaborative and problem-solving skills, and as advocates they should demonstrate an understanding of clients' needs and organizational factors (e.g., services offered by school systems). School psychologists working with interpreters should consider the extent of the interpreters' training and background experiences in fulfilling those roles so that interpreters are not asked to assume roles that they are unprepared to perform (Raval, 2003).

School psychologists, working jointly with other school personnel such as administrators and teachers, should collaborate to define the roles and functions of school psychologists within each school district. The roles and functions may include parent consultation, parent meetings and conferences, parent and student interviews, and student assessment sessions.

Trained interpreters, school personnel, and community members who have dual relationships with specific clients should not be placed in the position of providing translation services for those clients. As such, placing school children and family members in the roles of interpreters is not recommended (Lynch, 2004). The confidential and sensitive nature of the issues school psychologists discuss with children and parents precludes bilingual peers from acting as interpreters during interviews, conferences, and assessment situations. Peers and family members who are placed in the roles of interpreters may have difficulty delivering accurate translations because they may lack the language skills needed for the task. In addition, their personal involvement with the student and family may interfere

with their ability to remain objective during the translation process. As such, they may refrain from translating everything that is said because they do not agree with the content of the discussion or because they may wish to protect the student or family member they are helping.

Defining roles and functions of interpreters facilitates (a) communicating with interpreters as to expectations for their roles, (b) identifying interpreters with particular areas of expertise, and (c) planning training opportunities for interpreters. Role definition also facilitates the collaboration between school psychologists and interpreters, and the communication between school professionals, students, and parents.

Locating and Identifying Interpreters

When bilingual school psychologists are not available, school psychologists should work with interpreters who demonstrate the competencies outlined earlier in this chapter and in Table 1, including bilingual as well as bicultural competencies. Interpreters should be located using a variety of strategies (New York Task Force on Immigrant Health, 1997). For example, trained interpreters can be located by contacting local training institutions and universities, posting newspaper ads, and contacting nearby districts that have access to interpreters. School psychologists and other school personnel need to advocate for ELL students and their families within school districts to make sure that administrators provide funding to hire trained interpreters.

When professionally trained interpreters cannot be located, school psychologists may find themselves in the position of having to use bilingual school personnel with educational expertise to provide translation services. Among the bilingual school personnel who may provide assistance are teachers, social workers, counselors, teacher's aides, and trained paraprofessionals. Local directories should also be developed at the state and district levels so that districts are able to share interpreters who speak a variety of languages and who have expertise in working within a variety of professional situations (e.g., parent consultation, Individualized Educational Plan [IEP] meetings, student interviews).

Providing Training for Interpreters and School Psychologists

Given the many competencies needed by interpreters, school psychologists are well equipped to provide interpreters with knowledge and skills in how to provide translations within the contexts of educational and psychological services. Since trained interpreters may have little or no background working in school settings, school psychologists may need to provide interpreters with specific training pertinent to working within schools (e.g., intervention services available in districts, rights of parents, guidelines and regulations to receive prevention and intervention services, special education assessment practices and guidelines). School psychologists can also provide bilingual school personnel with the necessary training to prepare them for their roles as school interpreters. If bilingual school personnel are not available, school psychologists may want to locate individuals from the community who demonstrate bilingual proficiency and who are familiar with the cultural backgrounds of the students. Community members serving as school interpreters will require extensive training if they are unfamiliar with the educational and psychological issues that they will encounter in their roles as interpreters (Lopez, 2000). Research suggests that interpreters benefit from supervision within field-based sites where they are exposed to opportunities to observe the settings and situations in which they translate (Dean et al., 2003).

School psychologists are encouraged to carefully evaluate the particular scenarios in which they use interpreters and to work diligently to match the interpreters' competencies and skills with those of the situation in which the interpreters are required (Hsieh, 2006). For example, if an interpreter is needed to translate during a parent interview to plan for classroom interventions, that interpreter should have skills specific to that professional activity (e.g., translating terms related to students' behaviors and specific interventions, establishing rapport with parents). Interpreters who are required to translate during assessment sessions, for example, need to have extensive knowledge of the assessment process and the tools that they are translating. Consideration should be given to training interpreters for particular scenarios so that they have a range of knowledge and skills appropriate for a variety of professional functions and roles. School psychologists should interview interpreters in order to explore the extent of their background training and experiences. Although school psychologists can provide training to interpreters in areas specific to educational and psychological services, training pertinent to the process of translation and language skills should be conducted by professionals with expertise in training interpreters (Nida, 1964; Tribe & Raval, 2003).

Allocating Time

Providing psychological services through interpreters is time consuming because of the many barriers that are encountered during the process. Lopez (2000) reported that consultation activities took longer than expected because of the difficulties in locating qualified interpreters and the need to provide interpreters with adequate training to translate during consultation sessions. In addition, the time-consuming factor is inherent in the process of translation because all communication is filtered through a third party (i.e., the interpreter). School psychologists should acknowledge and expect that activities conducted through interpreters will take additional time. That factor should be shared with other school professionals involved in the activities where interpreters will be used so that time constraints are acknowledged early on during the process and steps are taken to prevent the violation of any explicit or implicit deadlines. Time should also be provided for interpreters to establish rapport with clients prior to the sessions in which interpreters will be used (Lopez, 2000). School psychologists should discuss rapport-building sessions with interpreters to establish the parameters of those preliminary interactions. For example, during those rapport sessions, interpreters should abstain from discussing any issues that will be brought up during conferences, interviews, or assessment sessions to avoid role confusion (e.g., parents becoming confused as to the roles of interpreters and school psychologists) and miscommunication, and to ensure that all pertinent information is discussed during the scheduled time with all the appropriate professionals.

Following Recommended Phases When Working With Interpreters

Three phases are recommended when working with school interpreters (Fradd & Wilen, 1990; Langdon, 1994). The first phase is referred to as briefing and entails devoting time to meet with interpreters prior to the translation session to prepare and set clear goals for the session. The second phase is the active phase and refers to the actual time during which school psychologists are working with interpreters to provide services to ELL students and their families. The third phase is the debriefing phase and involves school psychologists and interpreters meeting again to discuss and review the translation session. The Appendix provides an outline of the practices relevant to the three phases of working with interpreters.

The practices were adapted from the existing literature on interpretation and translation (Figueroa, Sandoval, & Merino, 1984; Fradd & Wilen, 1990; Langdon, 1994; Lopez, 2000; Lynch, 2004). It should be noted that the practices recommended during these three phases assume that the interpreters have adequate competencies and high levels of language proficiency in English and the second language.

Briefing Phase

Prior to working with interpreters, school psychologists should conduct briefing sessions with interpreters. If other school personnel are joining the school psychologist for activities such as meetings and interviews with parents, the briefing session should be conducted with all relevant personnel. Briefing sessions provide school psychologists with opportunities to discuss with the interpreters the background information needed to prepare for the translation session such as procedures that will be used (e.g., interviews, meetings, assessment) and topics that will be discussed (i.e., technical vocabulary). The briefing sessions are useful when school psychologists want to explore the cultural issues that they need to be aware of to work with ELL students from diverse cultural backgrounds.

Active Phase

This is the phase during which school psychologists and interpreters actively work together to communicate with ELL students and families. Practices recommended include making time to establish rapport with students and families via the interpreters, and using effective communication skills (e.g., avoiding the use of long chunks of communication and technical language, summarizing and reviewing information discussed to check for clarity of information).

Debriefing Phase

Debriefing sessions are held after translation sessions for school psychologists and interpreters to discuss issues and problems that surfaced during the translation process. This is the time when school psychologists and interpreters may discuss concepts that were difficult to translate and cross-cultural differences that may have influenced the translation session (e.g., differences in communication styles and perceptions of student's behaviors). The debriefing time is also conducive to exploring strategies as to how to improve communication with the students and families in future meetings.

Specific Recommendations Relevant to Problem Identification and Assessment

Consultation and prevention services (e.g., changes in instructional program) should be implemented to help ELL students to succeed academically. Within consultation and prevention frameworks, interpreters may work with school psychologists to communicate with students and parents during the problem identification stage. In addition to observations and teacher interviews, school psychologists may want to explore students' levels of language proficiency and academic functioning in the students' native languages by using informal tools such as newspapers, developmentally appropriate books, reading inventories, and structured language samples (Lopez, 2006). Interpreters will also play a pivotal role in helping school psychologists to communicate with parents about the parents' perceptions of school interventions and about planning and implementing home-based interventions. In general, efforts should be made to examine the classroom ecological variables that are having an impact on the ELL students' academic and behavioral functioning. Instructional and behavioral interventions should target ecological variables such as instruction and classroom management with interpreters used as resources to communicate with ELL students and families.

Bilingual school psychologists who are proficient in the students' native languages should assess ELL students who are referred for bilingual special education evaluations. The *Directory of Bilingual School Psychologists* (NASP, 2000) is a useful resource to locate school psychologists who speak a variety of languages. Trained interpreters should be used only when all resources have been exhausted to locate bilingual school psychologists and when a referral is imperative. Rhodes et al. (2005) recommend choosing interpreters who will become an integral part of multidisciplinary teams in order to facilitate relationship building and to encourage parent participation.

If an interpreter is needed to perform the evaluation, multiple procedures should be used to collect the assessment data, including observations, interviews, and formal as well as informal tools. When interviews are used as assessment tools, school psychologists should consult the practices discussed in the Appendix. On-the-spot translations of standardized achievement and cognitive tools are not recommended. The first choice should be using assessment tools that have been translated and validated for the population being tested. If such tools are available, school psychologists must provide the interpreters with training to assist in the assessment process (e.g., knowledge of standardization and assessment procedures). Interpreters should also have opportunities to familiarize themselves with the assessment tools and to practice administration of the assessment items. Once interpreters are familiar with assessment procedures, they are better able to understand the assessment process and to follow the school psychologists' directions.

Informal translations of cognitive assessment tools are not recommended. School psychologists assessing Spanish-speaking students via interpreters can utilize the Bateria III Woodcock-Muñoz (Woodcock & Muñoz-Sandoval, 2005) if they feel it is appropriate for the cultural and language background of the student being assessed. The Differential Ability Scales–Second Edition (DAS-II) includes a Spanish translation of the nonverbal subtests (Dumont & Elliott, 2007). The Bilingual Verbal Ability Tests (BVAT; Muñoz-Sandoval, Cummins, Alvarado, & Ruet, 1998) is another tool that school psychologists should consider when working with interpreters to assess students' language skills. The BVAT is available in 18 languages, including Arabic, Chinese (simplified and traditional), English, French, German, Haitian Creole, Hindi, Japanese, Korean, Polish, Portuguese, Russian, Spanish, Turkish, and Vietnamese. Interpreters who have competencies to translate during assessment sessions and who are familiar with the assessment instruments can administer the items in the language other than English under the supervision of, and in the presence of, the school psychologist. The Universal Nonverbal Intelligence Test is a recent cognitive assessment tool that provides school psychologists with the means to assess ELL students nonverbally (McCallum & Bracken, 2005). The instructions for the test are delivered through pantomime and do not require any verbalizations from the students, which means that translation is not necessary at all. If the students' academic skills must be assessed in their first languages and adequately normed tools are not available, school psychologists also have the option of working with bilingual teachers or other qualified bilingual personnel to develop informal curriculum-based assessment procedures such as informal reading inventories and writing sample tasks.

Any reports generated for the purposes of describing assessment data obtained through interpreters should include a number of points. In addition to any language and cultural data pertinent to the students' backgrounds, the report should clearly indicate that an interpreter was used. A clear description should also be included of the extent to which the interpreter was needed. The report should indicate the style of translation that was used (e.g., simultaneous, consecutive) and a clear description of any assessment procedures that involved the use of interpreters. A description should also be included of how the presence of the interpreter influenced the assessment sessions (e.g., establishment of rapport, comfort level of student) and outcomes. The report of any evaluation data collected through interpreters should address the validity and reliability of the findings. Scores should only be reported when the school psychologist worked with the interpreter to administer a validated version of the translated test, the test norms are representative of the student being assessed, and if the interpreter used had adequate skills to translate during the assessment sessions. If the results are not valid (i.e., the validated version of the test was not used and/or test norms were not representative and/or the interpreter did not have adequate skills) results should be presented in qualitative format only. All assessment data should be interpreted within the context of the students' cultural backgrounds. If the findings are questionable because the process of working with the interpreter did not yield valid assessment data, the assessment report should clearly state so and the recommendations should address the need for a bilingual evaluation by a qualified school psychologist or the collection of additional data using alternative assessment procedures (e.g., using a test-teach-test method over time to evaluate the student's response to interventions).

Systemic Recommendations

Blueprint III strongly argues that school psychologists have an important role in helping schools to build capacity by addressing systemic issues. The role of school psychologists as system consultants is relevant to the issue of interpreters because school psychologists are well equipped to act as leaders within schools to build and maintain a system to address the practices of hiring, training, and working with interpreters. Ultimately, building the school systems' capacity to implement an effective school interpret program will translate into improved services for ELL students and their families (e.g., better communication with ELL parents when implementing effective home–school interventions).

Plata (1993) proposed a management system to coordinate the services offered by school interpreters. He recommended that districts develop a roster of qualified interpreters, guidelines for outlining interpreters' roles, guidelines and procedures for selecting and working with interpreters, a system for monitoring the interpreters' practices, a plan for interpreter and school personnel training, a reward system for compensating interpreters, procedures to help interpreters to improve their performance, plans for conducting formative and summative evaluations relevant to the interpreters' programs, and a plan to employ bilingual school personnel to diminish the need to hire interpreters. School psychologists, other qualified school personnel, and school interpreters can work with district administrators to implement the management plan recommended by Plata. At the systems level, school psychologists can also advocate for ELL students and families by working with other school personnel to develop guidelines as to the kind of credentials, training, and experiences school interpreters must demonstrate.

Local school districts, school psychologists, and school psychology training programs need to work collaboratively with interpreter training programs in universities across the nation to develop preservice and inservice training programs for school interpreters. Interpreter training programs expose their trainees to a number of courses that target basic principles in translation, verbal expression, professional roles, and ethics (Tribe & Sanders, 2003). In addition, interpreter training programs offer courses that target setting specific situations such as translating during conferences and legal proceedings. The training programs use a variety of tools to sensitize interpreters to the psychological and social contexts of translation including practicum experiences, analysis of videotapes and audiotapes, and role playing. Given their expertise in educational and psychological issues, school psychologists have a pivotal role in training interpreters to deliver translation services to ELL children and families in schools. School psychologists can be instrumental in developing courses and workshop experiences to help interpreters acquire specific knowledge and skills to deliver translation services in schools. The use of role plays and the examination of videotapes and audiotapes of different situations where interpreters are needed should be helpful in training interpreters to acquire specific skills such as translating during clinical interviews and parent meetings. Practicum experiences can also be created for interpreters to receive practical experiences in working in school settings with a variety of professionals.

Evaluating the Process and the Information Obtained Via Interpreters

When working via interpreters, schools psychologists must be careful to evaluate the process and the information and/or data obtained. There are a number of questions that should be taken into consideration when evaluating the information obtained. The questions are organized into seven themes (see Figure 1):

- *Quality of the translation:* Were there problems with translating specific terms, concepts, or vocabulary? Did the interpreter possess high levels of language proficiency in English and in the other language? Does the interpreter have formal training in the process of translation? How did those translation problems have an impact on the validity of the information obtained?
- *Relational and social aspects:* Was rapport easily established? Was communication effective and conducive to positive interactions and relationship building? How did the process of working via an interpreter influence the establishment of rapport with the client? Did social differences in gender, religion, sexual orientation, and socioeconomic or educational factors influence the interactions between the school psychologists, interpreters, and clients?
- *Cultural responsiveness:* Were cultural differences acknowledged and addressed? Was there a match between the cultural background of the clients and the interpreter? Was the interpreter familiar with the cultural background of the clients and with the culturally diverse issues relevant to the situation? Was the information obtained helpful in pinpointing cultural differences and providing culturally responsive interventions?
- *Language differences:* Was there a match between the languages/dialects of the clients and that of the interpreters? Was there a match between the language styles of the interpreter and client (e.g., differences based on education)?
- *Professional context:* Is the interpreter trained? In what area is the interpreter trained? Is the school psychologist trained to work with language interpreters? Does the school interpreter have sufficient expertise to function as a cultural broker, cultural consultant, and/or advocate? Did the status of the interpreter influence the translation outcomes (e.g., family member or student translating, community member who may not be trusted because of confidentiality concerns)?

Figure 1. Evaluating the utility of the process and the data obtained via interpreters.

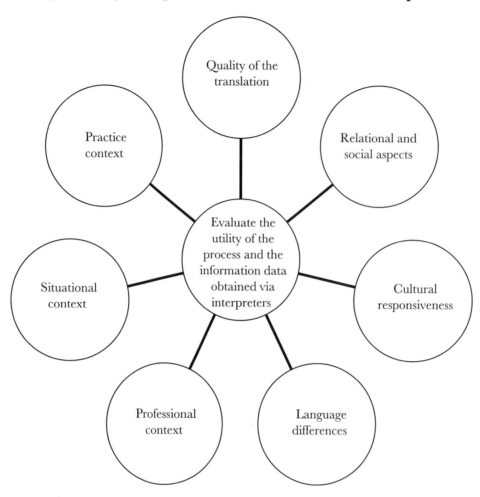

- *Situational context:* Does the school interpreter have training and/or experience in providing translation services during this professional activity (e.g., parent interviews, assessment of cognition, working with parents versus students)?
- *Practice context:* Were best practices followed in working with school interpreters? (See the Appendix.)

The responses to these questions should be helpful to school psychologists in terms of decision making. For example, if the match between the interpreter and the parent was poor because both were from different educational or socioeconomic backgrounds, the school psychologist may decide to reestablish contact with the family via a different interpreter or the school psychologist may work with the interpreter to approach future contacts using different strategies for communication and rapport building. Contacts or meetings in which rapport was not easily established may mean that school psychologists will have to create a variety of future opportunities to meet with the student and/or the family via the interpreter to establish better rapport. Assessment data collected via interpreters that are invalid may not be helpful in the process of data-based decision making and that may then require that the school psychologist make a case for a bilingual evaluation by a qualified school psychologist.

The responses to these questions should also help school psychologists evaluate the information and data obtained within the context of their utility for intervention and prevention purposes (Ysseldyke et al., 2006). For example, was there clear communication when discussing how to implement home-based interventions and ways to monitor intervention effectiveness?

SUMMARY

Providing educational and psychological services to ELL students and their families entails delivering a number of comprehensive services. These services include prevention programs, intervention plans designed to target instructional and behavioral problems, consultation services for parents and teachers, and problem identification efforts to identify ecological variables (e.g., instruction, classroom management) that need modifications. In an effort to provide such comprehensive services, school psychologists will most likely need to work with interpreters to communicate with the linguistically diverse population of ELL students and families.

This chapter makes a number of recommendations for school psychologists working with interpreters. Interpreters are defined as professionals who provide translation services in the context of spoken communication. In school settings, school psychologists work with interpreters during a variety of activities including interviews, conferences, consultations, intervention planning and implementation meetings, and assessment sessions. School interpreters facilitate the communication between school psychologists, ELL children, and their families.

The process of translation is complex and demanding. School interpreters must exhibit a number of important competencies and skills. Their bilingual and bicultural competencies are important because of their direct involvement in providing educational and psychological services to ELL students and families. School psychologists must also possess a wide range of knowledge and skills to work with interpreters.

The information provided here does not answer all the questions about the practices of working with interpreters. Literature relevant to the use of interpreters is scarce, and little research is available. Much work remains to be done in this area as this is a neglected topic in school psychology. The profession of school psychology needs to begin to establish a dialogue about the practice of using interpreters to provide educational and psychological services. Guidelines and policies must be developed at the national, state, and local levels to support the use of recommended practices when working with interpreters.

REFERENCES

American Educational Research Association, American Psychological Association, & National Council on Measurement in Education. (1999). *Standards for educational and psychological testing*. Washington, DC: Author.

Anderson, R. B. W. (1976). Perspective on the role of the interpreter. In R. Brislin (Ed.), *Translation: Application and research* (pp. 208–228). New York: Gardner Press.

Avery, M. B. (2001). *The role of the health care interpreter: An evolving dialogue*. Albany, NY: National Council on Interpreting in Health Care.

Barik, H. C. (1971). A description of various types of omissions, additions, and errors encountered in simultaneous interpretation. *Meta, 16*, 199–210.

Barik, H. C. (1973). Simultaneous interpretation: Temporal and quantitative data. *Language and Speech, 16*, 237–270.

Berk-Seligson, S. (2002). *The bilingual courtroom: Court interpreters in the judicial process*. Chicago: University of Chicago Press.

Bracken, B. A., & Barona, A. (1991). State of the art procedures for translating, validating, and using psychoeducational tests in cross-cultural assessment. *School Psychology International, 12*, 119–132.

Capps, R., Fix, M., Murray, J., Ost, J., Passel, J. S., & Hwewantoro, S. (2005). *The new demography of America's schools: Immigration and the No Child Left Behind Act*. Washington, DC: The Urban Institute.

Curtis, M. J. (2002, July). *The changing face of school psychology: Past, present and future*. Paper presented at the Future of School Psychology 2002 Invitational Conference, Indianapolis, IN.

Curtis, M. J., Hunley, S. A., & Grier, E. C. (2004). The status of school psychology: Implications of a major personnel shortage. *Psychology in the Schools, 41*, 431–442.

Curtis, M. J., Hunley, S. A., Walker, K. J., & Baker, A. C. (1999). Demographic characteristics and professional practices in school psychology. *School Psychology Review, 28*, 104–116.

Cushing, A. (2003). Interpreters in medical consultations. In R. Tribe & H. Raval (Eds.), *Working with interpreters in mental health* (pp. 30–53). New York: Brunner-Routledge.

Dean, R. K., Davis, J., Barnett, H., Graham, L. E., Hammond, L., & Hinchey, K. (2003). Training medically qualified interpreters: New approaches, new applications, promising results. *Views, 20*, 10–12.

Dumont, R., & Elliott, C. (2007). *Differential Ability Scales–Second Edition*. San Antonio, TX: Harcourt Assessment.

Esquivel, G., Lopez, E. C., & Nahari, S. (Eds.). (2007). *Handbook of multicultural school psychology: An interdisciplinary perspective*. Mahwah, NJ: Erlbaum.

Figueroa, R. (1989). Psychological testing of linguistic-minority students: Knowledge gaps and regulations. *Exceptional Children, 56*, 145–152.

Figueroa, R. A., Sandoval, J., & Merino, B. (1984). School psychology and limited-English-proficient (LEP) children: New competencies. *Journal of School Psychology, 22*, 131–143.

Flores, G. F., Laws, M. B., Mayo, S. J., Zuckerman, B., Abreu, M., Medina, L., et al. (2003). Errors in medical interpretation and their potential clinical consequences in pediatric encounters. *Pediatrics, 111*, 6–14.

Fradd, S. H., & Wilen, D. K. (1990). *Using interpreters and translators to meet the needs of handicapped language minority students and their families* (NCBE Program Information Guide Series No. 4). Washington, DC: National Clearinghouse for English Language Acquisition.

Geisinger, K. F. (1994). Cross-cultural normative assessment: Translation and adaptation issues influencing the normative interpretation of assessment instruments. *Psychological Assessment, 6,* 304–312.

Green, A. R., Ngo-Metzger, Q., Legedza, A. T. R., Massagli, M. P., Phillips, R. S., & Iezzoni, L. I. (2005). Interpreter services, language concordance, and health care quality: Experiences of Asian Americans with limited English proficiency. *Journal of General Internal Medicine, 20,* 1050–1056.

Haffner, L. (1992). Translation is not enough: Interpreting in a medical setting. *Western Journal of Medicine, 157,* 255–259.

Hale, S. (2002). How faithfully do court interpreters render the style of non-English speaking witnesses' testimonies? A data-based study of Spanish-English bilingual proceedings. *Discourse Studies, 4,* 25–47.

Harvey, M. A. (1982). The influence and utilization of an interpreter for deaf persons in family therapy. *American Annals of the Deaf, 127,* 821–827.

Hsieh, E. (2006). Understanding medical interpreters: Reconceptualizing bilingual health communication. *Health Communication, 20,* 177–186.

Kindler, A. L. (2002). *Survey of the states' limited English proficient students and available educational programs and services: 2000–2001 summary report.* Washington, DC: Office of English Language Acquisition, Language Enhancement, and Academic Achievement for Limited English Proficient Students.

Langdon, H. W. (1994, May). *Working with interpreters and translators in a school setting.* Paper presented at the Fordham University Bilingual Conference, New York.

Lopez, E. C. (1994, March). *Errors made by interpreters during on-the-spot translation of WISC-R questions.* Paper presented at the annual meeting of the National Association of School Psychologists, Seattle.

Lopez, E. C. (1995, August). *Survey of school psychologists: Training and practice issues in the use of interpreters.* Poster session presented at the American Psychological Association Conference, New York.

Lopez, E. C. (1999, August). *What competencies are needed for the delivery of psychological services through interpreters? Advances in the field.* Paper presented at the annual meeting of the American Psychological Association, Boston.

Lopez, E. C. (2000). Conducting instructional consultation through interpreters. *School Psychology Review, 29,* 378–388.

Lopez, E. C. (2006). Targeting English language learners, tasks, and treatments in instructional consultation. *Journal of Applied School Psychology, 22,* 59–79.

Lopez, E. C., & Rogers, M. R. (2001). Conceptualizing cross-cultural school psychology competencies. *School Psychology Quarterly, 16,* 271–302.

Lopez, E. C., & Rogers, M. R. (2007). Multicultural competencies for school psychologists. In G. Esquivel, E. C. Lopez, & S. Nahari (Eds.), *Handbook of multicultural school psychology: A multidisciplinary perspective.* Mahwah, NJ: Erlbaum.

Lopez, E. C., & Rooney, M. (1997). A preliminary investigation of the roles and backgrounds of school interpreters: Implications for training and recruiting. *Journal of Social Distress and the Homeless, 6,* 161–174.

Lopez, E. C., Sawyer, J., Biedenkapp, S., Irigoyen, M. A., & Mitchelle, J. (2007, May). *Survey of school psychologists working with interpreters.* Poster session presented at the annual meeting of the National Association of School Psychologists, New York.

Lynch, E. W. (2004). Developing cross-cultural competence. In E. W. Lynch & M. J. Hanson (Eds.), *A guide for working with children and their families: Developing cross-cultural competence* (3rd ed., pp. 47–89). Baltimore: Brookes.

McCallum, R. S., & Bracken, B. A. (2005). The Universal Nonverbal Intelligence Test. In D. P. Flanagan, J. L. Genshaft, & P. L. Harrison (Eds.), *Contemporary intellectual assessment: Theories, tests, and issues* (3rd ed., pp. 425–440). New York: Guilford Press.

McInstosh, D. E. (Ed.). (2004). Addressing the shortage of school psychologists [Special issue]. *Psychology in the Schools, 41.*

Messent, P. (2003). From postmen to makers of meaning: A model for collaborative work between clinicians and interpreters. In R. Tribe & H. Raval (Eds.), *Working with interpreters in mental health* (pp. 135–150). New York: Brunner-Routledge.

Morales, L. S. (2006). The impact of interpreters on parents' experiences with ambulatory care for their children. *Medical Care Research and Review, 63,* 110–128.

Muñoz-Sandoval, A. F., Cummins, J., Alvarado, G. G., & Ruet, M. L. (1998). *The Bilingual Verbal Ability Tests.* Chicago: Riverside.

National Association of School Psychologists. (2000). *Directory of bilingual school psychologists.* Bethesda, MD: Author.

New York Task Force on Immigrant Health. (1997). *Access through medical interpreter and language services: Report on research project.* New York: New York University School of Medicine.

Nida, E. A. (1964). *Toward a science of translating.* Leiden, Netherlands: E. J. Brill.

Ochoa, S. H., Gonzalez, D., Galarza, A., & Guillemard, L. (1996). The training and use of interpreters in bilingual psychoeducational assessment: An alternative in need of study. *Diagnostique, 21*(3), 19–40.

Plata, M. (1993). Using Spanish-speaking interpreters in special education. *Remedial and Special Education, 14*(6), 19–24.

Raval, H. (2003). An overview of the issues in the work of interpreters. In R. Tribe & H. Raval (Eds.), *Working with interpreters in mental health* (pp. 8–29). New York: Brunner-Routledge.

Raval, H., & Smith, J. A. (2003). Therapists' experiences of working with language interpreters. *International Journal of Mental Health, 32*(3), 6–31.

Rhodes, R. L., Ochoa, S. H., & Ortiz, S. O. (2005). *Assessing culturally and linguistically diverse students: A practical guide.* New York: Guilford Press.

Rogers, M. R., & Lopez, E. C. (2002). Identifying critical cross-cultural school psychology competencies. *Journal of School Psychology, 40*, 115–141.

Stansfield, M. (1980). Psychological issues in mental health interpreting. In F. Caccamise, J. Stangarone, & M. Mitchell-Caccamise (Eds.), *Century of deaf awareness* (pp. 102–114). Silver Spring, MD: Registry of Interpreters for the Deaf.

Tribe, R., & Raval, H. (Eds.). (2003). *Working with interpreters in mental health.* New York: Brunner-Routledge.

Tribe, R., & Sanders, M. (2003). Training issues for interpreters. In R. Tribe & H. Raval (Eds.), *Working with interpreters in mental health* (pp. 54–68). New York: Brunner-Routledge.

Woodcock, R. W., & Muñoz-Sandoval, A. F. (2005). *Bateria III Woodcock-Muñoz: Pruebas de Habilidad Cognitiva.* Chicago: Riverside.

Ysseldyke, J., Burns, M., Dawson, P., Kelley, B., Morrison, D., Ortiz, S., et al. (2006). *School psychology: A blueprint for training and practice III.* Bethesda, MD: National Association of School Psychologists.

Zhou, Z., Bray, M. A., Kehle, T., Theodore, L. A., Clark, E., & Jenson, W. R. (2004). Achieving ethnic minority parity in school psychology. *Psychology in the Schools, 41*, 443–450.

ANNOTATED BIBLIOGRAPHY

Lopez, E. C. (2000). Conducting instructional consultation through interpreters. *School Psychology Review, 29*, 378–388.

A qualitative investigation that explores the practice of using interpreters during instructional consultation activities. The findings address the facilitators as well as barriers encountered when using interpreters in consultation.

Lopez, E. C., Elizalde-Utnick, G., & Nahari, S. (2004). Interpreters for parent conferences with culturally and linguistically diverse families. In A. S. Canter, L. Z. Paige, M. D. Roth, I. Romero, & S. A. Caroll (Eds.), *Helping children at home and school II: Handouts from your school psychologist.* Bethesda, MD: National Association of School Psychologists.

Provides a practical handout for school psychologists working with school interpreters during parent conferences.

Lynch, E. W. (2004). Developing cross-cultural competence. In E. W. Lynch & M. J. Hanson (Eds.), *A guide for working with children and their families: Developing cross-cultural competence* (3rd ed., pp. 47–89). Baltimore: Brookes.

Provides guidelines for interventionists working with interpreters. Discusses the characteristics of effective interpreters, cautions in using family and non-family members as interpreters, stress factors for interpreters, and interpreter training guidelines.

Raval, H., & Smith, J. A. (2003). Therapists' experiences of working with language interpreters. *International Journal of Mental Health, 32*(3), 6–31.

A qualitative investigation designed to explore the process of providing mental health services via interpreters. Provides an excellent discussion of process issues and explores many barriers encountered by mental health clinicians focusing on communication, therapeutic style, intervention delivery, and interpreter–clinician relationship issues.

Rhodes, R. L., Ochoa, H. S., & Ortiz, S. O. (2005). *Assessing culturally and linguistically diverse students: A practical guide.* New York: Guilford Press.

Chapter 6 provides a discussion of practice-related issues focused on working with interpreters during assessment situations. Recommendations guide assessors in their work with interpreters. Helpful forms provide basic terms and concepts that often need translation, and criteria for the selection of interpreters.

Tribe, R., & Raval, H. (Eds.). (2003). *Working with interpreters in mental health.* New York: Brunner-Routledge.

Covers a variety of clinical issues that are relevant to school psychologists and other clinicians providing mental health issues. The topics are diverse and vary from general issues in working with interpreters to training, roles and functions, theoretical frameworks, and process issues. Case studies and summaries address multiple scenarios related to working with and via interpreters.

APPENDIX. RECOMMENDED PRACTICES FOR SCHOOL PSYCHOLOGISTS WORKING WITH INTERPRETERS

The following recommendations apply to such activities as interviews, conferences, consultations, and assessment sessions. The recommendations are made with the assumptions that the interpreters have adequate training to work in schools and demonstrate high levels of proficiency in English and the second language. The recommendations are organized following the three phases of working with interpreters: briefing, active, and debriefing.

During Briefing Sessions

- The school psychologist should establish sitting arrangements. Stansfield (1980) recommends that the clinician and the interpreter sit next to each other with the interpreter sitting slightly behind the clinician. According to Stansfield, this sitting arrangement allows the clients to see both the interpreter and the clinician, the client can look at both the clinician and the interpreter to receive verbal and nonverbal messages from both, and the clinician will be in a position of facing and directly talking to the client.

- The school psychologist should provide the interpreter with any information that the interpreter needs to understand the context of the situation. For example, the school psychologist might want to inform the interpreter of any unusual behaviors or verbalizations that may be characteristic of the student based on the diagnostic classification. The interpreter should be provided with an overview of the translation session. The overview includes a description of the activities that should take place such as interviews, discussions, and questions. The interpreter should also be appraised of the purpose of the translation session (i.e., to obtain information about the student's developmental background, to provide parents with feedback regarding the student's functioning).
- The school psychologist should discuss issues relevant to professional practices, address issues related to confidentiality, and describe boundaries of confidentiality.
- The school psychologist should make decisions about the practices that will be used during the translation sessions. The school psychologist should decide what type of oral translation will be used. Since the translation research supports the use of translation styles that provide frequent breaks for the interpreter to deliver messages with fewer translation errors, discontinuous consecutive translations may be most appropriate for school settings. Fradd and Wilen (1990) suggest developing an agenda to follow during the translation session. The agenda should list all the issues that will be covered during the session. The agenda should be reviewed by the school psychologist and the interpreter during the debriefing session. The school psychologist should discuss with the interpreter the expectation that everything will be translated to the client and that the interpreter should translate all communication from the client.
- The school psychologist should discuss technical terms that will be used during the session (i.e., diagnostic categories, special education terms, psychological terms) and encourage the interpreter to ask questions about any vocabulary or concepts that he or she needs more information about.
- The school psychologist should provide the interpreter with the opportunity to examine and translate any documents that may need translation during the session (i.e., IEP, letters).

- The school psychologist should discuss cross-cultural issues form the perspective of communication and behaviors. For example, the school psychologist may want to greet cross-culturally different families in ways that are culturally appropriate.
- The interpreter should review all assessment materials and should have the opportunity to ask questions relevant to the assessment materials prior to the assessment session if the appropriate tools are available. The school psychologist should also review with the interpreter concepts related to standardization, validity, reliability, and conduct during assessment sessions (e.g., do not coax students).

During Sessions When Interpreters Are Being Used

- The school psychologist should take time to establish rapport with the client. The interpreter should introduce himself or herself, the school psychologist, and any other school professional present during the session. If sitting arrangements have been predetermined, the school psychologist should be specific as to where everyone should sit. The school psychologist should speak directly to the client and direct attention to the client when the client is speaking. Avoid the ping-pong effect of darting eyes and attention back and forth from the client to the interpreter.
- Figueroa (1989) recommends the use of audiotapes during translation sessions. The audiotapes can provide the school psychologist and the interpreter with opportunities to review the session at a later point. If audiotapes are used, the school psychologist must obtain permission from parents and other participants. The permission should be obtained in writing. The decision to use audiotapes must be made taking into consideration that the presence of tape recorders may inhibit clients to discuss sensitive or confidential issues.
- The school psychologist should speak in short sentences and allow time for the interpreter to translate everything said during the session. The school psychologist should communicate to the client that he or she needs to stop periodically to allow the interpreter to translate the messages. The interpreter should be ready to ask the client to slow down or to speak in short sentences if the rate of speech is too fast

or if the client is not stopping frequently enough to allow the interpreter to translate the messages. In situations where the interpreter and the client become involved in long discussions, the school psychologist should be ready to interrupt the discussion to remind the interpreter and the client that all communications must be translated. Avoid idioms, slang, and metaphors because they are difficult to translate.

- The school psychologist and the interpreter should take notes relevant to any issues that need to be discussed during debriefing; for example, terms that were difficult to translate or cross-cultural issues relevant to communication.
- The school psychologist, during conferences and interview sessions, should periodically ask the client questions to establish that they understand the content of the communication. Asking clarifying questions is helpful in situations where information was lost as a result of the translation. The school psychologist should provide information more than once and review information if necessary to make sure that messages are clearly understood (Cushing, 2003). The school psychologist can check on the quality of the translation by asking the interpreter to back-translate the communication so that misunderstandings can be identified and clarified (Haffner, 1992). The ELL student and parents can also be asked to review the information to ascertain that it has been understood or can be asked about how they feel about the information or issue discussed as a way to monitor for understanding (Cushing, 2003).
- The school psychologist should carefully observe verbal as well as nonverbal interactions and discuss them during the debriefing session.

During Debriefing Sessions

- The school psychologist should discuss with the interpreter the outcomes of the translation session. In addition, the school psychologist should discuss any translation problems that may have surfaced during the session and their implications.

- The school psychologist should, after translation sessions, discuss with the interpreter cross-cultural issues relevant to the student's and parents' responses and behaviors.
- The school psychologist should encourage the interpreter to ask questions regarding the translation session. The school psychologist can also encourage the interpreter to discuss the interpreter's perceptions of the translation session and the cultural issues that surfaced during the session.
- The school psychologist should revisit issues or concerns during the session (e.g., observations of the client's nonverbal behaviors, situations during interviews that seemed to cause discomfort, discussions that led to positive outcomes) and explore shared understanding of the situation within the context of cultural specific issues (e.g., framework used fit a culturally responsive approach).
- The school psychologist should identify ways in which the interview, meeting, or assessment session could have been improved or changed within the contexts of culturally responsiveness and translation of communication (Cushing, 2003). In other words, learn from the experience. The school psychologist should discuss strategies with the interpreter to communicate more effectively during future meetings and sessions.

Evaluating the Process

- The school psychologist should evaluate the data that were obtained via the interpreter by taking into consideration the following issues: quality of the translation, relational and social aspects, cultural responsiveness, language differences, professional and situational context, and practice context (see Figure 1).
- The school psychologist should consider a variety of options in decision making including seeking additional contact with the student and/or family, working with a different interpreter during future contacts, obtaining additional data, or finding different means by which to obtain information (e.g., bilingual school psychologist).

111 Best Practices in Multicultural Counseling

Janine Jones
University of Washington

OVERVIEW

Serving children in schools is a noble, challenging, and important responsibility. School psychologists are trained to serve a wide range of children both with and without disabilities. They are trained to assess, counsel, and consult with other professionals regarding a variety of needs for children in schools and are also expected to serve all children, including children who come from a range of cultural and ethnic backgrounds.

The demographics of the United States are changing each year with increased proportions of people of color (e.g. race, ethnicity, and cultural differences). As the demographics have changed, the demographic of school psychologists, unfortunately, has not adapted to follow this trend.

According to the 2004–2005 National Association of School Psychologists (NASP) membership survey, 93 percent of school psychologists are White/Caucasian, 3% are Hispanic/Latino, 2% are Black/African American, and less than 1% are Asian American/Pacific Islander or American Indian/Alaskan Native (Curtis, Lopez, Batsche, & Smith, 2006), a disparity that is clear when, according to the 2000 U.S. census, we see that only 71% of U.S. citizens are White/Caucasian while 13% are Hispanic/Latino, 12% are Black/African American, 4% Asian/American-Pacific Islander, and 1% American Indian/Alaskan Native.

This pattern has existed for some time. For instance, Loe and Miranda (2005) conducted a study of ethnic incongruence using a sample of school psychologists in 1999. They found that 94% of school psychologists within their sample self-identified as Caucasian.

With this level of ethnic incongruence between school psychologists and children in schools, training in multicultural service delivery is necessary. To address this disparity, multicultural training continues to be one of the areas to be improved in most training programs (Loe & Miranda, 2005).

This chapter offers guidelines for school psychologists to provide multicultural counseling for children in schools. We will use documents from both NASP and the American Psychological Association (APA), which have developed ethical and professional practice standards to guide the practice of psychology, including how to serve students and families from diverse linguistic, cultural, racial, and social backgrounds. We will also use the expansive literature on counseling children and adolescents from culturally different backgrounds.

The focus of this chapter is to address the skills necessary for the school psychology professional to counsel such children. The skills include basic counseling skills (microskills), intrapersonal awareness, cultural competence/interpersonal awareness, cultural literacy, and multicultural intentionality. The application of the concepts within the chapter is presented in three levels: universal level, group level, and individual level. (These three levels parallel the three-tier model presented by Tilly, chapter 2, vol. 1.)

Although the emphasis of the chapter is on service delivery to multicultural populations, school psychologists will find that having the skills necessary for success with multicultural groups will also enhance their ability to serve all children. Thus, this chapter has relevance to the everyday professional lives of school psychologists.

BASIC CONSIDERATIONS

Culture

According to Banks and McGee Banks (2004), culture includes shared ideas, symbols, values, and beliefs

1771

between members of a group. It can encompass any of the following categories: race, socioeconomic status, language, ethnicity, disability, sexual orientation, and religious/spiritual identity. Culture affects everything we think, do, and feel in a given day; therefore, culture is the lens through which we view the world. Cultural worldview is a term to describe expressions of commonality among a group of individuals who share a common concept of reality (Jenkins, 2006).

School psychologists are faced with the challenge of not only understanding their own cultural worldview as it affects professional relationships and decisions, but also how the cultural worldview of the client affects how the client copes with stress. Thus, not only should school psychologists remain aware of their own cultural worldview, but, even more important, they should also have awareness and sensitivity to the cultural worldview of their clients. When school psychologists serve children and adolescents, they must understand that the cultural worldview of children and adolescents is formative and heavily influenced by the socialization provided by their parents. Consequently, school psychologists cannot serve children and adolescents in isolation, and nor can they see all children and adolescents as the same.

School psychologists fulfill a variety of roles including assessment provider, consultant to educational staff and parents, and provider of mental health counseling for students in need. Given the diverse nature of the histories and family context that students bring to the counseling relationship, school psychologists must be open and prepared for differences in worldview from their own.

The term *multicultural* applies to "a confluence of three or more coexisting and unintegrated cultures (e.g., those that differ by age, gender, race, ethnicity, social class, or sexual orientation) each of which displays patterns of human behavior" (Oakland, 2005, p 6). Behavior is guided by thinking and feeling, and the intergenerational transmission of the cultural worldview sustains it. Sue and Sue (2003) affirmed that in multiculturalism behavior can only be understood within the context that the behaviors exist. It honors human variation between and within groups; therefore, the term multicultural shall be used throughout this chapter to represent the potential incongruence between the multidimensional cultures of the client and the school psychologist as well the interaction of the cultures in the therapeutic process.

Training and Preparation

School psychologist expertise begins with their graduate-level training. They are trained to provide a range of services including psychological and educational assessment, consultation to staff and families, as well as counseling children. In a more traditional model of school psychology practice, there has historically been heavier emphasis on psychological assessment as the primary mode of service delivery. Given this history, the research literature has focused more on assessment and less on counseling competence of school psychologists. Regardless, counseling and crisis intervention are an important part of the profession and warrant attention.

Counseling Competence

In order to develop school psychologists who are competent in counseling, training programs include coursework that cover child psychopathology, child development, emotional and behavioral assessment and intervention, multicultural issues, and formal practica in counseling. Through these experiences, trainees develop a professional interpersonal awareness that is grounded in theory (i.e., theoretical orientation). Trainees learn empirically supported treatment approaches in the context of psychopathology and disorders and how to manage behaviors through communication and behavior modification techniques. In most counseling courses, the theoretical orientation that forms is based on a universal approach to counseling. Typically, in separate coursework, trainees begin to learn about cultural competence and are expected to integrate issues of culture into their current level of understanding within the newly developed theoretical orientation.

Cultural Competence

Cultural competence, on the other hand, is formed through specific training experiences that emphasize cultural self-awareness as well as multicultural experiences with clients and peers. According to Lynch and Hanson (2004), cultural competence is a process and includes the ability to "think, feel, and act in ways that acknowledge, respect, and build on ethnic, sociocultural, and linguistic diversity" (p. 43). Cultural competence includes intrapersonal awareness, or understanding one's own personal worldview, as well as awareness and sensitivity to the worldview of others. Training programs must provide experiences for trainees to evaluate themselves, develop an understanding of their cultural lens, learn more about the worldview of others, and develop an ability to integrate individual differences into their cultural worldview (Constantine, 2002; Pedersen & Carey, 2003; Reynolds, 1999; Sue & Sue, 2003).

Standards of Practice

APA, the Association for Multicultural Counseling and Development, and NASP have developed standards of practice to assist practitioners in providing the highest quality of services to clients. APA's set of guidelines specifically focuses on multicultural practice standards in education, training, research and practice (APA, 2002). Table 1 summarizes the six standards developed by APA.

Similarly, the Association for Multicultural Counseling and Development developed a basic set of multicultural competencies (Sue, Arredondo, & McDavis, 1992). The goals of the competencies are to address three areas: cultural self awareness, awareness of the worldview of the client, and developing culturally appropriate intervention strategies. Arredondo and Arcinega (2001) offer strategies for training counselors using these competencies.

NASP adopted six domains of culturally competent service delivery that include guidelines on legal and ethical issues, school culture, assessment and intervention, working with interpreters, and research (Rogers et al., 1999).

All of these standards are designed to cover the breadth of services provided by psychologists and school psychologists. To assist with the implementation of the standards of practice, NASP has a wide range of resources to assist practicing school psychologists in moving toward culturally competent practice. There are a variety of downloadable papers and presentations on NASP's website (www.nasponline.org) that cover topics such as cultural competence in crisis response, trauma, consultation, and assessment.

In addition to guiding practitioners in serving multicultural populations, NASP acknowledges the need to increase the diversity among practicing school psychologists. As mentioned previously, school psychologists of color are underrepresented in comparison to the population served. Therefore, NASP attempts to bridge the gap by addressing minority recruitment in a position paper as well as operating a scholarship program for students of color. The NASP-ERT Minority Scholarship Program has the goal of promoting diversity in the profession and enriching the school community. In addition, there are NASP committees and task forces that are devoted to the mission of diversifying the profession and addressing cultural issues within the school psychology service community. These include the Multicultural Affairs Committee, Minority Recruitment and Retention Task Force, Native American Task Force, and the NASP Multicultural Listserv. All of these efforts demonstrate a commitment to multiculturalism in school psychology service delivery. With the emphasis at the organizational level, it is the onus of the practitioner to access these resources and integrate the resources into everyday practice.

School Psychology: A Blueprint for Training and Practice III (Ysseldyke et al., 2006) outlines eight domains of competence that training programs must address in order to maintain program approval. One of the foundational competencies is diversity awareness and sensitive service delivery, which addresses the importance of developing the ability to recognize how issues of racial, ethnic, cultural, and linguistic differences manifest in the school community setting. According to *Blueprint III*, recognition of these issues, along with knowledge and skills for serving multicultural populations lead to effective intervention at all levels. The

Table 1. Summary of APA Guidelines on Multicultural Education, Training, Research, Practice, and Organizational Change for Psychologists

Guideline	Description
1	Psychologists are encouraged to recognize that, as cultural beings, they may hold attitudes and beliefs that can detrimentally influence their perceptions of and interactions with individuals who are ethnically and racially different from themselves.
2	Psychologists are encouraged to recognize the importance of multicultural sensitivity/responsiveness, knowledge, and understanding about ethnically and racially different individuals.
3	As educators, psychologists are encouraged to employ the constructs of multiculturalism and diversity in psychological education.
4	Culturally sensitive psychological researchers are encouraged to recognize the importance of conducting culture-centered and ethical psychological research among persons from ethnic, linguistic, and racial minority backgrounds.
5	Psychologists strive to apply culturally appropriate skills in clinical and other applied psychological practices.
6	Psychologists are encouraged to use organizational change processes to support culturally informed organizational (policy) development and practices.

Blueprint III conceptualization emphasizes that diversity is integrated and crosses over to the other domains of competence (Ysseldyke et al. 2006).

BEST PRACTICES

As presented in Tilly (chapter 2, vol. 1), the newest iteration of science-based practice in schools is a three-tiered model of service delivery. The three-tiered model should not only be used in curriculum and instruction but also in the application of academic and emotional interventions. In this chapter, we apply the three-tiered model to counseling intervention when serving multicultural populations.

Tier 1: Universal Approaches

Within the first tier are the universal approaches to counseling practice that school psychologists typically learn as trainees and beginning practitioners. This is the stage of primary prevention where school psychologists seek to reduce incidence of new referrals for behavior problems, emotional symptoms, or social impairments. The skills within this tier are applicable to all children with or without significant emotional impairment. Services may include social skills groups, mental health education groups, as well as parent, staff, and teacher training.

Microskills
Basic counseling skills, also referred to as microskills (Ivey, Pedersen, & Ivey, 2001; Corey, 2000), are the foundation for counseling practice. Microskills include using attending skills and influencing skills as well as the integration of the microskills into a particular theoretical orientation. Attending skills involve the use of open-ended questions, paraphrasing, encouraging, reflection of feeling, and summarization. These skills facilitate the development of a positive rapport (or relationship) between the school psychologist and the client. Influencing skills involve more advanced listening techniques including reframing, being directive, giving feedback, applying logical consequences, and knowing when to therapeutically use self-disclosure.

Cultural Self-Awareness
As mentioned previously, self-awareness is one of the initial components of developing cross-cultural competence. This self-awareness influences the school psychologist's ability to work with any child. Monitoring intrapersonal cultural awareness is an ongoing process

and requires intentional thinking (Reynolds, 1999). Sue and Sue (2003) indicate the importance of being aware of assumptions, values, and biases toward others. These biases can be related to race, ethnicity, socioeconomic status, family status, or any other human related context. *Blueprint III* echoes the necessity of self-evaluation: "These potential biases … will significantly affect the manner in which decisions are made, instruction is developed, behavior is evaluated, interventions are designed, and outcomes are influenced" (Ysseldyke et al., p. 16).

Every individual has some form of bias, and those who are aware of their biases are the most skilled at serving the public. School psychologists may develop in this area by using journaling as a technique for self-reflection, and the journal might include thoughts about individuals and personal reactions toward such individuals that may affect counseling skills and interventions. Another approach is to form multicultural consulting groups (workgroups, consultation meetings, or even ongoing dialogue through listserv communication) with colleagues to engage in regular dialogue about multicultural issues in counseling. At a minimum, psychologists should develop a list of professionals they may contact for consultation on multicultural issues. One example of a multicultural consulting interaction is a special populations consultation. In the state of Washington, all mental health providers in community agencies are required to request such consultations when they serve ethnic minority individuals and families. These consultations occur with professionals who have achieved training and experience working with specific ethnic minority groups in order to qualify for a Washington State Ethnic Minority Specialist credential. The consultation includes discussion about cultural factors that may influence treatment, and revisions to the treatment plan are sometimes necessary.

Other structured approaches to self-awareness analysis are also available. Several scales were developed to assist school psychologists in evaluating their level of self-awareness. Rogers and Ponterotto (1997) developed a scale for school psychologist training programs to evaluate the graduate's competence. This scale, the Multicultural School Psychology Counseling Competency Scale, consists of 11 items with broad questions to assess various levels of proficiency in self awareness, other awareness, comfort with racial differences, understanding the sociopolitical consequences of minority status, and communication styles. Although the scale was designed for use by training programs, school psychologists may also review the questions and rate themselves on the same domains. Even more pertinent to school psychology practitioners is the self assessment checklist adopted by NASP. The Self-Assessment Checklist for Personnel Providing Services and Supports to Children and their Families (Goode, 2002), includes 33 questions that provoke cognitive awareness of the values and practices that foster an environment for culturally competent practice. The checklist includes items in the following domains: physical environment, materials, and resources; communication styles; and values and attitudes. This checklist is particularly unique because it also includes attention to the nonverbal and environmental cues that school psychologists convey in their office. For example, a statement on the checklist might encourage a school psychologist to consider whether their office environment is reflective of different cultures (particularly those members of cultures who attend the school). Similarly, items remind the school psychologists to consider whether the counseling tools that are used (e.g. storybooks, games, puppets, dolls) are reflective of the ethnic background of the children and families served (Gil & Drewes, 2005).

These basic standards set the stage for a school psychologist to continue along the process of developing multicultural competence. Tier 2 includes more advanced skills and intentional thinking as school psychologists work in multicultural situations.

Tier 2: Group-Level Approaches

The second tier of the three-tier model includes specific group-level approaches to serving children in schools. The goal is to diagnose and treat problems early in the formation or to interrupt a cycle of preexisting problematic behavior, emotional symptoms, or social function impairments. School psychologists working at this level have the ability to identify risk and protective factors for particular cultural groups and have awareness of common cultural norms for a particular population such as religious beliefs or traditional practices. Ivey, DiAndrea, Bradford Ivey, and Simek-Morgan (2002) developed a theory of multicultural counseling and therapy, which includes an integrative perspective of theoretical orientations where the focus is on the individual in the context of family as well as culture. The individual is seen as part of a system where the psychologist should assess the combined influences of society, social justice, race, ethnicity, gender, and other cultural factors.

Cultural Literacy

Sue and Sue (2003) stress the importance of increasing cultural literacy, which includes learning more about specific norms within a culture so that school psychologists may develop a better understanding of the worldview of culturally diverse clients. As in Tier 1, cultural self-awareness analysis continues, but now the awareness is also in the context of other groups. For example, the psychologist might ask, "How are my beliefs affecting my relationship with _____?" "I have never known anyone of _____ ethnicity (the ethnicity of a new referral). How will I address my lack of cultural literacy about this group?" Sue and Sue (2003) and Paniagua (2005) both provide chapters to assist readers in increasing cultural literacy for African Americans, Native Americans, Asian Americans, and Hispanic Americans.

Communication style is a form of cultural literacy. Psychologists should be aware of the communication style of the client as well as the potential of a mismatch with their own communication style. Cultural literacy also includes staying current in the literature so that the political and social dynamics that affect the cultural norms within a particular group can be understood (Canino & Spurlock, 2000). Psychologists should be aware of appropriate language to use when referencing a group (e.g., African American versus Negro or colored). Similarly, identifying a person by referencing their skin color (e.g., Black or White) may be offensive to some and preferred by another.

Cultural literacy also includes developing understanding of the historical experiences that affect the worldview of the client's group. Greater awareness of the social, political, and historical challenges that fall in line with group membership increases the school psychologist's ability to understand the cultural worldview of the child and the family. Similarly, gaining understanding about the child's cultural literacy (e.g. the connection between cultural identity development and the child's awareness of how multicultural issues affect his or her life) is also essential. Developmentally younger children may not recognize the connection between treatment of other children and racism and prejudice to the same degree as a latency-age child or adolescent. Thus, practitioners who expect a child to articulate the connection during the rapport-building phase may overlook the true impact of multicultural issues with that particular child. Students in training may state, "Cultural issues are really not an issue for this child. The child said he or she doesn't think it makes a difference." However, this conclusion may better reflect the trainee's desire to avoid discussing issues of oppression and racism. It is important to note that children are socialized to believe that matching with dominant society is desirable and differences are not necessarily celebrated. Therefore, the child is more likely to adopt a preferred orientation of sameness and, in the absence of a strong rapport, will minimize the impact of culture to the novice school psychologist.

By increasing cultural literacy about a particular cultural group, school psychologists may gain insight into the child and family views toward counseling and therapy. They will also learn about common approaches to healing that are considered the first stop for getting help within the cultural group. Gaining an understanding about culturally acceptable forms of assistance, the school psychologist can also learn the expectations of the child and family. Further, increasing cultural literacy enables the school psychologist to recognize that some common theories of psychotherapy have historically reflected a host of biased values and beliefs that are not universal. There are culture-bound syndromes identified in the *Diagnostic and Statistical Manual of Mental Disorders* (4th edition, text revision; American Psychiatric Association, 2000) that should be considered as differential diagnoses. For example, *amok* is a dissociative episode common to Malaysia while *ataque de nervios* is an idiom of distress that is recognized by Latin Americans. By overlooking the fact that culture-bound syndromes exist, the school psychologist is less likely to develop a strong working rapport with the child and family because the school psychologist is unable to understand the family's interpretation of the symptoms. Thus, increasing cultural literacy is a key component to providing mental health services to multicultural populations. School psychologists who provide counseling services at this level are also considered to have developed a practice of "multicultural intentionality" (Ivey et al., 2002).

Multicultural Intentionality

School psychologists with multicultural intentionality have the ability to generate alterative approaches to a problem from different points of view. They are also able to communicate by looking at the child through a cultural lens, taking into account a variety of diverse groups as well as the complex interaction of the child's culture and their own. Both child and the school psychologist must have the opportunity to communicate within their own culture and learn how to understand other cultures (Ivey et al., 2002). School psychologists with multicultural intentionality can

also formulate plans that consider a range of options that exist within a culture and act upon those options. For example, when a child or adolescent becomes stuck in a pattern of the same behavior and responses to situations, the school psychologist with multicultural intentionality is able to consider the cultural worldview of the child that influences the behavior and then develop plans that may be effective within the context of the cultural worldview. Psychologists with multicultural intentionality will be aware of the trends and have the ability to explore these issues in an intentional clinical interview (Ivey et al., 2002).

Intentional Clinical Interviews

While there are countless options available for clinicians to use for collecting background information on clients, few offer the ability to collect information within the context of cultural mores and values. As a result, some techniques have been developed that are designed to assist practitioners in altering their clinical interviews to be more inclusive of culture.

Hardy and Laszloffy (1995) developed an approach to creating a "cultural genogram." The traditional genogram (McGoldrick, Gerson, & Shellenberger, 1999) development process is enhanced by 20 questions that assist the psychologist in gathering information about cultural issues. For example, "Under what conditions did your family/ancestors enter the United States?" "What has been your experience with racism and oppression and how does your family respond to it?" Similarly, Ivey et al. (2002) developed a technique of completing a "community genogram" as a strengths-oriented approach to viewing the self within the context of the community. This genogram assists the clinician in identifying the important groups that influence the everyday lives of the individual. The goal of the community genogram is similar to the traditional genogram in that it provides a visual image of the child within the family system. However, the community genogram adds the dimension of community relationships (church, school, neighborhood) and encourages the discussion of how the community influences the everyday decisions of the child and family. The graphic representation of the genogram is less structured and uses symbols generated by the child or family and encourages both to organize the relationships on the page as they feel appropriate. The goal is for the child and the psychologist to see the child and family in context. Consequently, this approach encourages open discussion about multicultural issues.

Another approach to conducting intentional interviews is using the RESPECTFUL model (Ivey, Pedersen, & Ivey, 2001). RESPECTFUL is an acronym for the dimensions that may relate to issues presented by clients in multicultural therapy. The multicultural issues represented in the acronym are religion/spirituality, economic class, sexual identity, psychological maturity, ethnic/racial identity, chronological challenges, trauma, family history, unique physical characteristics, language, and location of residence. This model encourages the exploration of these potential multicultural issues in the context of locus of control and level of cultural identity development.

Tier 3: Individual Level

The third tier of the model involves assessment and intervention at the individual level. This tier requires school psychologists to analyze and customize treatment while taking into account within-group variation and individuation. The emphasis is on improving daily functioning in the presence of a disability or significant emotional or behavioral impairment. School psychologists continue applying the skills used in Tiers 1 and 2 while integrating the ability to analyze within group differences and the individuality of the child. Tier 3 services are high intensity and also require the greatest level of clinical skills. The services are primarily for the highest need students where Tier 1 and 2 interventions were insufficient to improve functioning. Mental health interventions may include frequent (e.g., once or twice per week) individual therapy sessions, participation in a therapeutic group, and family collaboration with interventions. When working with a child or adolescent in a multicultural counseling situation, success is more likely to be associated with those school psychologists who have multicultural self-awareness and multicultural intentionality and who make significant efforts toward gaining multicultural expertise.

Multicultural Expertise

Clinicians with multicultural expertise have the ability to work with clients through a cultural frame of reference, to recognize the complexity of multicultural counseling, and to incorporate individual differences within the treatment planning. These clinicians continue the self-awareness process and practice with multicultural intentionality. Advanced skills develop over time as the Tier 1 and Tier 2 interventions become standard aspects of treatment. Multicultural expertise consists of a strengths-based focus on the client and ongoing dialogue

about the impact of cultural issues. Suggested approaches for obtaining multicultural expertise include conducting intentional multicultural interviews and involving the family in treatment planning and crisis intervention.

Intentional Multicultural Interviews

The initial clinical interview sets the stage for rapport building and future treatment planning. Too often mental health professionals jump directly into problem solving instead of taking a thorough history and learning more about the underlying perspectives of the child/adolescent and the family. While there are a variety of published structured clinical interviews, the interview questions typically have little emphasis on culture and systems level connections to worldview of the client. Jones developed the questions that appear in Table 2 (1999) as a means of facilitating discussion of cultural issues as they relate to stress and coping with children and adolescents.

The first category of questions addresses the family dynamics. The questions give the psychologist the opportunity to gather background information about the family unit that is deeper than basic demographics. Using these questions along with a community genogram or cultural genogram allow for collection of family-related information in the cultural context.

Questions about peer relationships are strategically placed after the family questions because the child or adolescent has just been primed to think from the perspective of family beliefs and relationships. Peer relations questions include both inquiries about support and conflict within the social network. When asking the questions about race, it is essential that the psychologist has a great sense of self-awareness and cultural literacy. The topics of race, racism, and oppression are frequently considered taboo in society. However, in multicultural counseling and therapy, these discussions are vital to the therapeutic process. Therefore, psychologists should be prepared for an open dialogue that will be revisited in numerous sessions and not just during the rapport-building stage. A psychologist with multicultural expertise sets the tone for open discussions on race and racial dynamics, and in future sessions these discussions will occur naturally as part of the treatment process.

The section on ethnicity includes questions that provide insight into values and norms within the child or adolescent's culture. The final section includes items that address the coping skills and communication style of the child and family.

Table 2. Multicultural Interview With Children and Adolescents

Domain	Questions
Family	• What do your family members call you (e.g., formal name, nickname)?
	• What name would you prefer for me to call you in front of your parents? In counseling sessions?
	• How do you define family? Who is in your family?
	• How and when did your family arrive in the United States? What were the circumstances of your family's arrival?
	• Where were you born? Where does most of your family live now?
	• Who makes decisions about your daily care (e.g., transportation, food, discipline)?
	• Who do you turn to when you are scared, sad, or worried about something?
	• When something bad happens what does your family do?
	• If you were to choose a job today, what would it be? Would your family approve of this job? Why or why not? What would your family prefer for you to do when you grow up? What is a job you would like to do but would never choose it? Why?
	• Describe the communication style of your family.
	• How does your family deal with feelings?
	• What does your family think about counseling? What do you think about it?
	• What are some things about your family that few people know?
Peers	• Who are your friends?
	• What are similar characteristics in all of your friends?
	• When there is conflict with peers at school, what is the usual cause?
	• Who supports you the most at school?
Race	• How do you identify yourself in terms of your race?
	• If you are multiracial, with which group to you identify the most?
	• How does your race affect your relationships with other people?
	• How does your race affect your performance at school?
	• What issues do you have with hair and/or skin color?
	• What experiences do you have with racial conflict?
Ethnicity	• What is your religious affiliation?
	• What church/mosque/synagogue does your family attend?
	• How does religion and spirituality affect your family everyday?
	• What do you believe are the responsibilities of women? Men?
	• What are some of the differences in how you relate to elderly family members?
	• What are some of the rules about your behavior in your house?
Personal	• What are your greatest strengths? Weaknesses?
	• When you are stressed or upset, how do you show it?
	• What situations are the most stressful for you?
	• What makes you angry? Happy? Sad? Afraid?
	• How do you help yourself feel better when you have _____ feelings ?

Note. Source: Jones (1999).

Although the questions are presented in a table format, it is not intended to be a structured one-session clinical interview. The intentional multicultural interview is to occur with psychologists who have well-developed self-awareness, cultural literacy, and multicultural intentionality. School psychologists at this level, with multicultural expertise, should add follow-up questions and move freely between the domains. Additionally, questions may be repeatedly addressed, particularly when coping skills increase or other contextual changes occur. The interview occurs with the child or adolescent and adapted questions are asked of the family. Thus, family involvement is another method of building multicultural expertise.

Family Involvement

Involving the family in the therapeutic process is often difficult when providing services in the school setting. If family members are not easily accessible, school psychologists are forced to collect information from the student's file and directly from the student once parent consent is obtained. Because services are provided in the school setting, it is not uncommon for school psychologists to offer individual therapy to students and have little or no involvement of the parents. This is not the best practice when providing multicultural counseling services.

Integrating the family into the treatment process is necessary to foster systemic change in the child or adolescent. At least one family member should be active in the process of determining needs, developing a treatment plan, and implementing interventions at home. If family members are perceived as necessary collaborators in the process, significant efforts are more likely to be made to foster involvement in the treatment process. School psychologists need to have a broad perspective and use creativity to make treatment planning accessible to the family. Creative approaches to involving the family include being open to home visits, evening phone calls, e-mail, and lunch meetings. Including family as collaborators in the process will also enhance the psychologists ability to support specific family needs rather than taking a general approach to counseling.

The questions from the intentional multicultural interview may be adapted to suit the adult members of the family. For example, "What is the best way to communicate with your family? How does your child communicate needs and feelings at home? What is the best way to make your child feel comfortable? What are your child's strengths? What are your concerns for your child? What are some of the factors that affect your child's learning and/or ability to get along with peers? How do issues of race affect your family?" Following this line of questioning will foster a relationship with the parent that reflects recognition that the influence of the child's culture and immediate environment are important aspects of treatment.

Strengths Perspective

School psychologists with multicultural expertise think from a strengths perspective rather than solely diagnosis. School psychologists are typically trained and socialized to find the problem, diagnose the problem, and treat the problem. Where interventions often fall short in multicultural counseling is when clinicians follow a Eurocentric paradigm for treatment. For example, some clinicians rigidly adhere to separating church and state when serving children in schools. When serving many families of color, the clinician may overlook the fact that spirituality and faith may be a primary source of support for that family and child. By learning about and exploring the strengths within a given culture, school psychologists are more prepared to serve children and families within the cultural framework. By using intentional multicultural interviews and other multicultural techniques, the school psychologist learns what supports are currently working, who is involved with providing support, and how to facilitate growth within the culture and the support network.

Crisis Intervention

By developing multicultural counseling and therapy skills, school psychologists are better equipped to respond to crises with multicultural populations. When increasing cultural literacy, psychologists will have general awareness of cultural perspectives on diagnoses as well as suicidal behavior. By conducting intentional multicultural clinical interviews, the psychologist will also be able to assess individual differences and formulate a treatment plan that is appropriate for that individual and the attached family system. Within a given ethnic group, there is individuation. In situations of suicidal thoughts and behavior, some parent responses may include denial of the meaning of the child's suicidal gestures. For example, the parent may perceive a suicidal statement as attention seeking rather than a true indication of the child's emotional state. Other families may be alarmed by the thought their child may consider suicide given the family's religious orientation. Simply creating a protection plan for the child without exploring the family worldview in context of the crisis may constitute a serious oversight on the part of the school psychologist.

Three-Tier Model for Multicultural Counseling and Therapy

Figure 1 is a graphic representation of the concepts presented in this chapter. It is presented as a pyramid shape to demonstrate the simultaneous interaction of the psychologist and the client variables.

As psychologists move up the pyramid, they demonstrate increasing levels of competence. As the client factors move up the pyramid, there are increasing levels of individuation that need to be addressed by psychologists. The bottom section of the pyramid includes Tier 1 interventions, the foundation for multicultural service delivery. For the psychologist, multicultural self-awareness is the entry level for developing multicultural skills. At this level, psychologists are becoming self-aware of multicultural issues while the client is imbedded in the culture and values of the family. The culture of the client may include easily recognizable characteristics as well as obscure ones. Psychologists who are self-aware yet conduct traditional clinical interviews and rating scales remain at the Tier 1 level of service delivery.

Moving up the pyramid, psychologists are becoming more intentional in multicultural service delivery. At Tier 2 they have increased cultural literacy about specific cultural groups and conduct intentional clinical

Figure 1. Three-tier model for multicultural counseling.

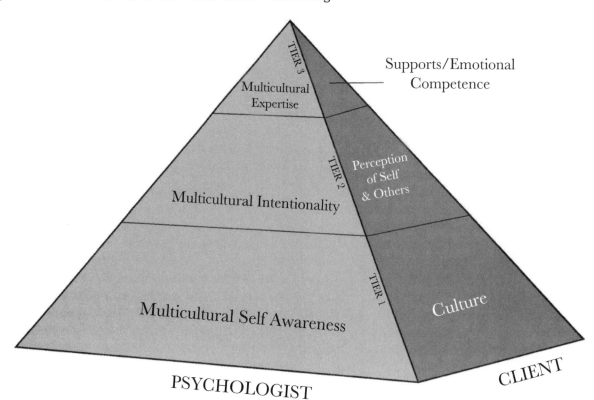

interviews with all clients. Psychologists with skills at this level act with multicultural intentionality and can generate alternative approaches to a problem through the lens of the client. They consider client characteristics such as the client's level of cultural literacy and cultural perceptions including the client's perception of himself or herself and of others.

At Tier 3 psychologists are demonstrating the highest level of skill in multicultural counseling, or multicultural expertise. Psychologists not only have self-awareness, cultural literacy, and multicultural intentionality, but they also have the ability to integrate individuation in therapeutic interventions. Psychologists at this level have the ability to work within the context of culture and integrate individual differences. Psychologists with multicultural expertise invite discussion about culturally related stressors as a context for the therapeutic process. Open dialogue about the issues allow for exploration of the client's individual differences in the cultural context. The psychologist is able to assess the client by gaining information about the client's emotional competence and culturally related strengths. As a result, treatment interventions are formulated specifically within the context of the culture and individual needs of the client.

Demonstration of the Three-Tier Model in Action

Lorena is a 14-year-old student in the eighth grade. She was referred to the school psychologist for counseling by her teachers because she has begun to lose focus in class (which was described as "spacing out"), has unexpected crying spells, and is withdrawing from activities that she normally enjoys. Lorena is cooperative with the teachers and poses no behavior problem. She is willing to participate in counseling, but she is reluctant for the school psychologist to call her parents to obtain permission.

Tier 1 response. The school psychologist reassures Lorena that permission is necessary to begin counseling and discusses with her the rules of confidentiality to try to increase her comfort level with the process. The school psychologist considers the fact that Lorena's parents speak Spanish while Lorena is bilingual. As a result, communication with the parents will not occur easily. Through the use of Lorena as an interpreter, the school psychologist obtains consent and begins the treatment process by using a standard clinical interview, rating scales (completed by the teachers), and observing Lorena's reactions to particular situations.

Tier 2 response. At Tier 2 the school psychologist is aware there may be cultural factors involved in Lorena's reluctance for the involvement of the parents and is also aware of limitations when working with non-English–speaking parents. Before seeking permission from the parents, the school psychologist discusses the potential impact of cultural factors with a professional peer. If the school psychologist is not bilingual, the assistance of an interpreter is sought that will allow the parents to ask questions and communicate more directly with the psychologist. The school psychologist is well aware of common communication styles and culture-bound syndromes for Latinos. An intentional interview using the RESPECTFUL model occurs with both Lorena and her parents, and a treatment plan is designed by the school psychologist and the family.

Tier 3 response. The school psychologist recognizes that Lorena may be having a reaction to a stressor that is manifesting itself in a culture-bound syndrome. Lorena is from Honduras and the referral was made on November 6. The school psychologist is aware that November 2 in Latino Catholic tradition is the Day of the Dead, where religious ceremonies focus on honoring the dead by decorating and visiting graves as well as by installing death altars for loved ones who have passed on. Lorena's reluctance to have the school psychologist communicate with her parents may lie in the fact that she knows her parents would prefer to seek support from an *espiritista*, or spiritist healer. The school psychologist addresses these ideas with Lorena and conducts communication with the parents as the Tier 2 psychologist did. The school psychologist then completes intentional multicultural interviews with both Lorena and her parents. The intentional multicultural interview consists of taking a cultural history and

includes Lorena's parents and the recommended spiritist in the treatment plan. The school psychologist recognizes that culturally related support systems are the foundation for coping, and the counseling interventions should supplement or enhance that context. The subsequent treatment is provided with ongoing collaboration with the family, always keeping the utmost respect for the culture and family norms.

SUMMARY

This chapter presents best practices in multicultural counseling with children and adolescents. School psychologists are overwhelmingly from Eurocentric backgrounds while the demographics of the United States are changing significantly. Multiculturalism is the wave of the future, and training programs must prepare practitioners to serve all children appropriately. Both NASP and APA and other mental health organizations have developed standards of practice to assist clinicians in understanding the factors that go into providing multicultural services, but very little structure is given to the process of engaging in such a relationship.

Using the three-tier model of service delivery, school psychologists will have greater self-awareness, better understanding of the cultural characteristics of groups, and will increase the likelihood of successful mental health support in the context of the client's culture. When the background between the psychologist and the client do not match, greater skill level is required for providing culturally appropriate services. This chapter offers a structure for developing multicultural expertise. Ideas for practitioners to develop better self-awareness, increasing cultural literacy and multicultural intentionality, as well as provide a framework for practicing with multicultural expertise were presented. Table 3

Table 3. Best Practice Tips for Psychologists Conducting Multicultural Counseling

- Continue exploring your own culture, beliefs, and values.
- Believe that you can serve individuals of a different race or ethnicity.
- Develop a list of professionals for consultation on multicultural issues.
- Engage in dialogue with colleagues and continue to increase cultural literacy.
- Complete intentional multicultural interviews.
- Always work with the child/adolescent systemically.
- Learn more about the culture of the child through the child and family.
- Alter your microskills based on the cultural norms and behaviors of the child and family.
- Assume there is heterogeneity within an ethnic group but the foundation of cultural values is likely to be homogenous.
- Have awareness of culture-bound syndromes and the meaning of the behaviors/symptoms to the client and the family.
- Keep the family active in the intervention planning and progress monitoring.
- Work from a strengths perspective.
- Continue exploring multicultural issues throughout the treatment process.
- Always strive for multicultural expertise.

summarizes some of the best practices presented in this chapter.

School psychologists must recognize that increasing competence in multicultural service delivery is a process. The process occurs along with experience and does not end with training in an academic program. Training programs with strong multicultural emphasis may take the psychologist to the level of Tier 3, or the ability to integrate individual cultural differences into the treatment of multicultural clients. However, this skill is honed only through experience with clients from a range of cultures and ethnicities.

REFERENCES

American Psychiatric Association. (2000). *Diagnostic and statistical manual of mental disorders* (4th ed., text rev.). Washington, DC: Author.

Arrendondo, P., & Arciniega, G. M. (2001). Strategies and techniques for counselor training based on the Multicultural Counseling Competencies. *Journal of Multicultural Counseling and Development, 29,* 263–273.

Banks, J. A., & McGee Banks, C. A. (Eds.). (2004). *Multicultural education: Issues and perspectives* (5th ed.). Hoboken, NJ: John Wiley.

Canino, I. A., & Spurlock, J. (2000). *Culturally diverse children and adolescents* (2nd ed.). New York: Guilford Press.

Constantine, M. G. (2002). Racism attitudes, White racial identity attitudes, and multicultural counseling competence in school counselor trainees. *Counselor Education and Supervision, 41,* 162–174.

Corey, G. (2000). *Theory and practice of counseling and psychotherapy* (6th ed.). Belmont, CA: Wadsworth.

Curtis, M. J., Lopez, A. D., Batsche, G. M., & Smith, J. C. (2006, March). *School psychology 2005: A national perspective.* Paper presented at the annual meeting of the National Association of School Psychologists, Anaheim, CA.

Gil, E., & Drewes, A. A. (Eds.). (2005). *Cultural issues in play therapy.* New York: Guilford Press.

Goode, T. D. (2002). *Promoting cultural diversity and cultural competency: Self-assessment checklist for personnel providing services and supports to children and their families.* Retrieved January 4, 2007, from http://www.nasponline.org/culturalcompetence/checklist.html

Hardy, K., & Laszloffy, T. (1995). The cultural genogram: Key to training culturally competent family therapists. *Journal of Marital and Family Therapy, 21,* 227–237.

Ivey, A. E., D'Andrea, M., Bradford Ivey, M., & Simek-Morgan, L. (2002). *Theories of counseling and psychotherapy: A multicultural perspective* (5th ed.). Boston: Allyn & Bacon.

Ivey, A. E., Pedersen, P. B., & Ivey, M. B. (2001). *Intentional Group Counseling: A microskills approach.* Belmont, CA: Brooks/Cole.

Jenkins, O. B. (2006). *What is worldview?* Retrieved January 4, 2007, from http://orvillejenkins.com/worldview/worldvwhat.html

Jones, J. M. (1999). *Multicultural interviews with children and adolescents.* Unpublished manuscript.

Loe, S. A., & Miranda, M. H. (2005). An examination of ethnic incongruence in school-based psychological services and diversity training experiences among school psychologists. *Psychology in the Schools, 42,* 419–432.

Lynch, E. W., & Hanson, M. J. (2004). *Developing cross-cultural competence: A guide for working with children and their families* (3rd ed.). Baltimore: Brookes.

McGoldrick, M., Gerson, R., & Shellenberger, S. (1999). *Genograms: Assessment and intervention* (2nd ed.). New York: Norton.

Oakland, T. (2005). Commentary 1: What is multicultural school psychology? In C. L. Frisby & C. R. Reynolds (Eds.), *Comprehensive handbook of multicultural school psychology* (pp. 3–13). Hoboken, NJ: John Wiley.

Paniagua, F. A. (2005). *Assessing and treating culturally diverse clients: A practical guide* (3rd ed.). Thousand Oaks, CA: SAGE.

Pedersen, P. B., & Carey, J. C. (2003). *Multicultural counseling in the schools: A practical handbook.* Boston: Pearson Education.

Reynolds, A. L. (1999). Working with children and adolescents in the schools: Multicultural counseling implications. In R. H. Sheets & E. R. Hollins (Eds.), *Racial and ethnic identity in school practices: Aspects of human development.* Mahwah, NJ: Erlbaum.

Rogers, M. R., Ingraham, C. L., Bursztyn, A., Cajigas-Segredo, N., Esquivel, G., Hess, R. S., et al. (1999). Best practices in providing psychological services to racially, ethnically, culturally, and linguistically diverse individuals in the schools. *School Psychology International, 20*(3), 243–264.

Rogers, M. R., & Ponterotto, J. G. (1997). Development of the multicultural school psychology counseling competency scale. *Psychology in the Schools, 34*(3), 211–217.

Sue, D., Arredondo, P., & McDavis, R. (1992). Multicultural counseling competencies and standards: A call to the profession. *Journal of Multicultural Counseling and Development, 20,* 64–88.

Sue, D. W., & Sue, D. (2003). *Counseling the culturally diverse: Theory and practice* (4th ed.). Hoboken, NJ: John Wiley.

Ysseldyke, J., Burns, M., Dawson, P., Kelley, B., Morrison, D., Ortiz, S., et al. (2006). *School psychology: A blueprint for training and practice III.* Bethesda, MD: National Association of School Psychologists.

ANNOTATED BIBLIOGRAPHY

Constantine, M. G., & Sue, D. W. (Eds.). (2005). *Strategies for building multicultural competence in mental health and educational settings.* Hoboken, NJ: John Wiley.

A comprehensive guide to applying the APA multicultural guidelines in a range of psychological practice settings. Addresses developing cultural competence when serving individuals schools, counseling centers, independent practice, private organizations, academic training, and research settings. The emphasis is on building competence by offering concrete strategies and case examples.

Frisby, C. L., & Reynolds, C. R. (Eds.). (2005). *Comprehensive handbook of multicultural school psychology*. Hoboken, NJ: John Wiley.

Offers practical information on the integration of culture into research and practice. Includes chapters that are grounded in empirical research and address commentary and dialogue on the definition of multiculturalism, cultural variation within American subgroups, school psychology practice, and training.

Ivey, A. E., D'Andrea, M., Bradford Ivey, M., & Simek-Morgan, L. (2002). *Theories of counseling and psychotherapy: A multicultural perspective* (5th ed.). Boston: Allyn & Bacon.

Provides an integrated presentation of multiculturalism in the context of different counseling theories. Emphasizes development of the clinician beyond the level of self-awareness and increasing cultural literacy. Provides a strong theoretical foundation to assist the clinician in integrating multicultural theory into practice.

Lynch, E. W., & Hanson, M. J. (2004). *Developing cross-cultural competence: A guide for working with children and their families* (3rd ed.). Baltimore: Brookes.

An excellent entry-level text for trainees in school psychology or special education. Assists the reader in increasing cultural literacy by providing extensive detail about history, traditions, family structure, values, beliefs, education, and other cultural factors of nine different cultural groups.

Sue, D. W., & Sue, D. (2003). *Counseling the culturally diverse: Theory and practice* (4th ed.). Hoboken, NJ: John Wiley.

The most cited reference in multicultural counseling and therapy. Utilizes a sound conceptual framework to guide clinicians in counseling interventions in the context of specific cultures. The emphasis is on increasing cultural literacy with a range of cultural groups.

WEB RESOURCES

American Psychological Association's Guidelines on Multicultural Education, Training, Research, Practice, and Organizational Change for Psychologists: www.apa.org/pi/multiculturalguidelines/

Anna's Toy Depot—Multicultural play therapy materials (Dollhouse families): www.annastoydepot.com/merchant2/merchant.mvc? Screen=CTGY&Store_Code=ATD&Category_Code=DFAD

Association of Multicultural Counseling and Development's Multicultural Counseling Competencies Guide: www.bgsu. edu/colleges/edhd/programs/AMCD/ProfStandards.html# Guide

Internet School Library Media Center's Multicultural Resources in Children's Literature: http://falcon.jmu.edu/~ramseyil/multipub. htm

National Association of School Psychologists: www.nasponline.org
- Six Domains of Culturally Competent Service Delivery: htttp://www.nasponline.org/culturalcompetence/sixdomains. html
- Promoting Cultural Diversity and Cultural Competency, Self-Assessment Checklist for Personnel Providing Services and Supports to Children and Their Families: http://www. nasponline.org/culturalcompetence/checklist.html
- NASP-ERT Minority Scholarship Program: htttp://www. nasponline.org/about_nasp/minority.aspx

112

Best Practices in Providing School Psychological Services in Rural Settings

Margaret Beebe-Frankenberger
University of Montana

OVERVIEW

Rural schools are small and are often the cultural heart of the community. Everyone knows everyone else, many teachers have taught the parents of their students, and community services and activities often take place at the school. Rural communities have generational roots that connect everyone with personal histories, and there is a sense of belongingness and support fostered by a small community, factors known to build social and academic competence and resilience in the face of risk factors (Shapiro, 2000). The power of close relationships fostered in rural communities is found in positive attributes of rural schools that support positive academic, social/behavioral, and mental health outcomes. The Community School Reform model is an example of how urban schools have recognized and emulated the idea of small community to promote a healthy sense of connectedness to community for urban students (Flaxman, 2001).

However, like their urban counterparts, rural schools continue to be faced with major challenges including high rates of poverty, high numbers of students with disabilities, an increasing number of English language learners, and high numbers of minority students disadvantaged by generations of racial and ethnic discrimination. Rural youth and their families are subject to the same stressors and temptations as their urban and suburban counterparts. Contrary to the commonly accepted idea of the "simple" rural life, the reality is that young people living in remote and rural areas are at similar or greater risk for alcohol and drug use and abuse, suicide, other high risk behaviors such as weapon carrying and unprotected sex, and are less likely to attend or finish college than urban and suburban youth (Frontier Education Center, 2003). The difference for rural areas, as compared to urban areas, is the apparent marginalization of rural communities and schools because they are "increasingly invisible in our mass society" (Rural School and Community Trust, 2005, p. 24). Most public policy is based on what is known about larger centers of population, as evidenced by a lack of public policy based on rural culture that would more specifically address the challenges faced by rural schools and communities. For example, current systemic changes in education are based primarily on poor outcomes for urban youth and designed to close the achievement gap by reorganizing partitioned programs in schools to a system of supports for all students. Ironically, many of the fundamental changes necessary to implement and sustain a seamless system of educational supports, such as shared responsibility by all educators for all student outcomes, are already found in rural schools (Jimerson, 2006). The smaller learning communities that rural areas provide offer the very assets that support a system of supports, and thus many of the components essential to tiered levels of service already exist in rural schools. Furthermore, rural school psychologists can help rural schools and their communities address major challenges by adopting an expanded role using problem solving to build greater internal and external collaborative partnerships to meet student needs.

What is rural? According to the most recent official definition (U.S. Census Bureau, 2000), rural areas comprise open country and settlements with fewer than 2,500 residents. Rural area is identified by default, that is of being neither an urbanized area nor urban cluster, which are described as greater than 50,000 population (urban area) or between 2,500 and 50,000 population (urban cluster). In 2000, 68% of Americans lived in 452 urbanized areas and 11% lived in 3,158 urban clusters. The 2000 census identified the total rural area population to be about 59 million, that is, 21% of the U.S. population lives in rural areas comprising about 75% of the total land area. Population densities in primarily rural states vary widely (e.g., Mississippi with 62 people per square mile and Wyoming with only 5 people per square mile).

The U.S. Department of Agriculture uses the Office of Management and Budget (OMB) description of rural as those counties identified as "nonmetropolitan" (75% of U.S. land) as compared to those identified as "metropolitan" (25% of U.S. land). In 2002–2003, 8.8 million children/youth, or 19% of all public school students, attended school in communities of fewer than 2,500 people. In addition, about 12.5 million students attended schools in small town communities with populations between 2,500 and 25,000.

Clearly, school psychologists who practice in rural areas continue to have a unique challenge given the sheer amount of travel time, sometimes in perilous weather conditions, to serve multiple school sites. However, with the advent of distance learning, university training and research web-based centers, web-based assessment data management systems, the professional development support of state school psychology and educational organizations, and the web-accessible information systems provided by national professional organizations such as the National Association of School Psychologists (NASP), rural school psychologists are in position to expand their role to serving schools and communities on a systems level while continuing to address the unique needs of students. The positive impact technology has had on education in rural areas cannot be overstated. The information and training now available to educators in isolated places is entirely due to information networks offered via technology. Importantly, the training and eventual competency in the area of informational technology is identified in *School Psychology: A Blueprint for Training and Practice III* (Ysseldyke et al., 2006) as a foundational competency to best practice as a school psychologist.

The primary purpose of this chapter is to discuss how school psychologists serving rural schools can use the problem-solving approach to both intervene upon and prevent identified school and student problems. Rural schools and communities have assets because of their smallness that support the notion of all educators for all children. When the problem-solving approach is used in conjunction with a continuum of curriculum and instructional supports and levels of student support services, school psychologists in collaboration with educators can meet the challenges rural schools and communities face today.

BASIC CONSIDERATIONS

An understanding of the rich history and complex dynamics of "simple" rural life in America today is essential to being an effective rural school psychologist. It is important to remember that there is great and rich diversity in the specific characteristics of rural areas across America, and it is critical for effective practice of school psychology to be based not only on best practices but also on the unique characteristics of the rural setting in which services occur (Helge, 1985; Jacob-Timm, 1995).

Rural Communities

It may be surprising to learn that rural areas exist in all 50 states, especially given the fact that the 79% of the population was identified as living in either urban areas or urban clusters in the 2000 census. Rural communities prior to the 1950s were historically composed primarily of individuals and families with generational roots in an area, the basis of the socially close knit and economically stable community. These rural communities are vital to the support and development of nonrural populations in the country as they provide the bulk of foodstuffs and building materials yielded by the work of rural populations in agriculture, ranching, mining, timber management, and fishing. During a period termed as the rural renaissance, which began in 1972 and continues today, rural communities changed dramatically from primarily farming to economies based increasingly upon small business, manufacturing, and resort activities (Helge 1985). Rural communities are heterogeneous and thus are difficult to describe. The following information pertains broadly to rural communities, but not necessarily to each one.

Two phenomena occurred since the 1950s that have affected the economic stability and close knit bonding of rural communities. First, many rural areas experienced an out-migration for various and complex economic and socio-political reasons not within the scope of this chapter. This decline in population resulted in much lower tax revenues, a decline in property values, lower enrollment in schools, and fewer employment opportunities that increased the likelihood that more people would leave the rural areas. A survival strategy many rural areas implemented was the consolidation of rural schools within an area into one location, sometimes very distant from a student's home. Although necessary for fiscal survival, this strategy continues to threaten a major asset rural communities provide their children, the sense of community and belongingness.

Second, migration back into rural areas. Since the mid-1980s, migration back to rural communities from urban and suburban areas has occurred by people of all ages. Several surveys about rural areas in the western U.S. found that "only about 10% percent of new migrants to rural areas are retirees over the age of 65 and that migrants are more likely to be young, highly educated professionals" (Rudzitis, 2001). Data from the same surveys indicate that about 75% of migrants either decrease or maintain their income to relocate in rural areas as a tradeoff for outdoor recreation, pace of life, scenery, and climate. In addition to these migrants, rural communities have also experienced an increase in immigrants from other countries who supply labor for production in the area. The increase in immigrants has resulted in an increase in English language learners in rural communities that, until recently, was not an issue in rural areas (Truscott & Truscott, 2005). Both migrant groups have an impact on the nature of rural communities and schools.

Other main issues include poverty, disproportionate numbers of children with disabilities, and increased rates of substance abuse. Poverty continues to persist in rural communities. Data provided by the U.S. Department of Education, National Center for Education Statistics

(NCES) in 2002–2003 report a mean per capita income for individuals residing in rural areas (U.S. Census Bureau, 2000) of $19,285, with a mean of 13.8% of rural children living in poverty. Students eligible for free or reduced-price meals in rural schools are reported at a mean of 37.4% nationally, with more than half of all rural students eligible in 11 states. "Poverty is the single strongest and most persistent threat to high student achievement" (Rural School and Community Trust, 2005, p. 6). Table 1 lists important rural community demographics, and from that table we can see the immense range of variability among rural communities by a comparison of the three highest and three lowest states in each category. For example, 13.8 % of rural children nationally are below the poverty level. However, only 2.7% of rural children in Connecticut are below the poverty level while 28% of rural children in Arizona and New Mexico live below the poverty level. These statistics exemplify the large variability in rural areas, thus serving as a caution to school psychologists to understand the unique characteristics and needs of a specific rural area.

Rural families experience stress because of high poverty rates, high unemployment rates, and low educational opportunities. These stressors contribute to higher rates of child abuse and neglect. The lack of mental health providers in rural areas to assist families experiencing domestic violence, depression, and abuse exacerbates stress and often results in substance abuse. The number of mental health providers in rural areas is critically low; that is, in excess of 85% of the 1,669 federally designated mental health professional shortage areas are rural. It is estimated that about two-thirds of

Table 1. U.S. Rural Community Demographics (2002–2003)

Community demographic	Mean	Highest three states		Lowest three states	
Rural per capita income	$19,285	CT	$33,428	WV	$15,177
		NJ	$30,905	MS	$15,242
		MA	$28,500	NM	$15,413
Percent of rural adults without a high school diploma	21.2	KY	32.4	CT	9.4
		MS	29.9	MA	9.8
		AL	29.4	CO	11.5
Percent of rural children (under age of 18) below poverty level	13.8	AZ	28.0	CT	2.7
		NM	28.0	MA	3.8
		WV	24.7	RI	4.6
Percent of rural children eligible for free/reduced meals	37.4	KY	76.4	CT	7.3
		NM	67.3	MA	10.1
		MS	65.6	RI	11.1

Note. Source: Rural School and Community Trust (2005).

individuals with mental illness symptoms receive no care, and of those who do receive treatment in rural areas, about 50% receive care from a mental health specialist and 45% from a general medical practitioner (U.S. Department of Health and Human Resources, 2005). Clearly, there is evidence that mental health services to rural families and their children are severely lacking.

Also associated with poverty are a higher proportion of disabilities among rural children as compared to urban, suburban, and nonpoverty children. Barriers to healthcare persist, particularly among culturally diverse, low-income, and rural families. Moreover, families of children with physical disabilities, including those children who are medically fragile, often must seek services outside their area, at both personal and financial cost. In spite of the fact that rural Americans account for a greater proportion of the population with disabilities than urban residents, they receive fewer specialized services, use a greater proportion of their income for healthcare, and generally receive poorer quality care (Offner, Seekins, & Clark, 1992).

Substance abuse in the form of alcohol and illicit drugs has been an ongoing issue in rural areas. Adolescent substance abuse rates in rural areas exceed those in urban areas for every drug except ecstasy and marijuana among tenth graders (Center on Addiction and Substance Abuse, 2000, in U.S. Department of Health and Human Resources, 2005). More specifically, rural eighth graders are more than twice as likely to smoke cigarettes, 70% more likely to smoke marijuana, 104% more likely to use amphetamines, and 50% more likely to have used cocaine than their urban peers. One study (Johnson, Bachman, & O'Malley, 2000, in U.S. Department of Health and Human Resources, 2005) found alcohol use prevalence rates among rural eighth graders to be 57%, compared with 50% among urban peers. Risk factors for rural and urban youth are similar in that, initially, adolescent substance abuse is primarily a social behavior rather than a response to addictive properties. Families can have either a direct or indirect influence on substance use, especially tobacco and alcohol. A youth is twice as likely to smoke if a parent smokes (direct influence), and children who believe their families are either unconcerned about substance use or have family conflict (indirect influences) are much more likely to use tobacco and/or alcohol (Oetting, Edwards, Kelly, & Beauvais, 1997, in U.S. Department of Health and Human Resources, 2005). Given the extent of poverty in many rural areas and the correlation between substance abuse and low socioeconomic status, rural youth are particularly vulnerable to substance abuse.

A relatively new issue is the drug production culture in the form of methamphetamine (meth) labs. The Center on Addiction and Substance Abuse, reported in 2000 that much of the meth production has become centered in sparsely populated areas of the west and midwest. According to state and local police records, in 1998 alone, 4,132 illegal drug labs, mostly meth, were seized. In 1998, the largest number of Drug Enforcement Agency (DEA) seizures was in seven west and midwest states, each of which experienced the seizure of at least 50 meth labs. In that same year, DEA seized 420 meth labs in four states with large rural and frontier populations (Frontier Education Center, 2003). Access and low cost of meth now plagues rural area youth to the extent that some primarily rural states have launched highly visible campaigns in rural communities against the use of meth. Prevalence rates are difficult to establish, especially in rural areas, although DEA (2002) reported that 12–14 year olds in small rural towns are 104% more likely to use meth than their urban peers. Emergency room admissions due to meth use increased 261% from 1991 through 1994 (U.S. Department of Health and Human Resources, 2005). Although there are no prevalence rates available relative to the specific use of meth by rural youth, the perception in many rural areas/states is that meth use is at epidemic levels.

In sum, rural communities across America offer advantages and disadvantages to those who live, work, and go to school there. The ways in which unique rural community assets, such as the sense of community and belongingness, can be used to increase prevention and intervention activities that address high needs in rural schools will be discussed in the Best Practice section of this chapter.

Rural Schools

Rural School Demographics
Data provided by the U.S. Department of Education, NCES, in 2003 report a mean of 19% (median 148,579) of all public school students enrolled in U.S. schools are in rural public schools (see Table 2). Note that a mean of 31% of all public schools are located in rural areas, while the mean percentage of state funding for rural school districts is only 18.5%. Although state funding percentages closely match student enrollment percentages, rural areas have the expense of maintaining almost twice the percentage of school buildings, a fiscal challenge that competes with all other community-funded educational expenditures. This is the basis for the consolidation movement since the 1980s whereby

Table 2. U.S. Rural School Demographics (2002–2003)

Demographic	Mean	Range			
		Highest three states		Lowest three states	
Percent of public students enrolled in rural schools in the state	19.1	VT	55.7	MA	4.7
		ME	53.1	CA	5.2
		SD	45.2	NV	7.4
Percent of public schools in the state located in rural areas	30.7	SD	77.6	MA	5.7
		MT	73.6	NJ	7.6
		VT	72.1	RI	10.0
Percent of state education funding going to rural schools	18.5	VT	61.2	CA	3.6
		ME	56.1	FL	6.3
		SC	50.2	UT	8.2
Rural student–teacher ratio (teacher per student)	15.0	CA	20.2	WY	11.4
		UT	19.6	ND	11.5
		OR	18.5	VT	11.5
Rural 4-year graduation rate	70.5	NE	90.5	SC	49.8
		IA	88.2	GA	50.2
		ND	86.5	AZ	50.9
Percent of rural students eligible for special education services	14.2	RI	18.8	HI	9.0
		NM	18.7	CA	9.2
		FL	18.5	CO	10.4
Percent of rural students who are minorities	22.2	HI	77.0	ME	2.5
		NM	70.6	NH	2.5
		AK	52.2	WV	2.7
Rural schools/students NAEP math and reading combined score for grades 4 and 8	499.2	CT	529.5	NM	465.0
		MA	527.5	MS	469.0
		NJ	521.5	AL	469.5

Note. Source: Rural School and Community Trust (2005).

small rural schools in an area were consolidated into one larger school.

Additional rural school demographics can be viewed in Table 2, which shows the national mean for each category as well as the range between the three highest and three lowest states in a category. Again, there is wide variability in rural areas. Overall, rural schools today are composed of a national mean percentage of 22.2% minorities. The national mean for rural teacher-to-student ratio in the classroom is 1:15, meaning smaller classes overall than urban schools. In respect to percent of students who graduate from high school, rural schools are below the national average, with a national mean percentage for rural schools of 70.5% compared to an overall national mean percentage of 80.4%. Rural schools have varied success in graduating students as reflected by a range of just half, 49.8%, in South Carolina rural schools to an impressive 90.5% in Nebraska rural schools. Academic achievement rates in rural schools are represented in the NCES data by National Assessment of Education Progress (NAEP) math and reading combined scores for grades 4 and 8,

and the national state mean score for rural schools is 499.2. Again, there is a wide spread of mean state scores among rural schools with a range of 465 in New Mexico to 529.5 in Connecticut. Factors outside the school's control, such as family poverty and parent or youth substance abuse, influence early school dropout and level of academic achievement. Fortunately, there are protective factors within the control of educators, such as a positive, safe school environment, evidence-based curriculum, and instructional methods, which also influence academic achievement and high school graduation rates. School psychologists in the twenty-first century will play a meaningful role in establishing and institutionalizing important prevention methods and programs in rural schools that will support increased student success. Finally, the national mean percentage of rural students eligible for special education services in 2002–2003 was 14.2%, with a range of 9% in Hawaii to 18.8% in Rhode Island. These rates have direct ramifications for how school psychologists, who are the primary assessors of students who are eligible for special education, spend their professional time.

Rural School Assets

Rural schools are embedded in small communities, are often the center of community activity, and can be described as a microcosm of the local culture. The strong sense of connectedness between members of the community translates into a sense of responsibility for each other. This is the very basis of the national movement to shift from a partitioned educational service delivery model (general education students, special education students, English language learner students, Title I students) to a shared responsibility model providing a continuum of services to all students (i.e., all educators for all children; see Tilly, chapter 2, vol. 1). Unfortunately, there is an ongoing struggle in rural communities across the nation because of the cost to maintain school buildings that serve a relatively small number of students. The very smallness that promotes shared responsibility has been viewed since the 1980s as a liability and fiscal burden. The solution has been school consolidation whereby a group of small rural schools in an area consolidate into one larger school for the region. Consolidation has been a fiscal solution but in many instances has been shown to create dysfunction in the community. The heart of the rural community, the school, is ripped away by consolidation. "Small villages that lose their schools lose more than a building—they lose their collective cultural and civic center" (Jimerson, 2006, p. 5). Moreover, students have less opportunity to identify with their own community and spend more time traveling, which competes with time to study and to participate in extracurricular activities. Rural schools and communities struggle with decisions about whether to save money by consolidation or to maintain the assets that smallness provides for the sake of community.

There are a host of assets that rural schools offer, some unique to a rural area, others more generalized to all small rural schools. Jimerson (2006) provides empirical evidence about the attributes of smaller schools that have a positive effect on student success. Appendix A lists 10 assets typically found in rural schools because of their small size and connectedness to community. Also listed are reasons why each asset has been shown to support school success. Noticeably, rural school asset outcomes are in alignment with essential components of educational tiered system supports, as well as federal mandates to close the achievement gap. Small class size that promotes personalized learning, positive social interactions, and greater collaboration among teachers are exemplars of methods that promote academic and social/behavioral success. The

recognition of these positive assets and outcomes of small rural schools has given rise to an alternative to school consolidation. Rural communities now consider administrative consolidation as a way to reduce costs while maintaining the small school culture within the rural community that so strongly provides the foundation for student success. Paradoxically, urban schools are actively setting up smaller learning communities within large urban schools to achieve the same outcomes found in small rural districts and schools. In spite of the positive assets typically found in small rural schools, they face many of the same challenges as urban schools.

Rural School Challenges

Research has suggested that adolescents in rural settings are just as at risk for substance abuse as their urban peers. A recent study (Shears, Edwards, & Stanley, 2006) examined the relationship between school belongingness (bonding), an established protective factor that is often found in rural schools, and substance abuse. Results suggest that although school bonding is a protective factor against substance abuse, school bonding is no more of a protective factor for rural adolescents against substance abuse, specifically marijuana and alcohol, than for their urban peers. However, results suggest the level of "rurality" moderates substance abuse. School bonding is more protective in more remote isolated rural areas than it is in less isolated rural areas located near more populated communities. Issues such as rural school consolidations and closures, long bus rides, and reduced funding decrease the likelihood that rural students can become involved in the very school activities that develop the sense of belongingness. Thus, rural schools and communities need to consider the impact to students when making decisions that minimize student's ability to engage in activities.

Meth production and use in rural areas is impacting rural school classrooms. There seems to be a sudden increase in the number of children entering school for the first time who have been prenatally drug exposed, and most specifically meth exposed. School psychologists, counselors, teachers, and administrators increasingly voice their concerns about the harmful effects on academic and social/behavioral success these young meth-exposed students are experiencing. The resources needed to support these often hard-to-teach students' school success is an obscure amount at present, but we can expect that the fiscal and personal cost to rural schools, families, and communities will climb.

With school psychologists taking on the expanded role of being agents of change, a final note about rural school governance and how it affects educational reform is important to understand. States have the primary responsibility for educating citizens. Education is regulated at both state and local levels. The autonomy of local school boards and administrators in rural communities is especially prized and, thus, guarded. The utility of a strong autonomous philosophy toward school governance can be a two-edged sword. Fiscal resources can be allocated in creative ways, choices in curriculum and instructional delivery can be made relatively quickly, and educational policy and procedures (e.g., disciplinary rules) can be established and enforced locally. The other side of a strong autonomous philosophy is that educational reform can be very difficult, especially when viewed suspiciously as being imposed upon the rural community and school. Moreover, because state policy makers seem to be making educational reform decisions based upon an urban understanding of school issues (Rural School and Community Trust, 2005), rural residents often believe educational reform comes at the expense of local control (Collins, 2001). That perceived loss of local control makes educational reform difficult but not impossible. Agents of change in rural schools work slowly and cautiously, first building both school and community buy-in and eventual ownership of important change (Merrell, Ervin, & Gimpel, 2006).

Rural School Psychology

Until the early 1980s, rural school psychological services developed very slowly and were based almost entirely upon the numbers of students with disabilities. The reasons for the slow acquisition of comprehensive school psychological services are the very characteristics prized by rural advocates, (i.e., small local schools and reduced population; Fagan & Hughes, 1985). An unintentionally prophetic statement made by Fagan and Hughes inspires and supports the idea of the paradigm shift in the practice of school psychologists today. They stated: "Had school psychology developed along lines of prevention, regular school programs, curriculum, and ability (as contrasted with disability), the situation in urban and rural areas may have been much different" (p.444).

The most prominent force in the development of more available and appropriate school psychological services in rural areas was the passage of federal legislation requiring all schools to provide school psychological services to children with disabilities, and as part of that service, to evaluate for eligibility for special education services. With the passage of Public Law 94-142 and later the Individuals with Disabilities Education Act (IDEA), rural areas increased the number of school psychologists. They adjusted to such barriers as isolation, difficult terrain, absence of service options, and sometimes mixed loyalties among closely knit rural communities and schools to deliver psychological services (Fagan & Hughes, 1985). The creation of regional units or agencies that employ school psychologists to serve a large rural area and their schools is one of the adjustments that facilitated improved services for students with disabilities. The collaborative nature of regional agencies has also helped overcome many of the perceived negative features of rural school psychology such as inappropriate or inadequate supervision, professional isolation, and few specialized service options for students with disabilities (Reschly & Connolly, 1990).

Although some rural school districts are large enough to employ a school psychologist, the majority of rural school districts typically contract with regional agencies for school psychologist and other specialist services. These independent contractors are known by various names such as Education Cooperatives, Board of Cooperative Education Services (BOCES), and Regional Education Service Agencies. This model of service delivery enables small rural districts to pool resources and thus provide levels of service that otherwise would be unavailable, insufficient, too expensive, or inefficient for one district. Thus, rural school psychologists are often employed by independent agencies rather than by school districts. In some models (e.g., BOCES), the regional agency participates in the governance of the school districts, but this is not the case in other service models (Benson, 1985). It is important for the rural school psychologist to understand the power base the education cooperative has in making local decisions, especially given the autonomy that rural school districts both revere and protect. Reschly and Connolly (1990) also warned that survey data based on "ruralness" may be skewed by the very fact that rural school psychologists are often organized in regional agencies/units, providing them with colleagues, increased professional development opportunities, and opportunities for more specialized practices, and, thus, may be more similar to their urban and suburban peers when examined as a group.

Rural School Psychology Demographics

A survey study (Hosp & Reschly, 2002) of 1,423 school psychologists with NASP membership (as of 1997) looked at regional differences in demographics, roles, job satisfaction, assessment practices, and system reform attitudes. The study did not look at differences based on rural, suburban, or urban settings, but rather divided the United States into nine regions. Table 3 lists the states located within each region, with many regions easily identifiable as composed of primarily rural states. Results of the survey indicated that all regions had more females than males, with a range of 53.6% in the mountain region to 78.4% in the west south central, although differences between the nine regions were not statistically significant. Curtis, Hunley, and Chesno Grier (2002) used survey data drawn from a national sample of school psychologists practicing in rural, urban, and suburban areas in the 1994–1995 school year to look at relationships among them in regards to demographics and professional practices. Results from the study correspond to the Hosp and Reschly (2002) findings. There are almost twice as many female as male

school psychologists in all three settings, but there is a slightly lower percentage of female practitioners in rural settings (67%) than in the urban (73%) and suburban (72%) settings.

Other important demographic data relevant to rural school psychologists, specifically psychologist-to-pupil ratios, salaries, and minority students served can be examined in Table 3, which combines data from two different studies. The table provides regional descriptions by states as well as national means and regional data on psychologist-to-pupil ratios, salaries, and percent majority school populations served. These data are crossed with data from the Rural School and Community Trust (2005), which ranks states as to level of need to address specific challenges in regard to poverty, other challenges, and major issues in rural education. "Other challenges" are operationalized by percentage of rural students who are English language learners, receive special education services, and are minorities, as well as rural adults without high school diplomas and family mobility. The states with the most urgent or critical need are listed in Table 3 under

Table 3. Hosp and Reschly (2002) Data Crossed With Rural School and Community Trust (2005) Data

Hosp and Reschly		Rural School and Community Trust			Hosp and Reschly		
Region	States in the region	Poverty	Other	Major issues	P:P ratio	Salaries	% majority
		(Challenges in education)					
Northeast	CT, MA, ME, NH, RI, VT	—	—	—	1,048.8	$54,168	79.9%
Mid-Atlantic	NJ, NY, PA	—	—	—	1,376.7	$55,271	70.8%
South Atlantic	DC, DE, FL, GA, MD, NC, SC, VA,WV	FL, GA SC, WV SC, VA	DE, FL GA, NC SC, WV	DE, FL GA, NC	2,329.0	$42,289	59.0%
East south central	AL, KY, MS, TN	AL, KY MS, TN	AL, KY MS, TN	AL, KY MS, TN	3,857.9	$43,525	72.9%
East north central	IL, IN, MI, OH, WI	—	—	—	1,816.2	$51,263	82.0%
West south central	AR, LA, OK, TX	AR, LA OK, TX	AR, LA OK, TX	AR, LA OK, TX	2,631.9	$39,228	58.0%
West north central	IA, KS, MN, MO, ND, NE, SD	MO, ND NE, SD	SD	MO, ND SD	2,119.5	$43,467	78.1%
Mountain	AZ, CO, ID, MT, NM, NV UT, WY	AZ, ID MT, NM UT, WY	AZ, ID NM, NV UT	AZ, ID MT, NM UT	1,667.2	$45,400	66.0%
Pacific	AK, CA, HI, OR, WA	AK, HI OR	AK, CA HI, OR, WA	AK, HI OR	1,963.5	$52,354	52.5%

Note. P:P = psychologist-to-pupil ratio; mean = 1,927.6; salaries mean = $48,346; percent majority mean = 69.5%. F ratio differences in nine U.S. regions: P:P ratio = F 9.23, $p < .01$; salaries = F 25.65, $p < .001$; percent majority (Caucasian) = F 12.30, $p < .001$. Source: Hosp and Reschly (2002); Rural School and Community Trust (2005).

"major issues". The source of data for the Rural School and Community Trust (2005) are merged databases from NCES and U.S. Census Bureau data, which was used to create variables for each school and district in the United States. The data were parsed out by population centers, defining rural areas as those of fewer than 2,500 persons as well as a school or district that is physically located in a place inside a metropolitan statistical area and has a population of fewer than 2,500. Using these data, the Rural School and Community Trust report looks at important key variables that have an impact on rural education in all 50 states and ranks them by level of need to be addressed. Although clearly rural areas in all 50 states have issues to be addressed, more than half of these rural areas rank either urgent or critical in variables that have an impact on education. Note that psychologist-to-pupil ratios are the highest in states and regions that also have the most urgent and critical levels of poverty, challenges, and major rural education issues. The mountain region is the exception, which is to be expected given the states in the mountain region have vast areas that are uninhabited or are identified as "frontier" (i.e., fewer than two persons per square mile). Conversely, where rural issues are not urgent or critical, psychologist-to-pupil ratios are lowest. This replicates earlier findings (Reschly & Connolly, 1990) in regards to higher psychologist-to-pupil ratios in rural schools. A second important variable is income for which the national average school psychologist salary is $48,346. Paradoxically, the states with the highest psychologist-to-pupil ratios and most urgent rural needs have the lowest mean salaries, while the states with the lowest psychologist-to-pupil ratios have the highest mean salaries and lowest rankings of rural areas with urgent needs. The only exception is the Pacific region with a mean salary of $52,354, where states have higher costs of living and also have urgent or critical rural issues primarily due to a high influx of immigrants and English language learners. This inverse relationship between salary and psychologist-to-pupil ratio also replicates earlier findings (Reschly & Connolly, 1990). Finally, a third variable identified by Hosp & Reschly (2002) is rates of minority and majority population within regions, illustrated in Table 3 by the percentage of majority (Caucasian) student population served by school psychologists in the nine regions. Again, with the exception of west north central and east south central, states with the most urgent and critical needs in rural education also have the lowest percentage of majority populations and conversely regions with lower needs in rural education have higher majority populations. The

two reports (Rural School and Community Trust, 2005; Hosp & Reschly, 2002) taken together offer convergent validity as to the challenges of working as a school psychologist in a rural area. These data also support the expanded role of school psychologists in rural areas as a facilitator of systems change that can ameliorate many of the challenges rural schools face.

Types of Settings and Professional Roles

In the past, studies suggested that the types of professional activities school psychologists engaged in varied according to the location and setting of their school district. In general, rural school psychologists were characterized as "generalists" in that they provided a wider range of services and were more likely to be involved at the systems level (McLeskey, Waldron, Cummings, & Huebner, 1988). Recent findings (Curtis et al., 2002) suggest only very small effect sizes between the type of settings and professional activities with slightly more initial evaluations completed in rural settings than in suburban or urban and fewer students served through consultation in rural settings than in suburban and urban settings.

Actual Roles

Hosp and Reschly (2002) examined differences between the nine regions described in Table 3 by estimations of hours per week currently spent in various types of services. Findings suggest that in general school psychologists averaged more than half of their time in assessment activities, with a national mean of 22.2 hours per week (SD 11.0), and there were significant regional differences. School psychologists in the east south central region spent 26.5 hours per week in assessment services and were among the highest regions in poverty indicators and leading regions with issues related to rural education, while school psychologists in the Mid-Atlantic region spent the least amount of hours in a week, 18.8 hours (SD 10.3) and was among the lowest regions in poverty indicators and least among regions with issues related to rural education. In respect to time spent in intervention the national mean was 7.6 hours per week (SD 6.5) and there were also significant differences among the nine regions, ranging from a high of 9.9 hours per week (SD 7.5) in the Mid-Atlantic region to a low of 6.5 hours per week (SD 6.2) in the south Atlantic region. This makes sense given the Mid-Atlantic region school psychologists spend less time in assessment and thus have time for intervention. The percentage of time spent in eligibility services was also significant between regions, with a national average of 60%, a range from 50.8% in the west south central, a region higher in issues related to poverty and rural education, to 65.6% in the east north central, a region lower in issues related to poverty and rural education. Actual time spent in individual consultation (teacher, parent, student), system-level consultation, and research was not significantly different among regions. Because these findings are based on data organized by regions and not necessarily by settings (rural, urban, suburban), we cannot make global assumptions specific to any type of setting. However, as illustrated in Table 3, some regions are composed primarily of rural states as compared to some regions more densely populated and comprised primarily of urban and suburban areas.

In the Curtis et al. (2002) study, rural settings were found to be significantly different from both suburban and urban settings in that rural school psychologists conducted more reevaluations and served fewer students through consultation. These findings must be cast in light of the fact that rural school psychologists in general have a significantly higher psychologist-to-pupil ratio and thus have higher special education case loads for reevaluation and less time for consultation. This fact alone predicts that more time may be needed for rural schools and school psychologists to fully engage in school systems change that creates and institutionalizes levels of service, prevention and intervention services, and broader roles as consultants.

Preferred Roles

Previous studies have historically found few differences between professional settings and preferred professional roles. More recently, Hosp and Reschly (2002) also examined differences between the nine regions described in Table 3 by estimations of hours per week professionals preferred they spend their time. None of the activity preferences varied significantly between regions, with the exception of marginal differences in assessment that can be explained by the differences in current assessment activities. Overall, findings from this study indicate that school psychologists across the United States, regardless of region, prefer to spend their 40-hour work week as follows: 12.8 hours in assessment, 11.4 hours in intervention, 9.0 hours in consultation, 4.3 hours in systems consultation, and 2.9 hours in research. In a symposium at the NASP annual meeting (Reschly et al., 2000), data were presented that compared current roles of school psychologists across the United States to those of school psychologists in Iowa, a primarily rural state. The comparison was made in order to illustrate the extent to which school psychologists' roles had changed given the use of the problem-solving method

within a tiered system of supports for student success. Ironically, the *actual* roles of school psychologists in the Heartland Area Education Agency 11 in Iowa corresponded very closely with the *preferred* roles of school psychologists reported in Hosp and Reschly (2002). Specifically, school psychologists in Iowa reported their work week spent as follows: 14 hours assessment, 9 hours direct intervention, 12 hours problem-solving consultation, 4 hours systems consultation, and 1 hour research. These figures signify the paradigm shift in the practice of school psychology toward an expanded role in schools that offer a tiered system of supports and problem solving to offer a balance of assessment, consultation, and prevention/intervention services. Moreover, these preferred roles are in direct alignment with those of the professional training guidelines described in *Blueprint III*.

Job Satisfaction

Previous studies have examined differences in job role and satisfaction between rural and nonrural school psychologists. These studies found no differences in overall job satisfaction (Reschly & Connolly, 1990), and a recent survey (Hosp & Reschly, 2002) looked at differences by regions of the country confirmed these findings. The Iowa Heartland AEA 11 school psychologists were compared to a national sample of school psychologists on job satisfaction (Reschly et al., 2000). Results suggest the school psychologists in the Heartland AEA 11, practicing problem-solving consultation within levels of services provided in the schools, scored equal to or higher than their peers across the U.S. on satisfaction with work, colleagues, supervision, pay, and promotion. Again, these data from a largely rural state bode well for rural school psychologists who are positioned in environments conducive to and in need of the expansion of school psychological services.

Professional Experience and Preparation

Reviews based on several studies in the 1980s of rural school psychologists described a gap in experience and preparation between rural and their urban/suburban counterparts. Rural school psychologists were described as younger, having less experience as either school psychologists or teachers, having fewer years in their current job, with fewer doctoral practitioners and more psychometricians in rural settings (Helge, 1985; Kramer & Peters, 1985). Data supported the role of the rural school psychologists as a generalist rather than a specialist in any one particular area (Huebner, McLeskey, & Cummings, 1984). However, subsequent studies have not confirmed these findings. Reschly and Connolly (1990) examined differences between rural, urban, and suburban school psychologists and found no difference in graduate education, certification, or licensure. Results also suggest that rural school psychologists were not more likely to be psychometricians and just as likely to have doctoral degrees as their counterparts. The study did confirm that rural practitioners were more likely to have slightly less experience, but the tradeoff was that they also were more likely to have had prior teaching experience than their urban and suburban colleagues. This suggests that rural practitioners are perhaps more likely to begin careers in education as teachers and subsequently respecialize as school psychologists, potentially for at least two reasons: to increase income and/or to fill a vacancy in their rural area. The study also found some support for the generalist role in that rural practitioners expressed a greater need for continuing education training in a variety of areas including intervention for regular education problems and remedial education programs. Reschly and Connolly summarized their findings as "school psychology appears to be far more the same than different in the city and the country" (p. 548). It may also be that in the time that elapsed between the two studies, rural communities made significant inroads in attracting equally qualified and prepared practitioners.

Summary

The preceding information provides a context for the delivery of rural school psychological services in the twenty-first century by defining rural, providing historical and current demographic information, an overview of the assets and challenges, as well as a historical and current look at the profession of school psychology in rural communities and schools. Clearly, the assets present in small rural schools, such as ownership by educators of all student outcomes, a sense of safety and connectedness, and small class size provide a sound foundation for developing a continuum of student supports for success. The rural school psychologist in the twenty-first century is well prepared to work in partnership with schools and external agencies to meet challenges using the assets rural schools and their communities provide to effect prevention and intervention practices that foster student success and community vitality.

BEST PRACTICES

In accordance with all other chapters in this edition of *Best Practices*, this section is designed to give an overview of best practices in rural school psychology with a focus on a problem-solving approach to providing school psychological services within a multitier model of service designed to match magnitude of need with appropriate level and nature of support services. As school psychologists of the twenty-first century expand their role from gatekeepers of special education to problem solvers at many levels of service, rural school psychologists have the opportunity to make significant progress toward finding solutions for the challenges found in rural America today. What Fagan and Hughes (1985) wrote in respect to these challenges still apply today: "The aspects of isolation, difficult terrain, absence of service options, mixed loyalties, etc., are not likely to disappear. They do not represent problems which we seek to eliminate but rather with which we seek better adjustment for the general improvement of services to children" (p. 450).

It is true that these challenges have not disappeared. However, changes in the way schools and school psychologists do business today by being proactive in frequently screening students to identify those at risk for academic, social–behavioral, and/or emotional concerns is one of those better adjustments to improve services to children/youth in rural schools. The problem-solving approach and continuum of supports along a multitier service level are consistent across settings, whether urban, suburban, or rural. Thus, this section will not repeat what is better described elsewhere in this edition of *Best Practices*. Rather what follows is a discussion about options and considerations for best practice in what is perhaps unique about rural school psychology.

The information presented in this section is offered for careful consideration in the practice of rural psychology. Just as with human individuality, each rural area is unique in the mix of strengths and weaknesses. The problem-solving rural school psychologist will use data-based evaluation to decide which assets are present that support change and which practices best match the unique needs of a rural area. The rural school psychologist works in partnership with rural school administrators, school nurses, guidance counselors, and curriculum directors within the school and with agencies and professionals outside the school to meet student needs.

Systems Change

The rationale for systems change in rural schools is the same for all schools and that is to increase the opportunities for students to be successful academically, socially, behaviorally, and emotionally, with the goal of reaching maturity with the best possible skills for success as an adult. The phases toward permanent systems change are the same described elsewhere: (a) create readiness/build capacity and support for change, (b) initial implementation with guidance and support structures in place, (c) institutionalization of the change with the infrastructure to sustain change regardless of personnel, and (d) ongoing evolution of reform via mechanisms that provide feedback about quality and support in the face of new challenges (Merrill et al., 2006). There are two aspects of rural schools and communities that make the approach to systems change necessarily different. First, and probably the biggest aspect, has been termed as "resistance to change and suspicion" (McLeskey et al., 1988, p. 93). Second, fewer fiscal resources are available. Rural schools face many of the same challenges as urban schools in the populations they serve with higher levels of poverty and resource inequities compared to their suburban counterparts (Voltz & Fore, 2006). Importantly, rural areas also provide an asset that can be used to overcome these challenges and support systems change, specifically the close-knit ties between school and community. Setting the stage for change requires rural school psychologists to use strategic planning with large doses of caution and patience in developing rural school and community relationships. The school psychologist works in partnership internally with administrators, school nurses, guidance counselors, and curriculum directors to effect change while also working externally with agencies and professionals to support the change. Best practice in facilitating systems change in rural areas necessitates an understanding of the psychology of power: (a) power bases in the school and community (i.e., know who makes decisions about what) and (b) the importance of referent power as a school psychologist.

Rural Power Bases

Rural school administrators and board members wield much power in the governance of schools. Rural school psychologists need to establish positive relationships with these decision makers who have great influence in the rural community, can reallocate funds and resources, support prevention and intervention programs, and help facilitate change among their staff. Once relationships are established, rural school psychologists readily become trusted resources to administrators for information on which to base their decisions. This expert power is important to guard. Remember the ethical duty to stay within competency boundaries to avoid the risk of misadvising and thus damaging the relationship. Appropriate referrals to sources of information are also deemed as expertise. Rural school psychologists should never underestimate the importance of these relationships with administrators, school board members, and other members of the community who can facilitate support.

Change mandated by state or federal policies and law can threaten local autonomy. Rural schools and communities feel a loss of local control under mandates (Rural School and Community Trust, 2005). Thus, best practice as a change agent is to help administrators identify a valid local catalyst for the change to shift the impetus for change back under the control of the rural school/community.

An example of a valid local catalyst from the author's own experience with school reform related to the learning disability definition and response to intervention is as follows. During initial training, administrators and staff identify at least one instance from experience when that person painfully struggled watching a particular student wait to fail only to watch that student not qualify for help, and then the subsequent downward spiraling of the student. Every person in education has had this agonizing experience, and it immediately justifies the need for change.

This gives the change a face and name, personalizing the need for change, empowering the person to make the change, and often providing the sustained energy to effect the change.

Referent and Expert Power

Referent power is the influence the school psychologist has with another person based upon that person's identification with the school psychologist on such parameters as values, attitudes, and behaviors. Expert power is the influence the school psychologist has with another person based upon that person's attribution of expertise to the school psychologist. Referent and expert power are not dichotomous but are interdependent. Effective rural school psychologists rely more heavily on referent power, maximizing the use of both (Fagan & Hughes, 1985; Jacob-Timm, 1995). The idea is that in rural areas, consultation is more acceptable from a school psychologist who identifies with the consultee who is not viewed as an outsider but who also has expertise. According to Fagan and Hughes (1985):

Referent power is based on identification and interpersonal attractiveness and results in more global influence. As a person is attributed higher levels of expertise, the person's overall interpersonal attraction declines. Given the generalist (expanded) role of the rural school psychologist and the importance of personal relationships in rural communities, the rural school psychologist is most likely to be a successful change agent if he or she establishes a high level of referent power (p. 447).

Rural school psychologists can have a significant impact on how schools promote student success through proactive prevention and intervention activities. By embracing the assets rural communities and schools provide in the close ties between schools and community, the need for interpersonal relationships, and the local autonomy in governance, school psychologists can influence the future. Understanding the power bases and the uses of referent versus expert power in the rural school and community is key to being an agent for systems reform.

Essential Practitioner Skills

School psychologists in the twenty-first century are not only assessors but are also consultants and interventionists (Merrill et al., 2006). Moreover, these same areas of practice are described as central to the practice and competency of school psychologists in the professional training guidelines described in *Blueprint III*.

This section discusses three key areas of school psychological services: assessment, intervention, and consultation. Best practices in these areas are the topic of other chapters in this edition of *Best Practices*, and thus only issues related to effective practice as a rural school psychologists will be discussed here.

Appendix B summarizes roles the rural school psychologist may take on in a multitiered delivery model. Note that many of the roles are ones that can be accomplished given the itinerant nature of rural school psychologists who may visit a school in their area once a week, twice a month, or only monthly. In any case, it is essential the school psychologist is a member of the problem-solving team.

Assessment

A key type of assessment that rural school psychologists must be competent with is curriculum-based evaluation. Formative assessment provides critical information about what specific skills to target in prevention and intervention, what to change about curriculum and/or instruction, progress monitoring, outcome evaluation, and Individualized Educational Plan goal writing.

At present, it is especially important that rural school psychologists be competent with formative assessment in the area of reading. It is essential to have an understanding of the process of learning to read as a basis for consultation with teachers and administrators. Owing to fewer resources in rural areas, many rural schools do not have a person who can function as a reading specialist for whom teachers can use as a resource for matching skills to curriculum and changes in instruction. Rural school psychologists are in a position to act as a resource in this area.

As an interventionist who links assessment to intervention and outcomes (see Batsche, Castillo, Dixon, & Forde, chapter 10, vol. 2), it is essential that school psychologists use formative assessment in their own evaluations. However, as suggested in Appendix B, rural school psychologists are encouraged to train teachers and other school staff on curriculum-based assessment so that teachers are empowered to use these effective tools to inform instruction, intervention, progress monitoring, and goal writing. Since, in most cases, rural school psychologists are not on a school campus daily, training school staff to implement and use formative assessment data is key to building the capacity for educators to make data-based decisions independently.

Adding skill in curriculum-based evaluation and measurement to the rural school psychologist's professional repertoire is critical and should be targeted for professional development if need be (see Howell, Hosp, & Kurns, chapter 20, vol. 2). This may be the case for many practitioners as a recent survey of school psychologists (Nelson & Machek, in press) found that few school psychologists feel prepared to take on an expanded role beyond traditional forms of assessment to intervention, prevention, and consultation about classroom instruction and that few were trained in or used curriculum-based measurement. Rural problem-solving school psychologists who have knowledge of reading skill acquisition and are competent in formative assessment provide critical information that result in data-based decisions.

A crucial part of assessment includes intervention outcome evaluation when decisions are made whether to continue, change, or discontinue intervention. The decision to discontinue intervention is made when a student reaches the goal(s) and is ready to be exited from intervention or special education services. School psychologists help educators design effective exit and transition strategies for these successful students, using outcome assessment to evaluate exit readiness and, perhaps, suggesting continued progress monitoring for a period of time to follow up on transition and continued academic success (see Powell-Smith & Ball, chapter 15, vol. 2).

Intervention and Prevention

In respect to prevention and intervention activities in rural schools, the keys are social validity and treatment acceptability by not only the interventionists but also by the student, the parents and family, and the community. Goals and methods of prevention or intervention activities must be shared clearly and be in alignment with family and community values. This reduces the likelihood of cultural biases and overcomes the suspiciousness factor found in rural communities. Intervention steps must also be acceptable to all stakeholders in order to ensure the integrity of intervention implementation. If the prevention or intervention is unacceptable, the likelihood that it will be implemented and then sustained for enough time to be effective is greatly reduced (Lane & Beebe-Frankenberger, 2004). Best practice for rural school psychologists is facilitating communication among all intervention partners, or to community leaders in the case of prevention programs, before, during, and after intervention. Communication among community leaders fosters collaboration and trust.

Communication with the rural community about prevention and intervention activities in the schools has a second benefit supported by the close-knit tie asset of rural communities. Private citizens and local businesses are much more likely to contribute to activities by volunteering, giving financial contributions, and or supplying community sites for implementing projects. This in turn supports the sense of belongingness to the school and community that is essential to the students' competence, good mental health, and overall development.

Consultation

As suggested in Appendix A, best practice by rural school psychologists includes consultation services for school administrators, teachers, staff, students, parents, and community, when appropriate. Although rural communities typically have close ties to the school, rural school psychologists want to promote healthy parent involvement with education and the school. The development of a school-based health center (SBHC) is another way rural school psychologists can provide consultative services to not only students but also families. Developing knowledge about both local and regional resources for purposes of referrals is critical to consultation in rural schools and in overcoming the fact that rural citizens needs for mental and physical health services are often not met.

Recommendations and Models for Rural School–Community Partnerships

The following recommendations and models are offered for consideration by rural school psychologists as ways to overcome the unique challenges of a rural area. The recommendations are made by consortiums on rural and frontier community life and are based on data and experience. The models are recommended as a result of empirical validation and/or positive program outcome evaluation.

Recommendations for School Improvement in Rural Areas

Recommendations are drawn from two comprehensive reports prepared by the Rural School and Community Trust Policy Program and the National Clearinghouse for Frontier Communities. The recommendations for school improvement are based upon aggregated data about current conditions of rural life and the challenges faced by schools and communities. These reports are listed in the annotated bibliography as a resource to rural school psychologists, school administrators, and policymakers. Appendix C lists selected recommendations from these reports and represent changes that can be facilitated by rural school psychologists. Note that many of the recommendations are consistent with best practice in enhancing opportunities for students to be successful (e.g., positive behavioral supports, team teaching).

Models for School Improvement

In a recent review of multicultural issues in urban and rural schools, Truscott and Truscott (2005) presented information about three school reform models for which there is strong empirical evidence for effectiveness in promoting academic success. There are other promising models that have not been as extensively examined, primarily because they are newer programs. These models are Expeditionary Learning Outward Bound, Modern Red Schoolhouse, and Roots and Wings. Only the three highly validated programs are briefly described here (Truscott & Truscott, 2005, p. 385).

- *Direct Instruction, S. Englemann, University of Oregon*: Designed to improve academic performance (K–6) so that by fifth grade, students are at least 1 ½ years beyond grade level. Direct Instruction features field-tested curricula, scripted lesson strategies, extensive writing, highly interactive instruction, flexible grouping, frequent assessments, and no pull-outs.
- *School Development Program, J. Comer, Yale University:* Designed to mobilize the entire community of adults to support students' holistic development and bring about academic success (K–12). The program features (a) three teams for school planning and management, student and staff support, parent teams; (b) three operations for comprehensive school, staff development, monitoring and assessment plans; and (c) three guiding principles described as no-fault, consensus, and collaboration.
- *Success for All, R. E. Slavin and N. A. Madden, Johns Hopkins University:* Designed to guarantee that every child will learn to read (preK–8). The program features research-based prescribed curriculum, one-to-one tutoring, family support team, cooperative learning, an on-site facilitator, and a building advisory team

The evidence-based features of these three models are ones that can be adopted in rural schools and are conducive to the multitier levels of service for which rural school psychologists advocate.

The remaining models reviewed here for school–community improvement are based upon four trends suggested in the literature about rural schools and communities (Collins, 2001):

- A healthy relationship between rural communities and their schools is crucial to school effectiveness and the communities' quality of life.
- Although it is impossible for rural communities to alter global changes that put them at risk, they can have broad-based local discussions, develop agreed-upon policies, and pursue educational, civic, and economic activities that enhance their sustainability and growth.
- Rural students must be prepared to work, learn, and live well, not only as participants in the global economy but also as citizens in their own communities.
- Rural schools, as central institutions in rural life, must assume a role in community economic development.

The school–community partnership builds on the context of local conditions and ideals to provide local solutions for local problems. Partnerships have a positive effect on student achievement, improve the quality of life in the community, and help students make successful transitions into adulthood. Rural school psychologists work internally within schools, but also in partnership with the external community and agencies.

Three models (see Appendix D) that are mutually beneficial to schools and the community include (Collins, 2005):

- The school as a community center, a lifelong learning center, and a vehicle for delivery of numerous services
- The community as curriculum, emphasizing the community in all of its complexities as part of students' learning activities in the classroom
- The school as a developer of entrepreneurial skills

Key factors common to successful school–community programs include forceful/energetic leadership; the ability to raise needed funds; the desire to improve the community's pride in, identification with, and support of the school; an emphasis on small-scale rural features to create a distinctively nonmetropolitan program; and recognition of the economic value of the school (Collins, 2001). Tapping the broader community resources and networks can benefit both the community and the schools. Rural school psychologists work with school administrators and civic leaders to identify community resources/assets that support and integrate with school programs for student success.

Finally, School Based Health Centers (SBHCs; Brown & Bolen, 2003) represent a fairly recent model for meeting the physical and mental health needs of rural students and their families. First developed in the early 1990s in urban schools to provide physical health care and teen pregnancy prevention programs, today SBHCs exist in 45 states and the District of Columbia and many are in rural schools. They provide immediate access to health care services by rural residents who may otherwise go unserved due to barriers of distance, transportation costs, and expense of time away from work for parents. SBHCs are developed through partnerships between schools and community agencies and programs. The essential elements include (a) a continuum of health and mental health prevention and intervention services, (b) services offered to all students (general and special education), and (c) services augment the work of school-hired mental health professionals (Weist,

Goldstein, Morris, & Bryant, 2003). SBHCs also provide peer support groups, grief counseling, assistance with classroom behavior management, and substance abuse prevention programs. Many SBHCs regularly provide psychosocial screening for students that allows for early identification and treatment for childhood emotional problems. The positive effects for students who use SBHC services include a 50% decrease in absences of students with psychosocial impairment, an increase in graduation rates, a 95% decrease in disciplinary referrals, a 31% decrease in failing grades, and a 32% reduction in absences from schools (Brown & Bolen, 2003).

School psychologists are trained to provide both mental health and psychosocial services and can broaden their role by providing consultation and intervention for students and their families as part of SBHCs. School psychologists can be an important link between the center staff and school staff, facilitating a collaborative system of care for students. "Participation in school-based health services delivery enables school psychologists to expand their role and broaden both their client population and the range of services they provide" (Brown & Bolen, 2003, p. 285).

The intention of this section was to provide best practices specific to the delivery of rural school psychological services and offer models for school improvement and school-community partnerships in raising children/youth of rural communities. Figure 1 is a model for how rural school psychologists build both internal and external partnerships in schools and community based upon the unique assets and challenges of the community. It represents an example of how one rural school used problem solving at a systems level to capitalize on community resources as it worked on internal school improvements to develop tiered levels of service to meet student needs. The school psychologist at this school met regularly by invitation with a community service club to report on how students were being successful with the new tiered services at their school. Club members visited the school to read and do math with the children in intervention. The school psycho-logist was on the school Positive Behavioral Initiative Team and successfully suggested and then recruited community businesses to post signs designed by students listing the three school-wide expectations (Be Responsible, Be Respectful, Be Safe) in their stores for students to see in the community. In this figure, the rural school psychologists work with school administrators and community leaders to identify the unique assets of the rural area that support programs designed to effectively meet identified challenges of the community

and school. The content at each level of service for both school and community are based upon the unique features of a rural town. Assets of this town include: (a) active civic and private clubs and organizations seeking philanthropic projects; (b) family and early-career business owners who support innovation; (c) an organized food and clothing bank for the needy; and (d) a sizeable retired population of former education, business, health, and other professionals. Challenges of this town include: (a) low SES, young, and single parent families population; (b) substance abuse issues; (c) out-migration of high school graduates who rarely return; (d) higher levels of adult depression and disabilities; and (e) high population of adults without high school education, many of whom would like to return to school.

The behavioral expectations are not only at school, but in the community. The school has implemented many other unique ideas and programs based on school and community assets to address the challenges the rural community faces. The school psychologist has the respect and trust of not only school colleagues but also the community, an instrumental piece toward building a collaborative rural school–community team.

SUMMARY

Rural schools provide a wealth of opportunity for children/youth to thrive. Rural communities have generational roots that connect everyone with personal histories, a sense of belongingness, and support. Attractive features of rural areas include space, healthy air, scenic beauty, and outdoor recreation. However, these very assets also bring challenges. Isolation, difficult terrain, fewer resources, stressed local economies, poverty, and higher rates of substance abuse, disabilities, and suicide among youth are difficult challenges to rural schools and communities. Rural consortiums study these challenges and continue to offer recommendations and models for rural school–community improvement. Factors within the control of educators, such as the school environment, curriculum, and instructional factors, influence academic achievement, prosocial behavior, and strong mental health. Rural problem-solving school psychologists can foster positive growth by using their skills in assessment, intervention, and consultation to support educators, students, and their families in rural life. The problem-solving approach within multiple tiers of academic, social/behavioral, and emotional services seems particularly well matched to the assets found in small schools while offering a systems

Figure 1. Internal and external partnerships build success in rural schools and communities.

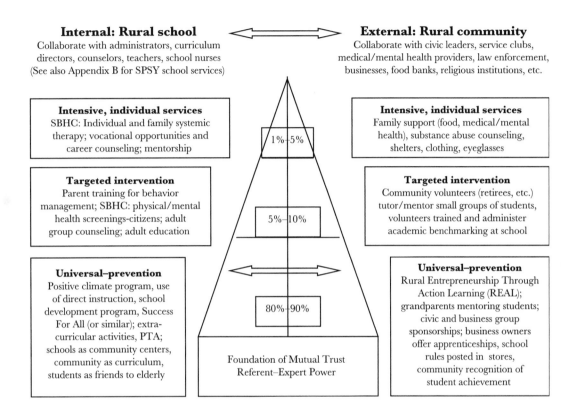

Rural School Psychologists Develop Internal and External Partnerships to Facilitate Preventative and Remediation Programs, Supports, and Services

Internal: Rural school
Collaborate with administrators, curriculum directors, counselors, teachers, school nurses (See also Appendix B for SPSY school services)

External: Rural community
Collaborate with civic leaders, service clubs, medical/mental health providers, law enforcement, businesses, food banks, religious institutions, etc.

Intensive, individual services
SBHC: Individual and family systemic therapy; vocational opportunities and career counseling; mentorship

Intensive, individual services
Family support (food, medical/mental health), substance abuse counseling, shelters, clothing, eyeglasses

1%–5%

Targeted intervention
Parent training for behavior management; SBHC: physical/mental health screenings-citizens; adult group counseling; adult education

Targeted intervention
Community volunteers (retirees, etc.) tutor/mentor small groups of students, volunteers trained and administer academic benchmarking at school

5%–10%

Universal–prevention
Positive climate program, use of direct instruction, school development program, Success For All (or similar); extracurricular activities, PTA; schools as community centers, community as curriculum, students as friends to elderly

Universal–prevention
Rural Entrepreneurship Through Action Learning (REAL); grandparents mentoring students; civic and business group sponsorships; business owners offer apprenticeships, school rules posted in stores, community recognition of student achievement

80%–90%

Foundation of Mutual Trust
Referent–Expert Power

approach through school–community collaboration to answer rural challenges. When students are engaged in their school and community, there is little time or need for destructive activities.

Rural school psychology began in a reactive mode; that is, the number of rural school psychologists was dependent upon the number of students with disabilities. New evidence-based curriculum, instruction, and intervention methods and systematic problem solving provide school psychology with a second chance. As Fagan and Hughes (1985) said: "Had school psychology developed along lines of prevention, regular school programs, curriculum, and ability (as contrasted with disability), the situation in urban and rural areas may have been much different" (p. 444). These words describe what rural school psychologists can help develop now. There are funding sources for rural programs, and school psychologists can be proactive in identifying specific funding opportunities that match a rural area's needs (see the Annotated Bibliography for funding resources).

Rural school psychologists in the twenty-first century play a meaningful role in establishing and institutionalizing important prevention methods and programs such as SBHCs, positive behavior support, and interactive school–community learning projects. By utilizing best practices in assessment, intervention, and consultation and keeping in mind the importance of relationships built on trust, rural school psychologists will help local school administrators overcome difficult challenges and enhance positive growth for children/youth and their families living in rural areas.

REFERENCES

Benson, A. J. (1985). School psychology service configurations: A regional approach. *School Psychology Review, 14*, 421–428.

Brown, M. B., & Bolen, L. M. (2003). School-based health centers: Strategies for meeting the physical and mental health needs of children and families. *Psychology in the Schools, 40*, 279–287.

Collins, T. (2001). Rural schools and communities: Perspectives on interdependence. *ERIC Review, 8*, 15–24.

Curtis, M. J., Hunley, S. A., & Chesno Grier, J. E. (2002). Relationships among the professional practices and demographic characteristics of school psychologists. *School Psychology Review, 31,* 30–42.

Drug Enforcement Agency. (2002). *Drug information.* Washington, DC: Author. Retrieved February 12, 2007, from http://www.dea.gov/concern/concern.htm

Fagan, T. K., & Hughes, J. (1985). Rural school psychology: Perspectives on lessons learned and future directions. *School Psychology Review, 14,* 444–451.

Flaxman, E. (2001). The promise of urban community schooling. *ERIC Review, 8,* 5–14.

Frontier Education Center. (2003). *Frontier youth: Living on the edge.* Ojo Sarco, NM: Author. Retrieved October 1, 2006, from www.frontierus.org

Helge, D. (1985). The school psychologist in the rural education context. *School Psychology Review, 14,* 402–420.

Hosp, J. L., & Reschly, D. J. (2002). Regional differences in school psychology practice. *School Psychology Review, 31,* 11–29.

Huebner, E. S., McLeskey, J., & Cummings, J. A. (1984). Opportunities for school psychologists in rural school settings. *Psychology in the Schools, 21,* 325–328.

Jacob-Timm, S. (1995). Best practices in facilitating services in rural settings. In A. Thomas & J. Grimes (Eds.), *Best Practices in School Psychology III* (pp. 301–310). Washington, DC: National Association of School Psychologists.

Jimerson, L. (2006). *The hobbit effect: Why small works in public schools.* Arlington, VA: Rural School and Community Trust. Retrieved February 12, 2007, from http://www.ruraledu.org

Kentucky Department of Education. (2000). Kentucky family resource and youth services center fact sheet. Frankfort, KY: Author. Retrieved August 21, 2006, from http://education.ky.gov/KDE/Instructional+Resources/Student+and+Family+Support/

Kramer, J. J., & Peters, G. J. (1985). What we know about rural school psychology: A brief review and analysis. *School Psychology Review, 14,* 452–456.

Lane, K. L., & Beebe-Frankenberger, M. (2004). *School-based interventions: The tools you need to succeed.* Boston: Allyn & Bacon.

McLeskey, J., Huebner, E. S., & Cummings, J. A. (1984). Issues in the delivery of psychological services in rural school settings. *Professional Psychology: Research and Practice, 15,* 579–589.

McLeskey, J., Waldron, N. L., Cummings, J. A., & Huebner, E. S. (1988). A descriptive study of psychological service delivery in selected rural school settings. *School Psychology International, 9,* 91–97.

Merrill, K. W., Ervin, R. A., & Gimpel, G. A. (2006). *School psychology for the 21st century: Foundations and practices.* New York: Guilford Press.

Nelson, J. M., & Machek, G. R. (in press). A survey of training, practices, and competence in reading assessment and intervention. *School Psychology Review.*

Offner, R., Seekins, T., & Clark, F. (1992). Disability and rural independent living: Setting an agenda for rural rehabilitation. *Human Services in the Rural Environment, 15,* 6–8.

Reschly, D. J., & Connolly, L. M. (1990). Comparisons of school psychologists in the city and country: Is there a "rural" school psychology? *School Psychology Review, 19,* 534–549.

Reschly, D. J., Ikeda, M. J., Tilly, W. D., III, Allison, R., Grimes, J. P., & Upah, K. F. (2000, April). *School psychology without IQ: Roles, assessment, satisfaction, supervision, and evaluation.* Symposium presented at the annual meeting of the National Association of School Psychologists, New Orleans, LA.

Rudzitis, G. (2001). Amenities increasingly draw people to the rural west. *Rural Development Perspectives, 14,* 9–13.

Rural School and Community Trust. (2005). *Why rural matters 2005: The facts about rural education in the 50 states.* Arlington, VA: Author. Retrieved October 19, 2006, from http://www.ruraledu.org

Shapiro, E. S. (2000). School psychology from an instructional perspective: Solving big, not little, problems. *School Psychology Review, 29,* 560–572.

Shears, J., Edwards, R. W., & Stanley, L. R. (2006). School bonding and substance use in rural communities. *Social Work Research, 6*(13), 1–18.

Truscott, S. D., & Truscott, D. M. (2005). Challenges in urban and rural education. In C. L. Frisby & C. R. Reynolds (Eds.), *Comprehensive handbook of multicultural school psychology* (pp. 357–393). Hoboken, NJ: John Wiley.

U.S. Census Bureau. (2000). *Census 2000 urban and rural classification.* Washington, DC: Author. Retrieved August 25, 2006, from http://www.census.gov/geo/www/ua/ua_2k.html

U.S. Department of Health and Human Services, Office of Rural Health Policy. (2005). *Mental health and rural America: 1994–2005.* Washington, DC: Author.

Voltz, D. L., & Fore, C., III. (2006). Urban special education in the context of standards-based reform. *Remedial and Special Education, 27,* 329–336.

Weist, M. D., Goldesten, A., Morris, L., & Bryant, T. (2003). Integrating expanded school mental health programs and school-based health centers. *Psychology in the Schools, 40,* 297–308.

Ysseldyke, J., Burns, M., Dawson, P., Kelley, B., Morrison, D., Ortiz, S., et al. (2006). *School psychology: A blueprint for training and practice III.* Bethesda, MD: National Association of School Psychologists.

ANNOTATED BIBLIOGRAPHY

Frontier Education Center. (2003). *Frontier youth: Living on the edge.* Ojo Sarco, NM: Author. Retrieved October 1, 2006, from www.frontierus.org

Provides in-depth information about youth at risk for emotional/behavioral issues who live in frontier communities. Provides the context of frontier life, data, and recommendations for prevention and intervention activities.

Jimerson, L. (2006). *The hobbit effect: Why small works in public schools*. Arlington, VA: Rural School and Community Trust. Retrieved February 12, 2007, from http://www.ruraledu.org

Synthesizes research-based evidence on the effectiveness of smaller schools, providing the rational argument against consolidation of several small rural schools into one larger school strictly for fiscal reasons. The 10 positive attributes of small schools described, and that urban schools are now emulating, are essential to the system of supports foundational to a response-to-intervention process.

Rural School and Community Trust. (2005). *Why rural matters 2005: The facts about rural education in the 50 states*. Arlington, VA: Author. Retrieved October 19, 2006, from http://www.ruraledu.org

Provides a comprehensive overview of the context and challenges of rural schools and communities. Provides data from national database (NCES and the U.S. Bureau of the Census), which is aggregated to earmark rural areas that are in urgent and critical need of assistance from policy makers.

U.S. Department of Education. (2001). Perspectives on urban and rural schools and their communities. *ERIC Review, 8*(2), 1–42.

Explores both urban and rural school–community relationships. Provides ideas about what urban and rural areas have in common as well as issues that are unique to each. Models for school improvement involving school–community partnerships are described in detail. Resources for funding and further information are included with contact information and website addresses.

U.S. Department of Health and Human Services, Office of Rural Health Policy. (2005). *Mental health and rural America: 1994–2005*. Washington, DC: Author.

Provides an epidemiological overview of mental health and substance abuse in rural America from 1994–2005 and information on mental health service delivery in rural areas, workforce development, and rural mental health in the twenty-first century. Includes information specifically about status of children/youth, school-based prevention programs. Has an extensive annotated bibliography and also provides lists of funding resources for rural programs.

APPENDIX A. TEN ASSETS AND POSITIVE OUTCOMES OF SMALLER RURAL SCHOOLS

Small school assets	Outcomes
Greater participation in extracurricular activities	• More positive attitudes about school and learning, higher self-esteem, better self-concept, higher expectations about going to college, lower dropout rates • Higher grade-point average, higher standardized test results, better rates of attendance • Better self-concept, lower dropout rates, greater school engagement
Safety	• Fewer violent incidents, less vandalism, theft, truancy, substance abuse, and gang participation • Students build relationships and skills to cooperate, disagree, and negotiate
Sense of belonging	• Small school climate equals belongingness or connectedness factor; therefore, less violence, substance abuse, suicidal thoughts, pregnancy, and dropout rates • Strongest in schools where students get along with and respect each other, correlates of small schools
Small class size; greater chance of individualized instruction	• Small class size, especially K–3, associated with higher academic achievement • Small classes allow teachers to individualize instruction; closer interactions with teachers and students, and more instructional time
Good teaching methods easier to implement	• Smaller learning communities provide greater opportunity for flexibility of scheduling and individualized learning experiences • Change easier to implement in smaller organizations that tend to be more efficient • Teachers have more autonomy and collaborate more often
Teachers feel better about their work	• Teachers tend to be more satisfied, have less absenteeism, collaborate more with colleagues, take greater collective responsibility for student learning • Teachers initiate innovative reforms more often on their own, have a stronger sense of professional community and teams, less teacher turnover
Mixed-ability classes avoid condemning some students to low expectations	• Smaller schools do not have the population to sort students that leads to tracking; incidence of tracking much lower in small schools • Less possibility of disproportionate representation of minorities and low SES • Heterogeneous grouping combined with high expectations and advanced curriculum leads to positive outcomes for all students
Multiage classes promote personalized learning and positive social interactions	• Research mixed, but majority of studies indicate positive impact on academic achievement, especially for children of color, males, and poorer students; students have more positive attitudes toward school, increased prosocial and fewer aggressive behaviors, greater leadership skills • Multiage classes have no negative outcomes and at the very least, high ability students are not held back in multiage classrooms as compared to single-grade classrooms
Smaller districts mean less bureaucracy	• Small districts are associated with higher academic achievement, especially for high poverty districts • Smaller districts have higher graduate rates • Smaller districts, especially those with two to three schools only, allow for greater school-level decision making which is associated with improved academic performance
More grades in one school alleviate many problems associated with transitions to new schools	• A wide grade span within a school building (e.g., K–8) has been found to have an impact on students both academically and socially; middle school students tend to do better academically, have lower dropout rates, and fewer discipline problems when grouped with elementary grades in comparison to high school grades • Transitions between schools (e.g., K–2 to 3–5 to 6–8 versus K–8) correlate with achievement loss; school transitions require social and psychological adjustment, which often results in more student stress

Note. Assets are ranked by the extent of evidence to support outcomes. Source: Jimerson (2006).

APPENDIX B. EXPANDED SCOPE IN PROVISION OF RURAL SCHOOL PSYCHOLOGICAL SERVICES

Role	Levels of service	Potential roles of rural school psychologists
Assessment	Tier 1: Primary/core/system (prevention)	• Be a member of the school-problem solving team • Coordinate triannual whole school screenings • Train local staff/volunteers on standardized data collection method • Conduct assessment integrity checks • Provide interpretation of screening data interpretation • Set up and train staff in data collection database
	Tier 2: Secondary/strategic	• Be a member of the Tier 2 problem-solving team • Train teachers and staff on CBE, CBA, CBM • Follow up booster trainings • Conduct CBM integrity checks • Set up systematic progress monitoring systems • Train staff in progress-monitoring data collection
	Tier 3: Tertiary/intensive	• Be a member of the Tier 3 problem-solving team • Conduct skills assessment to match with curriculum • Set up systematic progress monitoring systems • Conduct formal evaluation for entitlement to SPED supports • Train staff in progress-monitoring data collection
Intervention	Tier 1: Primary/core/system (prevention)	• Help design and implement school-wide prevention programs: positive behavior supports, social skills curriculum, crisis intervention plan, learning academies, antisubstance abuse, cultural awareness/tolerance • Help administrators evaluate evidence-based curriculum purchases • Facilitate school–family–community partnerships and involvement • Provide program outcome data interpretation and evaluation • Provide parent/community training programs (e.g., behavior management)
	Tier 2: Secondary/strategic	• Coordinate or provide group interventions for social skills, anger management, substance abuse, depression/anxiety, grief/loss • Facilitate implementation of an academic and/orbehavioral mentoring program • Link assessment data to strategic intervention
	Tier 3: Tertiary/intensive	• Link assessment data to intensive intervention • Facilitate support for and participate as practitioner in school-based health centers to meet mental health needs of students and their families
Consultation	Tier 1: Primary/core/system (prevention)	• Resource to school administrators • Resource to parents and the community on specific issues • Resource to teachers, staff • Facilitate parent involvement
	Tier 2: Secondary/strategic	• Facilitate home/school partnerships in changing student outcomes • Resource to interventionists • Resource to parents, students
	Tier 3: Tertiary/intensive	• Use problem-solving consultation with parent/teacher • Facilitate home/school collaboration and communication • Consult on type, duration, intensity of interventions • Consult with parent, student on social validity, family culture • Identify transition services for adult students • Identify/develop community apprenticeships for skill development

APPENDIX C. TIER 1 SYSTEMS LEVEL RECOMMENDATIONS FOR RURAL SCHOOL IMPROVEMENT

Recommendation	Rural issue	Systems level recommendation
Rural School and Community Trust (2005)	*Retain small scale of schooling:* Consolidation of rural schools: • Increases student travel time to school • Limits extracurricular activities • Disconnect from own community • Increased transportation costs	*Alternatives to school consolidation:* Multiage classrooms • Wider age span configurations (e.g., K–8) • Use of distance learning to pool students as well as faculty resources among clusters of small schools • Use school facilities in multiple ways (e.g., library, community center, meeting space) • Team teaching
	Reorganization standards: When consolidating and/or reorganizing, plans should result in an organizational structure that is accountable to standards that have interests of children and community in mind	• Maintain/improve small schools; more cost effective • Provide sufficient funding for each school to meet program and outcome standards; equal opportunity for each child to achieve • Retain schools within communities; avoid building schools in isolated places • Honor and reinforce policy of racial desegregation • Protect children from bus rides exceeding 30 minutes each way • Use regional resources for specialists
Frontier Education Center (2003)	*Reduce high risk behavior:* Promote and improve behavioral health within the rural school	• Maintain school discipline through positive classroom and school management • Refuse to tolerate aggression, specifically interpersonal violence and bullying • Make policies and display clear rules for appropriate behavior and the consequences of breaking the rules • Effective monitoring of high-risk students • Policies that are positive, communicate respect for students, and are not unduly harsh or punitive • Policies that improve the predictability of rewards for positive behavior and success
	Reduce high risk behavior: Frontier/rural school and community policies	• Conduct needs assessment in schools, develop solutions for at risk youth, develop action plans for providing mental health services, substance abuse prevention, violence prevention, and sexual awarenessprograms through schools • Create opportunities for staff/administration to learn about and visit other successful ruralfrontier programs • Develop alternative educational and mental health care delivery models • Create a single point of entry or focal point to coordinate services for at-risk youth • Begin prevention/awareness in preschool and elementary grades and continue through senior year, maximizing "peer power"

APPENDIX D. MODELS OF TIER 1 SYSTEMS LEVEL RURAL SCHOOL IMPROVEMENT

Model 1: Schools as Community Centers

- Provide public space for meetings and other activities
- Promote lifelong learning by establishing a learning resource center and offering adult education and literacy classes (e.g., GED and computer classes)
- Lead the networking, coordination, and delivery of family health services and other social services that enhance the community's social infrastructure
- Provide space for businesses to train employees or help businesses with their training

Other ideas for converting schools into community centers include opening schools early in winter so people can walk and exercise, sharing kitchen facilities with providers of food services for the community, and using school buses to transport the elderly.

Example. Kentucky's 1990 education reform set up Family Resource and Youth Services Centers in schools, with the long-term goal of raising student achievement. Each center has its own blend of program components depending on its location, available services, local need, and community input. In Kentucky schools with Family Resource Centers and Youth Services Centers, teachers report improved student-peer relationships and academic performance, and parents report greater satisfaction and involvement with schools (Kentucky Department of Education, 2000).

Model 2: Community as Curriculum

A place-based curriculum can provide an ideal bridge between the classroom and community development. Developing a place-based curriculum involves listing community assets that can be used in the classroom. These assets can be a springboard for positive partnerships and actions. A place-based curriculum can also help the community build a culture of education so both students and adults will become lifelong learners, with the school at the center of lifelong learning activities. Student learning is not limited to what goes on inside the classroom but extends into the community to embrace ecology, economic and civic involvement, spirituality, and living well in the community.

Place-based curricula look different in each community. However, there are four common themes:

- Attentiveness to students' home landscapes, which offers a solid grounding for interdisciplinary study
- Convergence of natural sciences and the arts through drawing, writing, identifying plants and animals, and studying processes of biological change
- Time spent outdoors doing systematic, experimental fieldwork that fosters exploration and attentiveness
- Human connections to the land that emerge out of exploring the cultural aspects of the community's relationship to its natural history across the generations.

Example. Rural school children in Alabama recorded the wisdom and life experiences of their elders and set the words to music. They created a CD, which was then distributed by Smithsonian/Folkways.

Model 3: Schools as Developers of Entrepreneurial Skills

School entrepreneurial programs are based on the idea that students who earn their keep in the community are less likely to out-migrate. Entrepreneurial students can prosper in the rural community by becoming business owners, creating a new segment of a revitalized middle class that supports lifelong community education and development while promoting sustainable economic diversity. Entrepreneurialism programs can be important in the vocational training of adolescents with disabilities. Options include school-based businesses, internships, and apprenticeships. Addresses educational, personal, and rural issues that contribute to poor vocational preparation and reduced independence.

Example. Rural Entrepreneurship Through Action Learning (REAL), now in 33 states.

Note. Source: Collins (2001).

113 Best Practices in Urban School Psychology

Antoinette Halsell Miranda
Julio C. Olivo II
The Ohio State University

OVERVIEW

"Improving urban education, in particular, has become one of the most prominent public policy issues in this country" (American Psychological Association [APA], 2005, p. 33). Without a doubt, a greater focus in education is on increasing the academic achievement of urban students and making schools work for the poorest children and children of color. In part, this is what the No Child Left Behind (NCLB) federal legislation seeks to accomplish. One of the major goals of the NCLB legislation is to close the achievement gap with accountability, flexibility, parental choices, and research-based reforms (Cicchinelli, Gaddy, Lefkowits, & Miller, 2003). The long-range goal is that all students will be proficient in reading and mathematics by the year 2014.

There is an acknowledgement that urban schools, urban students, and urban environments have characteristics that distinguish them from their rural and suburban counterparts. Unfortunately, much of the discussion around urban schools and settings in the past decade has been negative and pessimistic. The mass media has also portrayed urban schools and their students in a similar fashion. For most people in the United States this is the only image they see as they themselves have virtually no first hand experience with an urban population. As a result, stereotypes are rampant and difficult to dispel. Conversely, these images also harm urban students as they must struggle with negative stereotypes regarding their intellectual capability, character, behavior, and culture.

One of the greatest challenges facing researchers, practitioners, and others who are interested in understanding and working in urban settings is the complex nature of those settings. While there is no question that there are tremendous challenges, a focus on potential assets in these communities is often absent when working with urban populations. Understanding the strengths and assets can assist in overcoming the challenges presented in urban environments (APA, 2005).

In this chapter we will help the reader understand the complex nature of urban schools within urban settings and why one cannot be studied without the other. We will provide an overview of characteristics of urban schools, urban students, and urban environments and the interplay among the three as well as some of the most critical issues urban schools are facing.

BASIC CONSIDERATIONS

Urban Defined

As we attempt to provide a discussion around best practice in urban education, we believe it is first necessary to define the term urban and examine its characteristics. According to the U.S. Census Bureau (2006), the term *urban* refers to all territory, population, and housing units within an urban region. Such regions consist of a centralized location with adjoining units that have a total population of at least 2,500 residents for urban clusters or 50,000 residents for an urban area. Urbanized regions encompass 59.6 million acres of land in the United States (U.S. Department of Agriculture, 2002). Although urbanized regions make up only 3% of U.S. land, 79% of the population is housed within it.

Whereas, the term urban was historically used as a geographic concept, it is increasingly being used as a social or cultural construct to describe people and places (Noguera, 2003). Aside from population, urban territories are commonly characterized by stereotypes: structural, cultural, and immigration densities; high concentration of poverty and crime; complexities of transportation patterns; and inequities of healthcare, justice, and education (Lee, 2005). Such stereotypes are made even more explicit when references like inner city, ghetto, and slum are used to describe urban (Noguera, 2003). Although many urban areas experience these complex issues, many urban communities are pleasant and safe environments (Kopetz, Lease, & Warren-Kring, 2006).

The change in large urban centers has been occurring steadily since the 1950s. Large cities "have declined in importance as economic, political, and commercial centers.... In the 1950s, federal policies hastened the decline of cities as new highways were constructed, making it easier for the middle class to move out of cities to obtain a piece of the American dream" (Noguera, 2003, p. 23–24). A variety of other events, such as court-ordered busing, desegregation of housing, jobs moving to the suburbs, white flight, and the movement of minorities to the city all contributed to the transformation of big cities. Thus, for many cities the end result has been less power and influence and a disproportionate number of residents who are poor and non-white (Noguera, 2003). The schools in these communities also suffered tremendously from the changes that have occurred in the center cities that left them with large numbers of poor and minority students and limited resources. Hodginkson (2001) recently demonstrated that what used to be considered an "urban issue" is now spilling over to the suburbs. He states, "the inner city ring (where there is nothing between you and the city limits) will see a major increase in student diversity— more minorities, more immigrants, more students learning English as a second language … and more students from poverty" (p. 8). Thus, many of the issues that have characterized urban schools are now evident in suburban schools.

Characteristics of Urban Schools

Systemically, urban schools are different from suburban and rural schools in a number of ways (APA, 2005). Urban schools operate in political and financial milieu that is complex and at times contentious (Council of the Great City Schools, 2003). These environments typically have a declining tax base and fewer resources for a student population that requires the most support. In addition, the students themselves have fewer traditional resources to draw upon than their more affluent suburban peers. Urban schools are more likely to experience teacher shortages and have teachers working with emergency credentials (Urban Institute, 2002; Council of the Great City Schools, 2000; Anyon, 1997). Urban schools are usually defined as *public* schools marked with cultural diversity, poverty, limited resources, and minimal achievement (Weiner, 2006); however, this definition does not hold true for all urban schools. For instance, there are urban schools in which students academically excel, others are homogenously populated by ethnicity and race, and many schools are chartered or privatized. However, the academically excellent school, in large urban school districts, tends to be the exception rather than the norm.

Like all educational institutes, issues within urban schools are very complex and reflect the issues of the environment. Therefore, in order for the school personnel to provide best practice, they must understand the realities of urban America and accept the challenge of contributing to the solutions (Kopetz et al., 2006). It is clear that urban schools require highly skilled education personnel.

Urban schools and urban areas share the same attributes. Like urban areas, students in urban schools are *more likely* to be multicultural, children of low-income families, and non-English speakers (Council of the Great City Schools, 2003). Approximately 2.3 million students attending urban public schools had an expenditure per pupil below the state average. Since the national average includes urban schools outside of Great City Districts, which are schools in cities with a population more than 250,000 and a student enrollment of at least 35,000, it is projected that there is a larger discrepancy between all urban schools and the national average when it comes to monies spent per pupil. High poverty students need more and different resources than their advantaged peers (Predmore, 2004; Anyon, 1997). For example, urban schools generally require more facilities, have more programs to support, and have a larger percentage of students needing special services (Kozol, 2005; Anyon, 1997) Thus, some would argue (Kozol, 2005; Anyon, 1997) urban schools need more money than non-urban schools due to the lack of resources within the schools and with the students who attend those schools. Unfortunately, efforts to increases resources for urban school settings, most often through legislation, have not been successful (Kozol, 2005).

Owing to many of these ecological factors, urban school systems, as a whole, are experiencing many difficulties and facing significant challenges. Urban public school achievement is below the national average, the achievement gap between the privileged and underprivileged students still exists, and students of marginalized groups are dropping out at higher rates than Caucasian students (Council of the Great City Schools, 2003). In the academic year of 2003–2004, only 7 major city school systems out of 66 had half or more of their grade levels test better then their statewide average in mathematics, whereas 9 major city schools accomplished the same achievement in reading (Council of the Great City Schools, 2003). The educational system is failing to help low income, culturally diverse children within urban schools achieve.

Characteristics of Urban Students

According to the Council of Great City Schools (2003), 77.6% of students in Great City Schools are students of color when compared to the national average of 40.5%; 64.2% are eligible for federal free reduced lunch, compared to the national average of 35.2%; and 16.7% are English language learner students, compared to the national average of 8.4%. Nationally, the minority population will continue to grow with an estimation that minorities will account for 65% of the U.S.'s population growth in the next 2 decades, primarily from Latino and Asian ethnic backgrounds (Hodgkinson, 2001). Many of these students will continue to populate large urban school districts (Weiner, 2006; Kozol, 2005; Anyon, 1997).

For teachers to be successful in teaching urban students, they need to understand the conditions surrounding the lives of urban students (Kopetz et al., 2006). Having an understanding of these conditions is equally important for school psychologists who wish to practice in urban settings or with urban populations. The influence of home, neighborhoods, and families can negatively influence the school experience for many urban children. For many of these children, not only are they attempting to navigate and understand the requirements of school but they are also dealing with living in challenging families and neighborhoods that sometimes requires them to take on adult-like roles. Unlike their suburban counterparts, urban children are more likely to experience multiple safety issues, health risks, higher mobility rates, and engage in more risk-taking behavior (APA, 2005). Understanding the student from an ecological perspective recognizes the complex interaction of person variables within and across multiple systems. There needs to be a recognition that the student resides in multiple systems that have both direct and indirect influences on his or her schooling.

Achievement Gap

While there are a myriad of problems in urban schools, the issue that has been most vexing and has garnered the most attention is the achievement gap between minority and nonminority students. While there has always been a gap between African Americans and Caucasians and Latino and Caucasians, that gap started to close in the 1970s and 1980s (Lee, 2006). Unfortunately, in the 1990s it again began to widen. According to the National Assessment of Educational Progress, a standardized test administered to students throughout the United States, both African Americans and Latinos from central cities consistently perform below their Caucasian counterparts in reading, math, and science. In fact, scores have changed little since 1992 (Lee, 2006).

It has long been demonstrated that there is an inverse relationship between academic achievement and poverty. However, there are also other factors that have a demonstrated relationship with academic achievement, such as the mother's education level, early literacy in the home, and school variables such as class size and instructional practices.

It is important for school psychologists to have a better understanding of the achievement gap and the many factors that contribute to it. Many of these students are referred for possible special education because of their lack of academic achievement. Unfortunately, school psychologists in urban settings are viewed as limited in understanding urban students and contributing to the "overrepresentation" of minority students in special education (Haberman, 2003). Since 2001, a considerable amount of attention has been focused on closing the achievement gap. In fact, NCLB specifically addresses the achievement gap issue in its statement of purpose for Title I, which is to close the achievement gap between minority and nonminority students and between disadvantaged children and their more advantaged peers (Cicchinelli et al., 2003).

Over the years, a number of explanations have been posited to explain the gap; however, most researchers acknowledge that an explanation cannot be found in a simple theory (Singham, 2003). While most previous theories focused on child or sociocultural variables (Ogbu, 2002; Nieto, 2000) more recently researchers have begun to look at in-school factors that may contribute to the achievement gap as well as the interaction between various aspects of schooling and the characteristics of the student (Ferguson & Mehta, 2004).

Regardless of the reason, educators have the monumental task of closing the achievement gap, and thus there is a constant search for finding the "right" program. Unfortunately, too often urban schools engage in reform efforts by implementing programs that may have unrealistic expectations in which there will be quick and measurable results in student performance or requires too much overhaul in a large bureaucratic system (Henig, Hula, Orr, & Pedescleaux, 1999). For example, a large Midwestern urban school district that implemented Project GRAD, a national program that helps students in high poverty school districts reach graduation, ended their relationship with the national Project GRAD program because a report in 2006 could not prove the program worked in that school district (Richards, 2007). Unfortunately, the schools involved in the project had teachers that were less experienced and there was little stability due to high teacher and principal turnover in the schools implementing Project GRAD. These systemic factors ultimately had a negative impact on the project.

The failure of urban education reform, in large part, is also due to the implementation of too many programs without clear evidence of whether they work or not in the first place (Kopetz et al., 2006). The current movement is toward understanding the plethora of issues facing urban schools and implementing strategies that take these issues into account. It can be a daunting task because of the multiple issues that need to be considered.

Belief Systems

It is important for school psychology practitioners to explore their belief systems regarding children of color and academic achievement. Many practitioners, who are overwhelmingly Caucasian females, have little first-hand knowledge, about urban students, their culture, and the urban environments they exist in (Truscott & Truscott, 2005). That is not to say that just because a practitioner is from a minority group he or she will be a better clinician to minority students. It simply means that there is a population of clinicians who are less likely to have any first-hand experience with culturally diverse populations and life in urban settings.

It was not too long ago that the belief widely held by many was that African Americans were intellectually inferior. While that perception has waned greatly, there is still a lack of understanding by many in the education field as to why many minority populations struggle academically and the variables that contribute to the lack of academic success. For example, research has demonstrated that teacher's low expectation of minority students has an impact on the academic achievement of those children (Nieto, 2000; Howey, 1999). The low expectation generally is a result of teachers believing that poor minority children cannot meet high standards set forth by the teacher.

As advocates for children, school psychologists are in a position to challenge those belief systems that may be held by some education personnel.

While education personnel may have negative beliefs regarding students of color, these students themselves may internalize what they perceive as beliefs about their cultural group. For example, Steele and Aronson (1995) have explored what they call "stereotype threat" on the achievement of minority students in particular. They describe it as an effect where, if a person is challenged in an area he or she is concerned about, such as intellectual ability, the fear of confirming a negative stereotype can impair performance on a standardized test that person is taking. Steele and Aronson's research has demonstrated that African Americans who are informed prior to taking a test that the results of the test will be an indication of their intellectual ability perform less well than if they were told just to do their best on the test. Steele and Aronson readily acknowledge that this does not account for all low achievement but suggest there may be a social psychological predicament of race in a standardized testing situation.

School Psychologists in Urban Settings

Frankly, little has been written about school psychologists and their practice in urban schools. There is a fairly comprehensive piece by Truscott and Truscott (2005) in which they discuss the challenges faced by school psychologists in urban settings. But they acknowledge that very little has been written about urban school psychology in the discipline's top journals, which suggests that few academicians have "urban" as their research interest. There are several school psychology programs that have an emphasis or devote some of their training to urban issues (e.g., University of Wisconsin–Milwaukee, The Ohio State University, and Howard University), but far too few to develop a significant cadre of students prepared to go into urban settings. Some might even question if specialized training is even needed.

While school psychology has been noticeably absent when addressing the challenges of urban schools, APA has been, in comparison, at the forefront of addressing some of these issues. APA in 1997 convened a group of psychologists who joined educators in a conference in Washington, DC, to evaluate best practice as well as to determine effective practices that were already in place. There was a clear recognition that despite several decades of research on innovations that work in urban schools there was a wide gap between that knowledge and what actually happens in the classroom (http://www.apa.org/pi/urbaned/introduction.html). The group determined that psychology can use research, practice, and policy to improve America's schools. This is clearly an area where school psychologists could take a lead in researching innovative practices in urban schools that make a difference in the academic achievement of urban students, particularly given the profession's emphasis on the development of evidenced-based practices.

Urban school psychologists have tremendous demands placed upon them. While there has not been a comprehensive study conducted specifically evaluating the job demands of urban school psychologists, there have been studies that address concerns in urban areas as part of a larger demographic study (Curtis, Hunley, & Chesno Grier 2002). What has consistently been found in demographic studies is that urban school psychologists tend to have heavier assessment case loads, higher school psychologist-to-student ratio and a higher percentage of minority students in their population of students. Curtis et al. (2002) found that at least 25% of all school psychologists are working within the 1000:1 ratio recommended by the National Association of School Psychologists' (NASP) Standard for the Provision of School Services. The ratio of school psychologist-to-student has a substantial effect on the types of services provided to students (Reschly & Wilson, 1995). School psychologists serving large numbers of students are limited to providing specific psychological services such as initial and reevaluation services (Curtis et al., 2002). Hence, these services are more likely to be limited to traditional assessments, projective measures, and/or anecdotal behavioral observations (Hosp & Reschly, 2002). Presumably, a lower ratio would allow urban school psychologist to provide other services like interventions, consultation, and counseling (Curtis et al., 2002). However, the overwhelming needs and challenges of

urban schools may still keep school psychologists, who have a lower school psychologist-to-student ratio, spending the vast majority of their time in the special education classification process (Truscott & Truscott, 2005). If this pattern continues, in which urban school psychologists spend most of their time in special education classification, it is unlikely that they will have the time to provide best practices. More importantly, it will be very unlikely that the neediest children will be able to benefit from the full range of services that school psychologists can provide.

BEST PRACTICES

"The work of psychologists, like other professionals serving urban communities must become more culturally relevant to the realities of urban schools ..., urban life ..., and urban learners" (APA, 2005, p. 38). School psychologists have skills in research, consultation, and program evaluation that could be used to improve educational outcomes for urban students (Truscott & Truscott, 2005). This section will highlight ways that practitioners can meet the challenge of practicing in diverse, urban settings. Readers will note that there is not a section on assessment in this chapter. This is purposeful as assessment with diverse learners has been the one area where there has been research.

Understanding the Urban Population

Because urban settings are disproportionately minority, it is absolutely essential that school psychologists have a foundational knowledge about issues of diversity that prepares them to effectively practice with a population of students that most likely will be culturally, linguistically, racially, ethnically, and economically different from themselves. Howey (1999), in his discussion of preparing teachers for inner city settings, outlines a number of themes that should be interwoven through program preparation. While this chapter is not focused on preparation of school psychologists, the themes are worth citing and are viewed as appropriate for school psychologists as these themes speak to the knowledge and skills that need to become a part of best practice. It should be noted that these themes are consistent with *School Psychology: A Blueprint for Training and Practice III.* (Ysseldyke et al., 2006) as the field prepares for an increasingly diverse population and the challenges that legislation such as NCLB presents. Knowledge and skills essential for practice (Howey, 1999) are for school psychologists to:

- Understand and acquire first-hand knowledge of sociocultural/political factors that influence learning by youngsters in urban settings
- Immerse themselves in another culture and language for the purpose of examining their own cultural norms, references, and behavioral patterns, in relation to another culture; the urban environment is a good setting for this contrast
- Examine the interactions and relationships between language, learning, and culture in and outside of urban schools
- Become advocates for those who do not have equal educational opportunity
- Understand how the students' particular background experiences and lives outside of schools may have an impact on these students' school experience, performance on assessments, and performance in the academic curriculum
- Understand their own biases as well as others' biases and prejudices as they relate to social class, race, gender, religion, sexual preference, and other manifestations in school such as dress, physical appearance, ability, and behavior
- Demonstrate a commitment to the value of cultural pluralism, social justice, and equal opportunity for all

While this chapter is focused on urban settings, it is our opinion that much of what is presented is applicable to all students. Schools have become increasingly diverse in suburban and rural areas, and suburban schools are experiencing some of the same challenges regarding diversity that urban schools have been experiencing (Hodgkinson, 2001). Ideally, much of this knowledge about other cultures would be provided during preservice training. However, we recognize that formal university training is not always possible. Because of the rapidly changing demographics in the United States, issues related to urban education and diversity should be viewed as ongoing professional development. NASP and APA conventions are venues for these issues to be addressed. In addition, school psychology must have a greater commitment to addressing these issues in top-tier journals. Most important, school psychology must view this as a critical issue that must be at the forefront of promoting best practice for all children in education if substantial changes are to be made in the education of urban students.

Strength-Based Model

Because of the negative stereotypes that are generally coupled with the term urban, it is easy to approach urban students, schools, and communities from a deficit model. Professionals often fail to see the strengths and assets that not only the students bring with them to the school but the strengths that urban communities have to offer.

In recent years, there has been more emphasis on approaching school-based psychological services from a strength-based perspective (APA, 2005). A strength-based approach recognizes the tangible as well as intangible assets that students have. This perspective posits that students have inherent strengths but the strengths may not coincide with the belief systems that traditionally focus on middle class expectations.

Urban students have adaptive assets that are associated with skills in major life areas (APA, 2005). Practitioners often get mired in the many negatives that students bring to the school. When practitioners only focus on the negatives, it is often difficult to see the positive aspects that a student exhibits. Utilizing a strength-based perspective may more quickly lead practitioners to move toward a solution.

Assets in the Community

While urban school districts are often viewed as having problems, the communities these districts reside in may have a variety of resources that should be considered assets in the community. Traditionally, the religious institution in the inner city has been an important resource for poor families (Dilulio, 2002). Not only do these religious institutions provide spiritual guidance, but they often are able to supply necessities such as food and clothing and sometimes tutoring programs. Gardner et al. (2001) describe an effective partnership between a local university, a church, and an inner city elementary school that provided a tutoring program to African American males. A peer-mediated instruction intervention was implemented to improve the academic performance of these males in an after-school program. After 5 months, results demonstrated that all students made gains in reading and math facts.

School psychologists can assist schools in joining with community institutions and agencies to intervene in the cycle of failure that often plagues urban school districts. Partnering with community businesses, mental health agencies, local hospitals, and organizations such as the Urban League can provide not only monetary resources but people resources.

Culturally Responsive Practice: A Three-Tier Approach

As school psychologists strive to work more effectively with culturally diverse populations, there has been an increasing emphasis on engaging in culturally responsive practices. Culturally responsive practices are techniques and strategies that research has demonstrated work in increasing the academic achievement of underrepresented minority groups. These practices are based on the premise that diverse students will excel academically when they (a) have access to high quality professionals, (b) are provided with culturally relevant and respectful program curricula and resources, and (c) have professionals who value their culture and experiences and use them to facilitate their learning and development (Skelton, Kobayashi, Reyes-Rau, & Schaeffer, 2006). A three-tier model of culturally responsive practice can be useful in school psychology service delivery (Skelton et al., 2006). The first tier identifies five ways that educators at the school-wide level can engage in culturally responsive practice: (a) explicit instruction of academic and behavior skills; (b) clear, consistent, and frequent feedback about what is expected and what is the performance standard; (c) multicultural curricula; (d) research validated core curricula; and (e) confronting bias and stereotyping in classroom and nonclassroom settings.

Since urban settings are typically complex systems, it is probably not appropriate to think that just one of these practices can solve the problem. Thus, the use of a combination of the practices would probably be most appropriate.

The second tier includes the use of validated targeted programs that incorporate the elements of strong interventions, culturally relevant materials, and frequent progress monitoring.

The third tier involves the use of culturally valid intervention planning, ecological assessment, direct assessments, cultural brokers, cultural reciprocity, family participation, and the use of a response-to-intervention model to determine sufficiency of support services.

One of the potential challenges in culturally responsive practice is finding interventions that have been used with diverse or urban populations. A recent study by Freeman (2006) evaluated articles that focused on intervention outcomes in four leading school psychology journals during 1990–2004. While the studies did use diverse populations in their studies, they were not representative of the U.S. population. In other words, minority populations were less likely to be included in intervention studies. This does not mean these interventions will not work with urban populations. However, intervention studies conducted in urban settings that specifically address the myriad challenges that exist in those settings are needed.

While it is important to incorporate culturally responsive practices, it must also be understood that other environmental factors may work against the academic achievement of many urban youth. For example, students themselves must engage in practices that are conducive to academic achievement. Thus, part of culturally responsive practice is assisting students in developing skills and engaging in behaviors that are consistent with academic achievement (Ferguson & Mehta, 2004). In addition, the research on effective schools is important in providing information regarding common characteristics of schools that have been identified as effective in the education of urban students in particular (Reeves, 2003; Edmonds, 1979). School psychologists can engage in several of the activities that have been identified as common characteristics such as frequent assessment of student progress and assisting in designing performance assessments. Unfortunately, while school psychologists may not be able to control many of the negative variables in urban schools (e.g., poverty) they may still be able to be a catalyst to move the school in the direction of using culturally responsive practices.

Ecological Perspective

There is very little written about what constitutes best practice in urban school settings by school psychologists. However, several researchers believe the use of an ecological framework allows practitioners to view the child in a complex environment, understanding the interplay between these environmental factors and the effects the environment has on the child (Truscott & Truscott, 2005; see Miranda, chapter 109, vol. 5). Utilizing an ecological perspective moves the practitioner away from a deficit-oriented model, which has been the traditional outlook toward urban children. This perspective also fits well with a strength-based model of service delivery. The Urban Learner Framework (APA, 2005) advocates institutionalizing practices that will focus on the development of coping strategies and protective mechanisms that will ultimately increase the number of resilient students. While not directly focused on academic achievement, this framework suggests how school psychologists can focus on aspects of a child that may influence the child's developing increased academic achievement. The framework also implies that focusing on academics alone without recognizing other environmental variables that have an impact on urban students in the classroom may not be enough to increase academic achievement. In urban settings, school psychologists must look at the whole child.

Evidenced-Based Interventions to Improve Outcomes

The field of school psychology is at the forefront of advocating and instituting evidence-based interventions. The challenge is how to affect change in the urban educational setting by translating evidenced-based research into school based practices (APA, 2005). Thus, the use of a problem-solving model as a core aspect of school psychology service delivery is critical when implementing evidenced-based interventions.

One of the important features of a problem-solving model is the progress monitoring. In early research about effective schools, one important aspect identified as critical was the frequent monitoring of student progress (Edmonds, 1979). NCLB also advocates the frequent monitoring of students to affect change in academic achievement.

However, for many practicing school psychologists in urban settings, it will require them to move away from a "passive, bureaucratic approach to their job," which is inconsistent with the problem-solving model approach (Truscott & Truscott, 2005, p. 363).

Undoubtedly, more researchers are needed as well as practitioners to engage in applied research with respect to evidenced-based interventions. While the profession has a tendency to focus on quantitative studies, there needs to be more qualitative research that can evaluate many of the environmental issues, challenges, and nuances existing in urban schools that may have an affect on the successful implementation of evidenced-based interventions. The challenge for many urban school psychologists is how to move from the special education arena, which generally involves a heavy case load of assessment, and into an indirect service delivery model that utilizes a problem-solving framework.

The response-to-intervention movement, that utilizes a problem-solving framework, shows promise as a model that provides differentiated services that match students' needs with the appropriate level of services required for improved outcomes (see Tilly, chapter 2, vol. 1). There is research on evidenced-based practices that can assist school psychologists in urban settings to advance their

schools or school district in the direction of providing effective services within a tiered model. Research in urban schools utilizing evidenced-based interventions is critical in demonstrating validity evidence that these techniques are appropriate and effective for urban populations.

For example, positive behavior support (PBS) is an evidenced-based intervention that school psychologists can implement in urban school settings. Typical school-wide discipline approaches are often insufficient in addressing the needs of urban youth with behavior problems, and thus PBS can be seen as a viable alternative to address behavior concerns. Warren et al. (2003) implemented a school-wide PBS program in three inner city elementary schools. While their research demonstrated some encouraging outcomes, they also addressed critical issues and lessons learned with respect to implementation of such a program. Their observations and recommendations can be beneficial for school psychologists planning to implement PBS in an urban school. Research such as this addresses some of the unique and complex challenges in urban schools that might impede successful implementation of evidenced-based interventions.

Other evidenced-based practices that have been shown to be successful in urban schools are Dynamic Indicators of Basic Early Literacy Skills (Rouse & Fantuzzo, 2006) and curriculum-based measurement (Ysseldyke et al., 2001). School psychologists in urban schools who engage in activities that identify at-risk students early, utilize a prevention model of service delivery, and provide intensive intervention services in the early grades that are evidenced based will have a greater impact on improving the academic and behavioral needs of urban children than if they remain in the refer–test–place mode of operation.

SUMMARY

Urban schools are complex institutions that have many challenges. Little is written in the school psychology literature about best practice in urban settings. For school psychologists working in urban environments, it is critical to understand that urban schools "are intimately linked to and affected by the complex interactions of the force of urbanization" (APA, 2005, p. 33). This is probably the biggest difference between urban and suburban schools. Issues of poverty, the achievement gap, violence, lack of funding, and socio-political issues, to name a few, are system issues that significantly have an impact on what happens in urban school systems. Indeed, school psychologists have breadth and depth of knowledge to provide quality services to urban schools but they also need to understand the sociopolitical nature of urban settings as well as all of the complex system variables with urban students, their families, and the community. If all children are to succeed academically, the profession must give greater attention to solutions and practices that can assist in overcoming the challenges in urban education.

REFERENCES

American Psychological Association. (2005). *Toward an urban psychology: Research, action, and policy.* Washington, DC: Author.

Anyon, J. (1997). *Ghetto schooling: A political economy of urban education reform.* New York: Teachers College Press.

Cicchinelli, L., Gaddy, B., Lefkowits, G., & Miller, K. (2003). *No Child Left Behind: Realizing the vision.* Denver, CO: Mid-Continent Research for Education and Learning.

Council of the Great City Schools. (2000). *Urban schools face critical teacher shortage.* Washington, DC: Author.

Council of the Great City Schools. (2003). *Beating the odds III: A city-by-city analysis of student performance and achievement gaps on state assessments. Results from 2001–2002 school year.* Washington, DC: Author.

Curtis, M. J., Hunley, S. A., & Chesno Grier, E. (2002). Relationships among the professional practices and demographic characteristics of school psychologist. *School Psychology Review, 31,* 30–42.

Dilulio, J. J., Jr. (2002). Supporting black churches. In A. Thernstrom & S. Thernstrom (Eds.), *Beyond the color line: New perspectives on race in America* (pp. 155–164). Stanford, CA: Hoover Institution Press.

Edmonds, R. (1979, March/April). Some schools work and more can. *Social Policy,* 28–32.

Ferguson, R., & Mehta, J. (2004). An unfinished journey: The legacy of Brown and the narrowing of the achievement gap. *Phi Delta Kappan, 85,* 656–669.

Freeman, E. (2006, March). *Sample diversity across intervention studies published in school psychology journals.* Poster session presented at the annual meeting of the National Association of School Psychologists. Anaheim, CA.

Gardner, R., III, Cartledge, G., Siedl, B., Woolsey, L. M., Schley, G. S., & Utley, C. (2001). Mt. Olivet after-school program: Peer-mediated interventions for at-risk students. *Remedial and Special Education, 22*(1), 22–33.

Haberman, M. (2003). *Who benefits from failing urban school districts: An essay on equity and justice for diverse children in urban poverty.* Houston, TX: Haberman Educational Foundation. (ERIC Document Reproduction Service No. ED 477 530).

Henig, J. R., Hula, R. C., Orr, M., & Pedescleaux, D. S. (1999). *The color of school reform: Race, politics, and the challenge of urban education.* Princeton, NJ: Princeton University Press.

Hodgkinson, H. (2001). Educational demographics: What teachers should know. *Educational Leadership, 58,* 7–11.

Hosp, J. L., & Reschly, D. J. (2002). Regional differences in school psychology practices. *School Psychology Review, 31,* 11–29.

Howey, K. R. (1999). Preparing teachers for inner city schools. *Theory Into Practice, 38*(1), 31–36.

Kozol, J. (2005). *The shame of a nation: The restoration of apartheid schooling in America.* New York: Crown.

Kopetz, P. B., Lease, A. J., & Warren-Kring, B. Z. (2006). *Comprehensive urban education.* Boston: Pearson.

Lee, C. C. (2005). Urban school counseling: Context, characteristics, and competencies. *Professional School Counseling, 8*(3), 184–188.

Lee, J. (2006). *Tracking achievement gaps and assessing the impact of NCLB on the gaps: An in-depth look into national and state reading and math outcome trends.* Cambridge, MA: Civil Rights Project at Harvard University. Retrieved October 30, 2006, from http://www.civilrightsproject.harvard.edu/research/esea/nclb_naep_lee.pdf

Nieto, S. (2000). *Affirming diversity: A sociopolitical context of multicultural education* (3rd ed). White Plains, NY: Longman.

Noguera, P. A. (2003). *City schools and the American dream: Reclaiming the promise of public education.* New York: Teachers College Press.

Ogbu, J. U. (2002). *Black American students in an affluent suburb.* Mahwah, NJ: Erlbaum.

Predmore, S. R. (2004). Meeting the challenges of urban education. *Techniques, 79,* (pp. 1–2), Retrieved January 30, 2007, from http://www.acteonline.org/members/techniques/

Reeves, D. B. (2003). *High performance in high poverty schools: 90/90/90 and beyond.* Englewood, CO: Center for Performance Assessment. Retrieved October 30, 2006, from http://www.makingstandardswork.com/ResourceCtr/index.php#articles

Reschly, D. J., & Wilson, M. (1995). School psychology faculty and practitioners: 1986 to 1991 trends in demographic characteristics, roles, satisfaction, and system reform. *School Psychology Review, 26,* 74–92.

Richards, J. S. (2007, January 27). Slow progress downs Project GRAD. *Columbus Dispatch,* p. 3A.

Rouse, H. L., & Fantuzzo, J. W. (2006). Validity of the Dynamic Indicator for Early Literacy Skills as an indictor of early literacy for urban kindergarten children. *School Psychology Review, 35,* 341–355.

Singham, M. (2003). The achievement gap: Myths and realities. *Phi Delta Kappan, 84,* 586–591.

Skelton, S. M., Kobayashi, M., Reyes-Rau, C., & Schaeffer, K. (2005). *Promoting culturally responsive educational practices: Raising the achievement of all students.* Cleveland, OH: Ohio Integrated Systems Model Coaches Training.

Steele, C. M., & Aronson, J. (1995). Stereotype threat and the intellectual test performance of African Americans. *Journal of Personality and Social Psychology, 69*, 797–811.

Truscott, S. D., & Truscott, D. M. (2005). Challenges in urban and rural education. In C. L. Frisby & C. R. Reynolds (Eds.), *Comprehensive handbook of multicultural school psychology* (pp. 357–393). New York: John Wiley.

U.S. Census Bureau. (2006). *2000 census*. Washington, DC: Author. Retrieved March 14, 2007, from http://www.census.gov/

U.S. Department of Agriculture. (2002). *Urban and rural residential uses*. Washington, DC: Author. Retrieved March 14, 2007, from www.ers.usda.gov/publications/EIB14/eib14g.pdf

Urban Institute. (2002). *Absence unexcused: Ending teacher shortages*. Retrieved January 30, 2007, from http://www.urban.org

Warren, J., Edmonson, H. M., Griggs, P., Lassen, S. R., McCart, A., Turnbull, A., et al. (2003). Urban applications of school-wide positive behavior support: Critical issues and lessons learned. *Journal of Positive Behavior Intervention, 5*(2), 80–91.

Weiner, L. (2006). *Urban teaching: The essentials*. New York: Teachers College Press.

Ysseldyke, J., Spicuzza, R., Koscioleks, S., Teelucksingh, E., Boys, C., & Lemkull, A. (2001). *Using a curriculum-based instructional system to enhance math achievement in urban schools*. Minneapolis, MN: University of Minnesota.

Ysseldyke, J., Burns, M., Dawson, P., Kelley, B., Morrison, D., Ortiz, S., et al. (2006). *School psychology: A blueprint for training and practice III*. Bethesda, MD: National Association of School Psychologists.

ANNOTATED BIBLIOGRAPHY

Freedom Writers. (1999). *The freedom writers diary: How a teacher and 150 teens used writing to change themselves and the world around them*. New York: Broadway Books.

Provides an excellent detail of the ecological factors urban children experience. Erin Gruwell, a first-year English teacher, was faced with the challenge of trying to educate "troubled" teenagers from Wilson High School in Long Beach, CA. Gruwell challenged her students to keep a diary. The book is made up of student diary entries ranging with issues of teenage pregnancy to homelessness.

Kozal, J. (1992). *Savage inequalities: Children in American schools*. New York: Harper-Perennial.

Examines the inequalities that exist in the education system and concludes that racial segregation has been replaced by socio-economic segregation and that the education system is failing children of poverty; that is, children in poverty do not receive an efficient education. Students from inner cities, usually those of color, attend schools that are not equipped necessities such as heating and water.

Ladson-Billings, G. (2001). *Crossing over to Canaan: The journey of new teachers in diverse classrooms*. San Francisco: Jossey-Bass.

Describes the Teach for Diversity, a cultural-relevant pedagogy program at the University of Wisconsin–Madison. Follows members of the Teach for Diversity and notes their experiences and provides advice for school personnel to use while initiating multicultural education.

Noguera, P. A. (2003). *City schools and the America dream: Reclaiming the promise of public education*. New York: Teachers College Press.

Provides insight on how to improve urban schools for poor students and explains the role of the school in reducing racial inequality, unequal opportunities, and the need for safety in urban schools. Asserts that children of poverty need education the most. School personnel should read this book for advice on what it takes to improve urban schools.

Steinberg, S. R., & Kincheloe, J. L. (Eds.). (2004). *19 urban questions: Teaching in the city*. New York: Peter Lang.

Emphasizes the difficulty of urban education. Discusses answers to questions urban teachers should know before entering the field: Who are our urban students and what makes them different? What is urban education in the age of standardization? What does it mean to be in a gang? A must read for school personnel.

Thomas-El, S., & Murphey, C. (2003). *I choose to stay: A black teacher refuses to desert the inner city*. New York: Kensington.

Provides an inspirational story of an African American teacher who cares about his students and is faced with the challenge of leaving his teaching position at an urban school for an assistant principal position at an affluent school. Provides advice on how teachers can effect change.

Best Practices in Planning Effective Instruction for Children Who Are Deaf/Hard of Hearing

114

Jennifer Lukomski
Rochester Institute of Technology

J.T., a 7-year-old second-grade girl with a profound bilateral hearing loss, has been referred to the school psychologist. The etiology of her deafness is unknown. Both her parents are hearing. Her mother is an interpreter who is fluent in American Sign Language. Both her parents sign to her at home. Her cognitive abilities fall in the high average to superior range. She reads at the third-grade level, and her math/numerical concepts are at a fifth-grade level. Her early education programming was in a special program for deaf/hard of hearing students. Currently she attends a regular education program and receives a variety of related services. She works with the speech and language specialist, and the teacher for the deaf, and meets with the school counselor. She wears hearing aids, uses an interpreter, and uses an FM system. Her expressive language is primarily oral whereas she depends on sign language for her receptive language. Her classmates can understand 50% of her speech. She is easily distracted and has difficulty with personal space. She inappropriately touches her peers and frequently acts improperly in social situations. Her social skill performance is due to a performance deficit, not a skill deficit. She can explain and model to her counselor appropriate social behavior; however, frequently in large group situations, she is unable to perform the appropriate behavior. What will your course of action be as the school psychologist?

OVERVIEW

As an increasing number of children with deafness and hearing loss are educated in the mainstream setting, more school psychologists are being asked to provide services to these children. Planning effective instruction for deaf/hard of hearing children is complex. Owing to the heterogeneous nature of this population, fewer applicable generalizations apply to all children with a hearing loss, thereby making individualized educational programming necessary. For many deaf/hard of hearing children, instruction needs to be systematic, calling on an integration of information from multiple sources and involving an array of related service personnel with specialized expertise and techniques. Communication/linguistic, social, academic/learning, and identity issues are integrally interconnected and essential components that need to be examined when designing instruction for a child with a hearing loss.

This chapter is closely linked to the emerging school psychologist competencies and service delivery model outlined in *School Psychology: A Blueprint for Training and Practice III* (Ysseldyke et al., 2006). Four of the foundational competencies and three of the functional competencies are directly addressed in the content. These six competencies are: (a) interpersonal and collaborative skills; (b) diversity awareness and sensitive service delivery; (c) technological applications; (d) professional, legal, ethical, and social responsibility; (e) systems-based service delivery; (f) enhancing the development of cognitive and academic skills; and (g) enhancing the development of wellness, social skills, mental health, and life competencies. Data-based decision making is the guiding process of applying the content presented.

This chapter is written for school psychologists who have limited knowledge of working with children who are deaf/hard of hearing. The focus of this chapter is on the current themes related to deaf/hard of hearing children's formal and informal learning. The hope is that the school psychologist who is unfamiliar with the intricacies of the issues related to hearing loss will recognize the complexities and gain a working foundation of the issues. In addition, this chapter will provide practical suggestions that can support effective instruction for deaf/hard of hearing children.

BASIC CONSIDERATIONS

Specialized Training

Specialized training in the area of school psychology and deafness is highly recommended to accurately assess, diagnose, and treat deaf/hard of hearing learners. A critical element in the design and selection of educational instruction for a deaf/hard of hearing child is a comprehensive and ongoing assessment of the child's learning strengths and needs. Current law stipulates that a child must be assessed in the language normally used by the child (the 2004 reauthorization of the Individuals with Disabilities Education Act [IDEA]). Frequently for deaf/hard of hearing learners the native language is American Sign Language (ASL) and/or a combination of sign language and voice. For hard of hearing children whose primary mode of communication may be speech, a person knowledgeable with how a hearing loss affects learning and social/emotional functioning is recommended to assess the child's needs. Owing to the limitations of most of the current test instruments for use with deaf/hard of hearing children, the examiner needs to be sensitive and knowledgeable about the interpretation and integration of both the quantitative and qualitative information the child provides.

For assessment and diagnostic purposes, the best action for a school psychologist who does not have a background in deafness is to contact and consult with the school psychologist at the state school for the deaf. Some state schools provide a free-of-charge comprehensive diagnostic assessment as part of the state's special education services. Another resource that can provide direction regarding working with a deaf/hard of hearing child is the National Association of School Psychologists (NASP) deaf/hard of hearing interest Listserv (NAPS-IG-SchPsyDeaf-subscribe@yahoogroups.com).

All school psychologists need to take responsibility to recognize when, where, and how the issues of the child's hearing loss affect the child's academic and nonacademic learning. The school psychologist will need to collaborate with team members (e.g., teachers of the deaf, school psychologists who specialize in deafness, audiologists, interpreters, speech therapists, cochlear implant specialists, audiologists, family members, and the student). In addition, school psychologists need to apply their strong problem-solving skills and mental health knowledge to coordinate and implement social emotional supports for the child who is deaf/hard of hearing.

Heterogeneous Nature

A basic consideration regarding planning effective instruction with regards to deaf/hard of hearing children is the heterogeneous nature of this population. It is important to remember that the deaf/hard of hearing population is as diverse as the hearing population (e.g., religion, ethnicity, home languages spoken, intelligence, and sexual identity). In addition, there is considerable variability regarding each person's hearing loss characteristics such as the etiology of deafness and degree of hearing loss. Other factors include when the hearing loss was identified, when the loss actually occurred, the child's early language interventions, the family's hearing status and communication modes, the child's cultural identification, the child's language development, and whether the child's hearing is progressive or stable. Factors such as the child's use of speech, cued speech and/or sign language, and the child's use of hearing aids and/or cochlear implant also contribute to the uniqueness of each deaf/hard of hearing child. All of these variables (see Table 1) need to be thoroughly reviewed and considered when planning the child's instruction.

In many cases, the etiology of the hearing loss, such as viruses and prematurity, causes neurological damage to other parts of the brain. Prevalence estimates of secondary disabilities for deaf/hard of hearing children, such as learning disabilities, mental retardation, autism, and blindness, range from 20 to 40% (Knoors & Vervloed, 2003). In other words, a sensory deficit such as a hearing loss does not exclude the possibility of the presence of other disabilities.

Cultural Considerations

Because more than 90% of deaf/hard of hearing children are born to hearing parents, one unique aspect of the deaf culture is that the majority of deaf/hard of hearing children are not born into the deaf culture. Thus, hearing parents and deaf children seek the deaf culture out. This deaf cultural identification is not based on degree of hearing loss but rather on ASL fluency and interaction with the deaf community. Historically for many deaf/hard of hearing children, the state school for

Table 1. Background Information That Informs Instruction Planning for Deaf/Hard of Hearing Children

Hearing loss type • Conductive • Sensorineural • Mixed	Degree of hearing loss DB level/unilateral/bilateral • Sound awareness threshold • Speech awareness threshold • Aided and unaided hearing
Hearing loss • Progressive • Stable	Early language intervention services
Age loss was identified	Use of hearing aids
History of ear infections	Age first fitted with hearing aids

Postlingual/prelingual
  hearing loss
	Use of cochlear implant (age of
	  cochlear implant)

Etiology of deafness	Family's hearing status
Child's language development	Home communication modes
Child's cognitive ability level	Child's use and proficiency of speech, cued speech, ASL

Child's cultural identification	Child's use of assistive devices
	  (e.g., hearing aids, FM system,
	  blinking lights, TTY,
	  BlackBerry, CANT,
	  captioning, C-Print, CART,
	  TypeWell)

Other disabilities	Child's use of related services
	  (e.g., interpreters, speech/
	  language, audiologist, cochlear
	  specialist team)

the deaf was a focal place where the deaf cultural awareness was developed. Owing to a drop in the enrollment in these state schools, this identity exploration may not be fully initiated until adolescence when children participate in summer camps for deaf youth and/or when they are older and attend colleges such as Gallaudet University and the National Technical Institute of the Deaf.

Deafness is viewed by many as a distinct culture rather than a disability (Padden, 1980). From this cultural perspective, deaf individuals are viewed as different rather than as having a deficit. In addition, the hearing loss for many deaf individuals is, itself, less of an obstacle than society's attitudes and inability to provide full communication access (du Feu & Fergusson, 2003).

Some hard of hearing children may opt not to use ASL; however, many students in adolescence and emerging adulthood explore their identity and gravitate toward learning ASL, which is a principal characteristic of the deaf culture. School psychologists need to be knowledgeable about the options, the pros and cons of

each option for the specific child, and must listen to the parents' concerns and respect the parents' and child/ adolescent's position. School psychologists must learn about the child's cultural background and recognize that the child's first language may not be English. A language assessment in the child's primary language (i.e., ASL), in addition to English, may be warranted.

Sensitivity to these cultural nuances is essential for correct interpretation of the child's behaviors and support services. Deaf children's behavioral norms are often dictated by their communication mode. These behavioral examples include vigorous waving of a hand to get a person's attention, scanning the classroom periodically to see who is talking, use of peripheral vision to alert to the environment, maintaining intense and continual eye contact, touching another person to gain his or her attention, and use of animated sign language. When misinterpreted, these behaviors, the norm for children who are deaf/hard of hearing, can lead to misidentification of behavioral disorders in deaf/hard of hearing children (Morgan & Vernon, 1994).

Best Practices in Effective Instruction

There are three interconnected domains that need to be thoroughly addressed when designing instructional programming for the child who is deaf/hard of hearing: the child's communication needs, learning needs, and social interaction needs. Each of these domains is discussed in this section. The communication domain is segmented into the following domains: early intervention/family collaboration, learning environment, audiograms, speech and language, ASL, interpreters, assistive listening devices, and cochlear implants.

Communication

The best primary communication mode is still controversial. Questions exist regarding whether the child and/or adolescent should attend speech classes, have a cochlear implant, use a FM system, use sign language, or use cued speech. Most of these communication supports and communication modes are not exclusive approaches. Moreover, the use of sign language, the most naturally accessible language for deaf children, will not negatively delay the child's fluency in speech (Marschark, Lang, & Albertini, 2002).

Early Intervention/Family Collaboration

Since the 1990s, the technology to detect hearing loss in newborns has increased tremendously, and states now mandate universal newborn hearing screenings. These improvements in early detection, together with the technological improvements in cochlear implants, are promising advances for children who are deaf/hard of hearing. Until recently, many children with profound to severe hearing loss were not identified until a year old or older, whereas most hard of hearing children—mild to moderate loss—were not identified with a hearing loss until age 2 or 3 or older. Considering that many of the fundamentals of language acquisition are in place by age 3, the earlier the hearing loss is detected, the sooner intervention can begin.

Researchers agree that early childhood hearing loss identification, early amplification to take advantage of any residual hearing, and early intensive language intervention are critical components for deaf/hard of hearing children's learning (Yoshinago-Itano, 2006). That is, early identification of a child's hearing loss that leads to early intervention, including early amplification and early sign language use, can prevent significant language delays and related problems. Parents who participate in early education programming with knowledgeable professionals, who have a child who has average to above average intelligence, and who develop effective communication with their deaf/hard of hearing child can expect their child to achieve language and social skills commensurate with his or her hearing peers (Bodner-Johnson & Sass-Lehrer, 2003).

Necessary aspects to ensure early intervention effectiveness are involving, collaborating with, and supporting parents. Most hearing parents, when told they have a deaf child, are not prepared and typically lack the context necessary for fully understanding the issues related to this condition. These parents have limited knowledge about deafness and about the language and educational options available for their child. Complicating matters is that in the midst of the parents' grief regarding having a child with a hearing loss they may hear conflicting opinions about the most appropriate and effective communication and educational method for their child, such as having a cochlear implant, being educated in an oral setting, using cued speech, and using sign language. Thus, parents need unbiased information regarding hearing loss, assistive listening devices, communication and language development, and special education practices (Marschark et al., 2003). Professionals, in turn, need to collaborate with parents in evaluating the options for the child as a unique learner.

Earlier participation in intervention services translates into longer stays in early intervention programs, providing the parents with increased support to learn about the implications of their child's hearing loss and how to provide the best language development opportunities and experiences. An effective early intervention plan includes frequent assessments, collaboration with professions, and ongoing instruction of families. In addition, for children who have cochlear implants, parents are taught how to incorporate natural opportunities to teach listening skills and how to make listening and communicating fun and playful (Yoshinaga-Itano, 2006).

Learning Environment

When considering the appropriate school learning environment for a deaf/hard of hearing child, how the child communicates as well as how the environment supports the child's communication opportunities should be optimized. To determine the child's participation needs within a specific setting, an assessment must be made of the communicative demands required of the children within that setting (Ying, 1990). Frequently, hard of hearing children who are able to function orally in quiet one-on-one situations have communication breakdowns in a classroom setting where there are many speakers and the noise level is high. In addition, the child's communication needs in small group activities, auditorium presentations, classroom discussions, classroom lectures, physical education activities, and bus and cafeteria times can vary.

Most children who have cochlear implants or who wear hearing aids are sensitive to background noise. Any extraneous noise such as noisy heating/cooling systems or traffic outside the classroom can effect the child's concentration. The audiologist can take an audiometer reading in the classroom showing whether the reverberation and signal-to-noise ratio in the classroom is at acceptable or unacceptable levels (Seaver & DesGeorges, 2004). Carpets and acoustically treated ceiling tiles may need to be added to the classroom to create an effective instructional environment.

In the hearing world, the amount of language development and communication that occurs incidentally is significant. A hearing person learns about human interactions, family dynamics, cultural mores, and world affairs by overhearing conversations at home, school, and the community and by hearing announcements, overhearing phone conversations, and listening to the radio and television and the news. Deaf/hard of hearing children, in comparison, frequently miss out on these influential learning opportunities unless these incidental learning situations are made accessible.

For deaf/hard of hearing children who are not blind, the visual field will be the child's primary sense used to orient to the environment. Visual attention and visual orientation to the world has many ramifications. This reliance on the visual field influences the way deaf/hard of hearing individuals experience the world making their world experience different. Their dependence on visual information can also make deaf/hard of hearing children more prone to visual distraction than their hearing peers. This reliance on the visual field dictates that for instructional purposes, lighting and seating arrangements are of paramount importance. The classroom needs to be well lit, and glare on the windows and the positioning of the teacher in relation to the lighting needs to be examined. The child needs to be seated close to the teacher, so that the child can visually track the teacher without any visual obstructions. One of the best seating arrangements for the classroom is placing tables or seats in a horseshoe shape. When the seating arrangement is in a horseshoe, the deaf/hard of hearing child can visually locate other children who are participating in class discussion as well as track class activity.

Another consideration for children who are limited by the auditory input and rely on the visual field for communication is that the child's attention is divided among the various tasks presented in the classroom. To begin communication, the teacher first needs to gain the child's visual attention either by a tap on the child's shoulder, a hand movement in the child's visual field, or a flick of the overhead lights. Then the teacher needs to allow the child to orient visually to the teacher or object of discussion. The child has to shift visual attention from the environment to the communicator in order to receive a person's message. Often teachers present material and talk about the material at the same time. For example, teachers lecture while writing on the blackboard or explain points during a movie. For a deaf/hard of hearing child, this simultaneous presentation, rather than complementing the material presented, may compete with the salient information to be learned. Instead, the teacher should point to the visual material, pause and allow the child to scan the visual material, and then the teacher can discuss the material.

Taking lecture notes is another activity that can become a competing rather than a supplementing task for deaf/hard of hearing children. Daily interactions in the classroom, such as rapid rate of discussion, rapid turn taking, rapid change of topics, and more than one child talking at a time are also difficult for the deaf/hard of hearing child to follow (Stinson, Liu, Saur, & Long,

1996). To facilitate communication, classroom activities need to be structured in a manner that allows the child to fully participate. The best practice approach is for the teacher to limit simultaneous presentation of material, allow for pauses in presentation of activities, identify speakers, and monitor turn taking. In addition, depending on the child's age, some form of note taker may be necessary.

The school psychologist needs to be aware of the various environments that a child must function in and systematically observe the child, the environment, and the interactions of others with the child in the different settings. The child's communication plan should include strategies for handling communication breakdowns, handling the child's fatigue, training school personnel and classmates regarding communication strategies, and parent training in ASL.

Audiograms

The documentation that a child has a hearing loss is the child's audiogram. Audiograms should be completed and reevaluated annually to help determine the child's amplification needs. The audiogram, however, is a gross starting point to determine the child's communication needs. Two children with identical audiograms can have dramatically different functional hearing. Similarly, children with poorer auditory skills do not necessarily have the greater degree of hearing loss (Ying, 1990). In addition, frequent ear infections affects the child's language acquisition and access to learning opportunities. In general, many children with mild to moderate hearing loss benefit from amplification and speech training. Children with severe to profound hearing loss also can benefit from amplification and speech training; however, they frequently need sign language as their primary mode of expressive and receptive language.

Speech and Language

There is no single oral method of speech and language instruction. Rather, there is a group of methods that emphasize different aspects of the communication process (Beattie, 2006). Although there are 20 names for the various speech and language methods in North America, the oral methods most frequently used include auditory verbal, auditory oral, and cued speech (Beattie, 2006). The auditory verbal method focuses solely upon listening and restricting a child's access to lip reading during a therapy session and is used predominantly with children who have cochlear implants (Beattie, 2006). In comparison, the auditory oral approach allows children to lip read, develop their spoken language by combining auditory and visual cues, and is found in a range of educational settings. Cued speech is a speech system that visually represents English phonemes as different hand shapes that are positioned around the speaker's mouth to help a child become aware of speech sounds. Research conducted in France has shown that deaf children who used cued speech consistently at home and at school from an early age showed increased performance in reading skills (Marschark et al., 2002).

American Sign Language

For children with severe to profound hearing loss, exposure to spoken language usually is not sufficient for successful communication. For these deaf children, communication depends on ASL or other forms of manually coded English (Marschark et al., 2002). ASL is a natural language that has its own grammar and rules of syntax. In contrast, other manually coded sign languages use hands to convey language, yet are artificial signing systems that adopt and adapt ASL signs to fit the grammatical structure of English. The degree that these signing systems adhere to the grammatical structure of English lies on a continuum. Pidgin Sign English (PSE) falls in the middle of the continuum with its use of ASL structure as well as English word order. On the other end of the continuum are more rigid manually coded systems such as Signed Exact English (SEE1, SEE2). Total communication—using a combination of methods to communicate—is effective for facilitating communication; however, it is not a real language and does not develop a language base for the child.

Considering the varied language enrichment backgrounds of deaf/hard of hearing children, the assumption that deaf children will automatically learn and become fluent in ASL is optimistic and not correct. Interaction with ASL deaf role models facilitates the learning of ASL. Nonetheless, many deaf children who have limited exposure to deaf role models at early ages can benefit from formal instruction in ASL to enhance their communication/language skills.

Interpreters

Many deaf/hard of hearing children, with and without cochlear implants, require interpreting services for access to formal and informal learning experiences. The multiple visual stimuli, distractions, and variety of speakers in a classroom make it difficult for even a child with good speech reading skills and one-on-one conversational abilities to effectively participate in group situations. According to the IDEA regulations,

interpreting services include "oral transliteration, services, cued language transliteration services, sign language transliteration and interpreting services, and transcription services such as communication access real-time translation (CART), C-Print, and TypeWell."

For those children whose preferred mode of communication is sign language, an educational interpreter should be provided to facilitate communication. Often the function of the educational interpreter in the public school system is not clearly defined, and school personnel tend to misunderstand the role of the interpreter and who can interpret (Seal, 2004). The primary function of the interpreter is to be the voice and ears for the student and the voice of the teacher. The mere ability to sign does not qualify someone to be an interpreter. Especially in a formal setting, the interpreter must have specialized training and be certified by the state or national Registry of Interpreters for the Deaf. In addition, the interpreter must not only be a certified interpreter but also must be qualified to interpret in the sign language form used by the child. Another misunderstanding regarding the role of the interpreter pertains to when the interpreters' support is no longer needed. A deaf/hard of hearing child's success in the classroom does not mean that the child no longer needs the interpreter. One of the reasons why the child is successful is because the interpreter facilitates communication. Removing the interpreter eliminates the child's access to communication.

The other roles an educational interpreter may assume must be clearly defined with all members of the educational team. First and foremost, the interpreter is a facilitator of communication in and out of the classroom. This includes extracurricular activities. In the school setting, educational interpreters are also members of the educational team. Educational interpreters can assume other responsibilities if they have the qualifications, background, and time. School psychologists, understanding that some teachers may believe that the interpreter is either an interruption or a glorified teacher's aide, can facilitate the team's discussion regarding these misconceptions and help clarify roles.

When a classroom uses an interpreter, a few unique communication dynamics occur. The lag time between the spoken and signed message can affect the deaf/hard of hearing child's ability to fully participate in classroom discussion. In addition, the interpreter may need to further explain or define terms. Teachers, therefore, need to build in pauses, especially before calling on students, to allow for the deaf/hard of hearing child to catch up and be included in the discussion.

Unfortunately, educational interpreters frequently do not have the interpreting skills to work effectively in classrooms nor are they proficient enough to represent all aspects of conversation, discussion, dialogue, or lecture that have direct relevance to classroom instruction (Schick, Williams, & Kupermintz, 2005). Many interpreters, especially elementary interpreters, distort, omit parts, and simplify the teacher's message (Schick et al., 2005). In other words, the teacher's instruction that many deaf/hard of hearing children receive is not necessarily what the teacher delivers or what the hearing children receive. Confounding matters is that the interpreter is frequently the deaf/hard of hearing child's primary language model. School psychologists need to be aware of these issues when evaluating the child's instructional environment.

Assistive Listening Devices

There continues to be advances in the technology relating to assistive listening devices (ALDs) and other communication devices. The ALD goal is to aid the child to make the most of residual hearing and make speech or noises more audible, if not clearer. No device, however, restores the hearing to normal or typical hearing. In addition, a child's amplification requires ongoing management (Beattie, 2006). IDEA requires that the educational team considers whether the child requires assistive technology devices and services. The team must also ensure that the hearing aids and external components of a cochlear implant are functioning properly, which means regular checking of batteries and cords.

Most schools provide services that include electro-acoustic analysis of the hearing aid, real ear measurements, and/or listening checks. Schools usually perform troubleshooting services that include minor hearing aid repairs such a replacing batteries and unclogging earmolds. Daily listening checks of the implant, replacing coils, and performing auditory and speech perception measures to evaluate the effectiveness of the cochlear implant are other services that are necessary to perform.

The traditional ALDs are FM systems and hearing aids, which are used primarily by children who have moderate hearing losses to amplify the loudness and the clarity of the sender's voice. The teacher wears the microphone and transmitter and the child wears the receiver.

Other assistive technology that can be used to accommodate children with hearing losses are telecommunication devices (i.e., TDD, TTY), speech to text computer systems (e.g., C-Print, CART, TypeWell), video conferencing, captioned films and media

materials, and computers. Computer-assisted captioning technology such as C-Print, CART, and TypeWell requires a trained paraprofessional, either a C-Print captionist, CART stenographer, or a TypeWell transcriber. There are subtle differences between the various speech-to-text systems; however, the systems are basically set up the same way. The trained captionist is either present in the class or is connected via a telephone line. As the captionist types the presentation into the computer, the computer software translates the material into real-time captions that can be projected onto a laptop or other display monitor. The transcript can then also be printed as notes for the class eliminating the need for a separate note taker. Of course this technology is as only as good as the child's ability to read.

Another more omnipresent technological device that can be used for instruction as well as to facilitate communication and interaction among children is the computer and BlackBerry. The computer presupposes that these children have minimum literacy level and keyboard skills. Both of these skills can, however, be further developed as the child becomes more comfortable with the computer.

Cochlear Implants

As technology has advanced, cochlear implants have become more prevalent, and more parents are choosing implants for their children. Even though the cochlear implant acts as a powerful hearing aid in the IDEA regulations, a cochlear implant is explicitly defined as a medical device and not an assistive device or a related service.

In simplified terms, a cochlear implant has two internal and five external components. Surgery is required to place the internal stimulating electrode array inside the cochlea and to place a magnet under the skin to maintain contact between the externally worn components and the implanted electrode components. The external components consist of a microphone, sound processor, transmitter, transmitting cable, and battery. The sound in the environment is transmitted via the speech processor and converted to electrical impulses in the cochlea. The speech processor requires individual programming, called mapping, before use and may require remapping periodically. This first mapping typically occurs 1 month after the internal components have been inserted. Once the speech processor has been mapped the real work begins. The child receives explicit instruction and concentrated practice in perceiving and producing speech. An essential component for the success and effectiveness of the cochlear implant is the parents' and child's involvement and motivation in early auditory stimulation and sound comprehension.

Although there is a high degree of variability in the language performance and academic outcomes of children with cochlear implants, children who receive implants before age 5 tend to have language growth rates that are close to hearing children (Nicholas & Geers, 2006). Possible indicators of children who have success with cochlear implants are early implementation, the child's intelligence level and preimplant language base, realistic family expectations, strong parental commitment, family advocacy, and intensive speech and listening therapy (Christiansen & Leigh, 2002).

It is important that all team members understand that cochlear implants do not make the child hearing. For the most part, children with cochlear implants function more like hard of hearing children (Christianson & Leigh, 2002). Noisy situations, big group discussions, and interacting with strangers will be challenging situations. Children with cochlear implants still may need a variety of special education services. In addition to extensive speech and auditory therapy including auditory verbal therapy, children with cochlear implants may continue to benefit from FM amplification systems, open captions, note taking, and a sign language interpreter in the classroom.

Cochlear implantation, postsurgical maintenance, mapping, and replacement of the external or internal components are not the responsibility of the school district; however, the school district "must ensure" that the external components are functioning properly. In addition, school personnel are encouraged to monitor the child's behavior, to detect whether there is a change that may be due to hearing, and to recommend to the parents that remapping may be necessary. Someone on the child's educational team should be responsible for teaching the child how to change or recharge the batteries and replace broken or lost cords.

Learning Issues

Most of the academic lags that deaf/hard of hearing children experience are due to their poorly developed language skills from an early age (Marschark et al., 2002). The area that has to be first considered in developing these literacy skills is the child's language development. Many deaf/hard of hearing children are challenged to learn to read before they have acquired and internalized any formal language (McAnally, Rose, & Quigley, 1994).

Overall, deaf/hard of hearing individuals have average intellectual abilities. In contrast, their academic achievement, especially with regards to literacy, is below the level of their hearing peers. Fifty percent of deaf high school graduates read above the fourth-grade level and 50% read below the fourth-grade level (Marschark et al., 2002). No Child Left Behind accountability is an issue for many deaf/hard of hearing children. All too often deaf/hard of hearing children are allowed to get by with fewer requirements and lower standards and expectations than are required of hearing children (Marschark et al., 2002). Because most deaf/hard of hearing children do not learn the same way as most hearing children learn, it is of utmost importance that an instructional match be made between the child's specific skills, the instruction provided in the classroom, and the tasks that the child is asked to complete (Marschark et al., 2002).

Schirmer and McGough (2005) compared the National Reading Panel standards to the available research on deaf individuals' reading development and instruction and found that deaf readers are able to access phonological information, use finger spelling and sign language as visual codes for word recognition, and can learn to recognize words automatically. One area of concern was that the focus of teaching has been on teaching deaf/hard of hearing children the basic decoding skills of how to read, without encouraging active participation or teaching individual strategies for reading to learn for comprehension (Strassman, 1997). Instruction in mental imagery and inference making appears to improve reading comprehension for deaf/ hard of hearing children, whereas simplifying the syntactic structures in reading material does not improve deaf readers' comprehension (Schirmer & McGough, 2005). Instruction that focuses on basic skills such as using worksheets, answering teachers' questions, or memorizing vocabulary words without developing metacognitive knowledge of reading for meaning and authentic purposes is not effective. In addition, strategies that encourage attention to text elements as well as relations among those elements are most effective in optimizing text comprehension (Marschark & Lukomski, 2001).

It is possible for deaf children with profound hearing losses to achieve reading skills commensurate with those of their hearing peers. Although deaf/hard of hearing children of deaf/hard of hearing parents tend to read better than most deaf/hard of hearing children of hearing parents, many deaf/hard of hearing children of hearing parents who learn to sign also have reading abilities that are higher (Marschark et al., 2002). The crucial issue is that children who have access to a language at home and have more language experiences have an increased proficiency and automaticity in processing meaning from written work (Bebko & Metcalfe-Haggert, 1997).

Parents should be advised about the importance of reading with their young children and should be instructed on methods by which they can combine sign language and spoken language or sign-supported spoken language. Parents need to be taught how to be sensitive to their child's processing of verbal and visual information in a consecutive rather than a simultaneous manner. Early reading experiences can directly facilitate language development and literacy in children with a hearing loss. In addition, the parent and child relationship benefits from this structured interaction.

Unfortunately, the educational approaches over the last 150 years have focused on placing deaf/hard of hearing children in the regular education system to make them more like hearing children rather than in adapting instructional methods. The present field lacks validated instructional methods for deaf/hard of hearing children (Marschark, 2006). Possible instructional approaches to use are to borrow from those resources that are used with children who have difficulty with reading, such as strategies borrowed from the learning disability field (Marschark & Lukomski, 2001). Even for those deaf/hard of hearing children who do not have a secondary disability, the fact that deaf/hard of hearing individuals have a greater reliance on visual information than hearing peers, and in many situations process visual and verbal information consecutively rather than simultaneously, makes them different learners from hearing children. Strategies used with children who have reading disabilities involve interactive and direct instruction, emphasize pictorial materials, use repetition, and incorporate multisensory information sources, all of which enhance the learning experience for deaf/hard of hearing children.

Another component to interactive learning is teaching the deaf/hard of hearing child about his or her hearing loss. Similar to children who have learning disabilities, deaf/hard of hearing children need to be taught about their hearing loss and how it affects learning and the strategies needed to compensate for the differences. Their understanding of their learning strengths and needs encourages the child to become a self-advocate.

Social Interaction

School psychologists know how important friends are for mental health and overall adjustment. Children with positive social interactions in school tend to have higher academic achievement and are more likely to succeed in their careers (Marschark, 1997). The lack of close friendships for deaf/hard of hearing children in the mainstream setting has critical implications for program planning for their development. Coping with a hearing loss in the mainstream becomes more stressful without the variety of social interaction that can help combat some of the stress.

An essential aspect of the social emotional life of deaf/hard of hearing individuals is the communication barrier that leads to social isolation and limited opportunities to practice social skills (Calderon & Greenberg, 2003). Communication strategies in more intimate settings with parents and peers are key factors that support deaf/hard of hearing children to develop positive self-regard and to decrease the feelings of loneliness, depression, and social anxiety.

Another predictor of children's psychosocial adjustment hinges on teacher-related variables (Polat, 2003). For example, even though deaf/hard of hearing children were at age-appropriate social skill levels, hearing children were rated more socially mature than deaf/hard of hearing children in public schools by their teachers (Kluwin, Stinson, & Colarossi, 2002). One underlining theme is that, for a deaf/hard of hearing child, many of the social emotional issues are not inherent to deafness per se but rather directly linked to the environmental accommodations and understanding of the deaf experience by others. The teachers and hearing children need to learn about the strengths and needs of a deaf/hard of hearing child in their class and how to best communicate with that class member. The school psychologist can be instrumental in helping the teacher and other classmates understand the needs and perspective of their deaf classmate.

IDEA stresses the importance of providing access to nonacademic and extracurricular services to children who have a disability. Social interaction is not solely about having friends, socializing at school, and minimization of isolation or belonging to a group. Social settings provide rich learning opportunities for language development and also for incidental learning that illuminates the aspects of daily life (Yoshingao-Itano, 1997).

There is considerable overlap between communication, language, and social interaction. A shared language does not necessarily guarantee good communication; however, without a shared language, limited communication can happen, and without social interaction, language development is hampered. Social interaction activities such as teaching other children sign language or allowing children to use the FM system, and teaching deaf/hard of hearing children how to ask questions, take turns, and listen, can be planned in the deaf/hard of child's educational program. For the most part, small group activities are better than large social groups; dyad cooperative exercises are the best for an equal interaction to take place. Another possibility to increase friendships with other deaf/hard of hearing children is for the child to develop online interaction with other children who are deaf/hard of hearing. To have the most success in sustained peer interactions, specific strategies to address maintenance and generalization of these contacts needs to be built into the interventions (Anitia & Greenberg, 2003). Table 2 outlines some of these tips and additional tips for fostering the social–emotional development of deaf/hard of hearing children.

To foster and promote the deaf/hard of hearing child's social–emotional development, home–school collaboration is also critical. As with other disabilities, the family's coping and adjustment to the child's hearing loss is a good predictor of the child's adjustment. Some suggestions are to involve parents in the educational process and to provide the parents with resources regarding advanced ASL classes, family weekend retreats, exposure to deaf adults, and problem-solving groups to address deaf adolescent issues (Calderon & Greenberg, 2000). The importance of providing deaf/hard of hearing children opportunities to learn about cultural aspects of deafness and to socialize with other deaf/hard of hearing children and adults needs to be brought to the attention of the child's family.

Since long-term, intensive interventions for social–emotional opportunities are more effective than short-term interventions, some deaf/hard of hearing children may do best with an educational plan that recommends or supports different placements at different times during their development. Some deaf/hard of hearing children benefit from attending a separate program designed for deaf/hard of hearing children part of the day in addition to regular education classes for identified courses.

SUMMARY

School psychologists who are sensitive to the complex and interconnected nature of the communication, literacy, and socialization issues related to hearing loss can play a vital role in the planning of instruction. The purpose of this chapter was to provide a foundational resource for the school psychologist regarding the intricacies of working with deaf/hard of hearing children. The school psychologist can help provide the deaf/hard of hearing child with a more positive and effective school learning experience (see Table 3). A dominant theme and focus must be the child's language development. Early language intervention is a key element to foster early literacy skills. The school psychologist in the role of consultant can facilitate collaboration among the regular education teacher, special education teacher, interpreters, speech and language specialist, audiologist, family, and child/adolescent. Especially in the socialization domain, which addresses the deaf/hard of hearing child's social–emotional well-being, it is possible for school psychologists who are not deafness specialists to be proactive in advocating for the child's welfare.

In the case example presented at the beginning of this chapter, a recommended course of action for the school

Table 2. Tips for Fostering the Social–Emotional Development of Deaf/Hard of Hearing Children

- Create opportunities for successful social interactions.
- Invite deaf/hard of hearing speakers to the classroom to act as role models.
- Seek out opportunities for interactions with other children who have a hearing loss.
- Educate the child about his or her deafness through discussions about Individualized Educational Plans, individual strengths, and communication needs.
- Engage children in dyad activities that will create opportunities for social interactions within the classroom.
- Educate hearing peers about how to communicate with deaf/hard of hearing children and how to work effectively with an interpreter.
- Provide a structured opportunity for deaf children who sign to systematically teach signs to hearing children in the class.
- Perform a thorough functional behavioral assessment when a problem behavior occurs.
- Consider parent contributions and parenting issues when evaluating social–emotional difficulties in deaf/hard of hearing children.
- Implement a school-wide positive behavioral interventions and supports program.

Table 3. Tips for Creating a Supportive Instructional Environment for Deaf/Hard of Hearing Children

- Increase incidental learning experiences
- Limit divided attention tasks
- Reduce environmental noise
- Consider lighting and visual distractions
- Be sensitive to interpreter lag
- Slow down instructional pace
- Arrange specialized seating
- Supplement instruction with visual aids (i.e., notes, captioning, overheads, charts)
- Encourage dyad activities
- Increase sustained peer interactions
- Be sensitive to communication difficulties in large groups
- Plan for communication needs in the cafeteria, on the bus, and during recreational activities (i.e., playground, gym, swimming pool)

psychologist is to conduct systematic observations of J.T. in a variety of settings. After reading this chapter, the school psychologist should be more sensitive to the important factors when observing the teachers' instruction, the environmental setting, as well as J.T.'s and J.T.'s classmates' communication strategies. J.T.'s behaviors need to be examined in the context of her deafness and cultural norms. Based on the brief case background, J.T.'s primary needs appear to be in the social realm. The school psychologist should consult with J.T.'s team members (i.e., teacher for the deaf, regular education teacher, speech therapist, interpreter, school counselor, parents) to conduct a functional behavior assessment and develop a behavior plan for J.T. Owing to J.T.'s reliance on sign language, a psychologist who knows ASL and specializes in children who are deaf/hard of hearing may need to be consulted as well. Nonetheless, the school psychologist with team members can consider what tips on Table 2 could help foster J.T.'s social–emotional interactions.

REFERENCES

Antia, S. D., & Greenberg, M. T. (2003). Peer interactions of deaf and hard of hearing children. In M. Marschark & P. Spencer (Eds.), *Oxford handbook of deaf studies, language, and education* (pp. 164–176). New York: Oxford University Press.

Beattie, R. G. (2006). The oral methods and spoken language acquisition. In P. E. Spencer & M. Marschark (Eds.), *Advances in the spoken-language development of deaf and hard-of-hearing children* (pp. 103–135). New York: Oxford University Press.

Bebko, J. M., & Metcalfe-Haggert, A. (1997). Deafness, language skills, and rehearsal: A model for the development of a memory strategy. *Journal of Deaf Studies and Deaf Education, 2*, 131–139.

Bodner-Johnson, B., & Sass-Lehrer, M. (Eds.). (2003). *The young deaf or hard of hearing child: A family-centered approach to early education.* Baltimore: Brookes.

Calderon, R., & Greenberg, M. (2000). Challenges to parents and professionals in promoting socioemotional development in deaf children. In P. E. Spencer, C. J. Erting, & M. Marschark (Eds.), *The deaf child in the family and at school* (pp. 123–167). Mahwah, NJ: Erlbaum.

Calderon, R., & Greenberg, M. (2003). Social and emotional development of deaf children: Family, school, and program effects. In M. Marschark & P. Spencer (Eds.), *Oxford handbook of deaf studies, language, and education* (pp. 177–189). New York: Oxford University Press.

Christiansen, J. B., & Leigh, I. W. (2002). *Cochlear implant in children: Ethics and choices.* Washington, DC: Gallaudet University Press.

Das, J., & Ojile, E. (1995). Cognitive processing of students with and without hearing loss. *The Journal of Special Education, 29,* 323–336.

du Feu, M., & Fergusson, K. (2003). Sensory impairment and mental health. *Advances in Psychiatric Treatment, 9,* 95–103.

Kluwin, T. N., Stinson, M. S., & Colarossi, G. M. (2002). Social processes and outcomes of in-school contact between deaf and hearing peers. *Journal of Deaf Studies and Deaf Education, 7*(3), 200–213.

Knoors, H., & Vervloed, M. P. J. (2003). Educational programming for deaf children with multiple disabilities. In M. Marschark & P. Spencer (Eds.), *Oxford handbook of deaf studies, language, and education* (pp. 82–94). New York: Oxford University Press.

Marschark, M. (1997). *Raising and educating a deaf child.* New York: Oxford University Press.

Marschark, M. (2006). Intellectual functioning of deaf adults and children: Answers and questions. *European Journal of Cognitive Psychology, 18*(1), 70–89.

Marschark, M., Lang, H. C., & Albertini, J. A. (2002). *Educating deaf students: From research to practice.* New York: Oxford University Press.

Marschark, M., & Lukomski, J. (2001). Understanding language and learning in deaf children. In D. Clark, M. Marschark, & M. Karchmer (Eds.), *Context, cognition, and deafness* (pp. 71–86). Washington, DC: Gallaudet University Press.

McAnally, P., Rose, S., & Quigley, S. (1994). *Language learning practices with deaf children* (2nd ed.). Austin, TX: PRO-ED.

Morgan, A., & Vernon, M. (1994). A guide to the diagnosis of learning disabilities in deaf and hard-of-hearing children and adults. *American Annals of the Deaf, 139*, 358–370.

Nicholas, J. G., & Geers, A. E. (2006). The process and early outcomes of cochlear implantation by three years of age. In P. E. Spencer & M. Marschark (Eds.), *Advances in the spoken-language development of deaf and hard-of-hearing children* (pp. 271–297). New York: Oxford University Press.

Padden, C. (1980). The deaf community and the culture of deaf people. In C. Baker & R. Battison (Eds.), *Sign language in the deaf community: Essays in honor of William C. Stokoe* (pp. 89–103). Silver Spring, MD: National Association of the Deaf.

Paul, P. V., & Quigley, S. P. (1994). *Language and deafness* (2nd ed.). San Diego, CA: Singular.

Polat, F. (2003). Factors affecting psychosocial adjustment of deaf students. *Journal of Deaf Studies and Deaf Education, 8*(3), 325–339.

Schick, B., Williams, K., & Kupermintz, H. (2005). Look who's being left behind: Educational interpreters and access to education for deaf and hard-of-hearing students. *Journal of Deaf Studies and Deaf Education, 11*(1), 3–20.

Schirmer, B. R., & McGough, S. M. (2005). Teaching reading to children who are deaf: Do the conclusions of the National Reading Panel apply? *Review of Educational Research, 75*(1), 83–117.

Seal, B. C. (2004). *Best practices in educational interpreting* (2nd ed.). Boston: Pearson Education.

Seaver, L., & DesGeorges, J. (2004). Special education law: A new IDEA for students who are deaf or hard of hearing. In R. J. Roeser & M. P. Downs (Eds.), *Auditory disorders in school children* (4th ed., pp. 9–24). New York: Thieme.

Stinson, M. S., Liu, Y., Saur, R., & Long, G. (1996). Deaf college students' perceptions of communication in mainstreamed classes. *Journal of Deaf Studies and Deaf Education, 1*, 140–151.

Strassman, B. (1997). Metacognition and reading in children who are deaf: A review of the research. *Journal of Deaf Studies and Deaf Education, 2*, 140–148.

Ying, E. (1990). Speech and language assessment: Communication evaluation. In M. Ross (Ed.), *Hearing-impaired children in the mainstream* (pp. 45–60). Parkton, MD: York Press.

Yoshinaga-Itano, C. (1997). The challenge of assessing language in children with hearing loss. *Language, Speech and Hearing Services in School, 28*, 362–373.

Yoshinaga-Itano, C. (2006). Early identification, communication modality, and the development of speech and spoken language skills: Patterns and considerations. In P. E. Spencer & M. Marschark (Eds.), *Advances in the spoken-language development of deaf and hard-of-hearing children* (pp. 298–327). New York: Oxford University Press.

Ysseldyke, J., Burns, M., Dawson, P., Kelley, B., Morrison, D., Ortiz, S., et al. (2006). *School psychology: A blueprint for training and practice III*. Bethesda, MD: National Association of School Psychologists.

ANNOTATED BIBLIOGRAPHY

Christiansen, J. B., & Leigh, I. W. (2002). *Cochlear implant in children: Ethics and choices*. Washington, DC: Gallaudet University Press.

Provides an overview of cochlear implants and the process the family goes through with the decision making, the surgery, and the rehabilitation. The progress of language acquisition, school issues, and ethical issues are also discussed.

Marschark, M., Lang, H. G., & Albertini, J. A. (2002). *Educating deaf students: From research to practice*. New York: Oxford University Press.

Provides a research-based framework to summarize what is known about educating deaf students and what the implications for individuals who are involved in the education of deaf students. Some of the topics covered are the characteristics of deaf learners; language development; cognitive development; educational programs and philosophies; reading, writing, and literacy; teaching; and the curriculum.

Marschark, M., & Spencer, P. E. (Eds.). (2003). *Oxford handbook of deaf studies, language, and education*. New York: Oxford University Press.

A comprehensive and authoritative perspective on the social, educational, and linguistic aspects related to deafness. A reference volume consisting of a diverse group of contributors offering a wide range of discipline perspectives.

Schirmer, B. R. (2001). *Psychological, social, and educational dimensions of deafness*. Boston: Allyn & Bacon.

An examination of the major psychological, social, and educational issues affecting the lives of children, adolescents, and adults who are deaf/hard of hearing. Includes communication between parents and their deaf child, social integration and social skills, social status and roles, self-esteem, emotional and behavioral problems, intimacy, and sexuality.

Seal, B. C. (2004). *Best practices in educational interpreting* (2nd ed.). Boston: Pearson Education.

Chapters are organized by educational level with one lead chapter on the administrative aspects of educational interpreting services and a final chapter on the review of current interpreting research. Busy professionals especially administrators and teachers who work with interpreters can read the selected chapter that best fits their setting.

WEB RESOURCES

American Society for Deaf Children: http://deafchildren.org/resources.aspx
Provides links to information regarding decision making for parents, sign language use, amplification, alert systems, cochlear implants, and IDEA and provides links to various advocacy coalitions and partnerships.

Council for Exceptional Children, Division of Communicative Disabilities and Deafness: http://education.gsu.edu/dcdd/
Provides information about the council, including its mission statement to both help with the development and education of individuals with communicative disorders and to promote growth in professionals to better understand and work with these individuals. Also provides links to the group's journal and newsletters.

Hands & Voices: http://www.handsandvoices.org
Provides a variety of links about early intervention, education, and research for families and professionals working with children who are deaf/hard of hearing. Presents a number of instructional supports and some helpful products available for use.

Listen-Up: http://listen-up.org/implant.htm
Maintains a pro cochlear implant stance. Contains information regarding funding for implants, benefits of implants, tips for using implants, and links to position statements on the use of implants, as well as testimonials from individuals who have used them.

National Center for Hearing Assessment and Management, Utah Sate University: http://infanthearing.org

Has a wealth of information regarding infants and toddlers' hearing loss. Has detailed information on early hearing detection and intervention programs.

National Dissemination Center for Children with Disabilities: http://www.nichcy.org/states.htm
Provides contact information of state agencies, state chapters of disability organizations and parent groups, and of parent training projects.

National Institute on Deafness and Other Communication Disorders: www.nidcd.nih.gov
A resource for health information on hearing, balance, smell, taste, voice, speech, and language. Includes information and materials on American Sign Language, cochlear implants, and captioning.

Resource Materials and Technology Center for the Deaf and Hard of Hearing: www.fsdb.k12.fl.us/rmc/
Provides teachers with technology assistance, training, and consultation they need to successfully integrate assistive technology (interactive white boards, writing supports, Kurzweil software) into the classroom. Provides a large lending library of captioned and signed videotapes.

115 Best Practices for Instructing Students Who Are Visually Impaired or Blind

Sharon Bradley-Johnson
Sandra K. Morgan
Central Michigan University

OVERVIEW

Students with a visual impairment are a very hetero-geneous group because of differences in the severity and type of their vision loss, age at onset, and whether or not they have additional disabilities. Most of these students, even those classified as legally blind, are able to perceive light and see details to some extent. The interventions described in this chapter should be considered at each level of the three-tier service delivery model described by Tilly in chapter 2, vol. 1. Further, this chapter provides suggestions consistent with the National Association of School Psychologists' *School Psychology: A Blueprint for Training and Practice III* (Ysseldyke et al., 2006) by addressing strategies to enhance the development of cognitive, academic, social, mental health, and life skills. Working with these children will require strong interpersonal and collaborative skills, application of data-based decision making models, and an understand-ing of adaptive technologies.

The classification *legally blind* makes an individual eligible for government benefits. These individuals have a visual acuity of 20/200 or less in the better eye with correction or a restricted visual field with a diameter of no more than 20 degrees. Visual acuity describes distance vision measured with a standard eye chart, where 20 indicates the distance in feet at which vision is measured and 200 the distance in feet at which someone with normal vision could identify the largest symbol on the chart. A restricted visual field refers to the amount of visual field used to view something from the side. The amount is described in degrees, and typically the visual

field extends to 180 degrees (Sacks, 1998). Despite their vision loss, many of these individuals are able to use visual material.

Students who are legally blind are eligible for special education services under the classification of visually impaired, which includes students whose visual loss, even when corrected, interferes with their educational performance.

For clarity in this chapter, the term *blind* will be used to refer to students who in the classroom must use senses other than vision for learning. These students will need tactile and auditory input for instruction and will require special equipment and materials such as computer hardware and software with speech or braille output, talking calculators, recorded material, or raised line paper for writing.

The term *low vision* refers to students classified as visually impaired but who are not blind. These students have severe vision losses even after correction and need additional instructional adaptations. However, low-vision equipment and environmental changes can improve their vision. Examples of low vision equipment include book stands, magnifiers, and closed-circuit television (CCTV) where text is magnified electronically and displayed on a monitor. Some of these students may require large type whereas others may be able to read standard type. Even though some have sufficient vision for reading print, they also may require tactile and auditory material for instruction.

Thus, students classified as visually impaired require many different adaptations to enable them to function in the classroom.

Incidence

The following information is based on the Twenty-fifth Annual Report to Congress for the Office of Special Education Programs (2005). Based on 2001 data, students classified as visually impaired make up .4% of students who receive special education services: for ages 6–12, 57% are boys; and for ages 13–17, 53.5% are boys. In terms of inclusion, 28% of these students ages 6–12, and 47% of students ages 13–17, are included in regular classrooms 100% of the time. On standardized assessments, the percent of students with visual impairments who scored within the 61–100th percentile were as follows: for letter-word identification, 25%; for comprehension, 17%; and for calculation, 37%.

Etiology

Numerous and varied etiologies account for the many types and degrees of vision loss. Congenital vision losses can result from various conditions including prenatal damage, a genetic malformation, or an inherited condition. Examples include albinism and retinitis pigmentosa. A vision loss resulting from albinism involves abnormal pigment production in the eye. Classroom adaptations might include sunglasses because of light sensitivity, magnification, holding objects and materials close, and special lighting. Retinitis pigmentosa is an inherited condition involving degeneration mainly of light-sensitive cells in the retina, resulting in profound visual impairment. The symptoms are rarely evident to a large extent until at least late childhood. Adaptations may include use of CCTV, special lighting, and avoidance of glare.

Other losses are termed *acquired* or *adventitious* and frequently result from diseases or accidents including head injury, anoxia at birth, infection of the central nervous system (e.g., meningitis), or a reaction to medications. An example is cortical blindness resulting from injury, degeneration of occipital connections, or a tumor causing a lesion in the occipital lobe of the brain. The result is restriction of vision that usually requires some type of adaptation to enable a child to function in the classroom. Adaptations for adventitious vision losses might involve special telescopes to view material at a distance, magnifiers for desk work, high illumination, and CCTV.

Although most vision losses involve damage to the eye or optic nerve, one cause of children's visual impairment is cortical visual impairment (CVI) resulting from damage to the visual systems in the brain. Reduced flow of blood and oxygen to the brain is a primary cause, although head injuries from shaking or battery, or infection of the central nervous system, can cause the condition. CVI is a complicated condition with several educational implications. For example, these children typically have short attention spans, their visual ability is inconsistent and can fluctuate moment to moment, and often they use one sense at a time. For a detailed description of this condition and its educational implications see Palmer (2000).

The majority of students classified as visually impaired have one or more additional impairments. Consultation with a student's medical specialist, teacher, and the consultant for students who are visually impaired will help in understanding a student's condition. (Also see Lukomski, chapter 114, vol. 5, for information on students with a hearing loss and Powell-Smith, Stoner, Bilter, & Sansosti, chapter 76, vol. 4, for information on students with severe and low-incidence disabilities.) A multidisciplinary approach is essential to working effectively with these students.

Onset and Progression

Practitioners need to consider typical development to understand the impact of a vision loss on the development of cognitive, academic, and life skills. When the onset of a vision loss is after age 5, children typically retain visual memories such as memories for color and visual images. These memories facilitate learning language concepts and other skills. For example, learning the meaning of words such as *mountain, castle,* or *street* for sighted children usually is largely dependent on visual input. Whereas children who have a severe loss of vision prior to age 5 must depend on verbal explanations and definitions to understand such words. The reliance on verbal explanations may make it more difficult for them to acquire a complete understanding of certain concepts. Furthermore, some students with a vision loss may use certain concepts correctly in their speech, but do so only because they have learned to use them by rote. To ensure that these students have an adequate understanding of the concepts they use, it is wise to probe any questionable responses.

Whether the onset of the vision loss is gradual or sudden has implications for instruction. When the loss is gradual, teaching as much information requiring vision as possible while a student is still able to use visual input is important. For either type of onset, students and their families are likely to benefit from support and counseling to help cope with this change in their lives, understand the vision loss, recognize what adaptations can be made, and address their fears. Students with little usable vision will need to adapt to the use of tactile and auditory input for instruction and, in many cases, to a new mode for written expression.

BASIC CONSIDERATIONS

Multidisciplinary by Necessity

In nearly all cases, it is impossible to plan a comprehensive and effective instructional program for a student who is visually impaired without using a multidisciplinary approach. In addition to parents and teachers, school psychologists often must work with consultants certified in working with students who are visually impaired, medical specialists, and orientation and mobility instructors. A multidisciplinary approach with a high degree of cooperation among the members is critical in determining a student's strengths and difficulties, planning instruction, and ensuring the continuity of services.

Consultants certified in working with students who are visually impaired or blind may carry out a functional vision assessment and a media assessment, the results of which will include important recommendations for classroom instruction. How a particular student uses his or her vision when performing various academic and daily living tasks is assessed. Utley, Roman, and Nelson (1998) cited the example of a student with monocular dominance who needed to turn his head or position himself off center from a task to engage useful vision.

Uninformed members of a multidisciplinary team might choose the mid-line position as best for viewing the task because they lack an understanding of the effects of vision loss on learning. A consultant certified in this area, however, would be able to conduct an assessment that considers the student's type of vision loss and factors such as position, lighting, contrast, and glare. Based on these results the consultant could recommend positioning and environmental modifications to enhance visual efficiency.

Reports from functional vision assessments might include recommendations, for example, for intensity of illumination, position of the light source, and low-vision equipment. Results from a media assessment will suggest whether a child should be a print or braille reader, or both. However, this decision is often not clear until preschool because the recommendations are based on observations over time, perhaps several years (Koenig &

Holbrook, 2002). Functional vision assessments and media assessments are carried out with students ranging in age from infancy through adolescence.

If not properly trained, classroom teachers tend to rely on more traditional, less technological adaptations, even if more appropriate adaptations are available (Corn & Wall, 2002).

Reviewing medical reports is critical to understanding a student's loss of vision. Ophthalmologists' and optometrists' reports include a description of medical interventions needed, prescriptions, prognosis of progression, and any required restrictions on eye use. Reading a medical report can be daunting because of the terminology and abbreviations involved. Commonly used abbreviations and their meaning appear in Table 1.

Information in a medical report includes a description of visual acuity measured separately for each eye. Also, acuity will be measured with and without correction (with and without glasses). Usually such information is given for both near-vision and distance viewing.

Because vision conditions change frequently, resulting in changes in the needs of students, vision assessments should be current (no more than a year old). Hearing assessments also should be current. Students who are visually impaired or blind rely so heavily on what they hear that it is critical to ensure that their hearing ability is maximized.

Recommendations from a medical report, however, may not apply to the classroom context. Anxiety and the unfamiliar environment of a medical office may affect a student's use of vision during a medical examination. Thus, the recommendations from a functional vision assessment conducted within the school environment also are necessary to plan instruction. A functional vision assessment usually is carried out by a teacher of students with visual impairments.

An orientation and mobility (O & M) specialist has special training in facilitating safe, independent travel for students who are visually impaired or blind. The development of safe, independent travel skills will provide access to opportunities in a variety of settings. An untrained observer may think a student moves about quite well considering the vision loss. An orientation and mobility specialist making the same observations, however, may suggest several options that could increase independent functioning considerably. Thus, assessment and instructional planning by a specialist in this area is important. Training in orientation and mobility skills often begins in infancy (Leong, 1996).

Table 1. Commonly Used Medical Abbreviations

Abbreviation	Definition
C.C.	With correction
C.F.	Counts fingers; if unable to read letters on the eye chart, vision may be measured by the ability to count fingers held up at varying distances
H.M.	Hand movement; if unable to read letters on the eye chart or count fingers, vision may be measured by the ability to see hand movement at varying distances
L.P.	Light perception
N.L.P.	No light perception (totally blind)
N.V.	Near vision
O.D.	Ocular dexter (right eye)
O.S.	Ocular sinister (left eye)
O.U.	Oculi unitis (both eyes)
P.P.	Near point
P.R.	Far point
S., S.S., or S.C.	Without correction
V.A.	Visual acuity
V.F.	Visual field
W.N.L.	Within normal limits

An O & M assessment will include evaluation of a student's skills for moving about safely such as balance, posture, gait, and consideration of factors in the environment in which the student travels, such as obstacles, traffic flow, and the support received from others for the student's independence. An O & M instructor may teach a student directly, working on skills such as travel indoors or out, travel in both urban and rural areas, concept development, use of a cane, low-vision equipment, electronic travel devices, and public transportation. This specialist also may work with family members and other professionals who are able to help students practice skills, as well as arrange experiences where the skills will be needed (Fazzi, 1998).

Thus, to develop comprehensive, effective educational programs that maximize the benefit of services and ensure continuity for students who are visually impaired or blind, school psychologists must collaborate with other professionals. Work with teachers certified in this area is essential. Teaming with medical and orientation and mobility specialists also is necessary.

BEST PRACTICES

Working With Families

Adjusting to the diagnosis of a child's severe vision loss can be particularly difficult for family members who have had little or no contact with people who are visually impaired or blind. Family members may go through various stages of grieving when first informed of the condition. Parents may be frightened about the prospect of raising a child with a severe vision loss. Team members must consider the influence of the family's culture and consider the appropriateness of interventions. Working with other educational team members, school psychologists can help the family understand and adjust to the diagnosis, recognize ways to promote the child's independence, and aid in planning the child's educational program. When sharing information with students and their families, it is important to encourage conversation and provide an environment conducive to the students' asking questions. Preparing the student and family members to answer others' questions about the vision loss may be helpful (Sacks & Corn, 1996).

Besides providing support and counseling, school psychologists can arrange for family members to talk with adults who are visually impaired or blind. These adults can share their experiences, discuss concerns the parents have, and serve as role models for the families and the student. Arranging for the family to participate in parent support groups and talk with other families with children with severe vision losses also can be very helpful.

Because of vision loss, certain skills may be delayed in development, especially for young children. Some delays amount to only a few months, and some can be lessened or eliminated with instruction. If parents are aware that certain skills may take longer to develop for these children, they are less likely to be concerned when their child does not meet a developmental milestone at the age when sighted children do. Also, if parents are aware of possible delays, they can target these skills for practice, which should help minimize delays. Examples of developmental delays that may occur for these children include play and self-help skills that require fine motor movement (scooping food is particularly difficult); walking, which appears at approximately 20 months (Scott, Jan, & Freeman, 1985); social skills (discussed later in this chapter); and some language skills, including use of pronouns and recognizing one's name.

For children who will become braille readers, it would be beneficial if family members learned the basic braille components, including the alphabet and primary punctuation marks. Some family members may be willing to learn to read more braille, which would provide good models for children. Encouraging family members to observe their child in the classroom may help them better understand how their child functions in this setting and recognize how they can be of help. Discussing the importance of organization (covered later in this chapter) and different learning strategies may aid parents in helping children with homework.

Families also may benefit from information regarding computer technology, including voice input/output, scanners, and braille printers that help braille readers share information with others.

As Chen and Dote-Kwan (1998) suggested, "the simplest way to identify what is important for the family is to ask them" (p. 318). Parents must be closely involved in educational planning for their child, and their interests and concerns should be used in planning programs. Further, team members should consider the influence of the family's culture so that recommendations for interventions across domains will include appropriate etiquette and expectations of helping. Communication will be enhanced if school psychologists avoid using jargon when talking with parents.

Infants, Toddlers, and Preschoolers

Studies comparing interactions of parents of sighted infants and parents of infants with visual impairments indicate that often parents of infants with visual impairments need assistance in recognizing and interpreting their infants' signals (Chen, Friedman, & Calvello, 1990). Because infants with a severe vision loss do not make eye contact or direct their gaze toward someone speaking to them, parents may be disappointed or feel rejected in their attempts to interact with their infant. Lack of eye contact results in a decrease in the frequency of parents' visual and vocal responsiveness to their child (Rogers & Puchalski, 1984).

Another factor that may interfere with parent–child interaction is that smiles are difficult to evoke from infants who are visually impaired. Frequently, vigorous physical play is required to make these infants smile (Baird, Mayfield, & Baker, 1997). Without visual feedback, children's smiling behavior diminishes (Teplin, 1995). Verbal feedback and physical contact may reinforce smiling for some children.

Further, when auditory stimulation is present, infants with a visual impairment tend to decrease their movement. Parents may interpret this as a lack of interest in interaction. The motor inhibition, however, helps an infant attend to the auditory stimulation (Ferrell, 1985).

Consequently, parents of young children with a severe visual impairment must make considerable effort to evoke interaction with their infants. Often these parents need help in recognizing behaviors indicating that their infant is responding to their initiations, is signaling to initiate an interaction, or needs a break from interaction. These infant behaviors may be subtle and difficult to interpret. Other than eye contact and smiles, communicative behaviors can involve any fairly consistent change in behavior (e.g., quieting, squirming, changing facial expression, and other increases or decreases in activity level). Helping parents identify these responses, and modeling back-and-forth interaction with the baby, can facilitate responsive interactions between these parents and their infants. Such assistance can prevent a negative pattern of interaction where the infant's signals are ignored, the parent perceives the infant as disinterested in interacting, and initiations from both the parent and infant decrease.

Because some children are unable to see when someone is approaching, their parents may need guidance on how to avoid startling them when initiating an interaction. Reminding the parent to talk as he or she approaches the child will be helpful.

Physical contact contributes to the development of language, social skills, cognition, and motor skills, especially for young children with a severe vision loss. If young children with a visual impairment learn to find physical contact pleasurable, this will help prevent passivity and isolation. Thus, encouraging frequent physical contact between parents and infants or young children can be very beneficial. The use of sling carriers for infants makes providing physical contact easy for parents. The carriers also keep the infant in an upright position enhancing alertness and allowing the baby to be at a level where most activities occur.

Physical contact from parents in the form of guided exploration can be helpful for several reasons. Some infants with a visual loss may be quite passive as a result of extended hospital stays where they have been restrained for medical reasons. Passivity limits learning opportunities. Also, because infants and children with little or no useful vision are not enticed by visual stimulation, this may affect exploration of the environment. Furthermore, because these children cannot visually scan their environments, without assistance from others, they may be unaware of their choices and opportunities (Recchia, 1997). To familiarize children with various choices and opportunities, parents can physically guide their child to encourage movement, manipulation of objects, and search for objects that fall out of reach.

Whereas safety is an issue when vision is severely impaired, frequent interaction with the environment also is critical to reduce passivity and enhance learning. Hence, a balance needs to be found between encouraging exploration of surroundings and ensuring safety. Some parents of children with a disability tend to be overprotective and may inadvertently inhibit learning. Teaching these children to avoid hazards and to respond appropriately to "No" are critical skills to target for instruction.

Despite the loss of vision, exploratory behaviors of infants 12- to 23-months-old who are congenitally blind differ little from those of their sighted peers matched on age and mother's education (Bradley-Johnson, Johnson, Swanson, & Jackson, 2004). This study compared the two groups on 12 behaviors with toys, and no differences were found for 11 behaviors. The one difference observed was for pushing toys with wheels, which sighted infants did more frequently. Both groups of infants demonstrated a wide range of behaviors for exploration.

Providing appropriate toys facilitates active play. Large toys that make noise are easier for children with a severe vision loss to locate. Toys that respond to simple motor movements, such as roly-poly toys, wrist rattles, or bells on booties help an infant learn that his or her behavior affects the environment, an important lesson for a child with a physical or cognitive impairment.

Having a place for storing toys and other items belonging to the child, and teaching the child to put items back when finished with them, teaches organization skills. The sooner these skills are taught to children who are visually impaired or blind, the better. Besides helping children access toys and enhance their learning, developing the habit of keeping things organized will be particularly beneficial once children reach school age.

Because of vision loss, language development may be slower in some areas than for sighted children. Parents can help by routinely naming objects and describing their own actions, even with infants. Providing rich verbal descriptions of children's exploration of the environment can help integrate experiences in a meaningful way (Recchia, 1997).

Encouraging parents to use their child's name before saying something to the child is helpful for two reasons. First, these children often are delayed in learning their names. Frequent use of the child's name provides practice. Second, use of the child's name lets the child know that what is about to be said is directed to her or to him.

Social skills, unfortunately, are delayed for many children who are visually impaired or blind. Often these young children miss nonverbal cues such as gestures, facial expressions, and eye contact. Preschoolers with vision impairments have a tendency to spend most of the time playing alone. Their difficulty in interpreting nonverbal messages may cause a breakdown in communication with peers (Erwin, 1993). Rather than making eye contact, Chen and Dote-Kwan (1998) suggested that these children tend to use physical contact, which may not be positively received by their peers. Hence, social skills often may need instruction.

Another area where families of young children with a severe vision loss may require assistance is with sleep problems. While childhood sleep problems are relatively common in all children, children with visual impairments more frequently demonstrate difficulty falling asleep and sleeping through the night (Mindell & Demarco, 1997). Blind individuals are particularly prone to disturbances in circadian rhythms. Without visual input, circadian rhythms in body temperature, hormone levels, and alertness may not coincide with a 24-hour cycle. Sleep problems have been reported in from 34 to 80% of blind adults (Sack, Blood, Hughes, & Levy, 1998). Early intervention is important as sleep problems tend to continue into later childhood (Mindell, 1993). Behavioral interventions typically used with sighted children may help children with severe vision loss (Mindell, Goldberg, & Fry, 1996). Axelrod (2001) provided a framework for understanding sleep problems and suggested interventions for parents of children with visual impairments. Although a systematic review of interventions is not available, the establishment of consistent bedtime routines helps to cue the body that it is time to sleep (Ferber, 1987). Other behavioral strategies that have been helpful for sighted children include progressive delayed responding from caregivers (Ferber, 1987), crying it out, and scheduled awakenings (Rickert & Johnson, 1988). Oral doses of melatonin also have been shown to improve sleep of children with visual impairments (Stores & Ramchandani, 1999). School psychologists working with children with visual impairments can help to lessen the impact of sleep problems on families by working with parents to develop effective treatments.

School-Age Children and Adolescents

Classroom Behavior

Team members should consider the impact of the vision loss on student behavior for each intervention level. Strategies to address these difficulties should be universally applied. Students with a severe vision loss are likely to require more assistance from others than their sighted peers do. Consequently, they should be able to request help, accept help, and refuse help appropriately. If this is not the case, these behaviors should be taught. For some students developing and implementing a behavior plan to ensure that they are asking for help when needed, rather than sitting passively, may be beneficial.

To function efficiently, and avoid frustrating and unnecessary searches for materials, students who are visually impaired or blind need to be well organized. Using the Social Skills Rating System (Gresham & Elliott, 1990), Buhrow, Hartshorne, and Bradley-Johnson (1998) surveyed 21 regular-education teachers of elementary-level students who were blind. Teachers rated 81% of these students as having difficulty at least sometimes in keeping their desks clean and neat without being reminded. Teaching students to organize their desks and put things where they belong will enable these students to function more independently and more efficiently.

Because students with a severe loss of vision must rely heavily on auditory input, good listening skills are important. Yet, Buhrow et al. (1998) found that teachers rated 76% of the students who were blind as having difficulty sometimes or always in attending to teachers' instructions. Praising these students when they attend well, and asking them to repeat directions before beginning an assignment, should improve their listening skills.

Another teacher concern in the Buhrow et al. (1998) study was that 62% of students who were blind did not finish assignments in a timely fashion. This problem may be a result of several factors. First, braille reading usually takes about 2.5 times longer than reading regular type (Duckworth & Caton, 1986) and reading large type also takes longer than standard type. Fatigue is more of a factor when reading braille or large type. Some regular education teachers may be unaware of the amount of extra time needed and the fatigue involved and thus may set unrealistic time limits for these students. Problems with organization and listening may make these students less efficient in completing assignments. Teachers indicated that, at least on some occasions, 71% of the students who were blind were not using their time appropriately when waiting for assistance (Buhrow et al., 1998). If students who are visually impaired or blind are not completing assignments in a timely fashion, consideration of the appropriateness of teacher expectations, as well as the students' organization skills, listening skills, and ability to use time effectively while waiting for help, should assist in resolving problems.

Social Skills

Visual information helps in monitoring social interaction, especially when nonverbal communication (e.g., gestures and facial expressions) is used (Erwin, 1993). Thus, it is not surprising that for students with limited visual input, social interaction may sometimes be difficult. Results of several studies of adolescents with visual impairments indicate that these students have fewer friends than their sighted peers (e.g., Kef, 1997) and spend more time alone engaging in passive activity (Wolffe & Sacks, 1997). Because of these potential problems, instructional planning for these students should include an examination of both the frequency and quality of interaction with others.

Participation in clubs, sporting events, and other after-school activities should be encouraged as well. Ponchillia, Armbruster, and Wiebold (2005) demonstrated improved sports skills, attitudes, and motivation to participate in sports following short-term skill instruction in a camp designed to teach sports to children with visual impairments.

Several factors specific to students with a severe visual loss may contribute to social interaction problems. Students with little or no vision may need to be taught to face someone who is speaking. Without this skill, interactions will be awkward. Orienting to a speaker may be especially difficult when several people are speaking simultaneously.

The use of prompts, feedback, reinforcement, peer mediation, and modeling have been helpful in teaching students with a severe vision loss specific social skills including eye gaze, initiation of social interaction, and joining activities. These skills have generalized and been maintained over time (e.g., Raver, 1987; Sacks & Gaylord-Ross, 1989). In addition, well-researched social skill training programs for sighted students can be helpful, such as the Social Skills Intervention Guide (Elliott & Gresham, 1991), the ACCEPTS program (Walker et al., 1983), and the ACCESS program (Walker, Todis, Holmes, & Horton, 1988). Jindal-Snape (2004) used training in self-evaluation and recruitment of feedback to improve social interactions.

Although everyone engages in self-stimulation to some degree, students who are visually impaired or blind may self-stimulate at a higher frequency or engage in unusual behaviors. McHugh and Leiberman (2003) reported that of children with visual impairments, those who were totally blind or had retinopathy of prematurity, along with long hospital stays and surgeries early in life, were most likely to exhibit rocking. Self-stimulation is most likely to occur when a student is bored or stressed. Eye pressing and body rocking are the most frequent forms of self-stimulation for young blind children and they tend to be quite stable behaviors (Brambring & Troster, 1992). These behaviors interfere with learning. Because the behaviors can make a child appear strange to others, the behaviors may be perceived negatively by peers. If these behaviors are observed, intervention is needed. Brambring and Troster (1992) observed that when these behaviors occur in children over 4½ years of age, they are particularly stable, even if they occur at a low frequency. Thus, intervention to eliminate body rocking or eye pressing should begin as early as possible.

Eye pressing, which involves pushing on the eyes with one's fingers or thumbs, has been treated effectively using differential reinforcement of incompatible behavior (e.g., Raver & Dwyer, 1986), overcorrection using arm exercises (e.g., Wesolowski & Zawlocki, 1982), and time-out (e.g., Simpson, Sasso, & Bump, 1982). Likewise, different interventions have effectively eliminated body or head rocking including head-band mechanisms (e.g., Felps & Devlin, 1988), restraint and time-out (e.g., Barton & LaGrow, 1985), and verbal and physical prompts as well as praise (e.g., Ross & Koenig, 1991). Several studies (e.g., McHugh & Pyfer, 1999), suggest that vigorous physical activity can decrease the occurrence of such stereotypical behavior. Although these results are encouraging, long-term follow up, and studies with older students in integrated settings, are needed (DeMario & Crowley, 1994).

Effective procedures have been found for increasing positive behaviors to facilitate social interaction, as well. An extensive discussion of these procedures for different emotional and behavior problems for students who are visually impaired or blind is provided by Mar and Cohen (1998).

Oral Language

Students who are blind are not able to receive information conveyed by others through their facial expressions and gestures, and this problem can interfere with their learning and communication. Unless someone is speaking to them or touching them, students who are blind cannot tell when someone is attending to them.

As noted previously, a thorough understanding of some concepts learned primarily through visual input also may be lacking. Some students with a severe vision loss may have problems with articulation, and confusion with pronouns may occur for an extended time period.

Roland and Schweigert (1998) noted that sighted students use vision to monitor activities around them, but students without vision may use their speech for this purpose. They do so by using repetitive strategies (i.e., repeating words or phrases), by asking questions frequently (some of which may be off topic), and by using speech to attract others' attention. This occurs more often for these students than sighted students. Thus, the pragmatic aspects of speech may require instruction so that the students without vision can remain engaged in conversations.

Reading

An understanding of the development of reading skills in children with visual impairment will facilitate consultation and assist in the development of assessment strategies should specific concerns arise. Children who are blind require a broad range of life experiences to provide the background to enable them to be successful readers. Along with input from senses other than vision, they need rich, verbal feedback from others to acquire information that sighted children learn incidentally through vision.

Prior to formal reading instruction, all children benefit from exposure to books and reading with adults. These experiences are particularly important for children who are blind or visually impaired to enhance their language, listening, and early reading skills. Books written in print and braille allow sighted family members to read to the child, and the braille enables the child to tactilely experience the text. Because raised-line drawings do not convey the same meaning as objects, Miller (1985) suggested that real objects be used to substitute for pictures and that book bags be used to hold the objects. A number of print/braille books should be available so that children can choose those they enjoy for repeated reading.

Several programs can help parents and teachers support early literacy development for young children, including older children who are developmentally delayed. The Perkins Panda Early Literacy Program (www.perkinspublications.org) for children birth to age 8, includes storybooks by Odds Bodkin written in large print and braille with high-contrast illustrations, activity guides, cassettes, a stuffed panda, and a bag to hold objects for the story. A video from the American Printing House for the Blind (see Web Resources at the end of this chapter), *Discovering the Magic of Reading*, is for parents and teachers of children from birth to age 5, and presents methods for involving children in a story and choosing books of interest to children with a vision loss. Seedlings Braille Books (www.seedlings.org) also has many low-cost print/braille picture books.

Both braille and sighted readers must learn sound-symbol relationships to decode words, but braille readers must learn more symbols. Many contractions are used to increase reading speed and decrease the bulk of braille material. Braille characters are used for frequent letter combinations such as *er*; contractions for whole words such as *the*; and single-letter contractions are used as words, such as *c* for *can* (Steinman, LeJeune, & Kimbrough, 2006). In addition to the alphabet, the complete braille code includes 189 contractions and short-form words (Koenig & Holbrook, 2002). The three grades of braille vary in the number of contractions used: Grade 1 is uncontracted for beginning readers, grade 2 is most commonly used and involves many contractions, and grade 3 is used mainly by scientists and engineers and includes the most contractions.

To aid students in accurately recognizing frequently used braille characters, Wormsley and D'Andrea (2000) recommend using braille flash cards. Braille contraction cards are available from the American Printing House for the Blind. Patterns (Caton, Pester, & Bradley, 1980) is a basal braille reading program that begins with pre-braille skills and goes through the third-level reader. As Steinman et al. (2006) noted, once fluent in decoding, if braille readers have sufficient life experiences to aid comprehension, there is no reason to believe they perform any differently than sighted readers.

To monitor progress in braille reading (data-based decision making and accountability), a modified version of curriculum-based measurement (CBM) can be very informative. Morgan and Bradley-Johnson (1995) found that a modified CBM procedure with braille probes was as reliable and valid as the standardized CBM method is for sighted students. The modification involves use of a 2-minute rather than 1-minute probe, and use of 6 seconds rather than 3 seconds to prompt unknown words on probes.

Speed is a concern with braille reading. Trent and Truan (1997) found that the factor most related to reading speed is age at onset of blindness; that is, the later the onset, the slower the speed. They suggested that to develop speed, students need to read braille daily for a considerable amount of time, and that braille instruction should begin early, especially for students whose vision is such that eventually they will no longer be able to read print. Residual vision makes learning braille easier, and the sooner students begin braille, the more they will practice. Those who begin braille in grade 3 or later usually do not catch up to those who began braille reading upon school entry. Because braille typically takes 2½ times longer to read than regular print, even the fastest braille reader will not read at a rate commensurate with that of print readers. Because of the amount of required reading in regular classrooms, students with low or medium reading rates will require orally read material, audio taped material or both, as well as access to braille (Trent & Truan, 1997).

Students who can read large-type material can be taught with regular basal readers where magnifiers are used or print is enlarged. Although the appropriate size print for a student must be selected on an individual basis, standard print used with optical devices offers access to more visual material and results in a faster reading speed (Lussenhop & Corn, 2002). Gompel, Janssen, van Bon, and Schreuder (2003) found that children from the Netherlands with low vision are as accurate in decoding as their sighted peers, but they read slower. Further, their results indicated that the students' slower reading was a result of reduced visual input, not a lack of orthographic knowledge. Thus, they recommended that efforts to increase reading speed for these students focus on adapting visual input (e.g., print size, font, contrast) to meet each student's individual needs. As with sighted students, Layton and Koenig (1998) found that having students with low vision repeatedly read a short paragraph until they meet a fluency standard increased their oral reading fluency rate. To ensure that students with low vision are exposed to amounts of material that are similar to that of their sighted peers, adequate fluency is important. Despite the typically slower reading speed of these children, Gompel, van Bon, and Schreuder (2004) found that children with low vision from the Netherlands comprehended text as well as sighted children matched for educational age.

Arithmetic

Few studies have examined the development of arithmetic skills in children with a severe vison loss. Young children who are blind may be somewhat behind their sighted peers in arithmetical ability, but this difference seems to disappear by about ages 8–11 (Warren, 1994). Ahlberg and Csocsan (1999) found that 5- to 9-year-old children who were congenitally blind did not spontaneously use their fingers to solve arithmetic problems and had trouble showing a given number of fingers. This result was consistent with their prior study (Ahlberg & Csocsan,1994) indicating that children who are blind do not use their fingers to model numbers or count. They hypothesized that lack of finger counting occurs because children who are blind only perceive by touch the finger most recently counted without simultaneously experiencing the group of fingers. The authors suggested that grouping elements to be counted with both hands is important to the children's understanding of numbers so that they can experience the elements as units to compose and decompose.

Written Language

Students who have lost their vision after having learned to write may be able to use script writing on raised-lined paper, such as that available from the American Printing House for the Blind. Students who cannot use script writing may use a computer with speech, print, or braille output, an electronic notetaker, a brailler (similar to a typewriter, but for braille), or a slate and stylus.

Spelling skills of students who are blind seem to be very well developed. For example, Grenier and Giroux (1997) found that spelling skills of grade 9–11 students who were grade 2 braille readers were superior to those of their sighted peers. Although further studies are needed with larger samples, it appears that spelling skills of braille readers typically are well developed. Few studies have examined spelling skills for students with low vision. However, Gompel, van Bon, Schreuder, and Adriaansen (2002) found that the spelling skills of Dutch students with low vision and no additional learning problems were as strong as those of their sighted peers.

Besides considering each of the academic areas mentioned above, services for school-age students with

a vision loss also should include transition planning whenever these students are faced with a change in programs. Assistance in preparing for college or vocational pursuits also must be incorporated into their educational plans.

SUMMARY

Providing effective services for students with visual impairments requires many of the domains of competence identified in the *Blueprint III*. To provide effective interventions for students with visual impairments, considerable collaboration and planning is required. Team members must work together to understand the nature and impact of the vision loss, identify priorities for intervention, and develop a comprehensive intervention plan. Fortunately, several strategies have been shown to promote learning and adaptive life skills for these students. Interventions may be considered at each of the tiers within the three-tier service delivery model in both the academic and behavioral domains.

School psychologists are encouraged to take a developmental and culturally sensitive approach to working with students and families. For parents of infants or toddlers, sharing interventions designed to promote interaction and facilitate exploration of the environment are of particular importance. Providing experiences for concept development and early literacy are related to more positive outcomes. As children progress through school, interventions to promote organization, independence, and social skills are likely to be needed. Ensuring access to appropriate instructional materials, providing quality instruction, and sufficient practice and feedback will promote learning. Special attention to developing social skills also may be warranted.

REFERENCES

Ahlberg, A., & Csocsan, E. (1994). *Grasping numerosity among blind children* (Report No. 1994-4). Goteborg, Sweden: Institute for Special Pedagogy, University of Goteborg.

Ahlberg, A., & Csocsan, E. (1999). How children who are blind experience numbers. *Journal of Visual Impairment & Blindness, 93,* 549–560.

Axelrod, C. (2001). Helping you and your child get a good night's sleep. *See/Hear Newsletter, 6,* 8–14.

Baird, S. M., Mayfield, P., & Baker, P. (1997). Mothers' interpretations of the behavior of their infants with visual and other impairments during interactions. *Journal of Visual Impairment & Blindness, 91,* 467–483.

Barton, L. E., & LaGrow, S. J. (1985). Reduction of stereotypic responding in three visually impaired children. *Education of the Visually Handicapped, 16,* 145–151.

Bau, A. M. (1999). Providing culturally competent services to visually impaired persons. *Journal of Visual Impairment & Blindness, 93,* 291–297.

Bradley-Johnson, S., Johnson, C. M., Swanson, J., & Jackson, A. (2004). Exploratory behavior: A comparison of infants who are congenitally blind and infants who are sighted. *Journal of Visual Impairment & Blindness, 98,* 496–502.

Brambring, M., & Troster, H. (1992). On the stability of stereotyped behaviors in blind infants and preschoolers. *Journal of Visual Impairment & Blindness, 86,* 105–110.

Buhrow, M., Hartshorne, T., & Bradley-Johnson, S. (1998). Parents' and teachers' ratings of the social skills of elementary-age students who are blind. *Journal of Visual Impairment & Blindness, 92,* 503–511.

Caton, H., Pester, H., & Bradley, W. J. (1980). *Patterns: The primary braille reading program.* Louisville, KY: American Printing House for the Blind.

Chen, D., & Dote-Kwan, J. (1998). Early intervention services for young children who have visual impairments with other disabilities and their families. In S. Z. Sacks & R. K. Silberman (Eds.), *Educating students who have visual impairments with other disabilities* (pp. 303–334). Baltimore: Brookes.

Chen, D., Friedman, C. T., & Calvello, G. (1990). *Parents and visually impaired infants.* Louisville, KY: American Printing House for the Blind.

Corn, A. L., & Wall, R. S. (2002). Access to multimedia presentations for students with visual impairments. *Journal of Visual Impairment & Blindness, 96,* 197–211.

DeMario, N. C., & Crowley, E. P. (1994). Using applied behavior analysis procedures to change the behavior of students with visual disabilities: A research review. *Journal of Visual Impairment & Blindness, 88,* 532–543.

Duckworth, B. J., & Caton, H. (1986). *Basic Reading Rate Scale: Braille edition or large type.* Louisville, KY: American Printing House for the Blind.

Elliott, S. N., & Gresham, F. M. (1991). *Social skills intervention guide.* Circle Pines, MN: American Guidance.

Erwin, E. J. (1993). Social participation of young children with visual impairments in integrated and specialized settings. *Journal of Visual Impairment & Blindness, 87,* 138–142.

Fazzi, D. L. (1998). Facilitating independent travel for students who have visual impairments with other disabilities. In S. Z. Sacks & R. K. Silberman (Eds.), *Educating students who have visual impairments with other disabilities* (pp. 441–467). Baltimore: Brookes.

Felps, J. N., & Devlin, R. J. (1988). Modification of stereotypic rocking of a blind adult. *Journal of Visual Impairment & Blindness, 82,* 107–108.

Ferber, R. (1987). *Solve your child's sleep problems.* New York: Simon & Schuster.

Ferrell, K. A. (1985). *Reach out and teach: Meeting the training needs of parents of visually and multiply handicapped young children.* New York: American Foundation for the Blind.

Gompel, M., Janssen, N. M., van Bon, W. H. J., & Schruder, R. (2003). Visual input and orthographic knowledge in word reading of children with low vision. *Journal of Visual Impairment & Blindness, 97,* 273–284.

Gompel, M., van Bon, W. H. J., & Schreuder, R. (2004). Reading by children with low vision. *Journal of Visual Impairment & Blindness, 98,* 77–89.

Gompel, M., van Bon, W. H. J., Schreuder, R., & Adriaansen, J. J. M. (2002). Reading and spelling competence of Dutch children with low vision. *Journal of Visual Impairment & Blindness, 96,* 435–447.

Gresham, F., & Elliott, S. (1990). *Social Skills Rating System.* Circle Pines, MN: American Guidance Service.

Grenier, D., & Giroux, N. (1997). A comparative study of spelling performance of sighted and blind students in senior high school. *Journal of Visual Impairment & Blindness, 91,* 393–400.

Jan, J. E. (2004). Melatonin therapy for circadian rhythm sleep disorders in children with multiple disabilities: What have we learned in the last decade? *Developmental Medicine & Child Neurology, 46,* 776–782.

Jindal-Snape, D. (2004). Generalization and maintenance of social skills of children with visual impairments: Self-evaluation and the role of feedback. *Journal of Visual Impairment & Blindness, 98,* 470–483.

Kef, S. (1997). The personal networks and social supports of blind and visually impaired adolescents. *Journal of Visual Impairment & Blindness, 91,* 236–244.

Koenig, A. J., & Holbrook, M. C. (2002). Literacy focus: Developing skills and motivations for reading and writing. In R. L. Pogrund & D. L. Fazzi (Eds.), *Early focus* (pp. 154–187). New York: American Foundation for the Blind.

Layton, C. A., & Koenig, A. J. (1998). Increasing reading fluency in elementary students with low vision through repeated readings. *Journal of Visual Impairment & Blindness, 90,* 276–291.

Leong, S. (1996). Preschool orientation and mobility: A review of the literature. *Journal of Visual Impairment & Blindness, 88,* 145–153.

Lussenshop, K., & Corn, A. L. (2002). Comparative studies of the reading performance of students with low vision. *Review, 34,* 57–69.

Mar, H. H., & Cohen, E. J. (1998). Educating students who have visual impairments and who exhibit emotional and behavior problems. In S. Z. Sacks & R. K. Silberman (Eds.), *Educating students who have visual impairments and other disabilities* (pp. 263–302). Baltimore: Brookes.

McHugh, E., & Leiberman, L. (2003). The impact of developmental factors on stereotypic rocking in children with visual impairments. *Journal of Visual Impairment & Blindness, 97*, 453–474.

McHugh, E., & Pyfer, J. (1999). The development of rocking among children who are blind. *Journal of Visual Impairment & Blindness, 93*, 82–95.

Miller, D. D. (1985). Reading comes naturally: A mother and her blind child's experiences. *Journal of Visual Impairment & Blindness, 79*, 1–4.

Mindell, J. A. (1993). Sleep disorders in children. *Health Psychology, 12*, 152–163.

Mindell, J. A., & DeMarco, C. M. (1997). Sleep problems of young blind children. *Journal of Visual Impairment & Blindness, 91*, 33–39.

Mindell, J. A., Goldberg, R., & Fry, J. M. (1996). Treatment of a circadian rhythm disorder in a blind 2-year-old child. *Journal of Visual Impairment & Blindness, 86*, 162–166.

Morgan, S., & Bradley-Johnson, S. (1995). Technical adequacy of curriculum-based measures for braille readers. *School Psychology Review, 24*, 94–103.

Palmer, C. (2000). *Children with cortical vision impairment: Implications for education.* Retrieved October 20, 2006, from http://internex.net.au/~dba/papers.htm

Ponchilla, P. E., Armbruster, J., & Wiebold, J. (2005). The National Sports Education Camps Project: Introducing sports skills to students with visual impairments through short-term specialized instruction. *Journal of Visual Impairment & Blindness, 99*, 685–695.

Office of Special Education Programs. (2005). *25th Annual Report to Congress.* Retrieved October 26, 2006, from www.ed.gov/about/reports/annual/osep/2003/index.html

Raver, S. (1987). Training blind children to employ appropriate gaze direction and sitting behavior during observation. *Education and Treatment of Children, 10*, 237–246.

Raver, S., & Dwyer, R. C. (1986). Using a substitute activity to eliminate eye poking in a 3-year-old visually impaired child in the classroom. *The Exceptional Child, 33*, 65–72.

Recchia, S. L. (1997). Play and concept development in infants and young children with severe visual impairments: A constructivist view. *Journal of Visual Impairment & Blindness, 91*, 401–406.

Rickert, V. I., & Johnson, C. M. (1988). Reducing nocturnal awakening and crying episodes in infants and young children: A comparison between scheduled awakenings and systematic ignoring. *Pediatrics, 81*, 203–212.

Rogers, S., & Puchalski, C. B. (1984). Social characteristics of visually impaired infants' play. *Topics in Early Childhood Special Education, 3*, 52–56.

Roland, C., & Schweigert, P. (1998). Enhancing the acquisition of functional language and communication. In S. Z. Sacks & R. K. Silberman (Eds.), *Educating students who have visual impairments and other disabilities* (pp. 413–438). Baltimore: Brookes.

Ross, D. B., & Koenig, A. J. (1991). A cognitive approach to reducing stereotypic head rocking. *Journal of Visual Impairment & Blindness, 85*, 17–19.

Sack, R. L., Blood, M. L., Hughes, R. J., & Lewy, A. J. (1998). Circadian-rhythm sleep disorders in persons who are totally blind. *Journal of Visual Impairment & Blindness, 90*, 145–161.

Sacks, S. Z. (1998). Educating students who have visual impairments with other disabilities: An overview. In S. Z. Sacks & R. K. Silberman (Eds.), *Educating students who have visual impairments with other disabilities* (pp. 3–38). Baltimore: Brookes.

Sacks, S. Z., & Corn, A. L. (1996). Students with visual impairments: Do they understand their disability? *Journal of Visual Impairment & Blindness, 88*, 412–422.

Sacks, S. Z., & Gaylord-Ross, R. (1989). Peer-mediated and teacher-directed social skills training for visually impaired students. *Behavior Therapy, 20*, 619–638.

Scott, E. P., Jan, J. E., & Freeman, R. D. (1985). *Can't your child see?* Austin, TX: PRO-ED.

Simpson, R. L., Sasso, G. M., & Bump, N. (1982). Modification of manneristic behavior in a blind child via a time-out procedure. *Education of the Visually Handicapped, 14*, 50–55.

Steinman, B., LeJeune, B., & Kimbrough, R. (2006). Developmental stages of reading processes in children who are blind and sighted. *Journal of Visual Impairment & Blindness, 100*, 36–46.

Stores, G., & Ramchandani, P. (1999). Sleep disorders in visually impaired children. *Developmental Medicine & Child Neurology, 41*, 348–352.

Teplin, S. W. (1995). Visual impairment in infants and young children. *Infants and Young Children, 8*, 18–51.

Trent, S. D., & Truan, M. B. (1997). Speed, accuracy, and comprehension of adolescent braille readers in a specialized school. *Journal of Visual Impairment & Blindness, 91*, 494–500.

Utley, B. L., Roman, C., & Nelson, G. L. (1998). Functional vision. In S. Z. Sacks & R. K. Silberman (Eds.), *Educating students who have visual impairments and other disabilities.* (pp. 371–405). Baltimore: Brookes.

Walker, H. M., McConnell, S., Holmes, D., Todis, B., Walker, J., & Golden, N. (1983). *The ACCEPTS program: A curriculum for children's effective peer and teacher skills.* Austin, TX: PRO-ED.

Walker, H. M., Todis, B., Holmes, D., & Horton, G. (1988). *The ACCESS program: Adolescent curriculum for communication and effective social skills.* Austin, TX: PRO-ED.

Warren, D. (1994). *Blindness and children: An individual differences approach.* New York: Cambridge University Press.

Wesolowski, M. D., & Zawlocki, R. J. (1982). The differential effects of procedures to eliminate an injurious self-stimulatory behavior (Digito-Ocular Sign) in blind retarded twins. *Behavior Therapy, 13*, 334–345.

Wolffe, K., & Sacks, S. Z. (1997). The lifestyles of blind, low vision, and sighted youths: A quantitative comparison. *Journal of Visual Impairment & Blindness, 91*, 245–257.

Wormsley, D. P., & D'Andrea, F. M. (2000). *Instructional strategies for braille literacy*. New York: American Foundation for the Blind.

Ysseldyke, J., Burns, M., Dawson, P., Kelley, B., Morrison, D., Ortiz, S., et al. (2006). *School psychology: A blueprint for training and practice III*. Bethesda, MD: National Association of School Psychologists.

ANNOTATED BIBLIOGRAPHY

Palmer, C. (2000). *Children with cortical vision impairment: Implications for education*. Retrieved October 20, 2006, from http://internex.net.au/~dba/papers.htm

Provides a comprehensive overview of this condition and provides detailed educational considerations.

Sacks, S. Z., & Silberman, R. K. (1998). *Educating students who have visual impairments with other disabilities*. Baltimore: Brookes.

Describes research-based interventions. Because so many students with serious vision loss have additional impairments, this is a useful resource. Many topics are addressed including orientation and mobility, functional vision, transition planning, and use of technology.

WEB RESOURCES

American Foundation for the Blind: www.afb.org
Provides technical assistance to individuals who are visually impaired, to their families, professionals, and organizations. Also publishes books, periodicals, videos, and talking books.

American Printing House for the Blind: www.aph.org
Publishes educational and assessment materials, materials adapted and transcribed in braille or large type, and recorded books and magazines.

Blind Children's Center: www.blindcntr.org
Publishes booklets for parents of infants and preschoolers who are visually impaired or blind in English and Spanish. Some topics include play, language, and movement.

DBlink: http://www.tr.wou.edu/dblink
Federally funded service provides an extensive library of publications and products on vision loss and deaf blindness for birth through age 21.

116

Best Practices in Assessing and Improving English Language Learners' Literacy Performance

Michael L. Vanderwood
Jeanie Nam
University of California, Riverside

OVERVIEW

Since the 1990s, the population of English language learners (ELLs) in U.S. schools has risen dramatically. In 1994–1995, an estimated 3.2 million ELLs were enrolled in grades K–12 (National Clearinghouse for English Language Acquisition, 2005). By 2004–2005, the population of ELLs rose to 5.1 million students, representing approximately 10% of the total school enrollment (National Clearinghouse for English Language Acquisition, 2005) and consisted of students that represented at least 350 languages (Hopstock & Stephenson, 2003). In at least one state (i.e., California), the ELL population has grown to almost 25% of the total public school enrollment (National Clearinghouse for English Language Acquisition, 2005).

With the rapidly growing population of ELLs, school districts around the nation are faced with the challenge of teaching these students to speak, read, and write in English, and sometimes their native language, while also ensuring progress in acquiring content knowledge and content area literacy.

The purpose of this chapter is to provide school psychologists who work with ELLs a set of best practices in literacy assessment and intervention that are based on initial applications of the response-to-intervention (RTI) approach with this population and to help all school psychologists increase their knowledge in the *School Psychology: A Blueprint for Training and Practice III* (Ysseldyke et al., 2006) domains of Diversity Awareness and Sensitive Service Delivery, Data-Based Decision Making and Accountability, and Systems-Based Service Delivery.

A key factor for academic success is a solid foundation in literacy in the early grades. However, recent statistics indicate that approximately 76% of third-grade ELLs are performing below grade level in English reading (Zehler et al., 2003). Hispanic students constitute the largest group of ELLs and are twice as likely as non-Hispanic Whites to be reading below average for their age (Snow, Burns, & Griffin, 1998). Many ELLs are not adequately developing the skills necessary to become good readers, and, as a result, ELLs have become heavily overrepresented in special education programs (Case & Taylor, 2005) and a growing achievement gap is reflected on national and state tests (Snow & Biancarosa, 2003). Approximately 66% of ELLs with disabilities are served in programs for students with learning disabilities (Zehler et al., 2003), of which about 56% of ELL referrals are due to concerns about reading performance (U.S. Department of Education & National Institute of Child Health and Human Development [USDOE & NICHD], 2003).

One possible explanation for the disproportionate placement of ELLs in special education may be attributed to the lack of appropriate assessment tools to identify English learners who may experience reading difficulties (Wagner, Francis, & Morris, 2005). Consequently, these students may be denied the opportunity for early intervention. With the growing representation of ELLs in special education programs, validated identification tools are needed to determine whether students' academic difficulties reflect a learning disability, limited English proficiency, or other socio-cultural influences (Klingner, Artiles, & Barletta, 2006).

A lack of proficiency in English may often be misinterpreted as an intelligence deficit or learning disability (Langdon, 1989), which could affect the decision of whether a student should receive special education services. Artiles, Rueda, Salazar, and Higareda (2005) found that ELLs with low levels of proficiency in English were more likely to be placed in special education programs than their more proficient English-speaking peers. However, despite recent reports of the growing representation of ELLs in special education, there are very little data that can inform us in regard to the appropriateness of these placements (National Research Council [NRC], 2002). In addition, consensus does not exist about the most appropriate way to integrate cultural and language proficiency information into a special education eligibility assessment model. Without an accurate classification model that is sensitive to the language proficiency and cultural background of ELLs, language minority students may be inappropriately identified and misplaced in special education.

As the population of ELLs has increased in the public schools, the limitations related to personnel, procedures, and instruments to assess ELLs for special education eligibility have become painstakingly obvious (Gersten & Dimino, 2006; USDOE & NICHD, 2003). The traditional discrepancy approach has several limitations that apply to all students, including ELLs. NRC recommended that states look at alternatives to the discrepancy model because of the inherent wait-to-fail nature of the discrepancy approach (NRC, 2002). The limitations of the discrepancy approach presented by the NRC are compounded by the influences of culture and language differences for ELLs.

One obvious method to address service delivery concerns for ELLs is to examine the appropriateness of an RTI approach for this group. There is evidence that suggests this approach works well with monolingual students in early elementary grades (Burns, Appleton, & Stehouwer, 2005). The concepts of conducting screening assessment, intervening with a group of students identified in the screening process, and systematically monitoring progress with reliable and valid tools is considered by some authors as a potentially effective delivery model for ELL (Gersten & Dimino, 2006). RTI with ELL has the potential to address the limitations of the traditional aptitude–achievement discrepancy model and to reduce the impact of language proficiency and culture on evaluations of student performance.

BASIC CONSIDERATIONS

Although there is a substantial amount of research that indicates early assessment and intervention to address reading concerns for monolingual students can greatly reduce the number of individuals who need intensive supports (e.g., Wagner, Torgesen, Laughon, Simmons, & Rashotte, 1993), there is significantly less evidence about this approach with ELLs. Although there are some initial studies that will be presented later that indicate an RTI approach has significant potential with ELLs, several issues unique to ELL assessment and intervention must be addressed to ensure RTI is fully implemented with ELLs.

Assessment Tools for ELLs

The authors of the Standards for Educational and Psychological Testing (American Educational Research Association, American Psychological Association, & National Council on Measurement in Education [AERA, APA, & NCME], 1999) point out several unique tasks that need to be accomplished when developing and using assessment tools with students of diverse language backgrounds. The 11 standards in the chapter for testing individuals of diverse language backgrounds clearly apply to school districts and school psychologists who want to implement an RTI model or conduct individual assessments with ELLs. These standards apply whether testing is conducted with only one ELL or with statewide assessment of these students.

One of the biggest challenges to assessing ELLs is the need to document the equivalence between scores obtained by ELLs and those by monolingual students (AERA, APA, & NCME, 1999). For example, if scores from a reading assessment are going to be used to determine who should receive additional supports, which is a critical aspect of RTI, the scores on the test for ELLs should be able to predict future literacy performance to the same extent as they do for monolingual students. If the predictive coefficients are not as strong with ELLs as with monolingual students, that information should be noted in a test manual or other documentation that can be easily accessed by test users. In addition, if test data are used to suggest a student may have a disability, the scores should reflect a true deficit and not the impact of language differences.

Another challenge facing those who select assessments for ELLs is to ensure that ELLs are included in the validation and norming of the tests they select. Several of the most popular individually administered and group measures do not include ELLs in the norming and validation of the measure (Salvia & Ysseldyke, 2004). According to the test standards, the inclusion of a sample of ELLs is especially critical when the measure is used for critical education decisions like special education eligibility (AERA, APA, & NCME, 1999).

English Language Proficiency Assessments

The test standards also highlight the importance of assessing language proficiency (i.e., the ability to use language for academic and basic communication tasks; Cummins, 1984) in English and, if possible, in the student's native language to help interpret the results of other assessment activities. Second language learning is not an easy and automatic process for children and typically requires a significant amount of time to develop social and academic language skills (McLaughlin, 1992). Although research has shown that students who speak another language develop social proficiency, or basic interpersonal conversation skills (BICS), within the context of everyday living and without formal instruction, cognitive academic language proficiency (CALP) has been found to be reliant on formal schooling, taking about 5–7 years to develop (Cummins, 1984). BICS and CALP are used by many authors who investigate language proficiency, but the complete structure of the construct is viewed quite differently in the most popular measures, which can lead to significantly different scores across tests (Del Vecchio & Guerrero, 1995). In fact, early research in this area found that some of the most common language proficiency tests differed in the classification of whether students were limited English proficient (LEP) or fluent English proficient (FEP; Ulibarri, Spencer, & Rivas, 1981).

In a more recent investigation, the IDEA Proficiency Test (IPT), the Language Assessment Scales (LAS), and the Woodcock Language Proficiency Battery–Revised (WLPB-R) were examined to determine the extent to which the BICS/CALP distinction was reflected in the measures and to determine the extent of overall similarity between scores on the tests (Schrank, Fletcher, & Alvarado, 1996). The authors reported that BICS and CALP constructs were clearly evident in all three measures. Yet, a close examination of the correlation among subtests demonstrated that the tests were also measuring different aspects of language proficiency (Shrank, Fletcher, & Alvarado, 1996).

The most important point to take away from the current research in language proficiency assessment is that subtest comparisons across measures, even if the

subtests have similar names, are not currently justified. In addition, because the subtests are measuring different aspects, composite scores may also be affected. Finally, when selecting language proficiency measures, reliability and validity should be evaluated to ensure that decisions made with the test scores are as accurate as possible and adequately assess the variable in question (AERA, APA, & NCME, 1999).

In addition to using a language proficiency measure, individualized assessment of ELLs that may lead to special education eligibility or other intensive interventions should include a detailed educational history. A culturally sensitive examination of home literacy activities and prior exposure to literacy instruction is critical for putting an ELL's performance in context (Klingner & Edwards, 2006). For example, if an ELL were exposed to a substantial amount of literacy activities in his or her native language, but still has limited literacy skills in that same language, more intensive intervention is warranted than if the literacy concerns were only in English.

Language of Instruction

The debate about whether to provide literacy and other instruction in a student's native language or in English is beyond the scope of this chapter. Most research indicates that literacy instruction that can use or is paired with a student's native language is initially more effective than English-only instruction (Garcia, 1991). It is very clear that native language literacy skills can be transferred to and be used to help develop a second language (Cummins, 2003). This transfer across languages appears to apply to all languages, including languages that have distinct written forms (e.g., Chinese and English; Freeman & Freeman, 2002).

BEST PRACTICES

There is fairly strong evidence that a three-tier RTI model can be effective for native English-speaking students (McGuinness, 2004; Vellutino, Scanlon, & Tanzman, 1998). Initial research indicates the adoption of an early intervention and problem-solving approach will be just as, and possibly more, beneficial for struggling ELLs as it is for monolingual learners. Recent reports by the National Reading Panel (NRP; 2000) and NRC (Snow et al., 1998) indicate that implementing reading assessment and instruction across four key areas (i.e., phonological awareness, alphabetics, fluency, and comprehension) may provide the additional support struggling students need to acquire basic literacy skills. As will be shown, recent research examining literacy assessment and instruction for ELLs has found results similar to that of the NRP. The following sections use the NRP structure and provide assessment and intervention recommendations for implementing an RTI approach with ELLs to address literacy concerns.

Reading Assessment for ELLs

Assessment within an RTI approach is typically conducted for one of four purposes: screening, diagnosis (e.g., phonological awareness deficit versus phonics), norm-referenced comparisons (e.g., level), and progress monitoring (i.e., formative evaluation). In order to correctly identify ELLs who need Tier 1 and Tier 2 interventions, valid and reliable instruments must be used to screen for literacy concerns, and cut-off scores must be developed for differentiating ELLs who are at risk from those who are not at risk (e.g., Good, Simmons, & Kame'enui, 2001). As stated previously, the cut-off scores need to be developed with an ELL population if they are going to be used with that group (AERA, APA, & NCME, 1999). It is possible that by using cut-off scores developed for monolingual students, ELLs may fail to receive the additional supports that are imperative for their academic success or resources might be allocated to children who do not truly need remedial instruction. In addition, to appropriately evaluate interventions, evidence must be gathered that indicates which progress-monitoring tools can be used with ELLs and determines the expected growth rate on those measures. As the next section suggests, significant progress in addressing these questions for ELLs has occurred since 2000. Several recommendations based on the research presented next are provided in Table 1.

Phonological Awareness

It is clear that children at risk for reading failure, regardless of language differences, can be identified as early as kindergarten using measures of phonological

skills (Juel, 1988; Juel, Griffith, & Gough, 1986). There is also evidence that assessment tools can predict the future literacy performance of ELLs (Lindsey, Manis, & Bailey, 2003). Recent research clearly suggests phonological awareness is a general and not a language-specific skill involved in early reading. Therefore, once phonological awareness is developed in the child's native language, these skills may be applied in learning to read in a second language. Durgunoglu, Nagy, and Hancin-Bhatt (1993) examined the factors that predict the English reading development of Spanish-speaking first-grade ELLs. Measures of Spanish phonological awareness and word recognition were found to better predict performance on English word and pseudoword recognition tasks than measures of English and Spanish oral proficiency and English word recognition. First-grade students who displayed strong Spanish phonological awareness and word-decoding ability were better at decoding English words and pseudowords than students with poor native-language abilities. Quiroga, Lemos-Britton, Mostafapour, Abbott, and Berninger (2002) found further evidence supporting the cross-linguistic transfer of phonological awareness. In their study, both Spanish and English phonological awareness were found to predict English word reading.

Lesaux and Siegel (2003) found that second-grade ELLs who struggled with reading had low scores on measures of phonological awareness. Although measures of rapid naming, oral cloze performance, and letter identification in kindergarten accounted for a significant amount of variance in word reading ability, phonological awareness was the single best predictor of word reading ability in second grade for ELLs (Lesaux & Siegel, 2003). Given the strong correlation of phonological awareness across languages, as well as the prevalence of studies that have shown phonological awareness to be predictive of reading ability for ELLs, there is significant evidence that assessments of phonological awareness will assist educators in identifying students who may be at risk for reading disabilities.

Table 1. RTI With ELLs: Literacy Assessment Recommendations

- Ensure that language proficiency is assessed with reliable and valid measures.
- When possible, assess language proficiency in the student's native language as well as English.
- Complete an educational history to determine the extent to which the student has been exposed to instruction in his or her native language and in English.
- Conduct screening for phonological awareness, alphabetics, fluency, and comprehension in the language of instruction and, if possible, in his or her native language.
- All measures used with ELLs should have documented evidence that the measures can be used for the purpose selected.
- Progress monitoring should be conducted in the language of instruction using growth standards developed with ELLs.

Alphabetics

In a more recent investigation (Vanderwood, Linklater, & Healy, in press), a measure of alphabetics (Nonsense Word Fluency [NWF] on Dynamic Indicators of Basic Early Literacy Skills [DIBELS]; Good & Kaminski, 2002) collected in first grade was used to predict performance on three outcomes measures (i.e, curriculum-based measurement-reading [R-CBM] and Maze [from AIMSweb]; Shinn & Shinn, 2002; CAT/6) collected in third grade for 134 ELLs. The correlation between the 1-minute assessment in first grade and the assessments in third grade were at 0.65 (R-CBM), 0.54 (Maze), and 0.39 (CAT/6). More important, the NWF measure was able to identify 80% of those students who were above the 25th percentile on the outcome measures. NWF was not as accurate with students with the lowest level of English proficiency, which led the authors to conclude that NWF can be used as a screening device with ELL, but should be combined with other measures, including language proficiency.

Literacy Instruction and Intervention for ELL

Although there are clear guidelines in the test standards (AERA, APA, & NCME, 1999) that require the validation of assessment tools before using them with unique groups like ELLs, similar guidelines do not exist for the use of interventions. Yet, there is reason to believe that not all interventions that work with monolingual students will work with ELLs (Klingner & Edwards, 2006). School psychologists who work with teams to develop interventions should consider the issues of cultural sensitivity and language proficiency that were presented earlier in this chapter before implementing individual or group literacy interventions for ELLs. The remaining sections of this chapter review the research base with ELLs for interventions targeting the NRP (2000) targeted areas. See Table 2.

Phonological Awareness and Alphabetics

It is quite clear that exposure to a daily reading program can help ELLs acquire literacy skills (Elley & Mangubhai, 1983). It is also clear that regardless of

language status or ability, a balanced early reading program with small-group phonological awareness instruction has been found to remediate reading difficulties for language minority students. Lesaux and Siegel (2003) found that a model of early identification and intervention for ELLs at risk for reading failure was effective for children who entered kindergarten with little or no exposure to English. At-risk status was determined in kindergarten by measuring students on multiple skills related to early literacy, including syntactic awareness, rapid naming, and spelling. Regardless of language status or ability, the students were provided with small-group phonological awareness instruction in kindergarten, followed by phonics instruction in first grade. Classroom and resource teachers provided intervention three to four times per week, for 20 minutes per session. Measures taken in second grade indicated that the reading skills of ELLs were comparable to monolingual second-grade students. Although the ELLs had difficulties in kindergarten, by second grade many had caught up and, in some cases, performed better than their native English peers on various reading and spelling tasks. For example, on tasks of word reading, rapid naming, real word, and nonword spelling, ELLs performed significantly better than English-only students. These results indicate that given intense and explicit phonological awareness instruction, ELLs who are at risk for reading difficulties can make substantial gains in reading.

Healy, Vanderwood, and Edelston (2005) implemented an RTI approach with first-grade ELLs in an urban setting in southern California. The entire first grade was screened with measures of phonological awareness and phonics from DIBELS (Good & Kaminski, 2002), and the 15 lowest performers were selected for an intervention in English that targeted phonological awareness, phonics, and vocabulary skills. Students received the 30-minute intervention twice a week in groups of five and were monitored with DIBELS measures every week. Students were exited from the intervention after they achieved the benchmarks set by DIBELS. At the end of 20 weeks, only two students had not reached the goal.

Table 2. RTI With ELLs: Literacy Intervention Recommendations

- Offer a continuum of English language acquisition instruction.
- If possible, select a general education curriculum that is designed to address language and cultural diversity.
- If possible, select an intervention that has data suggesting it is effective for ELLs.
- Select interventions that are systematic and explicit, match the language of instruction, and address language diversity.
- Evaluate interventions routinely, and use evaluation data to improve the intervention.

Vaughn and colleagues also implemented an RTI model with first-grade students in English (Vaughn, Mathes, et al., 2006) and with a separate group in Spanish (Vaughn, Linan-Thompson, et al., 2006). The group that received the intervention in English was first screened for early literacy skills in English and in Spanish, and those who failed the screenings in both languages were placed in a literacy intervention. The group that received the intervention in Spanish failed a set of Spanish literacy screening measures. Participants in both studies received an explicit and systematic literacy intervention in either English (Vaughn, Mathes et al., 2006) or Spanish (Vaughn, Linan-Thompson, et al., 2006) over 7 months and were compared with local treatment comparison groups (i.e., literacy intervention already available at the school setting) that had received similar scores on the screening measures. Results of both studies indicated that the systematic and explicit intervention that focused on phonological awareness, phonics, vocabulary, and oral language created a stronger impact on literacy performance than the district-selected intervention.

Fluency and Comprehension

The ultimate goal of reading instruction is to help children acquire the skills necessary to derive meaning from text. A study by Garcia (1991) found that the reading comprehension abilities of fifth- and sixth-grade Spanish-speaking ELLs were greatly underestimated because of their unfamiliarity with English vocabulary. However, comprehending text requires more than a good vocabulary. It involves accurate and fluent decoding skills, as well as the ability to use syntax to anticipate words in a sentence, monitor context, and make inferences on the basis of background knowledge (McGuinness, 2004). Fluent readers are able to read text quickly and accurately. Thus, fluent readers expend less cognitive resources on decoding and have a higher capacity for comprehension.

Research by Calhoon (2005) suggests that the combination of phonological skill and comprehension training may not automatically generalize to reading fluency gains. Therefore, literacy instruction should incorporate explicit instructional strategies to build fluency. There are several empirically supported interventions that have been found to improve reading fluency for both monolingual English speakers and ELLs. Linan-Thompson, Vaughn, Hickman-Davis, and Kouzekanani (2003) found that a supplemental daily reading intervention for second-grade English learners significantly improved oral reading fluency and passage comprehension scores. The reading intervention included crucial elements known to remediate reading difficulties among struggling monolingual students, including intensive small-group instruction, explicit instruction combined with student-directed activities, and ongoing progress monitoring to allow teachers to tailor instruction toward mastery of key skills. The intervention was provided five times per week, for 13 weeks, and included instruction in fluent reading, phonological awareness, instructional-level reading, word study, and writing. Two follow-up scores, one at 4 weeks and one at 4 months, indicated significant gains in posttest reading measures, with the greatest gains seen in oral reading fluency.

Repeated reading is another instructional approach that has been found to improve reading fluency and overall reading achievement for students through at least fifth grade (NRP, 2000). A study by De La Colina, Parker, Hasbrouck, and Lara-Alecio (2001) found repeated reading activities to also be appropriate for ELLs, providing the practice needed to develop automatic recognition of English phonemes, high-frequency words, and word patterns. In this study, the authors examined the effectiveness of Read Naturally, a fluency-building program, for at-risk Spanish-speaking ELLs in first- and second-grade Spanish–English bilingual classrooms. Read Naturally combines three instructional methods: repeated readings, teacher modeling, and student self-monitoring. Students were selected for the intervention based upon their performance on initial screening measures, which included a measure of Spanish oral reading fluency, sight words, and beginning sounds. Low performance on these measures, along with their Individuals with Disabilities Education Act language proficiency (IPT) classification placed them at risk for reading difficulties. Students received the intervention 3 days per week, 45 minutes per session, for an 8–12 week period. All instructional materials were translated into Spanish so that students could receive instruction in their native language. Postintervention assessments of Spanish oral reading fluency and reading comprehension indicated that the Read Naturally program was effective in improving Spanish fluency and comprehension for at-risk bilingual readers.

The reciprocal teaching model is an approach to teaching comprehension strategies wherein students are taught to use thinking-aloud strategies to predict, summarize, generate questions, and clarify while reading text. Klingner and Vaughn (1996) investigated the effects of two interventions that targeted the reading comprehension skills of seventh- and eighth-grade ELLs with identified learning disabilities. The participants in this study were found to be adequate decoders, but had poor comprehension skills. Intervention students were randomly assigned to one of two groups: (a) reciprocal teaching in combination with cross-age tutoring and (b) reciprocal teaching in combination with cooperative grouping. In the cross-age tutoring groups, students worked together in tutor–tutee pairs, whereas students in the cooperative learning groups implemented comprehension strategies in groups of three to five students. The reciprocal teaching model in conjunction with either cross-age tutoring or cooperative peer learning strategies was found to improve the reading comprehension of middle-school English learners with learning disabilities. For those students who did not benefit from the intervention, initial reading level and oral language proficiency emerged as factors that affected their response to the intervention. Students who had decoding skills below a third-grade level and low English and Spanish oral language proficiency were least likely to show improvement.

Cummins (2003) suggested that the development of reading comprehension for ELLs is best supported by a program that combines phonological awareness and phonics instruction, strategies for decoding and comprehending text, as well as exposure to meaningful and varied texts. In addition, strategies including small-group instruction, repeated reading, progress monitoring, reciprocal teaching, cross-age tutoring, and cooperative grouping may assist ELLs in developing the fluency and comprehension skills needed to become successful readers. These results indicate that given a relatively short, yet intensive, intervention that includes the critical elements of reading instruction, ELLs can make significant progress in reading fluency and comprehension.

SUMMARY

Recent reports indicate that staggering numbers of ELLs are not learning to read and are far behind their monolingual peers (Zehler et al., 2003). There are also indications that the number of ELLs will increase across the country in the next decade to the extent that most education professionals will have to be able to serve this population (National Clearinghouse for English Language Acquisition, 2005). One approach to addressing literacy concerns for ELLs is to implement an RTI approach that is based on the targeted areas suggested by NRP (2000). Since 2000, research examining assessment tools and interventions that are necessary

to implement RTI with ELLs has produced results that provide initial support for using this approach in elementary school settings. There is a clear need to continue to investigate this approach and to examine methods to ensure assessments and interventions are culturally sensitive and to minimize the impact of the lack of English proficiency (Klingner & Edwards, 2006). School psychologists who want to include RTI information as part of their comprehensive assessments for special education eligibility should ensure that language proficiency is examined and that assessment information is, as much as possible, compared to other ELLs.

REFERENCES

American Educational Research Association, American Psychological Association, & National Council on Measurement in Education. (1999). Testing individuals of diverse linguistic backgrounds. In, *Standards for educational and psychological testing* (pp. 91–97). Washington, DC: Author.

Artiles, A. J., Rueda, R., Salazar, J., & Higareda, I. (2005). Within-group diversity in minority disproportionate representation: English language learners in urban school districts. *Exceptional Children, 71*, 283–300.

Burns, M. K., Appleton, J. J., & Stehouwer, J. D. (2005). Meta-analytic review of responsiveness-to-intervention research: Examining field-based and research-implemented models. *Journal of Psychoeducational Assessment, 23*, 381–394.

Calhoon, M. B. (2005). Effects of a peer-mediated phonological skill and reading comprehension program on reading skill acquisition for middle school students with reading disabilities. *Journal of Reading Disabilities, 38*, 424–433.

Case, R. E., & Taylor, S. S. (2005). Language difference or learning disability? Answers from a linguistic perspective. *The Clearing House, 78*, 127–130.

Cummins, J. C. (1984). *Bilingual and special education: Issues in assessment and pedagogy*. Austin, TX: PRO-ED.

Cummins, J. C. (2003). Reading and the bilingual student: Fact and fiction. In G. G. Garcia (Ed.), *English learners: Reaching the highest level of English literacy* (pp. 2–33). Newark, DE: International Reading Association.

De La Colina, M. G., Parker, R. I., Hasbrouck, J. E., & Lara-Alecio, R. (2001). Intensive intervention in reading fluency for at-risk beginning Spanish readers. *Bilingual Research Journal, 25*, 503–538.

Del Vecchio, A., & Guerrero, M. (1995). *Handbook of English language proficiency tests*. Albuquerque, NM: Evaluation Assistance Center-West, New Mexico Highlands University. Retrieved February 13, 2006, from http://www.ncela.gwu.edu/pubs/eacwest/elptests.htm#IPT

Durgunoglu, A. Y., Nagy, W. E., & Hancin-Bhatt, B. J. (1993). Cross-language transfer of phonological awareness. *Journal of Educational Psychology, 85*, 453–465.

Elley, W. B., & Mangubhai, F. (1983). The impact of reading on second language learning. *Reading Research Quarterly, 19*, 53–67.

Freeman, D., & Freeman, Y. (2002). Teaching English learners to read: Learning or acquisition? In G. G. Garcia (Ed.), *English learners: Reaching the highest level of English literacy* (pp. 34–54). Newark, DE: International Reading Association.

Garcia, G. E. (1991). Factors influencing the English reading test performance of Spanish-speaking Hispanic children. *Reading Research Quarterly, 26*, 371–392.

Gersten, R., & Dimino, J. A. (2006). RTI (response to intervention): Rethinking special education for students with reading difficulties (yet again). *Reading Research Quarterly, 41*, 99–108.

Good, R. H., III., & Kaminski, M. A. (Eds.). (2002). *Dynamic Indicators of Basic Early Literacy Skills* (6th ed.). Eugene, OR: Institute for the Development of Education Achievement.

Good, R. H., III, Simmons, D. C., & Kame'enui, E. J. (2001). The importance and decision-making utility of a continuum of fluency-based indicators of foundational reading skills for third-grade high-stakes outcomes. *Scientific Studies of Reading, 5*, 257–288.

Healy, K., Vanderwood, M., & Edelston, D. (2005). Early literacy interventions for English language learners: Support for an RTI model. *The California School Psychologist, 10*, 55–63.

Hopstock, P. J., & Stephenson, T. G. (2003). *Native languages of LEP students*. Arlington, VA: Development Associates.

Juel, C. (1988). Learning to read and write: A longitudinal study of 54 children from first through fourth grades. *Journal of Educational Psychology, 80*, 437–47.

Juel, C., Griffith, P. L., & Gough, P. B. (1986). Acquisition of literacy: A longitudinal study of children in first and second grade. *Journal of Educational Psychology, 78*, 243–255.

Klingner, J. K., Artiles, A. J., & Barletta, L. M. (2006). English language learners who struggle with reading: Language acquisition or LD? *Journal of Learning Disabilities, 39*, 108–128.

Klingner, J. K., & Edwards, P. A. (2006). Cultural considerations with response-to-intervention models. *Reading Research Quarterly, 41*, 108–117.

Klingner, J. K., & Vaughn, S. (1996). Reciprocal teaching of reading comprehension strategies for students with learning disabilities who use English as a second language. *Elementary School Journal, 96*, 275–293.

Langdon, H. W. (1989). Language disorder or difference? Assessing the language skills of Hispanic students. *Exceptional Children, 56*, 160–167.

Lesaux, N. K., & Siegel, L. S. (2003). The development of reading in children who speak English as a second language. *Developmental Psychology, 39*, 1005–1019.

Linan-Thompson, S., Vaughn, S., Hickman-Davis, P., & Kouzekanani, K. (2003). Effectiveness of supplemental reading instruction for second-grade English language learners with reading difficulties. *Elementary School Journal, 103*, 221–238.

Lindsey, K. A., Manis, F. R., & Bailey, C. E. (2003). Prediction of first-grade reading in Spanish-speaking English-language learners. *Journal of Educational Psychology, 95*, 482–494.

McGuinness, D. (2004). *Early reading instruction: What science really tells us about how to teach reading*. Cambridge, MA: MIT Press.

McLaughlin, B. (1992). *Myths and misconceptions about second language learning: What every teacher needs to unlearn*. Washington, DC: National Center for Research on Cultural Diversity and Second Language Learning.

National Clearinghouse for English Language Acquisition. (2005). *The growing numbers of LEP students: 2003–2004 poster*. Washington, DC: Author.

National Reading Panel. (2000). *Teaching children to read: An evidence-based assessment of the scientific research literature on reading and its implications for reading instruction*. Bethesda, MD: Author. Retrieved November 17, 2005, from http://www.nationalreadingpanel.org/Publications/summary.htm

National Research Council. (2002). *Minority students in special and gifted education*. Washington, DC: Author. Retrieved November 30, 2006, from http://newton.nap.edu/books/0309074398/html

Quiroga, T., Lemos-Britton, Z., Mostafapour, E., Abbott, R. D., & Berninger, V. W. (2002). Phonological awareness and beginning reading in Spanish-speaking ESL first graders: Research into practice. *Journal of School Psychology, 40*, 85–111.

Salvia, J., & Ysseldyke, J. E. (2004). *Assessment in special and inclusive education* (9th ed.). Boston: Houghton Mifflin.

Schrank, F. A., Fletcher, T. V., & Alvarado, C. G. (1996). Comparative validity of three English oral language proficiency tests. *Bilingual Research Journal, 20*, 55–68.

Shinn, M. R., & Shinn, M. M. (2002). *AIMSweb training workbook*. Eden Prairie, MN: Edformation.

Snow, C. E., & Biancarosa, G. (2003). *Adolescent literacy and the achievement gap: What do we know and where do we go from here?* New York: Carnegie Corporation of New York.

Snow, C. E., Burns, S. M., & Griffin, P. (Eds.). (1998). *Preventing reading difficulties in young children*. Washington, DC: National Academies Press.

Ulibarri, D. M., Spencer, M. L., & Rivas, G. A. (1981). Language proficiency and academic achievement: A study of language proficiency tests and their relationship to school ratings as predictors of academic achievement. *NABE Journal of Research and Practice, 5*, 47–80.

U.S. Department of Education & National Institute of Child Health and Human Development. (2003). *National symposium on learning disabilities in English language learners: Symposium summary.* Washington, DC: Author.

Vanderwood, M. L., Linklater, D., & Healy, K. (in press). Early predictors of future reading performance: An English language learner population. *School Psychology Review.*

Vaughn, S., Linan-Thompson, S., Mathes, P. G., Cirino, P. T., Carlson, C. D., Pollard-Durodola, S. D., et al. (2006). Effectiveness of Spanish intervention for first-grade English language learners at risk for reading difficulties. *Journal of Learning Disabilities, 39,* 56–73.

Vaughn, S., Mathes, P. G., Linan-Thompson, S., Cirino, P. T., Carlson, C. D., Pollard-Durodola, S. D., et al. (2006). Effectiveness of an English intervention for first-grade English language learners at risk for reading difficulties. *Elementary School Journal, 107,* 153–180.

Vellutino, F. R., Scanlon, D. M., & Tanzman, M. S. (1998). The case for early intervention in diagnosing specific reading disability. *Journal of School Psychology, 36,* 367–397.

Wagner, R. K., Francis, D. J., & Morris, R. D. (2005). Identifying English language learners with learning disabilities: Key challenges and possible approaches. *Learning Disabilities Research & Practice, 20,* 6–15.

Wagner, R. K., Torgesen, J. K., Laughon, P., Simmons, K., & Rashotte, C. A. (1993). Development of young readers' phonological processing abilities. *Journal of Educational Psychology, 85,* 83–103.

Ysseldyke, J. E., Burns, M., Dawson, P., Kelley, B., Morrison, D., Ortiz, S., et al. (2006). *School psychology: A blueprint for training and practice III.* Bethesda, MD: National Association of School Psychologists.

Zehler, A., Fleischman, H., Hopstock, P., Stephenson, T., Pendzick, M., & Sapru, S. (2003). *Policy report: Summary of findings related to LEP and SPED-LEP students.* Arlington, VA: Development Associates. Retrieved November 2, 2006, from http://www.devassoc.com/LEPdoclist.asp

ANNOTATED BIBLIOGRAPHY

Healy, K., Vanderwood, M., & Edelston, D. (2005). Early literacy interventions for English language learners: Support for an RTI model. *The California School Psychologist, 10,* 55–63.

Provides an example of how the RTI model can be applied to an ELL population by combining screening with high-quality measures, targeted interventions, and progress monitoring. First-grade students in a large urban school composed of over 90% ELLs were screened with English measures of phonological awareness and phonics from DIBELS. The 15 lowest performing students across the two measures received a small-group structured intervention in English for 16 weeks. At the end of the intervention period, only two students were still classified in the deficit category in phonological awareness and phonics.

Lesaux, N. K., & Siegel, L. S. (2003). The development of reading in children who speak English as a second language. *Developmental Psychology, 39,* 1005–1019.

Provides a model of early identification and intervention for ELLs at risk for reading failure. Examines the effects of a structured phonological awareness and phonics intervention for children who entered kindergarten with little or no exposure to English. Measures taken in second grade indicated that the reading skills of ELLs were comparable to those of monolingual English-speaking students following the intervention.

Vaughn, S., Linan-Thompson, S., Mathes, P. G., Cirino, P. T., Carlson, C. D., Pollard-Durodola, S. D., et al. (2006). Effectiveness of Spanish intervention for first grade English language learners at risk for reading difficulties. *Journal of Learning Disabilities, 39,* 56–73.

Examines the effects of a Spanish literacy intervention on Spanish reading and on English and Spanish oral language skills. An intensive literacy intervention was provided to first-grade ELLs who were at risk for reading difficulties. The language of instruction in the intervention program was matched to the language of instruction in the core reading program. The results of the study support the idea that intensive reading intervention for ELLs designed to match the language of core instruction can significantly improve student outcomes in the language of instruction.

Section VIII
Technological Applications

Volume 5 of *Best Practices in School Psychology V* supports an understanding of the *Blueprint III* competency emphasizing technological applications.

Description: School psychologists should be able to apply technology to improve outcomes and to support all other domains.

117

Best Practices in Digital Technology Usage by Data-Driven School Psychologists

Scott McLeod
Iowa State University
Jim Ysseldyke
University of Minnesota

OVERVIEW

The professional lives of school psychologists have changed dramatically over the past few decades. The role has evolved from correlational/predictive practices to experimental practices as first distinguished by Cronbach (1957). In the school psychology literature, these approaches have been labeled *traditional* and *alternative practice* (Reschly, 1988a, 1988b). Reschly and Ysseldyke (2002) described the shift over time toward services guided by problem solving and evaluated by the achievement of positive outcomes.

The overall goal of school psychological services is twofold: enhancing the competence of individual students and building the capacity of systems to meet students' needs (Ysseldyke et al., 2006; Ysseldyke et al., chapter 3, vol. 1). In order to accomplish these goals, school psychologists are increasingly expected to use electronic devices such as desktop computers, laptops, personal digital assistants, and digital voice recorders to do their work. School psychologists also are expected to use basic office software such as word processing, spreadsheet, and presentation programs to enhance their professional productivity and their communication with parents and other education professionals. Some school psychologists have access to electronic report writing tools. Others participate in professional learning opportunities through online e-learning systems.

It is safe to say that one of the biggest influences on the school psychologist's role is the increased prevalence of digital and online technology. *School Psychology: A Blueprint for Training and Practice III* (Ysseldyke et al., 2006) recognized the seismic societal and educational shifts that are occurring because of these technologies and so added "technology" as a specific domain in which school psychologists are expected to be competent.

In addition to these productivity and communication tools, many school psychologists are tapping into the wealth of resources available on the Internet and in other networks. Online resources include such websites as School Psychology Resources Online (www.school psychology.net), the Global School Psychology Network (www.dac.neu.edu/cp/consult), and PsychWiki (www.psychwiki.com) as well as the resources available from the National Association of School Psychologists (NASP; www.nasponline.org) and the American Psychological Association (www.apa.org). School psychologists also are using online library databases such as NASP EBSCO, PsycINFO, and ERIC. Many school psychologists are using e-mail, listservs, blogs, wikis, and other connective tools to stay in touch with each other and with the communities they serve.

As *Blueprint III* notes, one of the functional competencies for school psychologists is in the area of data-based decision making and accountability. The data-driven function of school psychologists has been enhanced by technological advances since the 1990s. A variety of databases, analytical software programs, data collection devices, and other tools now exist to help school psychologists with their assessment and progress-monitoring duties (McLeod, 2005; see Silberglitt, chapter 118, vol. 5). School psychologists must be aware of these various tools and the advantages that they provide.

This chapter describes the various technology systems that are available in schools and school districts for storing and analyzing student data. Suggestions for school psychologists are included throughout the chapter, as are various illustrative scenarios to help make the material more concrete and actionable.

BASIC CONSIDERATIONS

In order for school psychologists to understand how they might use various technologies to enhance their data-driven decision making, they must first have an awareness of the tools that are being employed in schools and school districts across the country. These tools fall into several main categories.

Not all of these tools will be present in every school system, and, indeed, lack of access to some of these tools by economically disadvantaged school districts is an important policy concern.

Student Information Systems

Most school districts have a student information system that serves as their central information repository. Student information systems originally were created to store student contact information as well as basic demographic variables. Today, student information systems also contain a variety of other student records, including attendance, discipline, and health records. Sometimes student information systems contain student outcome data such as grades, results from state assessments, or data from periodic formative assessments. Student information systems typically are accessed through a password-protected login screen that leads to a menu of options for viewing data and printing reports. Some student information systems are integrated with electronic grade book and parent portal software, thus allowing teachers and parents to share information about student grades, homework, academic progress, and other records.

Data Warehouses

Although student information systems can be powerful tools for data storage, they typically do not contain all of the data that can be valuable for a school system's decision making. For example, data from other software systems often are of interest to school decision makers, including data from library, course scheduling, food

service, special education/Individualized Educational Program (IEP) management, transportation, curriculum mapping, human resources, and financial programs. Another shortcoming of student information systems is that their analytical tools typically are not as capable as those found in other software programs.

To remedy these deficiencies, school districts increasingly are turning to data management and analysis (DMA) systems, also known as data warehouses, which are complex technology systems that allow educators to connect disparate data systems together so that they can then investigate questions that otherwise would be impossible to answer. Data warehouses link various school software systems through the use of student, employee, program, and building identification numbers.

Like student information systems, data warehouses usually are accessed through a password-protected login screen to protect confidentiality of student and employee data. Unlike student information systems, data warehouses typically also have comprehensive analytical interfaces that allow users to analyze and report data in a variety of useful ways, including cross-tabs, tables, and longitudinal graphs.

Scenario 1: Orchard High School receives a grant to set up an after-school remediation program for disadvantaged students struggling in math. Heather, the school psychologist, is part of the project team. Heather needs the following student information to set up the program: names, math grades, last year's scores on the state math assessment, free/reduced lunch status, ELL (English language learner) status, IEP and/or Section 504 status, and after-school bus route. While schools without a DMA system will find it difficult and time consuming to get this type of information together in one place, Orchard has a data warehouse. Within minutes, Heather has located and downloaded the information she needs to identify students and implement the school's newest academic intervention.

Although data warehouses are expensive and require sophisticated technological support and training, school systems are finding that the added value of these tools makes them well worth the expense. For example, data warehouses typically contain multiple years of data and are ideal for identification and analysis of longitudinal trends in student performance. Because data warehouses allow educators to combine data from student information systems, electronic grade books, parent portals, and other software programs, most school districts are using these tools to conduct powerful and interesting analyses, including evaluation of long-term progress toward the elimination of subgroup achievement gaps and examination of the relationships between academic or programmatic interventions and student learning outcomes. Many school districts are finding that comprehensive software systems to manage student learning data are necessary prerequisites for successfully closing student achievement gaps.

Instructional Management and Assessment Systems

As school systems augment their data-driven educational practices, they are paying greater attention to the importance of ongoing formative assessment. Although federal and state accountability systems are based on annual summative assessment practices, educators are finding that formative data from localized assessments are more helpful for instructional decision making. Instructional management and assessment (IMA) systems have emerged to help educators store, analyze, and report on the data from periodic student assessments.

IMA systems allow educators to quickly and easily administer formative assessments to students. Depending on the particular IMA system, the software and data may reside on a school network, a desktop computer, and/or a handheld computer. These systems typically come in two forms: (a) those that come with premade assessments or are modeled on existing psychometric assessments and (b) those that include item banks of questions that can be used to automatically or manually configure classroom-level assessments. Examples of the first type include the computerized assessments from the Northwest Evaluation Association, the curriculum-based measurements from AIMSweb, and Wireless Generation's handheld computer versions of the Texas Primary Reading Inventory and the Dynamic Indicators of Basic Early Literacy Skills. Examples of the second type include programs from a number of vendors, including Compass Learning, McGraw-Hill, Pearson Digital Learning, PLATO Learning, Renaissance Learning, and Scantron. In these latter systems, school psychologists and other educators can have the software program automatically generate random question sets or can choose individual questions or substrands of questions that are of interest.

Instructional management and assessment systems vary by periodicity. Some are designed to be administered once per quarter, once per trimester, or once per semester. Others are designed to be administered daily or weekly. Although some vendor systems only offer products at particular delivery frequencies, others offer suites of products that cover the full range of delivery possibilities.

Scenario 2: Westwood Middle School students take yearly state assessments in reading, math, and science. Because it was dissatisfied with the timeliness and frequency of the state's data collection and reporting, Westwood also has implemented a comprehensive formative assessment system to monitor its students' progress throughout the year. Teachers like the supplemental formative data system because it is easy to use and produces data that are more closely aligned to their daily instructional needs. The teachers also are pleased that the formative assessments can be taken quickly, which allow them to be administered frequently without having a negative impact on classroom instructional time. Westwood's school psychologist, Doug, works with departmental teacher teams to use the item banks to create modified assessments that are aligned with state standards and to then appropriately interpret the results from those assessments.

Instructional management and assessment systems also vary by their use of technology to deliver the assessments. Some systems are completely computerized and/or are online. Other systems require teacher input of data or use scannable student test forms. Most IMA systems align their item banks of questions with state curriculum standards. Some systems integrate with other software programs, such as curriculum mapping or lesson planning software.

Relational Databases and Spreadsheets

Many school districts cannot afford data warehouses or IMA systems. While sometimes these districts band together to cooperatively purchase these types of systems, often they turn to less-sophisticated tools for their data management needs. Small districts, in particular, often are reliant on relational database tools such as Microsoft Access or FileMaker Pro to link their data sets together. These tools require the manual connection of various data sources, which can be quite time consuming for district technical staff. Relational databases also typically reside on an individual hard drive rather than being accessible by multiple individuals through a shared network and lack the powerful analytical interfaces that are present in data warehouses. These characteristics make them less useful for educator decision making.

Like other educators, many school psychologists are using electronic spreadsheet software to track, analyze, and report student learning outcomes. The advantages of electronic spreadsheets are that they are easy to learn and that they have robust analytical and presentation features. The primary disadvantage of spreadsheets is that they are not designed to handle longitudinal data and are mostly useful for short-term progress monitoring (e.g., within a given year), at least for data at the student level. Other disadvantages of spreadsheets are that everything must be created manually, much like for relational databases, and that data files typically reside on individuals' computers rather than in shared spaces like grade-level folders in local area networks.

Scenario 3: The Minnehaha school district realizes that it needs the capacity in each of its high schools to organize and analyze raw student and school data. The district invests in advanced spreadsheet and relational database training for three to eight staff members from each school building. These teachers, media specialists, guidance counselors, technology integration specialists, school psychologists, and assistant principals form the core of each school's data team. These data managers then work with other staff in their buildings to download and analyze data from the district data warehouse, combine the warehouse data with school data in other locations, and/or create customized data collection and analysis tools.

Although used often by educators, spreadsheet software products have a number of powerful capabilities that largely go untapped. For example, most educators do not know how to sort, filter, apply conditional formatting, make graphs, or create pivot charts—features that allow educators to quickly identify data patterns and trends and thus facilitate meaningful monitoring of student academic progress. These skills and others can be easily taught to educators using screencasts such as those found at the UCEA CASTLE

School Data Tutorials website (www.schooldatatutorials.org), thus enhancing teachers' and administrators' ability to analyze and work with raw data instead of being dependent on preformatted reports from states, districts, and testing companies.

Computer-Assisted Instruction Systems

Computer-assisted instruction (CAI) systems complement or replace traditional, teacher-directed instruction. These interactive systems typically are focused on reading, writing, and mathematics skills. Most CAI systems use sound, graphics, animations, videos, and/or simulations to convey key concepts and then ask fixed-response questions to assess students' mastery of those concepts. Students proceed at their own pace and can work individually or in small groups. These systems maintain ongoing records of students' work and use reports and charts to display individual or classroom-level results.

Student Response Systems

Student response systems are tools that have recently emerged that may be of interest to school psychologists. Informally known as "clickers" because the devices look like television remote controls, student response systems allow educators to ask students fixed-response questions and instantly tally the results. Student response systems often can be integrated with electronic presentation software and/or can be utilized with a digital projector or electronic whiteboard. Student responses can be displayed in a variety of different ways, including bar and pie charts, and can be electronically archived for longitudinal analysis.

Summary

All of these tools facilitate the collection, analysis, and reporting of student learning data. The sophistication, comprehensiveness, and ease of use of their features vary widely. Even in school districts that possess data warehouses, many of these systems will remain disconnected from each other. School psychologists who wish to take advantage of the data from these tools thus must master multiple systems with different interfaces and features. Although some school psychologists will have access to many of these tools through their school systems, others may have to advocate for their use with local school leaders.

BEST PRACTICES

School psychologists have seen the importance of data collection and analysis grow steadily over the past few decades. The most recent iterations of the Individuals with Disabilities Education Act (IDEA) and Elementary and Secondary Education Act (i.e., No Child Left Behind) both place a heavy premium on the use of data for decision making. These and other accountability-related initiatives have spurred many state and local movements to better incorporate data into educational practice.

Perhaps the best mechanism for thinking about the intersections of data and technology for school psychologists is through the lens of the three delivery system tiers noted in *Blueprint III*. The various data systems described above can facilitate school psychologists' universal, targeted, and/or intensive interventions in productive and innovative ways. The examples that follow illustrate best practices and creative possibilities.

Universal Services

Data warehouses and student information systems contain a wealth of information that can be used to inform system-level services. In fact, most school districts are attempting to use their new data sources and technology tools to make system-level changes that will benefit struggling students. One example of this is the use of student performance results on yearly state assessments to help place students in appropriate learning environments. Although state-level assessment data typically are not detailed, they can be used to develop benchmarks as administrators, teachers, and school psychologists discuss appropriate placements for students with diverse learning needs. In some instances, state assessment data from district-level technology systems can be used as part of the initial screening process for new students.

In districts that have IMA systems or CAI systems, those data also can be used to inform general provision of services. For example, a district might administer a short reading assessment every 6 weeks to every elementary student. The assessment is designed to target key learning outcomes at each grade and to assess student readiness for the more comprehensive state assessment at the end of each year. The school psychologists in that district can work with administrators and teachers to use the results of the ongoing assessment to design academic and programmatic interventions for all students, grouping children as necessary for smaller scale instructional initiatives.

Scenario 4. Jenn, a newly hired school psychologist for a regional education service agency, works with teachers in a number of different preschool programs. The teachers who are now faced with federal mandates to track student progress ask Jenn to create data templates they can use to monitor a few key child outcomes. Fresh from her graduate training, Jenn uses her statistical and spreadsheet knowledge to create templates for teachers to track child development indicators from the Work Sampling System, the Creative Curriculum, and the Hawaii Early Learning Profile. Jenn then works with the teachers to utilize the results to inform instructional practice and to identify additional assessments that may be needed.

School psychologists can assist school districts by aiding the identification of useful school environment, instructional climate, and student behavior assessments. If districts can administer these assessments to the majority of their students and get the results into their student information systems and/or data warehouses, then they can use those data to improve student learning. One of the biggest challenges for school systems is mapping student learning and behavioral outcomes to instructional or programmatic interventions. School psychologists can help districts configure their data systems to conduct analyses that cut across multiple data domains (Bernhardt, 2004).

Another important role for school psychologists relates to interpreting the data that reside in district-level technology systems. As Rosenfield and Nelson (1995) note, "there are few others with training, experience, and expertise in assessment comparable to that of school psychologists" (p. 2). Teachers and administrators need assistance concerning interpreting and understanding the data that they have. Without proper guidance and training, educators often make overgeneralizations or incorrect interpretations of academic and behavioral analyses. School psychologists have specialized analytical expertise that often goes untapped within their school systems. Whether interpreting norm-referenced assessments that are being used for decisions about placement or helping teachers appropriately diagnose and classify individual students in other ways, school psychologists can be integral partners in districts' attempts to obtain maximum functionality from their data systems.

Scenario 5: Teachers at River Run Elementary would like to know the correlation between the scores that their students receive on the state reading assessment and their students' grades in reading. The school district, like most school systems, maintains two different datasets for these types of data. Before the advent of DMA systems, Keary, the school psychologist for River Run, either would have spent a great deal of time creating a combined data file by hand or would have told the teachers that they would have to forego the analysis altogether. Because Keary has access to the district's data warehouse, however, she can quickly and easily correlate the two variables of interest and break down the findings by grade level, classroom, and student demographics. The teachers thus are freed from the task of compiling the data and instead can spend their valuable time working with Keary to answer questions about the strength of the correlation, what to do when students do well in class but not on the state test, and what it means when students are successful on the state assessment but receive low class grades.

Targeted Interventions

There has been an explosion of new data collection and analysis tools since the 1990s. In addition to the tremendous growth in the use of data warehouses and student information systems, school systems increasingly are using one or multiple technology systems designed to facilitate formative assessment and ongoing progress monitoring of student performance.

There are literally dozens of IMA and CAI systems on the market. Making sense of these tools and identifying which have the greatest potential for improving student performance is a critical need for school districts. The evolving roles of school psychologists related to instructional assessment coincide with this important task.

Educators need help identifying appropriate assessments that can be used at the classroom or individual student level. Without appropriate guidance, administrators are susceptible to the latest pitch from commercial vendors, and history has proven that they are quite

apt to invest in assessment solutions that have little to no impact on student learning outcomes (e.g., *eSchoolNews*, 2005). School psychologists should be key members of districts' assessment purchasing teams in order to minimize the occurrence of such mistakes. All team members should ensure that they get answers to important questions such as these two: What evidence is there that use of these tools increases student achievement? Why are these assessment tools appropriate for the results we are trying to achieve?

Once appropriate assessments have been identified, school psychologists also can help districts identify which technology systems are best suited to administer, score, analyze, and report the data that are collected. One of the key mantras for any data-driven school system should be: If we expect educators to regularly collect student progress-monitoring data, we have to give them a place to put the data and a means to easily analyze the results.

Many a district assessment initiative has foundered because the school system failed to sufficiently invest in the technology necessary to make such initiatives happen.

Even districts that cannot afford an IMA system can use relational databases for data storage and electronic spreadsheets for data analysis and reporting. Although such an approach may be less costly, it also can be cumbersome and require significant amounts of time from technology support staff for system creation and maintenance.

Once an appropriate IMA or CAI system has been purchased, school psychologists are well suited to assist teachers in proper usage of such systems. Working alongside classroom educators, school psychologists can use the data from students' periodic academic and behavioral assessments to inform classroom instruction and behavior management. Although they may need some training in the specifics of the software tools, school psychologists likely are some of the best-trained personnel in the district when it comes to being able to interpret and use the data, reports, and charts generated by IMA and CAI systems. Modeling frequent and appropriate usage of assessment software to other educators can be an important role for school psychologists.

School psychologists' training programs prepare them to design and deliver targeted interventions for students who are unsuccessful under more universal approaches. School psychologists can help teachers determine which students need additional academic or behavioral interventions and which technology and assessment systems are best suited to monitor the progress of those particular students. Data from IMA and CAI systems often can be used to facilitate response to intervention (RTI) models by serving as pretest, posttest, and ongoing progress measures. Because most IMA and CAI systems have fairly robust analytical and reporting features, it usually is pretty easy for school psychologists and other educators to monitor the progress of students, either individually or in groups, on critical outcomes (Ysseldyke & Bolt, in press).

Scenario 6: Skip, a school psychologist serving Washington Junior High, helps teachers use a 15-minute computerized adaptive test to individually place students in leveled math instructional groups. The teachers then use the computerized assessments to periodically monitor students' math progress during the year and to help them individualize supplemental instruction. The software generates math problems that are individualized to students' skill levels and academic performance, ensuring that students continually function within their proximal zone of development. Once a week, Skip reviews teachers' daily status-of-the-class reports and assists teachers with their instructional planning. When individual students fail to make progress, alternative approaches are tried. If students' progress is too low for an extended time, they are referred for more comprehensive assessment.

The core components of an RTI approach are "the systematic … application of scientific, research-based interventions in general education; … measurement of a student's response to these interventions; and … use of the RTI data to inform instruction" (National Joint Committee on Learning Disabilities, 2005). Many IMA and CAI systems are based on research-based interventions, thus satisfying the first component of the RTI approach. These tools help educators monitor responsiveness to instructional interventions by tracking student performance and also help educators use the data for instructional decision making through the creation of various reports and progress charts. IMA and CAI systems thus should be viewed as important resources for facilitating educators' implementation of the RTI model (Ysseldyke & McLeod, in press).

Intensive Interventions

As instructional interventions become more individualized, the need for larger, system-level data collection and analysis tools diminishes. For many intensive interventions, spreadsheet software can be used for progress monitoring. For example, a team at the University of Minnesota created a variety of spreadsheets to facilitate student progress monitoring as part of the Osseo Area (MN) Schools Data Templates Project. Rather than teaching classroom instructors how to create formulas and make graphs from scratch, they simply handed them already-made spreadsheet templates into which they could enter periodic assessment scores. The district preloaded the spreadsheets with student names, identification numbers, and demographic data, and all the teachers had to do was drop in student scores. Data cells had conditional formatting rules built into them to facilitate teacher identification of struggling students. The spreadsheets also had drop-down buttons that allowed teachers to quickly see subsets of the student population. By clicking on tabs at the bottom of the spreadsheets, teachers could access a variety of premade, dynamic progress charts that generated themselves from the data entered by the teachers over the school year.

Similarly, Intervention Central (www.intervention central.org) is a website that provides free templates to school psychologists for ongoing progress monitoring as well as links to commercial progress-monitoring tools.

Spreadsheets can be a powerful replacement for local, paper-based, academic and behavioral monitoring systems.

Scenario 7: Guided by their students' results on the September iteration of the district's periodic standardized assessment, the fifth-grade teachers at Woodland Elementary decide to focus on math computation for the year. The teachers alternate creating a 20-question common math assessment that is taken by every fifth-grade student each month. The monthly assessment, which takes 8 minutes to administer, has five questions each related to addition, subtraction, multiplication, and division. Wiley, the school psychologist, helps ensure that the questions are statistically valid and reliable. Student results are entered once per month into a spreadsheet data template that was predesigned by Wiley. The team of teachers then analyzes its students' monthly progress and utilizes the pivot chart's drop-down buttons and drag-and-drop capabilities to disaggregate the data by teacher, student, or student minority status.

The key to the success of most of these technology and assessment initiatives is for teachers to spend as little time as possible on data entry and chart creation, thus freeing them for the more important tasks of data analysis, discussion, and formulation of instructional interventions. Although it may be valuable for school systems to train a few school psychologists and other educators to have the capacity to build such tools, most educators need only a few basic skills as long as they also have access to more sophisticated structures for support and assistance. Having a school psychologist or other designer create a spreadsheet template that can be used by many is much more efficient than having multiple educators each make their own individual templates.

Student response systems appear to have great promise for certain types of student assessments. Because student response systems require almost no training of student participants and can be used by students who are very young, they seem ideal for administering any kind of short, fixed-response assessment. The software that comes with most student response systems is easily learned by educators who are not technology savvy and usually has the capability of tracking student progress over time by identification number. Scenarios are easily imaginable in which school psychologists and teachers use student response systems to monitor student progress on a few key learning outcomes.

Finally, students can be taught to create spreadsheet tables and charts as early as the upper elementary grades. Some school psychologists and teachers have found it enormously empowering to teach students to monitor their own progress through the use of basic charting and graphing tools. Students who track their growth themselves appear to have strong buy-in toward continued progress, often regardless of their individual starting points.

SUMMARY

We now live in a technology-suffused, globally interconnected world. The technological revolutions that are radically transforming other sectors of society are gradually making their way into school systems and the professional lives of school psychologists. Increased expectations regarding data collection and analysis for improving student outcomes have been accompanied by a rise in the number and types of tools available to educators for assessment, data management, and reporting.

Although it is an exciting time for some, the rapid pace of technological change also makes it a difficult or an intimidating time for others. If school districts and professional associations expect school psychologists to use digital technologies for data-based decision making, then they must pay attention to the rational fears that many school psychologists have about technological transformations and must make significant investments in high-quality professional development initiatives in order to address and overcome existing concerns. As training efforts increase their skill at using technology systems for classification, evaluation, and intervention, school psychologists will be better able to maximize the potential of all students to be academically and behaviorally successful.

REFERENCES

Bernhardt, V. L. (2004). *Data analysis for continuous school improvement* (2nd ed.). Larchmont, NY: Eye on Education.

Cronbach, L. J. (1957). The two disciplines of scientific psychology. *American Psychologist, 12*, 671–684.

eSchoolNews. (2005). *$50M reading buy under fire in LA*. Bethesda, MD: Author. Retrieved July 27, 2007, from http://www.eschoolnews.com/news/showStory.cfm?ArticleID=5547

McLeod, S. (2005). *Technology tools for data-driven teachers*. Retrieved June 1, 2007, from http://www.microsoft.com/Education/ThoughtLeadersDDDM.mspx

National Joint Committee on Learning Disabilities. (2005). *Responsiveness to intervention and learning disabilities*. Retrieved June 1, 2007, from http://www.ldonline.org/?module=uploads&func=download&fileId=461

Reschly, D. (1988a). Special education reform: School psychology revolution. *School Psychology Review, 17*, 459–475.

Reschly, D. (1988b). Obstacles, starting points, and doldrums notwithstanding: Reform/revolution from outcomes criteria. *School Psychology Review, 17*, 495–501.

Reschly, D., & Ysseldyke, J. E. (2002). Paradigm shift: The past is not the future. In J. Grimes & A. Thomas (Eds.), *Best practices in school psychology IV*. Bethesda, MD: National Association of School Psychologists.

Rosenfield, S., & Nelson, D. (2005). *The school psychologist's role in school assessment*. Greensboro, NC: ERIC Clearinghouse on Counseling and Student Services. (ERIC Document Reproduction Service No. ED391985).

Ysseldyke, J., & Bolt, D. (in press). Effect of technology-enhanced continuous progress monitoring on math achievement. *School Psychology Review*.

Ysseldyke, J. E., Burns, M. K., Dawson, M., Kelly, B., Morrison, D., Ortiz, S., et al. (2006). *School psychology: A blueprint for the future of training and practice III.* Bethesda, MD: National Association of School Psychologists.

Ysseldyke, J. E., & McLeod, S. (in press). Using technology to enhance RTI progress monitoring. In S. Jimerson, M. Burns, & A. VanderHeyden (Eds.), *Response to intervention.* New York: Springer.

ANNOTATED BIBLIOGRAPHY

Chen, E., Heritage, M., & Lee, J. (2005). Identifying and monitoring students' learning needs with technology. *Journal of Education for Students Placed at Risk, 10,* 309–332.

Describes the beneficial uses of a web-based decision support tool, including timely identification of at-risk students, support for sound assessment practices, and facilitation of frequent assessment.

McLeod, S. (2005). *Technology tools for data-driven teachers.* Retrieved June 1, 2007, from http://www.microsoft.com/Education/ ThoughtLeadersDDDM.mspx

Describes a variety of technology tools that can be used for summative and formative data collection and analysis. The overview of data management and analysis systems is accompanied by links to free tools and templates for educators.

Mercurius, N. (2004). *Mopping and scrubbing dirty data.* Retrieved June 1, 2007, from www.techlearning.com/story/showArticle.php?article-ID=17000469

Discusses the importance of cleaning up dirty data. Describes clean data elements needed to facilitate data sharing across technology systems.

Sharkey, N. S., & Murnane, R. J. (2006). Tough choices in designing a formative assessment system. *American Journal of Education, 112,* 572–588.

Focuses on the difficult choices that educators face when choosing formative assessment systems and deciding how to use them. The experience of a large urban district is profiled in detail.

Wayman, J. C. (2005). Involving teachers in data-driven decision-making: Using computer systems to support teacher inquiry and reflection. *Journal of Education for Students Placed at Risk, 10,* 295–308.

Describes teacher use of technology systems that contain student learning data. Discusses the conditions that make data systems useful and helpful to educators.

WEB RESOURCES

Intervention Central: www.interventioncentral.org
Contains a number of resources for school psychologists, including innovative Internet applications for generating behavior report cards, reinforcer surveys, progress-monitoring charts, reading probes, and other useful tools.

School Data Tutorials: www.schooldatatutorials.org
Contains dozens of screencasts designed to enhance educators' ability to organize and analyze raw student learning data. Also includes example data collection and analysis templates for use by schools.

UCEA Center for the Advanced Study of Technology Leadership in Education: www.schooltechleadership.org
Contains a variety of resources related to data-driven education and other technology leadership issues, including articles, white papers, and podcasts.

118

Best Practices in Using Technology for Data-Based Decision Making

Benjamin Silberglitt

Technology and Information Educational Services, St. Paul, MN

OVERVIEW

The development of information and communication technology, and its potential for the field of education, has grown significantly in recent years (U.S. Department of Education, 2004). This expansion has occurred in a variety of workplace environments, and the education sector has been no exception (see Pfohl, chapter 119, vol. 5). Technology has become a focal point of training for school psychologists (National Association of School Psychologists, 2000), best exemplified by "technology applications" achieving status as a foundational competency in *School Psychology: A Blueprint for Training and Practice III* (Ysseldyke et al., 2006). These documents provide leadership and direction for the field of school psychology, emphasizing the notion that technology is an extremely broad domain, one that likely has an impact on almost every aspect of a school psychologist's daily practice. Given this breadth, more work needs to be done to outline the specific technological competencies that would best enhance the delivery of school psychological services.

School psychologists hold a unique role in the schools, one that enables them to provide leadership around the implementation of technologies that hold promise for improving student outcomes. In fact, a related functional competency in *Blueprint III* is "data-based decision making and accountability." The merger of these two areas of competence is an especially promising arena within which school psychologists can be well equipped to deliver solutions. Indeed, one of the successes and promising trends in today's schools described in *Blueprint III* is that "[i]ncreasingly, schools are using objective data, including those derived from technology-enhanced monitoring systems, to identify students who are not achieving critical academic benchmarks, and are putting in place systematic interventions to assist at-risk learners" (p. 7). This promising trend represents the nexus of two core competencies: technology applications and data-based decision making.

The goal of this chapter is to further describe ways in which school psychologists can use technology applications to support data-based decision making in schools. The applications described will be those that affect systems-based service delivery, as well as service delivery for individual children. The availability of technology tools that support data-based decision making has exploded in recent years, running the gamut from developing new uses of existing and widely available software to comprehensive web-based systems for analyzing and interpreting student performance data. This chapter will present a variety of available tools, providing information that will enable school psychologists to be informed consumers of these tools, both in terms of making decisions as to which tools to use and identifying keys to successful implementation.

Blueprint III proposes three levels of professional competency: novice, competence in some area, and expertise in one to two areas (Ysseldyke et al., 2006). While there is information in this chapter that would likely benefit a novice to these topics, this chapter focuses on refining skill development within the area of technology, leading to an expert level of application. Some basic considerations are presented, including some prerequisite skills (in addition to those likely acquired in a graduate program in school psychology) that would benefit the school psychologist interested in using technology for data-based decision making.

BASIC CONSIDERATIONS

This chapter will attempt to remain technology agnostic whenever possible, with the goal of not endorsing any specific product or tool. That said, in many cases certain tools may be better suited to a specific task, and those types of recommendations cannot be avoided. However, the author will also attempt to mention alternatives that serve parallel functions to any specific product.

The types of technology applications discussed will include spreadsheet software, relational database software, statistical analysis software, off-the-shelf web-based tools, and business intelligence/data warehouse tools. Spreadsheet software will focus on Excel, although AppleWorks is another well-known alternative. Relational database software will focus on the use of Access, although File Maker Pro is a well-known alternative. Statistical analysis software will focus on SPSS, although SAS and R are two well-known alternatives. In each of these three cases, while some specific methods within the software may be described, more general discussion of the context, strengths, and weaknesses of a type of tool will also be included, so that users who prefer a different but parallel software tool will still benefit. The chapter does not assume that the reader has an advanced understanding of any of these tools. However, a basic working knowledge of at least one example of each type of software tool is assumed for those sections of the chapter relevant to that tool.

In the cases of off-the-shelf web-based tools or business intelligence/data warehouse tools, no specific product will be endorsed or described. Discussion of these tools will focus completely on the contextual factors affecting their application in an educational setting. The chapter does not assume that the reader has any experience implementing these tools. However, some familiarity with examples of these tools would be helpful to the reader. Several examples of off-the-shelf tools for general outcome measurement (GOM) data include AIMSweb, DIBELS, EdCheckup, and Wireless Generation. Off-the-shelf tools for computer-adaptive assessments include NWEA and Scantron. Some examples of data warehouse tools include Cognos, SAS, and SchoolNet. For more information on data warehousing, see McIntire (2004).

A final caveat is that technology and the functionality of specific applications tends to change rapidly. It would be best practice when using this chapter as a resource to research any changes that may have happened since publication.

BEST PRACTICES

This section outlines some of the specific ways in which technology applications can support and enhance data-based decision making. These specific topics include linking student performance data to high-stakes outcomes, creating local norms, managing large student databases, and communicating and summarizing student data. While the focus of the chapter will tend to present examples related to assessment data, data from other domains of student performance may also be applicable.

Using Technology to Link Student Performance Data With High-Stakes Outcomes

Locally driven district or buildingwide assessments continue to grow in popularity. Many of these local assessments measure students in a way that allows for easy long-range tracking of student progress, a limitation of many group-administered or individually administered published norm-referenced tests (Salvia, Ysseldyke, & Bolt, 2006). Many schools are beginning to explore how local assessments such as curriculum-based measurement–reading (CBM-R) or computer-adaptive achievement tests such as the measures of academic progress (MAP) can be used to predict student performance on high-stakes outcomes. These measures provide the ability to measure both status and growth simultaneously, which distinguishes them from traditional forms of assessment that only measure status or relative standing. An approach that incorporates these measures takes advantage of the possibility of tracking progress across several years to measure growth toward a predefined long-term goal or high-stakes outcome. Statewide assessments that meet the requirements of No Child Left Behind (NCLB) or state-mandated tests required for graduation are two especially prominent examples of these high-stakes outcomes.

Linking performance on local assessments to high-stakes tests has recently received considerable attention in the literature, as well as in the K–12 education community (i.e., McGlinchey & Hixon, 2004; Stage & Jacobson, 2001; Kingsbury, Olson, Cronin, Hauser, & Houser, 2004). By linking local assessments to high-stakes tests, users are able to establish target scores on these local assessments, scores that divide students between those who are likely and those who are unlikely to achieve success on the high-stakes test. Target scores can be further developed to support a response-to-intervention (RTI) framework, in which students are divided into those requiring intervention at Tiers 1, 2, and 3 on the basis of their performance. (A specific example of using target scores within this framework is available in Gibbons & Silberglitt, chapter 133, vol. 6.)

Several studies have explored the relationship between local assessments and high-stakes tests, including many that specifically explore this relationship among CBM-R and other GOMs (McGlinchey & Hixon, 2004; Stage & Jacobsen, 2001). Interestingly, a study done by the Northwest Evaluation Association of their increasingly popular assessments examined the relationship between their assessments and state-mandated tests across a number of states in which their assessments are used. Kingsbury et al. (2004) found significant disparities across states, in terms of the percentile rank needed on a nationally administered assessment in order to predict a successful outcome on each state's particular statewide assessment. While this is enlightening information about the disparities in rigor across state tests developed to meet a common federal legislation, it also exemplifies the need for districts to refrain from simply adopting a set of national target scores, as these target scores may or may not be relevant to the high-stakes outcomes for which their students must be adequately prepared.

These linking studies all used a variety of statistical techniques for both exploring these relationships and setting target scores. Each of these techniques can lead to very different results, and one study in particular attempted to provide insight as to which technique might be most appropriate. Silberglitt and Hintze (2005) specifically examined several statistical techniques for this process, and discussed the benefits and concerns of each approach. A clear frontrunner in this study was a technique known as logistic regression (LR), which allows the school psychologist as data analyst to use one or more quantitative or categorical variables to predict a single categorical outcome (Neter, Kutner, Nachtsheim, & Wasserman, 1996). LR is especially valuable when looking at assessments such as CBM-R, where the distributions of scores are not always normal.

LR can essentially be used to link any assessment with any categorical outcome. In the example that follows, LR will be demonstrated in linking a single CBM-R assessment (an assessment given school or district-wide at a single point in time) and a single binary outcome (an outcome whose results can be dichotomized into two results; e.g., pass or fail, yes or no, meets grade-level standards, or does not meet grade-level standards). The outcome in this example will be success or lack of success in meeting grade-level standards on the state-wide assessment, an outcome that is especially high stakes for the school, as funding decisions may hinge on the results (NCLB).

While multiple logistic regression could be used to examine how several assessments predict a single outcome, several problems are encountered with this approach. Many of the predictive assessments are likely to be correlated with one other, introducing the problem of multicollinearity (Neter et al., 1996). The unique nature of the specific sample that is being studied can lead to results that suggest certain variables account for a greater degree of the variance in the outcome than others. However, this pattern may not be replicated with another sample. The process for establishing target scores, described below, does not generate reliable target scores when multiple assessments are simultaneously entered into the model as predictive variables. Instead, each predictive variable is analyzed separately, all predicting the common outcome, and a target score is then established for each variable.

Organizing Data

Prior to analyses, the school psychologist must organize a data file that captures, at a minimum, each student's scores on both the predictive measure and the outcome measure. Ideally, the data file would also include any other measures of interest, including other predictive measures that we plan to analyze, since building this data file all at one time is much more time effective. While we will not be entering more than one predictive variable into the model at a time, we may choose to set all of our target scores in one sitting by running the LR process repeatedly on each predictive variable of interest, each with a common outcome measure.

The data file should be organized horizontally, meaning that each row consists of every datum of interest on a specific student, and a specific student's data appear on only one row in the data file. Each column then represents a variable of interest, including any predictive variables, as well as the binary outcome variable (including actual scores on the outcome variable as well will allow us to create scatterplots of the bivariate relationship). See Figure 1 for an example data file. This file includes some basic information about each student, the scale score on the statewide assessment, whether or not the student reached grade-level standards (1 = yes; 0 = no), and several seasons of CBM-R data.

Figure 1. Example of an Excel data file in preparation for developing target scores.

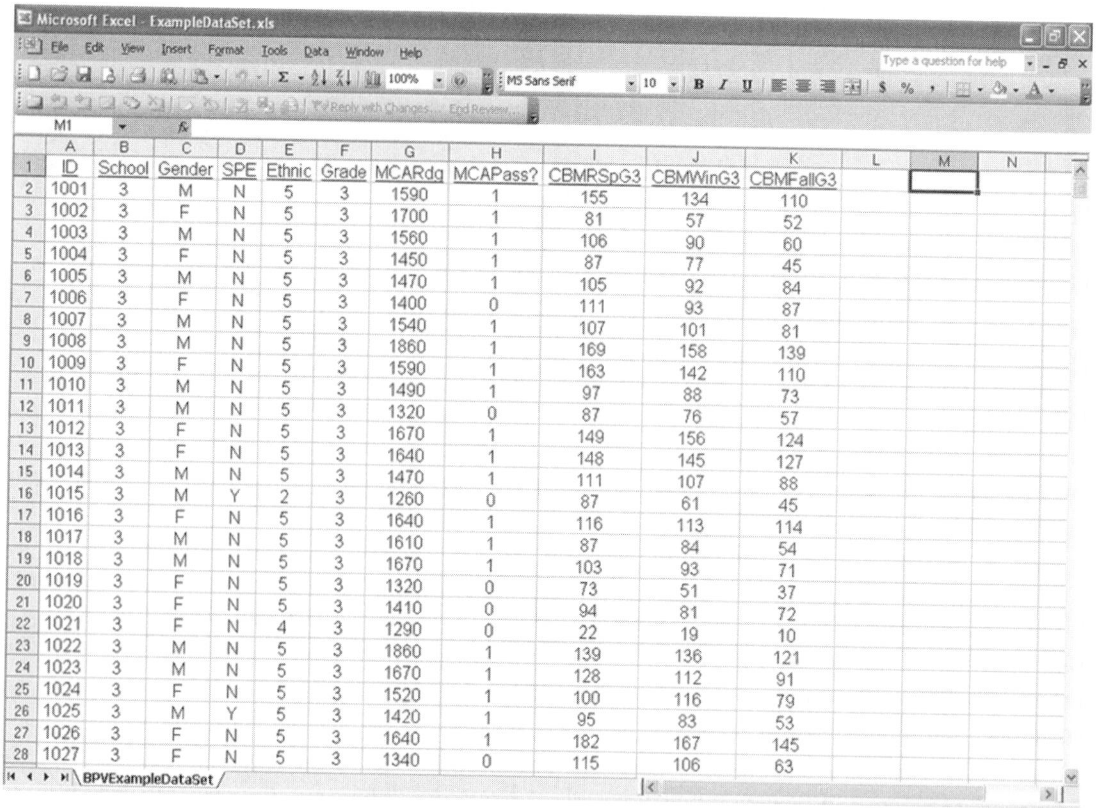

ID	School	Gender	SPE	Ethnic	Grade	MCARdg	MCAPass?	CBMRSpG3	CBMWinG3	CBMFallG3
1001	3	M	N	5	3	1590	1	155	134	110
1002	3	F	N	5	3	1700	1	81	57	52
1003	3	M	N	5	3	1560	1	106	90	60
1004	3	F	N	5	3	1450	1	87	77	45
1005	3	M	N	5	3	1470	1	105	92	84
1006	3	F	N	5	3	1400	0	111	93	87
1007	3	M	N	5	3	1540	1	107	101	81
1008	3	M	N	5	3	1860	1	169	158	139
1009	3	F	N	5	3	1590	1	163	142	110
1010	3	M	N	5	3	1490	1	97	88	73
1011	3	M	N	5	3	1320	0	87	76	57
1012	3	F	N	5	3	1670	1	149	156	124
1013	3	F	N	5	3	1640	1	148	145	127
1014	3	M	N	5	3	1470	1	111	107	88
1015	3	M	Y	2	3	1260	0	87	61	45
1016	3	F	N	5	3	1640	1	116	113	114
1017	3	M	N	5	3	1610	1	87	84	54
1018	3	M	N	5	3	1670	1	103	93	71
1019	3	F	N	5	3	1320	0	73	51	37
1020	3	F	N	5	3	1410	0	94	81	72
1021	3	F	N	4	3	1290	0	22	19	10
1022	3	M	N	5	3	1860	1	139	136	121
1023	3	M	N	5	3	1670	1	128	112	91
1024	3	F	N	5	3	1520	1	100	116	79
1025	3	M	Y	5	3	1420	1	95	83	53
1026	3	F	N	5	3	1640	1	182	167	145
1027	3	F	N	5	3	1340	0	115	106	63

We may choose to combine data across multiple school years or multiple buildings to generate a larger sample. Considerations regarding the representativeness of the sample are discussed later in this section. Also, there is no hard and fast rule for the number of students needed in order to conduct these procedures. However, having a small number of students poses some major concerns about the ability to use this sample to make an inference about a broader population (Howell, 2006). Smaller schools and districts may wish to consider combining their data with demographically, geographically, and/or instructionally similar sites that also use the predictive and outcome measures of interest.

The example shown in Figure 1 was created in Excel format, but formats such as tab-delimited and comma-delimited may also be acceptable. Since LR is a process that requires statistical software such as SPSS or SAS, it is important to choose a format that can be imported into the software that is planned to run the analysis.

Running LR in SPSS

Once the data are imported, we will want to run the LR procedure to establish estimates of the beta values. In SPSS, this is done by selecting *Analyze: Regression: Binary Logistic* in the graphic user interface. The *Dependent* variable is the binary outcome, and the *Covariate* is the predictive measure. In SAS, the procedure is probably easiest to run using PROC LOGISTIC, but also can be run using PROC GENMOD and other procedures. For this example, SPSS output will be described, since it is a popular product and it is assumed that users of SAS, R, or similar statistical software will be more familiar with both the procedures and their associated output.

Interpreting output. In SPSS, scroll down to Block 1 in the output file. At least two items of interest will appear there. The first is the Classification Table. See Figure 2 for an example. The overall percentage correct is the percentage of students correctly predicted by that target score that maximizes overall predictive accuracy. Note that this may not be the same as the target score we will eventually decide to implement. For now, we can compare the Overall Percentage Correct in this table to that percentage shown in Block 0. The overall percentage correct in Block 0 is the percentage of students we would have correctly predicted if we simply guessed the most frequently occurring result on the outcome measure (success or lack of success). This is the benchmark against which to establish that knowing the score on the predictive variable improves upon our

Figure 2. Example SPSS output from LR analysis.

Block 0: Beginning Block

Classification Table[a,b]

			Predicted		
			State test at or above grade-level?		Percentage Correct
Observed			No	Yes	
Step 0	State test at or above grade-level?	No	0	166	.0
		Yes	0	356	100.0
	Overall Percentage				68.2

[a.] Constant is included in the model.

[b.] The cut value is .500

Variables in the Equation

		B	S.E.	Wald	df	Sig.	Exp(B)
Step 0	Constant	.763	.094	65.898	1	.000	2.145

Block 1: Method = Enter

Classification Table[a]

			Predicted		
			State test at or above grade-level?		Percentage Correct
Observed			No	Yes	
Step 1	State test at or above grade-level?	No	83	83	50.0
		Yes	46	310	87.1
	Overall Percentage				75.3

[a.] The cut value is .500

Variables in the Equation

		B	S.E.	Wald	df	Sig.	Exp(B)
Step 1[a]	cbmspr	.038	.004	101.979	1	.000	1.039
	Constant	−4.045	.473	73.210	1	.000	.018

[a.] Variable(s) entered on step 1: cbmspr.

ability to predict the outcome measure. In this example, 68.2% of students reached grade-level standards on the statewide assessment, so this is the overall percentage of students correctly classified in Block 0. In Block 1, after including CBM-R scores in the model, the overall percentage correctly classified increases to 75.3%.

The second item of interest in Figure 2 is the table labeled "Variables in the Equation" in Block 1. This table contains the values of β_0 (in the B column, in the row labeled "Constant") and β_1 (in the B column, in the row labeled with the name of the predictive variable). In the output shown, the value of β_0 is −4.045 and the

value of β_1 is .038. Note that a significance test is conducted on each of these values to determine if they are significantly different from zero.

Considerations in establishing target scores.
If we would like to know the exact score SPSS selected to maximize overall predictive accuracy, it is possible to work backward from the classification table in Block 1 and compare the number of students predicted to be below grade-level standard to a frequency table of the predictor variable. However, the school psychologist is strongly discouraged from selecting this score as the

target score, so detailed instructions for this process has not been provided. Some problems with simply selecting the target score associated with maximum overall accuracy are presented below, followed by a preferred method for establishing target scores.

Problems with SPSS-generated target scores. There are three key reasons to select scores other than those that provided the best overall predictive accuracy. First, this procedure is using results from the sample, based on prior years' data, to generate target scores that will be used to make predictions for future years. So, there is likely to be some error in this process. Simply selecting the target score that provides the best diagnostic accuracy for a given sample does not ensure that it will work equally well with future samples (Swets, Dawes, & Monahan, 2000). This error is sometimes known as overfitting the data (see Babyak, 2004, for a discussion of this concept). While methods such as bootstrapping can be used to account for this, on a less technical level it is important to simply recognize that the target scores are somewhat coarse.

Second, consider whether the sample being used to generate target scores is representative of the population to which we are inferring. Shifts in curriculum, the student population, or in the difficulty of the outcome measure can have an impact on the quality of the prediction over time. For example, statewide tests in Minnesota were changed in the 2005–2006 school year. Targets set to the previous outcome measure (the previous version of the statewide test) might not be valid for predicting success on the new outcome measure. In another example, perhaps a district changed its basal reading curriculum in 2006–2007. This change may directly affect the way that students typically perform on both the local assessment and the statewide test, and it may also affect the relationship between these two measures among these students. As students reach the statewide test who have an increasing number of years of experience in the new curriculum, versus the previous curriculum, the school psychologist should consider reexamining the relationship between the local predictive measure and the high-stakes outcome.

Third, the school psychologist must consider whether the target score generated by SPSS will divide students in a manner that matches the level of resources and level of concern in the school or district. For example, while SPSS is concerned mainly with establishing the maximum overall predictive accuracy, the school may be more interested in ensuring that students who reach

target will in fact be successful on the outcome measure. They may be willing to sacrifice overall accuracy by incorrectly predicting some students to be of concern who will in fact be successful in order to limit the number of students who slip through without being identified (Macmann & Barnett, 1999). If the school has resources available to meet a wider range of students' needs, targets may be adjusted upward accordingly. A process is described below that recognizes to a greater degree the coarseness of these target scores, and provides this level of flexibility.

An alternate method for selecting a target score. Looking at a scatterplot will help in understanding the impact of selecting a specific target score. Figure 3 displays a scatterplot comparing scores on the statewide assessment (MCA) given in spring of grade 3 in Minnesota with scores on a districtwide CBM-R given in spring of grade 3 (Silberglitt & Hintze, 2005). These data include more than 2,000 students across 5 years of administering both tests. The horizontal line through the middle of the graph divides students who did and did not reach grade-level standards on the MCA. The vertical line divides students who were and were not predicted to reach grade-level standards, based on the CBM-R target score. These lines divide students into four quadrants by the relationship between their predicted and actual outcome. This process is analogous to a medical model; that is, we are screening for the existence of academic problems, just as in medicine we screen for disease. In either setting, positive is an undesirable result.

As the graph shows, increasing the target score will decrease the number of students who are false negatives, students who are expected to be successful who are not. However, it will also increase the number of false positives, students who are predicted to be of concern (and who may consume extra instructional resources) who actually are not. It is this adjustment, and the corresponding effect on the system, that is critical to the process of setting target scores.

While overall classification accuracy is an important statistic to consider, as discussed above, specific diagnostic accuracy statistics are also important to consider (Klecka, 1980; Huberty, 1994), especially in the aforementioned process of adjusting target scores to meet the districts' specific needs. These diagnostic accuracy statistics give, for example, the percentage of students predicted to be successful on the outcome measure who were actually successful (negative predictive power; NPP). Likewise, we could determine the

Figure 3. Scatterplot comparing scores on a statewide assessment with performance on CBM-R.

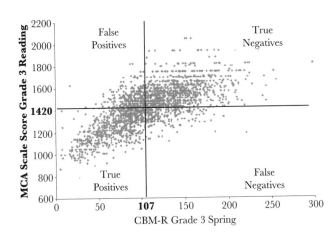

Figure 4. Example LR function.

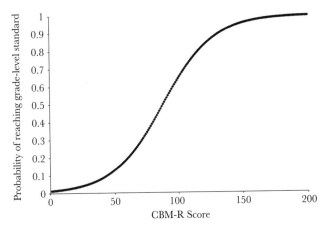

percentage predicted to be unsuccessful who actually failed to meet grade-level standards (positive predictive power; PPP). NPP and PPP are two of the more useful diagnostic accuracy statistics for this context of decision making (Landau, Milich, & Widiger, 1991). However, if the NPP is 0.85, meaning that 85% of all students above target end up achieving success on the outcome measure, this does not mean that both students just above target and students well above target have the same 85% likelihood of success.

A tool is available for providing an even greater level of detail for diagnostic accuracy by establishing the probability of success at each individual value of the predictive measure. This is known as the LR function (Neter et al., 1996). This function will graph a curve showing the probability of success across the range of scores on the predictive measure, based on the values of β_0 and β_1 found earlier. An example of this curve is found in Figure 4. The exact formula used to generate this curve is below:

$$E\{Y\} = [\exp(\beta_0 + \beta_1 X)] / [1 + \exp(\beta_0 + \beta_1 X)]$$

An Excel template was created that provides this curve, based on the beta values and names of the predictive and outcome measures that we choose to enter. The template is available at http://www.ties.k12.mn.us/DDDM.html.

Based on the results of this curve, schools can begin to establish target scores at a given probability of success. A consistent probability can be selected across multiple predictive measures, which provides consistency of target scores across these measures. For example, if the fall and spring CBM-R test both have these

consistent target scores, than a student who was below target in the fall and above in the spring can be said to have caught up. Without this consistency, it would be possible that the spring target was simply an easier target to reach, and we could not make a value statement about the student's growth relative to the desired outcome.

The curve can similarly be used to establish target scores separating Tiers 2 and 3. Consistency for these scores is equally important, and would allow the user to make decisions about the progress of individual students, as well as groups of students, being served at each of these levels within an RTI framework.

Throughout the process of setting targets using the LR function, it may be helpful to examine the diagnostic accuracy statistics of your new targets. This can be done in either Excel or SPSS, and involves setting up a cross tabulation of students above and below the target on the predictive measure (0 or 1) with students who succeed and do not succeed on the outcome (also 0 or 1), creating a 2 × 2 matrix. Once the number of students in each cell of the matrix is found, a useful tool for calculating the relevant diagnostic accuracy statistics can be found at http://www.public.asu.edu/~mwwatkin/Watkins3.html

Using Technology to Develop Local Norms

Understanding a student's performance in relation to his or her peers can be an essential piece of information to assist with instructional planning and decision making (Shinn, 1988; Deno, 2003). This peer group or comparison group can exist at a variety of levels, from national norms to classroom norms. Similarly, understanding a student or group of students' performance in relation to a benchmark criterion can also provide key information about individual interventions, staffing and resource decisions, and curriculum. Stewart and Silberglitt (chapter 13, vol. 2) provide an examination of local norms, within their context for decision making. This chapter will focus on the use of technology tools for creating local norms at the district, building, grade, or classroom level.

Local Norms in Excel

As mentioned in the earlier section on linking local assessments to high-stakes outcomes, creating a two-target system can allow the educator to divide a group of students into Tiers 1, 2, and 3, according to their current level of academic performance. Excel provides some useful possibilities for establishing and communicating both the number and percentage of students whose scores fall into each tier, as well as how those numbers and percentages change across the school year. A template for displaying and updating this information across the course of the school year was developed and is available at http://www.ties.k12.mn.us/DDDM.html.

This template displays students across three tiers of performance, summarizing data collected in the traditional fall-winter-spring benchmark assessment strategy. (An example of the display is provided in Gibbons & Silberglitt, chapter 133, vol. 6.) While the display is called the "Summary of Effectiveness Report," it is also affectionately referred to as the Chutes and Ladders chart, because it is reminiscent of the childhood game. It is designed to allow student scores and target scores to be entered, with the display updating to automatically reflect these data. With some more advanced level of programming skill, the chart could be enhanced to provide an interactive component (i.e., look ups when clicking on specific numbers in the chart). The author would like to encourage users to enhance the current template, and share these enhancements in the tradition of open-source applications of technology (see http://www.opensource.org/docs/osd). The author will post enhancements on this website, and provide appropriate credit to contributors.

In addition to criterion-referenced information, Excel can also provide norm-referenced information in the form of local norms. At the time of this writing, a free add-in is available in Excel that provides a variety of descriptive statistics. To access it, open Excel, and click on *Tools: Add-Ins,* and check the box for *Analysis ToolPak.* The tool will now be available under *Data Analysis* in the *Tools* menu. For calculating local percentiles, use the

Insert: Function: Statistical: Percentile to calculate any percentile from a range of data. The user could develop a spreadsheet that provided the score corresponding with each percentile rank from 1 to 99.

Excel is also capable of creating histograms and boxplots, although the process for doing so is somewhat involved, including many steps. However, several macros are available on the web that people have developed to complete these steps, turning these graphs into a simple point and click procedure. Simply use a search engine such as Google to look for the keywords "boxplots in Excel" or "histograms in Excel," and there will be several options. Please remember that, while the software itself may have changed since the time of this writing, spreadsheet software such as Excel are likely to continue to remain a viable tool for developing local norms.

Local Norms in SPSS

Another commonly used tool that can be helpful in developing local norms is SPSS. SPSS can provide descriptive statistics, as well as graphical analyses of a data set. These descriptive statistics and graphical analyses can easily be disaggregated by subgroup for further analysis. The user can also find percentile ranks for a set of test scores. To generate a list of scores corresponding to each percentile rank (1–99), choose *Analyze: Descriptives: Frequencies: Statistics* and in *Cut Points for ___ Equal Groups* enter 100.

Note that Excel and SPSS differ slightly in their methods for calculating percentiles. SPSS uses a formula known as weighted average, while, at the time of this writing, Excel does not similarly account for two individuals with the same score in a data set. Differences in percentile rankings would be especially prominent in smaller data sets, but otherwise are not substantial. Not surprisingly, there are competing arguments as to whether or not Excel is wrong for using a different method. See Cryer (2001) and Haiser (2007) for competing views.

Other Tools for Local Norms

While Excel and SPSS are helpful in providing local norms, many off-the-shelf tools provide the added benefit of student performance as compared to a broader norm group. Quite often, state or national user-norm data are made available, consisting of all data that has been entered into the product's database. However, a cautionary note in using these norms is that they may or may not have high-quality controls around the data that have been entered into the database, leaving users to question whether comparing their own data to those user norm data is appropriate. For example, were all the data in the user norm collected using best-practice administration conditions, including administrators who were properly trained? Can users be certain of the accuracy of demographic and other descriptive data about the user norm group? Assuming quality controls are in place, the flexibility of these products for providing norms around both level of performance and growth, as well as the capability to disaggregate norms by geographical region or student demographic, makes these products increasingly valuable uses of technology.

The web interface provides an added benefit of allowing easy access to these norms by stakeholders. A disadvantage of creating local norms in Excel or SPSS is that they sit on the computer of the school psychologist who completed the analysis. It is then the responsibility of this person or a team of staff to make these data available, either via posting on a secure district website or through e-mail or paper distribution. This can be an inefficient process (Wayman, 2005).

Business intelligence/data warehouse technology also provides an opportunity for efficient analysis and distribution of normative data. These technologies have the added benefit that broader state and national norms made publicly available by purveyors of assessment or data management technology may be captured and entered into the data warehouse, allowing for comparisons to these data.

Using Technology to Manage Large Student Databases

In both using technology to develop local norms and using technology to link student performance data with high-stakes outcomes, some data management skills are essential to the task. This is especially true in cases where local norms or linking studies are being conducted with large numbers of students, perhaps in large school districts or cooperatives, or when combining data across several years. Simply put, managing hundreds, thousands, or tens of thousands of records is a process whose efficiency and accuracy can be greatly improved by the use of technology (McIntire, 2002).

One example of the importance of using technology is in linking studies. In these studies, as described above, a school psychologist as data analyst attempts to collect information across two (or more) measures and link performance on one measure with performance on the other to establish and better understand the relationship

between the two. In many cases, the measures being linked will reside in multiple spreadsheets or databases. For example, the files may be two separate electronic spreadsheets on the user's computer hard drive, a file with statewide assessment data provided by the state and a file with local assessment data extracted from an off-the-shelf tool. Linking these two files requires some tools to enhance efficiency. Without such tools, the school psychologist is left to completing the task by hand, perhaps matching student names and other identifying information across data sources, in order to build a single table that contains every student's history of performance on the measures of interest.

Besides being unbelievably boring and time consuming, this task is fraught with potential for error. For example, a child may be identified as John Smith in one file and as Jonathon in another. Is this the same child? Answering yes when they are in fact two different individuals and answering no when they are the same child are both errors with concerning repercussions for the quality of the ensuing data analyses. Fortunately, there are several tools available to assist with this process, as well as strategies to reduce the potential for error.

First, using a unique identifying number that is already attached to the student is a key strategy for reducing error in linking information across spreadsheets and databases (McIntire, 2002). Most districts assign a unique identifying number to each student as part of their student information system. High-quality student information systems will ensure that this number is unique to the child throughout the child's educational career (i.e., across buildings within a district) and is never recycled. This prevents two different students from being assigned the same number, and ensures that a student who leaves the district and later returns is reconnected with the previous data.

The school psychologist can take advantage of this unique number by ensuring that it is similarly attached to any and all locations where student performance data are stored. For example, if a district chooses to create and manage class lists of student CBM-R data in Excel, it would save considerable time and improve flexibility of future data analyses to ensure that the students' unique identifying numbers were added to these class lists at the same time as their names. This identifying number might then be used to link any data in this file to any other performance data that are also connected to the student's identifying number, and could also be used, for example, to examine student demographic information, scheduling information, attendance information, and behavior data.

Studies that attempt to link student performance across multiple assessments are just one example of the many questions that can be asked of the data (Streifer & Schumann, 2005). Disaggregating the data, examining different demographic and other groups separately for comparison, is another common data question that schools would like to answer. How does the performance of the limited English proficient population compare to the rest of the students? How are student absences related to growth rates? These are just a couple of examples of questions that educators may want to answer. Multilevel disaggregation further divides subgroups for comparison. For example, how the performance of the limited English proficient population compares across ethnic groups and to the population as a whole would be an example of multilevel disaggregation.

However, the exact nature of which questions will become critical for the school or district to answer may not be known to those responsible for managing the data at the time they build their student database. Therefore, some advanced planning is needed, prior to gathering student data, to ensure that these types of surprise questions can be handled easily and without extensive time and effort spent finding and connecting data across data sources (McIntire, 2002). Below, three different tools are discussed for managing large student data sets: spreadsheet software such as Excel or AppleWorks, relational database software such as Access or File Maker Pro, and off-the-shelf web-based tools or data warehouse technology. The pros and cons of each strategy will be discussed. Based on my own level of experience with these products, I will focus, for example, on Excel rather than on AppleWorks (an alternative product). It is likely that any pros and cons to using Excel will be similar to those of alternative products with similar features.

Using Spreadsheet Software to Manage Student Data

Spreadsheet software such as Excel stores data into a series of single, flat-file spreadsheets. Each spreadsheet stores data in tabular form, and each table can be thought of as a page in a book of tables. There are several advantages to using spreadsheet software such as Excel to manage student data. The software is relatively inexpensive, readily available, and often school districts buy licenses in bulk, so a practitioner may already have access to it at no additional cost to the district. Excel is a

program that is also commonly used, so others are likely to be able to easily access and read the files. In addition, most other software programs, such as SPSS or SAS, can read and import data directly from Excel. Spreadsheet software is fairly simple to understand and use, and the basics can be accomplished with minimal training, although more advanced applications of the tool do become increasingly complex.

Despite these advantages, there are also some caveats to using spreadsheet software such as Excel to manage student data. First, because Excel stores data as multiple flat files, the files can only be linked to each other through a somewhat cumbersome linking procedure. This can be terribly inefficient when attempting to answer more complicated questions that require linking multiple spreadsheets of related data. However, this issue can be resolved with relational database software if the need arises. Second, Excel is limited in the number of rows (around 65,000) and columns (230) of data within a single spreadsheet, which can quickly be exhausted when storing longitudinal data for even a moderately sized group of students. Third, Excel allows data to take multiple formats within a column, so that data under a single field heading can be in both text and numeric formats. Especially with large files, it may be easy to overlook the fact that a subset of students is not included in an analysis simply because the score took on a text, rather than numeric, format. Fourth, while Excel does provide some analytic tools, more advanced statistical techniques require either a purchased plug-in or the use of other software. Finally, Excel data reside on a single server or computer hard drive, and it may be difficult to make either the raw data or summarized information readily available to key stakeholders.

Because of its lack of scalability, Excel is more useful in applications of data management where a very small number of students' data (less than 500) is being gathered over a relatively short period of time (less than 2 years) and where very few variables are being collected (fewer than 50). Attempts to manage larger data sets will likely result in frustrations around many of the caveats described above.

Excel does prove very useful as an intermediary between other tools, because of its ability to talk with many other software programs. For instance, extracting data from a data warehouse or relational database and cleaning and reformatting it for import to statistical analysis software tool is easily accomplished in Excel. Excel also may be a useful endpoint for producing graphical summaries of data extracted from other, larger data management tools.

Using Relational Database Software to Manage Student Data

Relational database software (such as Access) has several advantages over spreadsheet software (such as Excel) for managing student data. First, database technology allows the user to store data in a series of tables that are linked by common values. For example, 10 years of CBM-R performance data can be stored in 10 separate tables, all of which include a *Student ID* field. Rows of data with identical values for *Student ID* can be extracted from all 10 tables to produce a complete history of an individual student's performance. A separate table (or tables) of demographic data can also be stored, allowing the user to query the data on the fly to answer questions about performance at the group level across years.

Access and database software in general is much more efficient than spreadsheet software for linking student data from multiple sources, and database software also has capabilities for efficient sharing of data with software for analyzing and graphing. Further, database software generally is not limited in the number of rows allowed within a table, and especially long tables can also be broken into several tables linked through a relational model.

Additional advantages of database tools such as Access include the prevention of some common data entry and management errors. For example, Access allows only a single format for each column within a table. Further, Access also does not allow the user to sort only a portion of a table, which can often happen by mistake in spreadsheet software. Finally, Access also has some capability for providing a controlled interface for data entry, perhaps within a client/server relationship.

A few caveats related to using relational database software should be noted. First, database software is not as universally accessible as Excel, and use generally requires some training in relational database design, as well as in the specific software product. Access in particular is currently available only for Windows and not Mac; however, others such as File Maker Pro are available for both Windows and Mac. In addition, just as with spreadsheet software, with relational database software the data still reside on a single server or computer hard drive, in this case in their raw, unsummarized form. This requires individuals to retrieve and summarize these data in a timely fashion to allow users to answer questions, a responsibility that often falls on a single or small group of individuals within a school or district.

Access is probably most useful for managing databases of moderate size (roughly 500–5,000 students), and has the advantage of being able to store a very large number of related variables, using a structure that allows for efficient querying of the data to answer questions. Access is probably not a good solution when many different consumers wish to ask frequent questions of the data, especially when the data are dynamic (changing rapidly).

Other Tools for Managing Student Data

Off-the-shelf, web-based data management tools or business intelligence/data warehouse tools provide a means for both storing large quantities of data and presenting these data in raw or summarized forms. These tools pick up where relational database software like Access falls short. These tools can easily handle small, moderate, or large numbers of students, typically provide a web-based interface that allows for both entering and querying the data with a minimum of technical skill, and allow multiple users to answer questions of the data simultaneously, with a browser being the only software requirement at the user level (Wayman, 2005). This can be accomplished within a secure framework that ensures that users only have access to the data they are permitted to see while providing data in formats that are user friendly for all levels of user and summarized data in ways that are pertinent to specific users (i.e., teachers versus building principals versus superintendents and school boards; Wayman, 2005).

Off-the-shelf products are often designed to answer questions around a very specific set of information. For example, AIMSweb, DIBELS, EdCheckup, and Wireless Generation are four examples of off-the-shelf products designed to answer questions around GOMs such as CBM-R. They are more likely than other products to provide tools that are valuable for the specific types of analyses called for by these measures (i.e., drawing progress-monitoring graphs). However, they may not be able to answer other questions of interest that involve a broader range of data (e.g., summarizing student performance across several measures, including but not limited to GOMs) or users (e.g., allowing students to be assigned to and viewed by multiple teachers). Also, these for-profit companies may not be willing to develop additional, desired reporting features if they do not feel it will be a profitable enterprise.

Business intelligence/data warehouse tools can integrate multiple sources of data (that may currently be stored in multiple locations), can answer a very broad range of questions, and can often do so on the fly. By integrating with data sources such as student information systems, these tools provide a bridge between different domains of data (i.e., course assignments, grades, attendance, behavior, and test scores). This integration also provides a single point of access for the end-user, preventing concerns of users storing and tracking multiple passwords, concerns that relate both to security and usability.

These tools can often be purchased and then designed by local staff to meet the specific needs of the district. However, this customization process is relatively time intensive and requires a staff with specialized training who are dedicated to this task.

A significant caveat to both types of products is their expense. These tools are best for managing moderate to large dynamic data sets, where multiple users wish to access and summarize data frequently.

Using Technology to Summarize and Communicate Student Performance Data

Where the previous section on managing student data focused on the input, the following section on summarizing and communicating data focuses on the output. While these are discussed as separate sections in this chapter, decisions about each are inextricably intertwined. Data management must be accomplished with the end goal in mind: getting the data out in a manner and format that is fast, simple, and useful. However, data management is also concerned with expedient input of the data with a minimum of duplicated effort. If the school psychologist is responsible for managing both the data management and data analyses efforts, then this person can be certain that the needs of both sides of the equation are adequately met. If not, it is critical that constant communication occurs between data management coordinators and data analysts and evaluators (Cognos, 2007).

When to Graph
There are many times when a graph does not improve the quality of the information being described, and in fact may detract from it. In some cases, a simpler graph or perhaps even a table containing the raw numbers is both more efficient and more informative. Tufte (2001) captures this argument, explaining that the goal of communicating quantitative information is similar to the goal of any form of communication. The tenet is: maximize the amount of information communicated while minimizing the amount of ink used to display it.

For example, a bar graph displaying the percentage of students who were at or above target in the fall, winter, and spring on the local CBM-R benchmark assessments probably does not need to include three additional bars with the percentages below target at each time point, since this can be inferred. Presenting these additional bars may in fact detract from the overall message by breaking up the flow of what would otherwise be clear trends in the data. Similarly, adding colorful pictures and three-dimensional graphics often seem like a nice idea, but may serve only to confuse and/or distract the reader. (A much more extensive discussion of best practices in displaying data is presented in Hood, chapter 134, vol. 6.)

Summarizing and Communicating Data at the Group Level
Group-level data can be presented in a variety of settings and for a variety of purposes. Grade-level teams, building-level teams, administrative teams from a single or from multiple buildings, school boards, students, parents, and community members are several examples of potential audiences for presentations of group-level data. Each of these audiences may have a differing degree of familiarity with the measures being summarized, with the methods being used to summarize them, and with understanding and interpreting data. Similarly, the setting of the presentation can vary from a newspaper, perhaps accompanied by a written description, to an in-person presentation, accompanied by a verbal description. Understanding the audience and the presentation format are both important considerations when preparing to summarize data.

In any case, technology can provide some helpful tools for displaying data more elegantly. Figure 4 provides an example, created in Excel, of summarizing percent above target data to communicate a message around the effectiveness of an instructional program change. This figure shows the percentage of students scoring above target on a Kindergarten Early Literacy measure across six consecutive cohorts of kindergarteners for five different districts. Districtwide assessments are given in November, January, and May (note that 2.5 months of instruction occur before the first data point, in November). As can be seen in the chart, for all districts except District B, the percentage of students reaching targets in kindergarten has improved significantly over the 6-year time span. This chart was also used to help evaluate the effectiveness of All-Day Every-Day Kindergarten (ADED K) services. District B (shown by the circles) began ADED K prior to the 2000–2001 school year; District C (asterisks) increased instructional time in reading in the 2001–2002 school year, and moved to ADED K in 2002–2003; while District D (squares) moved to ADED K in 2004–2005. In each case, a substantial jump was seen in the percentage of students reaching target (compared to previous cohorts) as early as November. However, the remaining districts also demonstrated improvement across the years through improvements to early literacy instruction. Notably, these two districts had much lower levels of poverty than the three districts that moved to ADED K.

Summarizing and Communicating Data at the Individual Level

At the individual level, summaries of data are likely to be presented to a much smaller range of audiences, and are also more likely to be presented in a setting where there is a greater degree of latitude around supplementing the presentation of the data with a verbal and/or written description. Individual level data may include a profile of student performance across a variety of performance indicators (test performance, attendance, behavior, grades). Data may also include a more detailed summary of progress on a specific measure, as is done with individual progress-monitoring graphs of CBM-R performance. In either case, technology can again facilitate the storage and communication of this information.

Available tools. In the case of progress monitoring individual CBM data, several of the off-the-shelf web-based products mentioned earlier provide an interface that allows the user to enter a student's data, as well as the interventions they have received. These products will then produce a summary report including a graph of the data, with intervention lines and phase changes marked accordingly, as well as a written summary of the interventions attempted. A distinct advantage of these products over paper-and-pencil graphs is that the most current version of the student's graph is readily accessible to all individuals working with the student, preventing many potential issues with communication around current performance, interventions attempted, and accurate trend lines.

While it does not completely solve the above concerns in the way that an off-the-shelf web-based tool would, a less expensive alternative is to use one of many available Excel templates for generating progress-monitoring graphs. These templates ensure a clear and accurate presentation of the data, and electronic storage makes for easier (though not foolproof) communication of the most current graph for a student. The Intervention Central website (www.interventioncentral.org) includes several options, including a web-based application and Excel chart templates.

These types of homegrown templates also allow for more flexible application of the data. One example of

Figure 5. **Percentages of students above target on a kindergarten early literacy measure in five districts, across several school years.**

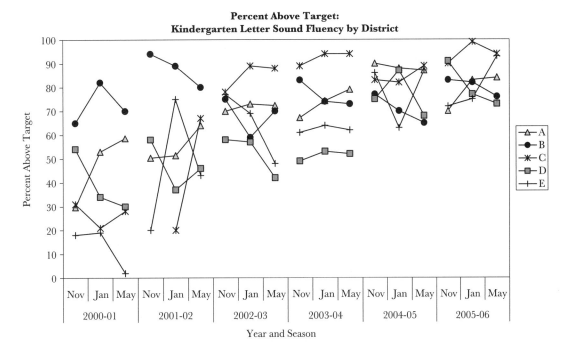

this is a template that attempts to account for measurement error, by providing a confidence interval around the student's aimline (http://www.measuredeffects.com/index.php?id=23).

Considerations. Individual student data and progress monitoring of student performance should be done in a broader context than simply tracking the growth of test scores (Bernhardt, 2006). As was mentioned earlier, a profile of student performance might include domains such as attendance, behavior, and classroom performance, in addition to test performance. These additional factors can also be very sensitive to changes in the student, allowing for a more complete analysis of a child's performance when considering, implementing, and evaluating an intervention. Data warehouse technologies can make use of the available data across these broad domains of performance (Bernhardt, 2006). These tools can summarize the data in ways that allow educators to obtain a more complete profile of student performance and may also be linked to recommendations for viable interventions based on a student's profile.

SUMMARY

Both data-based decision making and technology applications are key competencies for school psychologists (Ysseldyke et al., 2006). The recent proliferation of available technology tools and products designed to enable data-based decision making has made these two competencies both increasingly important and increasingly complementary to one another. Technology tools can provide fast, flexible, and straightforward access to student data in the form of individual student data, summaries of group-level data, and statistical analyses of educational data. These tools can also facilitate data-based initiatives, such as RTI (Ysseldyke & McLeod, 2007).

Expedient access to student performance data through the use of technology tools poses a new problem; that is, data can be made available at the click of a mouse, without any related support or instruction in their use and interpretation. It is important that schools and districts recognize that the efficiencies of technology bring along new challenges. School psychologists have the potential to be leaders in this arena.

School psychologists possess the understanding of assessment and measurement that is critical to guide proper decision making within a data-based context. By

developing their foundational competence in technology applications, school psychologists can be district or building leaders in adopting and/or developing new technology tools that enhance data-based decision-making processes in the schools. School psychologists can be flexible resources in the schools, providing leadership and assistance in deciding which tools to choose, ensuring that data management and transfer between tools is accurate and efficient, and providing necessary staff development around both the tool and the data-based decision-making process the tool was designed to facilitate.

REFERENCES

Babyak, M. A. (2004). What you see may not be what you get: A brief, nontechnical introduction to overfitting in regression-type models. *Psychosomatic Medicine, 66,* 411–421.

Bernhardt, V. (2006). *Using data to improve student learning in school districts.* Larchmont, NY: Eye on Education.

Cognos. (2007). *Data warehousing and decision stream "best practices"* (Technical Report). Ottawa, ON: Author.

Cryer, J. (2001). *Problems using Microsoft Excel for statistics.* Paper presented at the proceedings of the 2001 Joint Statistical Meeting. Retrieved April 18, 2007, from http://www.stat.uiowa.edu/%7Ejcryer/JSMTalk2001.pdf

Deno, S. L. (2003). Developments in curriculum-based measurement. *Journal of Special Education, 37,* 184–192.

Haiser, D. A. (2007). *Errors, faults, and fixes for Excel statistical functions and routines.* Retrieved April 18, 2007, from http://www.daheiser.info/excel/frontpage.html

Howell, D. C. (2006). *Statistical methods for psychology* (6th edition). Belmont, CA: Wadsworth.

Huberty, C. J. (1994). *Applied discriminant analysis.* New York: John Wiley.

Kingsbury, G. G., Olson, A., Cronin, J., Hauser, C., & Houser, R. (2004). *The state of state standards: Research investigating proficiency levels in fourteen states* (Technical Report). Lake Oswego, OR: Northwest Evaluation Association.

Klecka, W. R. (1980). *Discriminant analysis.* Beverly Hills, CA: Sage.

Landau, S., Milich, R., & Widiger, T. (1991). Predictive power methods may be more helpful for making a diagnosis than sensitivity and specificity. *Journal of Child and Adolescent Psychopharmacology, 1,* 343–351.

Macmann, G. M., & Barnett, D. W. (1999). Diagnostic decision making in school psychology: Understanding and coping with uncertainty. In C. R. Reynolds & T. B. Gutkin (Eds.), *Handbook of school psychology* (3rd ed., pp. 519–548). New York: John Wiley.

McGlinchey, M. T., & Hixson, M. D. (2004). Using curriculum-based measurement to predict performance on state assessments in reading. *School Psychology Review, 33*, 193–203.

McIntire, T. (2002). The administrators' guide to data-driven decision making. *Technology & Learning, 22*(11), 18–33.

McIntire, T. (2004). Eight buying tips: Data warehouses: Need a good place to store and manage all of your district's information? Here are some essentials for making the right decision. *Technology & Learning, 25*(1), 7.

National Association of School Psychologists. (2000). *Accreditation training standards.* Bethesda, MD: Author.

Neter, J., Kutner, M. H., Nachtsheim, C. J., & Wasserman, W. (1996). *Applied linear statistical models.* New York: McGraw-Hill.

Salvia, J., Ysseldyke, J. E., & Bolt, S. (2006). *Assessment: In special and inclusive education* (10th ed.). Boston: Houghton Mifflin.

Shinn, M. R. (1988). Development of curriculum-based local norms for use in special education decision making. *School Psychology Review, 17*, 61–80.

Silberglitt, B., & Hintze, J. M. (2005). Formative assessment using CBM-R cut scores to track progress toward success on state-mandated achievement tests: A comparison of methods. *Journal of Psychoeducational Assessment, 23*, 304–325.

Stage, S. A., & Jacobsen, M. D. (2001). Predicting student success on a state-mandated performance-based assessment using oral reading fluency. *School Psychology Review, 30*, 407–419.

Streifer, P. A., & Schuman, J. A. (2005). Using data mining to identify actionable information: Breaking new ground in data-driven decision making. *Journal of Education for Students Placed at Risk, 10*, 281–293.

Swets, J. A., Dawes, R. M., & Monahan, J. (2000). Psychological science can improve diagnostic decisions. *Psychological Science in the Public Interest, 1*, 1–26.

Tufte, E. R. (2001). *The visual display of quantitative information.* Cheshire, CT: Graphics Press.

U.S. Department of Education. (2004). *Toward a new golden age in American education: A national education technology plan.* Washington, DC: Author.

Wayman, J. C. (2005). Involving teachers in data-driven decision making: Using computer data systems to support teacher inquiry and reflection. *Journal of Education for Students Placed at Risk, 10*, 295–308.

Ysseldyke, J. E., Burns, M., Dawson, P., Kelley, B., Morrison, D., Ortiz, S., et al. (2006). *School psychology: A blueprint for training and practice III.* Bethesda, MD: National Association of School Psychologists.

Ysseldyke, J. E., & McLeod, S. (2007). Using technology tools to monitor response to intervention. In S. Jimerson, M. Burns, & A. VanDerheyden, A (Eds.), *The handbook of response to intervention: The science and practice of assessment and intervention.* New York: Springer.

ANNOTATED BIBLIOGRAPHY

McIntire, T. (2002). The administrators' guide to data-driven decision making. *Technology & Learning, 22*(11), 18–33.

Outlines key concepts and best practices in data management. These concepts are often presented alongside practical examples within the context of education.

Tufte, E. R. (2001). *The visual display of quantitative information.* Cheshire, CT: Graphics Press.

Examines the choices that are made in the visual presentation of data, providing historical examples of both excellent and poor displays of data, the ramifications of decisions made based upon these visual displays, and strategies for improving them.

Wayman, J. C. (Ed.). (2005). Transforming data into knowledge: Applications of data-based decision making to improve educational practice [Special issue]. *Journal of Education for Students Placed at Risk, 10.*

Presents six articles that examine data-driven decision making in schools. All articles examine direct applications of data-driven decision-making practices, and several of the articles focus especially on technology tools for facilitating these practices.

Ysseldyke, J. E., & McLeod, S. (2007). Using technology tools to monitor response to intervention. In S. Jimerson, M. Burns, & A. VanDerheyden, A (Eds.), *The handbook of response to intervention: The science and practice of assessment and intervention.* New York: Springer.

Provides a review of a wide variety of technology tools currently available that may enhance an organization's implementation of RTI. The chapter also provides some general considerations for using technology to support RTI and data-driven decision making.

WEB RESOURCES

Excel for statistical analysis: http://www.daheiser.info/excel/front-page.html
Provides tools and links for statistical analysis.

Intervention Central: http://www.interventioncentral.org
Provides tools and links to support data-based decision making.

Marley Watkins: http://www.public.asu.edu/~mwwatkin/Watkins3.html
Provides tools and links for statistical analysis.

SPSS tips and strategies: http://www.spsstools.net
Provides tools and links for statistical analysis.

TIES Data-Driven Leadership: http://www.ties.k12.mn.us/DDDM.html
Provides tools and links to support data-based decision making.

119 Best Practices in Technology

William F. Pfohl
Virginia A. Pfohl
Western Kentucky University

OVERVIEW

Integrated circuits, better known as computer chips, first made the scene in 1958. Chips form the foundation for nearly all modern electronic devices, from cell phones to supercomputers, enabling users to compute, catalog, access, and store information in ways scarcely imagined a half-century ago. The impact of this innovation may be comparable to or even surpass Gutenberg's invention of the printing press.

Computers, cell phones, personal digital assistants (PDAs), and other digital devices have greatly influenced our daily working lives. In the field of school psychology, these and other tech devices affect our practices, our professional careers, and our personal lives.

The purpose of this chapter is to address issues in technological usage among school psychologists; identify the best in current technology (especially computer technology); and give advice on how to select, purchase, and utilize appropriate technology. Issues involved in working with teachers, parents, and students will also be considered. It will also address how to minimize pitfalls posed by technology. This chapter will help school psychologists anticipate and meet their technological needs, use technology ethically, and develop a strategy for improving their knowledge to adapt to a world of rapid technological change.

This chapter, because it deals with technology, is time sensitive. Technology often readjusts itself to meet the demands of the moment, and, thus, specific terms and hardware and software, as well as companies and websites, may change or morph or combine. This chapter is meant as only a primer. See the Appendix at the end of this chapter for baseline considerations (as of December 2007) for buying a computer, both desktop and laptop.

BASIC CONSIDERATIONS

Computers and the rapid expansion of technology have made a significant impact on our personal and professional lives. Computer technology affects how we communicate, shop, eat, entertain, and inform ourselves. Professionally, we use computer scoring software, word processing programs, distance learning opportunities, and advances in educational mandates in assistive technology. The Internet, a worldwide array of computers linked via a web of connections, provides today's professional with access to a previously unimaginable range of databases, personal and professional services, communication, and educational opportunities.

Education has moved to embrace technology to help children learn and connect with a broader world. Computer literacy has been identified as a fundamental learning skill. In 1997, the International Society for Technology in Education pioneered the first set of National Educational Technology Standards in an attempt to define the new literacy and identify crucial technology skills for students and educators (McLester, 2007). The Association for the Advancement of Computing in Education, www.AACE.org, offers membership and an extensive library of journals concerning the use of technology in education.

Education reform movements in the United States (e.g., the No Child Left Behind Act of 2001) have increased the use of technology for primary education. Among school-age children, being connected and being computer literate are now expected norms. The U.S. Department of Education has a specialized Office of Technology, www.ed.gov/technology, whose responsibility is to lead, integrate information, and determine the uses of technology in education. Likewise, school psychologists are expected to develop competency in the use of technology (Ysseldyke et al., 2006).

School psychologists have been trained in technology use as part of their graduate programs since 2000 per the National Association of School Psychology's (NASP) Standards for Training and Field Placement Programs in School Psychology (NASP, 2000b). *School Psychology: A Blueprint for Training and Practice II* (Ysseldyke et al., 1997) merely mentioned the impact of technology on training and practice. The newer blueprint, *School Psychology: A Blueprint for Training and Practice III* (Ysseldyke et al., 2006), designates technology as a *foundational competence* for training and practice for all school psychologists.

This change is significant, especially for the experienced school psychologist, who may be less technologically adept than those recently joining the field. The frequent use and benefit of technology currently appears to be generational. The younger cohort is thought to be more comfortable with technology as a part of daily life (Paul & Stegbauer, 2007). However, school psychologists who have not grown up in the age of the personal computer must become educated in the use of technology and remain up-to-date in utilizing technology in their work.

In 1996, the U.S. Department of Education established four pillars, or principles, for guiding schools in the use of technology (Hughes, 2004): (1) All teachers will have the training and support they need to help students learn to use new technology; (2) all teachers and students will have modern multimedia computers in the classroom; (3) every classroom will be connected to the Internet; and (4) effective software and online learning resources will be an integral part of every school curriculum.

In 2000, the U.S. Department of Education revised these goals to reflect the need for research to find the best ways to use technology in schools and to help prepare children "for the intellectual and moral demands of technology" (Trotter, 2000, p. 32). In 2004, the U.S. Department of Education released its National Education Technology Plan (U.S. Department of Education, 2004).

Technology is widely used professionally and educationally in providing distance learning opportunities, interactive classrooms in remote locations, web-based classes, continuing education units (CEUs), and university course work.

Students with disabilities are also the beneficiaries of innovation. For instance, touch pads, voice-activated devices, electronic artificial limbs and devices, and electronic voice synthesizers make adapting to the home and educational environment much easier.

The transition from using traditional libraries to using interactive free access databases on the Internet has been largely completed. Search engines (Google, Yahoo, AOL, Windows Live, Ask) offer access to vast amounts of information from any computer connected to the Internet. Wikipedia, an online encyclopedia edited by its users, has become a resource for many who access the Internet in search of information. Many professional journals are online, including NASP's *School Psychology Review*.

Some school psychologists have struggled to keep pace with new technological innovations that affect their professional lives. Few, however, would return to the typewriter mode of report writing. Many school psychologists undoubtedly look forward to the day when they can dictate their reports and have them instantaneously printed out. Voice recognition software is still imperfect but evolving and offers the potential to someday be of great utility for the school psychologist.

Hardware

Technology changes rapidly. A person buying a computer today may feel that the purchase is growing obsolete within months of opening the box. In fact, a computer bought today will usually work well for 3–5 years before the components fall out of sync with updated versions of system software and peripheral devices that extend the computer's capabilities. To stay current, it is advisable to budget for a replacement computer at least once every 5 years.

To start, here are some basic definitions:

- *Computer:* An electronic device that uses silicon chip technology to process and store information.
- *Personal computer (PC):* The now ubiquitous computer used by most professional workers. The PC, first widely marketed by IBM, utilizes an operating system developed by Microsoft and has gone through constant development to become faster and more powerful and user friendly over the years. More than 70% of households with children under 19 years of age have access to PCs (U.S. Department of Commerce, 2004).
- *Desktop computer:* A computer designed to be used in an office or home setting. It typically includes a separate central processing unit (CPU), monitor, keyboard, and input device/mouse.

- *Laptop or notebook computer:* A compact computer, about the size of a textbook, which integrates the CPU, monitor, modem, keyboard, and input device/mouse into a single, portable unit.
- *PDAs:* These subnotebook-sized computers are handy for organizing information, such as calendars and phone lists, for storing photographs or documents, and for running a variety of applications typically found on larger computers. Increasingly, the functions of PDAs are also being incorporated into other devices, such as cell phones.
- *Hardware:* The tangible components that make up a computer system. At minimum, a computer system includes the CPU, which stores and processes data; a keyboard and mouse used to input data and navigate programs; a monitor for seeing the operation of the computer; and a printer to print documents. Typically, a computer also includes a modem (a device that allows the computer to connect via phone lines, satellite dish, or coaxial cable to the Internet).
- *Software:* Sets of instructions in computer code that tell the computer how to carry out tasks. Software can be further divided into two categories. Operating systems, which are supplied with individual PCs, tell the computer how to carry out basic functions (i.e., how to run applications, how to print, how to organize data into folders, how to find data on the computer's drive). Application software, which is specific software supplied with the computer or purchased separately, carries out specific work functions, such as word processing, desktop publishing, photographic manipulation, spreadsheet creation, psychological test scoring, and observation.
- *Network:* A series of interconnected computers that share information and data in a configuration known as a web. An individual PC may be connected to a network that includes peripherals (printers, document scanners, and modems), input devices (keyboard and mouse), a local area network (computers within a business, school, or organization), and the Internet, which includes billions of computers worldwide. (The Internet has six separate elements, with the World Wide Web being the graphic interface most commonly used.)

Making Purchasing Decisions

Knowledge about various computer systems will help in the selection of a computer for work or home. The first question is the budget. The second question concerns the tasks to be accomplished. The third question concerns compatibility issues that need to be addressed so that the computer functions with those of peers and within the school system.

In budgeting, a computer system must include both necessary hardware, including CPU, monitor, and printer, as well as relevant software for the desired task. Computers sold today frequently include not only the basic operating system (OS) software, but also applications software for a variety of standard business and leisure activities, such as word processing, digital photography, Internet connectivity, printing, music playing and management, spreadsheets, checkbook register, and address book.

When considering software and hardware needs, it is important to know if having multimedia (video or photo editing) capabilities or networking capability is necessary or if word processing for reports and scoring protocols is the primary use. The first two, multimedia and networking, will require a more powerful computer than word processing. Any computer available today will provide adequate word processing for reports or scoring of test protocols.

A CD-ROM is necessary for more capability, such as accessing books, and for installing large computer programs. A computer with a read/write drive (DVD-RW or CD-RW) will provide even more storage capability.

Currently, two computer choices exist: desktops or laptops, which include the newer ultraportable notebooks. Financial consideration may dictate the choice. Desktops are several hundred dollars less expensive than a laptop of the same capability. It is important to remember, however, that all laptops include a built-in monitor while a monitor for a desktop can be sold separately. The main issue is that if a computer is needed for outside appointments or if work needs to be shuttled between work and home, then a laptop is best. If all of the work is done in an office, then a desktop is best. A desktop, as we have said, is less costly than a laptop, offers the option of a larger screen, and generally gives more power and speed than a comparably priced laptop.

Desktops come in a wide variety of configurations depending on the needs of the user. Most new economy-priced desktops will meet the basic needs of Internet, e-mail, word processing, and test scoring. Many people choose to upgrade to more powerful computers because of the popularity of computer gaming, digital photo or video editing, DVD/CD copying, and large-scale research needs. Most premium computers are designed to be expandable for upgrading memory, while low-priced desktop computers are less likely to be expandable.

Prices of desktop computers vary widely but continue to drop. A flat-panel LCD monitor is recommended for a desktop because of its clarity and thin size. Hardware can be purchased locally, through school districts, at university bookstores, or through the Internet. A first-time buyer should buy locally, for the technical support and ease of return. Always find out the return policy. As comfort level increases, buying from the Internet or by phone is simple and frequently cheaper.

Laptops will soon outsell desktop computers as laptop prices continue to drop. Many users want a computer they can use to access the Internet anytime and anywhere. Restaurants, coffee shops, libraries, schools, and other public places frequently offer free wireless Internet access. Weight and durability will be important selection features for laptops. If laptops are dropped and broken, they are costly to repair. An extended warranty can be useful. Heat generated within the computer shortens its life. Laptop processing speed and short battery life are also factors to consider. Computer reviews report battery life results under ideal circumstances. Typically this is not what occurs in day-to-day usage. Maximize the battery life by turning on all the battery-saving features through the computer's OS. Upgrade to the best battery available for working away from the desk. Leaving the battery installed in the laptop while plugged into an AC outlet will shorten its life. Remove the battery if leaving the laptop plugged in for any extended period of time (more than 24 hours). Monthly, let the laptop battery drain completely and then fully recharge it. Laptops are easily stolen, with more than 600,000 thefts reported each year in the United States (Security4Laptops.com, 2005).

Whether shopping for a desktop or laptop, seek out name brands with good technical support services. Computers are reviewed on the Internet. C/net (www.cnet.com), a computer information resource, evaluates the market for computers regularly. *Consumer Reports* magazine and website likewise evaluates all major brand-name computers and their repair records. These and other consumer-level services are a good place to look when researching the purchase of a computer system and peripheral devices. Dell and Lenovo consistently are rated well. Apple's Macintosh brand of computers is considered to be extremely reliable.

Unfamiliar and less-established no-name-brand products can appear to be great bargains, but will become less so if the company goes out of business and cannot supply technical support or warranty repair service.

Having a computer built to order by some business supply stores can be tricky. It may be a good idea to ask around about the company's reputation before ordering. Make sure the warranty and return policy is understood and the computer is in the original carton before leaving the store.

Computer Compatibility

Apple introduced the Macintosh computer in the mid-1980s. These quirky computers gained a following among graphic designers, artists, and others in the creative fields, but were generally ignored by the business community. This is unfortunate, because the computers were typically better designed than competing PCs due to their integration of software and hardware. The Mac OS is very user friendly and powerful. It has a very low incidence of computer viruses and is considered reliable.

Today, Apple computers make up a small percentage of the overall marketplace, maybe 4 or 5%. However, their early introduction and promotion within the educational community has resulted in many schools utilizing the Mac as their basic computing platform. For years, this presented problems for computer system administrators trying to integrate Macs into larger networks of PCs and mainframe computers. Because the Mac OS is different than a PC OS, it is often difficult to get them to talk to each other, and applications cannot typically be shared across platforms.

However, in the last few years Apple has changed its computer OS to be more PC compatible. Newer generation Macs (post 2006) can run the Windows OS and can be purchased with Intel Pentium chip processors, the type used in most PCs. More and more software made for PCs can also run on the Mac platform.

If the school district extensively uses the Mac computer platform, then buying a Mac would be a wise choice. Macs are easier to use initially, are graphics intense, and have the basic software available to carry out most work-related tasks. Scoring software is more limited, however, which may be one factor that discourages the purchase of a Mac. Before looking at a Mac, be sure that there is accessibility to Mac-compatible scoring software or that the PC-based software will run on the Mac OS.

Microsoft's Windows OS has the most software compatibility for what school psychologists use daily. More software is developed for this platform than Mac due to the major difference in market share.

Selecting Hardware

As we have said, hardware is the tangible component that makes up a computer system. At minimum, a computer system includes the CPU, which stores and processes data; a keyboard and mouse used to input data and navigate programs; a monitor for seeing the operation of the computer; and a printer to print documents.

Printers

The two main choices in printers are laser or inkjet. A laser printer produces fast, top-quality black and white or color copies. Laser printers are initially much more expensive than inkjet printers but may offer savings in the long term as they typically print several thousand pages before the laser cartridges must be replaced (inkjet cartridges have much shorter print runs before the cartridges need replacement).

A high-quality inkjet printer produces near laser-quality copies. However, the images are less stable than laser copies and may run or smear if they get even slightly wet. Inkjets use more ink and thus may be more expensive in the long term if lots of printing will have to be done.

For reports, connecting to the district's computer network will give printer capability without having to buy a stand-alone printer. This network printer must be secure to protect confidentiality and privacy.

Printing of digital photos is popular but quality suffers on a lower priced inkjet. A better choice might be to upload digital pictures to Internet picture sites or take the memory card from the digital camera to practically any store that does photo printing and get pictures comparable in quality to a film camera. Portable printers, typically inkjet, are adequate but expensive to use due to the high cost of replacement ink cartridges.

PDAs and Other Portable Devices

Many school psychologists travel between school buildings and typically carry testing kits and other materials with them, including large (stuffed) appointment books. PDAs (e.g., Palm, Pocket PC) offer portable, affordable alternatives to carrying a large appointment book. School psychologists can use a PDA to write notes, keep appointments, track expenses, monitor Individualized Educational Programs (IEPs)/ Individualized Transitional Plans, write memos, do basic word processing, and track or assess student progress. A PDA can also provide extras such as e-mail, Internet access, MP3 music, global positioning (GPS), digital camera, and many other expanding capabilities.

PDA/hand-held computer devices have decreased greatly in size and increased in power. Smartphones integrate the features of the PDA and cell phone and Internet wireless service. Many have a keyboard built in for quicker e-mail and Internet usage. Both Palm and Windows Pocket PC OS are available for many of the units. BlackBerry devices offer other hardware and software options which have basic calendar capabilities and excel in e-mail and wireless communication. BlackBerry has a monthly subscription service fee and phone costs. All these portable devices provide password protection, which will keep information private and confidential, even if lost. Extensive reviews of these products are available online.

Storage Devices and Storage Peripherals

A scanner allows the copying of documents, pictures, and articles for storage on the computer hard disk. Scanned records allow for storage ease and later retrieval. A DVD-RW or CD-RW will allow for storage, backup, and ability to transport files. A USB flash drive (also called thumb drive, jump drive, or Universal Serial Bus [USB] memory drive), a tiny portable drive, is essential if there is no DVD-RW or CD-RW drive installed in the computer. Flash drives plug into the USB of any computer to access or transfer file information without any extra software required. Many USB drives come with encryption software for security protection of files. This will protect files from being read or copied by others.

Software

The OS software is provided by the computer hardware manufacturer and carries out the necessary functions to make the computer work. The most common OS, Windows, is manufactured by Microsoft and licensed for use by the majority of computer manufacturers today. Apple uses its own operating system, Mac OS, on its machines. A third operating system, Linux, was created as open-source software (meaning it can be used and adapted without charge) that can operate across a broad variety of computer platforms, including PCs and mainframe computers. It is used mainly in computer servers to control large networks of computers, including many universities.

Microsoft Windows XP as of this writing (September 2007) is the most common version of Windows being used. However, Microsoft released Windows Vista in

2007, and Vista will replace XP as the OS in all of the new machines. The change over may take several years for schools to adopt.

Linux OS and some Linux application software (e.g., word processing, databases, spreadsheets) are available for the technologically sophisticated. Many school, business, and university networks and Internet servers run on Linux software. There is no psychological scoring software available for Linux at this time, but Corel does have a Linux office suite.

Essential Work Applications

Application software carries out specific work-related tasks, such as word processing, spreadsheet creation, and accessing the Internet. Many of today's computers come with useful applications. Identify the software needed and determine which computer models or manufacturers supply the needed software package. Buying additional software can add significantly to the price of a computer, so be sure that the basic computer software needs are met when purchasing new hardware.

Software suites contain a number of programs—word processing, spreadsheet, database, e-mail, and media presentations—designed to work well together and share information easily. Standalone application programs are available but cost more than suites and are generally necessary only for intensive use of a specific task. The three most popular suites currently available for Windows are Microsoft Office, Corel WordPerfect Office, and IBM's Lotus Suite. All these suites work well and will handle any school psychologist's basic writing, storage, and presentation needs. Microsoft Works Suite is another option, but it is not compatible with other suites and thus sharing files across suites may be difficult if not impossible. Open Office is a free multiplatform and multilingual office suite that is compatible with all other office suites. Open Office is available for free download (www.openoffice.org).

Other suites are available on the Internet, but be cautious about support and reliability. If the computer hardware becomes inoperable due to bad software, the computer manufacturer may not honor its warranty.

Housekeeping

Another important software purchase is a utility program. These also come in suites, usually including antivirus and security software. McAfee (www.mcafee.com) and Norton's Internet Security (http://www.symantec.com/norton/index.jsp) can be downloaded and updated directly from the Internet. Other shareware and free security programs can be downloaded at www.download.com. These programs protect, maintain, and service security and virus problems with the computer. When using the Internet or e-mail, virus detection and spyware software is essential and must be kept up to date. Many of the popular web-based e-mail sites offer free virus scanners for e-mail received through their sites. Popular Internet Service Providers (ISPs) such as AOL also include free virus protection. These are not typically the full-featured stand-alone packages.

Some utilities come with maintenance software. Windows has some useful maintenance features built in (i.e., scan disk and defragmentation routines), but they are not the most current or capable versions available. These basic features can help the computer run more efficiently and prevent some problems.

Web Browsers and Internet Software

Since about the mid-1990s, the Internet has become an essential part of most computer users' working experience. Consequently, computer manufacturers have adapted computers to easily access the Internet using internal modem devices and software that helps the user to connect to the Internet via ISPs. The consumer chooses an ISP and then signs up for service charged on a monthly basis, usually subscribing to an annual or biannual contract.

In all likelihood, there is Internet access at the workplace. For home use, an ISP is contacted for the necessary cable connection or DSL service access. The ISP will supply the necessary software to utilize such functions as e-mail and web browsing. Most of the basic Internet software will be bundled with the computer, although the ISP may also have its own Internet bundle.

The ISP connects the computer to the Internet. Browser software allows the user to navigate it. Microsoft packages its Internet Explorer browser with the Windows OS. Mac uses its own web browser, Safari. Other good browsers, available for free download, include Mozilla Firefox and Thunderbird (www.mozilla.com) and Opera (www.opera.com). Some websites are tuned for a particular browser, so that all the site features may not be available for each browser. These browsers are also available for PDA/smartphones. AOL has a mobile version for an additional cost.

When connected to the Internet by DSL or cable modem, an Internet security/firewall program is essential to prevent others from accessing the computer. This software protects the computer and its contents. Some computer hackers take over a computer—without user knowledge—to send spam e-mails, monitor computer activity, steal personal information, or maliciously attack other computers. Microsoft has Defender, which is a free firewall Internet download. It only blocks incoming malware, but does not prevent outgoing malware/attacks if a virus or malicious program (worm, Trojan) is already on the computer. ZoneAlarm is a free computer security software program (www.zonealarm.com) for personal use. It is a two-way (incoming and outgoing) protection application and is updated regularly. All security programs must be updated regularly.

E-mail software is provided free by the ISP. Many websites, such as MSN, Gmail, AOL, and Yahoo, offer free software and an e-mail address that is accessed through their websites. These sites can offer a limited amount of storage for photos or other large files, and more storage is available for a charge.

Besides a web browser, two other software programs are helpful for using information or files downloaded from the Internet. One program is Adobe's free Acrobat Reader (www.adobe.com), which translates files that are written in PDF (portable document file) format. (Much of NASP's website uses PDF files.) The advantage of the PDF format is that it cannot be modified except by the author and when printed out it looks exactly like the printed page from which it was taken. Adobe Flash is free and also necessary to view some animations from the Internet.

The other program is called WinZip. Some files are zipped or compressed to make them easier and faster to download from the Internet or to place on a storage disk. WinZip is shareware and will open these files to their original format and size so they can be executed or run.

School psychologists often develop their own websites (e.g., www.InterventionCentral.com) to better communicate to clients and others about their services. Creating a website requires an ISP as well as software that will translate materials into HTML (Hypertext Mark-Up Language) format. The suites mentioned earlier can be used. Websites require HTML files (or equivalent), which these suites can translate. Many ISPs provide space for a personal web page. Many commercial or ISP-provided web-builder software programs are available. Microsoft's Front Page is the most popular commercial package, but many shareware packages exist for much less cost. Dreamweaver is the deluxe website builder. Pictures, clip art, graphics, text, and links are all contained in these packages.

Most computers today come with DVD-ROM drives to watch popular movies or to watch training DVDs directly on the computer. Some school psychologists teach high school psychology classes. The instructor's manual, test bank, and education resources provided by the textbook companies now come on CDs or DVDs.

Additional Software to Consider

A financial or tax accounting system (e.g., Quicken, TurboTax) is a time saver both personally and professionally for a school psychologist involved in grants or monitoring budgets. Printing cards and handouts or other graphics for presentations or professional training is simple with either PrintShop or PrintMaster.

Purchasing Software

University bookstores have an excellent price on all suite packages as well as academically focused software for eligible buyers. Specially packaged educator/student packages are full-performance versions for much lower prices. These are readily available in business supply and electronics stores, at university bookstores, and on the Internet via discount educational dealers. For educators and academicians, Academic Superstore (www.academicsuperstore.com) is a good source for reasonably priced software. Other sources of software are through the Internet, online services (such as AOL and Yahoo), local public libraries, and shareware sites.

Compatibility

The key element to software-hardware purchasing is *compatibility* (Pfohl, 2004). Read the sides of the boxes carefully and know the configuration of the computer hardware before shopping for software. Software has both minimum and recommended software requirements on the package. Minimum means that the software will work, but minimally; that is, not all of the software's capability will be used. The recommended system requirements will allow all the software's features.

Software Applications Specific to School Psychology

School psychologists have a wide variety of professionally focused software—scoring, observation, progress monitoring, test administration/assessment, report writers—available from book and test publishers. This software needs to be evaluated as carefully as inspecting a new technical manual from a test kit. The software must be error free and conform to the same high standards as testing technical manuals. Updating the software with each new version is essential for ethical practice.

These software packages are seldom perfect, particularly new versions just hitting the market. Report-writer programs can make mistakes and modify the school psychologist's writing style. Use a word processor to save various small files of your own typical text and explanations of the basic tests to keep in the spirit of individual reports; this will save retyping time. A template of the specific test and student performance description areas can be developed using a word processor. The tests, results, and descriptions can be updated and modified as new instruments come out.

Statistical packages, such as SPSS, are available for desktop and laptop computers for school psychologists who are collecting data or conducting research or program evaluation.

Neuropsychological testing software such as Continuous Performance Test (CPT) and Test of Visual Attention (TOVA) and personality tests (Millon Adolescent Clinical Inventory [Millon], Personality Assessment Inventory [PAI], Minnesota Personality Inventory–Adolescent [MMPI-A]) can now be administered on computers and scored. These tests and their technical characteristics need to be as carefully evaluated as hand-scored psychometric instruments. Currently, the Woodcock-Johnson is the only computer-scored test, but others may be as time goes on.

IEPs need to be individual. Some software developers of IEP packages do not have this goal in mind. The results are cookie-cutter IEPs that have similar or identical recommendations for different students. Some states (e.g., Kentucky) have developed software-based lists to help write IEPs. It is important to determine appropriate or individual goals rather than just choosing from an available list. Many of these suggestions may not be evidence based or research based just because they are included in a software package.

Software and hardware purchases take time and knowledge. Find a knowledgeable individual to help. Shop for features rather than by cost alone, and buy all the hardware together to help ensure compatibility.

Ethical practice requires awareness of the strengths and weaknesses of these scoring and writing products. Study the technical manuals that accompany these software packages just as you would new test materials and assessment technical manuals. Ethically, psychologists must continually update their software to the most current version.

The Internet Explained

The Internet is a collection of computers across the world that stores information on an array of topics. It was developed in the 1950s to help university and government research and communication. The original reason for the Internet's existence was to provide a form of communication in the event of a disruption of the normal methods of communication nationally, such as a war.

The Internet also allowed university researchers to communicate results to each other. However, the Internet has since expanded vastly to include worldwide forms of communication and information sharing that go far beyond the confines of the military or academia.

The Internet consists of six components: World Wide Web, Gopher, WAIS, ARCHIE, FTP (file transfer protocol), and Newsgroups/FAQ (frequently asked questions). The most commonly used are the World Wide Web, FTP (used for transferring files, especially large files), and Newsgroups, where people with similar interests share information.

All sites on the Internet are assigned a code that identifies them. On the World Wide Web, this identifier is called a uniform resource locator (URL) or address. URLs contain the prefix "http://" that tells a host computer to look for a specific web page, or location. Even without the exact address a search engine (Google, Yahoo, AOL, Windows Live, Ask) can be used to find web pages relevant to a specific topic. Use topical word descriptors (e.g., ADHD and stimulant medications) to search for websites containing those descriptors. Commonly used search engines can provide different results. Consider doing a search on more than one. A site's homepage, such as NASP's, can also have an internal search engine. A protected website, or membership-only website information, may not be found with a general search engine.

Almost everyone who has used a computer since the mid-1990s has surfed the web, the common euphemism for accessing and browsing the Internet via the World Wide Web. A recent survey (AskYahoo, 2006) indicated that more than 77% of Americans over age 12 are Internet users, up from 66.9% in 2000. They are online an average of 14 hours per week. According to Ask Yahoo, about 62 billion e-mail messages are sent per day around the world.

What makes the web so enticing is a process called hyperlinking, where one web page contains links/web addresses for others. Clicking on an address or word, typically highlighted in a different color and underlined, links the surfer to another page of related information without having to know or type out the specific URL. Moving from one topic to another can create unusual and often intriguing pathways, leading to the widespread adoption of the phrase "web surfing."

Listservs are another service on the Internet. Individuals can sign up to receive e-mail messages on a specific topic. Any topic is available and can be found by search engines. NASP has one for each special interest group. They are not interactive like a chat room, but an individual can respond and everyone can see the response. Some listservs can have hundreds of e-mails a day. Some offer a digest format to get all the messages in the e-mail bundled on a regular basis to read later.

Buying and selling merchandise is a popular feature on the Internet. Most large retailers have their own Web-based equivalent. Several sites developed in the late 1990s allow individuals to buy and sell merchandise from each other (e.g., www.eBay.com, www.craigslist.com, and www.amazon.com).

BEST PRACTICES

The Internet is changing from a place to look up bits of information to a place for integrated learning, such as distance learning opportunities. A high school diploma, college degree, advanced degree, and CEUs can now be obtained by completing coursework through the Internet.

The web has provided almost instant access to a vast amount of information that previously was available only at large research universities and medical centers. Parents and students now have access to much of the same information as school psychologists on various disorders and learning issues. Parents now use the Internet to gather information on various medical, developmental, and mental health conditions, and often bring printouts to the school psychologist's office or teacher's classroom. In some cases, this can lead to dubious findings, self-diagnosis, and misdiagnosis, which can cause problems.

Research and statistical analyses, previously performed only at university facilities, can be done on any computer in the district. The Internet is a tool to help enhance a school psychologist's knowledge base and provide better services. Professionally, the school psychologist should only access relevant websites while on company time.

Chat rooms and blogs are popular areas on the Internet to network, both socially and professionally, and share ideas and opinions. These are areas on the Internet where people can interact with others on a specific topic.

Web Databases

Various databases on the Internet store information useful to school psychologists. NASP's website

(www.nasponline.org) is a prime example of such a database. This site contains the entire collection of the journal *School Psychology Review*, *Communiqué* since 1996, parent and teacher handouts, CEU credits, conference and membership information, advocacy materials, and myriad other resource materials.

Some excellent U.S. government databases (indicated by the .gov ending) are valuable resources. A prime search engine is www.usa.gov. The U.S. Department of Education site (www.ed.gov) has extensive resources about education technology and child learning-related issues for the general public and educators (see also www.free.ed.gov). The National Center for Educational Statistics (www.nces.ed.gov) has any educationally related statistic collected by the government. Medscape (www.medscape.com) has medically related information. The National Parent Information Network (http://npin.org) is a full database on issues related to child rearing and child development from birth to teens. There are several links on this site to assistive technology under the learning disabilities heading. The Substance Abuse and Mental Health Service Administration (http://www.samhsa.gov) has extensive materials on mental health, substance abuse, and suicide.

The Office of the Surgeon General (www.surgeongeneral.gov) has many documents important to school psychologists on suicide, school violence, and child mental health. The Centers for Disease Control and Prevention (www.cdc.gov) has medically related information on healthcare and health education including mental health, as do the National Institutes of Health (www.nih.gov) and National Institute of Mental Health (www.nimh.nih.gov or www.mentalhealth.org). These are worthwhile sites to quickly find information to use for diagnostics, treatment recommendations, and various interventions.

Education Week has a special issue each fall on technology (Technology Counts) and is available on the Internet (www.edweek.org). This issue outlines the technological status of each state. The 2004 reauthorization of the Individuals with Disabilities Education Act (IDEA; Public Law 108-446) information is found at www.ideapartnerships.org and www.idea.ed.gov.

Internet Safety

Information on the web has no quality control. This is a serious problem. Anyone can create a website and post any information he or she desires, whether accurate or not. Parents may arrive with printouts of web information they have found, and all of that information has to be verified. Determine if information found on the web is current, accurate, from a reliable source, has knowledgeable authors, and is empirically valid. Too often, individuals think that since they found it on the web, it is accurate and authoritative. Never accept this information at face value.

When accessing e-mail or downloading information from websites, do not open an executable file (.exe) without knowing who sent it. Executable files may contain viruses that could wipe out valuable information on the computer. This also brings up the importance of backing up files on CDs or DVDs or portable hard drives to ensure that important information is not lost. Backing up the hard drive monthly is strongly recommended. A virus or other malware (worm, Trojan) accidentally downloaded with a file, program, e-mail, or while accessing a web page can wipe out valuable files on the hard drive. Thus, backing up files regularly gives a place to start to rebuild files.

Internet Privacy

Privacy on the Internet is a significant issue. The increase in e-commerce makes companies want to identify potential customers. Every time a computer connects to a website, it sends a code identifying the specific computer. This includes the specific user's username and computer's IP address.

This information is harvested in a variety of ways. Unscrupulous ISPs will sell their lists of usernames to companies, who can then send spam or unsolicited e-mails. This has become a trying annoyance as computer mailboxes become overwhelmed with unwanted solicitations. Many computers and some ISPs offer spam filters, so companies have devised other methods of identifying who accesses their specific sites.

It is important to note that e-mail is not a secure method for sending personal or professional information. It can be intercepted and read without the user even knowing it has been read. E-mail can also place vicious web files/code on the computer if the computer is not security protected. These rogue programs allow others to take command of the computer. The school psychologist's responsibility is to protect the client's records and identity and also his or her own personal information. Phishing (soliciting personal information by e-mail) or vishing (soliciting personal information by voice means) for personal information is done also for profit and identity theft. Never reply to an unsolicited spam or e-mail solicitation. It confirms that the address is accurate. Never click on an embedded address in the

e-mail URL or link. By clicking on the link, another computer may access your machine and begin copying data that are not secure. Always retype it in the address line of the browser and check its source. Some companies (such as AOL) will help with spam and junk solicitations. Misspellings can be a tip that it is not a legitimate site.

With the rise of Internet shopping, identity theft is also increasing. Before releasing private information, make sure the commerce site is secure. If a site starts with https:// in the URL, it is currently thought to be secure. Many online retailers now use encryption to ensure safe transactions. It is advisable only to deal with reputable, established web retailers that use identity protection systems. When connecting to a secure site, a lock icon should be visible in the locked position on the taskbar. If not, the connection may not be secure.

Tracking web pages visited can be done through cookies. A cookie may hold a customer's password and username, credit card information, or items previously purchased. Shopping will require a cookie for the purchase as it stores the transaction information. School psychologists may also encounter cookies when registering for a conference or making hotel, airline, or other travel arrangements.

Browser software allows a user to control cookies by adjusting software preferences. Options range from completely blocking cookies to accepting all of them. An intermediate approach is to have a browser alert when a cookie is coming to make an active choice to accept or reject it. Cookies remember login information, so retyping it each time is eliminated. For public or work computers, this may compromise security. Cookies can be deleted periodically through security software or the web browser. Most of the cookies are harmless but can be easily removed. A no-frills freeware cookie cruncher is available (www.rbaworld.com). For more on cookies and security, go to www.cookiecentral.com and www.zdnet.com.

Software harvesting companies profile web users and give or sell information to other e-companies. Some web pages include banners, click-on boxes, or similar ads from different companies, which all send a cookie for their product. Be cautious about clicking on these. They may take you to an unsecure or phishing site.

Most individuals want to protect their privacy. Internet use may make a person more visible and vulnerable than desired. There are complicated ways to hide an identity but usually a footprint or history is left when using the Internet.

The end of an e-mail message will tell where it came from and how it got there. All of this is public information. E-mails sent or received on a work computer can legally be read by the employer. E-mails that are personal, confidential, humorous, or potentially libelous should be avoided. Deleting them does not erase their footprint.

When software is registered using the Internet, the host site keeps a record of its identifying information. Read all privacy policies carefully upon entering the registration site. They are important. Microsoft has been particularly bad with its security, and there is a hole in their website that can allow for anyone's registration information to be harvested by outsiders.

Microsoft's software is very vulnerable to privacy and virus problems; this has been an ongoing problem, and fixes are continually in progress. Microsoft Word, Outlook, and Outlook Express have been targeted most by viruses. Microsoft Word documents are vulnerable to transporting viruses through e-mail attachments. Viruses are also targeting Apple for the first time as part of downloading music for iPods.

Privacy is a significant issue for Internet users and especially school psychologists working with confidential information. Protecting secure personal and business information is worth careful consideration. Privacy and encryption software to help can be found at www.zdnet.com or www.download.com.

Social Ramifications of the Internet

Many people socialize through the Internet, especially high school and college students. MySpace and Facebook have enabled individuals from across the world to get acquainted and keep in touch with friends. Unfortunately, young people can access chat rooms and be contacted by predators. Research supports the addictive nature of the Internet, particularly games and chat rooms or blogs (Beard & Wolf, 2001; Young, 1996). Many graduate students have failed to finish their education due to web addiction, and undergraduates spend hours each day checking their Facebook pages. Cautioning teachers, parents, and children about these potential pitfalls is important.

With increasing Internet use in schools, there has been a corresponding rise in cyberbullying. Cyberbullying is similar to face-to-face bullying except it takes place through various technological means, including e-mails, text messages, or instant messages. Cyberbullying is bullying on the emotional level rather than the physical level. Cyberbullying can include harmful comments, threats, or spreading rumors that may hurt an individual.

As we have said, many students, especially teenagers, have their own websites on popular sites such as MySpace or Facebook. These can be perceived as popularity contests in which students compete to see who can have the most "friends." These websites contain identifiable information as well as sometimes provocative pictures posted by teens. Inappropriate pictures or comments can also be viewed by colleges, graduate schools, or potential employers. Teens also leave comments on each other's pages that can be hurtful or be quickly spread as rumors because many teens check this website multiple times a day. Posting hurtful or embarrassing pictures or video clips on websites can be as damaging as written comments.

Many teens' social lives are just as involved on the Internet as face-to-face interaction. Many school psychologists and parents are not aware of the abuse that is going on because it is essentially underground from adults.

When cyberbullying is involved, it is hard to determine when the school is responsible. Cyberbullying may happen from computers at school or at home as well as from cell phones. Many schools, including colleges, have banned in-school use of popular websites such as MySpace because of its possible harmful effects to individual students.

Ethics and Technology

Both NASP (2000a, 2000b) and the American Psychological Association (APA; 1993, 1995, 2002) have ethical standards concerning the use of technology. Harvey and Carlson (2003) offer a comprehensive overview of ethical issues and technology.

The Standards for Educational and Psychological Testing (APA, 1999) includes guidelines and cautions about the use of computers in assessment. Computer and technological advances lead to a growing reliance on technology for daily work. This area is becoming a significant legal and ethical issue for school psychologists.

McMinn, Buchanan, Ellens, and Ryan (1999) surveyed 1,000 APA members about technology awareness and practices related to ethical practice, including use of telephones, faxes, and computer storage of data. The results revealed concerns about data loss and storage, confidentiality, computerized reports, and technology failure (e.g., lightning striking the computer, failure of the hard drive, a computer disk not working, a phone message machine breaking down, a virus infecting the computer). The study's authors posed this ethical question in their survey: "What if a computer hacker broke into a network and had access to confidential files. Is this an ethical violation?"

Questions of this sort are not clearly covered under existing ethical guidelines, nor do existing ethical guidelines clarify how to resolve difficult ethical problems relating to technology. As more psychological reports, computerized testing data results, and IEPs are stored on computer disks, CD/DVD media, flash drives, or school networks, it is the responsibility of the school psychologist to safeguard these materials. School psychologists who do computerized billing for Medicaid will have this additional valuable and identifying information on the computer. Most of the work done by school psychologists is confidential.

Advances in e-mail, faxing, and cell phones have made information instantly available. These new innovations in technology, however, can make information more open and available. Cell phone conversations, for example, can be monitored by scanners. Faxes can go to unsecured fax machines or the wrong number. An e-mail, which is not secure unless encrypted, may be sent to the wrong person or may have the wrong attachment with confidential information. Careful training of school personnel about web-based record confidentiality is essential. Whenever a computer or its files can be used or accessed, there is a high potential for ethical or legal violations. Computers connected to networks that are *shared file* enabled are particularly vulnerable to others accessing files.

Some confidential breaches are due to carelessness. Computers that are left on may have a report or testing data on the screen, or a storage media disk/USB flash drive may be left in a computer. Storage media, such as CDs, DVDs, and flash drives, can be easily lost. The computer or electronic device may be stolen or hacked into by another individual.

School psychologists must have their computers password protected so that no other individual can access them. Password protection through Windows is often the only access protection available but may not be enough to protect from a professional computer thief.

These scenarios demonstrate the myriad ways in which sensitive information can fall into the wrong hands. If an ethical complaint is filed, the school psychologist will have to provide careful documentation of efforts made to secure and protect student/client information. Password protecting the computer or using a fingerprint identification device is now considered the minimum standard to protect data and a client's identity.

Ninety-four percent of the general population fear identity theft, yet 81% lack adequate protection against it. Most individuals do not do anything to update or upgrade security software after they start using their computer (U.S. Department of the Treasury, 2005).

It is the school psychologist's ethical obligation to use the most current and accurate professional software available. Some cognitive tests are available for administration on a computer directly, as are a variety of personality/behavioral assessments. These results are left on the computer. Careful consideration of confidentiality and protection of the student's identity and records are ethically required. School psychologists should password protect the data files or computer in general. This solution is simple compared to deleting record information, which may be needed later for due process or parent records. USB drives where student data or files are stored must be password protected to protect files and data.

Another expanding use of technology with ethical ramifications especially benefits rural areas. The TeleHealth technology—video, Voice over Internet Protocol (VoIP)—may help with case consultation, supervision, and peer-to-peer professional contact. However, with it comes concerns about legal and ethical transmission of privileged information and data. There are few good strategies yet. TeleHealth is defined as "the use of telecommunications and information technology to provide access to health assessment, intervention, consultation, supervision, education, and information across distance" (Nichelson, as cited in Reed, McLaughlin, & Milholland, 2000).

Issues in Education and Technology

Despite rapidly dropping costs, there is still an uneven distribution of technology. White, middle class, and college-educated people have the greatest access to technology at home and work. Minority, less educated, and lower socioeconomic status individuals have more limited access. The data reveal that the digital divide—the disparities in access to telephones, computers, and the Internet across certain demographic groups—still exists and, in many cases, has widened significantly (National Telecommunications and Information Administration, 2006).

Students in poorly achieving schools have benefited from state and federal funding and the 1998 Technology Related Assistance Act. E-cost accounts (government-subsidized Internet) provide low-cost Internet access in schools. However, many students do not have computers at home to do their homework, as some teachers prefer. In Kentucky, for example, schools have 100% access to the Internet while 42% of the students lack computers at home, and more than half the homes lack Internet access (Kentucky lags, 2005). More affluent districts provide computers to their students for learning opportunities (Finneran, 2000).

In addition, little research has been done to evaluate the best way to use educational technology to help students learn and to evaluate its effectiveness. A recent U.S. Department of Education study compared educational technology software packages in teaching basic reading and math. Results indicated no test score advantage in using software compared with classroom teaching (Dynarski et al., 2007).

There continues to be a lack of trained personnel to help educators understand the complexity of technology. Schools and educators need help with setting up networks of computers. Only about 20% of teachers have been trained in technology and its uses in facilitating learning. Often students are showing teachers how to use the classroom technology (Metze, 2007).

Assistive Technology

Understanding assistive technology is important to all school psychologists. Under IDEA, technology is mandated to help enhance learning opportunities for students with handicaps or disabilities. Two elements are defined in IDEA for assistive technology: devices and services. Devices are equipment related, while services involve modification of environments, adaptation of assessment procedures, or training others to work with the child. Pfohl and Craycroft (1999) outline the various components for using assistive technology with students with handicaps or disabilities. The guidelines need to start at the low tech modification and then become more high tech as individual cases dictate.

Using computers or adapting the environment are both examples of assistive technology. Whether modifying a pencil, pen, or assessment instrument, or providing a voice synthesizer for a nonverbal child or a child with cerebral palsy, assistive technology can be relatively easy with today's technological advances. The computer can be modified easily with Windows by accessing the Control Panel and clicking on the Accessibility (handicapped) icon. These functions may help a visually- or hearing-impaired child or a child who

has motor control problems to have the keyboard modified.

Assistive technology, devices and/or services, must be outlined in the student's IEP (Cunningham & Kelly, 1998). The amount of time, type of services, and specific device to be modified or used needs to be indicated. If the assistive device is a computer, it can also be used to collect the evaluation data for goal(s) attainment, as required for response to intervention.

Technological advances for hearing-impaired and low-vision students have made learning more accessible and efficient. Auditory implants, audio books, large print books, and adjustments for computer fonts are some examples. Some useful sites are Internet4-Classrooms (http://www.internet4classrooms.com/assistive_tech.htm); Family Guide to Assistive Technology (http://www.pluk.org/AT1.html); and the U.S. Department of Education, for laws, grants, and resources (http://www.ed.gov/programs/atsg/index.html).

Distance Learning

Distance learning is exploding across the world. Individuals can take courses for college credit, continue professional development, or get an entire degree. There are many options for learning new techniques or intervention strategies. Webcasts and podcasts provide either real-time presentations or can be stored for future viewing. Often these opportunities can be interactive with faculty. Cybercounseling and cyberlearning (Bloom & Walz, 2000) illustrate the potential in using the Internet as a mental health service delivery tool. An advanced configured computer with high-speed Internet connection will likely be necessary to take full advantage of these distance learning offerings (Alterkruse & Brew, 2000).

SUMMARY

Changes in society and education due to technology will be permanent and extensive. Technology is involved in every facet of our society as well as our personal and professional lives. With the information explosion of the Internet, excitement about technology has grown, along with a vast new vocabulary and services. Conversations now include gigabytes, RAM, gigahertz, processing speed, flash drives, CD-ROM, and URLs. Abbreviations used for text messaging and Instant Messaging are starting to show up in everyday language.

There appears to be no limit to what technological innovations are being developed. It is a matter of what individuals will buy. Technology is becoming more auditory, more visual, and more kinetic. It now needs to move and be heard to be learned. Even toys for infants and toddlers embrace technology. Music is now stored digitally in a sound chip, not just on a CD (or cassette, or 8-track, or LP). Computer games are as realistic as life. Digital cameras are replacing film. Wireless e-mail and Internet services are available and widely used in business, schools, and at home. Houses can be monitored for heat/air conditioning, lights, and conservation. Cars have mobile computer technology with the capability to self-diagnose and call for help in an emergency. GPS units use satellites to give precise location and directions. Devices are available to perform extraordinary medical procedures that are technology based. Voice activated devices are available. The list is really endless.

School psychologists have professional responsibility to keep up with changes in technology as it affects their professional lives. Ethical and legal practices continue to be redefined, so school psychologists must keep current on the latest developments. Changes in assessment and intervention methodology, record/data management, and confidentiality of student information are specific examples. The expansion of technology into classrooms may be equally influential on learning and the students. Research about technology's impact on learning will be necessary, and school psychologists can assist in this research and program evaluation.

The technology revolution may have the same global impact on society as the Industrial Revolution and development of the printing press. Technology is changing how people work, interact, learn, and are educated. Educators have the massive challenge to use but not abuse technology. School psychologists can play an important part in this revolution. They will have to think outside the kit to accomplish this. School psychologists, along with educators, will be challenged to keep pace with technology as it evolves.

REFERENCES

Ask Yahoo. Retrieved November 27, 2006, from http://ask.yahoo.com/20060324.html

Alterkruse, M. K., & Brew, L. (2000). Using the web for distance learning. In J. W. Bloom & G. R. Walz (Eds.), *Cybercounseling and cyberlearning: Strategies and resources for the millennium* (pp.129–141). Washington, DC: American Counseling Association.

American Psychological Association. (1993). Record keeping guidelines. *American Psychologist, 48,* 984–986.

American Psychological Association. (1995). *Services by telephone, teleconferencing, and the Internet: A statement by the Ethics Committee of the American Psychological Association.* Washington, DC: Author.

American Psychological Association. (1999). *Standards for educational and psychological testing.* Washington, DC: Author.

American Psychological Association. (2002). Ethical principles of psychologists and code of conduct. *American Psychologist, 57,* 1060–1073.

Beard, K. W., & Wolf, E. M. (2001). Modification of the proposed diagnostic criteria for Internet addiction. *CyberPsychology & Behavior, 4,* 377–383.

Bloom, J. W., & Walz, G. R. (Eds.). (2000). *Cybercounseling and cyberlearning: Strategies and resources for the millennium.* Washington, DC: American Counseling Association.

Cunningham, L., & Kelly, R. M. (1998). Assistive technology: A handout for teachers. In A. Canter & S. Carroll (Eds.), *Helping children at home and school: Handouts from your school psychologist* (pp. 535–537). Bethesda, MD: National Association of School Psychologists.

Dynarski, M., Agodini, R., Heaviside, S., Novak, T., Carey, N., Campuzano, L., et al. (2007). *Effectiveness of reading and mathematics software products: Findings from the first student cohort.* Retrieved June 11, 2007, from http://ies.ed.gov/ncee/pdf/20074005.pdf

Finneran, K. (2000). Let them eat pixels. *Issues in Science and Technology.* Retrieved June 9, 2007, from http://www.issues.org/16.3/editorsjournal.htm

Harvey, V. S., & Carlson, J. F. (2003). Ethical and professional issues with computer-related technology. *School Psychology Review, 32,* 92–107.

Hughes, J. (2004). Technology learning principles for preservice and inservice teacher education. *Contemporary Issues in Technology & Teacher Education, 4,* 345–362.

Kentucky lags behind other states in computer ownership. (2005, November 14). *Lexington Herald Leader.* Retrieved August 31, 2007, from http://www.kctcs.edu/todaysnews/index.cfm?tn_date=2005-11-14#2190

McLester, S. (2007). Technology literacy and the Myspace generation. *Techlearning.* Retrieved June 9, 2007, from http://www.techlearning.com/showArticle.php?articleID=196604312

McMinn, M. R., Buchanan, T., Ellens, B. M., & Ryan, M. K. (1999). Technology, professional practice, and ethics: Survey findings and implications. *Professional Psychology: Research and Practice, 30,* 165–172.

Metze, L. (2007). *Western Kentucky University's e-Train Express Project goal: To increase the number and quality of new teachers who are highly skilled in using technology to improve instruction.* Bowling Green: Western Kentucky University. Retrieved June 12, 2007, from http://etrainexpress.com/about.htm

National Association of School Psychologists. (2000a). *Principles of professional ethics: Professional conduct manual.* Bethesda, MD: Author.

National Association of School Psychologists. (2000b). *Standards for training and field placement programs in school psychology.* Bethesda, MD: Author.

National Telecommunications and Information Administration. (1998). *Falling through the net II: New data on the digital divide.* Washington, DC: Author. Retrieved November 28, 2006, from http://www.ntia.doc.gov/ntiahome/fttn99/part1.html

Paul, G., & Stegbauer, C. (2007). *Is the digital divide between young and elderly people increasing?.* Retrieved August 31, 2007, from http://www.firstmonday.org/issues/issue10_10/paul/index.html

Pfohl, W. (2004). Computer software for children: Guidelines for parents. In A. S. Canter, L. Z. Paige, M. D. Roth, I. Romero, & S. A. Carroll (Eds.), *Helping children at home and school II: Handouts for families and educators* (pp. S217–S219). Bethesda, MD: National Association of School Psychologists.

Pfohl, W., & Craycroft, L. (1999). IDEA-97 and assistive technology. *Communiqué, 28*(4), 21–22.

Reed, G. M., McLaughlin, C. J., & Milholland, K. (2000). Ten interdisciplinary principles for professional practice in telehealth: Implication for psychology. *Professional Psychology: Research and Practice, 31,* 170–178.

Security4Laptops.com. (2005). *How many laptops are stolen each year?* Retrieved August 31, 2007, from http://security4laptops.com/how-many-stolen

Trotter, A. (2000, May 24). Ed department revising its priorities for school technology. *Education Week,* p. 32.

U.S. Department of Commerce. (2004). *A nation online: Entering the broadband age.* Washington, DC: Author. Retrieved November 28, 2006, from http://www.ntia.doc.gov/reports/anol/NationOnlineBroadband04.htm

U.S. Department of Education. (2004). *Toward a new golden age in American education: How the Internet, the law, and today's students are revolutionizing expectations.* Washington, DC: Author. Retrieved August 31, 2007, from http://www.ed.gov/about/offices/list/os/technology/plan/2004/site/docs_and_pdf/NationalEducation_Technology_Plan_2004.pdf

U.S. Department of the Treasury. (2005). *The use of technology to combat identity theft.* Washington, DC: Author. Retrieved August 31, 2007, from http://www.treasury.gov/offices/domestic-finance/financial-institution/cip/biometrics_study.pdf

Young, K. S. (1996). Internet addiction: The emergence of a new clinical disorder. *CyberPsychology & Behavior, 1,* 237–244.

Ysseldyke, J., Burns, M., Dawson, P., Kelley, B., Morrison, D., Ortiz, S., et al. (2006). *School psychology: A blueprint for training and practice III.* Bethesda, MD: National Association of School Psychologists.

Ysseldyke, J., Dawson, P., Lehr, C., Reschly, D., Reynolds, M., & Telzrow, C. (1997). *School psychology: A blueprint for training and practice II.* Bethesda, MD: National Association of School Psychologists.

APPENDIX: DESIRABLE PERFORMANCE CHARACTERISTICS AND FEATURES FOR PERSONAL COMPUTERS

This information is current as of December 2007. Of course, technology changes rapidly, but this should give the interested school psychologist a baseline.

Desktop computers

- Pentium or ADM 64 operating chip or better
- 2 GB (gigabyte) of memory RAM or more
- 160 GB (gigabyte) or larger hard drive
- 128 MB (megabyte) graphics card or higher
- DVD-RW/CD-RW; DVDs offer 10 times larger backup capacity than CDs
- USB hookup: two ports are standard; more is better
- 17–19 inch monitor or larger
- Advanced multimedia speaker card and speakers
- 56K modem (cable modem or DSL modem as needed); network card or network connection port for schools
- Wireless connection capability (broadband wireless cards for desktop and laptop computers are available to allow connection to local wireless networks and telephone services)
- High quality surge protector, with phone or broadband cable protection
- A portable or external hard disk drive to back up files

Laptop/notebook computers

- Pentium Centrino Mobile Processor with 1.5 MHz rating or better
- 1–2 GB of RAM memory
- 60 GB hard drive or larger; buy an external back up hard drive to store extra files and to do regular back ups
- A portable hard disk drive to back up files and the computer
- DVD-RW/CD-RW; DVDs offer 10 times larger backup capacity than CDs
- USB hookup: at least two ports and buy an extra USB 2.0 hub for more connection points
- Active matrix screen: 15 inches or larger (if it is being used for desktop replacement); wide screen is best for DVD movies and video games but not necessarily for word processing; some 12- or 13- inch monitors on the ultraportables are sharp and clear for limited hours of use
- Network card: built in (if network access is desired) or wireless network card (or capability)

- High-quality surge protector, with phone protection and security cable
- No more than 8 pounds total with battery and AC adapter; ultraportables weigh under 3.5 pounds
- Lithium ion battery: get the *long life* battery if available
- Padded case or computer sleeve
- Purchase the extended warranty for the laptop

AUTHOR NOTE

Special thank you to Gavin Ehringer and Susan Pasko for their extensive and helpful editing assistance on this chapter. Special thank you to Janice Erlewine, who helped research and contribute references to this document.